W9-AUU-048

THE STANDARD
KNIFE
COLLECTOR'S
GUIDE

FOURTH EDITION

IDENTIFICATION
&
VALUES

Roy Ritchie and Ron Stewart

COLLECTOR BOOKS
A Division of Schroeder Publishing Co., Inc.

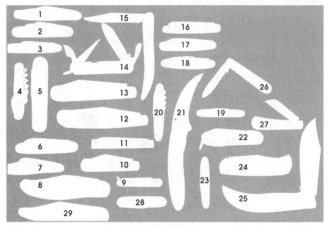

1. Case
2. Merrimac Cutlery Co.
3. Holley
4. Anheuser Busch
5. Remington Bushpilot
6. Buffalo Cutlery
7. Case Stock Knife
8. Kabar
9. Bates & B Empire Fob
10. Russell Barlow

11. Case Doctor's Knife
12. Remington Bullet
13. Robeson Daddy Barlow
14. Imperial
15. Winchester "Toothpick"
16. McPherson
17. Fairmont Cutlery Co.
18. "92"
19. Schrade-Walden Push
    Button

20. Brückmann
21. Smith & Wesson
22. Victorinox Shuttle Knife
23. Joseph Rodgers
24. Buck w/Yellowhorse handles
25. Case Buffalo
26. Wostenholm I-XL
27. Fight'n Rooster
28. Schrade-Walden
29. Kinfolk

COLLECTOR BOOKS
P.O. Box 3009
Paducah, Kentucky 42002-3009

www.collectorbooks.com

Copyright © 2003 Roy Ritchie and Ron Stewart

The current values in this book should be used only as a guide. They are not intended to set prices, which vary from one section of the country to another. Auction prices as well as dealer prices vary greatly and are affected by condition as well as demand. Neither the authors nor the publisher assumes responsibility for any losses that might be incurred as a result of consulting this guide.

Searching for a publisher?

We are always looking for people knowledgeable within their fields. If you feel that there is a real need for a book on your collectible subject and have a large comprehensive collection, contact Collector Books.

⊰ Contents ⊱

⊰ Dedication ⊱

This book is dedicated to our wives, Bethel Ritchie and Christine Stewart, and to Shadron, Shane, and Marsha, and in memory of Reginald B. Ritchie and Rollie W. Yoder.

⊰ Acknowledgments ⊱

There are always more persons involved in writing a book of this kind than appear on the cover as authors. Among the people and organizations that we owe a special note of thanks are (alphabetically): Delbert Adkins, American Historical Foundation, John Bartlett (Sheffield Museum), Finley Begley, Camillus Cutlery, Canadian Knife Collector's Club, Frank Centofante (Knifemakers Guild), Chicago Cutlery, Earl B. Christy (Christy Knife Co.), Pete Cohan, C.V. Cooper III, Christy Culpepper (MOP Co.), Ed DeCoursey, Roy Ehrhardt, Ed Fitz (Fitz Cutlery), Jim Frost (Frost Cutlery), William "Bill" Gorman, Joseph Green, Jim Hart, Carl and Henry Heimerdinger (Heimerdinger Cutlery Co., Inc.), Blair Howard, Ka Bar Collector's Club, Linda Kerr, Sherman Lamb (Belknap Hardware), Stewart Linham, Miniature Knifemakers Association, National Knife Collector's Association, Alvin Norlin, Herman Owens, Frank Phelps, Houston Price (Knife World), Luther Ritchie, Barry Robinson, A.G. Russell (The Knife Collector's Club), William Shockley, Lloyd Stewart, Stewart A. Taylor (Taylor Cutlery), Bob Troiano, Tera Warner, T.A. Whitemore (Cutler's Hall, Sheffield), G.C. Williams (Alliance of Local Knife Clubs), Bill Wright, Rollie W. Yoder, and Mark Zalesky.

The earlier editions and price revisions of this book have been well received. It has again been a challenge to revise the book beyond value adjustments. Our readers have helped with useful suggestions and information. For this, we say THANKS!

We have included new information on knife history and manufacturers in an effort to help the collector be better informed. We have expanded the RBR Evaluation Scales to help the collector follow our appraisal criteria. The appendix pricing and commemoratives have been expanded, re-evaluated, and updated as appropriate.

We have received correspondence from almost every state and from around the globe. When inquiries have been accompanied by a self-addressed, stamped envelope, we have attempted to respond. Correspondence and inquires tell us that the hobby of knife collecting is expanding and the demand for collectible cutlery is still growing.

Computer and auction sites on the Internet have added new twists to collecting. A little persistence and eBay often combine to make available almost any knife your heart may desire. This new marketplace makes it even more important that the collector be knowledgeable and have a dependable reference guide readily available with which to calculate values.

Our updated "RBR Evaluation Scales" continue to provide readers with tools to become their own "expert" in determining knife values. We continue to believe that this driving formula is the most valuable resource in our book.

The expanded sections on handle materials, blade designs, and knife patterns are in response to collector interest in these topics.

We hope you find this new edition useful and enjoyable.

Good collecting,

Roy B. Ritchie
Ron Stewart

Cover design by Beth Summers
Book layout by Mary Ann Hudson
Illustrations on pages 4, 27, 54 by Harold Deaton, Jackson, Kentucky

In the Midsouth among the easy living villages of Kentucky and Tennessee, the collecting of pocketknives became a serious hobby, in the modern technical sense, during the late 1950s. In the relatively short period of time since then, the hobby has grown into an international pastime.

The man who got it all off the ground and into print was a folksy columnist for the *Louisville Courier-Journal* newspaper named Allen Trout. He has since become the recognized "Dean" of serious knife collectors. Although he collected all sorts of antiquity and folk art, his specialty was the old Barlow pocketknife made by the John Russell Cutlery Company.

The *Courier-Journal,* one of our country's great newspapers, was a natural outlet for Trout's column. He stirred wide interest in collecting pocketknives and knife trading by organizing the "Barlow Bearcats." There were no dues, and the group was open to all who could produce proof that they owned a Russell Barlow. The names of new members were mentioned in the column, and the club grew rapidly. It became the first nationally recognized pocketknife collectors club and made the old Russell Barlow king of collectibles for many years.

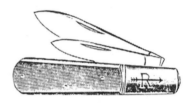

The Russell Barlow

Ownership of this knife served as the membership requirement of the "Barlow Bearcats" club. The club encouraged in its members a pride in and appreciation for fine old knives.

The "Barlow Bearcats" was the most widely recognized knife collectors club in the country until Roy Scott, a Tennessee collector, and publisher of a small tabloid called *The Blue Mill Blade,* succeeded in organizing The National Knife Collector's and Dealers Association. This organization has since rapidly grown into an international association, with thousands of members and branch clubs in this country and abroad. Today it is "the" organization to which all self-respecting knife collectors belong.

When you become a member, you will receive a monthly newletter that will keep you posted on what is happening in the world of cutlery.

Although knife collecting as a serious hobby is considered to be still in its infancy, casual knife trading and collecting definitely are not new. Knives have been used as an item of barter for centuries. A recent survey showed that knife collecting is growing by leaps and bounds. There are tens of thousands of collectors in the United States and a growing number abroad.

New York Knife Co., Ivory, Office pen knife.

Knives have been used as an item of trade and barter longer even than money. After all, knives have been carried around longer than money. It appears that the common ornery old pocketknife is indubitably man's most useful and cherished tool. It is the only gadget a man will allow to stay in his pockets day after day. There are so many types and styles of knives available that one can always be found which is adaptable to personal or professional needs. A person can even choose a style which suits his fancy alone. It is doubtful that the popularity of the pocketknife will diminish with time or be replaced by another invention in the forseeable future.

The knife's ancestry dates from the early stone ages when stone knives and hand axes gave the cave man an "edge" of superiority over the beasts of the jungle. Archaeologists are finding, from digs throughout the world, that as man progressed, he became very adept at improving the blade edge. In one European dig during the 1970s, a knife was found which had an edge "sharp enough to shave the hair off your arm." According to *Omni Magazine* (January 1982), surgeons may soon be using stone age obsidian (volcanic glass) knives similar to those used by the Mayans of Central America and Mexico. According to Pacon Sheets, an anthropologist from the University of Colorado who has been studying the Mayan find, "The fractured glass edge (of the obsidian knives) is vastly sharper than anything commercially available with a honed edge." Sheets also points out that the use of obsidian knives can be traced to 2000 B.C., making the knives approximately 4,000 years old. Currently, obsidian pocketknives are being marketed by at least one U.S. company and several custom knifemakers.

The ancient Romans are credited with making the ancestor of what is today known as the folding or pocketknife. Roman knives were made of bronze, and according to Plato, who was a Roman captive at one time, "they made the blade to fold back into the handle," making it safer to carry in a pocket or pouch.

Later in their reign, the Romans began the use of iron ore for making their blades and armor. Whether they discovered its use themselves or adapted it from the Hittites of Asia Minor is an open question.

Roman clasp knife, 1st Century AD, note hinged/folding blade. Photo courtesy of Blair Howard, Simon Moore collection.

It is almost certain that the source of the first iron ore used for knives was melted-down meteorites. They were abundant then, as they are now in isolated areas of the earth.

Although the pocketknife has been refined greatly, the principle of its construction has remained basically the same. The handle, which doubled as a carrying case, made the knife a safer, more useful tool. Naturally, this tool became an item of trade or barter.

Whether or not our historians mention it, knives and hatchets were major items used by our earliest settlers in trade with the Indians. Early traders found that the Indians were willing to pay dearly for cutlery tools. The Indians found that the white man's knives were much more adept for practical uses, as well as for lifting settlers' scalps, than were their own crude flint equipment. These early import trade knives were generally designed for both fighting and rough work. They were the predominant cutlery trade items until our own famous Russell "Green River" came along in the 1830s. The Russell was the knife to win the West and to add the phrase "Up to Green River" (meaning to stick it all the way in) to our vocabulary.

An early Russell "Green River Works" knife.

Folding knives with backsprings crossed the channel from Europe to England during the 1500s and rapidly became popular. Evidence that the backspring mechanism probably originated in France is established by the legendary "Jacques de Liege" (Jack of Liege) knife. An old knife bearing this inscription was discovered in Liege, France, during the 1500s. It established the origin, name, and pattern of the "Jack Knife." About a century later, 1667, an English cutler, Obadiah Barlow, supposedly lengthened the bolsters of his knives for strength, making the Jack Knife pattern, the "Barlow."

Records of early English commerce attest to the popularity of both the Jack Knife and Barlow patterns with the colonists and Indians. The more popular Barlow became the most accepted trade pattern the world has ever known.

The use of knives as a medium of trade and barter is not a new fad, as is collecting for the purpose of display. You would miss the mark to think that knife trading began with the typical crowd of "mule beaters" gathered around county courthouses. The closeness with which knives are associated with trade is illustrated by the fact that ancient Chinese used "knife money," a bronze coin with a blade protruding from its edge, many years before the West was civilized. One might even say that pocketknives have been the closest thing to pocket money since "grandpa's great grandpa was a pup."

Recently a new dimension has been added to this trade media. This addition is the sport and recreation of knife collecting. Many features, components, and characteristics now must be considered in determining the value of knives. The hobby has grown to such an extent that large amounts of money are exchanged by those seeking to improve their collections. With the economy the way it is, one needs a lot of technical know-how to participate in the knife trading/collecting game to make it more interesting and, of course, profitable.

Collecting, trading, and learning about knives is a fun game! With some knowledge of the game, you can develop a serious interest in the hobby, build a collection, stay "even," and perhaps make a profit. Some collectors with experience in investment fields maintain that knives are safer and many times more profitable than stocks and bonds.

Also, there is a tremendous range in the market value of knives. This provides everyone an opportunity to take part in the hobby, according to their financial means. While some rare old brands have reached very high market values, there are other brands which may be acquired for only a few dollars. Then there is always the "sleeper" awaiting discovery, which lures the collector and investor. A sleeper may be bought for a song and resold for enough to buy the concert hall. Every collector is looking for one of these. Luck, of course, plays a role in making a find. Knowledge and experience are even more important in determining whether or not the collector recognizes the find and takes advantage of it.

Definite collecting trends and changes are always surfacing of which both the new and experienced collector should be aware. Since original and antique knives are rarely seen in great condition on today's market, "new" or "mint" knives, such as the bicentennial commemoratives, reproductions, replicas, some counterfeits, limited productions, souvenirs, and custom-made knives are finding a place on the collector market. Because prices are still rising, inexperienced collectors can lose their socks if they do not invest wisely and selectively.

It is certainly worthwhile to read a few good books, subscribe to current literature, and become generally knowledgeable before wading in too deep. Many knives, as most experienced collectors have learned, are not destined to quickly increase in value. The amount you invest in a knife depends on the purpose for which it is being purchased. Knives bought to be resold are in one category. Those purchased to beef up a collection or as a long-term investment are in an entirely different category. It is always useful to know the seller, the market, and of course the collector value of a knife which you are planning to purchase.

The prominent trends in the new millennium will most likely be specialization in specific patterns, brands, or styles. Many veteran collectors have already moved in this direction. They are selling many rare old knives from their collections to buy specific patterns and/or brands. Some dealers are catering to the collectors' trade by buying and breaking up some nice collections, putting them back into circulation. Watch for this. It gives collectors an opportunity to examine, and perhaps even acquire, some old masterpieces which they've only been able to read about or look at in displays. However, don't get upset with the dealer if the price of one of these knives seems high. He is in business to make a profit and probably had to drop a bundle in order to get the collection which contained the knife which interests you.

Always be on the look-out for the old "boogie man," the counterfeit. Although they are rather obvious to the collector with even a little experience, they are still on the market. Don't expect them to go away. As long as collectors are willing to pay the high dollar for the rare "mint" knife, there will be someone who is willing to supply it. While there is no defense for the counterfeiter, his actions are shared by those who blindly pay the price for his products. Reputable dealers will generally stand behind their product, if you have reason to doubt its authenticity.

There has been such a strong demand from collectors in recent years that many new cutlery firms, new producers, distributors, and dealers have begun to surface. Very few of these new firms actually manufacture their own knives. Most of them have their knives made abroad. The Orient has become a most popular source of this new cutlery. Japan, for example, makes knives with skill and artistry which equals and sometimes exceeds the products of Western manufacturers. The quality of Oriental knives, as that of other modern products being made there, can no longer be blindly sneezed at. So, unless brand, age, and tradition are main factors in your collection, you can buy Oriental knives with confidence.

A current bright spot for the knife collector is the renewed use of natural handle materials which have not been on the market, in many cases, since the early 1950s. Of course, quantities may be limited and the prices will be high, but for materials such as genuine stag, bone, pearl, and abalone, they will be worth it! Plastics, such as gold and silver glitter, swirls, candy stripe, and Christmas tree, are available again. These add color to one's collection as well as to the market place.

This knife is an excellent example of Japanese crafts-manship. Note the hand filework on the blades and backsprings. The beautifully fitted mother-of-pearl handles and the polished and fitted nickel silver bolsters and dividers further enhance the knife. (Distributed by United Cutlery)

We recommend these new knives with natural handle material, quality steel, and workmanship as good potential investments. In our unpredictable economy, the prices of quality cutlery with natural scales will surely increase, regardless of brand or where they are made. So what about that inflation hedge everyone is looking for?

As you read the following chapters, we suggest that you pay attention to the characteristics that make knives collectors' items, the methods used to determine brands, conditions, and the histories, however brief, of companies and their stampings. These will help you to identify the good buys, as well as the overpriced knife, and will make collecting more fun. Visit trade marts, flea markets, junk and antique shops, estate auctions, and whenever possible, knife shows. Talk to dealers, collectors, and traders, and learn from them. You will find them to generally be among the nicer people with whom you have an opportunity to associate. Ask for their advice. Most everyone will be more than willing to share their opinion with you. The bottom line, however, is to *never* pass up an opportunity to learn!

Knife collecting can be a very addictive hobby. It can take up a disproportionate amount of time and energy. For this reason, you should share your interest with your spouse. You could easily find your interest in knife collecting becoming a part of shopping trips and vacations on which you are accompanied by your spouse. You may find that he/she too is adept at trading and collecting. Some of the best traders you encounter at knife shows and flea markets can be women. So if the opportunity for consuming time is there, perhaps you should consider ways to combine your hobbies in a mutual interest affair. One author (Roy) relates how he did so successfully. His example follows:

> *I had promised my wife for years that I would take her on vacation to Europe to see some of the scenes I remembered from World War II days. Finally, in the spring of 1969, I decided to live up to the promise. We spent a very pleasant month roaming the cities and hamlets of several European countries in our rented Volkswagen. I haunted the cutlery shops and knife factories, while my better half pursued her interest in antique and Bavarian china shops. It turned out to be not only a very enjoyable vacation, but a real education as well. Since then we have made many such trips and never failed to enjoy them.*

Isn't such a trip intriguing? Exceptionally fine quality knives are still being manufactured in Germany, England, Switzerland, France, and several other European countries. It is possible to find some of the fine natural scale materials such as European stag, fine woods, and mother-of-pearl, too. However, in spite of the economy of the 2000s, prices continued to increase. The collector/buyer who is looking for bargains in new knives should look to the Orient and to former Communist bloc countries which are economically and politically working toward market economies. The efforts of these countries to become competitive will soon result in finely made cutlery products.

The average collector/trader will doubtlessly become interested also in related items, such as sheath knives and razors, in spite of himself. Among all those pocketknives one looks at, there are bound to be some beautiful sheath knives which were made by highly respected old firms such as Winchester, Kinfolk, Cattaraugus, etc. There will be a temptation to add them to your collection. Yield to it! These old sheath knives can add interest and value to your collection. Hunting or sheath knives have a collectible value comparable to some pocketknives of the same brand and condition.

A current trend of many sportsmen is to buy their hunting knives custom made. Many artisans are working in this field and turning out some exquisite works of art. These may seem somewhat expensive. How-

7-Day set from the Rollie Yoder collection.

ever, like other works of investment grade art, they are likely to increase rapidly in value. This is a good field for the collector/investor, but it does involve high finances to collect knives made by the top ranking artists. Still, you may want to buy one or two, even though you can't afford to collect them.

Old razors, too, have become popular items to collect along with knives and other cutlery items. Many of our outstanding knife makers once manufactured them, and some still do. A number of collectors now specialize in razors. In fact, the popularity of razor collecting has grown to the point that we have written a separate book on the subject. If you have an interest in razors, we urge you to pick up a copy of *The Standard Guide to Razors, Identification and Values, 2nd Edition* by Roy Ritchie and Ron Stewart. The chapter on straight razors in this book draws heavily on that guide.

Finally, in the related field of cutlery are those marvelous old kitchen carving knives and carving sets that were once the pride and joy of every household. These were the knives that cutlery firms once deployed their top artisans to design. Many of them are elegant and efficient works of art in sterling, stag, pearl, and bone. Really, they are the masterpieces of cutlery art that collectors have largely overlooked. It would be extremely unwise to pass them up.

A good pocketknife is, in reality, a precision instrument which can be compared to a fine watch. It has springs which must apply just the right tension and moving parts that are expected to wear for generations, when properly maintained. Quality blades are forged from the best steel the age of science produces and then enclosed in a brass or nickel silver framework. This magnificent tool is then covered with scales, or handles, made from some of nature's most beautiful and durable materials. Among the more attractive of these are stag, bone, mother-of-pearl, abalone, rosewood, cocobolo, walnut, and jacaranda. Even precious metals are sometimes used in the handles of pocketknives. Although beautiful handles do not increase the quality of the knife, you can bet that they make them a darn sight more valuable. True quality is built into a knife by the experienced hands of a craftsman, performing numerous hand operations. It is then enhanced by the pride of the manufacturer in his product. Machines, though helpful in speeding up production, cannot make premium pocketknives. The W.R. Case Cutlery Company and Queen Cutlery insist that over 200 hand operations go into every Case pocketknife it produces. The blades, backsprings, bolsters, shields, and handles of a quality knife will usually have a scintillating polished finish. The springs will be flush with the edges of the bolster, handles, and liners. The blades will come to their open and shut positions with a snap that the old timers called "talking to you." Delicate adjustments, which enable the movements to be as smooth as they would if they turned on ball bearings, require the work of the human hand, the experience and skill of a craftsman, and the appreciative eye of an artist.

Unfortunately, the establishment of tradition and the possession of know-how does not always ensure quality, one of the first things one should look for in a knife. In a society like ours, the desire for profit and the demand for a product can sometimes short-circuit quality controls. During the first quarter of the twentieth century, for example, these factors had an observable effect on cutlery produced by some firms in the United States. Some manufacturers during the 1920s and '30s found the costs of automation and mass production to be threats to their profit margins and began producing shoddy, novelty-type knives instead of the quality cutlery upon which their reputations were built. The schoolboy's rhyme, "Tin handles and pewter blades, Best ole knife that ever was made," had a ring of truth that should have been embarrassing to a self-respecting cutler. Pride in these products was impossible! Many were stamped only with "Made in U.S.A." The public rejected these knives because of the careless manner in which they were made. This rejection, accompanied by the hard times that came with the Depression, caused many of these companies to go under.

Some firms, however, did not yield to this temptation but continued to carry on the traditions of fine cutlery which had been established by their founders. When the pendulum of public demand swung again toward quality, they were ready and willing to meet the demand. Of course European firms were also ready to help out, and the number of imported knives began to increase again during the 1950s.

Inflation is a culprit with which our cutlery firms always have to contend. It has taken its toll in the form of cutbacks on natural handle materials and a severe restriction in the variety of patterns available. At this time, Oriental cutlery firms are rising to the occasion. They are producing quality knives for cheaper prices. Of course, a large number of factors, including the value of the dollar on foreign markets, the oil shortage, and the cost of labor, must be considered when commenting on today's market. In spite of this, some American cutlery firms will survive and continue to produce quality cutlery.

A bright light found amid all the current problems is the attention cutlery is receiving from the general public. Knife collectors and connoisseurs are greatly responsible for this. Their interest has sparked new life into the business and art of pocketknife manufacture. A willingness on the part of the consumer to pay a fair, if somewhat higher, price for quality cutlery has been recognized by many of our major companies, and they are working to adjust to this standard. Perhaps in the near future we can look forward to production knives which emphasize marks of art and excellence instead of "hold the price down" cutlery.

For many years there has been a general consensus that the finest cutlery in the world are the premium quality, hand forged pocketknives made in England, Germany, or the United States. These countries have long-standing traditions of manufacturing quality products to back up their brands. Other countries make some fine knives, but they either lack experience in the area of pocketknives or are latecomers. They have not yet built the reputation for products that cutlers must traditionally maintain. This tradition is very important for maintaining consistency in cutlery products.

The availability of quality steel has always played an important part in determining the standards of a product. The cutlers of England and Germany went to great lengths to obtain steel that would maintain the standards upon which they had built their reputations. The steelmaker of the nineteenth century, because of the technology of his time, needed the highest grade of iron to turn out steel adequate for cutting instruments. The best ores of that time were obtained from Sweden and India. Knife firms which had built their reputations on fine cutlery went to great lengths to obtain this ore. They recognized its importance and used the metal's origin to help sell their cutlery. It is not unusual to find the products of an English or German knifemaking firm with "Swedish Steel etc.," added to their brand name. An example of this usage, common to most collectors, was the "John Primble, India Steel Works" knife.

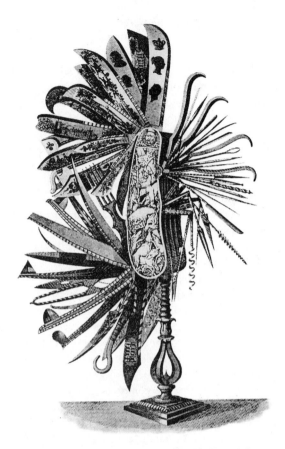

This knife, on display at Cutler's Hall in Sheffield, is known as "The Norfolk Knife." It was made by Rogers for the 1875 Exhibition. It was auctioned during the 1960s, purchased by Cooper Bros. (silverplate firm), and placed on permanent loan at Cutler's Hall, a must-stop for any knife collector visiting England.

Modern technology and steel refining techniques have made the source of extremely high-quality ore less important than it was in the earlier days. This technology has also enabled steel manufacturers to introduce a more high carbon and rust resistant (stainless) steel to knife manufacturers around the world. Improvements in these metals have made them more acceptable to the consumer, so most modern companies have incorporated them into their cutlery lines. Today a new knife from any country that is making an effort to produce a quality product will be made of superior metals.

However, in the marketplace, the traditions built by the older cutlery firms are still recognized by the consumer. These reputations were not easily built nor are they easily forgotten. Sheffield steel has long been a recognized name in the world of knives. The name comes from one of the great industrial cities in England. It is located in Yorkshire, on the northern perimeter of England's "black country." Coal and iron ore lie so close together there that they sparked the Industrial Revolution. Access to these materials enabled this city to build a fine reputation for quality which dates back to the 1300s. Even during the days of knighthood, swords, and armor, Sheffield steel and fine handcrafted cutlery were legendary around the world. Today, the city's superb craftsmen still strive to keep the tradition alive by using the best of the old and tested hand-finished methods to turn out their beautiful "Made in Sheffield, England" knives.

"Solingen, Germany" is also a name linked to superior quality knives which still enjoys its traditional reputation. Solingen is the name of a city located in the Industrial Ruhr Valley of Western Germany. Since before the Crusades, the traditional occupation of its people has been making swords, knives, and other cutting instruments. Most of Solingen's steel comes from Sweden, where some of the finest steel making ore in the world is still mined. The heavy process of milling and forging is done in the cities' large plants. However, as has been the tradition, much of the fine detailed work in grinding, tempering, and hand finishing is done by cottage industry or in small factories. The quality has been maintained and is evident in the flawless perfection found in the better grade pocketknives imported from Solingen.

The United States, a relative newcomer, took a short cut in the process of building tradition. We directly inherited century-old skills when many of Europe's great cutlery artists migrated to this country. They played an important role in establishing the colonies' new industries. The Russell brothers, for example, recruited craftsmen from England and combined their skills with more modern industrial techniques of production to develop superior cutlery products. Other examples include the New York Knife Company, which was started by a group of cutlers from Sheffield in 1854, and the Camillus Cutlery Company which was formed by A. Koster and Brothers, a family of importers from Germany. The Koster brothers started their firm in 1875.

"Charter Oak" souvenir knife. Holley Manufacturing Company was the first to mass-produce pocketknives in the United States.

16

Knives made in America had to be darn good to compete with the English and German imports of the nineteenth century. This competition and our imported craftsmen helped our cutlery firms to establish a tradition of producing pocketknives which were of quality equal to the world's best. It is significant that we were able to attract European craftsmen to our country to help us build the industry. Pocketknives and other fine cutlery cannot be produced by amateurs. It takes time, skill, and training to become a master cutler. The apprentice knife maker begins learning his trade by making sheath knives or butcher knives. From these, he progresses to a more polished and better finished blade. Finally, he "graduates" to the most complicated of the line, the pocketknife. In this manner, quality is perpetuated to build knives that will be genuine collector items for years to come.

So remember that quality, tradition, and rareness go hand in hand. As quality is a prime consideration to the collector, perhaps the best place to look for it is in some old American brands.

Now, just what should you look for that might be worthy of investment potential? The categories of knives which fall under this heading will vary, depending on who is advising you. One of the most common of these, however, is the knife which has been made by a company that is no longer in business. There are literally hundreds of these old companies. Many of them made quality cutlery, but because of lack of demand, poor management, merger, depression, and any number of other reasons, they went under. These knives will probably increase in value, to paraphrase Will Rogers, "cause they ain't making any more of them." Even so, the knife of a relatively unknown brand may bring less money than one half its age about which a lot has been written. The market will often vary on these, simply because of available information about the knife's history.

Another common investment category includes knives with a discontinued pattern or stamping design made by a company which is still in production. The Case XX is an excellent example of this. These knives, whether Case or some other brand, will have a value that is influenced by the current popularity of the brand. Generally speaking, these too have more information available on them than do those from companies which are now out of business.

Sometimes a knife's shield, which indicative of high quality and rareness (Remington Bullet, Dog-head Kabar, etc.), will make a knife more valuable as a collector's item. Often these shields are of the profile type, connotating the knife's general use.

Knives of historical significance are in a special group of their very own. The variety of this kind of collection is limited only by the imagination of the collector. Sometimes only one or two knives can make a valuable collection. Just imagine the worth of a knife which was used for whittling by Abraham Lincoln or Jefferson Davis, and such knives do exist. Of course, documentation for this kind of collection is significant, perhaps more so than any other type. Some knives do

17

not have to have belonged to a famous person to be of historical significance. They may have been found on a battlefield or in an estate auction which would serve to date them. There are thousands of metal detectors around these days which people use to locate artifacts. Knives are not uncommon finds. If this should happen to you, a bit of advice concerning documentation is to use a camera to record your find. A knife found on the Wilderness Road or on the Santa Fe Trail, for example, could be worth a great deal if properly documented. A find like this will probably be rusty and perhaps in poor condition. If you are a handy man who likes to restore things, please don't "restore" it unless you want to destroy its historical value. Of course, you may do some light cleaning so long as you do not detract from the age or the look of the tool it was designed to be. If you are unsure, it would be better to make a duplicate of the knife and leave the original alone. Then you would have two collector items.

Since before the American Revolution, soldiers and sailors have been required to carry pocketknives as part of their survival equipment. A person interested in military knives can make one heck of a collection out of them. These knives were not designed to be used as combat weapons like swords, sheath knives, and bayonets, but in some cases may have served such a purpose. Some may have been acquired from old soldiers and can have an interesting history. If so, it is advisable to document the tool in the same way as you would one of other historical significance.

The military knife collector has a wide variety from which to choose. He will find military pocketknives somewhat different from others he has seen in that they usually have scales made of materials which are designed only to be durable and not decorative.

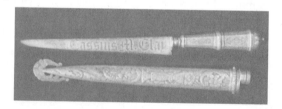

This knife is an excellent example of a knife of historical significance. Czar Alexander II presented it to Cassius M. Clay (U.S. Minister to Russia under Lincoln, Johnson, and Grant) at the end of his ministry in 1869. Clay and the Czar had become close friends during Clay's service to Russia. The choice of this gift, made by a Russian artisan especially for Clay, is evidence of the Czar's awareness of Clay's appreciation of fine cutlery. The estimated value of this knife is between three and five thousand dollars. (Photo by M. Lincoln)

Stampings may only have the country of origin or branch of service marked on them. For example, typical knives used in World War II were stamped U.S.A. or U.S.N. with no mention of the company which manufactured them. Others may have no identification at all. This does not affect their quality because they generally were designed specifically for armed forces survival kits. However, the absence of a company stamping will reduce the value of the knife.

The person attracted to the military knife may be interested in collecting custom-made knives which were ordered by soldiers. Many of these are of superb quality and were made by reputable knife makers. The Randall knife is an excellent example of a custom-made knife that has been going into combat since World War II and has proven itself over and over. They are of excellent steel and are tempered so well that they can cut some metals as well as wood. In 1944, President Ronald Reagan (then Captain Reagan of the U. S. Army Air Corps) ordered a custom knife from W. D. "Bo" Randall. There are any number of directions to take in building a collection of military knives and related items.

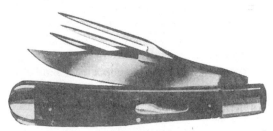

Knives similar to this diner's knife have been a part of a soldier's equipment throughout history.

Mostly in a group by themselves are the silver fruit knives from the nineteenth century. Designed specifically for cutting fruit, their blades, and handles usually, are made of silver alloy to prevent rusting. Some blades have also been made of gold.

English silver fruit knife, the type which was very popular in the 1800s. (See others on pages 531 and 539.)

Needless to say, these attractive knives were a favorite of the ladies, and the artful embellishments of engraving and sculpture work on handles and blades were done to please them.

Of course, with the coming of stainless steel, these knives had served their purpose and were phased out. However, they made their mark in the collecting field and have become a highly collectible class of cutlery with a likewise high collector value.

In the same context, those knives made by our major gun manufacturers are among the most desirable collector items in the field. Notably Winchester, Remington, and Marbles, all of which have discontinued their line of pocketknives, command premium prices. Knives with the old gun company trademark are reappearing as authorized reissues/reproductions/limited editions, commemoratives, etc. These new knives are generally of good quality, as were their namesakes. Also, during the 1970s some other gun companies adopted lines of knives, usually manufactured by other makers, stamped with their brands. These are collectible, but generally are highly priced for new knives.

For the person who is interested in the smaller, pretty, and generally unusual knife, the novelty knife is worth his or her consideration. Particular groupings of novelty knives are now re-emerging in specialized collecting fields. Although they may overlap in style and purpose, they can be classified roughly as advertisers, souvenirs, commemoratives, and figurals. Many of the older ones such as "The Brown Shoe Company," "Anheuser Busch," and original "Coca-Cola," are higher than a piggy-bank's roost.

Another classification of knives that are collector items with a wide range of values, and which we will endeavor to define, is the field of "art knives," knives that have been given special treatment by the manufacturer or craftsman to make them more attractive or appealing than other knives of similar types.

This is, in general, a broad classification that includes knives in most other categories, such as fruit knives, figurals, and souvenirs, where they are above the average in esthetic appeal.

However, art knives should not be considered as a new cult collectible or classification. Since before King Arthur's time, swords have been decorated with gold, silver, and precious stones. The Romans, who possessed the first known folding knives, carved their handle material to resemble figures of men or beasts. (See photo, page 7.)

In later years cutlers used semi-precious, natural material such as tortoise shell, pearl, abalone, and ivory to beautify and handle their knives. Synthetics, such as celluloid and plastics, were used as colorful goldstone, sparkle, Christmas tree, and picture handles. These were more modern decorations, and sailors developed the art of scrimshander or scrimshaw (carving on whale ivory) during their long passages at sea.

Today what are considered true art knives are more closely defined and usually originate in the custom knife field. They generally consist of eloquent designs with engraving, sculpture, scrimshaw, file work, etching, etc.

Art knives of today are often embellished with semi-precious stones such as turquoise, onyx, and coral. A wide variety of exotic woods may be included in the artist's knife handle. It is not unheard of to find dinosaur bone or mastodon ivory being used as knife scales. In the hands of a craftsman, these materials can be used to create true beauty. The custom knifemakers working in this arena are truly turning the concept of the art knife into a field of genuine knife artistry.

These knives are expensive, as should be expected. However, like all works of art, their value will almost surely increase with age.

Remember though, generally speaking the older knives are the ones to seriously consider. They are symbols of the past. Some of the shiny, new reproductions are a dime a dozen (or should be) and are being stamped out by the thousands. Many of them are of such low quality that they are practically worthless. Modern collectors have a tendency to forget, however, that while the old souvenir and commemoratives, such as those once sold at World's Fairs and tourist meccas, are below average in quality, they are great collector's items! This is simply because of their age and origin. An original "Von Hindenberg" com-

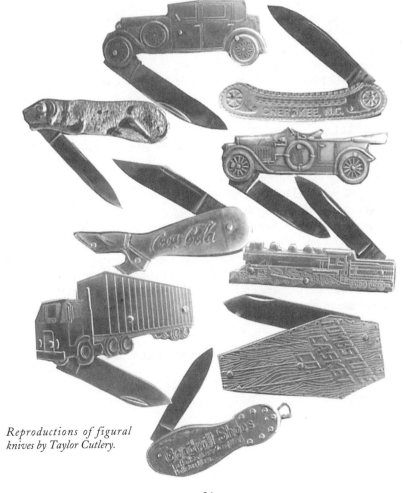

*Reproductions of figural
knives by Taylor Cutlery.*

21

memorative or an old "Royal Canadian Mounted Police" souvenir knife, which sold only a few years ago for between eight and ten dollars, now may easily bring several times that amount.

Since the knife collecting boom began, many people began collecting recently made commemoratives, limited edition and reproduction knives. This too can be considered as a separate category. Some of these knives like "The Kentucky Rifle" and "Case Bicentennial" have increased in value many times the original price. Club knives too have grown in value at a rapid rate and may be considered in this grouping. However, all commemoratives and limited editions have not seen increased values. Many may be purchased now at less than half the issue price. So don't be taken in just because it is a limited edition. Study the quality of the cutlery, its handle material, and its manufacturer, and compare the price with others before you buy. It may take some time and you may not get in on the "ground floor," but your efforts may prevent you from becoming the proud owner of a "turkey."

We mentioned the custom knife earlier and advised that, if your interests lay in their collection, you should be prepared with a rather fat bank roll. These knives are often works of art and should be appreciated as such. They are worthy of the investment they require. After all, if an artisan works on his products as long and as hard as these fellows must, in order to produce the outstanding cutlery that they do, then they should have adequate compensation. We do not advise the purchase of custom knives as short-term investments but instead as pieces of art which you can keep and appreciate over the years. If anything can produce that kind of enjoyment, it is well worth the investment.

The theme of the 1939 World's Fair is easily identified on the handles of these World's Fair knives. (The Lloyd Stewart collection)

The last type of collecting category we will discuss is the figurals. These knives are made in the general shape of some object such as a fish, bird, animal, gun, shoe, etc. The older of these are generally very expensive. They were not usually well made and were designed to catch the tourist trade. However, many of them, like the previously described advertising knives, bear inscriptions of objects and events that indicate their dates. They provide a wide variety of unusual knives for collecting, and many veteran collectors do specialize only in these knives.

Perhaps by now you have gathered that knife collecting as a sport or hobby can be educational, mind expanding, and recreational. There are so many interesting facts and facets involved in knives' becoming collector's items that the possibilities are almost unlimited. If you become involved, you can't help learning something about an awful lot of things. You will pick up bits and pieces of knowledge from history, geography, mathematics, science, art, and a lot of other subjects that weren't taught in school. Big Ed DeCoursey, an Eastern Kentucky mountain man and long-time knife trader, perhaps properly summed it up by saying, "I'm just an old country boy and there's enough here to bust my head!"

After all the justifications for knife trading and collecting have been used and all the rational arguments exhausted, if you really want to know why knife collecting will be around for quite a while as a hobby, ask someone who has been at it for years. He'll tell you, "It's plain fun!"

Custom-made knives such as this can be appreciated for their workman-ship and as works of art, as well as their utility potential. This knife was made by Gene Baskett, Elizabethtown, Ky. (From the Barry Robinson collection)

EXPLODED VIEW OF POCKETKNIFE PARTS

Pivot (or bolster pins)

Handle (or scale)

Bolsters

Shield

Small Blade

Master Blade

Liner

Caplift & Screw Driver

Bolster

Backspring

Divider

Punch

Back Spring Pin

Bolster

Backspring

Liner

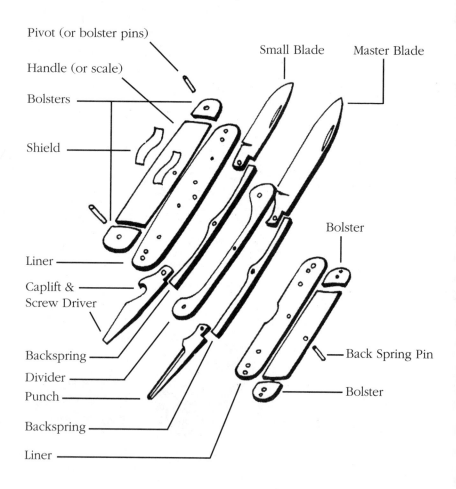

Few people in today's world ever take the time to speculate as to why an ordinary, simple pocketknife, in addition to its essential parts, should have a shield on the handle. What's its purpose? Is it just another useless piece of decoration which adds expense to a manufacturing process? Just another cost that is passed on to the customer?

In order to understand something as important as the shield, it is necessary to look at its origin or history. The knife shield is little more than an anachronism from medieval days when the bold Knights of the Round Table emblazoned their battle shields with symbols and slogans signifying their dauntless feats of arms in battle. These added legend and glory to their family names. Later, these much decorated battle shields were to become their personal family "Coat of Arms," "Crest," or "Escutcheons" and were passed on, along with the family's history, to the descendants of the knight.

This family symbol was a method of identification and was affixed to finger rings and seals, decorative plaques, stationery, and most every item of family pride. This would eventually include items of armor and cutlery. The first application of this family symbol to swords and large fighting knives was in the form of engravings and etchings on the blades. Later, and more permanently, the "escutcheon" was applied to the handles or scales as small plaques. These retained the shape of the battle shield or crest. Sometimes a "Monk-Scroll" design was used with the family name inscribed lengthwise on it. This, then, was the origin of the term "escutcheon" which is used today to describe those used on fixed-blade knives. The term "shield" is used more commonly in reference to the symbol on the folding or pocketknife.

The family shield or coat of arms is the ancestor of the shield found on many pocketknives. Many collectors do not consider a knife to be fully dressed without a shield.

The English folding knifemakers did not generally attach shields to their early 16th century products. Cutlers were not long, however, in discovering the effectiveness of the little gadgets for eye-catching sales appeal. The shield soon became a symbol of pride in workmanship and of the skill and "tender-loving-care" that went into the knife's making. A token of quality, this tradition has lingered through centuries and seems to still be around today.

Some manufacturers will tell you that the shield is nothing but an expensive bauble that is non-functioning and as useless as "teats on a boar hog." Some have dropped them from their line of cutlery. However, public reaction to this type of change quickly convinced those who are still in business that perhaps the shields aren't such a bad idea.

Seldom does a cutlery buff look at a knife without immediately noticing the shield. They find them to be both attractive and a means of identifying the brand or maker. To many, the shield is one of the most important distinguishing features of the knife. Some collect knives because of the shield design alone. The collector who has an appreciation of shield designs gets a deep, gut-burning desire when he sees one of those old "Dog-head Kabars," the "Silver Bullet" shield of a Remington, or the Utica "Buffalo Head" shield. In addition to these, other shields like the Remington "Acorn" and the Western "Bullhead" have a reputation of directly affecting the value of knives. They push their value beyond the point where they can be appraised on a standard scale for other knives of the same pattern. Since there are "Variations" close-up, you will find them listed separately alongside other knives of the same brand.

During the current rebirth of cutlery, the shield is again receiving special attention. It is often an outstanding feature of commemorative knives which proliferate the market. While we cannot actually say that these new shields increase the quality or usefulness of these modern cutlery instruments, they do give the average collector a measure by which he may separate them from common mill production.

Shields often contribute to the value of knives. The profile-type shields seem to be most notable in this respect. Because they can add to the value, we think it is important for you to recognize their different classifications and nomenclature as indicated.

The following are the six most common geometric patterns with examples of how each may vary.

Profile	Medallion	Oval	Scroll	Crest	Bar

The origin of bone's use as a handle material for knives is buried so deeply in ancient history that probably the first use of it for this purpose can never be accurately determined. Through speculation we can perhaps safely assign responsibility for its initial use as a handle material to the first tool makers who used the bone of some dinosaur, pterodactyl, mastodon, or even sabre toothed tiger to handle his flint or jasper knife or his ax blade. Perhaps the idea of this utilization came along because of his previous use of a splintered bone for a cutting edge of sorts. In any event, surely the availability of this material, its characteristics of being durable and workable, and the relative ease with which it could be sawed or shaped made the use of bone for knife handles a logical choice of our earliest tool makers.

To move from the time of the first tool makers to the Industrial Revolution is quite a jump. However, after making that leap, you find the characteristics that early man found attractive about bone as a knife handling material were still, at that time, held in esteem by knife makers. Availability, durability, and the relative ease for shaping all stood time's test to insure the material's continued and wide use. The early English and American cutlers had little difficulty in securing suitable bone for their knife-handling materials.

When the Industrial Revolution began in England, slaughter houses and meat packing firms had already become a prominent feature of the urban landscape. Bone was considered a waste product, and these early butchering houses would almost pay for having it hauled away. Cutlers, as a result, used bone almost exclusively.

Early bone scales primarily had sawed or smooth finishes. Occasionally, the handles of a knife were carved to represent animals or men but they seldom were dyed or colored. As the industry developed, cutlers branched out to using stag and shell for their more fancy handle patterns. Of these, they discovered that stag handles were very well liked because of the rough, warm feel it has in the hand. This preference prompted the introduction of jigged bone in an effort to simulate the look and feel of stag.

The era of abundant bone ended abruptly, however, when the need to feed an expanding population demanded that fertilizers be used to enrich the soil. Ground bone or bone meal became a principal part of many fertilizers. Slaughter houses quickly learned it was more profitable to sell bone waste to fertilizer factories than to process it for the cutlery trade. This cut sharply into the supply of bone for cutlery purposes.

If the fertilizer market was not enough to complicate matters, the use of bone as an additive in the manufacture of materials such as light-sensitive camera film certainly was! Competition became so stiff that cutleries began importing bone from less industrialized areas, such as Argentina, where one of the chief national products is the production of beef. Here, knife companies found suppliers willing to boil the meat from bones and export them to North America. This new source of supply helped, but it did not completely alleviate the shortage which still continues. According to our information, the W.R. Case Cutlery Company negotiates a special trade agreement with Eastman Kodak to insure a limited supply of bone for their knives.

Since the factory production of clasp knives and pocketknives began, the leg or shin bone of cattle has been the most commonly used handle material. This is likely because a good supply has always been available. It does not mean, however, that bone from other animals has not been, and is not being used. "Bullet" brand knives from Pakistan often use camel bone as their primary handle material. We have seen some recent specialty knives handled in mastodon bone.

We were especially amused by a somewhat macabre item which appeared in a New York knife auction — a Tibetan prayer knife, with handles purportedly made from the bone of a Tibetan monk! (We have yet to figure how to include that one in our evaluation scales!) Nevertheless, the bulk of industrial bone scales has always been from domesticated cattle.

Although South American bone supplies have frequently been interrupted when "Hoof and Mouth" disease has struck South American herds, the most severe shortages came about during World Wars I and II when German submarines made sea lanes hazardous to shipping between North and South America. During these times, cutleries searched frantically for suitable substitutes for bone.

Early plastics were made and test marketed. Celluloid, an early type of plastic, was found to be inexpensive and very easy to make, mold, and color. Clear celluloid provided a see-through window under which could be placed pictures and advertising. This became the favorite material for many novelty and, of course, advertising knives. However, celluloids were extremely flammable and became unstable with age.

Hard rubber was marketed under such trade names as Gutta Percha and Bakelite. This handle material was not as pretty as celluloids but was non-flammable and more durable. It was also used extensively during the war years. This rubber-based material closely resembled black-dyed bone when it was jigged. Collectors now refer to it as "rough black" when it is jigged and "slick black" when it is smooth and polished. Because they are reasonably rare, these old materials currently fetch premium prices.

The hardships encountered by cutlery firms in securing and maintaining adequate supplies of bone gave rise to companies whose sole purpose was to supply this product. Two of the most notable of these were the Winterbottom

Materials Company and the Rogers Material Company. They furnished handle materials for many of the cutlery firms in operation at this time.

Winterbottom bone is perhaps easiest to recognize because of its long, lengthwise groove design which somewhat resembles the roughness of stag. Their chief customer was Queen Cutlery. Rogers bone, on the other hand, is characterized by irregular, short but heavy jigged pits, with the rounded top surface polished down for a smooth firm grip.

The Rogers bone style is perhaps the most extensively used of all jigging styles. Neither of these styles was original with these two companies, as a little study of very old cutlery catalogs will quickly show.

After these firms ceased operations, cutlery firms that used material from them continued these jigging styles. Queen Cutlery, for example, even carried the Winterbottom style over to their Delrin line. Case's jigging style is very similar to Rogers bone.

Cutlery firms which had not used Winterbottom or Rogers bone extensively developed different styles of jigging for their knives. Schrade, for example, developed a "peach seed bone" which had a more elite or dense type of jig pattern. Camillus Cutlery used a jigging style resembling wrinkled tree bark or light, rough stag.

Most companies also began dyeing bone at about the same time they began their own jigging. Dark brown was the preferred color, but they found bone did not always take colors in a predictable manner. This can be aptly illustrated by examining age lines of knives made by the W.R. Case Company. Case purportedly has always used the same dye, but many Case handles made during the 1940s have a distinctively green tint, while many of those of the 1950s appear to be a rather deep red. Of course, age and sunlight can be responsible for the fading of almost any dye, but most of the beautiful old green, red, and honeycomb from these years were created, unintentionally, by unstable dyes.

Were handle color inconsistencies a handicap for the cutlery market? Shucks, no! The public loved the unusual variations in color that made the knives they purchased one-of-a-kind items. Collectors still appreciate them and use handle color as a clue in determining the age of some knives.

Some companies endeavored in a deliberate way to dye their knife handles colors which could not be considered as natural. Outstanding among these were the Queen Winterbottom Green and the Robeson Strawberry Red. These old knives have become prizes for collectors. They were dropped during the 1950s to be replaced with plastic imitations. The collector's market has brought them back! Authentic reproductions of many fine old Winchesters, Remingtons, Schatt and Morgans, Cases, Cattarauguses, and others are making the old styles and handle materials available to collectors today. Fortunately, most of these knives are marked or dated so they will not be mistaken for their older cousins. Because of the care given to their accurate re-creation and identification as such, these knives will also enter the collector's market and become sought after.

In the decades following World War II, from 1950 to the 1970s, it looked as if bone-handled pocketknives would become a thing of the past. They were being supplanted by new and improved types of plastics with trade names like Delrin and Micarta. These new plastics were good. They had little tendency to crack, check, or shrink. They were practically indestructible. However, instead of their lustre and patina improving with age, they tended to grow dull and less attractive. Seemingly, a love affair had developed between collectors and the flaws associated with genuine bone. Many of the things once complained about by collectors became treasured quirks of the trade and "increased the value" of the knives.

This preference for genuine bone was recognized by knife companies and is probably responsible for the abandonment of some of the trend toward bone substitutes as knife handle material. Case has gone back to using bone almost exclusively for handles. Most of the other old companies are using bone at least in their limited edition knives and commemoratives. New companies too have gotten in on the game. Import companies such as Taylor Cutlery and Frost Cutlery have knives made to their specifications in Japan and use bone extensively, especially on their fine reproductions and the sleek new custom-like designs, which they are marketing today. In short, bone is back! We predict it is here to stay!

The use of smooth bone, as opposed to jigged bone, began a comeback with the introduction of Case's highly successful "Appaloosa." It is no longer uncommon to see this style scales on knives today. Smooth bone is used extensively on import knives from the Orient. It is also used by many U.S. cutlery companies and some English and German ones. It is often dyed in a variety of colors and maintains the same characteristics of other type bone we have already described.

Currently, a large variety of dyes are being used to impregnate bone in such ways that you can find bone handles in every color of the rainbow. The stability of these colors is amazing, when compared to the dyes used just 20 or so years ago. Also, you should not be surprised to find dinosaur bone used in knife handles today. Even though it is generally a novelty, the MOP Company, which is a major surplus of knife handle materials in this country, shows dinosaur bones in its current line.

So, can increasing one's knowledge of the history of bone-handled knives be used as a reliable means for identifying old knives with worn-away brand stamping? It can at least be helpful, but remember that cutlers used different styles of jigging at different periods and that dye effects were extremely varied.

A working knowledge of bone can be very useful in spotting counterfeits and rehandled knives. Knife brand and age identification based on handle material alone are very tricky. When used, these should be combined with other methods for determining positive identification.

Bone as a handle material has earned its reputation in use and has stood the test of time. So long as it is available, we expect it to play an important part in the knife industry. It was here yesterday, and it will be here tomorrow.

All knife patterns are logical or were when they were first designed. When you think about them and the way they were constructed, you can see that each pattern was created to increase efficiency and convenience for a particular task. As a result, we believe the common old pocketknife, when chosen to meet the particular needs of the owner, imparts greater satisfaction and pride than any other tool ever acquired.

In the early days of the Roman Empire when the first folding knives were created, the innovators were not thinking of design or patterns. Their concern was how to get those darn razor-sharp blades tucked away from their tender and extremely vulnerable hides in such a way they could be carried safely and even slept with. Thus, the first crude folders consisted of only three parts: blade, hinge (or pivot) pen, and a slotted handle for the blade to fold into. This became the most durable and basic of all pocketknife patterns. The concept of all folding knives made since then have their roots in this Roman design. Of course there have been innovations, changes, and additions, many of which we will discuss, but the folding concept dates back to this Roman folder.

If you are around knives very much, you will doubtlessly see direct descendants of these early knives. Designed like a straight razor, they are perhaps made by some tinker who doesn't care for backsprings. These knives, without backsprings, have only a stop in the open position for the blade to rest against. They stay closed because of a snug, gripping action of the slot into which the blade closes.

Until the introduction of the spring knife during the 16th century, this was the only folding pattern known. For centuries in England and other European countries, it sold for the worth of a big English penny or less. For this reason it was dubbed the "Penny Knife" or "Penny Pattern." It is still a principal pattern which can be found in the markets of many non-industrialized countries. In India, street merchants peddle the simple brass "sikes" and in the West Indies or Caribbean, the "Banana Knife" or crude Navaja pattern with curved blades from 2" to 10" long is still very much in use.

Jack Knife.

The "backspring" folder originated somewhere in Europe. If we can believe the "Jacques de Liege" legend, it originated in or around the French city of Liege. Even if this was not the first, it surely as the monkey's tail was responsible for naming the "Jack Knife" pattern. This pattern, with its backspring design, quickly replaced the Penny knife with a safer and more sturdy tool that is still standard today. The primary distinguishing feature of the Jack pattern is that it has a blade, or blades, hinged on only one end of a backspring. For each additional blade, an additional backspring must be added to the knife frame. Experience has shown that when a knife has more than two backsprings, it appears somewhat out of proportion, bulky, and unbalanced. The addition of several backsprings and blades makes the knife feel heavy like a rock in one's pocket and about the same in the hand.

Office Pen Knife.

As with so many inventions, necessity became the mother of the "Pen Knife" pattern during the Victorian period. This small dainty pattern has blades hinged on both ends of the same backspring. It was made for the ladies and gentlemen of the court and first used for such menial tasks as trimming goose quill pens, fingernails, etc. So, it is easy to see how it acquired its name. In our present society, it is usually dubbed "Office Knife," "Fob Knife," or "Sunday Knife." As you may have already deduced, there is a bit more skill involved in the manufacturing of opposed blade knives. The blades must be so ground and angled that they pass each other and fit snugly in the same frame. Therefore when compared with jack knives of equal size and quality, the pen knife will be a bit more expensive.

Pen Knife by Holley Manufacturing Company.

The "Pen Knife" pattern's greatest contribution is that it opened the way to add more blades to a knife's framework without significantly increasing the thickness and weight. The Jack and Pen patterns are the basic or parent patterns from which the myriads of other patterns available today have evolved. Most have been developed through only slight changes or modifications of the originals. These changes generally have come in the form of an additional blade, change in blade style, alteration of size, or modification of the framework which has made the knife more suitable for a specific task.

Folding Dirk/Stiletto (Kissing Crane).

When the Jack Knife pattern evolved to where the blade was 4½" to 5" and was slender and pointed, it became the "Dirk" or "Stiletto" pattern. This design was used for fighting or self-protection. It appears that such a weapon was necessary during medieval times. This same type knife, with thicker stronger blades, became known as the "Trapper" and eventually the "Folding Hunter." As necessity demanded, changes were made to deal with ever-changing environmental needs. The name of the "new" pattern was generally determined by either the job for which it was designed or the shape or appearance of the knife itself.

Among the small and medium size two blade Jack patterns which are common today are the "Dog Leg," "Peanut" or "Serpentine," "Gunstock," "Barlow," "Physician" or "Pill-buster," "Copperhead," and "Game." The Jack pattern seems to have reached its peak in number of blades with the "Farrier's" or "Horseman's" knife. It had approximately eight blades which varied in type and included such items as hooks, gouges, and flem blades. It was so large that the owner had need for a leather pocket to carry it.

The Jack pattern became the most common, popular, and sturdy pattern of all time when it was changed by the English cutler named Barlow. He lengthened the bolsters of the Jack pattern for added strength and renamed it the "Barlow." For years, and sometimes today, this pattern was referred to as the "Jack Barlow."

Meanwhile, the little Pen Knife, with its two opposed blades and one backspring, grew and evolved into what are now known as the "Senator" and "Congress" pens, the "Pumpkin-seed," the "Canoe" and "Baby Canoe," the "Flatfish," the "Sunfish" or "Elephant's Toenail," "Rope Knife," "Moose," and all other patterns which have two opposing blades and one backspring.

With the addition of an extra backspring and three or more blades, the evolution continued with the introduction of patterns such as the "Cattle," the "Stockman," the "Warncliffe," "Whittler," "Congress" (4 blade), "Scout," and "Utility." We are sure that there are some that you can add to this list, but these are the basic ones.

It appears that when a folding knife has more than two backsprings, it loses much of its appeal to the buying public.

Farrier's Knife.

Some patterns, such as the "Lobster Pen," have used inner springs with blades hinged on both sides to avoid increasing the thickness of the knife. Some "Utility patterns," such as the "Swiss Army," have recessed the backsprings and hinged extra blades/tools (like corkscrews, punches, screwdrivers, toothpicks, etc.) in the central portion where they will half open and do not significantly increase the size. This pattern with light but durable handles and aluminum liners is gaining in popularity in many parts of the world, especially Europe, because of its versatility.

At some time or other, almost every small tool known has been added to the folding knife in addition to its customary cutting blades. Some examples that have been tried include button hooks, pliers, wrenches, and hatchets. Even small caliber, bullet firing, pistol-knives were marketed before they were ruled illegal. But in general, knife patterns have remained logical and have been designed to meet the needs of the times during which they were made. As a result, patterns are always important in determining the value of a knife.

Although some patterns have become obsolete in our changing society, their antiquated designs are clues that speak to us in knife collector language of another time and mode of living. These are fine collector items because new ones, more appropriate for the present, are taking their place. While age and rareness are tangible factors in determining a knife's value, the pattern is of major importance. And, as generally conceived, the collector value goes up with a pattern as the knife's size increases. Because of this, knife patterns are definitely a major component for appraising a knife's collector value. Any collector worth his salt should give serious consideration to the evolution of pocketknife patterns and the skill and logic behind every design. You will find on the following pages outline charts illustrating the most basic patterns and blade designs.

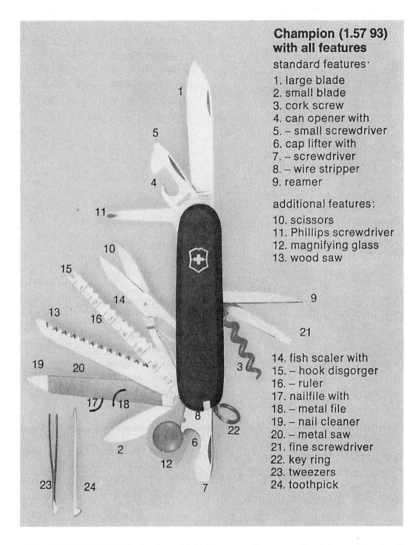

Champion (1.57 93)
with all features
standard features·
1. large blade
2. small blade
3. cork screw
4. can opener with
5. – small screwdriver
6. cap lifter with
7. – screwdriver
8. – wire stripper
9. reamer

additional features:
10. scissors
11. Phillips screwdriver
12. magnifying glass
13. wood saw

14. fish scaler with
15. – hook disgorger
16. – ruler
17. nailfile with
18. – metal file
19. – nail cleaner
20. – metal saw
21. fine screwdriver
22. key ring
23. tweezers
24. toothpick

This VICTORINOX "Swiss Army Knife" is an excellent example of the variety of tools which can be included on a knife. A knife similar to this is part of the tool kit issued to U. S. space shuttle astronauts.

35

PATTERN CHART

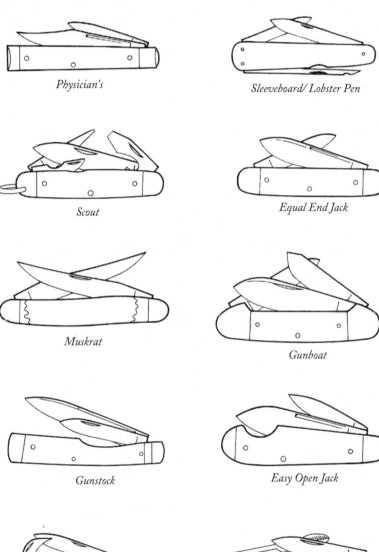

Physician's

Sleeveboard/ Lobster Pen

Scout

Equal End Jack

Muskrat

Gunboat

Gunstock

Easy Open Jack

Champagne or Bartender's

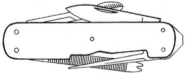

Fly Fisherman

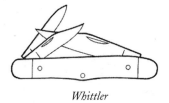

Whittler

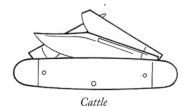

Cattle

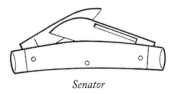

Senator

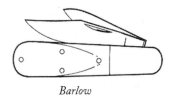

Barlow

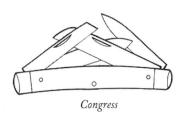

Congress

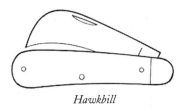

Hawkbill

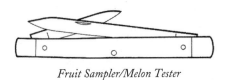

Fruit Sampler/Melon Tester

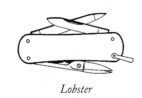

Lobster

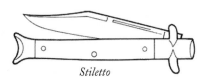

Stiletto

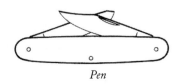

Pen

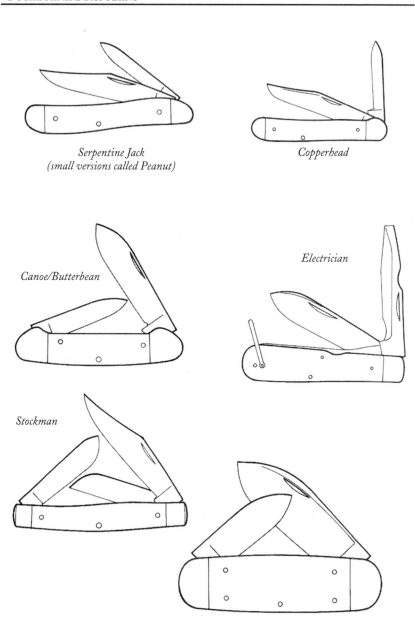

Serpentine Jack
(small versions called Peanut)

Copperhead

Canoe/Butterbean

Electrician

Stockman

Elephant's Toenail or Sunfish

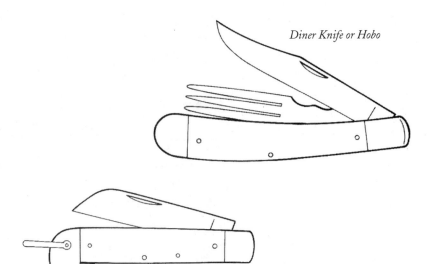

Diner Knife or Hobo

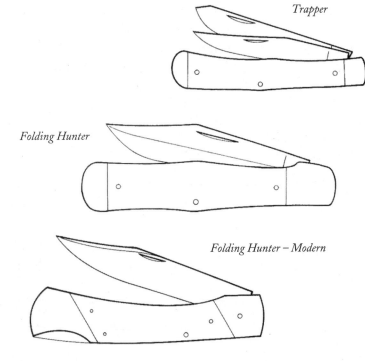

Marlin Spike or Rigger's Knife

Trapper

Folding Hunter

Folding Hunter – Modern

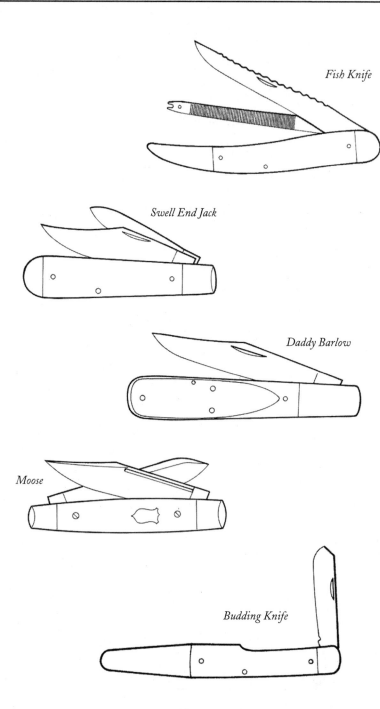

Fish Knife

Swell End Jack

Daddy Barlow

Moose

Budding Knife

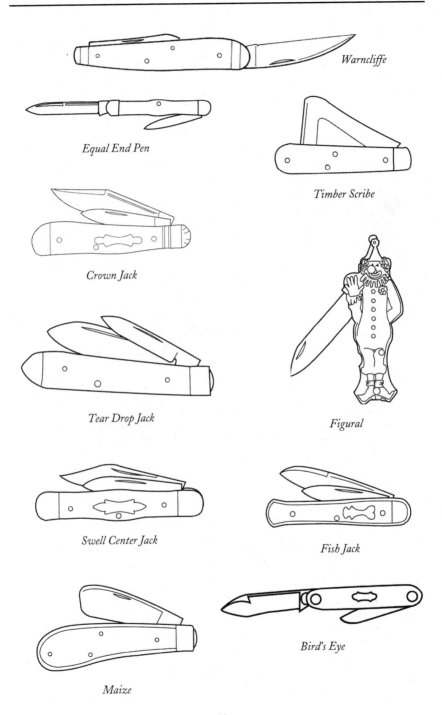

Warncliffe

Equal End Pen

Timber Scribe

Crown Jack

Tear Drop Jack

Figural

Swell Center Jack

Fish Jack

Maize

Bird's Eye

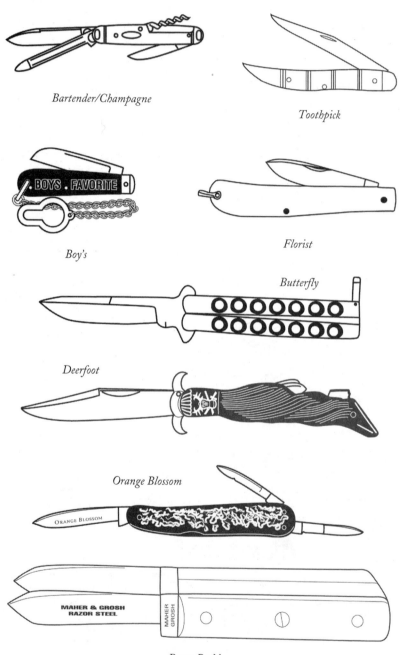

Bartender/Champagne

Toothpick

Boy's

Florist

Butterfly

Deerfoot

Orange Blossom

Pecan Budder

42

Grizzly or Clasp

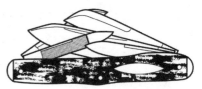

Humpback Congress

Spring Knife, automatic, switchblade

Sow Belly

Cotton Sampler

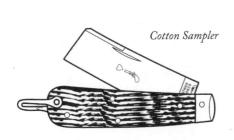

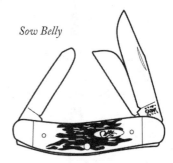

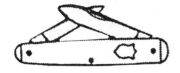

Sleeveboard Pen

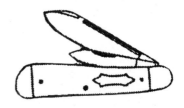

Dogleg Jack

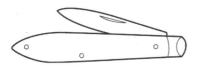

Quill/Pen

45

COMMON POCKETKNIFE BLADES

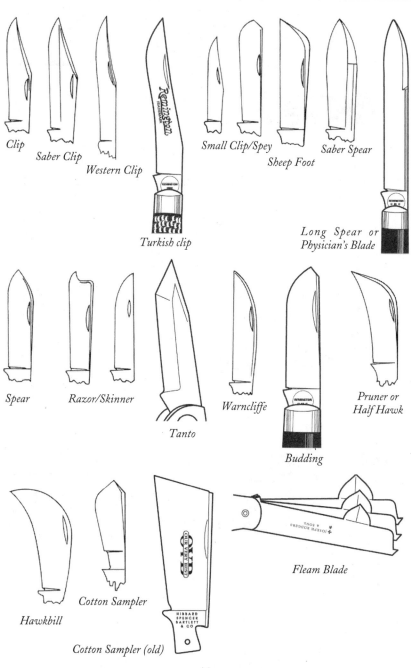

Clip

Saber Clip

Western Clip

Turkish clip

Small Clip/Spey

Sheep Foot

Saber Spear

Long Spear or
Physician's Blade

Spear

Razor/Skinner

Tanto

Warncliffe

Budding

Pruner or
Half Hawk

Hawkbill

Cotton Sampler

Cotton Sampler (old)

Fleam Blade

46

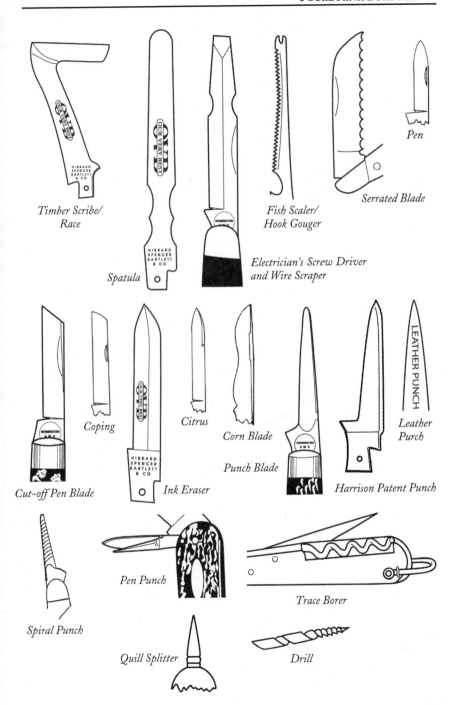

Timber Scribe/
Race

Spatula

Electrician's Screw Driver
and Wire Scraper

Fish Scaler/
Hook Gouger

Serrated Blade

Pen

Cut-off Pen Blade

Coping

Ink Eraser

Citrus

Corn Blade

Punch Blade

Harrison Patent Punch

Leather
Purch

Spiral Punch

Pen Punch

Trace Borer

Quill Splitter

Drill

47

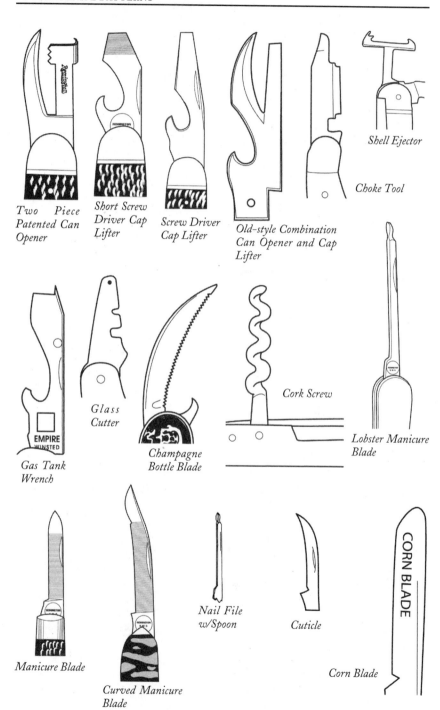

Two Piece Patented Can Opener

Short Screw Driver Cap Lifter

Screw Driver Cap Lifter

Old-style Combination Can Opener and Cap Lifter

Shell Ejector

Choke Tool

Gas Tank Wrench

Glass Cutter

Champagne Bottle Blade

Cork Screw

Lobster Manicure Blade

Manicure Blade

Curved Manicure Blade

Nail File w/Spoon

Cuticle

Corn Blade

48

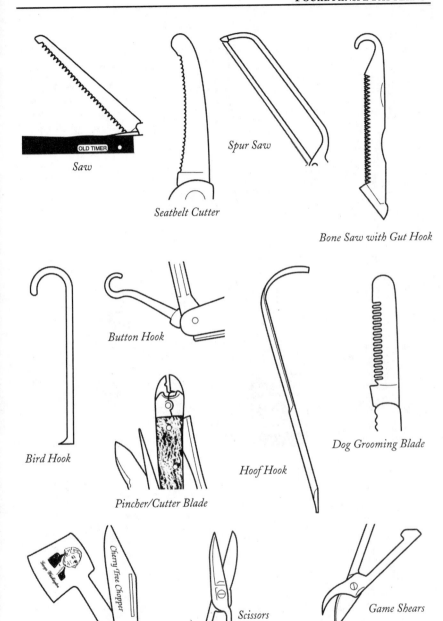

Saw

Seatbelt Cutter

Spur Saw

Bone Saw with Gut Hook

Bird Hook

Button Hook

Pincher/Cutter Blade

Hoof Hook

Dog Grooming Blade

Hatchet or Ax Blade

Scissors

Game Shears

49

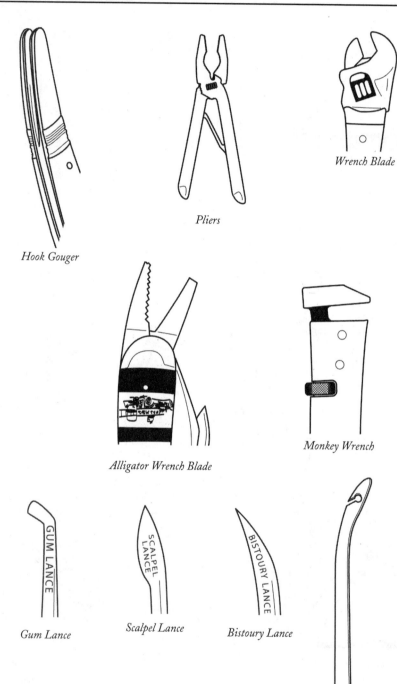

Hook Gouger

Pliers

Wrench Blade

Alligator Wrench Blade

Monkey Wrench

Gum Lance

Scalpel Lance

Bistoury Lance

Reed Hook

50

We have encouraged you to acquire as much experience as possible before jumping headlong into the knife collecting game. To succeed in this sport like any other, you must practice and learn. The more proficient you become, the better player you will be. But how does one learn?

A mountain school teacher, who was near and dear to his students' hearts, used to point out that, "Experience is always the best teacher . . . or at least as good a method as any for pounding knowledge into a cadaver's head." We might add though that experience can sometimes be expensive, unless one proceeds in the right direction.

So, since none of us really wants to be out excessive expense for learning or to become knife trading cadavers, let us look at other methods. The most obvious is simply consulting one's "common sense" for a method of weighing or measuring the value of knives before buying them for a collection. Immediately you may say to yourself, "A good price guide will do this for me," but we suggest a measure of caution here, too. It does seem that many price guides place great value on Mint condition knives and too little on old, used knives. Possibly we are biased, but we do have experience to back us up. We suggest you use common sense here, too.

We have advised you about many common pitfalls and errors which face the beginning trader, as well as the veteran collector. Now we will go beyond this and suggest a system for appraising knives which will provide you with specific collector value. This system has been used and standardized by the RBR Cutlery for more than 20 years. It consists of four charts; the last three are percentage values. In short, they are called the "RBR Evaluation Scales." We have included them in the following chapters and believe you will enjoy using them.

As a collector and trader you can (and should) place whatever personal value you desire on your knives . . . but the RBR Evaluation Scales will protect you from paying too much for the knives you buy.

The obvious things to consider in establishing a knife's value are brand, quality, age, and rareness; pattern, size, number, and type of blades; handle material; shield; and of course, condition. Each of these factors has a bearing on the value of the knife. We have already discussed them casually. Now, since there is a need to shorten the listing to make them more workable, consider that quality, age, and rareness generally are associated with the manufacturer's brand stampings. The common shield is also generally regarded as another trademark of the brand. The knife's size, number, and type of blades are usually indicated by the knife's pattern. So this leaves us four major component parts to work with to determine a knife's value: *brand, pattern, handle material,* and *condition.*

In a convenient way, the RBR Evaluation Scales have packaged each of these major components in four charts. The first is a general listing for identification and base price. The last three are for computing values by percentages. First, though, before you begin using the charts in a professional way, we urge you to follow through and learn thoroughly how each component affects the overall collector value of the knives. In doing so, you can become your own expert. Thus, the likelihood of becoming a more competitive sportsman is much greater.

BRANDS: Their relationship to value, Chart 1 (pgs. 64 – 139)

Brands (trademarks, tang stampings, etc.) are the most important components for determining the collector value of most production knives. The first thing a novice learns is that a Russell, Winchester, or Remington is worth much more than a modern creation from Pakistan or China. There is also a tremendous range in value between knives made in our own country even when they are of the same approximate age and of identical design.

Brands are determined by the company's name, trademark, or logo that is generally stamped on the blade tang of the knife. This is the simplest way of identifying the knife which the collector has available. When a knife company changes the design or form of its stamping, it serves to date the knife for the period of time the design is used. This often causes knives of the same brand (such as Case XX) and same pattern to differ very much in collector value. The tang markings then, in more ways than one, play an important role in determining the value of a knife.

However, like the cowboy who believes "nothing he hears and only half of what he sees," there is reason for caution even in this component category. The number of mint Winchesters, Remingtons, Case XX's, Cattarauguses, Marbles, Pine Knots, etc., which have appeared on the market is absolutely amazing. It is even more amazing that many of these have been produced by the most modern techniques available to knife makers of Germany, Japan, and even the United States. To put it another way, **there are abundant numbers of counterfeits available which will be sold at a handsome profit to the unwary.** Anyone with "walking around sense" should be suspicious of the rare knife which is in too good a condition at a price that is just too reasonable. The older brands were mostly made of high carbon steel which tends to stain, rust, pit, and deteriorate in a number of other ways. The effects of aging take their toll on handles, pens, and other parts too. This is not to say that it is impossible to find a rare old "mint" knife. It is, however, unlikely that there are many of them around. Natural aging should not be considered to greatly reduce the value of an old knife. Instead, it should be used to authenticate it as being original.

Careful consideration of other components can reveal more clues for authenticating brands. Never overlook the value of the advice of an experienced collector. Most of them will be glad to share their opinion with you. To further assist you in identifying and evaluating the older knives, we have included a general listing of all brands (Chart 1), which provides you with a high and low pattern value range for knives made by a particular company. This may be used as a quick reference price guide in determining value. Every collector occasionally encounters a brand with which he is somewhat unfamiliar. When you have this experience, we suggest that you check pages 149 – 322, which contains the brief histories of many major knife companies.

PATTERNS: THEIR RELATIONSHIP TO VALUE, CHART 2 (pgs. 140 – 143)

Patterns play an important role in determining value. Often, the value will increase with the size of the knife. There has been little change in basic design over the years, but patterns are made in different variations and sizes. Many have changed in popularity because of usage. Collectors determine their value based on rareness, size, and type.

It seems contradictory that some small pen patterns, such as an older "office knife," will out-rate on a value scale many larger and more practical patterns of the same brand. These so-called "Sunday Knives" were generally small pen patterns which were reasonably rare even when new and easily lost. The handles were often made of the most expensive materials available, such as ivory, mother-of-pearl, and precious metals.

Of the current production knives, the larger three blade knife in the whittler, cattle, or stock patterns is commonly the best seller. These are even preferred by many collectors over the four blade congress patterns.

On the collector market, top prices are being paid for the bigger knives, which are in the folding hunter category. These may have one or two blades. Their popularity is due to their sturdiness, size, and the variety of patterns in this category. These patterns range from ordinary jackknives and daddy barlows to more refined lockback patterns such as those made by Buck, Browning, Case, and Schrade. Almost every major knife company is now producing some variation of this pattern.

We believe that a contributing factor to the popularity of the folding hunter patterns is that they can be carried in a belt case and with the lockback design, opened blades are considered as safe as sheath knives. Television, too, has had its effect. In the T.V. series "The Dukes of Hazzard," the two principal characters, Bo and Luke, were often seen carrying a knife in a belt case. These are also common in current movies.

Present attitudes are greatly responsible for the almost unbelievable prices which are being paid by collectors for the older folding hunters which were made by famous firearms companies. Two leaders in this category are the Winchester No. 1920 (the big "Coke" pattern), and the Remington Bullet series, specifically pattern R1123. Although these knives have not been produced since the 1940s, the quality of one of these knives which has been cared for will equal or surpass any new knife on today's market.

The "old timers" method of classifying a knife as a folding hunter was simple and to the point. It had to be a large knife which was strong enough to skin and dress large game. The blade was at least four inches, broader than average, and strong enough to split the ribcage of a full-grown deer. If you have never dressed a deer, this may leave you somewhat at a loss for comparison purposes. However, after you have examined a few of these knives, you will see what it takes to be classified as a "folding hunter."

Of course, if we don't mention that perennial, ever popular pattern, the Barlow, we will be liable for expulsion from the infamous "Barlow Bearcats Club." Again, we must give credit to Allan Trout, formerly of the *Louisville Courier-Journal*, for originating this world renowned society. From its beginnings in 1950, no dues were charged for membership except that each member own at least one genuine, original Russell Barlow. Upon receiving proof of ownership, Trout initiated each new member by a notation in his column. This kicked off the "great Barlow collecting fad" that increased the value of all the older brand Barlows.

The Barlow, which is simply a modification of the old jackknife pattern, has never lacked in popularity. The bolster, which is about one-third of the total length of the frame, makes it among the most sturdy and dependable knives available. It is also one of the least expensive patterns to manufacture.

The Barlow has, at one time or another, been almost every American boy's dream knife, his "flaming Excalibur." We're told that a Sheffield cutler, Obadiah Barlow, made the first pattern in his home workshop in 1667. It immediately caught on and has been popular ever since. The basic design of the pocketknife, referring to those with backspring mechanisms, has not changed over the past two centuries. Different patterns, however, have evolved from the first single blade jackknife. Styles of varying size, shape, arrangement, and type and number of blades have been developed to accommodate the needs of different professions.

For example, in medieval days when the scholar and literate gentry did most of the writing, the pen knife pattern came into its own. This was a small two-blade knife which was used for trimming goose quill pens. It had two opposing blades, which hinged on a single backspring. From this pen knife pattern came the office knife, various Sunday knives, the canoe, and even the big sunfish or elephant toenail pattern. Perhaps of most importance, this pattern enabled the maker to add more blades to a knife without significantly increasing its weight or thickness.

In the same manner, almost every other original pattern has undergone changes and refinements. These have resulted in literally thousands of patterns which have different names but great similarities. All these can be classified and identified as offspring of no more than a half-dozen old basic patterns. So, the first thing to look for when identifying a pattern is the number, type, and arrangement of blades. After doing this, shape, form, and framework should tell the rest of the story.

Since patterns are significant in their relationship to value, the collector needs enough expertise to identify them on sight and often by more than one name. You will find many illustrations and pictures of different patterns throughout this book to assist you in learning them.

HANDLES: THEIR RELATIONSHIP TO VALUE, CHART 3 (pgs. 144, 145)

Another important feature of pocketknives is the handles or scales. These will tell the collector much about the knife and its value. From the handles alone, it is possible to identify the brand, approximate age, and general condition of the knife. If the collector is really good, he can quickly recognize the type material of which the handles are made and whether they are genuine or artificial.

Handle material determination can be darn difficult! Some of the modern materials simulate nature so closely they can fool many "experts," unless they take time to test them.

This is indeed a plastic age. Every material man has found in nature and used for knife handles is being reproduced in plastic. Included are pearl, stag, bone, wood, and tree bark. Imitations may look better, be cheaper, and last longer, but darn it, things should be what they really appear to be!

For example, the old celluloids never tried to be anything other than what they were. You could take them or leave them. They appeared on knife handles in all the colors of the rainbow and in fanciful designs. This forerunner of plastic was used by many firms to create genuine beauty in design and form. Today, years later, they are still the most beautiful of all plastics, and many are true works of art. Modern "Space-age" plastics would be as attractive, if enough time and care were taken in its production and if it were not used to imitate natural materials.

Since the likelihood of knife companies restricting the use of plastics to non-imitating handle designs is nil, it becomes even more important for the collector to "know his handles." Some of these artificial materials can simulate nature so closely that even the experienced collector will want to test them in order to make positive identification.

If a knife has handles of genuine mother-of-pearl, when held at different angles, iridescent shades of pink, purple and green can be seen. When checked under a magnifying glass, different layers and flakes of material, formed during the different growth periods of the shell as a living organism, can be seen. These are characteristics which have not yet been duplicated in plastics. However, you may rest assured that since especially the larger pearl handles are becoming increasingly rare, the technology boys will keep up their effort.

One must look closely at late model knives to detect the difference between genuine stag or bone and current synthetics. Stag, bone, and ivory look similar when worn or dressed down to a smooth finish. However, stag is rarely used in this polished state for pocketknife handles. Its natural rough state is preferred for scales and has not been successfully duplicated with synthetics. Bone, cut to look like stag, has had only limited success. The difference in jigged bone made to look like stag and the real stag is readily apparent.

Synthetics can generally be identified by their perfection. They tend to discolor and fade less than their natural counterparts. Ivory yellows with age, dyed stag and bone fade to a yellow honeycomb or greenish yellow hue, and each develops tiny hairline cracks which can be detected with a ten-power magnifying glass. Stag has detectable growth layers along the edges while bone contains tiny grain pits where living cells once grew. When compared to the edges of cross sections of synthetic materials which have not been dyed, it is easy to see the even color which is as smooth as glass. Nature just doesn't work with such perfection.

In order to properly identify old, exotic woods which were used for handles, one needs experience and a color and grain chart. The older wood handles usually turn black, but the natural grain and color can be seen if you smooth off a section with a fine emery cloth. Once identified, you can more accurately determine value based on rareness and condition.

All handles of natural material such as bone, ivory, wood, or antlers go through changes as they age. This process may be compared to the aging or seasoning of an old Stradivarius violin or the yellowing of a good meerschaum pipe. This ripe and mellow patina that can be attained only by age and good care both authenticates and enhances the value of the knife's scales.

Since handle or scale materials have such an effect on the collector value of knives, it is definitely helpful to be able to recognize and appreciate the beauty of them. Chart 3 is designed to give you an idea of the difference in value between the common handle materials.

CONDITION: Its relationship to value, Chart 4 (pgs. 146, 147)

Our trading and collecting experiences have led us to believe that most dealers, traders, and collectors use a type of condition grading scale which is somewhat flexible and more attuned to the current market than any we've seen in print. This scale, we suspect, is used unknowingly and seems to be based on pure horse-sense. Although we use a four category series of charts for determining a knife's total value, many traders apparently use only brand and condition as a quick reference for value determination. However, a little probing reveals that they do use all four factors for their final appraisal.

This condition reference scale, though, seems to have five categories that we hereby classify as MINT, EXCELLENT, GOOD, FAIR, and JUNKER. Of these, the middle three are most often used in knife trading, especially if they are dealing in old or discontinued knives.

The grade FAIR refers to a knife which is definitely in used condition, with up to 20% wear on working parts and flaws which include tarnish, some pitting, shrinkage, and cracked handles because of both use and natural aging. Blade etching has probably disappeared, and handles, if bone or stag, are worn practically smooth. Even some chipping and dubbing of the blades is permissible, but the knife is still complete in parts and is useable. The brand stamping can still be read. A top brand knife in this FAIR condition is not a junker, just a semi-retired veteran.

The grade GOOD includes some knives which have been whetted, honed, and used, but not nearly to the extent as described above. The original design and contour of the blades and handles should show no more than 10% wear, at the most. Tarnish and fading can be forgiven, but rust pits too deep to be removed by expert buffing cannot. Conspicuously cracked or chipped blades too deep to hone out are not acceptable in this category. The springs play a role in that they should be strong enough to snap the blades shut and to stand them open with no obvious disalignment or "bow back." The grade GOOD means a good used knife that has just been broken in.

The grade EXCELLENT consists of knives that are as close to being new or MINT as is possible for really old knives, and not exceeding more than 15% wear. We specify "as nearly as possible" because a pocketknife made over 40 years ago, unless it has been stored under ideal climatic conditions and never taken from its original wrapper, is sure as heck going to show some signs of some natural aging effects. Since serious collecting started with these older knives, most collectors have assigned a value to them which is usually higher than is reserved for those MINT knives that are being currently produced. Due to this, the minor flaws which may be attributed to aging may be forgiven and if any old knife has been used so little **that it does not show to the naked eye,** it should lose little if any value because of it. Other than these minor flaws and natural aging effects, perfection should be expected in this EXCELLENT category.

The grade MINT, of course, means the knife must be in "as new" condition. We recognize that there are some of the older knives in MINT condition, but these are extremely rare and are generally very expensive, if you could buy them. The financial circumstances of many collectors limit their pursuit of older mint knives, and indirectly because of this they end up buying reproductions or outright counterfeits. Most MINT knives on the market today are those of either current or relatively current production, such as Case USA. If you happen to be a "MINT bug," you can collect to your heart's desire in this group. However, if you are after a really old knife that is in MINT (as new) condition, **expect to pay three to four times** what you have to pay for the same knife which qualifies as 99% EXCELLENT on the RBR Evaluation Scales. We caution you in this pursuit: There are many skilled mechanics who can restore old knives to apparent mint condition. **A restored or buffed knife may qualify for the 99% Excellent category but it should never be considered to be MINT.**

Occasionally a collector may encounter a unique knife in "as new" (Mint) that is over 40 years old. This knife, if authenticated as original, **may command a price of as much as three or four times our 99% Excellent scale.** If you encounter such a knife, please proceed with extreme caution. As is often the case, if it looks too good to be true, it probably is too good to be true.

The grade JUNKER, for sure, is on the opposite end of the condition scale, in worse condition than the grade FAIR. In this group are the knives with broken blades, cracked or missing scales, etc. Still, there are collectors who are looking for knives in this grade for they are often repairable or contain many good useable parts. If you happen to be interested in restoring knives, though, take a little advice and always be sure that you use only parts from an identical knife of the same brand. A properly repaired knife can be considered restored and reintroduced in the market.

A related problem beginning to surface is knives with welded blades. Perhaps this was done as a sincere effort to restore a broken blade for which a replacement could not be found. However, these welded blades are generally weaker than the original blade, and the welding can be detected with just a little experience.

The repairman with honest intentions will mark the knife in some way to show that repair has been made. This can be done by scratching the initials of the person doing the work just inside the center section of the liner (similar to the way early watchmakers marked the inner back of the watches they repaired). These scratches should also include the date and some indication as to what repair was done. This will not detract from the looks or value of the knife and the repairman/trader cannot be accused of fraud. Since many welded blades are beginning to surface, we advise collectors to stay on the look-out and become expert enough to recognize a welded blade or backspring. It is not likely that anyone else or any organization will do this for you.

We have discussed some of the topics mentioned above because faking and counterfeiting are directly connected to a knife's condition, and condition is a big factor in determining the knife's collector value.

In previous discussions, we have described the parts of the knife and their relation to value. It is important that you understand the role of each of the following charts and how each helps in determining the collector value of pocketknives.

The percentage scales found in these charts have been most carefully standardized by using a wide segment of markets extensive enough, in both this country and abroad, to insure that the percentage of error is small enough to protect your investments when buying or selling knives.

The market in pocketknives, like most other collectibles, varies from area to area. It is possible to buy knives in some areas for a little less and resell them in other areas for a little more. It is also true that every collector or dealer has a buying and a selling price. So if the prices computed on the RBR Evaluation Scales seem a little low if you are wishing to sell a particular knife or a little high if you are wishing to buy a particular knife, just remember that the computed price is to be used as a guide. This variance is what knife collecting and trading is all about! There would be little interest in the sport if it were not this way.

We believe that it is important for you to familiarize yourself with the use of these facts and the use of the following charts in order to thoroughly enjoy knife collecting. Today, you can no longer approach knife collecting as a hit or miss proposition. Any collector needs to develop expertise in appraising knives. Otherwise, you may find yourself getting in "too deep" before you realize what it's all about.

Since Charts 2, 3, and 4 require the use of basic math in figuring percentages, we recommend using a small calculator to help speed up your calculations and make it possible for you to appraise collections in the field or at swapmarts. These little computers are very inexpensive and well worth the investment.

Chart 1 is a Master Chart or General Listing of knife manufacturers, their brands and stampings, and a recognized range of values. Additionally, listed with most companies is an "example knife," the price of which is calculated by the scales. Use of this "example knife" and the range of values can provide the experienced collector with an excellent, quick reference guide with which he can approximate the value of various patterns of a particular brand.

However, when you seek to make a more accurate evaluation of a specific knife, the information in Chart 1 is essential for discovering its current collector value. You should note the date of the company's beginnings and the time it ceased production (included when it is known). The dates are usually good indicators of the knife's age and rareness. Following the dates, there is a range of value, from low to high. These were established from the catalogued patterns the company is known to have produced and from actual sales records rather than from the "asking prices" or dealer prices. Both the high and low values are calculated on *mint* knives.

As collectors have discovered, although most knife brands used numerous patterns, some brands were made on only one or two patterns. If only one pattern of a brand is known, the high and low values will obviously be the same. Of course, there is always the chance that some lucky collector will turn up a rare, heretofore unknown pattern. The value of such a find will rest greatly with the collector, his willingness to part with it, and his customer's desire to own it.

To the far right of the Value Range is another number in parentheses. This is not some magic number which we drew from a hat. It is, as indicated, a "Code" value, computed by percentage from the list value of the "example knife" for the particular brand. This was possible because the "example knife" is fully specified.

This "Code" value represents the most average, expensive, sales leading knife pattern the company could have made, with common bone handles. It is essential to finding the overall collector value of your knife because this is the value you take from Chart 1 to Chart 2 for use in finding the pattern value of your knife. Chart 2 is a listing of numerous knife patterns and a breakdown, by percentage, of their relative values as they relate to collector knife pricing.

To the right of each percent is the name of the basic pattern to which it applies. This is followed by alternate and descriptive names, size, number of blades, etc. If your knife does not seem to fit a basic pattern, try the alternate names. If there is still doubt, check to see if you have identified it correctly. Then by studying the knife's shape, size, and number of blades and their arrangement, try matching it to the pattern that it most resembles.

Many alternate and descriptive names for old basic patterns have recently been added to our knife vocabulary. If you are not familiar with this new terminology, it may help to re-read the pattern section, pages 31 – 50.

Once you have identified your knife's pattern and found its correct percentage on the scale, simply multiply this percentage by the "Code" value from Chart 1. This gives you the Pattern Value for your knife.

Now, proceed with the Pattern Value to Chart 3 and find the value of your knife's Handle Material.

Chart 3 is a listing of numerous knife handle materials and a breakdown by percentage of their relative values to pocketknife collectors.

Directly to the right of each percentage is the common (or trade) name of Handle Materials. Following this will be specifications of type, age, color, etc.

Since the handle material of a pocketknife plays an important role in determining its value and since there is such a wide range in values of this item, we cannot overly stress the importance of being able to make correct identifications of this material (pages 503 – 541). When you are sure of the identification of the handles on your knife, find the percentage indicated on Chart 3 and multiply it times the total Pattern Value from Chart 2.

However, if your knife has been used, sharpened, or damaged in any way, you must take the Chart 3 value to Chart 4 "Condition Grade" to find its final collector value.

Chart 4 is a percentage breakdown of visible wear and other damages that your knife may have sustained. This chart is very important when evaluating any used or damaged knife that shows more than 1% wear or damage. Chart 4 also contains a quick reference guide which may be used by first making a categorical evaluation of the condition of your knife and then placing it in the proper grade bracket such as Excellent, Fair, Junker, etc., and then multiplying the grade bracket percentage times the Chart 3 value.

Chart 4 is in two parts; part one will help you determine the percentage wear your knife has sustained. The second section, part two, will help you accurately determine the damages indicating the wear percentage that should be subtracted from 99% Excellent. They are a list of identified damages your knife may have sustained. A total of these percentages subtracted from the 99% excellent value should place your knife in one of the four "Bracket Grades" we have listed. You can use the percentage derived here to find your knife's Condition value. Simply multiply the Chart 3 value times the percentage subtotal you have derived from Chart 4 and you have the approximate *collector value* of your knife.

Estimating your knife's Wear Percentage from part two of Chart 4 is the most difficult task you will face. In most cases you must visualize the original appearance of the knife's blades, handles, etc., as they appeared when new or in mint condition. This is most deceptive with older knives that one has never seen in new condition. However, a method that has proven helpful and which we will refer to later as "the extended profile check" is to lay the blade flat on a piece of paper and draw an extended outline that appears to fill out the blade's original fullness. Then by observing the space between the blade's edge and the extended outline, you can make a more accurate estimate of the percentage of wear.

Damage percentages are easier to estimate because they require only close scrutiny of your knife. They are clearly specified in the lower section of this chart. All damages you find must be totaled and combined with wear percentages (be honest!). When the combined percentages are totaled and subtracted from 100% (Mint value), you will have the figure to place in the Chart 4 bracket. This Condition Percentage times the Chart 3 value will give you your knife's *Total Appraisal Collector Value.*

Directions in Brief

Chart 1: Identify the knife, its brand, and value range. Note the Code value. (Remember this is the highest possible value of the company's knife with bone handles.)

Chart 2: Identify your knife's pattern. Find the pattern percentage value indicated on Chart 2 for your knife. Multiply this percentage times the Code value from Chart 1.

Chart 3: Identify the handle material of your knife. Find the percentage value indicated for this material on Chart 3. Multiply this percentage times the value you brought from Chart 2. (Note: If your knife is excellent condition, you now multiply by .99 and you have the total collector value of your knife. If not, take this final value to Chart 4.)

Chart 4: If your knife is not EXCELLENT (99%), find its percentage of wear by use of the "extended profile check." Then add this to the total of percentage of damage it has sustained, using the bottom part of the chart. Subtract this total from 99% EXCELLENT for its place in the condition bracket.

FINAL STEP: Multiply your final Chart 4 percentage times the Chart 3 value. You now have the "Total appraisal collector value" of your knife.

*If your knife is indeed in 100% mint condition, it will be worth three to four times your Chart 3 value.

Walk Through

The knife you wish to appraise is a Syracuse by Camillus. It is a two blade, 3½" Sleeveboard pen with genuine mother-of-pearl handles. It is only slightly worn. Close examination reveals that there are three scratches on the main blade and a couple of pit marks which are hardly visible, caused by rust. The brand stampings are easy to read. Examination reveals two hairline cracks around the center rivet on the right handle of the knife. The backsprings are in good shape, and the blades will "walk and talk" when closed. The bolsters look tarnished, but you determine that with a little polish they can be restored to mint so there will be no scratches on them.

To appraise this knife, first look up Syracuse/Camillus Company in the Chart 1 General Listing. It says: Syracuse Knife Co. NY (c. 1904-), the range of prices is $25.00 – $250.00. The Code value is $150.00. Move to Chart 2.

Look up the Sleeveboard Pen pattern on Chart 2. The 3½" length closed makes it fall into the "large" pen category. To the immediate left you find the percentage value, which is 40%. Multiply the code value from Chart 1 times .40. ($150 x .40 = $60) Take this value to Chart 3. Find the pearl percentage value on Chart 3. Now, note the percentage value which is 170%. Multiply this percentage times the Chart 2 Value. (Chart 2 value ($60) x 1.70 = $102.00) Take this value to Chart 4.

Chart 4 has a number of stages which need your attention. First determine the wear of your knife. It is slightly worn, approximately 5%. Keep this figure in mind. Secondly, re-examine the damages. They are three scratches on the primary blade. Look at the lower part of the chart. You find that these scratches are judged at 3% each, totaling 9%. Next there are two rust pits which are hardly visible worth 3% each totaling 6%. The brand stamping is Okay. 0%. The backsprings are strong and there are no apparent damages to the bolsters. So, now we total the damage and wear percentages of your knife:

Wear overall	5%
Blade scratches	9%
Blade pitting	6%
Brand stamping	0%
Handles	0%
Backsprings	0%
Bolsters	0%
Total of wear and damage	20%

Subtract this total from 99% (EXCELLENT) = 79%
Multiply the Chart 3 Value ($10.20) x .79 = $80.58
The collector value of your knife is $80.58

CHART 1

POCKETKNIFE MANUFACTURERS MASTER LIST
(Brand Code x Pattern x Handle Material x Condition = Collector Value)

Brand Marks & Stampings (Dates)	Value Range		
	Low	High	Code
A.A. FISHER CO., New York, NY (c. 1900 – 15)			
*3" 2 bl. Jack, bone hdls. $51	$10	$75	($133)
A-I NOVELTY CUT. CO., Canton, OH (c. 1879 – 1948)			
*Large 3 bl. Whittler, cel hdls. $75	20	150	(125)
A. BARRETT & SONS, Piccadilly, Eng.			
*3½" 2 bl. Dog leg jack, bone hdls. $50	10	80	(100)
A. BURKINSHAW, Pepperill, MA			
*3" 2 bl. Pen pat. pearl hdls. $53	10	90	(122)
ACCO, Atlanta, GA (c. 1970 –) USA			
*3" 2 bl. Pen pat. pl. hdls. $11.50	10	20	(50)
A.C. PENN., New York			
*3½" 2 bl. Swell end jack, Bone hdls. $55	15	70	(95)
ACME (F. Westpfal c. 1884 – 1928) Ger.	8	50	(60)
ACE CUTLERY CO. Fremont, OH			
*3" 2bl. Pen, Pearl hdls. $65	15	70	(106)
ADAMS & SONS Ivy (c. 1860 – 1890)			
*4" 2 bl. Jack, Wood hdls. $50	25	100	(120)
A'DINCER, Kaiserslautern, Ger.			
*3½" 4 bl. Pen, Pearl hdls. $60	20	95	(95)
ADOLPH BLAICH, San Francisco, CA, Ger.			
*2½" 2 bl. Pen Pat. Cel. hdls. $30	12	65	(72)

Brand Marks & Stampings (Dates)	Value Range Low	High	Code

ADOLPH BUSCH, Ger. Bartender (orig. Peep-hole adv)
*3¼" 3 bl. w/corkscrew, metal hdls. $150   60   150   (300)

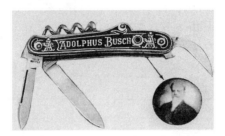

Chart 1 Code Value		Chart 2 Pattern Value		Chart 3 Handle Value		Chart 4 Condition		RBR Collector Value
300	x	.40	x	.80	x	.99	=	$95.00

ADOLPHIUS CUT CO., Sheffield, Eng. (c. 1882 – 1891)
*4" 3 bl. Stock pat. Bone hdls. $70   12   80   (100)

ADD-KNIFE Made in USA   8   20   (50)

A.E. MERGOTT & CO., Newark, NJ
*3" 2 bl. Equal end Jack, Bone hdls. $18   10   40   (60)

AERIAL CUT. MFG. CO., Marinette, WI (c. 1912 – 1944)
    15   250   (250)

Chart 1 Code Value		Chart 2 Pattern Value		Chart 3 Handle Value		Chart 4 Condition		RBR Collector Value
250	x	.80	x	1.25	x	.99	=	$247.50

A.E. BANISTER & CO, Newark, NJ
*3" 3 bl. Pen Pat. Bone hdls. $35   10   65   (95)

A. FIELDS & CO., Eng.
*3½" 3 bl. Stock pat. Bone hdls. $35   15   65   (75)

A. FIELDS & CO., Ger.
*3½" 3 bl. Stock pat. Bone hdls. $30   10   50   (50)

Brand Marks & Stampings (Dates)	Value Range		Code
	Low	High	
A. FISHER, Solingen, Ger.			
2½" 2 bl. Pen pat. Wood hdls. $8	8	40	(66)
A.J. JORDEN CUT. CO., St. Louis, MO **(c. 1887 – 1890)**			
*4" 3 bl. Stock pat. Bone hdls. $83	20	45	(85)

Chart 1 Code Value		Chart 2 Pattern Value		Chart 3 Handle Value		Chart 4 Condition		RBR Collector Value
150	x	.45	x	1.75	x	.99	=	$116.82

A. KASTOR BROS., New York-Ger. (c. 1876 – 1947)			
*3½" 4 bl. Bartender pat. Pearl hdls. $120	10	85	(150)
A & K KLASS, Solingen, Ger. (c. 1834 –)			
*4" 3 bl. Stock pat Bone hdls. $35	12	60	(65)
A.K.C. CO., Ger. (American Knife Co)			
*4" 2 bl. Slim jack pat. Bone hdls. $15	8	40	(40)
ALAMO, Japan			
*4" 2 bl. Melon Tester Jack. Cel. hdls. $10	5	18	(20)
ALAS CO., Solingen, Ger.			
3½" 2 bl. Jack pat. Wood hdls. $7	8	30	(40)
ALEXANDER, Sheffield, Eng.			
*4" 2 bl. Jack pat. Stag hdls. $50	12	75	(85)
AKRON CUT. WORKS, Akron, Oh (c. 1911 – 1928)			
*4" 2 bl. Trapper pat. Stag hdls. $65	30	80	(80)
ALBERTSON CO., Kane, PA (c. 1930 – 1938)			
*3" 2 bl. Med. Jack, Bone hdls. $20	20	75	(70)
ALERT (c. 1936 – 1937)			
*3" 2 bl. Pen pat. Wood hdls. $12	8	25	(45)
ALFRED BLACKWELL, Sheffield, Eng.			
5" 1 bl. Dirk pat. Stag hdls. $300	80	200	(165)

Brand Marks & Stampings (Dates)	Value Range		
	Low	High	Code
ALFRED & SON, CELEBRATED CUT., Eng.			
*4" 3 bl. Stock pat. Stag hdls. $75	90	150	(100)
ALOISE, Ger.			
*3" 2 bl. Jack pat. Wood hdls. $5	8	15	(30)
ALLEN CUT. CO., Newburg, NY (1919 – 1925)			
*3½" 2 bl. Gun stock pat.			
Bone hdls. $71	20	90	(100)
ALTENBACK, Swanwerk, Ger.			
*3" 2 bl. Equal end Jack, Cracked Ice hdls. $22	10	50	(55)
ALLMAN, Ger.			
*2½" 2 bl. Jack pat., Metal hdls. $8	7	30	(40)
AMBASSADOR (COLONIAL) Prov., RI (c. 1951 – 1961)			
*3½" 2 bl. Pen pat. Inlay pl. hdls. $20	8	30	(90)
AMERICAN ACE, USA. (c. 1919 – 1920)			
*3" 3 bl. Pen pat. Cel. hdls. $45	9	75	(90)
AMERICA'S BEST (CAMILLUS), NY			
*4" 3 bl. Stock pat. Sl. black hdls. $60	10	80	(130)
AMERICAN CUTLERY CO. USA (c. 1879 – 1920)			
*3¼" 3 bl. Whittler pat. Bone hdls. $80	12	100	(100)
AMERICAN CUTLERY CO., Ger.			
*3" 2 bl. Jack pat. Wood or Pl. hdls. $20	7	25	(70)
AMERICAN CUTLERY CO., Japan			
*4" 2 bl. Trapper pat. Bone hdls. $20	7	30	(60)
AMERICAN KNIFE CO., Thomaston, CT (c. 1849 – 1965)			
*3½" 4 bl. Cattle pat. Bone hdls. $82	12	100	(110)
AMERICAN KNIFE CO., Plymouth, MA			
*4" 3 bl. Stock pat. Bone hdls. $65	10	65	(100)
AMERICAN KNIFE CO., Winstead, CT (1919 – 1965)			
*3" 2 bl. Jack pat. Bone hdls. $31	10	50	(80)

Brand Marks & Stampings (Dates)	Value Range		
	Low	High	Code
AMERICAN KNIFE CO., Japan *3½" 2 bl. Stock pat. Bone hdls. $15	7	20	(30)
AMERICAN IMPORT CO., Ger. (Arrow Brand) 3½" 2 bl. Stock pat. Bone hdls. $18	8	30	(40)
AMICO, Japan *2½" 2 bl. Pen pat. Comp. hdls. $7	6	12	(35)
AMERICAN SHEAR & KNIFE CO., Haydenville, CT *3½" 4 bl. Cattle pat. Bone hdls. $58	15	75	(80)
AMERICAN MAID (Utica Cut. NY c. 1949 – 52) NY *4" 2 bl. Jack pat. Bone hdls. $50	15	80	(85)
ARM & HAMMER (New York Knife Co. c. 1856 – 1931) *4" 3 bl. Stock pat. Wood hdls. $120	20	175	(266)
AMERICAN VETERAN (c. 1945 – 1947)	40	75	(80)
AMES CUTLERY CO., MS (1829 – 1900)	90	150	(200)
ANHEUSER-BUSCH., Ger. (adv) (c. 1900 – 1922) *3½" 3 bl. w/corkscrew & peep hole Embossed pearl handles. $125	50	150	(150)
ANVIL (Colonial c. 1974 –) *3" 2 bl. Serp. Jack pat. Del. hdls. $15	7	30	(60)
ANTELOPE, Ger. *3¼" 3 bl. Pen pat. Cel. hdls. $20	8	19	(40)
ANTON WINGER, JR., Ger. *3" 4 bl. Utility pat. Bone hdls. $16	10	30	(40)
ARNEX, Solingen, Ger. *3" 4 bl. Utility pat. Comp. hdls. $10	8	20	(50)
ARROW BRAND, San Francisco USA (Adolph Blaich c. 1885 – 1954) *3" 2 bl. Jack pat. Bone hdls. $33	10	70	(75)
ARGYLE CUT. COMPANY, Ger. (Brown Bros) *3½" 2 bl. Jack pat. Cel. hdls. $20	10	65	(70)

Brand Marks & Stampings (Dates)	Value Range		
	Low	High	Code
ARISTOCRAT (McCrory Stores c. 1932 – 1953) *3" 4 bl. Pen pat. Comp. hdls. $30	10	60	(85)
ARMSTRONG CUTLERY CO., Ger. *2½" 2 bl. Pen pat. Cel. hdls. $15	10	30	(35)

Chart 1 Code Value		Chart 2 Pattern Value		Chart 3 Handle Value		Chart 4 Condition		RBR Collector Value
75	x	.35	x	.80	x	.99	=	$20.79

ARMSTRONG CUTLERY CO., USA (c. 1901)
*3" 1 bl. Jack pat. Metal hdls. $21   10   60   (75)

ARTISAN, Chicago (c. 1937)
Slide blade "vest pocket" knife
w/imitation tortise celluloid hdls. $16   10   50   (25)

Chart 1 Code Value		Chart 2 Pattern Value		Chart 3 Handle Value		Chart 4 Condition		RBR Collector Value
25	x	.25	x	1.30	x	.99	=	$15.46

ATCO, Japan
*2½" 2 bl. Pen pat. Comp. hdls. $5   5   11   (30)

Chart 1 Code Value		Chart 2 Pattern Value		Chart 3 Handle Value		Chart 4 Condition		RBR Collector Value
75	x	.45	x	1.10	x	.99	=	$36.63

ATLANTIC CUTLERY CO., Ger. (c. 1900 – 1914)
*4" 2 bl. Easy open jack
Old smooth bone hdls. $37   10   75   (75)

ASK, (C. Knotte, c. 1929)
*3½" 3 bl. Cattle pat. Comp. hdls. $36   10   60   (65)

| Brand Marks & Stampings (Dates) | Value Range | | Code |
	Low	High	
AUTOPOINT, Chicago, IL (c. 1950) *3" 3 bl. Sleeveboard pat. Pl. hdls. $14	9	50	(65)
AUGUST HERMES, Solingen, Ger. *3" 2 bl. Jack pat. Bone hdls. $15	8	18	(50)
AUG MULLER SOHNE, Solingen, Ger. 2½" 2 bl. Jack pat. Wood hdls. $6	5	15	(40)
ART KNIFE CO., Nicholson, PA	30	30	(50)
A.W. BRADSHAW & SONS, Eng. *4" 3 bl. Sailors pat. Wood hdls. $30	15	90	(133)
A. WRIGHT & SONS LTD., Shef. Eng. *3" 3 bl. Cattle pat. Bone hdls. $40	12	60	(72)

A.W. WADSWORTH & SONS, 3⅞" Jack, bone hdls. $75

Chart 1 Code Value		Chart 2 Pattern Value		Chart 3 Handle Value		Chart 4 Condition		RBR Collector Value
120	x	55	x	1.10	x	.99	=	$71.87

Brand Marks & Stampings (Dates)	Low	High	Code
A.W. WADSWORTH & SONS, Austria (c. 1905 – 1917)	15	150	(120)
A.W. WADSWORTH & SONS, Ger. (c. 1905 – 1917) *4" 3 bl. Stock pat. Stag hdls. $85	12	100	(110)
BABE RUTH (Old Schrade Adv.)	50	300	
BABY RUTH (Old Remington Adv.)	150	350	
BADGER STATE KNIFE CO., Ger. *4" 2 bl. Trapper pat. Bone hdls. $52	15	100	(90)
BALDWIN CUT. CO., Tidioute, PA (c. 1913 – 1919) *4½" 1 bl. F. Hunter pat. Bone hdls. $140	30	125	(100)

Brand Marks & Stampings (Dates)	Value Range		
	Low	High	Code
BANNER KNIFE CO. *2½" 2 bl. Pen pat. Bone hdls. $12	10	20	(60)
BANNER CUTLERY CO., Austria *3" 2 bl. Jack pat. Bone hdls. $21	10	30	(70)
BARNETT TOOL CO. HHH, Newark, NJ *4" 2 bl. Stock pat. Wood hdls. $68	25	150	(150)
BARON, Solingen, Ger. *3" 2 bl. Serp. jack, Comp. hdls. $18	8	30	(50)
BARNSLEY BROS. CO., Rochester, NY *4" 2 bl. Jack pat. Wood hdls. $31	15	75	(70)
BARNSIF BROS., Monett, MO *3½" 3 bl. Stock pat. Bone hdls. $42	15	80	(85)
BARRY & CO., Ger. *3½" 3 bl. Stock pat. Comp. hdls. $15	8	25	(50)
BARTLETT TOOL CO. (c. 1915 – 1916) *3½" 4 bl. Utility pat. Bone hdls. $40	20	75	(85)
BARTON BROS., Sheffield, Eng. *3½" 3 bl. Cattle pat. Bone hdls. $37	10	60	(65)
BASSETT, Derby, CT *3½" 2 bl. Elec. pat. Wood hdls. $20	10	50	(115)
BASTWICK BROWN CO., Toledo, OH *3" 2 bl. Pen pat. Metal hdls. $18	15	20	(75)
BATES & BACON, St. Paul, MN	12	40	(80)

Brand Marks & Stampings (Dates)	Value Range		Code
	Low	High	

BATES & BACON, 11 John St., NY
*2½" 2 bl. Pen pat. Sil. hdls. $50 — 75 — 50 — (65)

Chart 1 Code Value	Chart 2 Pattern Value	Chart 3 Handle Value	Chart 4 Condition	RBR Collector Value
150 x	.50 x	1.50 x	.99 =	$111.37

BATTLE AXE, Ger.
(Hardin Wholesale, Kenova, WV)
3¾" 3 bl. Stock pat. Stag hdl. $115 — 40 — 80 — (150)

BAY STATES, Worcester, MA
*3" 3 bl. Equal-end pat. Bone hdls. $73 — 40 — 200 — (140)

B & B CO., St. Paul, MN — 12 — 12

BEAR MGC CUTLERY, Jacksonville, AL — 50 — 100 — (120)

BEAVER FALLS, PA (c. 1867 – 1886)
*4" 2 bl. Op. end jack pat. Bone hdls. $85 — 30 — 200 — (145)

BELK & SONS, Shef., Eng.
*3" 4 bl. Congress pat. Horn hdls. $30 — 9 — 20 — (75)

BELKNAP HARDWARE CO., Louisville, KY (c. 1840 – 1986)
*3½" 2 bl. Barlow pat. Bone hdls. $70 — 7 — 150 — (135)

BELMONT KNIFE CO. USA
*3½" 2 bl. Flatfish pat. Stag hdls. $50 — 10 — 70 — (70)

BENCH MARK, USA (Gaston, NC) — 20 — 125 — (210)

*BENCH MARK-Rolox-1 bl. Stag. $250

BENGALL (Cadman, c. 1748 – 1926)
*4" Op. end jack, 2 bl. Bone hdls. $44 — 20 — 80 — (75)

Brand Marks & Stampings (Dates)	Value Range		
	Low	High	Code
BEN HUR, (Van Camp, c. 1927 – 1954) 3½" 4 bl. Congress pat. Stag hdls. $55	25	100	(70)
BERKSHIRE CUTLERY CO., Eng. *4" 2 bl. Big jack pat. Bone hdls. $40	15	65	(75)
BERTRAM (Hen & Rooster) Solingen, Ger. (c. 1872 – 1983) 4 bl. Congress, European Stag. $185	40	300	(250)

Chart 1 Code Value		Chart 2 Pattern Value		Chart 3 Handle Value		Chart 4 Condition		RBR Collector Value
250	x	50	x	150	x	.99	=	$185.62

BERTRAM HEN & ROOSTER (c. 1993 – present) Stag/stock pattern. $65	50	150	(150)
BETA BOS'N	20	35	
BIG HORN MARK, Italy (H. Willis Co. Louisville, KY c. 1971 – 1975) 4" 3 bl. Stock pat. Bone hdls. $40	20	50	(80)
BIG HORN MARK, Italy (Grawolf Trading Co. c. 1976 –) 4" 3 bl. Stock pat. Bone hdls. $35	15	40	(70)

BIG HORN MARK, Equal end jack, Medium stag. $145

Chart 1 Code Value		Chart 2 Pattern Value		Chart 3 Handle Value		Chart 4 Condition		RBR Collector Value
210	x	45	x	1.50	x	.99	=	$140.33

Brand Marks & Stampings (Dates)	Value Range		
	Low	High	Code

BINGHAM CO., Cleveland, OH (c. 1841 – 1930)
Equal End Jack, Medium Stag. $145.00

25   250   210

Chart 1 Code Value		Chart 2 Pattern Value		Chart 3 Handle Value		Chart 4 Condition		RBR Collector Value
500	x	.60	x	1.60	x	.99	=	$475.11

BLACK MOUNTAIN, KY
5" 1 bl. Barlow F.H. pat. Stag hdls. $475

85   500   (500)

BLAKE & LAMB, Utica, NY
*3½" 2 bl. Muskrat pat. Bone hdls. $90

30   110   (150)

BLISH, MIZE & STILLMAN, Atch., KA
4" 4 bl. Stock pat. Bone hdls. $125

30   250   (150)

BLUE GRASS (Belknap, c. 1898 – 1986)
Barlow, 3½", Roughsawed bone hdl. $120

40   350   (230)

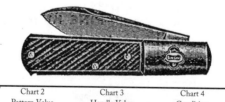

Chart 1 Code Value		Chart 2 Pattern Value		Chart 3 Handle Value		Chart 4 Condition		RBR Collector Value
130	x	40	x	130	x	99	=	$118.80

BLUE RIBBON CUT CO.
*3" 3 bl. Pen pat. Cel. hdls. $32

50   50   (70)

BLUE MOON of Ky. (c. 1987 –)

15   50   (95)

BOKER, HEINR, Ger. (c. 1867 –)
*4" 3 bl. Stock pat. Bone hdls. $90

20   100   (150)

Brand Marks & Stampings (Dates)	Value Range		
	Low	High	Code
BOKER, Solingen, Ger. Alamania (c. 1867 –) *4" 3 bl. Stock pat. Bone hdls. $80	20	85	(160)
BOKER, Ger. (c. 1867 –) 4" 3 bl. Stock pat. Del. hdls. $40	10	75	(115)
BOKER, USA (c. 1867 –) *4" 3 bl. Stock pat. Comp. hdls. $35	10	35	(70)
BONSA, Solingen, Ger. *4" 3 bl. Stock pat. Bone hdls. $35	12	35	(70)
BON KNIFE CO	10	10	(40)
BONTGEN & SABIN, Ger. *3" 3 bl. Stock pat. Stag hdls. $40	15	40	(60)
BOSTWICK BRAUNN CO., Toledo, OH (c. 1873 –) *3" 2 bl. Canoe pat. Bone hdls. $59	20	180	(95)
BOWEN, KNIFE CO., Atlanta, GA (c. 1973 –) *4½" 1 bl. Rem. bullet pat. Del. hdls. $55	20	75	(75)
BOWER, F.A. IMP. CO., Ger. *5" 1 bl. Daddy Barlow pat. Rough-sawed bone hdls. $58	15	100	(75)
BOWIE KNIFE, Newark, NJ *5" 1 bl. Springer pat. Bone hdls. $235	40	200	(150)
BOZORGZADEH, Tehran	25	25	
BRACH D. C. R. F., Ger. *3" 3 bl. Pen pat, Pearl hdls. $35	20	75	(60)
BRADLEY, L. & CO., Naugatuck, CT (c. 1844 – 1896) *3½" 3 bl. Whittler pat. Stag hdls. $95	25	150	(125)
BRAMHALL ELLISON, Carlisle Works, Eng. 4½" 2 bl. FH pat. hdls. $200	30	150	(125)

Brand Marks & Stampings (Dates)	Value Range		
	Low	High	Code
BRANDA D. R . PATENTO	20	20	(65)
BRANTFORD CUT. CO. USA *4" 2 bl. Trapper pat. Stag hdls. $75	20	80	(90)
BRESDUCK INC., New York (1930 – 1952) *3" 2 bl. Pen pat. Pearl hdls. $45	15	70	(70)
BRESNICK, CARL E., NY (c. 1927 – 1947) *4½" 4 bl. Cattle pat. Bone hdls. $68	20	125	(105)
BRIDDLE, CHARLES D. INC., Crisfield, MD *3" 2 bl. Jack pat. Comp. hdls. $19	10	75	(95)
BRIDGE CUTLERY CO., St. Louis, MO (c. 1915) *3½" 2bl. Jack pat. Bone hdls. $115	50	250	(200)
B.G.I. CO., Bridgeport, CT *4" 2 bl. Physician pat. Bone hdls. $58	20	130	(100)
BRIGHTON WORKS, Ger. 3" 2 bl. Pen pat. Art metal hdls. $25	15	50	(75)
BRISTOL LINE, Ger	18	18	(60)
BRIT-NIFE, St. Louis, MO	25	50	(75)
BROCH & THEIBES CUTLERY CO., St. Louis, MO (c. 1882 – 1892) *3½" 2bl. Jackpat. Rosewood hdls. $40	10	75	(100)
BROOKS & CROOKS, Shef., Eng. (1859 – 1947) *3¼" 3 bl. Whittler pat. Pearl hdls. $165	10	240	(150)
BROOKLYN CUT. CO., New York *4" 3 bl. Sailor pat. Wood hdls. $40	40	100	(150)
BROWN & PHARR, Norcross, GA (c. 1975 – 1981) 3½" Sowbelly pattern Rosewd. hdls. $65	50	100	(120)

Brand Marks & Stampings (Dates)	Value Range		Code
	Low	High	
BROWN SHOE CO., St. Louis, MO Lady's boot knife, medium, colorful celluloid. $85	75	75	(70)

Chart 1 Code Value		Chart 2 Pattern Value		Chart 3 Handle Value		Chart 4 Condition		RBR Collector Value
150	x	45	x	125	x	.99	=	$83.53

BROWNING ARMS CO. USA (c. 1969 –) 5" 1 bl. FH Pat. Rosewd. hdls. $300	75	300	(370)
BROWNING ARMS CO. USA (c. 1969 –) *3½" 3 bl. Stock pat. Wood hdls. $80	90	150	(200)
BROWNING, Germany *3½" 3 bl. Stock pat. Wood hdls. $20	20	75	(60)
BRUCKMANN, Ger. (c. 1890 – 1956) *3" 4 bl. Pen pat. Pearl hdls. $218	100	200	(250)

Chart 1 Code Value		Chart 2 Pattern Value		Chart 3 Handle Value		Chart 4 Condition		RBR Collector Value
150	x	.45	x	.90	x	.99	=	$60.14

BUCK CREEK, Solingen, Germany (c. 1968 –) *3¾" 2 bl. Stock pat. "Copperhead" Micarta hdls. $60	25	150	(150)
BUCK, El-Cagon, CA (c. 1965 –) 4" 3 bl. Stock pat. Del. hdls. $70	20	150	(150)
BUCKEYE CUT. CO., Dayton, OH *4" 3 bl. Whittler pat. Cel. hdls. $70	20	100	(80)

Brand Marks & Stampings (Dates)	Value Range		
	Low	High	Code
BUFFALO CUT. CO. *5" 1 bl. Coke F/h pat. India stag hdls. $210	35	125	(120)
BULLDOG BRAND, Ger. (Johnson City, TN) 3¾" 2 bl. Gunstock pat. Bone hdls. $40	55	150	(90)
BULLET, Pakistan (c. 1973 –) *4" 3 bl. Stock pat. Bone hdls. $20	10	40	(40)
BUHL & SONS CO., Detroit, MI *3½" 3 bl. Cattle pat. Bone hdls. $40	18	100	(70)
BURKINSHAW KNIFE CO., Pepperell, MA (c. 1853 – 1920) *3" 2 bl. Pen pat. Ivory hdls. $98	25	100	(75)
CALDWELL CUT. CO, Indpls., IN (Ger) *3½" 3 bl. Warncliffe pat. Bone hdls. $58	20	120	(90)
CAMBRIDGE CUT. CO., Shef., Eng. *4" 3 bl. Stock pat. Stag hdls. $80	35	100	(100)
CAMCO (Camillus) USA *3" 2 bl. Jack pat. Comp. hdls. $23	7	50	(65)
CAMCO, MUMBLEY PEG (Camillus) *3" 2 bl. Equal jack pat. Comp. hdls. $75	60	60	(215)
CAMILLUS CUTLERY CO., Camillus, NY (1902 –) *4" 3 bl. Stock pat. Bone hdls. $110	24	150	(150)
CAMILLUS, New York, NY (c. 1902 –) *4" 3 bl. Stock pat. Del. hdls. $35	15	75	(100)
CAMILLUS SWORD BRAND, NY USA *4" 3 bl. Stock pat. Del. hdls. $40	20	100	(115)
CAMDEN CUTLERY CO., Ger. *3" 2 bl. Jack pat. Wood hdls. $15	8	60	(60)
CAMP BUDDY USA (Thornton) *3¼" 4 bl. Utility pat. Comp. hdls. $20	15	60	(40)

Brand Marks & Stampings (Dates)	Value Range Low	Value Range High	Code
CAMERON KNIFE CO. *4" 2 bl. Trapper pat. Stag hdls. $66	20	75	(80)
CANASOTA KNIFE CO, NY (c. 1874 – 1895) *4", 3 bl., stock, bone hdls. $200	80	240	(310)
CANDCO, Switzerland *2½" 2 bl. Pen pat. Nickel hdls. $17	8	25	(60)
CANTON CUTLERY CO., Canton, OH (1879 – 1930) *3⅞," Equal end whittler, clear picture celluloid $140	20	175	(200)

CANTON CUTLERY CO.,
CANTON, OHIO,
JAN 1st. 1901.

Chart 1 Code Value		Chart 2 Pattern Value		Chart 3 Handle Value		Chart 4 Condition		RBR Collector Value
200	x	.55	x	1.25	x	.99	=	$136.12

Brand Marks & Stampings (Dates)	Low	High	Code
CAPITAL CUTLERY CO., Indpl., (Van Camp c. 1904 – 1948) *3½" 3 bl. Stock pat. Cell. hdls. $83	15	50	(85)
CARL SCHLIEPER, Solingen, Ger. ("Eye") *4" 3 bl. Stock pat. Bone hdls. $75	15	150	(100)
CARL SCHMIDT, Ger.	30	50	(75)
CARBO-MAGNETIC, (Griffon Cut. 1895 – 1906) *4" 2 bl. Jack pat. Bone hdls. $40.	15	60	(90)
CARRIER CUT. CO., Elmira, NY	25	30	(50)
CAR VAN STEEL, Canton, OH (c. 1911 – 1930) *3" 4 bl. Pen pat. Cel. hdls. $50	15	80	(100)
CARTER, Scottsville, KY (c. 1969 – 1974) *4" 4 bl. Congress pat. Pearl hdls. $110	20	120	(100)

Brand Marks & Stampings (Dates)	Value Range		Code
	Low	High	
CARTWRIGHT & YOUNG, Pittsburgh, PA (1847 – 1860)			
*5" 1 bl. L/back FH pattern Stag hdls. $200	30	200	(120)
CCC (Cattaraugus c. 1880 – 1963)			
*5" 1 bl. Barlow pat. Sawed bone hdls. $195	45	400	(250)
CASE BROS., Little Valley, NY (c. 1889 – 1905)			
*4" 2 bl. Jack pat. Wood hdls. $200	80	900	(500)
CASE BROS., Springville, NY (c. 1900)			
*4" 2 bl. Jack pat. Bone hdls. $200	50	600	(450)
CASE XX TESTED, Bradford, PA (c. 1905)			
*3½" 3 bl. Whittler pat. Stag hdls. $300	50	400	(310)
CASE XX, W.R. & SONS, Bradford, PA (c. 1950 – 1965)			
*4" 3 bl. Stock pat. Stag hdls. $200	40	350	(250)
CASE USA, W.R. & SONS, Bradford, PA (c. 1965 – 1969)			
*5" 1 bl. Bulldog			
Recent/common FH pat. Stag hdls. $265	25	300	(150)
CASE USA, W.R. & SONS, (W/Dots-c. 1970 – 1979)			
*4" 3 bl. Stock pat. Bone hdls. $65	16	150	(130)
CASE USA, W.R. & SONS (Angle letters/dots, c. 1980 –)			
*3½" 3 bl. Stock pat. Bone hdls. $36	16	100	(80)
CASE USA Bradford, PA (c. 1880 – current)			
No dot – Parker Cut. Co. "Case Classics" Reproductions			(60)
CAST STEEL, LA	20	25	(60)
CATSKILL KNIFE CO., NY			
*4" 3 bl. Stock pat. Bone hdls. $118	20	125	(150)
CATTARAUGUS CUTLERY CO., Little Valley, NY (c. 1880 – 1954)			
*5¼" 1 bl. Coke FH pat. Bone hdls. $897	30	650	(550)
CENTAUR CUTLERY, Sperry & Alex (c. 1893 – 1913)			
*3½" 3 bl. Stock pat. Wood hdls. $50	14	75	(80)

Brand Marks & Stampings (Dates)	Value Range		Code
	Low	High	
CENTRAL CITY KNIFE CO., Phoenix, NY (c. 1880 – 1892)			
4" 3 bl. Stock pat. Bone hdls. $113	50	150	(175)
C.B.S., Solingen, Ger.	12	30	
CELEBRATE CUT. CO., Solingen, Ger. (c. 1895 – 1927)			
*3" 2 bl. Game pat. Bone hdls. $45	12	50	(100)
CHALLENGE CUT. CO., Bridgeport, CT (1867 – 1928)			
*3½" Swell end jack, bone. $70	20	100	(150)

Chart 1 Code Value		Chart 2 Pattern Value		Chart 3 Handle Value		Chart 4 Condition		RBR Collector Value
150	x	.45	x	1.10	x	.99	=	$67.49

	Low	High	Code
CHAMPION KNIFE (c. 1925 – 1932)			
*5" 2 bl. Fish pat. Comp. hdls. $25	10	50	(55)
CHARLTON, Shef., Eng.	15	50	(70)
CHATILLON, JOHN & SONS, NY (c. 1894 – 1937)			
*3½" 2 bl. Warncliffe pat. Stag hdls. $93	35	150	(90)
CHAPMAN, HAND FORGED			
*4" 3 bl. Whittler pat. Bone hdls. $92	40	70	(95)
CHICAGO KNIFE WORKS, (c. 1911)			
*3½" 3 bl. Stock pat. Bone hdls. $45	20	75	(70)
CHICAGO POCKET KNIFE CO.			
*3½" 4 bl. Equal end pen pat. Picture hdls. $70	20	85	(100)
CHIPAWAY CUT. CO. (E.C. Simmins, c. 1891 – 1907)			
*3" 3 bl. Pen pat. Ebony adv. hdls. $50	35	90	(140)

Brand Marks & Stampings (Dates)	Value Range Low	High	Code
CHERO-COLA CO.			
*3" 2 bl. Jack pat. Picture hdls. $45	25	70	(80)
CHRISTIANS			
Lobster pattern, Medium, Mother-of-Pearl. $37			(70)

Chart 1 Code Value		Chart 2 Pattern Value		Chart 3 Handle Value		Chart 4 Condition		RBR Collector Value
225	x	.40	x	1.75	x	.99	=	$155.92

CHRISTIANS, Solingen, Ger.   (225)

Chart 1 Code Value		Chart 2 Pattern Value		Chart 3 Handle Value		Chart 4 Condition		RBR Collector Value
50	x	.35	x	.80	x	.99	=	$13.86

CHRISTY KNIFE CO., Fremont, OH (c. 1890 –)
3" Slide blade, Pen pat. Met. hndls. $14   10   25   (50)

C. J. HERBERTZ, Ger.
*3" 3 blade Lob Pen pat. Pearl hdls. $60   35   90   (100)

C. J. & C., Shef. (Christopher Johnson & Co. c. 1865 –)
*4" 3 blade Stock pat. Stag hdls. $75   45   100   (85)

C.K. CO.   30   30   (60)

C. KUNBE & SONS, Dresden
*4½" 1 blade Jack pat. Comp. hdls. $20   30   65   (50)

	Value Range		
Brand Marks & Stampings (Dates)	Low	High	Code
CLARK BROS., Kansas City, MO (1895 – 1925) *4" 4 blade Congress pat. Bone hdls. $70	20	90	(100)
CLAUBERT CUTLERY CO., Ger. (1847 – 1875) *4" 3 blade Warncliffe pat. Bone hdls. $65	25	100	(100)
CLAUSS, Fremont, OH (c. 1847 –) *3½" 4 blade Cattle pat. Bone hdls. $70	30	75	(127)
CLAY-ANDERSON, NY USA	20	50	(60)
CLEAN CUT (Dunham, Corrigan & Hayden c. 1884 – 1906) *4" 3 bl. Stock pat. Wood hdls. $60	50	75	(90)
CLEMENTS, Shef., Eng.	30	50	(50)
CLEVELAND CUT CO. 2½" 3 bl. Pen pat. Cel. hdls. $33	20	75	(75)
CLOVER BRAND, Syracuse, NY (Kastor Bros. c. 1941) *3" 2 bl. Pen pat. Bone hdls. $50	20	40	(120)
CLYDE CUTLERY CO., Clyde, OH (c. 1935) *5" 1 bl. Fish pat. Cel. hdls. $50	30	100	(125)
COAST CUT. CO., Portland, OR (c. 1922 –) *4½" 3 bl. Stock pat. Stag hdls. $114	20	150	(95)
COCA-COLA, Atlanta, GA (c. 1973 –) Adv. + old. *3½" 4 bl. Utility pat. Metal hdls. $90	90	90	(85)
COFWANOE WORKS, Phila., PA *4" 2 bl. Jack pat. Bone hdls. $41	35	75	(90)
COHELLE	35	35	(50)
COLES, New York – Germany (c. 1969 –) *4" 3 bl. Stock pat. Stag hdls. $64	30	90	(85)
COLONEL COON, Columbia, TN 4" 3 bl. Stock pat. Bone hdls. $75	20	80	(150)

Brand Marks & Stampings (Dates)	Value Range		
	Low	High	Code
COLONIAL CUTLERY CO. Providence, RI (c. 1926 –) *4" 3 bl. Stock pat. Stag hdls. $90	15	150	(100)
COLONIAL, Providence, RI (c. 1938 –) *3" 2 bl. Jack pat. Tin shell hdls. $14	4	20	(55)
COLT, Ger. (c. 1968) *4" 3 bl. Stock pat. Stag hdls. $75	20	75	(100)
COLT ARMS CO., (Woods Design) Hartford, CT (c. 1969) *4½" 1 bl. Swing hdls. FH pat. Micarta hdls. $550	150	400	(610)
COLUMBIA CUT. CO., Worcester, MA (c. 1898 – 1905) *4" 2 bl. Gunstock pat. Stag hdls. $105	30	150	(120)
CONTENTO, Made in Germany	16	16	(40)
CONTINENTAL CUT. CO., New York *3½" 3 bl. Equal end jack Cel. hdls. $36	20	70	(65)
COOK BROS., Shef. Eng. *4" 3 bl. Warncliffe pat. Stag hdls. $125	30	85	(120)

Chart 1 Code Value		Chart 2 Pattern Value		Chart 3 Handle Value		Chart 4 Condition		RBR Collector Value
95	x	.40	x	1.30	x	.99	=	$48.90

COPPEL, Ger. (c. 1884 – 1892) NY 3" Barlow Bone hdls. $50.00	25	80	(95)
CORA, Ger.	12	15	(40)
CORLISS CUT., Ger.	20	20	(40)
CORNWALL KNIFE CO., New York *4" 2 bl. Jack pat. Bone hdls. $72	30	65	(100)
COVINGTON, Nashville, TN (c. 1945) *4" 2 bl. Muskrat pat. Cracked ice hdls. $40	12	50	(95)
C. PLATT & SONS (see Platt Bro's)			

Brand Marks & Stampings (Dates)	Value Range		Code
	Low	High	
CRAFTSMAN, (Sears Roebuck & Co) *4" 2 bl. Stock pat. Del. hdls. $30	10	75	(95)
CRANDELL CUT. CO., Bradford, PA (c. 1905) *4½" 2 bl. Trapper pat. Bone hdls. $75	14	150	(136)
CRESCENT CUT. CO. (c. 1917) *3½" 4 bl. Congress pat. Bone hdls. $65	14	50	(90)
C. R. LINDER, Solingen, Ger.	8	8	(30)
CRIPPLE CREEK USA, Lockport, IL 4" 2 bl. Trapper pat. Bone hdls. $101	65	200	(225)
CROOKES & SONS, Shef., Eng. (c. 1827 – 1907) 4" 4 bl. Stock pat. Bone hdls. $146	35	350	(150)
CROWN CUT. CO., New York/Prussia *5" 1 bl. Coke pat. FH, Stag hdls. $206	30	150	(110)
CRUCIBAL KNIFE CO., New York (c. 1926 – 1929) *4" 3 bl. Stock pat. Bone hdls. $52	20	75	(80)
CRUSADER, Trademark, USA	12	25	(60)
CUMBERLAND CUT. CO., Shef., Eng.	30	40	(60)
CURLEY BROS., New York (1902 – 1903) *4" 2 bl. Jack pat. Bone hdls. $60	30	70	(90)
CURTIN & CLARK, St. Joseph, MO (c. 1898 – 1909) *4" 2 bl. Trapper pat. Stag hdls. $95	40	125	(126)
CUSSIN & FERN CO. USA (1931 – 1941) *3½" 4 bl. Congress pat. Bone hdls. $40	15	80	(80)
CUTINO CO., Kansas City	20	30	(60)
CUT SURE, (Kruse & Bahlmarr c. 1894 – 1962) *4" 1 bl. Springer pat. Comp. hdls. $40	20	80	(66)
DAHLIA, Ger.	10	30	(60)

Brand Marks & Stampings (Dates)	Value Range		
	Low	High	Code
DASCO, Rockford, IL	12	25	(50)
DAWES & BALL, Shef., Eng. *3½" 4 bl. Congress pat. Bone hdls. $50	15	75	(100)

Chart 1 Code Value		Chart 2 Pattern Value		Chart 3 Handle Value		Chart 4 Condition		RBR Collector Value
300	x	1.10	x	1.10	x	.99	=	$359.37

D. BARNETT TOOL CO., Newark, NJ *4½" Farrier's tool pat. Bone hdls. $365	30	150	(300)
DEBORE & BACH (D & B), Ger. (c. 1916 – 1917) *3" 4 bl. Pen pat. Bone hdls. $30	15	65	(75)
DECORA, Germany	12	25	(50)
DEE CEE, USA	15	30	(60)
DELETTRES, (Vadsco c. 1927 – 1932) *4" 4 bl. Utility pat. Comp. hdls. $25	10	60	(50)
DEWEY, England 3⅝" 2 bl. Large Jack pat. "Mechanic's knife" bone hdls. $25	6	23	(50)

Chart 1 Code Value		Chart 2 Pattern Value		Chart 3 Handle Value		Chart 4 Condition		RBR Collector Value
150	x	.45	x	1.10	x	.99	=	$73.50

| | Value Range | | |
Brand Marks & Stampings (Dates)	Low	High	Code
DIAMOND EDGE, (Shapleigh Hdw. Co. c. 1902 – 1960)			
*4" 2 bl. Jack pat. Bone hdls. $75	30	200	(150)
DIAMOND EDGE, (Val-Test c. 1960 – 1965)			
*4 3 bl. Stock pat. Del. hdls. $35	15	90	(100)
DIAMOND KNIFE CO., Ger.	20	50	(65)
DIAMOND EDGE, (Imperial c. 1967 –)			
*4" 3 bl. Stock pat. Del. hdls. $30	12	50	(85)
DICKINSON, Shef., Eng.			
*4" 2 bl. Physician pat. Stag hdls. $82	25	125	(115)
DISSTON, E.W. & Sons, Germany	25	150	(125)
DISSTON, E.W. & Sons			
3³/₄", Crown jack, Old bone. $39			(70)

Chart 1 Code Value	Chart 2 Pattern Value	Chart 3 Handle Value	Chart 4 Condition	RBR Collector Value
125 x	45 x	1.30 x	.99 =	$72.38

	Low	High	Code
DIXIE KNIFE CO.			
*4" 2 bl. Trapper pat. Bone hdls. $50	30	75	(90)
DIXON CUTLERY CO., USA-Ger.			
*3" 2 bl. Pen pat. Pearl hdls. $60	20	75	(100)
DODSON, Chicago, IL			
*3½" 4 bl. Cattle pat. Comp. hdls. $45	20	80	(85)
DOLLAR KNIFE CO., Titusville, PA (Schatt & Morgan c. 1926)			
*3½" 2 bl. Serp. jack pat. Bone hdls. $56	20	75	(125)
DOMAR CUTLERY CO., Oklahoma City	50	50	(60)
DOUBLE COLA	50	50	(90)

Brand Marks & Stampings (Dates)	Value Range		
	Low	High	Code
DOUGLAS WA USA, Brockton, MA (Shoe adv.) $75	40	40	(75)
DRAKE HDW. CO. (Ulster)	40	40	(60)
DWIGHT DIVINE & SONS, USA (c. 1876 – 1941) *5" 1 bl. Coke FH pat. Stag hdls. $176	30	175	(100)
DORIC (S. E. Kress c. 1932 – 53) *3½" 2 bl. Jack pat. Wood hdls. $36	30	80	(90)
DREIZACK, Ger.	20	65	(50)
DUKES, FATHER OF BARLOWS	120	200	(150)
DUNN BROS., Providence, RI	10	45	(50)
DUBL-DUCK (C. Bresnick c. 1927 –) *3½" 3 bl. Pen pat. Pearl hdls. $60	20	75	(90)
DUANE CUT CO., Ger	10	15	(50)
DUNHAM, CORRIGAN & HAYDEN CO., San Francisco (c. 1849 – 1927) *4½" 1 bl. Lockback FH pat. Stag hdls. $180	40	200	(96)
DUPONT, (c. 1933 – 1934) *4½" 2 bl. Jack pat. Bone hdls. $267	30	125	(165)
E.A.A., Solingen, Ger.	12	12	(40)
EAGLE POCKET KNIFE CO., New Haven, CT (c. 1916 – 1919) *3½" 2 bl. Jack pat. old Metal hdls. $38	25	90	(130)
EAGLE, Japan (c. 1974 –)	10	20	(40)
EAGLE PENCIL CO., New York (1883 –) *4" 1 bl. Screw-push pat. Metal hdls. $75	40	75	(80)
EAGLETON KNIFE CO. USA *3½" 2 bl. Barlow pat. Bone hdls. $78	30	100	(150)
E. A. HERDER & SONS, Solingen, Ger. *4" 2 bl. Jack pat. Wood hdls. $20	20	75	(70)
EDGAR MASTER, USA	12	15	(50)

Brand Marks & Stampings (Dates)	Value Range		
	Low	High	Code
EDGE, Solingen, Ger. (c. 1974 –) *4" 3 bl. Stock pat. Wood hdls. $36	15	75	(80)
EDGE MARK, Japan (c. 1976 –) *3½" 3 bl. Stock pat. Wood hdls. $35	12	60	(75)
EDWARD WEEK & SONS, New York *3½" 4 bl. Cattle pat. Stag hdls. $70	15	100	(80)
E. F. & S., Eng. (Enos Furness) *3½" 2 bl. Barlow pat. Bone hdls. $83	20	90	(160)
E. FELSENHELD, Ger.	20	20	(60)
E. F. WALTERS & CO. GUARANTEED *4" 4 bl. Congress pat. Bone hdls. $76	30	90	(90)
EDITH WERKS, Solingen, Ger.	18	18	(50)
ED. WUSTHOFF, Solingen, Ger. *3½" 3 bl. Warncliffe pat. Wood hdls. $35	18	65	(60)
EIG, Germany/Italy/Japan *4" 3 bl. Stock pat. Wood hdls. $35	10	50	(65)
EISENSTADT MFG. CO. (c. 1907 – 1954) *4" 2 bl. Open end jack pat. Bone hdls. $47	18	45	(80)
EKA, Eskilstuna, Sweden *3" 4 bl. Pen pat. Art. Metal hdls. $55	15	105	(170)
E. K. TRYON CO. *3" 4 bl. Cattle pat. Bone hdls. $71	20	90	(100)
ELDER & CO., Ger.	20	20	(50)
ELECTRIC CUT. CO., Walden, NY (c. 1873 – 1901) *5" 1 bl. Lockback FH pat. Stag hdls. $315	30	300	(190)
ELECTRIC, France *4½" 2 bl. Pliers pat. Metal hdls. $60	40	40	(110)
ELEPHANT MARK	20	20	(60)

Brand Marks & Stampings (Dates)	Value Range Low	Value Range High	Code
EL GALLO, Solingen, Ger. (c. 1968 – 1970) *4" 3 bl. Stock pat. Bone hdls. $45	25	80	(75)
ELLINVILLE KNIFE CO. (D. Devine-c. 1876 – 1920) *3½" 3 bl. Equal end pat. Pearl hdls. $60	25	90	(85)
ELGIN AM MFG. CO, USA	25	70	(90)
ELKISCH KADISON, Ger.	15	15	(50)
ELLIOT CUT. CO., Ger. (Czech) *3" 2 bl. Op. end jack pat. Wood hdls. $15	12	40	(70)
ELLIOT, WM. & CO., New York (c. 1880 – 1908) *3" 3 bl. Whittler pat. Bone hdls. $86	35	90	(120)
ELOSI, Ger.	12	12	(50)
ELYTE, Ger.	12	12	(40)
ENGLEWERK, Ger. *3" 3 bl. Pen pat. Pearl hdls. $75	35	35	(126)
ENGLISH STEEL, Shef., Eng. *3½" 3 bl. Stock pat. Comp. hdls. $30	20	80	(60)
ENDERS MFG. CO., St. Louis, MO (c. 1908 – 1913) *3½" 2 bl. Muskrat pat. Old green bone hdls. $80	30	90	(100)
EMMONS-HAWKINS HDW. CO. (c. 1910) *3¼" 2 bl. Gunstock pat. senator Bone hdls. $70	30	80	(95)

Chart 1 Code Value		Chart 2 Pattern Value		Chart 3 Handle Value		Chart 4 Condition		RBR Collector Value
95	x	55	x	130	x	.99	=	$67.24

Brand Marks & Stampings (Dates)	Value Range		
	Low	High	Code

EMPIRE KNIFE CO., Winstead, CT (c. 1856 – 1930)
3½" Electrician jack pat. Ebony wood hdls. $80   50   300   (250)

Chart 1 Code Value		Chart 2 Pattern Value		Chart 3 Handle Value		Chart 4 Condition		RBR Collector Value
250	x	.35	x	.90	x	.99	=	$77.96

EMPIRE KNIFE CO., Ger.
*3½" 3 bl. Whittler pat. Stag hdls. $63   20   90   (70)

ENTERPRISE CUTLERY CO., St. Louis
Jack medium, Celluloid hdls. $35   (100)

Chart 1 Code Value		Chart 2 Pattern Value		Chart 3 Handle Value		Chart 4 Condition		RBR Collector Value
100	x	35	x	1.00	x	.99	=	$34.65

ENTERPRISE KNIFE CO., St. Louis (Ger.)
*3½" 3 bl. Stock pat. Bone hdls. $55   20   75   (100)

ERN, Ger. (1916 – 1926)
*3¼" 3 bl. Stock pat. Bone hdls. $32   15   70   (65)

ERVIN CUT. CO., Ger.   18   18   (35)

ESKILSTUNA, Sweden (1865 – 1949)
*3" 4 bl. Pen pat. Art Metal hdls. $40   20   150   (130)

ESSEX CUTLERY CO.   15   15   (20)

ETCHED, LIC., NY (c. 1933)   25   80   (70)

Brand Marks & Stampings (Dates)	Value Range		
	Low	High	Code
EVERKEEN (see John Pritzlaff Hardware Co.)			
EVERSHARP CUTLERY CO. USA (c. 1923 – 1925) *4" 2 bl. Muskrat pat. Bone hdls. $65	15	100	(131)
EXCELSIOR KNIFE CO. (c. 1880 – 1884)	20	100	(100)
EXECUTIVE, USA *3" 2 bl. Pen pat. Crk. Ice hdls. $21	12	40	(80)
EYE, CARL SCHLEIPER, Solingen, Ger. *3½" 3 bl. Stock pat. Comp. hdls. $65	15	150	(125)
EYE BRAND, Solinger, Ger. *3½" 3 bl. Stock pat. Comp. hdls. $65	15	150	(125)
EYE WITNESS, Eng. (See-Taylor's Eng.)	25	125	(100)
FABICO, Ger. & Japan	6	20	(40)
F & L CELEBRATED CUTLERY CO. (Freidman & Lauterjung, c. 1873 – 1881) *4" 4 bl. Congress pat. Bone hdls. $81	30	150	(125)
F. A. BOWER DIST. CO., Solingen, Ger. *5" 1 bl. Barlow pat. Bone hdls. $44	15	95	(110)
FABYAN KNIFE CO., New York *4" 3 bl. Stock pat. Comp. hdls. $31	15	45	(95)
F. A. KOCH & CO., New York	20	40	(50)
FAIRMONT CUTLERY CO., NY *3½" 3 bl. Pen pat. Stag hdls. $60	20	75	(100)
FARWELL-OZMUN-KIRK & CO., St. Paul, MN (c. 1881 – 1959) *4" 3 bl. Stock pat. Bone hdls. $75	40	125	(150)
FAULKHAINER & CO., Ger. *4" 3 bl. Stock pat. Bone hdls. $35	40	65	(70)
FAVORITE KNIFE CO., Ger. *3" 3 bl. Pen pat. Metal hdls. $15	8	30	(60)

Brand Marks & Stampings (Dates)	Value Range		
	Low	High	Code
FAYETTEVILLE KNIFE CO. (c. 1911) *3¼" 2 bl. Barlow pat. Bone hdls. $62	20	80	(120)
FEDERAL KNIFE CO., Syracuse USA (c. 1927) *3½" 2 bl. Serp. Jack pat. Bone hdls. $55	20	80	(110)
FEIN STAHL, Ger.	10	20	(40)
FEIST & CO., Ger. (c. 1903 – 1948)	10	20	(40)
FIDELITY KNIFE CO., New York *3½" 2 bl. Jack pat. Bone hdls. $50	12	40	(85)
FIFE CUTLERY CO., Mt. Sterling, KY (c. 1968 – 1974) *4" 4 bl. Congress (H&R pat. G & T Imp) Stag hdls. $135	20	150	(130)
FIGHTIN' ROOSTER (Frank Buster) Ger./USA 3½" 3 bl. Stock pat. artistic plastic hdls. $90	35	200	(200)

Chart 1 Code Value		Chart 2 Pattern Value		Chart 3 Handle Value		Chart 4 Condition		RBR Collector Value
200	x	.50	x	.90	x	.99	=	$89.16

FILLMORE CUTLERY CO. *4" 4 bl. Congress pat. Bone hdls. $71	10	80	(85)
FINEDGE, Solingen, Ger.	12	20	(60)
FIELDS, A. & CO. 3½" 3 bl. Stock pat. Bone hdls. $46	10	75	(80)
FLAGG CUT. CO., New York (c. 1886) *4" 2 bl. Jack pat. Bone hdls. $52	30	80	(85)
FLETCHER HDW. CO., Detroit, MI *3½" 2 bl. Game pat. Bone hdls. $34	15	50	(75)

Brand Marks & Stampings (Dates)	Value Range		
	Low	High	Code

FLORAWERKS CUT. CO., Ger.
*3" 3 bl. Pen pat. Pearl hdls. $61 — 20 — 100 — (99)

FLYLOCK KNIFE CO., Bridgeport, CT (Challenge Cut. Co. c. 1916 – 68)
*4½" 1 bl. Springer pat. Bone hdls. $225 — 30 — 250 — (340)

Chart 1 Code Value		Chart 2 Pattern Value		Chart 3 Handle Value		Chart 4 Condition		RBR Collector Value
340	x		x		x	.99	=	$262.35

FLOYD & BOHR, Louisville, KY
*4" 4 bl. Congress pat. Bone hdls. $62 — 20 — 80 — (95)

FORD MEDLEY, Eng.
*4" 2 bl. Physicians pat. Stag hdls. $61 — 20 — 100 — (85)

FOX CUTLERY CO., Milwaukee, WI (c. 1884 – 1955)
*5" 1 bl. Folding hunter pat. Stag hdls. $315 — 40 — 300 — (190)

FRANK BUSTER CUT. CO., Ger./USA
(See Fightin' Rooster) — 35 — 200 — (200)

FULTON CUTLERY USA, NY
*3½" 2 bl. Jack pat. Comp. hdls. $28 — 15 — 95 — (95)

GAMBLE STORES
*3" 4 bl. Pen pat. Comp. hdls. $21 — 10 — 40 — (80)

Chart 1 Code Value		Chart 2 Pattern Value		Chart 3 Handle Value		Chart 4 Condition		RBR Collector Value
150	x	.35	x	1.75	x	.99	=	$90.95

GARDEN CITY CUTLERY, Austria
2½" Pen pat. Pearl hdls. $95 — 8 — 60 — (150)

Brand Marks & Stampings (Dates)	Value Range		Code
	Low	High	
G. C. COMPANY, Italy (1969 –) *5" 3 bl. Stock pat. Horn hdls. $45	12	75	(102)
GARLAND CUT. CO., Ger. (c. 1913)	10	30	(65)
GENEVA CUTLERY CO., Geneva, NY (c. 1902 – 1935) *4" 4 bl. Cattle pat. Bone hdls. $94	30	150	(120)
GERMANIA CUT. WORKS, Ger. *3½" 2 bl. Jack pat. Bone hdls. $30	15	40	(65)
GERBER, Portland, OR (c. 1939 –) *5" 2 bl. Folding Hunter pat. Stag hdls.$220	20	200	(155)
GERLACH, Portland, OR	20	85	(65)
GEO. SCHRADE KNIFE CO., Bridgeport, CT (c. 1925 – 1945) *4" 1 bl. Springer pat. Bone hdls. $200	30	250	(140)
GESCO, Japan or Ireland	8	15	(45)
GERSON CO., Ger.	10	50	(50)
GIT'S RAZOR NIFE, Chicago, IL (1938 – 1950)	15	90	(90)
GRAFRATH (G) *5" 1 bl. Gravity pat. Comp. hdls. $90	40	50	(125)
GIBBERSON & CO., Shef., Eng./Scotland *4" 4 bl. Pen pat. Tortoise hdls. $375	30	400	(234)
GLOBE CUTLERY CO., Ger.	20	30	(65)
GUARANTIE, Ger. (Stahl)	10	30	(10)
GUTMAN CUT. CO. (c. 1960 –) *4" 4 bl. Congress (H&R) pat. Stag hdls. $78	20	100	(75)

Brand Marks & Stampings (Dates)	Value Range		
	Low	High	Code
GOLDEN RULE CUT. CO., Chicago, IL (1911 – 1924)			
Jack medium, Picture celluloid hdls. $72	30	250	(128)

Chart 1 Code Value		Chart 2 Pattern Value		Chart 3 Handle Value		Chart 4 Condition		RBR Collector Value
128	x	45	x	125	x	.99	=	$71.28

Brand Marks & Stampings (Dates)	Low	High	Code
GOLD SEAL, Shef., Eng.	20	40	(80)
GRAEF & SCHMIDT, Ger. (c. 1888 – 1943)			
*4" 2 bl. Gunstock pat. Stag hdls. $58	20	100	(80)
GRAY & CO.	20	40	(50)
GRIFFON XX, Worchester, MA (1919 – 1946)			
*5" 1 bl. FH pat. Bone hdls. $165	30	150	(120)
GRIFFON, Ger.	30	40	(65)
GUSTAHL, Ger.	20	30	(50)
GUST HAKER, Ger.	20	30	(50)
G. WOODHEAD, Sheffield			
*3½" 3 bl. Warncliffe pat. Stag hdls. $99	20	125	(95)
HACKMAN PUUKO, Finland			
*3¼" 1 bl. Jack pat. Comp. hdls. $22	15	50	(75)
HALBARD (F. A. Clauberg, c. 1912 – 1914)			
*3" 2 bl. Jack pat. Horn hdls. $27	12	70	(95)
H. A. DREER, Phila. USA			
*3" 4 bl. Pen pat. Comp. hdls. $20	15	40	(95)
HALL, USA	15	40	(65)

Brand Marks & Stampings (Dates)	Value Range		
	Low	High	Code
HALIGARD, Eskilstuna, Sweden *5" 1 bl. FH. pat. Wood hdls. $71	20	90	(81)
H. & J. KING, WARRANTED *4" 4 bl. Congress pat. Stag hdls. $100	30	150	(95)
HAMILTON KNIFE CO., St. Louis, MO *3½" 3 bl. Whittler pat. Bone hdls. $75	20	80	(100)
H. A. MACK CORP., Boston-Italy	15	45	(60)
HAMMER BRAND, (New York Knife Co. c. 1878 – 1931) Large Jack. "Large" Cocobolo hdls. $140	30	300	(350)

Chart 1 Code Value		Chart 2 Pattern Value		Chart 3 Handle Value		Chart 4 Condition		RBR Collector Value
350	x	45	x	.90	x	.99	=	$140.33

	Value Range		
HAMMER BRAND (Imperial Cut. Co. c. 1936 –) *4" 3 bl. Stock pat. Comp. hdls. $49	10	60	(100)
HARRIS BROS., Chicago, IL *3½" 2 bl. Elec. pat. Comp. hdls. $22	20	60	(75)
HART CUT. CO., NY (1909 – 40) *2½" 2bl. Pen pat. Pearl hdls. $45	15	70	(76)
HARTKOPE & CO., Solingen, Ger. *3" 4 bl. Pen pat. Abl. pearl hdls. $63	25	90	(80)
HATCH CUTLERY CO., Bridgeport, CT (c. 1892 – 1898) *5" 2 bl. Fold-hunter pat. Bone hdls. $172	20	150	(200)
HAWTHORN CUTLERY CO., Ger. *4" 4 bl. Flatfish pat. Stag hdls. $105	20	80	(95)
H & B MFG. CO., New Britain, CT (c. 1852 – 1895) *3½" 2 bl. Jack pat. Cel. hdls. $53	20	95	(85)

Brand Marks & Stampings (Dates)	Value Range		
	Low	High	Code
HAYWOOD & CO., Shef., Eng.	12	50	(60)
HEATHCOTE, Eng.	15	65	(65)
HEINZ, Solingen, Ger.	20	20	(65)
H. KESCHNER, Solingen, Ger.	10	30	(60)
H. LITTLEWOOD CELEBRATED CUT., Ger. *3½" 3 bl. Flatfish pat. Cel. hdls. $37	15	75	(65)
HELLER BROS. CO., Newark, NJ (c. 1900 – 1930) *4" 3 bl. Cattle pat. Wood hdls. $55.	12	75	(95)
HENKEL & JOYCE HDW. CO. USA *3½" 3 bl. Whittler pat. Bone hdls. $85	25	90	(120)
HENCKELS, J. A., Ger. (c. 1931 –) *4" 3 bl. Stock pat. Stag hdls. $98	30	150	(125)
HENCKLES, PAUL A. 3½" 3 bl. Stock pat. Bone hdls. $32	12	75	(70)

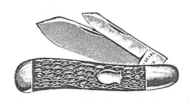

Chart 1 Code Value		Chart 2 Pattern Value		Chart 3 Handle Value		Chart 4 Condition		RBR Collector Value
150	x	.35	x	1.00	x	.99	=	$51.97

HEN & ROOSTER, Spain (Unauthorized stamp) *4" 3 bl. Stock pat. Bone hdls. $90	50	125	(180)
HENRY SEARS & SONS (1865) 3⅜" 2 bl. Dog leg jack pat. Jigged celluloid hdls. $55	35	250	(150)
HERDER & CO., Solingen, Ger. (1887 –) *5" 1 bl. Lockback FH pat. Stag hdls. $99	12	45	(60)

Brand Marks & Stampings (Dates)	Low	Value Range High	Code
HENRY W. MASON & CO., Shef., Eng. *4½" 2 bl. Physician pat. Bone hdls. $73	20	80	(125)
HERDER, FREEDR. ABR., Solingen, Ger. (c. 1925 –) *4" 1 bl. Lockback pat. Wood hdls. $25	12	60	(65)
HERMITAGE CUTLERY CO.	15	60	(65)
HERMITAGE, Ger.	12	40	(50)
HERMES, Ger.	8	12	(60)
HIBBARD, SPENCER & BARTLETT (c. 1855 – 1960) 3⅝" Cattle/old spear. Pearl hdl. $200	15	150	(150)

Chart 1 Code Value		Chart 2 Pattern Value		Chart 3 Handle Value		Chart 4 Condition		RBR Collector Value
150	x	75	x	1.75	x	.99	=	$194.90

HICKORY, USA (J. H. Sutcliffe Co., Louisville, KY) Sway back jack. Large Cocobolo hdls $50	20	45	(100)

Chart 1 Code Value		Chart 2 Pattern Value		Chart 3 Handle Value		Chart 4 Condition		RBR Collector Value
100	x	55	x	90	x	.99	=	$49

HICKOK MFG. CO., Rochester NY (c. 1937 – 1951)
*5" 2 bl. Folding hunter pat. Stag hdls. $262   30   250   (140)

Brand	Low	High	Code
HILGER & SONS, CELEBRATED CUT., Eng. 3" 4 bl. Pen pat. Bone hdls. $41	12	90	(90)
HILL BROS. *4" 3 bl. Stock pat. Bone hdls. $55	60	75	(85)

		Value Range		
Brand Marks & Stampings (Dates)	Low	High	Code
H & L MFG. CO., New Britain, CT *3½" 2 bl. Serp. jack pat. Ivory hdls. $100	30	90	(95)
HINDENBURG SCHNEID, Solingen, Ger. *4" 3 bl. Whittler pat. Stag hdls. $90	20	70	(100)
HIT, USA	20	30	(55)
HOFFRITZ, N.Y., Germany *4" 3 bl. Stock pat. Stag hdls. $65	20	140	(85)

Chart 1 Code Value		Chart 2 Pattern Value		Chart 3 Handle Value		Chart 4 Condition		RBR Collector Value
450	x	.55	x	1.25	x	.99	x	$306.90

HOLLEY MFG. CO., Lakeville, CT (c. 1843 – 1930) 3¼" closed, Swell center whittler pat. Waterfall celluloid hdls. $310	35	400	(450)
HOLLINGER, Fremont, OH *3½" 3 bl. Stock pat. Bone hdls. $58	20	70	(100)
HOLLINGSWORTH, Kane, PA (c. 1916 – 1930) *4" 3 bl. Stock pat. Cel. hdls. $72	25	75	(115)
HOLUB, Sycamore, IL	20	50	(70)
HOMF., USA	20	75	(80)
HONK FALLS KNIFE CO., Napanoch, NY (1921 – 1929) *3" 4 bl. Pen pat. Pearl hdls. $185	45	300	(300)
HORYIBIN (W & S) Shef.	40	150	(120)
HORIZONT, Ger.	20	20	(45)
HORNES CUT CO., Ger.	15	30	(65)
HOWARD BROS., Ger. *4" 3 bl. Whittler pat. Comp. hdls. $55	15	90	(73)
HOWARTH, Eng. (c. 1920 – 1951) *4" 4 bl. Utility pat. Bone hdls. $26	20	70	(75)

Brand Marks & Stampings (Dates)	Value Range		
	Low	High	Code
HUBERTS, Ger. (Wheel)	20	20	(50)
HUDSON KNIFE CO., USA	15	35	(70)
HUMPHREYS, Shef., Eng. *4" 2 bl. Jack pat. Stag hdls. $51	15	70	(75)
HUNTER (Radigan-Rich c. 1905 – 1907) *5½" 1 bl. Lock back FH pat. Stag hdls. $300	30	90	(166)
HUNTER CUTLERY CO., Ger. *3½" 2 bl. Serp. jack pat. Bone hdls. $46	20	45	(80)
HYDE MFG. CO., Southbridge, MA (c. 1875 –) *4" 2 bl. Elec. pat. Wood hdls. $25	12	65	(102)
H. VILLE KNIFE CO. *3" 2 bl. Pen pat. Ivory hdls. $85	20	90	(138)
IBBERSON, G., Shef., Eng. (c. 1700 –) *4" 3 bl. Whittler pat. Tortoise hdls. $390	40	400	(150)
IBBOTSON, C. & CO., Sheffield (c. 1868 – 1896) *3½" 2 bl. Senator pen pat. Ivory hdls. $225	30	300	(155)
IDEAL K. CO. USA (c. 1898) *3" 2 bl. Barlow pat. Bone hdls. $32	20	45	(80)
IDEAL, USA *3" 2 bl. Jack pat. Metal shell hdls. $11	5	15	(125)
I.K. CO. USA	5	10	(60)
IMPERIAL KNIFE CO., Providence, RI (Circle, c. 1917 –) *4" 3 bl. Stock pat. Bone hdls. $58	8	200	(90)
IMPERIAL, Prov., RI (c. 1936 –) *3½" 3 bl. Cattle pat. Metal shell hdls. $15	8	60	(70)
IMPERIAL, Mexico/Germany *3½" 2 bl. Serp. jack pat. Comp. hdls. $14	8	60	(50)

Brand Marks & Stampings (Dates)	Value Range		
	Low	High	Code
ILLINOIS CUTLERY CO., Chicago (c. 1911 – 1912) *3" 2 bl. Jack pat. Cel. hdls. $81	15	110	(200)
I.N.C. CO., Keota	15	50	(65)
IPAYA, Spain	10	40	(45)
IROKA, Ger.	5	70	(50)
IROQUOIS, Utica, New York *3" 2 bl. Pen pat. Bone hdls. $49	10	80	(95)
IROS KEEN, NY *4" 3 bl. Whittler pat. Cel. hdls. $60	10	75	(100)
IRVING CUT. CO., Ger.	10	60	(50)
IVY (Leaf stamp), Ger. (S. Hecht & Son c. 1900 – 1901) *3½" 2 bl. Jack pat. Comp. hdls. $16	10	80	(70)

Chart 1 Code Value		Chart 2 Pattern Value		Chart 3 Handle Value		Chart 4 Condition		RBR Collector Value
175	x	.45	x	1.50	x	.99	=	$116.93

	Low	High	Code
I-XL GEORGE WOSTENHOLM & SON, Eng. (1890 –) 3½" 2 bl. Crown Jack pat. Stag hdls. $120	25	200	(175)
I-XL GEORGE WOSTENHOLM, Shef. (Oil the Joints) *4" 3 bl. Stock pat. Bone hdls. $52	25	125	(105)
IXL, Japan (I-XL in Triangle) *4" 3 bl. Stock pat. Bone hdls. $30	10	70	(60)
INTERNATIONAL CUTLERY CO., Fremont, OH (Clauss, c. 1890-1907) *4" 2 bl. Jack pat. Bone hdls. $65	15	100	(111)
JACK KNIFE BEN, Chicago, IL (c. 1887 – 1929) *4" 4 bl. Cattle pat. Bone hdls. $215	30	150	(300)
JACOBY & WESTER, NY (Wester Bros. Ger. c. 1891 – 1904) *3½" 3 bl. Stock pat. Bone hdls. $49	20	80	(75)
JAEGER BROS., Marinette, WI (Aerial Mfg. Co. c. 1912 – 1944) *3½" 3 bl. Pen pat. Cell. hdls. $90	20	90	(250)

Brand Marks & Stampings (Dates)	Value Range		
	Low	High	Code
JACKSON, Fremont, OH (Stacy & Smith, Shef., Eng.)			
*5" 1 bl. FH. pat. Stag hdls. $156	30	125	(95)
JUDSON CUTLERY CO., New York City			
5¼" Swell centered F.H. Green bone hdls. $359	40	500	(225)
KA-BAR, Olean, NY (c. 1919 –)			
5" 1 bl. Grizzly (Springer) FH pat.			
Stag hdls. $1672	100	500	(950)

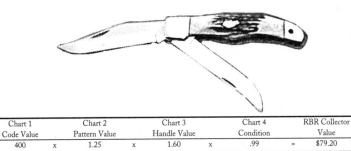

Chart 1		Chart 2		Chart 3		Chart 4		RBR Collector
Code Value		Pattern Value		Handle Value		Condition		Value
400	x	1.25	x	1.60	x	.99	=	$79.20

KA-BAR, Olean, NY (c. 1919 –)			
5" 1 or 2 bl. FH pat. (w/Dog head Shield)			
Stag hdls. $800	45	900	(400)
KA-BAR, Olean, NY. (c. 1919 –)			
4" 3 bl. Stock pat. Stag hdls. $399	50	275	(400)
KA-BAR, Olean, NY (c. 1950)			
4" 3 bl. Stock pat. Bone hdls. $75	12	136	(150)
KABAR, USA (c. 1960 –)			
4" 3 bl. Stock pat. Delrin hdls. $44	10	70	(125)
KEYSTONE CUTLERY, Milwaukee, WI (c. 1925 – 1938)			
*3½" 2 bl. Jack pat. Cel. hdls. $42.	30	50	(75)
KINFOLKS, Little Valley, NY (1927 – 1948)			
*5¼" 2 bl. FH pat. Bone hdls. $450	50	350	(260)
KINGSTON, USA (Devine & Ulster c. 1915 – 1945)			
*4" 2 bl. Jack pat. Comp. hdls. $35.	12	50	(62)

Brand Marks & Stampings (Dates)	Value Range Low	High	Code
KINGS QUALITY *4" 2 bl. Gunstock jack pat. Ivory hdls. $112.	50	150	(100)
KISSING CRANES (Robert Klass c. 1834 –) *4" 4 bl. Congress pat. Stag hdls. $84	50	115	(100)
KLICKER USA	10	40	(65)
KLOSTERMEIR BROS., Atchison, KA *4" 3 bl. Stock pat. Stag hdls. $80	40	100	(90)
KNECHT, Ger. (c. 1880)	20	80	(75)
KEOLLER & SCHMITA CUT. CO.	30	30	(70)
KORTEN & SCHERT, Ger. *4" 2 bl. Jack pat. Bone hdls. $35	30	75	(71)
KORIEN, Ger.	10	30	(50)
KRUSE HDW. CO., Cincinnati, OH *4" 2 bl. Muskrat pat. Bone hdls. $58	30	80	(100)
KRUSIUS BROS., Ger./N. Y. (c. 1889 – 1927) *4" 4 bl. Flatfish pen pat. Bone hdls. $44.	9	65	(75)
KUNDE & CIE, Remcherd, Ger.	30	40	(60)
KUTMASTER, Utica, N.Y. (Utica Cut. c. 1937) *4" 3 bl. Stock pat. Del. hdls. $49	10	55	(110)

Chart 1 Code Value		Chart 2 Pattern Value		Chart 3 Handle Value		Chart 4 Condition		RBR Collector Value
110	x	.60	x	2.50	x	.99	=	$163.35

KUTWELL, Olean, NY	30	150	(150)
KWIK CUT, USA (c. 1921 – 1926) *4½" 1 bl. Slim-Jim jack pat. Cel. hdls. $30	20	65	(80)

Brand Marks & Stampings (Dates)	Value Range Low	High	Code
LABELLE *4" 2 bl. Jack pat. Bone hdls. $40	20	65	(100)
LACKAWANNA CUTLERY, Nicholson, PA (1915 – 1930) *4" 2 bl. Coke jack pat. Picture hdls. $85	40	200	(150)
LA GROSSE, Ger.	20	30	(50)
LAFAYETTE CUT. CO., Ger. (c. 1909 – 1910) *4" 3 bl. Warncliffe pat. Wood hdls. $50	10	100	(90)
LAKESIDE CUTLERY CO. *3½" 2 bl. Gunstock jack pat. Stag hdls. $145	30	150	(150)
LAMSON & GOODNOW MFG. CO., Shelborn Falls *3½" 2 bl. Stock pat. Bone hdls. $43	20	90	(95)
LATT & SCHMIDT, N.Y.	15	60	(65)
LANDER, FRARY & CLARK, AETNA WORKS (c. 1865 – 1950) *3¼" 2 bl. Equal end jack pat. Bone hdls. $99	20	95	(200)
L.F. & C., New Britain, CT (1898 – 1950) *3¼" 2 bl. Equal end jack pat. Cel. hdls. $81	18	80	(200)
LANGSTAFF HDW. CO., Prussia	20	60	(75)
LATOMA, Italy	9	45	(50)
LAUFER TRADING CO., Ger. 4" 2 bl. Trapper pat. Bone hdls. $45	15	80	(75)

Chart 1 Code Value		Chart 2 Pattern Value		Chart 3 Handle Value		Chart 4 Condition		RBR Collector Value
100	x	1.10	x	.80	x	.99	=	$87.12

LE SABOT, Fontenville, France 4½" F.H. Deerfoot pat. $90	15	100	(1,000)
LAWTON CUT. CO., Chicago (c. 1895)	15	75	(90)
LAYMAN CAREY CO.	15	70	(60)

Brand Marks & Stampings (Dates)	Value Range		
	Low	High	Code
LEADER, USA	10	30	(50)
LEE CUTLERY CO., Hotchkissville *4" 3 bl. Stock pat. Cel. hdls. $75	10	100	(120)
LEE, HDW. CO., Salina, KS *3½" 3 bl. Stock pat. Bone hdls. $46	9	80	(80)
LEGAL, USA *3¼" 2 bl. Equal end jack pat. Cel hdls. $45	15	60	(75)
LENOX CUT CO., Ger. (c. 1909 – 1914) *3" 2 bl. Jack pat. Wood hdls. $15	10	40	(60)
LEONARD, Piqua, Ohio *4" 3 bl. Whittler pat. Picture hdls. $125	20	95	(133)
LEVERING XXX KNIFE CO., New York *4½" 2 bl. FH jack pat. Open end. Bone hdls. $200	20	250	(130)
LIBERTY KNIFE CO., USA	15	70	(65)
LIGRIAM MFG. CO., Chicago, IL	15	50	(60)
LIFETIME, (Bresnick c. 1928 – 1948) *3½" 2 bl. Equal end jack pat. Cel. hdls. $60	20	75	(90)
LINCOLN HDW. CO. (D. H. Lory c. 1924 – 1928) *4" 2 bl. Stock pat. Stag hdls. $80	30	120	(100)
LINCOLN NOVELTY CO.	20	80	(85)
LIPIC USA	9	20	(50)
LION CUTLERY CO., Shef., Eng.	20	40	(65)
LIPSCOMB & CO., Nashville, TN (1891 – 1913) *4" 2 bl. Fish pat. Bone hdls. $50	20	80	(110)
LIPSCHULTZ (H&R), Solingen, Ger. *4" 4 bl. Congress pat. Bone hdls. $76	30	80	(90)
LISH, Ger.	10	40	(40)

Brand Marks & Stampings (Dates)	Value Range		
	Low	High	Code
LITTLE VALLEY CUTLERY ASSOCIATION, NY (c. 1900)			
*4" 4 bl. Cattle pat. Bone hdls. $292.	75	350	(300)
L.L. BEAN, INC., Freeport, MN			
*5" 1 bl. FH pat. Stag hdls. $178	12	200	(125)
LITTLEWOOD CELEBRATED CUTLERY, Eng.			
	30	90	(100)
LOCKWOOD BROS., Shef., Eng.			
*4" 4 bl. Fourmaster pat. Stag hdls. $122	40	150	(125)
LSZ (BLACK FOREST) GER.			
*4" 4 bl. Utility pat. Horn hdls. $32	30	75	(90)
LUKE OATS	40	100	(90)
LUBLIN, Ger.	20	60	(80)
LUBOT, Cincinnati, OH	9	30	(80)
LUNAWERKS, Ger.	10	70	(70)
LUX, Solingen, Ger.	8	15	(50)
LUXRITE, Hollywood, CA	20	60	(75)
LYON CUTLERY CO.			
*3¼" 2 bl. Barlow pat. Comp. hdls. $22	15	50	(85)
MADDEN & SONS, Shef., Eng.			
*5" 1 bl. Daddy Barlow pat. Bone hdls. $85	30	100	(110)
MAGIC (Eagle Pencil Co. c. 1883 – 1935)			
*Novelty pencil knife. Screw-out blade $30	15	40	(100)
MAGNETIC CUT. CO. (J. Nones c. 1933 – 1936)			
*2¼" 3 bl. Lobster pen pat. Pearl hdls. $45	10	40	(75)

Brand Marks & Stampings (Dates)	Value Range		
	Low	High	Code
MAGNETIC CUTLERY, Ger. (c. 1910)			
*4" 4 bl. Utility pat. Wood hdls. $25	10	50	(75)

Chart 1 Code Value		Chart 2 Pattern Value		Chart 3 Handle Value		Chart 4 Condition		RBR Collector Value
100	x	.45	x	.90	x	.99	=	$40.01

MAJESTIC CUTLERY CO., Ger.			
3½" Balloon jack pat. Ebony hdls. $40	12	60	(100)
MANIAGO, Italy			
*3½" 3 bl. Pen pat. Horn hdls. $25	8	20	(75)
MAHER & GROSH, Toledo, OH (1877 – 1963)			
*4" 4 bl. Congress pat. Bone hdls. $145	40	175	(175)
MAHER & GROSH, Clyde, OH (1963 –)			
*4" 4 bl. Congress pat. Del. hdls. $41	25	75	(90)
MANOS CUTLERY CO., Ger.	15	30	(55)
MAPPIN BROS., Shef., Eng.	20	40	(60)

Chart 1 Code Value		Chart 2 Pattern Value		Chart 3 Handle Value		Chart 4 Condition		RBR Collector Value
800	x	1.25	x	1.20	x	.99	=	$1,188

MARBLES, Gladstone, MI (c. 1898 –)			
*5½" 1 bl. Safety FH pat.			
Rough black hdls. $1,200	80	1600	(800)
MARBLES, Gladstone, MI (c. 1898 –)			
4" 3 bl. Stock pat. Bone hdls. $325	80	1000	(500)
M.S.A., Gladstone, MI (Marbles 1898 –)	90	650	(500)
MARCEL H&R (Bertram Cut. Ger.)	10	60	(90)
MARGO, Shef., Eng.	10	30	(65)
MARSH BROS., Shef. Eng. (1904 – 1947)			
*4" 2 bl. Physicians pat. Stag hdls. $90	20	100	(125)

Brand Marks & Stampings (Dates)	Value Range		
	Low	High	Code
MARSHALL FIELDS & CO., Ger.			
3" 2 bl. Pen pat. Metal hdls. $24	15	75	(75)
MARSHALL WELLS HDW. CO. (1893 – 1963)			
*4" 2 bl. Jack pat. Bone hdls. $95	40	200	(150)
MARTIN BROS., Shef.			
*4" 3 bl. Cattle pat. Stag hdls. $79	60	100	(90)
MARX, Ger.	20	75	(80)
MASON & SON, Shef.	30	75	(70)
MAUSSNER, Ger. (Magnetic Cut. 1910)			
*4" 2 bl. Elec. pat. Wood hdls. $18	30	70	(70)
M.C. CO. (MC inside pyramid)	10	20	(70)
MCINTOSH HEATHER, Cleveland, OH (1903 – 11)			
*4½" 2 bl. Trapper pat. Bone hdls. $93	20	150	(130)
MCLEAN & SON, Chicago, IL			
3" 2 bl. Electrician pat. Wood hdls. $18	15	60	(75)
MCNITOR KNIFE CO.	10	70	(70)
MCFADDEN, JH, Mt. Vernon, SD (c. 1924)			
*3" 3 bl. Pen pat. Bone hdls. $35	20	60	(75)
MEHAN, Ger.	20	20	(65)
MELROSE CUTLERY CO., Ger.			
*4" 3 bl. Stock pat. Comp. hdls. $35	20	50	(70)
MELKA, Ger.	10	50	(70)
MERCATOR, Ger.	20	60	(70)
MERIDEN, CUTLERY CO., Meriden, CT (1855 – 1925)			
3½" 2 bl. Half whittler pat. Bone hdls. $170	40	200	(200)
MERIDEN KNIFE CO. USA (1917 – 1932)			
*4" 3 bl. Stock pat. Bone hdls. $125	20	100	(227)
MERRIMAC CUTLERY CO., Ger.			
*3½" 2 bl. Barlow pat. Bone hdls. $56	20	100	(95)

Brand Marks & Stampings (Dates)	Value Range		Code
	Low	High	

METROPOLITAN CUTLERY CO., Ger. (Twin/cranes 1940 – 1951) NY
*4" 4 bl. Congress pat. (fourmaster)

Bone hdls. $80	15	75	(95)
MITSUBISHI, Japan	15	150	(150)

MILLER BROS. CUTLERY CO. Meriden, CT (1863 – 1926)
*4" 2 bl. Whittler pat. Bone hdls. $180 40 280 (250)

Chart 1 Code Value		Chart 2 Pattern Value		Chart 3 Handle Value		Chart 4 Condition		RBR Collector Value
250	x	55	x	130	x	.99	=	$176.96

M. KLEIN & SONS, Chicago, IL
*4" 2 bl. Elec. pat. Wood hdls. $18 10 20 (205)

MONTGOMERY WARD, Chicago, IL (1928 –)
*4½" 3 bl. Stock pat. Bone hdls. $98 10 100 (100)

MONROE CUT. CO., Ger. 10 30 (65)

MONUMENTAL CUTLERY CO. (1864 – 1893), Eng.
*4" 2 bl. Physician's pat. Rough blt. $51 20 75 (95)

MOORMAN USA 15 30 (65)

MORLEY & SONS, Ger. (1913 – 1927)
*5" 2 bl. Barlow pat.

Bone hdls. $90. (XLNT on bol.)	30	90	(115)

Chart 1 Code Value		Chart 2 Pattern Value		Chart 3 Handle Value		Chart 4 Condition		RBR Collector Value
115	x	45	x	1.75	x	.99	=	$89.65

Brand Marks & Stampings (Dates)	Value Range		
	Low	High	Code
MORRIS CUTLERY CO., IL. USA (1882 – 1930) *4" 3 bl. Cattle pat. Bone hdls. $122	30	150	(125)
MUMBLEY PEG USA (Camillus Cut. c. 1937 – 1948) 3½" pen pattern, Rough black handles $65	60	125	(85)
MURCOTT, Ger.	20	30	(60)
MUTUAL CUTLERY CO., Canton, OH	20	60	(75)
MUTT LIBSCHUTZ, Ger. *3½" 3 bl. Stock pat. Pearl hdls. $75	20	95	(85)
NAGLE REBLADE KNIFE CO., Poughkeepsie, NY (1912 – 1916) *4" 2 bl. Jack pat. Comp. hdls. $600	250	600	(NS)
NAGBAUR USA	10	25	(65)
NAPANOCH KNIFE CO., Napanoch, NY (c. 1905 – 1938) *4" 4 bl. Senator pen pat. Pearl hdls. $385	50	500	(300)
NATIONAL CUT. CO., New York-Ger.	20	40	(65)
NAUGATUCK CUTLERY CO. (1872 – 1888) *4½" 1 bl. Pruner pat. Wood hdls. $100	40	250	(200)
N. B. KNIFE CO. USA	9	15	(65)
NEEDHAM BROS., Shef., Eng. *4" 2 bl. Jack pat. Wood hdls. $40	50	150	(100)
NEFT SAFETY KNIFE 5½" 1 bl. FH pat. Bone hdls. $245	70	200	(180)
NELSON KNIFE CO.	20	40	(55)
NEW BRITAIN	20	40	(65)
NEW CENTURY CUTLERY CO., Germany *4" 2 bl. Jack pat. Metal hdls. $33	15	70	(65)
NEW ENGLAND CUTLERY CO., Wlfrd., CT (c. 1860) *4½" 4 bl. Whittler pat. Wood hdls. $135	20	100	(200)

Brand Marks & Stampings (Dates)	Value Range Low	Value Range High	Code

Chart 1 Code Value		Chart 2 Pattern Value		Chart 3 Handle Value		Chart 4 Condition		RBR Collector Value
350	x	.45	x	1.1	x	.99	=	$171.50

NEW YORK KNIFE CO., Walden, NY (c. 1852 – 1931)
3½" Equal end Jack pat. Bone hdls. $175   35   400   (350)

NEW YORK CUTLERY CO., (Rowe*Post c. 1875 – 1876)
4" Stock pat. Bn hdl. $97   40   85   (150)

NIAGARA CUT CO.
4½" 2 bl. Open-end jack pat. Bone hdls. $71   30   95   (100)

NIFTY KNIFE CO., St. Louis, MO   8   15   (75)

NIPPES & PLUMACHER, Ohligs, Ger.
*4" 3 bl. Cattle pat. Bone hdls. $61   20   70   (85)

NORMARK, Finland
*4" 1 bl. Jack pat. Comp. hdls. $20   8   30   (70)

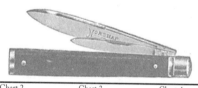

Chart 1 Code Value		Chart 2 Pattern Value		Chart 3 Handle Value		Chart 4 Condition		RBR Collector Value
208	x	.45	x	.80	x	.99	=	$74.25

NORSHARP (Norvell-Shapleigh) St. Louis, MO
3⅝" 2 bl. Physician's pat. Buffalo Horn hdls. $75   40   350   (208)

NORTHFIELD KNIFE CO., CT (c. 1858 – 1964)
*3½" 3 bl. Whittler pat. Wood hdls. $170   20   200   (250)

NORTHHAMPTON CUTLERY CO., MA
*5½" 1 bl. Barlow pat. Bone hdls. $120   30   140   (125)

NORVELL-SHAPLEIGH HDW. CO., (Shapleigh Hdw. c. 1902 – 1920)
*5" 2 bl. Coke FH pat. Stag hdls. $355   40   350   (200)

NORWICH CUTLERY CO., USA   15   65   (80)

Brand Marks & Stampings (Dates)	Value Range		
	Low	High	Code
NOVELTY CUTLERY CO., Canton, OH (c. 1879 – 1948)			
*4½" 2 bl. Jack pat. Picture hdls. $225 (N.C. Co.)	15	200	(400)
NOVELTY CUTLERY CO., Brooklyn, NY (c. 1929 – 1930)			
*3½" 3 bl. Whittler pat. Picture hdls. $104	20	90	(110)
OAK LEAF, (WM Enders c. 1911 – 1913)			
*3½" 4 bl. Cattle pat. Bone hdls. $92	20	60	(95)
OAKLAND CUT. CO., USA	10	30	(50)
OHIO CUTLERY CO., Massillon, OH (1919 – 1923)			
*3½" 2 bl. Pen pat. Bone hdls. $47	25	85	(90)
OLBUS, Germany	10	25	(60)
OLCUT (Union Cut. 1911 – 1914)			
*4" 4 bl. Cattle pat. Stag hdls. $276	40	340	(230)
OLD FAITHFUL (A.J. Jordon c. 1888 – 1889)			
4" 3 bl. Stock pat. Bn hdl. $58	40	95	(90)
OLD HICKORY (Ontario Knife Co. c. 1971 –)			
*4" 4 bl. Stock pat. Del. hdls. $30	10	45	(70)
OLD KENTUCKY, (Miller Bros. c. 1920)			
*4" 3 bl. Cattle pat. Bone hdls. $250	70	200	(413)
OLIMPIC CUTLERY CO., New York	20	45	(70)
O.N.B. Ger. (Germania Cutlery Works c. 1901 – 1913)			
*3½" 2 bl. Barlow pat. Bone hdls. $45	20	70	(100)
OLSON KNIFE CO. Howard City, MI (Ger.)			
*4½" 2 bl. Trapper pat. Bone hdls. $75	20	80	(125)
O'NEIL & THOMPSON, Ireland	20	40	(75)
ONTARIO KNIFE CO. (True Edge)	15	50	(90)
OMOR, Ger. or Pakistan	9	20	(50)
OPPENREIMER, Italy	10	40	(65)
OPINEL, France (Twistlock Bolster)	15	50	(80)

Brand Marks & Stampings (Dates)	Low	Value Range High	Code
OSBORNE, KEENE & CO., USA *4" 4 bl. Congress pat. Bone hdls. $105	20	75	(95)
OSTISO, FINE EDGE *4" 1 bl. Stiletto pat. Cel. hdls. $32	20	50	(85)
OTHELLO, Solingen, Ger. *4" 1 bl. Switch blade pat. Comp. hdls. $64	20	125	(85)
OTTO HAAG, Solingen, Ger.	15	40	(75)
O. V. B. (Hibbard, Spencer & Bartlett c. 1884 – 1960) *3½" 1 bl. Jack pat. Cel. hdls. $67	15	125	(150)
OVERLAND, Solingen, Ger.	20	50	(70)
OWL CUTLERY CO., Shef., Eng. *5" 2 bl. Coke FH pat. Wood hdls. $135	30	150	(135)
PACIFIC HDW & STEEL CO. (Stiletto) *4" 1 bl. Trapper pat. Bone hdls. $79	12	35	(80)
PAKISTAN, Pakistan	6	20	(65)
PAL CUTLERY CO., Plattsburg, NY (c. 1935 – 1953) *4" 2 bl. Jack pat. Old faded-out bone hdls. $88	35	250	(150)

Chart 1 Code Value		Chart 2 Pattern Value		Chart 3 Handle Value		Chart 4 Condition		RBR Collector Value
150	x	45	x	1.30	x	.99	=	$86.87

Brand Marks & Stampings (Dates)	Low	High	Code
PAL BLADE CO. (Same as above)	35	250	(150)
PAL CUT. CO. (With Remington stamped blades) 4½" 2 bl. Bullet sh. FH pat. Bone hdls. $972	70	1000	(600)
PAL BRAND, Ger. *3½" 3 bl. Stock pat. Bone hdls. $44	10	60	(75)

Brand Marks & Stampings (Dates)	Value Range		
	Low	High	Code
PANZER MESSER, Ger. (Shooting Blade, Springs)	60	80	(75)
PARIS BEAD CO., Chicago, IL			
*3" 4 bl. Swell-center pat. Board Pen Picture hdls. $75	20	150	(150)
PARISIAN NOV. CO., Chicago, IL (Same as above)	20	150	(120)
PAPE THIEBES, (Ger) St. Louis (1903 – 1920)			
*4" 3 bl. Whittler pat. Stag hdls. $81	20	125	(90)

Chart 1		Chart 2		Chart 3		Chart 4		RBR Collector
Code Value		Pattern Value		Handle Value		Condition		Value
100	x	.45	x	.70	x	.99	=	$31.18

	Low	High	Code
PARKER-FROST CUTLERY CO. (Chattanooga, TN 1974 – 1978)			
3½" 2 bl. Trapper pat. Del. hdls. $32	10	75	(100)
PARKER CUT. CO. (1978 –)			
*4" 2 bl. Trapper pat. Bone hdls. $44	8	40	(80)
PAUL VON HINDENBURG, Ger.	20	40	(85)
PAULS BROS., New York (1887 – 1892) Ger.			
*3½" 2 bl. Barlow pat. Bone hdls. $46	20	50	(90)
PAXTON & GALLAGER & CO., Omaha (1864 – 1959)			
*4" 4 bl. Stock pat. Bone hdls. $71	20	80	(110)
PERLESS USA	15	30	(55)
PEARLDUCK, INC., New York (c. 1947 – 1952)			
*3" 3 bl. Sleeveboard pen Pearl hdls. $75	15	110	(110)
PENN CUTLERY CO., Tidioute, PA (1909 – 1913)			
3½" 2 bl. Jack pat. Bone hdls. $67	20	120	(115)

Brand Marks & Stampings (Dates)	Low	Value Range High	Code
PENNSYLVANIA KNIFE CO.	20	40	(80)
PERES. D., Germany (c. 1885 – 1929)	20	35	(75)
PERMISSO, Italy	9	30	(20)
PETERS BROS. CUT., St. Louis, MO (c. 1876) *4" 2 bl. Trapper pat. Stag hdls. $75	40	125	(110)
PHARUS (F. Herder c. 1922 – 1931) *3" 2 bl. Pen pat. Cel hdls. $32	12	35	(65)
PHOENIX KNIFE CO., Phoenix, NY (1892 – 1916) *3½" 2 bl. Barlow pat. Bone hdls. $91. (WE-XL on bols)	20	200	(175)
PIC, Ger. *4" 3 bl. Stock pat. Bone hdls. $35	10	90	(70)
PIC, Japan	7	25	(50)
PINE KNOT, JAS. W. PRICE (Belknap Hdw. c. 1930 – 1934) *4" 3 bl. Stock pat. Cel. hdls. $121	50	300	(275)

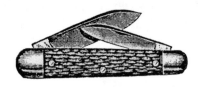

Chart 1 Code Value		Chart 2 Pattern Value		Chart 3 Handle Value		Chart 4 Condition		RBR Collector Value
275	x	.40	x	1.10	x	.99	=	$119.79

PLATT & SONS, Andover, NY
*4" 2 bl. Gunstock pat. Stag hdls. $100   30   150   (200)

Chart 1 Code Value		Chart 2 Pattern Value		Chart 3 Handle Value		Chart 4 Condition		RBR Collector Value
200	x	.40	x	1.25	x	.99	=	$.99

Brand Marks & Stampings (Dates)	Value Range Low	Value Range High	Code
P. KAMPHUS, Ger.	15	40	(70)
POTTS, Ger. 4" 3 bl. Stock pat. Bone hdls. $45	10	45	(70)
POTTERY-HOY HDW. CO., USA *4" 2 bl. Florist pat. Wood hdls. $30	40	70	(90)
POWR-KRAFT, (Montgomery-Ward Co.) *5" 2 bl. FH lock pat. Bone hdls. $127	20	150	(105)
POWELL BROS. Ger.	10	30	(60)
PREMIER CUT. CO., NY (c. 1921 – 1955) Ger.	20	45	(70)
PRENTISS KNIFE CO., New York *4" 2 bl. Open end jack pat. Bone hdls. $44	20	75	(75)
PRESIDENT (Loeb-Phillips c. 1929)	40	60	(90)
PRESS BUTTON KNIFE CO., Walden, NY (1900 – 1928) *4½" 1 bl. Springer Jack pat. Bone hdls. $312	40	250	(400)
PRADEL, France	20	40	(70)
PRESTO (George Schrade c. 1925 – 1945) *4½" 1 bl. Springer Jack pat. Comp. hdls. $125	40	200	(150)

PRITZLAFF, JOHN, HARDWARE CO., (JPH), Milwaukee, Wisc., (1850 – 1957)
5¼" Folding hunter, Cocobolo hdls., $180

Chart 1 Code Value		Chart 2 Pattern Value		Chart 3 Handle Value		Chart 4 Condition		RBR Collector Value
150	x	1.25	x	.90	x	.99	=	$167.06

| PROV. CUT. CO., Prov., RI (c. 1917 –)
*5" 1 bl. Fish knife pat. Metal shell hdls. $11 | 9 | 40 | (80) |

Brand Marks & Stampings (Dates)	Low	Value Range High	Code
PUKKO, Finland	20	45	(65)
PUMA, Solingen, Ger. *4" 3 bl. Stock pat. Wood hdls. $135	20	175	(200)
PUTNAM CUT. CO., Putnam, CT (c. 1887 – 1909) *4½" 2 bl. Open end jack pat. Stag hdls. $247	40	250	(150)
QUAKER CITY CUT CO.	20	60	(90)
Q. C. Mfg. Co., Massillon, OH	20	60	(90)
QUEEN CITY, Titusville, PA (c. 1922 – 1924) in script *4½" 2 bl. Jack pat. Bone hdls. $130	20	200	(250)
QUEEN CITY, Titusville, PA (c. 1922 – 1925) in block *4½" 2 bl. Open end jack pat. Stag hdls. $225	20	250	(240)
QUEEN CUTLERY, Titusville, PA (c. 1925 –) (W/Q's and Crown Stampings) *4" 3 bl. Stock pat. Del. hdls. $34	20	100	(95)
QUEEN STEEL (1945 – No stamping)	10	100	(90)

Chart 1 Code Value		Chart 2 Pattern Value		Chart 3 Handle Value		Chart 4 Condition		RBR Collector Value
115	x	.65	x	.70	x	.99	=	$51.80

QUEEN
3½" Congress pat.
Imitation stag (delrin) hdls. $55 15 80 (115)

	Low	High	Code
QUEEN 3½" Congress pat. Imitation stag (delrin) hdls. $55	15	80	(115)
QUICK POINT, St. Louis (1920 – 1940)	30	60	(80)
QUICK POINT, (Winchester or Remington on back of tang) *3" 2 bl. Pen pat. Cel. hdls. $125	40	350	(250)
QUICKUT, Inc. Fremont, OH *4" 3 bl. Serpentine jack pat. Cel. hdls. $51	20	85	(90)

Brand Marks & Stampings (Dates)	Low	Value Range High	Code
RACE BROS. CELEBRATED CUTLERY, Eng. *4½" 4 bl. Whittler pat. Tortoise hdls. $480	40	500	(200)
RADIGAN, RICH & CO., New York (c. 1905 – 1907) *4" 2 bl. Trapper pat. Bone hdls. (Hunter-stamp) $130	40	190	(150)
RAINBOW, (Colonial Cut. Co. 1933 – 1954)	15	40	(90)
RAND, Ger.	15	30	(75)
RANDALL HALL & CO.	20	40	(75)
RANGER, (Colonial Cut. Co. 1938 – 1951)	11	20	(80)
R. A. SIMMONS, Chicago *3½" 2 bl. Whittler pat. Bone hdls. $65	15	50	(80)
RATHER & CO., Ger.	20	60	(65)
RANSOM, Toledo, OH (c. 1890 – 1892)	20	50	(70)
RAOLA CUT. CO.	20	50	(65)
RAY (TOM RAY) CUT CO., Kansas City, MO (1905 – 1910) *4" 4 bl. Cattle pat. Bone hdls. $165	40	150	(200)
R. C. KRUSHEL, Duluth, MN	20	70	(70)
RED DEVIL, S&H CO., New York (Smith & Hemingway c. 1900 – 1906) *4½" 2 bl. Trapper pat. Stag hdls. $148	30	80	(150)
REC-NOR CO., Boston, MA	15	60	(65)
RELIANCE CUT. CO., Ger. (Natenberg-Strauss c. 1922 – 1924)	20	40	(75)
REMINGTON, Ilion, NY (Straight line c. 1920 – 1939) *3½" 2 bl. Barlow pat. Comp. hdls. $132	30	225	(200)
**REMINGTON UMC, (Circle stamp c. 1920 – 1939) *5¼" 1 bl. Daddy Barlow pat. Bone hdls. $405	50	500	(610)
**REMINGTON UMC (c. 1920 – 1939, Circle stamp) 4" 3 bl. Stock pat. Bone hdls. $433	50	600	(525)

Brand Marks & Stampings (Dates)	Value Range		Code
	Low	High	
**REMINGTON UMC, (Circle w/bullet shield 1920 – 1939) *5½" 1 bl. Lockback FH pat. Bone hdls. $2437 (The rare R1176 or "Baby Bullet") $1250	150	2000	(1300)
REMINGTON UMC (Mumbly-peg stamped 1920 – 1929) 3½", Equal End pat. Bone hdls. $260	75	550	(525)
REMINGTON UMC, Quickpoint, St. Louis, MO *3" 2 bl. Pen pat. Cel hdls. $200	50	300	(400)
REMINGTON, Germany *4" 4 bl. Congress pat. Bone hdls. $81	25	150	(125)
RENSHAW (T) & SON, Shef., Eng. *4½" 3 bl. Whittler pat. Bone hdls. $100	30	200	(130)
RESISTANT (L, F&C c. 1916 – 1950) *3½" 2 bl. Serpentine Jack pat. Comp. hdls. $38	20	75	(130)
REPUBLIC	15	50	(80)
REV-O-NOC, (Hibbard, Spencer & Bartlett 1905 – 1960) *4" 2 bl. Open end Jack pat. Bone hdls. $70	40	100	(150)
REX, Solingen, Ger.	9	30	(65)
RICHARDS CO., USA (1862 – 1908) Southbridge, MA *4½" 1 bl. Budding pat. Wood hdls. $50	40	80	(100)
RICHARDS & CONOVER HDW. CO., Kan. City, MO (1894 – 1956) *4" 3 bl. Stock pat. Bone hdls. $62	35	80	(90)
RICHARTZ BROS. & SONS LTD. Ger.	20	65	(75)
RICHMOND CUT. CO.	10	45	(70)
R.J. RICHTER, Ger.	20	40	(65)
RIC-NOR Boston, USA (Prov. Cutlery)	20	50	(75)
RIVAL CUT. CO., Ger.	10	20	(60)
RING CUTLERY, Ger. & Japan	10	20	(70)

Brand Marks & Stampings (Dates)	Value Range		
---	Low	High	Code
RIVINGTON WORKS, Shef., Eng. *4" 3 bl. Whittler pat. Stag hdls. $93	30	100	(105)
ROBERT KLAAS Solingen, Ger. (1834 –) *4" 4 bl. Congress pat. Bone hdls. $65	20	124	(100)
**ROBESON CUTLERY CO., Rochester (1894 – 1965) *4" 3 bl. Stock pat. Bone hdls. $152	30	350	(235)
**ROBESON CUT. CO., Suredge (1922 – 1965) *4" 3 bl. Stock pat. Bone hdls. $115	25	175	(175)
ROBESON, Germany *4" 3 bl. Stock pat. Bone hdls. $45	20	80	(90)
ROBINSON BROS. & CO., Louisville, KY (1880 – 1925) *3½" 3 bl. Whittler pat. Bone hdls. $98	20	100	(160)
ROGERS CUTLERY Shef., Eng. (c. 1724 –) *4" 3 bl. Stock pat. Stag hdls. $125	30	300	(165)
ROGERS (WM) CO., Hartford, CT *3½" 2 bl. Gunstock jack pat. Bone hdls. $93	30	150	(130)
ROMO, Ger. or Japan	10	20	(60)
ROTGENS SUPERIOR CUT. 3½" 6 bl. Congress pat. Pearl hdls. $137	30	200	(120)
ROYAL BRAND CUT. CO. USA *3½" 4 bl. Cattle pat. Bone hdls. $78 (Sharpcutter)	20	150	(110)
ROYAL OAK (EXTRA)	15	75	(100)
RUF N TUF (Union Cut. c. 1924 – 1929) *4" 2 bl. Trapper pat. Bone hdls. $162	90	250	(250)
RUSSELL GREEN RIVER WORKS, MA (1875 – 1941) *4½" 1 bl. FH lockback pat. Stag hdls. $1,869	200	2000	(1,150)
RUSSELL GREEN RIVER WORKS, MA (1875 – 1941) *3½" 2 bl. Jack pat. Bone hdls. $380	75	900	(650)

Brand Marks & Stampings (Dates)	Value Range Low	High	Code
RUSSELL, J. CUTLERY CO. (c. 1875 – 1941) 5" 1 bl. Daddy Barlow pat. (old) Sawed Bn. hdls. $495	75	300	(500)

Chart 1 Code Value		Chart 2 Pattern Value		Chart 3 Handle Value		Chart 4 Condition		RBR Collector Value
500	x	.40	x	1.30	x	.99	=	$257.40

RUSSELL, J. CUTLERY CO. (c. 1875 – 1941) 3¼" 2 bl. Barlow pat. (old) Sawed bn. hdls. $260	50	200	(500)
RUSSELL (c. 1974, 100 year commemoratives) USA 3½" 2 bl. Barlow pat. Bone hdls. $150	135	150	(250)
RUSSELL, Germany (c. 1968 – 1971) *5" 1 bl. Barlow pat. Bone hdls. $72	30	80	(120)
RUSSELL, Canada	20	60	(80)
RUSSELL, (AG) Springdale, AR (c. 1974 –) Ger. *3½" 2 bl. Pen pat. Horn hdls. $32	15	90	(100)
S&A CO. NY (Sperry & Alexander c. 1893 – 1913) *3" 4 bl. Pen pat. Pearl hdls. $110	15	75	(180)
SACCO	10	40	(60)
SABITIER, Rue St. Honore, Paris, France	15	40	(90)
SABRE, Ger.	8	35	(55)
SABRE, Japan	7	35	(50)
ST. LAWRENCE CUT. CO., St. Louis (Schmactenburg Bros. c. 1886 – 1916) Ger. *4" 2 bl. Ez. open jack pat. Bone hdls. $125	30	100	(110)
SALM, Torrence, CA (c. 1918 – 1935) & "Deluxe" stamp *3" 4 bl. Pen pat. Pearl hdls. $110	15	70	(130)
SAYNOR, COOK & RIDAL	15	40	(70)
SAMCO, Nashville, TN *3½" 2 bl. Flatfish pen pat Cel. hdls. $70	30	80	(110)

Brand Marks & Stampings (Dates)	Value Range		Code
	Low	High	
SANDERS MFG. CO., Nashville, TN			
*4" 2 bl. Muskrat pat. Bone hdls. $75	40	90	(130)
SANDERSON BROS., Shef., Eng. (c. 1860 – 1933)			
*4" 2 bl. Trapper pat. Bone hdls. $64	20	80	(110)

Chart 1 Code Value		Chart 2 Pattern Value		Chart 3 Handle Value		Chart 4 Condition		RBR Collector Value
150	x	.35	x	1.50	x	.99	=	$77.96

	Low	High	Code
SYRACUSE, USA			
3¼" Pen pat. Stag hdls. $80	25	250	(150)
SAVOY CUT, Ger.	10	35	(60)
SAXONIA CUTLERY, Ger.			
*3½" 2 bl. Ez. open jack pat. Bone hdls. $44	15	60	(75)
S.B. CO.	10	30	(60)
SCHMIDT & ZIEGLER, Solingen, Ger. ("Bull Brand")			
*4" 3 bl. Stock pat. Bone hdls. $45	15	75	(90)
SCHATT & MORGAN, Gowanda, NY (1890 – 1895)			
*5" 1 bl. FH Coke pat. (old)			
Bone hdls. $406 (S&M stamp)	40	500	(250)
SCHATT & MORGAN, Titusville, PA (1895 – 1928)			
*5" 1 bl. FH Coke pat.			
Bone hdls. $325 (S&M Stamp also)	30	300	(200)

Chart 1 Code Value		Chart 2 Pattern Value		Chart 3 Handle Value		Chart 4 Condition		RBR Collector Value
200	x	40	x	1.30	x	.99	=	$102.96

	Low	High	Code
SHOFIELD, Ger. (Atlas Brand)	15	35	(55)
SCHRADE CUT. CO., Walden, NY (c. 1904 – 1948)			
*4" 3 bl. Stock pat. Bone hdls. $150	30	180	(150)

Brand Marks & Stampings (Dates)	Value Range		
	Low	High	Code
SCHRADE-WALDEN, NY (c. 1948 – 1973) *4" 3 bl. Stock pat. Del. hdls. $45	14	85	(90)
SCHRADE, NY (c. 1973 –) *4" 3 bl. Stock pat. Del. hdls. $30 (Note: See Geo. Schrade Knife Co. B. Port, CT)	15	80	(65)
SECO WORKS, New Orange, NJ	15	40	(60)
SEGERSTROM, Sweden	20	50	(75)
SENA J, Ger. *4" 3 bl. Stock pat. Stag hdls. $49	20	75	(65)
SENECA CUT. CO., Utica, NY (Utica Cut. c. 1932) *3" 2 bl. Pen pat. Bone hdls. $60	15	70	(115)
SEYMOUR CUT CO., NY (1909 – 1917)	20	75	(90)
SHAPLEIGH HDW. CO., St. Louis, MO (1840 – 1960) *3½" 2 bl. Serp. Jack pat. Cel. hdls. $115	40	300	(200)
SHEFFIELD STEEL, Eng.	10	45	(60)
SHUMATE CUT. CORP., St. Louis, MO (1901 – 1907) *4" 2 bl. Gunstock jack pat. Bone hdls. $82	30	100	(140)
SHUR-SNAP, Prov., RI (Colonial Cut. c. 1948 – 1950) *3½" 2 bl. Jack pat. Rough black hdls. $49	20	100	(90)
SIMMONS HDW. CO., St. Louis, MO (1868 – 1960) Stockman/Old-Speared & blade, Mother-of-pearl, fiery white, $330	40	300	(150)

Chart 1 Code Value		Chart 2 Pattern Value		Chart 3 Handle Value		Chart 4 Condition		RBR Collector Value
250	x	.75	x	1.75	x	.99	=	$324.72

Brand Marks & Stampings (Dates)	Value Range		
	Low	High	Code
SIMMONS-WARDEN-WHITE, Dayton, OH (1937 – 1946)			
*3½" 4 bl. Utility pat. Comp. hdls. $28	20	100	(95)
SIX STEEL EDGE CUT., Ger.	20	95	(80)
SKIFFMAN, Ger.	15	20	(60)
SMITH & HEMENWAY, Utica, NY (c. 1896 – 1906)			
*4½" 2 bl. Trapper pat. Stag hdls. $72	30	80	(100)
SMITH & WESSON (1974 –)			
*5" 1 bl. Lockback FH pat. Wood hdls. $125	40	180	(150)
SNOW, J.P. & CO. Chicago, IL (c. 1861)	15	50	(70)
SOLINGEN CUT. CO. Ger.			
*4" 3 bl. Stock pat. Bone hdls. $35	20	80	(70)
SOL. WEYERSBURG & CO., Ger. (Military)			
*6" 2 bl. Drop-loc pat. (Gravity WWII)			
Wood hdls. $175	150	150	(200)
SOUTH BEND	10	60	(80)
SOLIDUS	10	20	(60)
SOUTHERN & RICHARDSON, Shef. (c. 1846 – 1941)			
	15	30	(65)
SOUTHERN CUT. CO., CT (1865 – 1905)			
*4½" 2 bl. Physician's pat. Bone hdls. $94	30	150	(160)
SPEAR CUT. CO., Ger. (c. 1907)	15	60	(75)
SPRATTS, Eng.	20	50	(70)
SPRING CUT. CO., Shef., Eng.	15	40	(65)
SSP 1942 BRITISH ORDNANCE	50	60	(75)
SPRING STEEL BARLOW CO., Prussia	30	45	(75)
STAINLESS CUTLERY CO., NY (Hibbard, Spencer & Bartlett c. 1927)			
*3" 2 bl. Pen pat. Cel. hdls. $55	20	70	(110)
STAINLESS CUTLERY CO., Ger.	10	30	(65)

Brand Marks & Stampings (Dates)	Value Range		
---	Low	High	Code
STANDARD KNIFE CO., NY (W.R. Case c. 1920 – 1923) *4½" 2 bl. Trapper pat. Stag hdls. $180	100	300	(250)
STANDARD CUT. CO., Shef., Eng.	20	75	(70)
STAR, Japan (Star Sales, Knoxville, TN) 3½" 3 bl. Whittler pat. Bone hdls. $45	10	100	(80)
STAUFFER, Made in Eng.	20	50	(65)
STAY SHARP	20	75	(90)
STERLING CO., Ger.	10	40	(50)
STERLING, Chicago-Japan	15	50	(50)
STILETTO (Miller, Sloss & Scott c. 1896) 4" Slim Jim jack pattern Bone handles $31	30	75	(80)
STILETTO CUTLERY CO., NY (Baker, Hamilton & Pacific Co. c. 1926) *4" 2 bl. Physician's pat. Bone hdls. $75	30	125	(125)
S.T.T. CO., Louisville, KY *4½" 2 bl. Eq. end jack pat. Bone hdls. $125	30	100	(175)
STRATCO (Stratton & Terstegge Hdw. c. 1937 – 1938) *4" 2 bl. Muskrat pat. Bone hdls. $56	30	125	(95)
STRAUMAN, Ger.	15	35	(60)
STRAUSS BROS & CO., Ger., NY (c. 1909 – 1910) 4" Stock pat. Bone handles $78	15	45	(80)
STURDY USA	10	60	(50)
SUMMIT CUTLERY (Pavian-Adams c. 1906) 4" 3 bl. Stock pat. Bone $90	20	75	(90)
SUPERIOR CUTLERY 4" 3 bl. Stock pat. Bone hdls. $65	20	75	(85)
SUPPLE HDW CO., Phila. (c. 1905 – 1906)	20	60	(65)
SUPREME USA	20	50	(65)
S.W. CO., USA (Simmon-Worden)	20	80	(75)

Brand Marks & Stampings (Dates)	Value Range		Code
	Low	High	
SWAN WERKS CUT CO. Ger. *3½" 3 bl. Pen pat. Pearl hdls. $75	20	75	(90)
SWANK, USA	10	35	(55)

Chart 1 Code Value		Chart 2 Pattern Value		Chart 3 Handle Value		Chart 4 Condition		RBR Collector Value
110	x	1.10	x	.70	x	.99	=	$83.85

SWORD BRAND Folding Hunter 1 bl. Side lock Indian Stag hdls. $85.00	15	130	(110)
SWORD BRAND (Camillus 1902 –) *4" 4 bl. Cattle pat. Bone hdls. $106	15	130	(110)
SWORD & SHIELD, Ger.	20	30	(75)
SYRACUSE KNIFE CO., NY (c. 1904 – Camillus) *3½" 2 bl. Flatfish Pen pat. Bone hdls. $70	20	130	(120)
TAC, Italy	10	30	(55)
TARRY (Lizard on Blade)	20	90	(85)
TAMPA HDW. CO., Tampa, FL (c. 1910 – 1912) *4" 2 bl. Ez. Open jack pat. Bone hdls. $70	15	80	(95)

Chart 1 Code Value		Chart 2 Pattern Value		Chart 3 Handle Value		Chart 4 Condition		RBR Collector Value
105	x	.40	x	1.10	x	.99	=	$45.74

TAYLOR CUT. CO., Kingsport, TN (c. 1975) 4" Canoe, Bone hdls. $46	10	125	(105)
TAYLOR CUT. CO., Kingsport, TN (c. 1975 –) (Maker of Bearcreek and Elkhorn knives) 3½" 2 bl. Copperhead pat. Stag hdls. $62	10	125	(105)
TAYLOR (EYE) WITNESS, Shef., Eng. (Needham, Veal & Tyzack c. 1836 – 1967) *3½" 2 bl. Dog-leg jack pat. Bone hdls. $48	20	100	(151)

127

Brand Marks & Stampings (Dates)	Value Range		
	Low	High	Code
TEJA & ROSA, Italy	10	40	(60)
TELL, Ger. *4½" 1 bl. Lock back pat. FH pat. Bone hdls. $110	15	40	(100)
TERRIER CUTLERY CO., Rochester, NY (1910 – 1916) *4" 3 bl. Stock pat. Bone hdls. $71	20	90	(110)
THOMAS MFG. CO., Dayton, OH (c. 1907 – 1911) *3" 3 bl. Pen pat. Cel. hdls. $55	40	75	(110)
THOMASTON KNIFE CO., Thomaston, CT (c. 1887 – 1930) *3½" 4 bl. Cattle pat. Bone hdls. $117	20	180	(120)
T/C (in circle) (Thompson/Center Arms Co. c. 1972) *4" 3 bl. Stock pat. Rosewood hdls. $61	45	75	(135)
THORNTON USA	10	35	(65)
TIC, Italy	9	20	(50)
TIDIOUTE, PA. (c. 1919)	15	75	(90)
TIFFANY & CO., NY (c. 1900 – 1928) *3½" 4 bl. Pen pat. Pearl hdls. $90	25	100	(151)
TIGER CUTLERY CO., Ger. (O. Barnett Tool c. 1915) *4" 2 bl. Muskrat pat. Bone hdls. $71	30	100	(154)
TINA	8	12	(55)
TIP TOP (Camillus Cut. c. 1904 – 1941) *3¼" 2 bl. Barlow pat. Comp. hdls. $23	30	50	(100)
TOLEDO CUT. CO., Ger. *3" 2 bl. Dogleg jack pat. Bone hdls. $38	20	40	(85)
TOMRAY CUT. CO., (See Ray Cut. Co)	30	90	(130)
TOM THUMB (Imperial c. 1933 – 1949)	10	40	(110)
TOOTHILL	20	110	(90)
TORNADO (c. 1911 – 1952)	10	35	(100)

Brand Marks & Stampings (Dates)	Value Range		
	Low	High	Code
TORREY (J.R) & CO., Worcester, MA *4" 2 bl. Physician's pat. Bone hdls. $76	30	150	(130)
TOWER BRAND (J. Holler c. 1867 – 1906) *3½" 2 bl. Barlow pat. Bone hdls. $70	40	90	(135)
TOWIKA, Ger. & Ireland *4" 3 bl. Stock pat. Comp. hdls. $34. (Ger.) *4" 3 bl. Stock pat. Metal shell hdls. $15. (Ireland)	10	30	(75)
TOWNLEY, Kansas City (c. 1884 –) *3½" 3 bl. Stock pat. Comp. hdls. $39	15	45	(90)
TRAIN SHARE	15	25	(65)
TROUBLESOME CREEK, Owens Cutlery (Hindman, KY) 4" 2 Bl. Trapper Bone handles $33	15	25	(75)
TROUT HDW. CO., Chicago	12	30	(65)
TRUE VALUE, Chicago, IL (Hibbard, Spencer, & Bartlett) *4" 2 bl. Serp. Jack pat. Cel. hdls. $56	15	40	(100)
20TH CENTURY CUTLERY CO.	20	40	(75)
TWENTY GRAND, Prov., RI (Colonial cut)	20	35	(85)
TWO EAGLES	20	60	(100)
TYLER & CO., Eng. (1869 – 1877) Theile & Quack	20	50	(85)
U. C. CO. (Union Cutlery Co.) *(See Union Cutlery)	30	200	(150)
U.D. CO. MADE IN USA	15	75	(65)
ULRICH, Ger.	12	20	(50)
ULERY (U.J) CO., NY (c. 1902 – 1906) *3" 2 bl. Ez. open Jack pat. Bone hdls. $79	20	100	(175)
ULERY, NY USA (Nappanoch Knife Co., c. 1917 – 1919) *4" 2 bl. Jack pat. All metal hdls. $79.	20	75	(180)

Brand Marks & Stampings (Dates)	Low	Value Range High	Code
ULSTER, DWIGHT, DEVINE & CO., Ellenville, NY (1876 – 1941) **& ULSTER KNIFE CO.** Ellenville, NY (c. 1876 – 1941) *5" 1 bl. Lockback, FH Coke pat. Stag hdls. $305	40	300	(165)
ULSTER USA NY (c. 1941 –) *4" 3 bl. Stock pat. Bone hdls. $71	10	100	(110)
UNCLE HENRY (Schrade Cut. Co), Walden, NY *4" 3 bl. Stock pat. Del. bone hdls. $35	20	60	(100)
UNION CUTLERY CO., Chicago, IL (c. 1887 – 1888)	40	350	(500)
UNION RAZOR CO., Tidioute, PA (c. 1898 – 1909)	20	250	(700)
UNION CUTLERY CO., Tidioute, PA (1909)	20	175	(650)

Chart 1 Code Value		Chart 2 Pattern Value		Chart 3 Handle Value		Chart 4 Condition		RBR Collector Value
600	x	.40	x	1.00	x	.99	=	$237.60

	Low	High	Code
UNION CUTLERY CO. *3½" Office pen pat. Smooth bone hdls. $240	25	400	(600)
UNION CUTLERY CO., Olean, NY (1910 – 1951) *4" 2 bl. Sunfish pat. Pearl hdls. $610. (Makers of KA-BAR)	40	900	(435)
UNITED, Grand Rapids, MI (1942 – 1943)	25	100	(120)
UNITED, Ger.	10	40	(60)
UNIVERSAL KNIFE CO., New Britain, CT *5" 1 bl. Barlow pat. Bone hdls. $79 (O.N.B. on bols.)	20	100	(95)
UNITED CUTLERY CO., Austria (c. 1901 –) 4" 3 bl. Cattle pat. Bone hdls. $108	10	150	(110)
UNITED STATES CUTLERY CO. (c. 1930)	30	100	(95)

Brand Marks & Stampings (Dates)	Value Range		
	Low	High	Code

UTICA CUTLERY CO., Utica, NY (1929 – 1937)
*5" 2 bl. FH "Remington Bullet" pat.
(W/Buffalo head Shield) Bone hdls. $850   30   900   (523)

UTICA KNIFE CO., Utica, NY (1923 – 1937)
*4" 4 bl. Cattle pat. Bone hdls. $232
(Makers of Kutmaster)   30   300   (310)

VADSCO, New York (1927 – 1932)   12   40   (70)

VALLEY FALLS CUTLERY CO.
*4" 2 bl. Gunstock Jack pat. Bone hdls. $70   30   80   (311)

VALLEY FORGE CUTLERY CO., Newark, NJ (c. 1892 – 1950)
Plier knife, Old washed-out bone hdls. $180   30   250   (210)

Chart 1 Code Value		Chart 2 Pattern Value		Chart 3 Handle Value		Chart 4 Condition		RBR Collector Value
210	x	65	x	130	x	.99	=	$175.67

VALOR, Ger., Japan, Miami, FL (c. 1970 –)
*4" 1 bl. Lock-back FH pat. Wood hdls. $52   10   60   (67)

Chart 1 Code Value		Chart 2 Pattern Value		Chart 3 Handle Value		Chart 4 Condition		RBR Collector Value
125	x	.35	x	1.30	x	.99	=	$56.30

VAN CAMP, Indianapolis, IN (c. 1876 – 1960)
3⅜" Jack pat. Jigged bone hdls. $60   20   100   (125)

VAN CAMP HARDWARE, Indianapolis, IN (c. 1876 – 1960)
*3", 3 bl. Stock pat. Bone hdls. $82   20   150   (125)

Brand Marks & Stampings (Dates)	Value Range		
	Low	High	Code
VAN CAMP USA (Capital Cut Co. c. 1904 – 1948) *3" 2 bl. Serp. Jack pat. Bone hdls. $45	15	80	(100)
VAN CAMP, Ger. (Also-V. Camp Cut. Co., V.C.C. & Vanco)	15	75	(75)
VANCO, Indpls. (c. 1876 – 1960) *3" 3 bl. Stock pat. Cel. hdls. $62	20	100	(125)
VERITABLE PRADEL (Anchor) *4" 2 bl. Sailors pat. Wood hdls. $22	20	30	(90)
VICTORINOX, Switzerland 3½" 8 bl. Swiss Army Utility pat. Del. hdls. $52.50	15	75	(150)
VIGNOS CUT CO., Canton, OH (c. 1879 – 1948) *4" 2 bl. Jack pat. Picture hdls. $231. (Canton Cut. Co)	30	150	(160)
VIKING USA (E. Wedemeyer c. 1933 – 1934)	30	100	(120)
VOLORT CUT, Shef., Eng.	15	35	(70)
VOM CLEFF & CO., NY-Ger. (c. 1887 – 1913) *4" 4 bl. Congress pat. Bone hdls. $80	20	80	(95)
VOOS (Arrow) USA *3½" 2 bl. Ez. open jack pat. Bone hdls. $68	20	95	(115)
VOSS CUT. CO., Solingen, Ger. (c. 1920) *4" 3 bl. Stock pat. Stag hdls. $85	30	150	(100)
VOSS CUT. CO., Solingen, Ger. (H&R) Stamp (c. 1920 –) *4" 4 bl. Congress pat. Stag hdls. $115	40	150	(110)
VULCAN KNIFE CO., Ger.	10	30	(60)
VULCAN CUT CO. (T. Ellin Co. c. 1846 –) W (in a triangle), Ger.	20	50	(75)
WAGG, CELEBRATED CUTLERY, Shef., Eng. *6" Bone 1 bl. Folding dirk pat. Bone hdls. $1,137			(700)

Brand Marks & Stampings (Dates)	Value Range		
	Low	High	Code
W. A. & CO., Shef., Eng.	10	20	(75)
W & A CO., Prov., RI	15	45	(75)
WABASH CUT. CO., Terre Haute, IN (c. 1921 – 1935) *4½" 2 bl. Trapper pat. Picture hdls. $100.	35	125	(89)
WADE & BUTCHER, Shef., Eng. (1819 – 1974) *6" 1 bl. Dirk folder pat. Stag hdls. $1,300 (Cross & Arrow)	40	1400	(650)
WADE & BUTCHER, Ger. *4" 3 bl. Stock pat. Bone hdls. $81	20	90	(125)
WADE BROS. CELEBRATED CUTLERY (Theile & Quack c. 1866 – 76) *4½" 2 bl. FH jack pat. Bone hdls. $178	50	300	(125)
WADSWORTH, Ger. (A.W. Wadsworth & Sons c. 1905 – 1917) *3⅞" Folding hunter, Bone hdls. $180	15	70	(125)

Chart 1 Code Value		Chart 2 Pattern Value		Chart 3 Handle Value		Chart 4 Condition		RBR Collector Value
125	x	110	x	130	x	.99	=	$176.96

WAGNER (WILH), Solingen, Ger.
*3½" 3 bl. Stock pat. Bone hdls. $50   20   45   (85)

WALDEN KNIFE CO., Walden, NY (c. 1870 – 1923)
*2¼" solid green gold hdls. $32   50   250   (225)

Chart 1 Code Value		Chart 2 Pattern Value		Chart 3 Handle Value		Chart 4 Condition		RBR Collector Value
100	x	.20	x	1.60	x	.99	=	$31.68

Brand Marks & Stampings (Dates)	Value Range		
	Low	High	Code
WALDENAR KNIVES	20	65	(100)
WALKER CUT. CO., Solingen, Ger.	20	40	(65)
WALKILL RIVER WORKS, Walden, NY (NY Knife Co. c. 1928 – 1931)			
*4" 4 bl. Cattle pat. Bone hdls. $270	30	250	(327)
WALL BROS., Shef., Eng.	20	90	(90)
WALTCO USA (Safe-T-Sheath)	11	25	(75)
WALTER BROS., Ger.			
3½" 2 bl. Jack pat. Metal hdls. $15	10	25	(75)
WALTHAM CUTLERY CO., USA-Ger.	9	25	(75)
WANDY, Milan, Italy	9	20	(70)
WARDS USA			
*4" 4 bl. Fourmaster pat. Bone hdls. $122	20	150	(387)
WARDLOW CUTLERY CO., Walden, NY			
*4" 3 bl. Stock pat. Bone hdls. $78	30	90	(120)
WARREN, JOSEPH & SONS, Eng.			
Cattle knife, Matured bone hdl. $150	25	250	

Chart 1 Code Value		Chart 2 Pattern Value		Chart 3 Handle Value		Chart 4 Condition		RBR Collector Value
250	x	.55	x	1.10	x	.99	=	$149.24

WARREN, MADE IN AKER, OR	25	95	(90)
WARWICK KNIFE CO., (c. 1907)	20	90	(100)
WASHINGTON CUT. CO., Milwaukee, WI (c. 1898 – 1903)			
*4½" 2 bl. Trapper pat.			
Bone hdls. $96 (Village Blacksmith)	40	150	(135)

Brand Marks & Stampings (Dates)	Value Range Low	High	Code
WASHINGTON CUTLERY, Ger.	15	70	(65)
WATAUGA, Nashville, TN (H.G. Liscomb) 4" 2 bl. Jack, Royal black bone hdls. $60	20	80	(110)

Chart 1 Code Value		Chart 2 Pattern Value		Chart 3 Handle Value		Chart 4 Condition		RBR Collector Value
110	x	45	x	120	x	.99	=	$58.80

WATERVILLE CUT. & MFG. CO., Waterville, CT (c. 1843 – 1899)

Pen, Pearl hdls. $200	40	200	(300)

Chart 1 Code Value		Chart 2 Pattern Value		Chart 3 Handle Value		Chart 4 Condition		RBR Collector Value
300	x	35	x	175	x	.99	=	$191.00

	Low	High	Code
WATKINS-COTTREL CO., Richmond, VA (c. 1901) *4" 4 bl. Cattle pat. Bone hdls. $87	20	65	(90)
WEBSTER SYCAMORE WORKS, USA	15	40	(85)
WECK, New York (c. 1893 – 1943) *3½" 4 bl. Pen pat. Wood hdls. $35	20	75	(95)
WEDGEWAY CUTLERY CO., (Morley Bros. c. 1887 – 1933) *3½" 3 bl Pen pat. Bone hdls. $46	20	85	(90)
WEILAND, (C) New York	10	60	(70)
WENGEN, Switzerland	10	50	(75)
WENGER DELAMONT, Switzerland *3½" 6 bl. Swiss Army pat. Del. hdls. $42	15	45	(133)
WEST BROS., Shef., Eng.	15	40	(85)

Brand Marks & Stampings (Dates)	Value Range		
	Low	High	Code
WESTACO, USA (Western Cut)	25	150	(150)
WESTCO, Boulder, CO. (Western Cut. c. 1911 – 1951) *4" 1 bl. Hawkbill pat., Wood hdls. $36	20	100	(150)
WESTER & BUTZ, Solingen, Ger. (c. 1832 – 1966) *4" 2 bl. Open end jack pat. Bone hdls. $60	15	65	(85)
WESTER BROS., New York, Ger. (1904 – 1967) *3" 3 bl. Whittler pat. Bone hdls. $97	20	250	(135)
WESTER-STONE MC, New York (1904 – 1930) *4" 2 bl. Ez. open jack pat. Bone hdls. $71	20	95	(100)
WESTERN CUT., New York-Ger. (Wiebusch & Hilger c. 1876 – 1914) 4" 3 bl. Stock pat. Bone hdls. $125	30	150.	(130)
WESTERN SHEAR CO. (c. 1911)	20	100	(120)
WESTERN STATES, Boulder, CO (c. 1911 – 1951) *4" 3 bl. Stock pat. Stag hdls. $150	30	180	(200)

Chart 1 Code Value		Chart 2 Pattern Value		Chart 3 Handle Value		Chart 4 Condition		RBR Collector Value
200	x	55	x	130	x	.99	=	$141.70

WESTERN STATES, Boulder, CO *This variation is the rare Cattle pat., 4 bl. Bone hdls. with "Bull-head Shield" $400	100	400	(410)
WESTERN, Boulder, CO (c. 1951 – 1978) *4" 3 bl. Stock pat. Del. hdls. $85	15	75	(243)
WESTPFAL (A) CUT CO., NY-Ger. (1920 – 1951) 4" 3 bl. Stock pat. Bn. hdls $49	15	60	(75)
WHALE DESIGN, Ger.	15	60	(60)
WHITTLECRAFT, Little Valley, NY (Cattaraugus c. 1931 – 1963) *4" 3 bl. Whittler pat. Bone hdls. $210	40	200	(255)

Brand Marks & Stampings (Dates)	Value Range		Code
	Low	High	
WHITEHOUSE	20	50	(95)
WHITON HDW. CO., Seattle, WA (c. 1903 – 1908)	15	35	(85)

Chart 1 Code Value	Chart 2 Pattern Value	Chart 3 Handle Value	Chart 4 Condition	RBR Collector Value
125 x	.45 x	1.30 x	.99 =	$72.38

Brand Marks & Stampings (Dates)	Low	High	Code
WILBERT CUT. CO, Chicago (Sears-Roebuck c. 1908) *3½" Easy open jack. Jigged bone hdls. $75	20	100	(125)
WILD W & SONS, Shef., Eng. *6" 1 bl. Dirk pat. Ivory hdls. $1,050	100	1050	(350)
WIHL-WAGNER, Ger. *4" 3 bl. Stock pat. Bone hdls. $49	20	75	(75)
WILKINSON (NY) CUTLERY CO., Shef., Eng. *4" 2 bl. Pen pat. Metal hdls. $80	20	150	(250)
WILL & FINK, San Francisco (c. 1863 – 1930) *5" Fork & knife diner combo. Big jack pat. Bone hdls. $152 (Most pocketknives made in Germany)	30	190	(307)
WILLIAM ROGERS, Shef., Eng. *4" 4 bl. Pen pat. Pearl hdls. $328	30	200	(250)
WILSON BROS. USA	20	75	(75)
WILSON CUTLERY CO., Ger.	20	40	(65)
WILSON, Shef., Eng. *3½" 3 bl. Whittler pat. Tortoise hdls. $360	30	350	(150)
WILTON, Eng. or Ger. (Horse & Rider-Stamping) *4" 4 bl. Cattle pat. Bone hdls. $88	20	120	(90)
WINCHESTER, Trademark, Made in USA (c. 1919 – 1942) 4", 3 bl. Stock pat. Bone hdls. $375	40	250	(535)

Brand Marks & Stampings (Dates)	Value Range		
	Low	High	Code
WINCHESTER, Trademark, Made in USA (c. 1919 – 1942) 5½" 1 bl. FH Pat. 1950 Lockback. Bone hdls. $2,238	275	1,000	(1,235)
WINCHESTER, Trademark Made in USA (c. 1919 – 1942) *5½" 1 bl. FH 1920 Coke pat. Bone hdls. $1,605	60	1,500	(1,235)
WINCHESTER-QUICKPOINT, St. Louis *3" 2 bl. Pen pat. Im. tortoise hdls. $140	50	500	(320)
WINCHESTER, Trademark, Germany (1970 –) *6" 1 bl. FH pat. Bone hdls. $165	30	200	(150)
WINGEN, Solingen, Ger.	20	50	(75)
WISMAR, Ger.	10	40	(55)
WOLF & CO., Solingen, Ger.	20	65	(70)
WOOD, BARRY (Mark I, 1974 – 1975) Folding hunter, Micarta hdls. $525			(550)

Chart 1 Code Value		Chart 2 Pattern Value		Chart 3 Handle Value		Chart 4 Condition		RBR Collector Value
650	x	90	x	90	x	.99	=	$520.24

WOSTENHOLM-WASHINGTON WORKS, Shef., Eng. (1848 – 1890)
*3" 3 bl. Jack pat. Mother-of-pearl hdls. $265   40   250   (275)

Chart 1 Code Value		Chart 2 Pattern Value		Chart 3 Handle Value		Chart 4 Condition		RBR Collector Value
275	x	.55	x	1.75	x	.99	=	$261.80

Brand Marks & Stampings (Dates)	Value Range		Code
	Low	High	
W.R.B., Terre Haute, IN & Shef., Eng.	20	60	(75)
WUSTHOF (CARL), Solingen, Ger. *4" 3 bl. Cattle knife pat. Bone hdls. $57	20	75	(50)
WUSTHOF (ED), Solingen, Ger. (Trident Stamping) *4" 4 bl. Champagne knife, Mother-of-pearl fiery white hdls. $275	15	35	(350)

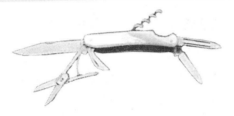

Chart 1		Chart 2		Chart 3		Chart 4		RBR Collector
Code Value		Pattern Value		Handle Value		Condition		Value
350	x	.45	x	1.75	x	.99	=	$272.25

WYETH'S CUTLERY, St. Joseph, MO (c. 1884 – 1907) *4" 3 bl. Stock pat. Bone hdls. $65	20	100	(100)
WYOMING (c. 1974 –)	20	55	(95)
YALE BRAND CUT. CO. (c. 1894 – 1919 Son Bros.) 3½" 3 bl. Pen pat. Bone hdls. $48	10	30	(80)
YANKEE CUT. CO., USA & Ger.	12	35	(100)
Y.B. CIGARS, USA (Adv.)	15	30	(70)
YORK CUTLERY CO., Ger. (1970)	10	30	(60)
ZAK, Ger.	15	35	(45)
ZENITH, (Marshall Wells Hdw. (c. 1894 – 1963) *3½" 4 bl. Cattle pat. Bone hdls. $97	30	150	(100)
ZIPPO, Bradford, PA (c. 1970 –) *2½" 3 bl. Lobster pat. Stainless hdls. $30	15	35	(107)
ZOPPIS, Italy	15	75	(75)

*Denotes example pattern
**See Appendix

CHART 2

PATTERNS — PERCENTAGE VALUES

Brand (Code) x Pattern % x Handle Material % x Condition % = Collector Value)

Percent	Patterns	Alternate Names	Blades
125	Folding Hunter	(Old/Special)	1 or 2 blade
125	Folding Hunter	(Old/Special/Grizzly/ Coke Bottle)	1 or 2 blade
120	Folding Hunter	(Antique Dirk)	1 or 2 blade
110	Folding Hunter	(Old/Common)	1 or 2 blade
110	Farrier's Knife or Tool	(Med/Lrg./Old)	3 to 6 blade
110	Cartridge Puller		2 blade
100	Deerfoot		1 blade
90	Trapper	(Old/Special)	2 blade
90	Folding Hunter	(Common/Recent)	2 blade
80	Folding Hunter	(Common/Recent)	1 blade
80	Sunfish, Elephant's Toenail	(Rope, etc)	2 blade
80	European Style Folding Hunter		1 blade
75	Gunboat	(Old/Special)	3 blade
75	Large Physician, Doctor's	(Old/Special)	1 or 2 blade
75	Stockman	(Old/Special)	4 or 5 blade
75	Whittler	(Old/Special)	3 blade
75	Cattle	(Old/Special)	3 or 4 blade
75	Sowbelly	(Old/Special)	3 to 5 blade
75	Congress	(Large)	4 blade
75	Fourmaster	Large 3½" – 4½" (Stock)	4 blade

Percent	Patterns	Alternate Names	Blades
70	Warncliffe	(Old/Special)	2 or 3 blade
65	Adjustable Wrench w/pliers		1 or 2 blade
60	Moose		2 opposed
60	Sowbelly	Large (Recent 3½" – 4½")	3 to 5 blade
60	Springer	(Common-type)	1 blade
60	Daddy Barlow	(Old/Special)	1 or 2 blade
60	Canoe	(Old/Special)	3 blade
60	Whittler	(Large 3½" – 4½")	3 blade
60	Stockman	(Old/Special)	3 blade
55	Cattle	(Old/Special)	3 or 4 blade
55	Senator pen		2 blade
55	Big Jack or Big Trapper	(Giant-5")	2 blade
55	Whittler	(Medium)	3 blade
55	Pistol Grip Jack	Large	1 blade
55	Musican Large		
50	Stockman	(Large 3½" – 4½")	3 blade
50	Congress	(Medium)	4 blade
50	Scout (Lg. Utility/Swiss Army etc.)		3 to 8 blade
50	Timberscribe		1 or 2 blade
50	Muskrat		2 opposed
50	Tanto		1 blade
50	Jack/Trapper	(Large 3¼" x 4¾")	2 blade

Percent	Patterns	Alternate Names	Blades
45	Canoe	(Medium-2½"-3½")	2 blade
45	Board	(Large/Flatfish, etc)	2 opposed
45	Jack	(Med./Physician, Easy Open, Gunstock, Crown, Dogleg, Lady's Boot, Toothpick, Copperhead, Game, Sailor, Swell End, Teardrop, Cigar, Serpentine, Balloon, Equal End, Swell-center, etc)	2 blade
45	Stockman	(Medium)	2 or 3 blade
45	Warncliffe		2 blade
45	Trapper		2 blade
45	Scout	(Avg. Utility, Swiss Army, etc)	3 to 8 blade
45	Orange Blossom	Medium	3 blade
45	Texas Jack		2 blade
45	Cotton Sampler	Medium/Large	1 blade
45	Large Bartender		
40	Whittler	(Small)	3 blade
40	Barlow	Standard Old	1 or 2 blade
40	Pen	Office, Sleeveboard, Canoe Lobster, Senator, Congress Half Whittler, Bartender, Champagne, etc.	2, 3, or 4 blade
40	Fish Knife		1 or 2 blade
40	Daddy Barlow	(Common-Recent 3½" – 4")	1 or 2 blade
40	Barlow	(Standard Old)	1 or 2 blade
40	Barlow	(Old/Special 2½" to 3½")	1 or 2 blade

Percent	Patterns	Alternate Names	Blades
40	Dog Groom		2 blade
40	Razor Knife		1 blade
35	Stockman	(Small)	3 blade
35	Congress	(Small)	4 blade
35	Pen	(Medium) Office, Sleeveboard, Lobster, Senator, Canoe, Half Whittler, etc	2 or 3 blade
35	Barlow	(Standard) Peanut	1 or 2 blade
35	Jack	(Medium-Electrician, Boy's, Florist, Dogleg, Mechanics, Pruner, Butterfly, Hawkbill, Seaman, etc)	1 or 2 blade
35	Barrel		2 blade
35	Castrator		1 or 2 blade
30	Jack	(Medium/Slender-Fish, Melon Tester, Stiletto, Slim Jim, Serpentine etc.)	1 or 2 blade
25	Jack	(Small-Peanut, Dogleg, Boy's, Baby Copperhead)	2 blade
25	Slide Blade		1 blade
25	Cigar Cutter		1 blade
20	Pen	(Small)	2 blade
20	Pen	(Very Small) – fob etc.	
15	Jack	(Very Small)	1 blade

TERMS

Old – Made before 1965±
Special – Something unique about the knife

Giant – 5"+
Large – 3½ – 4¾"±
Medium – 2½ – 3¼"±
Small – 1¾" – 2¼"
Very Small – ½" and under

CHART 3

HANDLE MATERIAL — PERCENTAGE VALUES

Percent	Material	Type, Description, Etc.
400%	Tortoise Shell	Genuine
'375	Ivory	Fossil or very old
250	Ivory	Recent
175	Pearl	Abalone, Black or Stained
175	Pearl	Fiery White
170	Pearl	White, Pink, common
160	Stag	Sambar, or India
160	Gold	Solid gold handles
150	Stag	European or American
145	Bone	Old-Green, Honeycomb, winter bottom, etc.
140	Bone	Old-Red, Cherry, Strawberry, etc.
130	Bone	Old-Faded, Washed Out, Rough Sawed, etc.
130	Stag	Old-Second Cut, Jigged, etc.
125	Celluloid/Composition	Old-Gold Flake, Christmas Tree, Candy stripe, Picture, Waterfall, etc. (plain – 100%)
120	Rough Black	Old-Hard Rubber, Gutta Percha, Bakelite, etc.
115	Slick Black	Old-Hard Rubber, Gutta Percha, Bakelite, etc.
110	Bone	Matured / worn, not faded or discolored
100	Smooth Bone	Recent-Natural or stained

Percent	Material	Type, Description, Etc.
100	Celluloid/Composition	Old/plain – jigged
100	Jigged Bone	Recent-Common Brown, Black, etc.
90	Wood	Fancy or Exotic-Cocabolo, Rosewood, Walnut, Redwood, Maple, Ebony, etc.
90	Artistic Plastics	Modern, Cracked Ice, Imitation Pearl
90	Micarta, etc.	Plain or colored-Imitation Ivory, Ebony, Wood Grain, other Modern Synthetics
80	Horn	Natural or Stained
80	Deer Hoof	With hair
80	Metal	Solid & Heavy-Brass, Nickel Silver, Stainless Steel, Pewter, Gold Plate, Gold-filled, etc.
70	Delrin	Colored or Simulated Bone, Stag, Ivory, etc.
70	Wood	Common Hardwood Hickory, Beech, Oak, etc.
65	Metal	Solid & Heavy, Iron, Cast Iron, Steel, etc.
65	Plastic	Recent Colored or Simulated Christmas Tree, Candy Stripe, Picture, etc.
65	Plastic	Plain, Common, Low Grade Composition Fiber, etc.
50	Wood	Common Softwood Popular, Boxwood, etc.
40	Metal	Recent, Common Brown, Black, etc.
25	Metal	Tin Shell Strap-on, Plastic or Paint-covered

NOTE: Handle materials containing precious metals or stones such as turquoise, onyx, silver, gold, etc., must be appraised separately, from the chart, by quantity of same; and art-worked scales by both quality and esthetic appeal. (See note following Chart 4.)

CHART 4

CONDITION — PERCENTAGE VALUES

Percent	Grade	Condition
*100%	Mint	"As new," with all original polish, etching, engraving, stamping sharp, clear and intact.
85-99	Excellent	Natural aging, light tarnish, handle and etching fade, etc. . . (Total damage excluding wear cannot exceed 15%.)
65-84	Good	Maximum 10% wear in one area, or 20% overall. Wear should not change original shape or work-order of parts. . . (Total damage cannot exceed 24%.)
40-64	Fair	Maximum 15% wear in one area, or 30% overall. Must retain all parts. . .(Total damage cannot exceed 35%.)
15-39	Junker	Excessive wear. Breakage and distortion damage over 40%. . . May still retain some value as historic or nostalgic relic, or source of parts for knives of similar brand and pattern.

*This grading should only apply to knives made after the 1965-1970 era. Knives made prior to this time will rarely be found in "as new" condition. Knives polished or buffed to "as new" should NOT be considered in this category. Older knives which DO fit the "as new" description may actually be valued three to four times the 99% EXCELLENT grading value (see page 57).

IMPORTANT: For accurate grading: First determine percent of wear only, by use of extended profile check, and combine with total percent of damages, below. Subtract combined total from 100% (Mint) as in Chart 4 of Condition Value Ratings. You now have your knife's condition percentage value.

SUGGESTED DAMAGE PERCENTAGES
(Total and subtract from rating determined from Chart 4.)

BACKSPRINGS:

Broken . . . . .50% ea.
Slow . . . . .20% ea.
Hinge Rivet:
Broken . . . . .35% ea.
Loose . . . . .25% ea.
Poor Blade:
Alignment . . . . .25% ea.

BLADES:

Broken . . . . .40% ea.
Scratched . . . . .3% ea.
Gapped to ¹⁄₁₆" . . . . . .5% ea.
Gapped to ¼" . . . . . .10% ea.
More than ¼" gap . . .25% ea.
Dubbed to ¼ . . . . . . .5% ea.
More than ¼" dub . .35% ea.

BOLSTERS:

Missing . . . . .35% ea.
Slightly battered . . . . . .5% ea.
Badly battered . . . . . . .25% ea.

BRAND STAMPINGS

Hardly visible . . . . . . .5% ea.
Magnified, only . . . . .10% ea.
Totally erased . . . . . .25% ea.

HANDLES:

Cracked, Checks & Hairline:
Not through . . . . .4% ea.
Through . . . . .25% ea.
Loose . . . . .10% ea.
Shrunken:
Hardly visible . . . . . . .4% ea.
Disfiguring . . . . .25% ea.

RUST PITTING:

Hardly visible . . . . . . .3% ea.
Quite visible . . . . . . .10% ea.
Disfiguring . . . . .25% ea.

NOTE: Although many years of experience, study, and information gleaned from others along the way have gone into the formulation of these scales, you may find your first experience in using them to be somewhat awkward, and, of course, nothing is perfect. But as you become more familiar and with a little routine practice, you will soon be amazed and gratified with the results.

Remember: **These charts are meant only as a guide,** and 100% accuracy is an impossibility.

You will soon learn to make adjustments for those odd-ball knives and knives that vary from the basic pattern designs by fitting them in with knives that have similar component parts. Art knives, advertising knives, and even those knives containing precious metals can be evaluated by our scales, up to a certain point. However, all art work, such as scrimshaw, carving, inlay, etc., must be independently evaluated according to its quality and type. Advertising knives are evaluated more on age and rareness, plus the current popularity of the items the knife is advertising. Because precious metals must be weighed by quantity and current value, it is always best to consult with an expert in that field before buying. Finally, while fixed-blade knives and sheath knives are not considered our specialty, we believe it is quite helpful to use Charts 3 and 4, after you have established a base price for your knife, to determine their final values.

A knowledge of the history of our most important knife makers and the approximate dates of the stampings of their knives should be very helpful and interesting to any genuine collector. Many find it almost as interesting to collect these historical facts as they do to collect the knives. It is not an easy task to obtain information on many of our older companies because they have long since been closed or have lost interest in the production of fine cutlery. With the passage of time, many records and much useful data have been lost.

The exact dates of many changes, methods, patterns, and brand stampings are either unverified or lost. For this reason you may be unable to specifically identify the time of a change. A knowledge of the general time period of such changes, however, is usually adequate for collecting and trading purposes.

Another topic the collector should be aware of is the numbering systems that knife companies use to identify and keep track of the different patterns of their knives. These coded numbers were listed in their catalogs and stamped on the boxes of knives that were ready for shipment. Most older pocketknife manufacturers made more patterns than companies do today, and some found it useful to expand their numbering systems to code numbers to indicate type of handles, number and type of blades, bolsters, liners, etc. Since different patterns were continually getting mixed up in shipment, some companies began stamping the numbers on the back tang of their knife's master blade. Though pattern numbers were not intended for collector's use, when they were discovered and decoded by collectors, they gave knife collecting an extra boost. The smart collector who understands the systems can make a more definite identification of a knife's pattern and check its authenticity for having the correct number and type of blades and handle materials. In this way he can tell whether the knife (even though original) has been faked or tampered with. This is only possible if the manufacturer used an expanded numbering system that indicated materials and stamped the complete number on the blade of his knives. Most cutlery companies did, and still do, have pattern numbering systems, but few have the expanded systems, or go to the extra trouble and expense of stamping them on their knives. Thus, they are of little use to collectors. It would be useless to include such systems in this book.

The collector's option is to become familiar with the manufacturer's pattern styles. We have included those companies with good numbering systems for collector use and urge you to become familiar with them.

JOHN RUSSELL CUTLERY COMPANY
GREEN RIVER WORKS
TURNERS FALLS, MASSACHUSETTS, U.S.A.

AERIAL CUTLERY MANUFACTURING COMPANY
Marinette, Wisconsin C. 1901 – 1945

This company was founded in Duluth, Minnesota, in 1901 by Thomas Madden, and Chris, Richard, and Fred Jaeger. They supposedly conceived the name "Aerial" from the lofty, soaring spans of the St. Louis Bay Bridge located near their Duluth factory. There were so many Jaegers in the firm, it is natural that some of their knives were also stamped "Jaeger Bros."

In 1912 the company moved to Marinette, Wisconsin. Knives continued as their main line of business until the mid-1920s when they switched to barber and beauty supplies. By the mid-1940s they had ceased producing pocketknives altogether.

Aerial knives are usually of high quality. Some were handled in natural materials, such as bone and mother-of-pearl. They are most noted, however, as early makers of "picture handle" knives which were manufactured in all patterns and sizes. Additionally, it should be pointed out that some of their knives were handled in other synthetic materials.

In 1972 the company discovered a large cache of mint Aerial knives which had been stored and forgotten in their warehouse. They were marketed at current prices and were responsible for quite a drop in the value of the old collector quality knives. But as of now, prices of Aerial knives are close to normal again. A word of caution, though, is that some of the 1972 knives were used to fake other knife brands such as Pine Knott, Winchester, and Cattaraugus.

Collectible rating: High
Stampings used by Aerial were:
Aerial Cutlery Mfg. Co., Duluth, MN
Aerial Cutlery Mfg. Co., Marinette, WI
Jaeger Bros, Marinette, WI
Aerial Cutlery Co., Marinette, WI
Current stamping: None (discontinued)

AERIAL KNIVES

General
An unusually well-made knife. Bolsters heavy and large. One large bevel shaped spear blade, one small spear, and one file blade.

Chieftain
A thin model fairly large knife. Large spear in one end and small spear in other.

Craftsman
A very neat, smooth finished, rounded equal ends, sunk jointed knife. One large bevel shaped blade and two small spears.

Champion
One large clip, one large spear, and two small spears.

Hawkeye
This knife has a well-rounded pyralin handle without severe edges that are uncomfortable to the hand. One large clip and one small spear blade.

A.G. RUSSELL

The A.G. Russell Company was started by custom knife maker A.G. Russell in 1970. It was responsible for having the Kentucky Rifle knife produced, which was one of the most successful early commemoratives. This was followed by the Russell Barlow commemorative and the Knife Collector's Club.

The company owned the Bertram Hen and Rooster manufacturing facilities and brand from 1975 until 1980. During this time the knives with the A.G. Russell trademark, as well as Hen and Rooster knives were manufactured in this German plant.

Currently the A.G. Russell Company markets most of its products through the Knife Collector's Club. Each year they produce a number of informative catalogs through which offer a variety of interesting knives, knife products, and collecting advice to their members. Their products include top quality custom made knives, and products from the most reputable cutlery manufacturers available.

Knives purchased directly from the A.G. Russell Company carry the strongest money back guarantee existing in the cutlery industry.

Stamping: A.G. Russell

Collectible rating: Very high

Model 340 Lockback. Top, smooth bone; middle, stag; bottom, black pearl.

One Hand Knife with scales.
Clockwise, from far left: mammoth ivory scales; elephant ivory scales; brown jigged bone scales; India stag scales; black rucarta scales; coral (red) rucarta scales; ivory rucarta scales.

Smoked pearl, pearl, smooth bone, India stag.

ALLEN CUTLERY COMPANY
Newburg, New York C. 1917 – 1925

This firm was established in 1917 in Newburg, New York, by Benjamin Allen to manufacture pocketknives. These knives were unusual as they used a fold of sheet metal to form handles and frame in one piece. The firm went out of business in 1925 when Mr. Allen moved to Scarsdale, New Jersey. However, he had obtained a patent on the construction of his knives, which "Ulery" brand knives, made by Napanoch Cutlery, used for the construction of some of their knives.

Although these knives were made for rugged use, they are rather rare due to the short period of their production.

Collectible rating: Very Good
Stamping: Allen Cut. Co., Newburg, NY
Current stamping: None, discontinued 1925.

AMERICAN KNIFE COMPANY
Thomaston, Connecticut C. 1849 – 1865

This firm was started in 1849 by Mr. Daniel Catlin who moved into an old clock factory on Reynolds Bridge Road and began manufacturing pocketknives. This proved to be a thriving concern and at one time employed more than a hundred workers.

However, the Northfield Knife Co. of Northfield, Connecticut, secured control of the firm in 1865, and the factory was shut down.

Collectible rating: Very Good
Stampings: American Knife Co., Thomaston, CT
Current stamping: None, discontinued 1865.

AMERICAN KNIFE COMPANY
Winstead, Connecticut C. 1919 – 1955

Established in 1919 and incorporated about one year later in Winstead, Connecticut, this was a small firm. The business was moved in 1947 from Boyd Street to Lake Street and renamed the Kendall Mfg. Co. The name changed once again that same year to Bukar Mfg. Co. Then the Great Flood of 1955 hit the area and the entire business was washed away.

Knives made by this firm are of good quality, and they are rare because of limited production. The Kendall Mfg. Co. stamp is extremely rare. It is unlikely that any knives were ever stamped with Bukar Mfg. Co. brands.

Collectible rating: Very Good
Stampings:
    American Knife Co., Winstead, Conn.
    Kendall Mfg. Co., Winstead, Conn.
Current stamping: None, discontinued 1955.

AMES CUTLERY COMPANY
Chelmsford, Massachusetts C. 1791 – 1935

The Ames Cutlery Co. was first established in 1791 in Chelmsford, Massachusetts, by Nathan P. Ames, a blacksmith who made small tools and cutlery. His two sons, Nathan and James, learned their father's trade, and in 1829 the family moved to Chicopee Falls where they set up business. In 1834 they renamed their firm the Ames Mfg. Co.

Although they manufactured other items, including the brass casting of cannons, bells, and bronze statues, the Ames family is most noted as America's first sword, bayonet, and dagger makers.

They produced many types of fixed-blade knives, some of which were shipped abroad for military use, but there is no record of them having manufactured folding or pocketknives.

Collectible rating: Top Priority (Because of their historical significance)
Stampings used:
    Ames Cutlery Co., Chelmsford, Mass.
    Ames Mfg. Co., Chicopee Falls, Mass.
Current stamping: None, discontinued in 1900.

BALDWIN CUTLERY COMPANY
Tidioute, Pennsylvania C. 1913 – 1919
Jamestown, New York C. 1919 – 1932

This company was established in 1913 in Tidioute, Pennsylvania, by Harry D. Baldwin, who moved his firm to Jamestown, New York, in 1919 and continued the firm's business until 1932.

The firm produced mostly large patterns of well-made knives.

Collectible rating: High
Stampings used:
    Baldwin Cut. Co. Tidioute, PA
    Baldwin Cut. Co. Jamestown, NY
Current stamping: None, discontinued 1932.

Four blades, Congress shape, stag handle, iron lined, fluted steel bolsters, polished blades.

BATTLE AXE
Hardin Wholesale, Kenova, West Virginia C. 1975 – 1990

This company first began importing knives in 1975. All knives are made in Solingen, Germany, and appear to be top quality. They are made almost exclusively in limited numbers and collector sets in which the knives have different handle materials, such as one Stag and one Bone. However, it is sometimes possible to buy the knives individually at the same price as included in the sets.

Collectible rating: Good

Current stamping: Battle Axe (over two crossed axes)

Battle Axe, Gunstock

Battle Axe, Congress Whittler

Battle Axe Folding Hunter, The Conqueror

The Gambler, Canoe

BEAVER FALLS CUTLERY COMPANY
Beaver Falls, Pennsylvania
(See Cattaraugus Cutlery)

BELKNAP HARDWARE COMPANY
Louisville, Kentucky C. 1840 – 1986

This firm was founded in 1840 by W. B. Belknap. It dealt mainly in wagon, carriage, and blacksmith supplies. Soon knives and other types of cutlery, along with farm equipment, were added to their line. Belknap sold knives made by Russell, IX-L, Robinson, Winchester, and others but also included their stock knives made to their own specifications and stamped with their own brand. Belknap grew to be the largest hardware company in the world. However, in 1986, the firm closed its doors and went completely out of business.

Their brands, first introduced about 1890, include the following:

Pine Knott, J. C. Price, discontinued about 1930.

Blue Grass, a name conceived from the rich bluegrass region of central Kentucky, discontinued about 1950 except on a standard Barlow pattern with plastic handles.

John Primble, a brand, current at closing, dating back to the late 1800s.

John Primble, India Steel Works, named because made in Sheffield, England, of a special imported India steel. The George Wostenholm Cutlery firm held this contract. (See following illustrations from the 1913 Belknap catalog.)

John Primble, Germany, produced in the early 1900s, probably by the H. Boker Cutlery firm in Germany.

John Primble, with a star under the stamping, was most likely made by Camillus until 1965. This stamping, without the star, was by Schrade Cutlery Company on knives made for Belknap.

The collector will also find some knives stamped J. Primble and with only Primble on the tag. These knives are generally old, and the manufacturing company and dates are unestablished. But recent knives stamped in this manner may have a blade stamped Schrade-Walden.

When Belknap Hardware closed its doors in 1986, Blue Grass Cutlery Corp. of Manchester, Ohio, acquired the rights to reproduce some of their patterns and brand stampings, so the trademark continues.

Collectible rating: High

Stampings: As described above.

157

JOHN PRIMBLE INDIA STEEL WORKS POCKET KNIVES

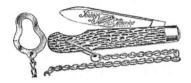

Boy's Knife
No. 4804S. Chain, stag handle, brass lining, steel bolster, half polished, 3³/₁₆" long, chain 21" long.

Jack
No. 4814R. Redwood handle, steel lining, steel bolster, glazed blade, 2⁷/₈" long.

No. 56155. Stag, tip handle, half polished, 3" long.

Pen/Quill
No. 5434W. White bone handle, brass lining, steel bolster, glazed blade, 3" long.

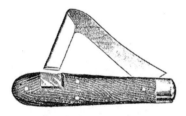

Timber Scribe
No. 5103R. Carpenter's race knife, redwood handle, steel lining, steel bolster, 3½" long.

Cotton Sampler
No. 5105R. Cotton Knife, cotton sampling, redwood handle, steel lining, steel bolster, half polished, 4" long.

Florist's Knife
No. 5231S. Budding, stag handle, stag scale lining, half polished, 3⁷/₈" long.

JOHN PRIMBLE INDIA STEEL WORKS POCKET KNIVES

Hawkbill
No. 5106R. Pruning Knife, rosewood handle, steel lining, steel bolster, half polished, 4" long.

One Arm Barlow
No. 5014S. With razor blade, steel handle and steel lining, German silver bolster, half polished, 3⁷⁄₁₆" long.
No. 5008S. With clip blade instead of razor blade.
No. 5010S. Spear blade instead of razor blade.
No. 5012S. With sheepfoot blade instead of razor blade.
No. 5018S. Spaying blade instead of razor blade.

Easy Open Balloon Jack
No. 5175R. Redwood handle, easy opener, brass lining. German silver bolster, cap, and shield, half polished, 3⅝" long.

Lobster
No. C3-967. 3" long; manicure file, pen and spear pocket blades and scissors all stainless; nickel silver linings and tips; blades full polished, mother-of-pearl handle.

Swiss Style Army/Camp Knife
No. C2-01008G. 3½", 8 stainless steel blades; pen large, pen small, scissors, can opener, crown opener, screwdriver, saw, cork screw, and punch. Brass lining, red ball on handle.

JOHN PRIMBLE INDIA STEEL WORKS POCKET KNIVES

Scout

No. C3-7593. 3⅝", genuine bone stag handle, large spear, frosted etching "Tree Brand," small clip, screwdriver and cap lifter, can opener, corkscrew, punch blade and shackle. Mirror polished, hand honed. Nickel silver bolsters and lining.

Boy's Jack

No. C3-460. 3⅛", clip and pen blades, white pyralin and imitation stag handles, nickel finish bolsters, brass lining.

Congress Pen

No. C1-5228S. 3¼", improved stag handle, full polished and etched pen and sheepfoot blades, nickel silver bolsters and shield, milled brass lining.

Fish Knife

No. C1-795R. Stainproof fishing knife; closed length 5". Stainless steel blades and springs; one long clip blade and a combination hook disgorger, fish scaler, and caplifter blade; patented beer can opener made of tempered steel and corrosion-proof plated. Brass lining, nickel silver bolstered. Blades full mirror polished. Red pyralin handles.

Castrating Knife

No. C3-1612. All metal construction for submersion in sterilizing bath. Fine cutlery steel blades, spay and hoe shapes, stainless steel handle, 3½" long. Excellent for both farmer and veterinarian.

BENCH MARK KNIVES
Gastonia, North Carolina, C. 1976 – 1984
Bench Mark Knives, USA 1984 – 1991

Bench Mark Knives were introduced sometime in the later 1970s as a division of the Jenkins Metal Corporation of Gastonia, North Carolina. The president of the firm was R. B. Jenkins, Jr.

Sheath knives were their first staple. Later the company introduced their Rolox System of enclosed blade knives. The Rolox System incorporates a blade that slides from a fixed, locked position inside the handle to a locked, open position. When the release is triggered, the blade glides back into the handle.

Handles were in a choice of stag, buffalo horn, or white micarta and woods. There were four models of this knife, and Bench Mark later released a fixed-blade, all stainless, utility knife that carried its own blade cover piggyback, so to speak. It was called the S.O.S. due to this safety factor.

The earlier knives were designed by "Blackie" Collins, a custom knifemaker, who founded the company. They were produced by the Jenkins Metal Company and are held in highest esteem by collectors.

The company was sold to Gerber Legendary Blades in 1985 who continued to market the knives, until the parent company was acquired by Fiskars in 1987.

Collectible rating: Excellent

Stamping and logo: Bench Mark Knives (through a circle)

Bench Mark "Rolox" Knives designed by Blackie Collins.

BERETTA USA
Knife Dept., Accokeek, Maryland, C. 1978

The "Beretta U.S.A., Arms Corp." began manufacturing side arms in the United States at the above address in 1977, and was awarded a contract by U. S. Armed Forces in 1985 to provide them with the Model M9 side arm to replace the heavy Colt 45 in most branches.

Since then, the company expanded rapidly and later began releasing a lock blade folding hunter knife as a companion piece to their popular side arm. This knife, designated the Model K-92, was their first knife (several later models have been released) and since it is a quality piece of workmanship, has become so popular that it is not easy to obtain.

Collectible rating: High

Current stamping: Beretta, USA

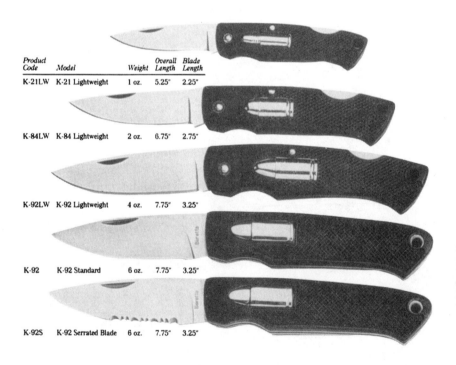

Product Code	Model	Weight	Overall Length	Blade Length
K-21LW	K-21 Lightweight	1 oz.	5.25"	2.25"
K-84LW	K-84 Lightweight	2 oz.	6.75"	2.75"
K-92LW	K-92 Lightweight	4 oz.	7.75"	3.25"
K-92	K-92 Standard	6 oz.	7.75"	3.25"
K-92S	K-92 Serrated Blade	6 oz.	7.75"	3.25"

BERTRAM (C) CUTLERY COMPANY (HEN & ROOSTER)
Solingen, Germany C. 1872-

This small cutlery firm was first established in 1872 by Carl Bertram, a noted fancier of poultry, and the famous "Hen & Rooster" logo was adopted to symbolize the high grade quality of their knives. The firm was run by members of the family until 1975 when it was purchased by A. G. Russell of Springdale, Arkansas.

Until sold, the firm made many contract knives for other firms with the Hen & Rooster logo on one side of the blade and the contract firm's name on the other side. Under the A. G. Russell leadership, the firm continued to make some contract knives and some special design patterns for Russell to sell in the United States.

In 1983 the firm was liquidated, and the trademark and Bertram name were acquired by James Frost of the Frost Cutlery, Chattanooga, Tennessee, and Star Sales of Knoxville, Tennessee. Although Hen and Rooster knives continue to be made on contract with other German cutlery firms, they are not made in the original C. Bertram factory, which somewhat diminishes their collector value.

Collectible rating: Very Good
Original stamping: (Hen & Rooster)
   C. Bertram Cutlery, Solingen, Germany
Current stamping: (Hen & Rooster)
Bertram Cut.

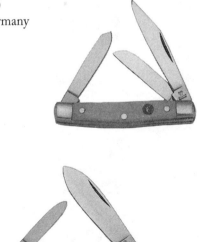

HEN & ROOSTER CURRENT PRODUCTION

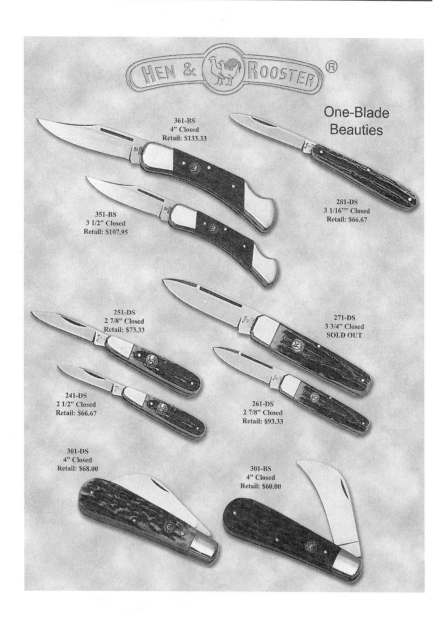

HEN & ROOSTER ®

One-Blade Beauties

361-BS
4" Closed
Retail: $133.33

351-BS
3 1/2" Closed
Retail: $107.95

281-DS
3 1/16"" Closed
Retail: $66.67

251-DS
2 7/8" Closed
Retail: $73.33

271-DS
3 3/4" Closed
SOLD OUT

241-DS
2 1/2" Closed
Retail: $66.67

261-DS
2 7/8" Closed
Retail: $93.33

301-DS
4" Closed
Retail: $68.00

301-BS
4" Closed
Retail: $60.00

164

HEN & ROOSTER CURRENT PRODUCTION

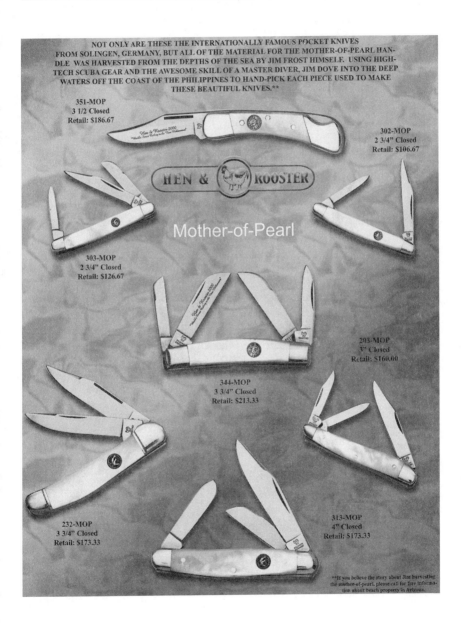

NOT ONLY ARE THESE THE INTERNATIONALLY FAMOUS POCKET KNIVES FROM SOLINGEN, GERMANY, BUT ALL OF THE MATERIAL FOR THE MOTHER-OF-PEARL HANDLE WAS HARVESTED FROM THE DEPTHS OF THE SEA BY JIM FROST HIMSELF. USING HIGH-TECH SCUBA GEAR AND THE AWESOME SKILL OF A MASTER DIVER, JIM DOVE INTO THE DEEP WATERS OFF THE COAST OF THE PHILIPPINES TO HAND-PICK EACH PIECE USED TO MAKE THESE BEAUTIFUL KNIVES.**

351-MOP
3 1/2 Closed
Retail: $186.67

302-MOP
2 3/4" Closed
Retail: $106.67

Mother-of-Pearl

303-MOP
2 3/4" Closed
Retail: $126.67

293-MOP
3" Closed
Retail: $160.00

344-MOP
3 3/4" Closed
Retail: $213.33

232-MOP
3 3/4" Closed
Retail: $173.33

313-MOP
4" Closed
Retail: $173.33

**If you believe the story about Jim harvesting the mother-of-pearl, please call for free information about beach property in Arizona.

165

HEN & ROOSTER CURRENT PRODUCTION

BINGHAM (W.W.) COMPANY
Cleveland, Ohio C. 1841 – 1946

The W.W. Bingham Co. was one of the large, old hardware firms, established in 1841. They carried mostly contract knives bearing their own brand and made to their specifications by the best cutlery manufacturers. They also carried many knives, alongside their own, with the other cutlery firm's brands. These included such brands as Miller Brothers and Winchester. By doing this, they gave the customer a choice, proving in some cases that their contract knives excelled the brand names.

Collectible rating: Very Good
Stampings and logos:
W. Bingham & Co., B.B.B. (Bingham's Brand)
XLCR (for Excelsior)
XLCR (With arrow through letters)
Current stampings: None, discontinued 1945

BLUE GRASS (Brand-Stamping)
(See Belknap Mfg. Co.)

BLUE GRASS CUTLERY CORPORATION
304 W. 2nd Street
Manchester, Ohio C. 1987

This company is outstanding for their high quality and limited reproductions of famous discontinued old brand knives. When Belknap Hardware Company of Louisville, Kentucky, closed their doors in 1986, Blue Grass Cutlery obtained the rights to reproduce their original "John Primble, India Steel Works," brand knives.

They also secured the authorized rights to reproduce all of the original patterns of the Winchester Arms Co. knives and were licensed by Olin Corporation, owners of the Winchester trademark.

As of this date, all of their knives are manufactured in the United States, using original dies from the factories of bygone days.

These are truly high-quality knives, with fine old Roger Bone handles and both shields and handles attached with hand-hammered rivets as were the originals. The blades are of the best available high-carbon steel, and both blade etching and tang stampings are original company markings.

Pattern numbers are also original and stamped on the reverse tang, and the tang also includes (clearly stamped) the year the knife was manufactured.

Collectible rating for The Blue Brass Cutlery Corp. reproduced John Primble, India Steel Works: Very High.

Winchester Trademark: Very High.

Illustrated with Winchester trademark.

BLUE GRASS CUTLERY

H. BOKER & COMPANY, GERMANY AND BOKER USA
C. 1867 – Present

This firm was founded in 1867 by Heinrich Boker in Remschied, Germany. They adopted a tree as their trademark. During the same year, other members of the Boker family came to the United States and started Herman Boker & Co. USA. The early USA firm did not manufacture knives themselves but were the sole US importer and distributor of German Boker knives.

In 1917 they acquired the Valley Forge Cutlery Co. of Newark, New Jersey. At this plant, they began producing Boker USA knives. They continued the Valley Forge brand stampings along with their own until about 1950. They remain the exclusive importers of Boker, Solingen, Germany. In 1969, Boker USA became a branch company of J. Wiss & Sons. The firm's address was changed to Maplewood, New Jersey.

In 1978 the firm was purchased by a North Carolina tool manufacturing corporation called the Cooper Group, but in 1986 the company once again became a part of the Heinrich Boker Company of Germany. It now has a headquarters in Golden, Colorado.

Most collectors and users place a higher value on the Solingen-made knives with the following stampings:

Heinr. Boker & Co.

H. Boker & Co. Cutlery

H. Boker Improved Cutlery

Boker Alemania, Ger.

Boker, Solingen, Ger. (current)

Henry Boker (around stamping of pelican, non-U.S. import)

Collectible rating: High

Stamping for the Boker Cutlery Co., Maplewood,

New Jersey brand: Boker, USA

Collectible rating: Good

Current stamping: Boker Cutlery Co. Golden, Colorado

1869 – 1900   1900 – 1924   1924 – 1935   1935 – 1947   1947 – 1974   1974 –

BOKER POCKETKNIVES

BO-2040. Ceramic Titanium Dela, 4¼" closed lockback. Custom styling. 3½" ceramic clip blade. Titanium handles.

BO-4474. Stockman. 4" closed. 440C stainless blades. Genuine deer stag handles.

BO-414. Gentleman's Knife. 3⅜" closed. Sculptured metal handles with wildlife scenes. Stainless steel blades.

200. Canoe nickel silver bolsters perfectly compliment this canoe's handsome gray bone handles. 440A stainless steel pen and spear blades. 3½" closed.

2005. 3⅛" folding Damascus blade, set in handles of mother-of-pearl. Bolsters are polished nickel silver.

BOKER POCKETKNIVES

7474 SS. A Stockman knife with stainless steel blades and red bone handles. 4" closed.

Today, Boker continues to be on the "cutting edge" of technology. It was the first company to offer knives with titanium handles and ceramic blades.

BOWER (F.A.) IMP. & DIST. COMPANY
Solingen, Germany

The F.A. Bower Import Co. has made the "Bower" stamped knives a reputable and familiar brand in the U.S.A. and other countries because they have been around so long. Bower knives were of good comparative quality that usually retailed for a little less because they were import knives. Most Bower knives are made in familiar patterns, with shields stamped "Bower," and the bolsters on the Barlow patterns were also stamped with the Bower brand.

The firm began importing their fine knife from Solingen, Germany, very early in the 1900s, and they seem to have measured up very well against our own fine domestic brands.

Collectible rating: Very Good

Stampings: "Bower" Solingen

"Bower Imp. Co." Solingen, Ger.

"F.A. Bower Dist. Co." Solingen, Ger.

BROWNE & PHARR MANUFACTURING COMPANY
Norcross, Georgia (C. 1976 – 1981)

In the mid-1970s the Browne & Pharr Mfg. Co. introduced two new pocketknives to the market designed specifically as high-quality functional tools for use by many tradesmen. By removing screws, these knives could be easily disassembled, cleaned, and parts restored, if necessary. From all indications, Browne & Pharr knives were not designed with collectors in mind, and they were more expensive than most knives. Still, they were quite distinctive and add a touch of class to any collection.

Collectible rating: Very Good

Stamping: "Browne & Pharr" Atlanta, GA

BROWNING ARMS COMPANY
Gunnison, Utah (Knives C. 1969 –)

The Browning Arms Co. of Gunnison, Utah, decided to expand their line of sporting goods to include knives in 1969. Having noted, no doubt, that knives made by arms companies were rated top priority by sportsmen and collectors, they proceeded to introduce a line of four hunter models. Three of these were sheath knives, or fixed blade, and the other a lockblade folder with belt sheath. All of these were designed by Gil Hibben, an outstanding custom knifemaker and designer. These knives were an instant success, and it should be noted that the sleek, new design lines of the Browning/Hibben folding hunter were mostly duplicated by the Case "Shark Tooth" folding hunter.

In 1970 Browning introduced two stock pattern pocketknives to their line, both purportedly made on contract with the Kabar Cutlery of Olean, New York. These pocketknives, pattern numbers 2518 USA, and 3018 USA, were well made with the look of quality, but for some reason, perhaps production cost, only about 7,000 were made in the USA in 1970 and the contract was transferred to an unknown German firm in 1971. Due to this shifting of nationality, these two patterns with the rare USA stamping are now top collectibles.

However, since Browning has recently added some new patterns and some of these are being manufactured in the USA once again, this may prove to be confusing to some collectors unless pattern numbers and country of origin are closely checked.

At the present time there are numerous patterns of Browning knives being produced with different patterns manufactured in the USA, Germany, and Japan.

Collectible rating: High

Current stampings: Browning USA, Browning (Country
  of Origin), BAR (Country of Origin)

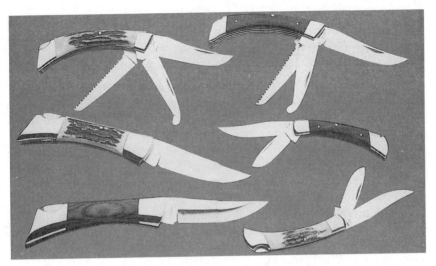

Folding hunter lockback. Double edge Damascus Hunter.

BRÜCKMANN, (E) CUTLERY
Oligs-German C. 1920 – 1956

Ernest Brückmann established this company in 1920 and manufactured all types of cutlery until 1956 when he passed away. The trademark was an arched bridge over "Mann."

Brückmann pocketknives are of excellent quality, and the large stock remaining when the firm closed is still selling in various areas. For a more complete sampling of Brückmann Knives, see *The Big Book of Pocket Knives* (Collector Books, 2000).

Collectible rating: Good

BUCK CREEK
Burns & Company, London, Kentucky (C. 1968 – 1985)
Taylor Cutlery, Kingsport, Tennessee (C. 1985 – present)

Buck Creek brand knives were initiated and made in Germany for Millard Burns of Burns & Company of London, Kentucky. The company began importing knives in 1968 with one yellow delrin handle stock knife pattern with "Buck Creek" stamped on the tang of each blade. The back tang places the origin as Solingen, Germany, where the knives were made to the Burns specifications by the Heinrick Kaufmann & Sohnne Co.

The name Buck Creek was later enclosed by antlers and became a trademark easily recognized by collectors. The origin of the Buck Creek name is a mountain stream in Eastern Kentucky, near London.

The majority of the numerous patterns of the Buck Creek brand pocketknives are made in Germany. However, one pattern was made in Japan and another's blades were made in England while the additional parts were made and the knife assembled in Pakistan.

Handle materials are of all varieties. They include stag, horn, bone (both cow and camel), wood, pearl, and delrin. Buck Creek was the first modern U.S. company to reintroduce the "Christmas Tree" handle. A note of interest to collectors is that the material used for this first "Christmas Tree" knife was from an undiscovered cache made prior to World War II.

Dating of Buck Creek knives is difficult at best. The key, however, is in the shield design. Between 1968 and 1972, the shield design was either smooth oval or smooth crest. From 1972-1975, a crest design was used which had crossed swords and the word "Solingen" beneath them. From 1976 to the present, the crest shield with antlers imprinted has been used on their standard line of knives. On their Owl's Head and Indian Head Penny lines, a profile, circular shield was used. Exceptions to these designs are the Bob Cat large congress pattern, which has used a bent bar shield, with Buck Creek stamped on it, since its introduction in 1974. The 1981, slim congress, pearl handle pattern has no shield.

Buck Creek knives have a reputation of quality and reliability. Their price has always been considered to be reasonable. Because of their slowness to make pattern changes and to introduce new patterns, they are becoming popular with collectors who wish to collect complete pattern sets of a particular company.

In the spring of 1985, Mr. Burns passed away and the Buck Creek trademark was purchased by Stewart Taylor of Taylor Cutlery, Kingsport, Tennessee. Mr. Taylor continued the quality and designs that made Buck Creek a respected brand.

In 1990 he began having the year of manufacture etched on the face of the master blade of each Buck Creek knife. In 1991, the shield design was changed on knives with the "official" style shield, and Stewart A. Taylor Co. was added to the back of the blade tang. Between 1991 and 1993, some special runs of knives were made with a special celluloid handle called Rohoid. This is especially tough, and as a result, these handles did not have shields embedded in the handles as did other Buck Creek knives.

In 1996, rights to use the Buck Creek trademark were acquired by Frost Cutlery of Chattanooga, Tennessee. It is the intent of Frost Cutlery to continue the Buck Creek line and expand it. Another German company has been contracted to produce the knives in many of the same patterns and trademark variations as before.

Our contract at Frost Cutlery says, "Buck Creek knives will still be made in Solingen, Germany, with hard to find carbon steel blades. The Buck Creek name has long been recognized for top quality and is highly desirable among top collectors. We intend to keep it that way."

The first shipments of the knives produced under Frost Cutlery supervision include the Diamondback; Whittler; Bear & Bull, 2 & 4 blades; Bob Cat; and Baby Diamondback. These knives were made with a variety of handle materials.

The collector will want to compare the new Buck Creek with the old one to see if there are differences in quality, stampings, patterns, etc. Regardless, we believe this new direction will serve to enhance this brand as a valued collectible.

Collectible rating: Very Good
Stamping and logo:
Buck Creek
Buck Creek (enclosed by antlers)
Buck Creek (above two owl head etchings)
Buck Creek (above two Indian head etchings)
Bear & Bull (Wall Street style Bear & Bull, "Buck Creek" on shield

(See Apendix 1 for a detailed Duck Creek price guide.)

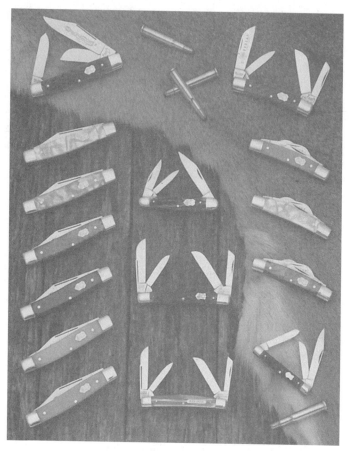

These are the first of the Buck Creeks made under Frost Cutlery supervision.

BUCK KNIVES, INC.
P.O. Box 1267
El Cajon, California C. 1961 –

. Buck Knives, Inc. was established in 1961 by Alfred Buck, the son of H.H. Buck, a blacksmith, who had begun forging sheath knives in his shop much earlier. H.H. had experimented with tempering farm implements to the point of producing a superior edge-holding steel. He presented many of his earlier knives to friends and supplied our servicemen of WW II with a large number, thereby establishing a fine reputation for their dependability and edge-holding ability.

176

When H. H. died in 1949, Alfred and his two sons continued the family business as Buck Knives, Inc., and in 1965 they produced their first folding knife: a lockblade, folding hunter with a belt sheath. This first Buck model, with its heavy brass bolsters and blade, was a tremendously strong folder and proved itself an equal to most moderate size fixed-blade knives. Furthermore, this initial pattern seemed to set the styling trend for most of the lock blade knives made today, plus the popular habit of carrying them in belt sheaths.

In 1968 Buck added pocketknives to their line and now has a wide variety of patterns. Although most Buck knives are still being constructed for the toughest kind of use, the older models are growing in popularity as collector items. Of interest is a note from Al Buck, which is included with Buck knives, that reflects the Christian attitudes of Buck management. It says in part:

The fantastic growth of Buck Knives, Inc. was no accident. From the beginning, management determined to make God the Senior Partner. In a crisis, the problem was turned over to Him, and He hasn't failed to help us with the answer. Each knife must reflect the integrity of management, including our Senior Partner. If sometimes we fail on our end because we are human, we find it imperative to do our utmost to make it right. Of course, to us, besides being Senior Partner, He is our Heavenly Father also, and it's a great blessing to us to have this security in these troubled times. If any of you are troubled or perplexed and looking for answers, may we invite you to look to Him, for God loves you.

Collectible rating: Very Good
Current stamping: "Buck" Made in USA

BUCK KNIVES

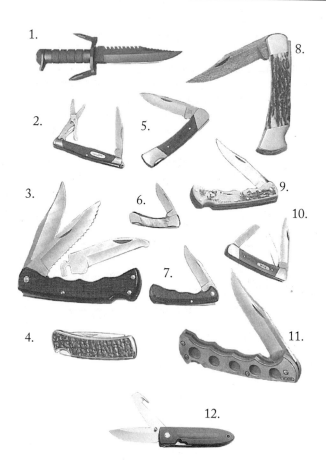

1. *Parkerized Buck Master*
2. *Clipper Series*
3. *The Selector, w/Interchangeable blade*
4. *Buck Skins Series*
5. *Prince, Model #503, 500 Slimline Series*
6. *The Ultima Model #507, Executive Series*

7. *Bucklite*
8. *Folding Hunter, w/Damascus Blade*
9. *Scrimshaw Series, Model #4265 w/Mallard Duck Scene*
10. *Bronco/Model #701*
11. *XLTI Titanium, Model #560*
12. *Cross Lock Hunter*

BULLDOG BRAND
Bulldog Knife Company
Johnson City, Tennessee C. 1980 –

This company first began importing knives in 1980. Their line includes top quality, limited edition collector sets. The first five sets imported sold quickly. The reason for Bulldog's popularity is perhaps the materials used. Most are made of high grade carbon steel. Some, however, were made of stainless or surgical steel. The varieties of scaling materials vary greatly, including genuine pearl, India stag, jigged bone, and delrin in a variety of colors. Bulldog knives were imported and distributed solely through the Bulldog Knife Company's office in Johnson City, Tennessee.

However, the trademark was sold to the Parker Collection Service of Chattanooga, Tennessee. The line has since expanded, and the logo has changed. The earlier knives, with the trademark below, have become sought-after collectibles.

The quality of the new knives indicates that they too will become sought-after in the future.

Collectible rating: Good

Stamping and logo: Bulldog Brand (under two fighting pit bulldogs)

Current stampings: A single bulldog

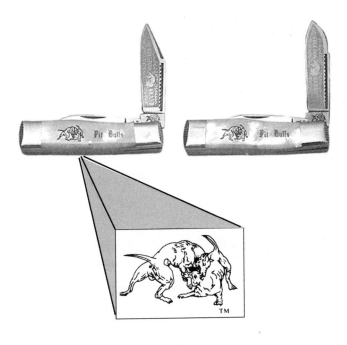

BULLDOG BRAND POCKETKNIVES

Moose. 3⅝" long, Abalone Swirl handle.

5 Blade Sowbelly. 3⅝" long, Abalone Swirl handle.

6 Blade Congress. 3⅞" long, Genuine Stag handle.

Muskrat Dog & Coon. 3⅞" long, Coonstripe handle.

Cattleking. 4¼" long, Greenbone handle.

Trapper. 4⅛" long, Abalone Swirl handle.

BURKINSHAW KNIFE COMPANY
Pepperell, Massachusetts C. 1853 – 1923

This company was established in 1853 by Aaron Berkinshaw, a Sheffield cutler who immigrated to the USA in 1848.

The firm produced pocketknives of a very high quality for many years. When Mr. Berkinshaw passed away, his two sons, Fred and Charles, continued to run the company until it closed in the early 1920s when mass-produced knives cornered the market.

Collectible rating: Very Good

Stampings: A. Burkinshaw Knife Co., Pepperell, Mass.

Current stampings: None, discontinued 1923

CAMCO
(See Camillus Cutlery Company)

CAMILLUS CUTLERY COMPANY
54 Main Street, Camillus, New York C. 1902 –

Adolf Kastor & Bros. began their cutlery import business about 1875. In 1902 they purchased the Camillus Cutlery Co. of Camillus, New York, from Charles Sherwood and began producing their own knives using the Camillus stamping. They also manufactured many high-quality contract knives for large hardware and distributing companies. These firms had their own brands and trademarks stamped on their knives. Some exceptionally high-quality cutlery was produced under contract by Camillus. Among these were the following:

Keen Kutter of E.C. Simmons Hdw. Co., St. Louis, Mo.

Diamond Edge of the Norvell-Shapleigh Hardware Co., St. Louis, Mo.

Henry Sears No. 1865, St. Paul, Minn.

John Primble of Belknap Hardware & Manufacturing Co., Louisville, Ky.

Today Camillus is still one of the giants in the business. They still produce a number of contract knives, but their own brands have made an impact in the knife world.

Collectible rating: Very Good

Stampings were:
  A Kastor & Bros., New York-Germany
  Camillus Cutlery Company, Camillus, New York USA
  Camco
  Camillus, Sword Brand
  Syracuse Federal
  Tip Top
  Mumbly Peg
Current stampings: Camillus (underlined) New York USA

SWORD BRAND
CAMILLUS CUTLERY

ACTUAL SIZE CLOSED 3⅛" (Muskrat)
Sportsman's knife has two skinning blades, genuine Cabone handles.

ACTUAL SIZE CLOSED 3⅛" (Trapper)
Sportsman's knife – Mirror polished sabre clip and spay blades, genuine Cabone handles.

ACTUAL SIZE CLOSED 4⅜₆"
*Large **equal end jack** with mirror polished spear and pen blades, genuine grain white handle.*

ACTUAL SIZE CLOSED 5"
*Sword Brand Deluxe bench-made **Angler's knife**. Features Indian Stag handles. Stainless steel sabre clip blade with serrated tip. Combination hook disgorger-fish scaler blade with cap lifter.*

ACTUAL SIZE CLOSED 4"
***Utility knife** with Hawkbill blade, steel linings. Brass lock keeps blade from closing when in use. Extra heavy steel bolsters. Unbreakable handle has hole for lanyard.*

ACTUAL SIZE CLOSED 3⅞"
Sportsman's knife *(Trapper) – Mirror polished sabre clip and spay blades, genuine maize handles.*

ACTUAL SIZE CLOSED 3⅜"
Office knife *– Mirror polished spear and eraser blade, genuine white grain handle.*

ACTUAL SIZE CLOSED 3¼"
Electrician's knife *with spear blade. Screwdriver has insulation scraper and brass lock to keep it from closing when in use. Unbreakable handles.*

ACTUAL SIZE CLOSED 3⅝"
Sword Brand Deluxe – OUTDOORS-MAN'S bench-made knife. Features Indian Stag handles, gleaming nickel silver parallel slant bolsters. Spear blade of Sword Steel, can opener, punch, screwdriver-cap lifter.

ACTUAL SIZE CLOSED 3⅝"
Carpenter's & Whittler's knife *has mirror polished sabre clip, pen clip, and coping blades, genuine Cabone handles.*

ACTUAL SIZE CLOSED 4½"
Marlin Spike *knife has stainless steel blade and spike. Spike locks in open position for safety. Solid Ebonite handles, rosette riveting.*

ACTUAL SIZE CLOSED 4¼" (Stock)
Sword Brand Deluxe – Bench-made knife features Indian Stag handles, gleaming solid nickel silver, parallel slant bolsters – mirror polished clip, sheepfoot and spay blades of Camillus high carbon cutlery Sword Steel.

CAMILLUS POCKETKNIVES

ACTUAL SIZE CLOSED 3⅞"
Premium Stock – Has clip, sheepfoot, and spay blades of famous Razor Edged Stainless Sword Steel. All hand made using finest materials – solid brass linings, solid nickel silver bolsters, genuine Cabone handles.

CAMILLUS POCKETKNIVES

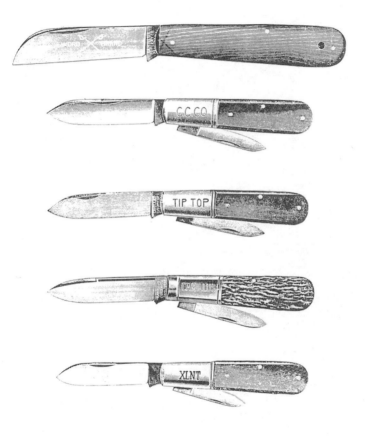

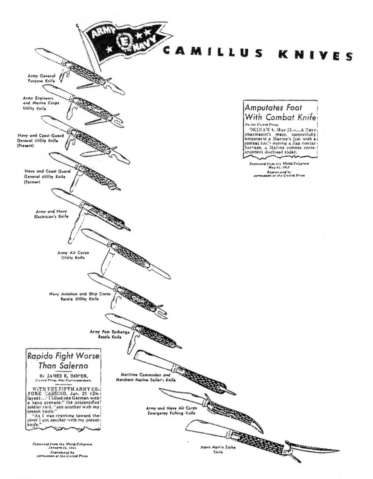

CAMILLUS KNIVES

Army General Purpose Knife

Army Engineers and Marine Corps Utility Knife

Navy and Coast Guard General Utility Knife (Present)

Navy and Coast Guard General Utility Knife (Former)

Army and Navy Electrician's Knife

Army Air Corps Utility Knife

Navy Aviation and Ship Stores Resale Utility Knife

Army Post Exchange Resale Knife

Maritime Commission and Merchant Marine Sailor's Knife

Army and Navy Air Corps Emergency Fishing Knife

Navy Marlin Spike Knife

Amputates Foot With Combat Knife

By the United Press.

OKINAWA, May 25.—...A Navy pharmacist's mate, successfully amputated a Marine's foot with a combat knife during a Jap mortar barrage, a Marine combat correspondent disclosed today.

Reprinted from the World-Telegram May 26, 1945
Reproduced by permission of the United Press

Rapido Fight Worse Than Salerno

By JAMES E. ROPER,
United Press War Correspondent.

WITH THE FIFTH ARMY BEFORE CASSINO, Jan. 23 (Delayed)... "I killed one German with a hand grenade," the unidentified soldier said, "and another with my trench knife."

"As I was crawling toward the river I got another with my pocket knife."

Reprinted from the World-Telegram January 24, 1944
Reproduced by permission of the United Press

During World War II the military demand for pocketknives and fighting knives grew continually — like a snowball rolling downhill. Towards the end of the war, the requirements of the Armed Forces far exceeded the production capacity of the entire industry. That the knives made were needed as part of the essential equipment of soldiers, sailors, marines, and coast guardsmen, and used many times under life or death circumstances is attested by the clippings reproduced here. These are just a few of many reported instances.

Manufacturing knives for the military was an old custom at Camillus — beginning with those made during World War I, knives were continually supplied to the Army and Navy. When World War II made greater and greater demands, more and more of their production was turned over to the manufacture of war knives until practically the entire plant capacity was devoted to the furtherance of the war effort.

that went to war !

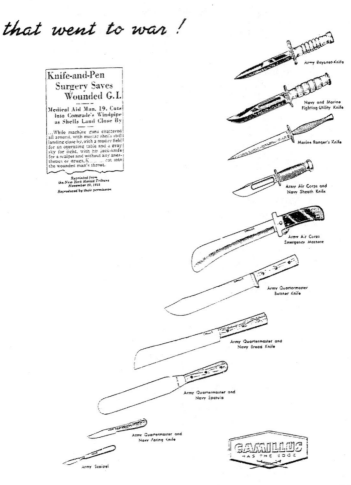

The efficiency and excellence of this production were recognized by the War Department when on August 17, 1943, the Army-Navy "E" was awarded. This — the first such honor in the pocketknife industry — was awarded when less than 2½% of all eligible war plants had received it. Three stars for continued excellence were added as Camillus' war production matched contract demands. When the fighting had stopped, almost 12,000,000 pocketknives and over 2,000,000 fighting and other sheath knives had gone to war from the Camillus factory . . . a record unequalled in the industry.

This intense production not only helped our war effort — but also you — by quickening the development of the finest factory for the manufacture of quality pocketknives and hunting knives America has ever seen, a factory that now serves you with top efficiency, modern manufacturing methods, and war-tempered skill.

187

CANTON CUTLERY COMPANY
Canton, Ohio C. 1879 – 1930

Established in Canton, Ohio, in 1879, with William S. Carnes as president from 1910 to 1930, when they ceased production of pocketknives. At first Mr. Carnes bought an interest in the company, but soon became sole owner, and also sole owner of the Car Van Steel Products Company of the same address. The firm is chiefly noted for having introduced the transparent handle cutlery of the "Picture Window" handle knife. The use of this material on most all patterns for advertising and depicting memorable events, places, and times quickly caught the public's fancy.

Canton Cutlery knives were of good quality, and some were large folding hunter patterns that are rare and highly prized by collectors.

Collectible rating: High

Stampings: Canton Cutlery Co., Canton, Ohio

    C.C.C. Canton, Ohio

    Car-Van, Canton, Ohio

Current stamping: None, discontinued 1930 (*Note: See Novelty Cutlery Co., Canton, Ohio*)

CASE BROS., Little Valley, New York C. 1889 –
W. R. CASE AND SONS, Bradford, Pennsylvania C. 1905

Case Bros. Cutlery was founded in 1889 in Little Valley, New York, by John, Jean, and Andrew Case. They adopted the now famous trademark "Tested XX" about 1895. When their factory in Little Valley burned in 1905, a nephew of the founders, Russell Case, took over and consolidated the firm's holdings as W. R. Case & Sons, Bradford, Pennsylvania. This purchase also included the Springville, New York, branch of the Case Bros. In 1922 W. R. Case & Sons bought the Crandell Cutlery Company in Bradford.

Case Cutlery was family owned until 1972 when it was acquired by American Brands, Inc. Even afterwards, the Case family, managers, and workers who remained with the new company retained a great deal of influence on the company and its direction for the next decade.

In 1989, Case Cutlery was acquired by Parker Cutlery of Chattanooga. This change in ownership fostered some major changes in Case Cutlery. Emphasis was placed on producing knives for the collector's market. The availability of damascus steel, from the Parker knife factory in Alabama, made it possible for collectors to see the first Case damascus line of knives (an innovation which was quite unique). Rights to reproduce discontinued Case patterns and trademarks were leased to a branch of Parker Cutlery, and knife patterns which had only been seen in books by many collectors began to again appear on the market (these knives are easily identified and marked as reproductions). The Parker Knife Collector's service still distributes many of these reproductions.

Case Cutlery Company changed its logo several times over the years. These logo changes have well served collectors as a method of dating the knives. The most famous of Case logos was the "Case Tested XX." This meant that the blades had been heat treated and tested twice. That logo was used at some time or the other on almost every pattern of Case knives produced.

Around 1940, Case introduced the "CASE XX" stamp which served the company for the next 25 years. In 1965, Case XX, U.S.A. replaced the Case XX stamping.

Then in 1970, perhaps in response to collector interest, Case introduced its dotting/dating system. This system enabled the buyer to identify the year the knife was made by the dots on the logo. (In 1970, for example, in addition to the Case XX, USA logo, there were 10 dots beneath it. One dot was dropped for each year that followed.) In 1980, a new dotting/dating system was introduced with the Case "lightning S" logo. This time the dots were located in a line between the CASE XX and U.S.A. Again, one dot was dropped as a year passed. In 1989, the dotting/dating system was dropped and replaced with a system which stamps the year of manufacture on the tang of the blade.

Case Cutlery changed hands again in 1991 when it was acquired by the Three Rivers Investment group of Chattanooga. Its last ownership turnover came in 1995 when ownership was passed to the Zippo (Lighter) Corporation.

Case knives continue to be made in Bradford, Pennsylvania, by the same craftspersons who built Case's reputation.

Collectible rating: High

Stampings: Case XX, Bradford, PA (with date on opposed tang)
   CASE XX
   19USA96
   Bradford, PA

(See Appendix 2 for a detailed Case price guide.)

The Case Limited Lifetime Warranty

We warrant every Case knife to be free from defects in workmanship and materials for the life of the owner. (Case does not warrant against normal wear, and the warranty does not cover misuse.) If your Case knife has a manufacturing defect, mail it with a description of the problem to:

Repair Center
W.R. Case & Sons Cutlery Co.
Owens Way, Bradford, PA 16701

If your knife cannot be repaired, Case will replace it with the currently manufactured knife that most closely matches the one you sent in for repairs.

If you knife was damaged by misuse, send it in and we'll repair it for a reasonable price.

Case Repair Policy

As stated in our warranty, Case will attempt to repair any knife that may have a defect in materials or workmanship. If repairs cannot be made in such cases, we will offer you a new knife. However, if the knife holds sentimental value or is a collector's item and cannot be repaired, Case is not responsible for offering a replacement or repayment that is equal in value. Case will furnish a currently manufactured item that most closely matches the item sent in for repair.

Case Stampings

CASE'S
BRADFORD

W.R. CASE & SONS
CUTLERY CO
BRADFORD, PA

1920(?) and before

1915(?) and before

CASE & SONS
BRADFORD
PA

*1920(?) and
before*

CASE XX

*1920(?) and
before*

CASE
BRADFORD
PA.

*1920(?) and
before*

STANDARD
KNIFE CO

1920 – 1923

CASE
TESTED XX

1920 – 1940

Case

1920 – 1940

Case
25¢

1935 – 1940

CASE XX
METAL STAMPINGS
LT.D.

1935 – 1940

CASE'S
TESTED XX

1940 – 1950

CASE
TESTED XX

1920 – 1940

CASE
XX

1920 – 1940

CASE'S
STAINLESS

Late '40s to early '50s

CASE
XX

1940 – 1965

CASE XX
STAINLESS

1940 – 1965

CASE XX
U.S.A.

1965 – 1970

CASE XX
STAINLESS
U.S.A.

1965 – 1970

CASE XX
U.S.A.
....

1970 – 1979

CASE XX
STAINLESS
U.S.A.
....

1970 – 1979

CASE XX
....
U.S.A.

1980 – 1990

CASE XX
····· §§ ·····
U.S.A.

1980 – 1990

CASE XX
USA
•••••

1990 – 1993

· X · X ·
CASE XX
X · X · X

2000 – 2009

CATTARAUGUS CUTLERY COMPANY
Little Valley, New York C. 1886 – 1963

This company was founded in 1886 by J. B. Champlin and his son, Tint. In that same year the senior Champlin, who had been a jobber, engaged as associates four brothers-in-law from the Case family, W. J., Jean, John, and Andrew Case. Although the Case relatives left the company soon thereafter, the Champlins purchased the Beaver Falls Cutlery Company of Beaver Falls, Pennsylvania, and enlarged their firms in 1890.

During its heyday, Cattaraugus produced almost every pattern known and some of the world's finest cutlery. They made knives for our Armed Forces during WWI and WWII. The high esteem in which the knives were held is demonstrated by the fact that the Byrd Polar expedition used Cattaraugus cutlery.

During the 1950s, when the cutlery business was declining drastically, they sponsored a national whittling contest, with prizes of up to $50,000, in hopes of stimulating interest and sales. Despite these efforts, they went out of business in 1963. Collectible rating: Very High

Stampings:

    Cattaraugus Cutlery Company, Little Valley, NY

    CCC (on Barlow bolsters)

    3C (inside a circle, used during the 1950's)

    Whittle Craft

*Current stampings: None, discontinued 1963

(See Appendix 3 for detailed Cattaraugus price guide.)

*In 1985, A.G. Russell Cutlery of Springdale, Arkansas, began reproducing some Cattaraugus patterns with Cattaraugus stampings.

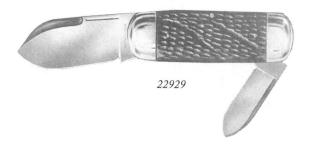

22929

CATTARAUGUS KNIVES

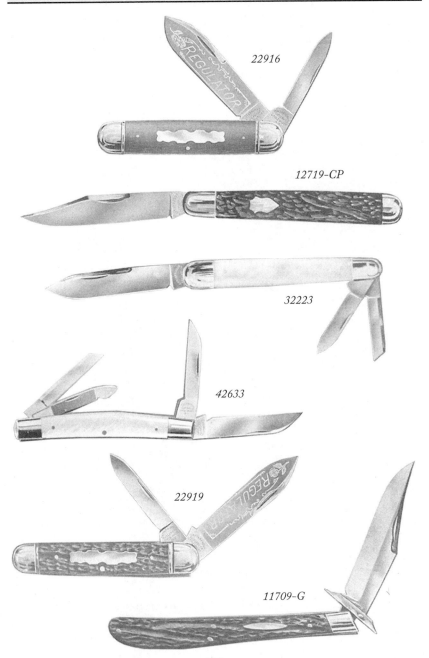

22916

12719-CP

32223

42633

22919

11709-G

193

CENTRAL CITY KNIFE COMPANY
Phoenix, New York C. 1880 – 1916

This firm was founded by Charles Avery in 1880 in Phoenix, New York. The plant was located on an island in the Oswego River. In 1892 the firm name was changed to Phoenix Knife Co., and their knives were stamped accordingly. Knives were high quality.

In 1916 the company was destroyed by fire.

Collectible rating: High

Stampings:

Central City Knife Co., Phoenix, N.Y.

Phoenix Knife Co., Phoenix, N.Y.

Current stamping: None, discontinued 1916

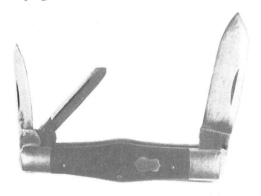

(Photo courtesy National Knife Collector's Magazine)

CHICAGO CUTLERY
Minneapolis, Minnesota C. 1932 – Present

Chicago Cutlery was founded in 1930 as a knife rental and sharpening service for professional butchers. The business evolved into a company which manufactured and supplied a full line of knives for meat processing plants, butchers, and chefs across the United States.

In 1969, Chicago Cutlery entered the retail market and through the use of attractive displays in a variety of department stores, hardware stores, etc., became well recognized by the general public. Recognition and merchandising, however, are only effective in terms of initial purchases. To sustain a business, a reputation must be established to attract repeat customers. As with their professional supply business, Chicago Cutlery has managed to establish a reputation for quality with consumers.

In 1971, Chicago Cutlery introduced the first wooden knife blocks, which are now in service on countertops in literally hundreds of thousands of kitchens across America.

In 1982, the Biocurve 19-degree handle, ergonomically designed to fit the natural contours of the hand, was made available on a line of their kitchen cutlery.

In 1979, an impressive line of pocketknives became a part of Chicago Cutlery's line. Patterns included pen, stock, and folding hunter lock-backs. This folding line also included a line of lock-back fish knives which were acclaimed nationally in fishing magazines.

Collectible rating: Especially good for the new or young collector who might be interested in building a long-range collection of "all the folding knives" of one company.

Stamping: Chicago Cutlery, (the pattern number) U.S.A.

CHRISTY KNIFE COMPANY
Fremont, Ohio C. 1890 –

The firm was founded in 1890 by Russ J. Christy in Fremont, Ohio. They specialized in a new type of razor blades and domestic kitchen cutlery. Russ Christy was a journeyman machinist and inventor. He designed and made his own machining and equipment. He held a number of patents on knives and razors including a scalloped edge bread knife (1890 – 1891). He patented the first single edge safety razor in 1909 (called, interestingly enough, the hoe razor). At the turn of the century, the Christy Company had 75 home kitchen items in its catalog. Production of domestic cutlery was curtailed with the advent of World War I, around 1917. It did not resume after the war.

Safety razor manufacture was the primary Christy product from 1909 when a Patent Referee determined the points of patent which were assigned to Russ J. Christy and to King Gillette, his chief competitor. This determination resolved litigation on the issue of the safety razor patent rights. The Christy firm was the larger of the two firms until Gillette went conglomerate with worldwide advertising and international sales. Christy manufactured safety razors from 1909 until 1959.

When Russ Christy retired in 1920, he moved to Florida. He left a son, D. L. Christy, in charge of the company. One night, following encouragement from a neighbor to design a knife in which the opening wouldn't break fingernails, the elder Christy had a dream of a knife with a sliding blade. Not being one to ignore inspiration, he awakened and made a sketch of the knife in his dream. Early the next morning, and over the following months, he carved a number of wooden models of it. As the design was perfected, the models were sent to his son in Fremont.

By 1936, the Christy sliding blade knife was on the market. The design and construction are unique and simple. It consists of a slotted rod, bent inward around the outer perimeter of a blade that slides in and out through an open slot in the end. A locking mechanism secures the blade at the desired length. It is an economical, yet efficient, cutting instrument. This little knife found a ready market during the depression years and is still being manufactured.

The Christy Knife Company ceased production in 1971, but was reactivated in 1974 by Earl B. Christy, a grandson of Russ Christy. Earl Christy assures us of plans to be a viable manufacturer for generations to come.

Collectible rating: Good

Stampings and logos:

Christy

Christy Knife Co. (inside double circle with XYT in center)

Christy (with long tail of "C" underlined)

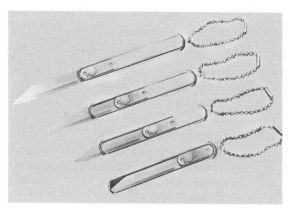

The Christy Sliding Blade Pocketknife

"THOSE WONDERFUL CHRISTY KNIVES"

COLONEL COON
Tennessee Knife Works, Inc.
Columbia, Tennessee C. 1978 – 1988

The Tennessee Knife Works was established in 1978 in Columbia, Tennessee, by Adrian Harris, a knifemaker and repairman. He first produced one standard Barlow pattern for which he adopted the brand "Colonel Coon." The Barlow was made in a choice of stag, bone, or genuine pearl.

The firm later added Muskrat, Congress, Stock, and Folding Hunter patterns to its line. All "Colonel Coon" knives were of top quality and pridefully advertised as "Made in Tennessee, by Tennesseans."

Collectible rating: Very Good

Stamping and logo: "Colonel Coon" (with a standing coon etched on the blades)

COLONIAL CUTLERY COMPANY
Providence, Rhode Island C. 1926 –

This company was founded in 1926 by Fredrick Paolentonio and two brothers. Experienced cutlers from Frosolone, Italy, a town famous for its bladesmiths, they immigrated to the U.S. and worked for Empire Knife Company and Miller Bros. Cutlery Company until they started the Providence Cutlery in 1917.

In 1925 the Providence Cutlery Co. was sold, and the three brothers started the Colonial Cutlery Company, Providence, Rhode Island, in 1926.

Al Paolentonio is the current president.

Collectible rating: Very Good

Current stampings:

    Colonial Cutlery Co., Providence, Rhode Island
      Ranger
      Colonial, Prov. USA
      Old Cutlery
      Anvil Brand
      Coyote

CL-CY14. Green handles with Coyote logo. Lockback. 4" and 5" closed. Comes with belt sheath.

CL-923. 3-blade Medium Stockman. 3⅛" closed. Available in black, yellow, and white.

COLT
Colt Arms Company
Hartford, Connecticut 1969 – 1973

Colt Arms Company of Hartford, Connecticut, although a legend in our nation's history, entered the cutlery field late in the game. In 1969 they contracted with the veteran knife maker, Barry Wood, to produce for them an unusual swing-frame, folding hunter. Approximately 15,000 of these were made and stamped with the "Rampant Colt" and "Colt, Hartford, Conn."

During their short entry in cutlery, Colt also produced several patterns of sheath hunting knives, of which some were made in England. All Colt knives are top collectibles and eagerly sought by collectors today, but the Wood/Colt folding hunter is the top prize.

Collectible rating: Very High

Stamping and logo: Colt, Hartford, CT (with the "Rampant Colt" in a circle)

Woods Colt

*CT8. Colt Dagger.
10¼" overall.*

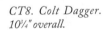

*CT7. Serengeti Skinner. 4¾"
blade. 10⅟₁₆" overall.*

*6831. Colt Bowie. 12⅜"
overall, 8" blade.*

199

CRIPPLE CREEK, U.S.A.
Cargill Knives
Old Fort, Tennessee

Cripple Creek U.S.A. knives were manufactured by Cargill Knives of Old Fort, Tennessee.

Cripple Creek knives were, as advertised, all American-made by expert craftsmen of the finest material. Each knife had a lifetime guarantee. The year of manufacture was stamped on the shield of each knife.

Collectible rating: Very Good

Stamping: Cripple Creek, U.S.A.

THE EAGLE POCKETKNIFE COMPANY
New Haven, Connecticut
C. 1916 – 1919

The company was founded in New Haven, Connecticut, 1916, by three Hemming brothers. Their main talent was in devising means to simplify and speed up production so as to produce practical and affordable pocketknives, at much less cost.

Since their primary product was an all-metal knife with wrap-around handles, they invented machines that made it possible to manufacture knives of this type on an assembly line basis.

In addition to the all-metal knives, they made other knives of the usual hand-made patterns, with scales of black fiber, bone, and even stag. Some of these knives are of a quality that are on a par with other top-notch brands, and these are premium collectibles today. However, collectors should use extreme care not to confuse knives made by this company with those made by others, such as: Eagle Cutlery (Eagle Pencil Co), Eagle, Philadelphia (G. Creutzburg), and Eagle Brand (Parker Cut. Co.).

In 1919 The Winchester Arms Co. purchased this firm to gain control of the Hemming — designed and patented machinery — to modernize their own cutlery manufacture. The machines became widely used, and some are used even today.

Collectible rating: Very High.

Stampings: Eagle Knife Co. Pat Pend.
Made in U. S. A.

EMPIRE KNIFE COMPANY
Meridian, Connecticut 1856 – 1930

This company was founded in 1856 by two brothers named Alvord. By 1920 the company was hard pressed due to the beginning of the Depression. It was acquired by George Brill, who converted the plant to more modern techniques. Still, the Empire Knife Co. closed production about 1930. This firm left a complete sample display of their knives in the Winstead Museum. Upon Mr. Brill's death, his son sold the collection to a West Liberty, Kentucky, collector. Most of the collection of approximately 80 fine knives are supposedly still somewhere in Kentucky.

Collectible rating: High

Stamping: Empire Knife Co., Winstead, Conn.

Easy Open Jack

EYE BRAND KNIVES
CARL SCHLIEPER CUTLERY
51-59 Burger Landstresse
Solingen, Germany C. 1898 – Present

The Carl Schlieper Company was established in Remscherd, Germany, in 1898 as a part of the Schlieper Tool (and Cutlery) Company. The principal owner at present is Hans Peter Schlieper, a member of the family which has now owned the company for six generations.

In 1952, the company's cutlery division moved into separate facilities at 51-59 Burger Landstresse in Solingen where they, as have other cutlery firms in that area, utilized the city's well-established network of cottage industry in the manufacture of their products.

The Schlieper firm currently makes kitchen cutlery, scissors, hunting knives, and pocketknives. Their export markets are located in Canada, Australia, South Africa, Saudi Arabia, Thailand, Malaysia, and the United States. The U.S. is the primary market for pocket cutlery products.

The exclusive U.S. importer of Carl Schlieper and Eye Brand products is Mark Cruse of Knife Importers, Inc., Austin, Texas.

Collectible rating: Good

Stampings and logo: Eye (sketch with Carl Schlieper, Ger. written over and below)

Eye (sketch only, Solingen below or on back tang)

Carl Schlieper, Solingen, Germany (two lines)

El Gallo, Germany (two lines)

Jim Bowie, Germany (two lines, J. Bowie in script)

Fan Co., Solingen Germany (with a small fan logo to the left of the name)

Fan logo only on tang of blade

202

Stock
350-DS. 3½" closed, carbon steel, genuine stag handles.

Folding Hunter
Regal-DSL. Lockback, 3¾" closed, surgical steel blade.

Copperhead
GX-DS. 3¾" closed, genuine stag handles, carbon steel.

56-DS. 3½" closed, Congress pattern, genuine stag handles, carbon steel.

Trapper
J-DS. 4" closed, carbon steel, genuine stag handles.

54-DS. 3½" closed, carbon steel, genuine stag handles.

"FIGHT'N ROOSTERS"
(Frank Buster Cutlery Company)
Sugar Flat Road
Lebanon, Tennessee C. 1977 – Present

This firm was established in 1977 by Frank Buster in Lebanon, Tennessee. Mr. Buster was a knife dealer and trader. He became aware of the growing market potentials for collector knives early in the game, and decided immediately to import and sell knives under his own brand.

Thus, in keeping with his plan, he chose the logo of two fighting cocks in profile, a logo remarkably similar to the famous German "Hen and Rooster" brand knives.

In keeping with the trend, Frank Buster selects only the highest quality knives made of the most fashionable materials for his "Fight'n Roosters" brand. Each pattern is strictly limited in quantity so as to insure them as collector items.

Although most "Fight'n Roosters" knives are made in Solingen, Germany, some are made in Sheffield, England and in other countries with a tradition of high quality.

Mr. Buster's goal of producing only collector knives and his unique method of advertising mostly "sold out" stock, have apparently paid handsome dividends.

Collector rating: High

Current stamping: A profile of two "Fight'n Roosters"

Gold Blade Whittler, 15th Anniversary Blade Knife. 4½", genuine pearl handle.

Jack Knife. 3", Genuine stag handle, colored blade etch, old stamp.

204

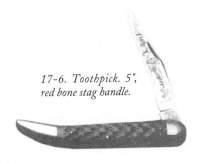

*17-6. Toothpick. 5",
red bone stag handle.*

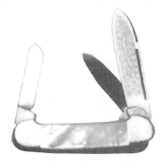

*17-9. Palmetto Canoe 1977. 3¼",
genuine pearl handle, gold etched
– engraved "mfg. by Fight'n
Rooster."*

Pen
*16-9. Coal Miner. 3", brass relief
handle.*

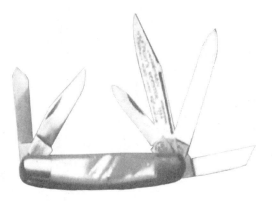

15-9. 6 Blade Stockman. 4", gold etched.

FROST CUTLERY
Chattanooga, Tennessee C. 1978 –

Frost Cutlery was established in 1978 in Chattanooga, Tennessee, by Jim Frost, who had been a knife collector, trader, and distributor since 1972. He was also a full partner in the Parker-Frost Cutlery and shared in the design and production of the fine collector sets produced there.

Jim Frost was appointed business manager for the NKCA in 1974 and is credited with increasing the membership and bringing the organization into national prominence.

Frost knives made on contract, and imported mostly from Japan, are strictly specified to his own designs to assure top quality workmanship and materials. Frost has a full line of cutlery. The following illustrations are a sampling of their products. Collectible rating: Very Good

Stamping & logo: Frost Cutlery (over striking falcon)
  (Surgical Steel-Japan)
  (Note: See Parker-Frost Cutlery)

Little Warrior, 3" closed.

Range Rider, 3¼" closed.

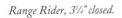

Gambler II, 3½" closed.

Hawkeye, 4" closed.

Quicksilver™ stainless with pocket/belt clip, 4¼" closed.

Bullet Trapper I, 3½" closed.

Mini Muskrat, 3¼" closed."

1940 Ford™ pick-up die cast replica with 17-105HCB Frost Little Peanut, 2¼" closed.

Wrangler II, 4" closed.

207

GERBER LEGENDARY BLADES
14200 SW, 72 Avenue
Portland, Oregon C. 1939 –

The firm of Gerber Legendary Blades was started in 1939 in Portland, Oregon, by Joseph Gerber, for the manufacture of home and kitchen cutlery. However, in 1950 they began production of hunting, fishing, and outdoor knives, and their line included lockblade folding hunters. Some of the blades of the early folders show that they originated in Germany. Today most of their small folders are made in Japan. All Gerber knives are of very high quality, and most of the early ones are considered fine collector items.

In 1978, the firm began production of Paul Poehlmann's patented "Paul" folding knife. These, too, are considered collector items, because they deploy a new concept of opening and closing.

Collector rating: Very Good

Stampings: Gerber, Portland, OR

Dark blade.

Silver Knight Schooner. 3¾" closed. Stainless steel locking drop-point blade, stainless steel bolsters.

Gator. 8¼" open.

L.S.T.® Camouflage. 3½" closed.

Presentation 400CG, Cushiongrip. 10½" overall.

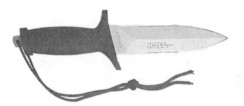

Tac II. 11" overall, double-edged blade with serrated edges.

The Paul Knife, 3¼" closed.

Applegate Combat Knife, 5⅝" closed.

209

GUTMANN CUTLERY CO., INC.
Mt. Vernon, New York C. 1950 –

Gutmann Cutlery Co. was founded in the 1950s by Kurt Gutmann to import and distribute "Hen & Rooster" knives from the Bertram Cutlery works in Solingen, Germany. These knives were stamped "Gutmann, Ger." on one side of the tang, and have the "Hen & Rooster" logo and Solingen on the opposite side. Although higher priced than other Hen & Rooster imports, the Gutmann brand did quite well in the U.S. market.

In 1957 the Gutmann Company picked up the "Puma" brand knives of Puma-werk, Lauterjung & Sohn of Solingen, about the time when the ancient firm was changing over to a more modern line of functional outdoor knives for hunters, farmers, and, of course, collectors. These early Pumas were modestly priced, but that was in the 1950s and early 1960s. With inflation and a persistent advertising campaign by the Gutmann Company, prices soared.

While Gutmann no longer imports and distributes either Hen & Rooster or Puma knives, the older models they did import now have a higher value to collectors than the current models.

Collectible rating: Very High

Stampings: Gutmann on back tang of Hen & Rooster (not on Puma knives)
    None current

(Note: See Puma-werk, Lauterjung & Sohn & Bertram Cutlery.)

Gutman currently distributes Wenger Swiss Army knives, Opinel knives, and a variety of designs under the "Explorer" trademark.

"The Alamo" Bowie Knife, 14¾" overall.

"The Huntsman," 10¾" overall.

Guthook Damascus, 8" overall.

HEIMERDINGER CUTLERY COMPANY
Louisville, Kentucky 1861 – present

This company was established in the Butchertown section of Louisville in 1861 by German immigrant August Heimerdinger. During this time the shop primarily supplied cutlery to meat cutters.

Like so many cutlery concerns, the company was a family business. It still is in the family. As it grew, it diversified into razors, shears, sewing machines, and an expanded line of home kitchen knives. A number of inventions are credited to the company, including the following: the Sorosis Safety Corn Razor, double-edged reversible scissors, grass shears, razor whetting machines, and a technique of mating iron handles and Sheffield scissor blades. They also contracted work for Belknap and Sears for cutlery items produced with those companies' trademarks.

Today, under the management of Carl E. Heimerdinger (5th generation), the company continues to provide for the cutlery needs of Louisvillians. Their shop is a classy retail outlet in the St. Matthews section of Louisville, 4207 Shelbyville Road. A visit to the store is well worth your time!

Collectible rating: Very High, company did not produce pocketknives. Look for stampings on kitchen cutlery, scissors, and razors.

Stampings:

A.E. Heimerdinger Co., Louisville, Ky.

W.C. Heimerdinger Co., Louisville, Ky.

W.C. Heimerdinger Co., Inc. Louisville, Ky. (beginning 1922)

Current stampings: None

HENCKELS, (J.A.)
Solingen, Germany C. 1731 – present

Peter Henckels established the firm in Solingen, Germany, in 1731. We have yet to discover why he chose the curious "Henckels Twins" trademark (two small men) that has become famous all over the world.

In 1816, the firm came under the management of Johann Abraham Henckels, a direct descendant of the founder, who greatly enlarged the sales and production by the use of very advanced technology. Not only did he enlarge the firm's production capacity, but by establishing showrooms in major cities and using modern day type advertising, he made the Henckels Twins brand of cutlery the most famous in the world. The company still uses J. A. Henckels as the firm's name.

We do not know the date, or under what circumstance, the firm was transferred out of the Henckels family's hands, but in 1884 Friedrich Beckmann was the sole owner. A branch office was opened in the United States about that time. Then in 1919, the company, ironically, almost lost their famous trademark when after WWI, our government seized the rights from Henckels and assigned it to John Detjens of Stapleton, New York. It was only after a long period of lengthy difficulties the Henckels firm of Solingen regained the use of their famous logo in 1928.

The firm has always produced a quality product and is still one of the finest, and oldest, producers of pocketknives in the world. The Henckels brand can be found in almost every country in the world and they are not difficult to collect. As far as we know, there has been no detailed research done of material, pattern, stampings, etc., for determining age and rareness.

Collectible rating: High

Stampings:

J. A. Henckels, Zillingswerk, Germany (with Henckels Twins logo)

J. S. Henckels, Ger. (Henckels Twins)

HENCKELS

HENRY SEARS & SONS
Rockford, Illinois 1865 – 1959

This company was founded in Rockford, Illinois as Henry Sears & Company. In 1879 it became the Henry Sears Manufacturing Company. In 1883 the name was again changed to Henry Sears & Son, and in 1885 the company was moved to Chicago.

In 1897, the St. Paul Company, Ozmun-Kirk & Co. Hardware, purchased Henry Sears & Sons and began using the trademark Henry Sears & Sons 1865 and used this trademark until 1959.

For almost a hundred years, a variety of quality knives were made with this trademark. This has created a rather large body of knives available as collectibles, the most recent of which are 40 years old. This brand has great potential as an investment grade collectible.

Collectible rating: High

Stampings: QUEEN, 1870 +/-

Henry Sears & Co. 1865, 1897 – 1959

HIBBARD, SPENCER, BARTLETT & CO.
Chicago, Illinois 1855 – 1960

This company grew to be one of the nation's largest hardware and wholesale firms. It was founded in Chicago, Illinois, in 1855. The three family members who gave it its name used many different trademarks and stampings on their cutlery. Most of their knives were made for them by Ulster and Camillus Cutlery Companies.

Their pocketknife cutlery division was closed about 1960.

Collectible rating: High

Stampings: Hibbard, Spencer, Bartlett & Co., Chicago, Ill.

OVB (initials for Our Very Best)

Ajax

Black Diamond

Rev-O-Noc

Hibbard

HibSpeBar

Current stamping: None

(discontinued 1960)

HIBBARD, SPENCER, BARTLETT & CO.
CHICAGO.

For Lasting Service   American Made Pocket Cutlery   For Cutting Quality

FULLY WARRANTED

HIBBARD, SPENCER, BARTLETT & CO.

Cattle
3⅝", genuine bone stag handle. Four blades; clip, sheepfoot, spay, and Harrison punch.

Stock
4", Nupearl handle. Three blades; clip, spay, and spiral punch.

3⅝", Scout. Genuine bone handle. Four blades; spear, cap lifter, can opener, and spiral punch. Shackle.

3⅛", Congress. Nubuck stag handle. Four blades; 2 sheep foot and 2 pens.

Cattle
3⅛", marble horn celluloid handle. Three blades; clip, spay, and Harrison punch.

3⅝", Easy Open Jack. Genuine bone stag handle. Two blades; spear and pen.

HOFFRITZ
New York-Germany

Hoffritz is one of the great old import-export cutlery trading companies with branches in New York, U.S.A. and Solingen, Germany. Their boast is "Great blades from the world's best sources" and, "Each blade is handcrafted from the finest material that bears the world famous Hoffritz name." This is very true, because Hoffritz collectors will tell you that Hoffritz knives, whether from Germany, France, or Japan, are no less than top quality.

While Hoffritz chiefly noted as importers and distributors of fine Solingen-made knives, they also seem to select the best from every nation in the world.

Collectible rating: Very High

Stamping and logo: Hoffritz (Country of Origin)

4 Blade, Congress, pearl

4 Blade, Congress, stag

HONK FALLS
(See Napanoch Cut. Co.)

HOLLEY MANUFACTURING COMPANY
Lakeville, Connecticut C. 1844 – 1936

This firm was established in 1844 by Alexander Holley on a site where Ethan Allen, hero of our War of Independence, had a blast furnace. It may well be, as acclaimed, the first truly American pocketknife manufacturing company.

It is recorded that Alexander Holley hired a group of skilled Sheffield cutlers who were failing in their efforts to start a successful factory in Waterbury, and moved the workers, machinery, and stock to his Lakeville site, where they began manufacturing pocketknives of fine quality.

By 1850 Holley acquired two partners, Nathan W. Mervin and George B. Burrell, and incorporated in 1854 as the Holley Manufacturing Co.

All Holley knives were remarkably well constructed. From the first they were marketed with brass linings, nickel, silver, bolsters, stag, horn, bone, and ivory handles, assembled by the best handcrafting methods. And the guarantee was to replace any worn-out knife with a new one free when it was presented to any salesman of the company.

By the early 1900s the slow method of handcrafting could not compete with mass production. Pocketknives were dropped from production about 1936, and the factory was converted into a ski factory during WWII.

The most famous Holley knife was doubtlessly the "Charter Oak" knife, with handles made of wood from the Connecticut Charter Oak. This was also the first notable, and intentionally limited production, commemorative knife that we know.

Collectible rating: Very High

Stampings: Holley Mfg. Co., Lakeville, Conn.

(Note: Perhaps the finest collection of Holley knives in the world was owned by the late Alvin P. Norlin of Imlay City, Michigan. Mr. Norlin was also the finest authority to whom we are indebted for the Holley information and pictures contained in this publication.)

HOLLEY KNIVES

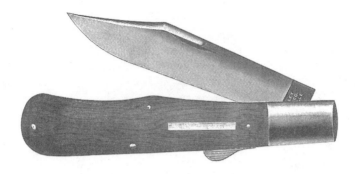

Rip Van Winkle. Folding Hunter lockback, brass lined, 5½" closed.

Small Warncliffe Whittler, brass lined, 3⅜" closed.

Excelsior Whittler Pen, brass lined, 3¼" closed.

HOLLEY KNIVES

Small Congress. Brass lined, 2⅞" closed.

Senator. Brass & German Silver lined, 3¼" closed.

Combination Knife and Cigar Cutter. German silver handle. 3¼" closed.

Jack. Steel lined, 3⅜" closed.

Pocket Budder. Steel lining, 3¼" closed.

220

HOLLEY KNIVES

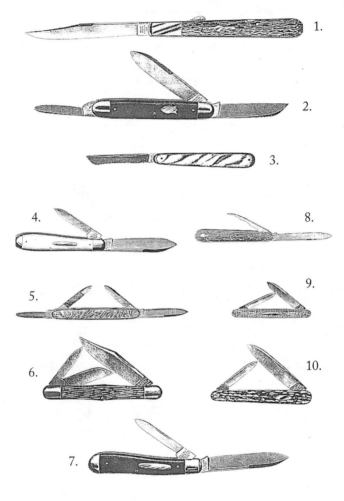

1. *Lock Back Dirk–Brass lined, Lock Back length closed 4¼"*
2. *"Cattle Knife"–Brass lined w/sheep foot blade, length closed 3¾"*
3. *Corn Knife–German, silver lined, length closed 3⅛"*
4. *"Balloon Capped" Jack–Brass lined, length closed 3½"*
5. *"Large Senator Octagon" –German silver lined, length closed 3⅛"*
6. *"Bull Frog"–Whittler pattern, brass lined, length closed 3⅝"*
7. *"Capped Dog Leg"–Brass lined, length closed 3½"*
8. *"Fruit Knife"–Silver plated throughout, length closed 3⅛"*
9. *Dress pen Knife–Sterling silver handle, length closed 3¼"*
10. *"Sleeveboard"–German silver lined, length closed 3"*

HOLLINGSWORTH KNIFE COMPANY
Kane, Pennsylvania C. 1916 – 1930

This firm succeeded the former Kane Cutlery Co. of Kane, Pennsylvania, remaining in business for about 14 years, and was acquired by the Albertson Co. in 1930.

It is believed the Albertson Company discontinued knives to produce other products.

Collectible rating: Good
Stampings: Hollingsworth, Kane, Pa.
Current stamping: None, discontinued 1930
(Note: See Kane Cutlery Co.)

IBBERSON (GEORGE) & COMPANY
Sheffield, England C. 1700 –

This company was founded by George Ibberson in Sheffield, England in 1700 and still manufactures a full line of cutlery. In this modern age, they are outstanding for the line of beautiful "chased" art-worked knives they produce. For commercial producers, these worked-back springs and blades are almost a lost art. Ibberson's quality workmanship in this area still remains. They also still use the finest handle materials available on their knives.

An interesting footnote is that Ibberson was the first company to use stainless steel for their knife blades. Their first use of this metal was in 1913.

Although Ibberson has used many marks and logos during their long existence, the most outstanding ones are their first and the current one. Their first logo was an "S" over a "T." Their current logo, granted as a trademark in 1880, is their now famous "Violin" logo.

Collectible rating: Very High
Stampings: "S" over "T"
Violin

IMPERIAL KNIFE COMPANY
Providence, Rhode Island C. 1917

The brothers Michael and Felix Mirando, whose parents were cutlers from Frosilona, Italy, founded the firm in 1917. They had just finished an internship of working for the Empire Knife Company of Winstead, Connecticut. Their early knives were well made and from good quality materials. But in order to speed up production in the beginning years of the Depression, they developed the tin shell-handled knife, an inexpensive stamped-out cover that replaced both handles and bolsters and was strapped to the frame by extruded metal bent under at the bolsters. Blades and liners too were often stamped out from low grade metals.

When the New York Knife Co. went out of business in 1931, Imperial acquired the rights to their "Hammer Brand" trademark. From 1933 to the early 1970s these shell-handled knives were the mainstream of production, and Imperial was producing knives at the rate of 10,000 per day. While firms producing quality handmade knives were struggling to stay in business during the Depression years, the inexpensive shell-handled knives were selling. By 1940 Imperial was rated the largest cutlery firm in the world.

In 1947 they purchased the Ulster Knife Company of Ellenville, New York, and in 1948 the Schrade-Walden Cutlery Co. of Walden, New York. In 1957 they proceeded to move the Schrade factory to Ellenville and combined the two under the leadership of "Uncle Henry" Baer; hence the "Uncle Henry" line of Schrade knives.

In 1977 Imperial gained control over the Rodgers-Wostenholm (I-XL) Cutlery Co. of Sheffield, England; hence the Schrade I-XL brand knives. All are now under the Imperial Knife Associated Companies, Inc., and are still producing knives with their original brand stampings.

Meanwhile, since the demand for high-quality cutlery has definitely returned, the Imperial Knife Company is once again producing well-made, quality knives in a wide variety of old and new brands.

Collectible rating: High
Stampings:
    Imperial Knife Co., Providence, RI
    Tom Thumb
    Jack-Master
    Shorty
    Kamp King
    Frontier
    Diamond Edge (on shield)
    Rodger-Star & Cross (on shield)

Motorman's Tool Kit. File, cap lifter/can opener, chisel, screwdriver, pocketknife, reamer.

IMPERIAL KNIVES

Stock. Three blades–Clip, sheep foot, and spay. Length closed 4".

Muskrat. Two skinning blades. Length closed 4".

Angler. Large clip and fish/hook disgorger blade. Length closed 4⅛".

Stock. Two blades–Clip and pen. Length closed 4".

Stock. Three blades–clip, spay, and pen. Length closed 3¼".

JAEGER BROS.
(See Aerial Cutlery)

JEAN CASE
(See Kinfolks, Inc.)

KA-BAR CUTLERY COMPANY
Olean, New York C. 1898 – present

The KA-BAR Cutlery Company was established in 1898 as the Union Razor Company of Tidioute, Pennsylvania by W.R. Brown, a grandson of Job R. Case. As the company grew, it began producing a variety of cutlery products in addition to razors. In January of 1909, the "Union Razor Company" trademark was dropped and was replaced by the "Union Cutlery Company" trademark.

In 1912 the firm moved to Olean, New York. The KA-BAR logo was first used around 1919. It has been suggested that the name was devised to sound like Case Brothers. However, the company claims it was adapted from the poor spelling in a trapper's letter about how he had used one of their knives to "kil a bar." Regardless of the name's origin, the KA-BAR stamping, which was used mostly on larger knives, became more popular than the Union Cut. Co. stamping. In 1951 the company changed its name to KA-BAR Cutlery Company. The KA-BAR stamping was subsequently changed to Ka-bar.

During World War II, the company used the "M-2" design to make a great number of KA-BAR sheath knives for the Navy and Marines. These are currently highly valued by collectors.

Although the firm's line of genuine stag and bone patterns were on par with those of Case Cutlery, they were discontinued around 1955 because of declining sales.

In 1966 the company was purchased by Cole National Corporation of Cleveland, Ohio. By 1977, KA-BAR had ceased to produce its own knives. However, the Ka-bar trademark is still being used on quality cutlery produced to KA-BAR's contracted specifications and standards.

On May 31, 1996, Alcas Cutlery purchased the KA-BAR trademark. Alcas had been producing cutlery for KA-BAR since its production facilities closed in 1977. They will continue producing quality cutlery under the KA-BAR name. Both operations and manufacturing are again located in Olean, New York.

Collectible rating: Very High

Stampings:

UNION RAZOR CO., Tidioute, Pa.

UNION CUTLERY CO., Tidioute, Pa.

UNION CUT. CO., Tidioute
Union Cut. Co., Olean, N.Y.
Union Cut. Co.
KA-BAR
KA-BAR, Olean, N.Y.
Olcut
Current stampings:
    Kabar, U.S.A.

2179. Grizzly Pressbutton.

61106. Dogshead Folding Hunter.

661. Fish Knife.

KANE CUTLERY COMPANY
Kane, Pennsylvania C. 1910 – 1916

This company had its beginning about 1910, and the name was changed to Hollingsworth Knife Co. in 1916. We have very little other information on this company at this time.

Collectible rating: Good
Stamping: Kane Cutlery Co., Kane, Pa.
Current stamping: None, discontinued 1916
(Note: See Hollingsworth Knife Co.)

KINFOLKS, INC.
Little Valley, New York C. 1926 – 1958

This company was started in 1926 by three cousins, Tint C. Champlin, Dean Case, and Russell Case. All these men were directly related to the head families of Case and Cattaraugus Cutleries. Because of this, "Kinfolk" was chosen as the firm's name and logo. Their main operation was supplying the Case and Cattaraugus Cutleries with sheath knives. However, by 1929, Dean Case and his father, Jean Case, purchased the company from the other members. As a result, the "Jean Case" logo was introduced into the firm along with the "Kinfolks" logo.

During WW II the company manufactured sheath knives and machetes for the Armed Forces. The Kinfolk line of folding knives was not extensive, and their pocketknives are rare. The rarest of the line are those with the "Jean Case" stampings.

In 1950 Robeson hired Emerson Case from Kinfolk and acquired the Kinfolk trademark. They proceeded to manufacture Kinfolk knives and market them through Kinfolk dealers for several years until they introduced their "strawberry" handles.

The company went out of business in the late 1950s.

Collectible rating for Kinfolk and Jean Case: Very High

Stampings: Kinfolks, Little Valley, New York
   Jean Case, Little Valley, N.Y.

Current stamping: None, discontinued 1958.

(Note: See Robeson Cutlery Company)

KLAAS, ROBERT
Solingen, Germany C. 1834 – present

This firm was established in Solingen, Germany, by Robert Klaas in 1834. In 1896, Max Klaas opened an import office in New York under the name Max Klaas Company, but by 1940 Crane Brands were owned by the Metropolitan Cutlery Company of New York with Emil Goldman owner of the firm.

All Klaas knives have been made in Solingen, Germany, under a variety of brand and stampings, the most familiar and well known being the "Kissing Crane" logo.

A major distributor of Klaas knives in the United States at this time is Star Sales Company, Inc. of Knoxville, Tennessee.

Collectible rating: High

Stampings:

Robert Klaas (two cranes touching bills) Solingen,
    Germany
R. Klaas, Prussia
Klaas (through crown)
R. Klaas, Solingen, Ger. (under golf clubs)

Deer Hunter, etched blade, 9¼"

Lockblade (2219). 4⅛"
closed. Genuine bone
stag handle.

Whittler (3135). 4"
closed. Genuine deer
stag handle.

Congress (1446).
3½" closed. Yellow
Lifetime handle.

Whittler (3235). 4⁵/₈"
closed. Genuine deer stag
handle.

Congress (1746). 3¾"
closed. Yellow Lifetime
handle.

Copperhead (2026).
3¾" closed. Yellow
Lifetime handle.

Fourmaster (2346). 3¾" closed.
Yellow Lifetime handle.

Mini Canoe (2926).
3" closed. Yellow
Lifetime handle.

Canoe (2626). 3⁵/₈"
closed. Yellow Life-
time handle.

KUTMASTER, USA
Utica, New York C. 1925 –

This is the current stamping
or trademark of the Utica
Cutlery Company. *(See Utica.)*
Collectible rating: Good

LANDERS, FRARY & CLARK
New Britain, Connecticut C. 1865 – 1950

This firm was established in 1865 in New Britain, Connecticut, when two small manufacturing companies, Landers & Smith and Frary & Carey, joined with James D. Frary as president and Clark as the firm's attorney. In 1866 they purchased the Meriden Cutlery Co. and began manufacturing cutlery. In 1897 they adopted the trademark "Universal" and became one of the largest producers of cutlery in the world. In 1912, they also purchased the Humas & Beckley Mfg. Co. and made their cutlery in that plant. They also used the "H & B" trademark along with their "L. F. & C." trademark.

In 1950 their cutlery division was discontinued. All their additional assets were sold to the General Electric Corporation in 1965.

Collectible rating: High

Stampings:
Universal
L. F. & C.
H & B

Current stampings: None, discontinued 1950

PEN KNIVES

No. 02185–3⅛" stag handles, large spear & pen blades, half polished. Nickel silver bolsters, brass lined.
No. 42185–Buffalo ivory handles.

No. 0265–3⅝" stag handles, large spear & pen blades, half polished. Nickel silver bolsters, nickel silver lined.

No. 0216–3¼" stag handles. Large sheep foot & pen blades, fine glazed finish. Steel bolsters, brass lined.

No. 0218–3¼" stag handles, large sheep foot & pen blades, half polished. Nickel silver bolsters, brass lined.

*No. 02618¾ – 3⅝" stag handles, large
clip & spay blades, half polished. Nickel
silver bolsters, nickel silver lined.*

*No. 02480 – 3⅞" stag handles, large clip
& pen blades, half polished nickel silver
bolsters, brass lined.*

LACKAWANNA CUTLERY COMPANY
Nicholson, Pennsylvania C. 1915 – 1930

The Lackawanna Cutlery made two unsuccessful starts between 1915 and
1917 before it was taken over by the firm of Walt and Reese, a construction firm
for the railroad.

In 1917 Mr. Layton Wallace, who had managed a factory in Kane, was
placed in charge. With Mr. Wallace and better financing, Lackawanna became a
successful concern until the plant was destroyed by fire in 1923. Walt and Reese
left the business, but Mr. Wallace opened a factory in an old garage where he
continued to assemble knives under the same name and produced six patterns,
all with transparent handles. In 1930 he took a job as postmaster and the Lackawanna Cutlery closed its doors for good.

Collectible rating: Very Good

Stampings: Lackawanna Cut. Co., Nicholson, Pa.

Current stamping: None, discontinued 1930

MAHER AND GROSH CUTLERY COMPANY
Clyde, Ohio C. 1877 –

The Maher and Grosh Cutlery Company is perhaps the oldest cutlery company
in the United States which is still in existence and handling cutlery. The company
was formed as a mail-order firm in 1877 dealing in "hand forged, razor steel,
pocket cutlery razors, shears, axes, hatchets, butcher knives, etc."

In their 1900 catalog, they state that "our business has increased from year
to year so that our goods, since we began in 1877, have penetrated to every post
office in the United States, and are today well known for their reliability." Their
knives were shipped postpaid and warranted "so that you can sit in your chair
and see what is on our shelves." The range of their knife patterns rivaled those of

Remington, Winchester, and even Case, all of which were latecomers by comparison. They also assured customers that their order would be filled the same day the order was received.

In addition to the standard patterns common to older knife companies, Maher and Grosh was rather innovative in design in its earlier days. Examples of their knives as seen in their 1900 and 1929 – 30 catalogs are shown on the following two pages. If you are interested in sales techniques and the pride the company had in its knives, read the fine print describing the patterns.

This pride seemed to be well deserved as is evidenced by the fact that notables such as Henry M. Stanley, the explorer who led the expedition into Africa searching for Dr. David Livingston, carried a Maher and Grosh pocketknife on the expedition. There is also some indication that a pattern was made to order for Teddy Roosevelt.

The reputation and prolific production of knives by this company have eroded with time, as often happens with companies. However, they are still in business and have moved from Toledo, Ohio, their location until 1963, to Clyde, Ohio, where they sold, under the Maher and Grosh name, knives that were made by American manufacturers such as Schrade.

In 1992 the company officially closed its mail order operation and no longer sells knives.

Collectible rating: High

Stampings: Maher and Grosh, Toledo, OH
Maher and Grosh, Clyde, OH

Henry Ford's Favorite, No. 65.

Maher & Grosh Cutlery Co., Toledo, Ohio 7

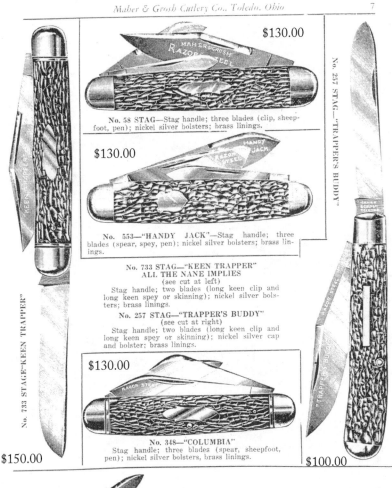

$130.00

No. 58 STAG—Stag handle; three blades (clip, sheepfoot, pen); nickel silver bolsters; brass linings.

$130.00

No. 553—"HANDY JACK"—Stag handle; three blades (spear, spey, pen); nickel silver bolsters; brass linings.

No. 733 STAG—"KEEN TRAPPER"
ALL THE NANE IMPLIES
(see cut at left)
Stag handle; two blades (long keen clip and long keen spey or skinning); nickel silver bolsters; brass linings.

No. 257 STAG—"TRAPPER'S BUDDY"
(see cut at right)
Stag handle; two blades (long keen clip and long keen spey or skinning); nickel silver cap and bolster; brass linings.

$130.00

No. 348—"COLUMBIA"
Stag handle; three blades (spear, sheepfoot, pen); nickel silver bolsters, brass linings.

$150.00

$100.00

$120.00

No. 305
CARPENTER'S KNIFE

Ebony handle; three blades (spear, sheepfoot, and pen); nickel silver bolsters and shield; brass linings.

233

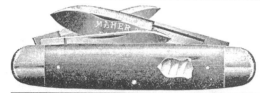

$90.00

No. 222

Ebony handle; three blades (spear and two pen); nickel silver bolsters and shield; brass linings.

$90.00

No. 54

Ebony handle; three blades (spear and two pen); nickel silver bolsters and shield; brass linings.

$150.00   No. 357
GENUINE STAG HANDLE

Genuine stag handle; three blades (spear and two pen); nickel silver bolsters and shield; brass linings

$115.00

No. 444

Stag handle; four blades (two sheepfoot and two pen); nickel silver bolsters and shield; brass linings.

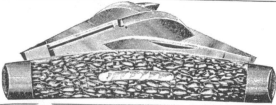

$150.00

No. 326
"BIG BRONCHO"

Stag handle; three blades (spear, sheepfoot, and pen); nickel silver bolsters and shield; brass linings.

$90.00

No. 324—STAG
"BIG HORN"

Stag handle; two blades (large spear and pen); nickel silver cap, bolsters and shield; brass linings.

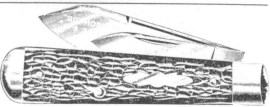

MARBLE ARMS & MANUFACTURING COMPANY
Gladstone, Michigan C. 1898 –

This firm was established in 1898 in Gladstone, Michigan, by W. L. Marble as the Marble Safety Ax Company. Knives were added to their line in 1902. At first, only two models of sheath knives were produced. These were "Ideal" and "Dall DeWeese." Four years later, a line of pocketknives was added. In 1911 the company's name was changed to Marble Arms & Manufacturing Company.

Many of the Marble brand knives were sophisticated in design and patent. They were used by Teddy Roosevelt and the Perry Arctic expedition. Although most of the Marble patents ran out after 1920, their designs were contracted by the government to other companies during WWII and are still being produced.

In addition to the innovative design of Marble knives, this company seems to have originated the numbering system which was adopted by Case. An explanation of the Marble's numbering system is found in their 1907 catalog. It states under "KEY TO KNIFE NUMBERS: The last two figures indicate the number of the pattern. The second figure indicates the number of blades. The first figure indicates the kind of handle as follows: Figure 8, Pearl; Figure 5, Genuine Stag; Figure 6, Bone Stag." It is indeed unfortunate for collectors that Marble did not see fit to stamp these numbers on their knives.

The company discontinued production of pocketknives around 1950 but still produces some hunting knives.

Collectible rating: Top Priority

Stampings used by Marble:

    Marble, Gladstone, Mich.

    Marble, Gladstone, Mich. USA

    MSA Co., Gladstone, Mich.

Current stampings: Marble, Gladstone, Mich. USA (for only sheath knives)

Jack
No. 5111. One 3½" blade. Spring lock. Genuine stag handle.

235

MARBLE KNIVES

Physican
No. 5206. One 3" and one 2¼" blade. Genuine stag handle.

Whittler
No. 5392. One 2⅝" and two 1¼" blades. Genuine stag handle.
No. 8292. One 2⅝" blade and one 1¼" blade like lower blade.

No. 6228. Easy opener. One 2¼" and one 1¼" blade. Bone stag handle.

No. 6203. Jack. One 2⅞" and one 2⅛" blade. Bone stag handle. Steel bolsters and lining.

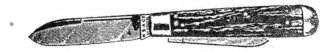

Jack
No. 5213. One 2⅝" and one 2" blade. Genuine stag handle. Steel bolsters.

MARBLE KNIVES

Congress/Senator
No. 8468. One 2" and three 1¼" blades. Pearl handle.

Warncliffe Whittler
No. 5354. One 2¼", one 1½", and one 1⅜" blade. Genuine stag handle.

Marble's Safety Hunting Knife
No. 85. Blade, 5"; weight, 6 ounces.

MILLER BROTHERS CUTLERY COMPANY
Meridian, Connecticut C. 1886 – 1925

This New England firm was established about 1868 by two brothers, George and William Miller, at Yalesville, Connecticut. Two years later, in 1870, they moved their plant to Meridian, Connecticut.

The Miller brothers produced an extensive line of well-made cutlery for many years. They stamped their Barlows with a monogram MBC on the bolsters.

The company closed production of pocketknives about 1925.

Collectible rating: Very High

Stampings: Miller Bros. Cut. Co., Meridian, Conn.

Current stampings: None, discontinued 1925.

MILLER BROTHERS

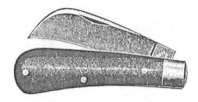

*One-Blade Pruning Knife. Length 4",
ebony handle, steel lining and bolster.*

*Standard Scout Knife. Length 3⅝", celluloid
handle, four blades, spear, punch, can opener,
screwdriver and cap lifter, brass lining, nickel
silver bolsters and shield, shackle.*

*Lobster
Length 3¼", two blades and nail file, pearl handle,
nickel silver lining.*

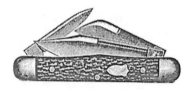

*Length 4", Premium Stock Knife, clip,
sheep foot and pen blades, stag handle,
brass lining, nickel silver bolsters and
shield.*

NAPANOCH KNIFE COMPANY
Napanoch, New York C. 1900 – 1934

The Napanoch Knife Co. was a proud cutlery firm which believed that quality advertised itself. It was founded in the early 1900s by William Horenbeek and Irving Carmen in Napanoch, New York. Later in 1919 it was purchased by the Winchester Arms Company. The Napanoch name, along with its skilled workmen, moved to New Haven, Connecticut, where Napanoch knives continued to be made in the New England pocketknife plant of the old Eagle Knife Co. which had been acquired by Winchester just prior to the move.

Meanwhile, the deserted Napanoch plant was purchased by former Napanoch employees who produced knives stamped "Honk Falls" until 1929 when the old plant burned.

When Winchester withdrew from the knife business, it allowed one of the former employees, Irvin Carmen, to produce "Napanoch" brand knives in his private plant in Napanoch, New York. This company operated until the death of the owner in 1939.

Collectible rating: Very High

Stamping:

Napanoch Knife Co., Napanoch, N.Y.

Napanoch USA

Current stamping: None, discontinued 1939

(Note: See Winchester Arms Company)

Congress Pattern No. 440. Length closed 3¼", stag handles, nickel silver shield and bolsters.

Dogleg Jackknife No. 2570. Length closed 3½", stag handles, nickel shield and bolsters.

239

COMMON NAPANOCH PATTERNS

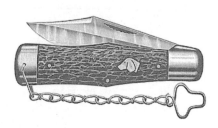

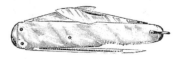

Sleeve Board Lobster Pattern No. 3312-S. Length closed 3⅛", pearl handles, German silver bolsters, lining, and swivel.

Folding Hunter, Pattern X100X. Length closed 5⅜", stag handles, brass lining, nickel silver bolsters and shield.

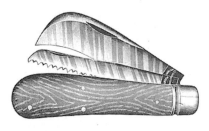

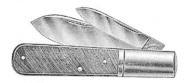

Pruning Knife, Pattern No. 010 (with saw blade). Length closed 4", cocobola handle (wood), steel bolster, steel lining.

Barlow Pattern No. 2270. Length closed 3½", stag handle, steel lining and bolster.

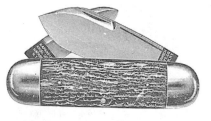

Jack Knife Pattern No. 2020. Length closed 3⅝", stag handles, steel bolsters, brass lining, and silver shield.

Sawfish or Elephant Toenail No. 2250, 2 heavy blades. Length closed 4¼", 1½" wide, stag handle, steel bolsters, and brass lining.

NEW YORK KNIFE COMPANY
Walden, New York C. 1852 – 1931

In the year 1852 a group of cutlers from the struggling Waterville Mfg. Co. of Waterbury, Connecticut, left that firm and started the New York Knife Company in Matterwan, New York. In 1856 they relocated in Walden, New York. Thomas W. Bradley was president, and under his able management the firm became and remained the largest of its type in the world until he died in 1879.

Bradley's son, Thomas J. Bradley, who was a Medal of Honor winner during the Civil War, then took over and maintained the company until it was sold to C.B. and J.E. Fuller in 1903.

Knives made by this firm were among the highest quality in the world until it closed shop in 1931. Like many other firms producing top quality knives, the combination of the Depression, cheap imports, and low quality knives on the market was too much with which to compete.

Collectible rating: Top Priority

Stampings and Logos:

"New York Knife Co." Matterwan, N.Y.

"New York Knife Co." Walden, N.Y.

"Hammer Brand" (under arm with hammer)

"Wallkill River Works" Walden, N.Y.

Current stamping: None, discontinued 1931

(Note: Imperial Knife Co., Providence, R.I., has used the "Hammer Brand" stamping and logo on a cheap line of shell handled knives.)

NORMARK COMPANY
Minneapolis, Minnesota C. 1959 –

This firm was founded in 1959 by Ron Weber and Ray Ostrom in Minneapolis, Minnesota. The firm gained early prominence by the introduction of the Rapala fishing lure and fillet knives following Norwegian designs. Later they introduced some styles of single blade folding knives with removable screw-set handles that were easy to clean and replace.

Collectible rating: Good

Current stampings: "Rapala" Minneapolis, Minn.

"Normark" Minneapolis, Minn.

NORTHFIELD KNIFE COMPANY
Northfield, Connecticut C. 1858 – 1964

This company was incorporated in 1858 with John S. Barnes as president. In 1865 they acquired a group of top quality English cutlers from the Waterville Manufacturing Company of Waterbury, Connecticut, and began production of high quality knives. Franklin H. Catlin then became president.

In 1865 they also acquired control of the American Knife Company of Thomaston, Connecticut, and in 1885 the Excelsior Knife Company of Torrington, Connecticut, expanding their capacity for production to over 1,000 styles of knives. They won prizes and awards at several World's Fairs, including the Chicago and Paris expositions.

Perhaps it was the lowering sales of high-quality knives that prompted this firm to sell their stock to the Clark Brothers Cutlery of St. Louis in 1929. The Clark Brothers dropped the Northfield stampings for their own and sold the land to the state of Connecticut for a state park.

A Mr. Gill purchased the buildings and equipment and moved it off the property. He proceeded to continue producing Northfield knives in a very small quantity until about 1964.

Collectible rating: High

Stampings & logos: "Northfield Knife Co." Northfield
"UN-X-LD" Northfield, Conn.

Current stamping: None, discontinued 1964
(See American Knife Company)

Northfield Jack Knife.

NOVELTY CUTLERY COMPANY
Canton, Ohio C. 1879 – 1944

This firm was founded in 1879 by Augustus Vignos, a Civil War veteran and former postmaster of Canton, who had lost an arm during the war.

Mr. Vignos secured the rights to manufacture transparent handle knives from the inventors Henry and Rubin Landis who were also residents of Canton.

In so doing, they shared honor and competition with the Canton Cutlery Company, also of Canton, by introducing the popular handle material to the public. No other connections other than this existed between the two firms, yet both produced patterns that were very similar.

When Mr. Vignos died in 1925, his son, Alfred A. Vignos, carried on. They ceased making knives in 1944.

Collectible rating: High

Stampings and logos:

    Silver Tip (with bear in oval)

    N. C. Co., Canton O.

    Vignos

Page twenty   **NOVELTY CUTLERY COMPANY, CANTON, OHIO**

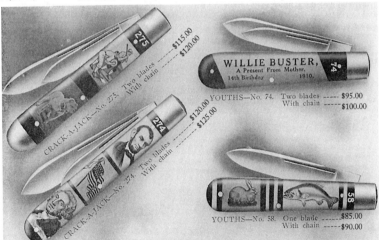

CRACK-A-JACK—No. 275. Two blades ------ $115.00 With chain ------ $120.00

CRACK-A-JACK—No. 274. Two blades ------ $120.00 With chain ------ $125.00

WILLIE BUSTER, A Present From Mother, 14th Birthday 1910.

YOUTHS—No. 74. Two blades ----- $95.00 With chain ----- $100.00

YOUTHS—No. 58. One blade ----- $85.00 With chain ----- $90.00

BOYS' KNIVES—This page shows two styles of Boys' knives in which the material and temper is not wanting, but the finish is not what may be expected in our other knives. They are good values for the price, and will serve the youths as well as a more highly finished knife.

OAK LEAF
(See E.C. Simmons Co.)

OBADIAH BARLOW COMPANY
Campo Lane, Sheffield, England C. 1667 – 1798

This cutlery established in 1667 by Obadiah Barlow is included here because of the historical significance of this knife's pattern. Although several Sheffield companies made Barlow pattern pocketknives during the 1600s and some even duplicated the "BAR" trademark, the Obadiah Barlow Company is credited with the design, development, and production of the first pocketknife of this design.

The Barlow pattern was developed as an export item with the American Colonies in mind as the targeted market. Because of this, the knives had to be strong and utilitarian enough to satisfy pioneer requirements, while at the same time they had to be produced at the most economical level. The result was a knife with blades forged of the best high carbon steel, bone handles (generally unpolished), and steel bolsters that were increased to an uncommonly long length (approximately ⅓ the length of the handle) for added strength. Most early Barlows were one blade.

The Barlow was met with enthusiasm when it reached the American shores. It quickly became the most popular knife of the era and has continued to hold a high position throughout America's history.

The Obadiah Barlow Cutlery Company is not included in our price guide because it would be almost impossible to find a knife of this brand in any condition today. To discover such a rarity would be a truly historical find, since our sources indicate that not even the Sheffield City Museum (claimed to have the largest cutlery collection in the world) or the Smithsonian Institution has a genuine Obadiah Barlow pocketknife.

Collectible rating: Top Priority

Stampings and logo: BAR (also on bolsters)

OLD TIMER
(See Schrade Cutlery)

OLSEN KNIFE COMPANY
Howard City, Michigan
1950 – 1985

The Olsen Knife Company has, for the past several years, primarily imported contract pocketknives from Germany. Exceptions to this have included contracts with manufacturers in the United States and Japan. Additionally, the Olsen brand could be found on hunting fixed-blade knives and kitchen cutlery which were made in their Howard City plant.

After several years of declining business, severe competition from abroad, and a generally depressed economy, this company declared bankruptcy. However, by the summer of 1983, the company was back in business. It was purchased by two former employees and a regrouping-rebuilding process began. Fate did not smile on the new venture though, and by 1985 the doors of the Howard City plant closed again.

Collectible rating: Good
Stamping: "Olsen Knife Co." Howard City, MI

German-made giant single blade Lockback, 6" closed, 11" open. Genuine bone handles. Mint condition. $85.00 each.

ONTARIO KNIFE COMPANY
Franklinville, New York C. 1889 –

This firm was established in 1889 in Franklinville, New York, and manufactured kitchen cutlery only. It was acquired by Servotronics, Inc., in 1970 as a sister company to Queen Cutlery which is also owned by Servotronics, and began a line of pocketknives labeled "Old Hickory" in 1971.

The "Old Hickory" brand was adopted from their line of kitchen cutlery.

Collectible rating: Good
Stamping: "Old Hickory" Ontario Knife Co.

OPINEL
1890 – Present

Since Joseph Opinel began making knives in 1890, the people of the Alps have used them for heavy work. The knives all have a hardwood handle and are equipped with a safety device that locks the blade open. They carry the hallmark of the Crowned Hand, La Main Couronnée, a symbol of quality that has been in use in Europe for more than a century.

The knives come in a variety of sizes but just one pattern. They are not fancy, but being French country knives, they are not meant to be.

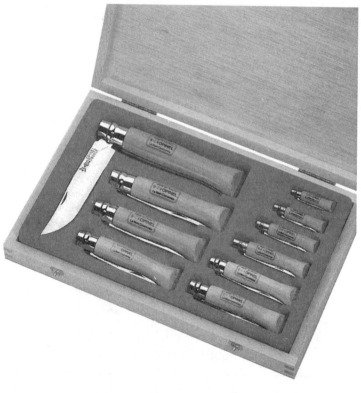

SINCE 1890

PAL CUTLERY COMPANY
Plattsburg, New York C. 1925 – 1950

Pal Cutlery was established about 1925 as the Pal Blade & Tool Company, Plattsburg, New York. Their principal operation during the 1930s was the manufacture of inexpensive tools and safety razor blades. However, they did make M3 trench knives for the Armed Forces during WWII and purchased the cutlery equipment of the Remington Arms Co. when it dropped its cutlery line.

Afterwards they changed their company's name to Pal Cutlery Co. and continued making pocketknives until late in 1950. Unlike Remington, they did not produce a large variety of patterns, but what they made were very similar to the Remington designs.

Some of their early knives did contain Remington stamped blades. The "Pal" Bullet pattern knives are rare collector prizes.

Collectible rating: Very High

Stampings: Pal Blade Co., Plattsburg, N.Y. USA
    Pal Blade Co. USA
    Pal Cutlery Co. USA

Current stamping: None, discontinued 1950

(Note: See Remington Arms Company)

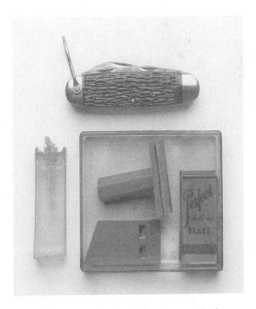

Traveler's set. (Delbert Adkins collection)

247

PARKER CUTLERY COMPANY
Chattanooga, Tennessee C. 1978 –

The James Parker Cutlery Association was formed in 1978 in Chattanooga, Tennessee, immediately after the partnership of Parker-Frost Cutlery Co. was dissolved, and has its location at the same address. James Parker, the owner, had been a credit manager for Sherwin-Williams Paint Company and a gun trader, so it was natural for him to become interested in collecting and dealing in knives during the late 1960s.

The story is that Mr. Parker borrowed $5,000 to finance a distributorship in dealing with the knives of various companies. Then in 1976 Parker joined in partnership with Jim Frost, another distributor, to establish the Parker-Frost Cutlery Co. which grew rapidly into one of the largest of its kind. Importing knives from Japan and establishing their own Eagle Brand line, they produced a notable number of bicentennials, commemorative sets, and limited edition sets. After Jim Frost left to start his own Frost Cutlery, the company's name was changed to James Parker Cutlery Association. The firm continued to grow and offers its customers over 500 patterns of cutlery from which to choose. James Parker has demonstrated to the cutlery field that with very little capital it is still possible to turn a pleasurable hobby such as knife collecting into a large and lucrative business.

Collectible rating: Good

Stampings & logos: Parker Cutlery Co. (over flying eagle)
    Surgical Steel (country of origin)
    Parker Brothers (over flying eagle)
    Chattanooga, TN.
    Parker USA Cutlery
    Parker–Edwards (Damascus Steel)
    Jacksonville, Alabama
(Note: See Parker-Frost Cutlery Co. and Frost Cutlery)

PARKER KNIVES

Folding Hunter. 5¼", smooth bone handle.

Silver Roller Lockback. 3½", metal handle.

Folding Hunter. 5", genuine bone handle.

Folding Hunter. 4¼", second cut stag handle.

Whittler
Celebrated Dirk. 4", genuine pearl handle.

Jack
Palmetto. 3½", genuine pearl handle.

PARKER-FROST CUTLERY COMPANY
Chattanooga, Tennessee C. 1976 – 1978

The Parker-Frost Cutlery Company was established in Chattanooga, Tennessee, in 1976 by James Parker, a former paint company employee and gun trader, and James Frost, a chemical company worker. Both men grew interested in knives through traveling together to shows and trading and selling knives with their fellow workers. Mr. Parker is said to have borrowed $5,000 to expand his stock, and eventually both Parker and Frost became distributors for many of the leading U.S. cutlery firms. Then in 1976 they combined the two independent distributing firms in the short-lived partnership of Parker-Frost Cutlery Company.

The partnership of Parker-Frost Cutlery Company lasted for only about two years, but during this time introduced a large number of fine collector sets and bicentennial commemoratives along with their own "Eagle Brand" line. While the majority of Parker-Frost knives were made in the Orient as contract knives, strict specifications elicited the highest quality and the best of materials.

When Parker and Frost dissolved partnership in 1978, Mr. Parker retained most of the collection pieces and the line carrying the Parker-Frost brand except for those made in Japan. Parker's new company at the same address is The James Parker Cutlery Association. Frost's new company became the Frost Cutlery Company at a new location.

Collectible rating: Very Good
Stamping and logo:
   Parker-Frost (flying eagle) (country of origin)
Current stamping: None, discontinued 1978
(Note: See Parker Cutlery and Frost Cutlery)

PHOENIX KNIFE COMPANY
Phoenix, New York C. 1892 – 1916
(See Central City Knife Co., Phoenix, New York)

PINE KNOTT
(See Belknap Mfg. Co.)

PUMA-WERK, LAUTERJUNG & SOHN
Solingen, Germany C. 1769 –

Lauterjung & Sohn was established in 1769 by the Lauterjung family in Solingen, Germany. They produced razors, hunting knives, table knives, shears, scissors, and swords and daggers for the military. In 1947 Baron Von Frandenburg, a son-in-law of a Lauterjung descendant, took over the management of the firm. Von Frankenburg was a noted big game hunter and launched the firm on a course of producing modern and more functional hunting knives for the sportsman, such as the Puma "White Hunter" and the "Scale Knife."

In 1957 the Gutmann Cutlery Corp. of Mt. Vernon, New York, introduced Puma knives in general to the United States. Then, in early 1991, after 35 years, the exclusive distributing rights for Puma knives in the USA changed hands from Gutmann to Coast Cutlery Co. of Portland, Oregon.

Since the Puma and Gutmann names have, after so many years, become so closely associated, it will be difficult to recognize one without the other.

Today there are many stock models in the Puma line, and many additional types of cutlery, including pocketknives, razors, hog spears, and survival knives.

Collectible rating: High

Stampings: Puma, Solingen, Ger. (Logo: Outline head of puma)

4-STAR DROP POINT FOLDING KNIVES

No. 16-725
Length closed 4"
Contoured handle of durable wood laminate with Puma shield. Mirror polished German nickel silver bolster and pins, satin finish blade.

No. 16-700
Length closed 3"
Contoured handle of Jacaranda wood with Puma shield. Brass lining. Mirror polished German nickel silver bolster and pins.

PUMA KNIVES

4-STAR DROP POINT FOLDING KNIVES

No. 16-745
Length closed 4"
Contoured handle of select India stag horn.
Mirror polished brass bolster. German nickel
silver pins, satin finish blade.

No. 16-740
Length closed 3"
Contoured handle of select India stag horn.
Brass lining. Mirror polished German
nickel silver bolster and pins, satin finish
blade.

No. 16-715
Length closed 4"
Contoured handle of ivory micarta with
Puma shield. Mirror polished brass bolster
and pins. Mirror polished blade.

No. 16-730
Length closed 3"
Contoured handle of stainless steel with satin
finish and Puma shield. Satin finished blade.

"400 SERIES"
FOLDING HUNTING KNIVES
PUMA-LITE GREEN HANDLES

No. 16-455 Puma Rambler.
Length closed 3".

No. 16-955 Puma Gentleman.
The baby of the Puma family,
closes to only 3".

No. 16-460 Puma Cadet.
Length closed 3¼".

No. 16-960 Puma Cub.
Closes to compact 3½".

FOLDING LOCKBACK
HUNTING KNIVES
JACARANDA WOOD HANDLES

No. 16-465.
Length closed 4¼".

No. 16-965 Puma Deer Hunter.
Handy size for hunting, camping or
backpacking, 4¼" closed.

No. 16-470 Puma Master.
Length closed 5".

No. 16-970 Puma Game Warden.
Most popular size folding knife.
5" closed.

PUMA KNIVES

UTILITY KNIVES

*No. 16-536 Puma Pocket Friend.
Length closed 4".*

*No. 16-644 Puma Work Knife
Length closed 4⅛"*

FIXED-BLADE
HUNTING KNIVES

*No. 16-397 Puma Hunter's Pal.
4" Blade.*

*No. 16-394 Hunter's Companion.
5" Blade.*

FIXED-BLADE KNIVES

*No. 16-378 Outdoor.
5" Blade.*

*No. 16-382 Trail Guide.
5" Blade.*

*No. 16-393 Skinner.
5" Blade.*

*No. 16-375 White Hunter.
6" Blade.*

*No. 16-396 Bowie.
6½" Blade.*

QUEEN CUTLERY COMPANY
Titusville, Pennsylvania C. 1918

The Queen City Cutlery Company was founded in 1918 by six highly skilled employees of the Schatt and Morgan Cutlery firm which had moved from Gowenda, New York, to Titusville in 1895 *(see Schatt and Morgan)*. Since all of its production capacity was devoted to contract manufacturing, the company had no official name until 1922.

Titusville was known at the time as the "Queen City" because of Drake's oil well. Queen City was selected as the tang stamp of the new company.

Queen City prospered during the '20s. Schatt and Morgan, greatly weakened because of the void left by the loss of skilled employees, did not. By 1930, Schatt and Morgan went broke.

In 1932, Queen City purchased Schatt and Morgan and moved their operations into the Schatt and Morgan factory building. They made knives throughout the '30s and early '40s using their traditional carbon steel blades.

In the early '40s, the company began to experiment with stainless steel, and in 1945-46 began to replace carbon steel blades with stainless steel. When the public balked at the use of stainless steel for knife blades, the company replaced the stainless stamping with "Queen Steel" (registered as a trademark in 1947). This marketing strategy seems to have worked, as the knives were accepted as "Queen Steel," even though the blade material was stainless. The Queen City Cutlery Company changed its name to Queen Cutlery Co. in 1947. Stampings were changed from Queen City to markings which included a larged crowned "Q." This stamping was used until about 1955 when tang stamping was dropped in favor of blade etching.

In 1969, Queen Cutlery became a subsidiary company of Servotronics, Inc. Soon afterward, they began stamping their knives again with a crowned "Q." The first was a Barlow with "1922" on the left side and "1972" on the right. This was used to commemorate Queen City's Drake oil well as well as their own 50 years of business.

Queen's operations today have not significantly changed. They proudly point out that "Queen Cutlery takes pride in using many of the original hand operations utilized by both Schatt and Morgan and Queen City" and "over 150 hand operations are required to make the average Queen pocketknife and about 200 operations are required to make the Schatt and Morgan reproductions."

Collectible rating: Very Good

QUEEN CUTLERY

1890 – 1930

1918 – 1947

Circa 1932 – 1955

QUEENCUTLERYCO
TITUSVILLE, PA.

Circa 1932 – 1950

Circa 1946 – 1950

STAINLESS

Circa 1946 – 1950

Circa 1949 – 1958

1972 only

1976 only

Marking instituted in 1947, continuing to the present.

256

QUEEN CUTLERY

Push Button Lockback. 5¼", brown jigged Delrin handle with Queen shield.

Muskrat. 4", jigged Delrin handles, stainless blades.

Paul Revere Lockback. 5", polished brown pakkawood handles.

Button Lock. 3¾", chipped bark handle.

Toothpick. 5", burnt white bone handle.

Copperhead, 3¼", jigged Delrin handles.

REMINGTON ARMS COMPANY
Ilion, New York C. 1918 – 1940

Established in 1816 by Eliphalet Remington, the Remington Arms Co. of Ilion, New York, is one of our oldest and most reputable arms manufacturers. Although they made bayonets during WWI, they did not begin the manufacture of pocketknives until 1920. With an established reputation for quality, plus the tremendously wide range of patterns and styles, Remington became an almost instant leader in the cutlery field. They were especially noted for their big folding hunters with the bullet shields.

Because Remington had previously merged their holdings with another company, the Union Metallic Cartridge Co., their tang stamping retained both "Remington" and "UMC" inside a circle with "Made in U.S.A." inscribed outside the circle. The circle represented the primer end of a cartridge. Some stampings, however, do not contain the "UMC." The later ones are marked "Remington" (no circle) inscribed in a straight line across the tang.

With the approach of WWII, Remington's government contracts for arms increased to the point that around 1940, they ceased knifemaking. After the war, they sold their cutlery machinery to Pal Cutlery Company which continued knifemaking until 1950.

Presently Remington is producing an updated version of its Bullet patterns. These are aimed primarily at the collector's market.

Collectible rating: Top Priority

Stampings:

    Circle, Remington UMC, Made in U.S.A.

    Circle, Remington, Made in U.S.A.

    Remington (straight line)

Current stampings: None, discontinued 1940

(See Appendix 5 for detailed Remington price guide.)

258

REMINGTON NUMBERING SYSTEM

While Remington's numbering system is stamped on nearly every knife they made, the amount of information it provides about the knife's make-up is limited.

The letter "R" which precedes all numbers simply denotes that the knife is a pocketknife, but don't be surprised if you also find one is a small sheath knife. There is no figure in the pattern to indicate the number or type of blades, but the last figure in the pattern number does indicate the handle material as follows:

1. Redwood
2. Black Comp.
3. Genuine Bone "Stag"
4. Genuine Pearl
5. Pyremite, or Celluloid

6. Genuine Stag
7. Ivory or White Bone
8. Cocabolo Wood
9. Metal
10. English Buffalo Horn

The figures R1 to R2999 indicate Jack knives, R3000 to R5999 indicate knives in such classes as Cattle, Stock, Mechanic, etc., while R6000 to R9999 indicate Pen knives.

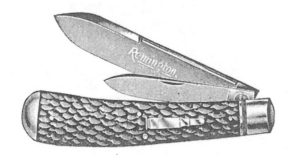

No. R1273. Hunters' Favorite. Stag handle, two blades, one long spear, crocus polished and etched; one pen, blue glazed, nickel silver bolster, cap and cartridge shield, brass lining. Length closed 5¼".

No. R1263. Hunters' Favorite. Stag handle, two blades, one long clip, crocus polished and etched; one pen, blue glazed, nickel silver bolster, cap and cartridge shield, brass lining. Length closed 5¼".

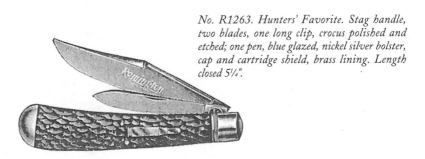

259

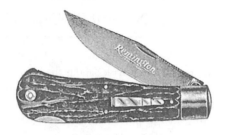

No. R1306. Lockback Hunting Knife. Genuine stag handle, one blade, sticking and skinning, crocus polished and etched, nickel silver bolster, cartridge shield and lining, hole in end for leather thong or lanyard. Length closed 4½".

No. R1253. Lockback Hunting Knife. Stag handle, one blade, large sabre clip, crocus polished and etched, nickel silver bolster, cap and cartridge shield, brass lining. Length closed 5¼".

No. R293. Trappers and Sportsmen's Knife
Stag handle, two blades, one large sabre clip, crocus polished and etched; one long curved spay (surgical), blue glazed, nickel silver cap, bolster and shield, brass lining. Length closed 3¾".

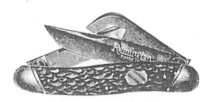

No. R4083. Stockmen's and Sheepmen's Knife
Stag handle, three blades, one large sabre clip, crocus polished and etched, one sheep foot and one spay (surgical), both blue glazed, diagonal nickel silver bolsters, nickel silver shield, rivets, lining and full milled center scale. Length closed 3⅞".

No. R4383. Scouts' Knife "Junior" Size
Stag handle, four blades, 1 large spear, crocus
polished and etched, one combination bottle
opener and screwdriver, one can opener, both
blue glazed, one punch, blued inside, polished
back, nickel silver bolsters, shackle, rivets and
shield nickel silver lining, milled center scale
& reinforced lining on punch blade side.
Length closed 3⅛".

No. R4393. Scouts' Knife
Stag handle, four blades, one large spear,
crocus polished and etched, one combination
bottle opener and screwdriver, one can
opener, both blue glazed, one punch, blued
inside, polished back, nickel silver bolsters,
shackle, rivets and shield, brass lining,
milled center scale and reinforced lining on
punch blade side. Length closed 3¼".

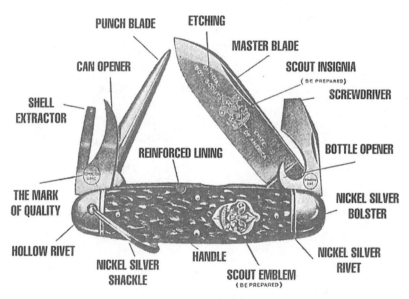

Scout or Camp Pattern
No. RS333. *Official Knife of the Boy Scouts of America. The Boy Scouts of America have
authorized the Remington Arms Company Inc., to manufacture the "Official Knife of the Boy
Scouts of America." The Remington is the genuine official knife. Every official Scout knife bearing
the Remington trademark is equal in quality and workmanship to the master exhibits submitted
to and approved by the U.S. Government Bureau of Standards.*

261

"Moose"
No. R4013. General Purpose Knife.
Stag handle, two blades, one large
clip, crocus polished and etched, one
spear, blue glazed, nickel silver bolsters, shield and rivets, brass lining.
Length closed 3⅝".

Stiletto
No. R653. Dagger Knife. Stag handle,
one blade, long clip, crocus polished and
etched, nickel silver cap, bolster with
guard and shield, brass lining. Length
closed 4".

Humpback Whittler
No. R6836. Carpenters' and
Mechanics' Favorite. Genuine
stag handle, three blades, one large
sabre clip, etched, one pen and one
cut-off pen, all full crocus polished,
threaded nickel silver bolsters,
nickel silver shield, rivets, lining
and milled center scale. Bolster
and lining are one piece. Length
closed 3⅛".

Humpback Whittler
No. R6816. Lock Back Knife. Genuine
stag handle, three blades, one large sabre
clip, etched, one pen and one cut-off pen,
all full crocus polished, threaded nickel
silver bolsters, nickel silver shield, rivets,
lining and milled center scale, bolsters
and lining are one piece. Length closed
3½".

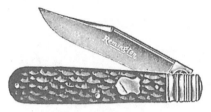

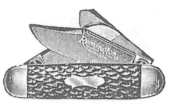

No. R1143. Camp or Fishermen's Knife.
Stag handle, one blade, large clip, crocus
polished and etched, nickel silver bolster
and shield, brass lining. Length closed 4⅛".

No. R3203. Farmer's Knife. Stag
handle, three blades, one large
clip, etched, one spay (surgical)
and one sheep foot, all blue glazed,
polished steel bolsters, nickel silver
shield and rivets, brass lining.
Length closed 3½".

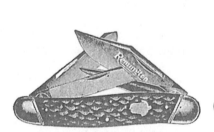

No. R3713. Farmers' and Threshers'
Knife. Stag handle, four blades, one large
clip, crocus polished and etched, one long,
cut-off pen and one spay (surgical), both
blue glazed, one punch, blued inside,
polished back, diagonal nickel silver bolsters,
nickel silver shield, rivets, lining and full
milled center scale. Length closed 3⅛".

No. R3143. General Utility Knife.
Stag handle, five blades, one large clip,
crocus polished and etched, one sheep
foot, one pen and one spay (surgical),
all blue glazed, one punch, blued inside,
polished back, nickel silver cap, bolster
shield and rivets, brass lining and full
milled finished scale. Length closed 3⅞".

REMINGTON BULLET POCKETKNIVES

Folding Hunter Trapper
R1123

Folding Hunter Trapper
R1128

The Remington Cutlery Company may not have known they were producing a future collector's item when they designed the Bullet, but they knew they were producing a quality product, and they were proud of their handiwork. In their 1923 Catalog No. 107, they describe Bullet models R1123 and R1128 as being "Built to withstand rough, hard usage. An excellent all-purpose knife. (The) Joints are flush and square when the blades are closed, preventing dirt, twigs, etc., from interfering with the proper action of the blades. Convenient to carry. (It has) Sturdy, strong, sharp cutting edges (and) non-slip grips.

"(The) Knife has (a) shield (and a) brass lining. (It also has a) Hole in (the) butt for (the) use of (a) leather thong or lanyard."

When one holds either of the Remington Bullet models in his hand for the first time, he can literally feel the quality and balance which result from the marriage of materials through a technique respectfully referred to as the cutler's art.

The Remington Bullet Pocketknives are among the most sought after pocketknives ever produced. These were Remington's "top of the line." They were expensive in their day and were considered by many to be well worth the investment. However, the knife was limited in production to what the market would bear and in the '20s and '30s, that market did not bear a great many expensive quality knives.

Even so, a surprising number have survived and are available to collectors. The vast majority of these knives have seen use and some even abuse. However, there are some which even qualify as "mint" which are still around. The collector who can find a true Remington Bullet in excellent or better condition, and can afford the price, is indeed lucky. Those of us who may not be able to afford the rarer of the surviving Bullets can take heart, for even Remington Bullets which fall into the good and fair category can serve to enhance a collection.

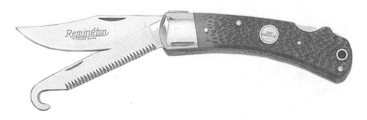

RE-3. 5", Folding Hunter with large clip blade and utility saw blade with rip hook, Delrin imitation bone handles.

RE-6. 8⅛" fixed blade, Skinner. Sawback blade, imitation stag handles.

ROBESON CUTLERY COMPANY
Camillus, New York C. 1894 – 1977

This company was founded in the year 1894 in Camillus, New York, by Millard Robeson, a former cutlery salesman. In 1895, he acquired the Rodchester Stamping Works and changed the name of that firm to Robeson, Rodchester Corporation.

Mr. Robeson died in 1903. After his death the firm did not prosper until 1940 when Emerson Case was hired as manager. He later became president of the company, and Robeson became more progressive.

Robeson Cutlery Company used top quality natural materials in their knives. Scales were made of stag, mother-of-pearl, and bone. Their earliest bone scales were green, which later were replaced by a brown bone. The latter bone was to become famous as "strawberry red."

Early in 1950, they dropped the genuine bone and replaced it with a reddish plastic material that resembled their "strawberry red" bone. They also acquired Kinfolks Cutlery, Inc. about this time.

In mid 1960, Robeson was acquired by Cutler Federal Inc., and Emerson Case retired. This same year, Robeson ceased making their own knives, but continued to sell Robeson brand contract knives which were made by Camillus Cutlery Co.

In 1971, the Ontario Knife Co. bought Robeson and continued use of the trademark until 1977, when the Robeson brand was discontinued.

Collectible rating: Very High

Stampings:

   Robeson, Made in USA

   Robeson, Pat. Applied For

   Robeson USA

   Robeson

   RCC (on the bolster of old daddy barlows)

   Whittle Craft (on shield)

   Pocketeze (on shield)

   Robeson Suredge

Current stampings: None, discontinued 1977

(See Appendix 4 for detailed Robeson price guide.)

Robeson Numbering System

Robeson's numbering system is excellent, perhaps the best. It is stamped on all Robeson-made knives except for some of the late contract knives.

The first figure in the number indicates the handle materials used. The second indicates the number of blades, while the third indicates materials used in liners and bolster types. Numbers following are pattern numbers only.

Handle materials are coded as follows:

1. Black Composition
2. Rosewood
3. Yellow
4. White
5. Genuine Stag (or metal)

6. Bone
7. Genuine Pearl
8. Mottled Composition
9. Gun Metal

Lining and bolsters are coded as follows:

1. Steel liners and bolsters
2. or 6. Brass liners, nickel silver bolsters
3. Nickel silver liners and bolsters
9. Stainless or chrome, liners and bolsters

RODGERS (JOSEPH) & SONS
Sheffield, England C. 1724 –

This firm was established in 1724 by Joseph Rodgers at No. 6 Norfolk Street, Sheffield, England. Their trademark of a Star and Cross was granted in 1764 and has been in continuous use ever since.

This firm was appointed as the official cutlers of six British kings and queens, by U.S. President Grant and by 27 maharajahs. When one considers the function of tradition, as it relates to knifemaking, the Joseph Rodgers Company provides an excellent example of its effect.

In 1971 Rodgers took over the George Wostenholm firm and became the Rodgers-Wostenholm firm. In 1977 the firm was purchased by Schrade Cutlery Co., a division of Imperial Cutlery Co. of Providence, Rhode Island.

They are still producing cutlery.

Collectible rating: High

Stampings:

Joseph Rodgers & Sons, Sheffield, Eng.
Joseph Rodgers & Sons, Shef., Eng. (Star & Cross on back tang)
Rodgers Cutlers to His Majesty
Rodgers Cutlers to Their Majesties, No. 6 Norfolk St., Sheffield
Rodgers-Wostenholm, Sheffield
Imperial Rodgers (Star & Cross) Shef., Eng.

(Note: See George Wostenholm Cutlery, Schrade Cutlery, and Imperial Cutlery.)

Congress
4" closed, stag handle, four cutting blades.

Whittler
3" closed, pearl handle, four blades, German silverplate.

Senator or Congress Pen
3¼" closed, stag handle, four blades, German silver bolster.

Whittler
*No. 21860ST–Genuine stag
handle, brass lining, 3⅛" long.*

Congress
*Genuine stag handle, steel lining
and bolsters.
No. 22445-3¼" long, with file
blade as illustrated.
No. 22445-3½" long, with file
blade as illustrated.
No. 22445-3½"–With tobacco
blade instead of file blade.*

Sleeveboard
*Brass lining, 3⅛" long.
No. 21797-ST–Genuine stag
handle.
No. 21797-IV–Ivory handle.*

Congress Whittler

No. 22445-3B–Genuine stag handle, steel lining and bolster, 3⅛" long.

Congress

Genuine stag handle, steel lining and bolsters, 3¾" long.
No. 24489–With file blade as illustrated.
No. 24489TOB–With tobacco blade instead of file blade.

Congress

No. 12091–Genuine stag handle, steel lining and bolsters, 3¾" long.

Congress

Genuine stag handle, brass lining, German silver bolsters, 3½" long.
No. 12753–With file blade as illustrated.
No. 12753TOB–With tobacco blade instead of file blade.

Coke Bottle Jack

Genuine stag handle, steel lining and bolster, 3½" long.
No. 19923-1BLSP–1 large spear point blade.
No. 19923-1BLSF–1 large sheep foot blade.
No. 19923-2BLSP–1 large spear point blade and 1 pen blade.
No. 19923-2BLSF–1 large sheep foot blade and 1 pen blade.

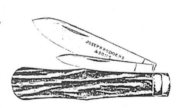

JOHN RUSSELL CUTLERY COMPANY
Southridge, Massachusetts C. 1832 – 1932

The John Russell Cutlery Company was established in 1832 in Deerfield, Massachusetts (now Greenfield, Mass.), on the banks of the Green River. The founders were John and Francis Russell. They used the river's power and resources in the manufacture of their knives. Later they became the first cutlery firm to use steam power and the trip hammer in forging steel.

Their first factory was destroyed by a flood in 1936. However, it was rebuilt on the same site and christened the "Green River Works." Again, in 1864, the factory was destroyed, this time by fire. The firm then moved to Turner Falls, Massachusetts, where they built the largest factory in the world.

Although Russell produced tremendous quantities of pocketknives in many patterns, the Russell Barlow was the pattern for which the company is now famous. This Barlow had an "R," pierced by an arrow, on the bolsters.

The company ceased making pocketknives in the early 1930s. In 1936 they merged with the Harrington Cutlery Company and moved to Southridge, Massachusetts, where they are presently producing kitchen cutlery.

In 1974, the company introduced 12,000 Russell Barlow commemoratives. These knives were made with the original equipment but with stainless steel blades. They were not manufactured by the Russell Company, but it is assumed they were made, on contract, by Schrade.

Collectible rating: Top Priority

Stampings:

J. Russell & Co., Green River Works

Russell (arching over an R and pierced by an arrow)

Russell (arching over an "R" and flanked by a diamond on each side) Russell (written straight across the tang)

In some earlier models, G.R. can be found under the stamping indicating "Green River Works."

Current stampings: None, discontinued in 1932 except for commemoratives, reproductions, and kitchen cutlery.

A VARIETY OF RUSSELL KNIVES

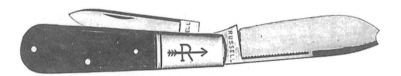

Barlow
No. 10. 3⅜", iron handles.

Barlow, Easy Open
No. 68. 3⅜", bone handles.

Granddaddy Barlow
No. 600. 5", bone handles.

Cotton Sampler
No. 2194. 4¼", cocoa handles.

271

A VARIETY OF RUSSELL KNIVES

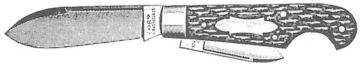

Easy Open Jack
No. 2780. 3¼", bone handles.

Hunting Knife
No. 80. 6" fixed blade, ivory handles.

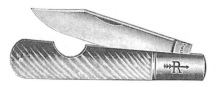

Barlow
No. 6000. 5", bone handle, clip blade.

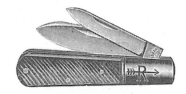

Barlow
No. 62. 3⅜", bone handle, spear and pen blades.

Spatula
No. 3. Pocket Spatula, 2½" blade, ebony handle.

SAYNOR
1738 –

Samuel and John Saynor began this knife manufacturing company in 1738, and it continues today. The company went through a number of name changes through the years, including Saynor & Cooke (1861 – 1877) and Saynor, Cooke & Ridal (1877 – present). Prior to 1810 Saynor was the largest cutlery firm in England. Over the years they used the trademarks of "Rainbow," "Depend," and "Pioneer," producing all types of cutlery, including Bowie knives.

Pruner, 3¼", knife is from the Jim Varney (Ernest) Estate. Photo courtesy Stewart Linham.

SCHATT & MORGAN
Gowanda, New York C. 1890 – 1895
Titusville, Pennsylvania C. 1895 – 1928

While this firm was originally founded in Gowanda, New York, in 1890, they moved to Titusville, Pennsylvania, in 1895. The founders were J.W. Schatt and C.P. Morgan, both men having had previous experience in the cutlery trade.

The firm enjoyed vigorous growth from the beginning and was credited with producing cutlery of the highest quality, and by 1906 they had gained national reputation and high respect for their products. They guaranteed unconditional satisfaction for every knife whether the price was 50¢ or $50.00, and made knives with genuine stag, pearl, silver, and gold handle materials.

In 1911 C.P. Morgan bought out J.W. Schatt and became sole owner of the firm, but in 1922, a group of foremen left the firm to form a separate company — the Queen City Cutlery Company — leaving Schatt & Morgan shorthanded in skilled craftsmen. They ceased operation in 1930, and the Queen City Cutlery Company purchased their stock and facilities in 1932.

Collectible rating: Very High

Stamping and logos:

"Schatt & Morgan" Gowanda, N.Y.

"Schatt & Morgan" Titusville, Pa.

"S&M" Titusville, Pa.

"S & M" (with flying cross between) Titusville, Pa.

"Dollar Knife" Atlanta

(See Queen Cutlery Company)

SCHATT & MORGAN

Schatt & Morgan reproduction knife by Queen Cutlery: Jumbo Folding Hunter. 5¼" closed.

Titusville Plant, circa 1905.
(Photo courtesy of National Knife Collector's Magazine)

EXAMPLES OF SCHATT & MORGAN
REPRODUCTION KNIVES BY QUEEN CUTLERY

Trapper. 3½" closed.

Barlow. 3½" closed.

Reverse Gunstock. 4¼" closed.

Trapper. 4⅛" closed.

SCHRADE CUTLERY COMPANY
Walden, New York C. 1904 –
&
GEORGE SCHRADE CUTLERY COMPANY
Bridgeport, Connecticut C. 1916 – 1950

The Schrade Cutlery Company was established in Walden, New York, in 1904 by George and his brother Louis Schrade. George left the Walden firm to work on his own inventions around 1916 and founded the George Schrade Cutlery Company of Bridgeport, Connecticut, where he pioneered in the manufacturing of switchblade knives.

Both companies were active in filling government contracts for knives during WWII. The older bone handled knives with "peach seed" jigged bone are very desirable collector's items. The George Schrade "Presto" and "Press Button" switchblades are also prime items in the collector market.

The Schrade Cutlery has made contract knives for other companies throughout its history, and today the firm makes more commemoratives and reproductions than most other companies.

Both companies switched from genuine bone to Delrin plastics during the late 1940s, about the time the Schrade company of Walden switched stampings to Schrade-Walden, USA. In 1948, Schrade-Walden was purchased by Ulster Knife Company and moved in 1957 from Walden, New York, to Ellenville, New York. In 1973, the stamping was changed once again from Schrade-Walden, USA to Schrade, USA.

In 1977, through their association with Imperial Knife Co., Schrade took control of the George Wostenholm (I-XL) Knife Co. of Sheffield, England, and began manufacturing the new Schrade-I-XL line of knives in the English factory. Today their "Old Timer," "Uncle Henry," and "Schrade, I-XL" trademarks are their main lines.

Collectible rating: High

Stampings:

Schrade Cutlery Co., Walden, New York

Schrade-Walden, U.S.A.

Schrade, USA (current)

Schrade, I-XL, Sheffield, Eng. (current)

The George Schrade Cutlery Company of Bridgeport, Conn., went out of business about 1950.

Collectible rating: Very High

Stampings:

George Schrade Cut. Co., Bridgeport, Conn.

Press Button

Presto, USA

Current stampings: None, discontinued 1950

(Note: See Imperial Knife Company)

No. C2041SD. Electrician's Knife. Cocabolo handles.

No. C1824W. Corn Knife. Celluloid handles.

SCHRADE CUTLERY POCKETKNIVES

No. P2066. Smoker's Knife.
Nickel silver handles.

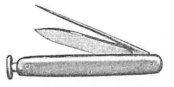

No. 20145. Easy Opener Jack.
Imitation tortoise shell handles.

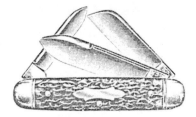

No. 8173. Cattle Knife. Bone handles.

No. 8116B. Sleeveboard-Whittler.
Mother-of-pearl handles.

No. 9463. Boy Scout
Knife. Bone handles.

No. 2157. Barlow. Bone handles.

No. 07564. Office Knife. Celluloid handles.

SCHRADE CUTLERY POCKETKNIVES

No. 2202. Jackknife. Ebony handles.

No. 7606. Lobster Pattern. Mother-of-pearl handles.

No. 2223³/₄. Serpentine Jackknife. Bone handles.

No. 9753. Congress Pattern. Bone handles.

No. 9146T. Senator. Mother-of-pearl handles.

No. 8813. Stock Pattern. Bone handles.

SUPERIOR POCKET KNIVES

SCHRADE SAFETY PUSH BUTTON KNIFE

THE ONLY AUTOMATIC KNIFE WITH A SAFETY LOCK— DOUBLE LOCKED WHEN SAFETY IS IN ACTION.

Operated With One Hand.

No Breaking of Finger Nails.

Will Not Open in Your Pocket.

Will Not Close on the Fingers When In Use.

THE Schrade Safety Push Button Knife, of which we are the exclusive manufacturers, is rapidly becoming the leading knife on the market because of its many advantages over the ordinary pocket knife. Being easily operated with one hand it is far more convenient than the old style pocket knife which necessitates the use of both hands to open and frequently results in broken finger nails. The greatest care has been exercised in the development and manufacture of this knife and to-day it is one of the outstanding achievements of the cutler's skill.

This novel knife is especially suitable for a gift or souvenir, as it is something out of the ordinary, very useful, and when furnished with one of our attractive handles makes an ideal gift.

Our Safety Push Button Knives are manufactured in five sizes, in a great variety of handles and styles, illustrations of which, are shown on the following pages.

"SCHRADE Safety Push Button Knives are the pioneer SAFETY Knives, and do not infringe the patent rights of anyone."

TRADE EVERLASTINGLY SHARP MARK

279

SCHRADE SAFETY PUSH BUTTON KNIVES

No. 7405SD
Executive pen, sterling silver handles,
3⅜".

No. 7403
Pen, bone handles, 3⅛".

No. 7404 Blue
Pen, abalone pearl, Pyralin, 3⅛".

No. 7404S
Pen, mottled green celluloid, 3⅛".

No. 7503
Pen, bone, 3¼".

No. 7504 GP
Pen, golden pearl celluloid, 3¼".

SCHRADE SAFETY PUSH BUTTON KNIVES

No. 7503B
Pen, bone, 3¹/₄".

No. 7523B
Pen (moose), bone, 3¹/₄".

No. O1514K
Stiletto, Pyralin, 4".

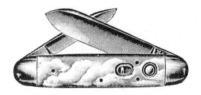

No. 7506B
Pen, pearl, 3¹/₄"

No. 1613³/₄
Folding hunter, bone, 4⁷/₈".

No. 7533
Pen, bone, 3¹/₄".

SHAPLEIGH HARDWARE COMPANY
AND E. C. SIMMONS COMPANY
St. Louis, Missouri C. 1863 – C. 1869

These two great hardware companies have interwoven histories. They originated and distributed many famous brand knives. Shapleigh Hardware Company of St. Louis, Missouri, was organized by A. F. Shapleigh in 1863. It adopted the "Diamond Edge" brand for its superior line of cutlery. This brand became a favorite during that time. It was manufactured by current companies such as the Camillus Cutlery Company of New York, to the specifications of Shapleigh. Shapleigh Hardware Company ceased business in 1960 when they sold their stock to the Val Test Distributors, Chicago, Illinois.

Collectible rating for original Shapleigh: High

Val Test knives: Average

Stampings:

A diamond with D.E. enclosed and Shapleigh Hdw. Co., St. Louis, Mo. written around the diamond

Norvel-Shapleigh Hdw. Co., St. Louis, Mo.

Current stamping: None, discontinued

NOTE: The Imperial Knife Co. of Providence, Rhode Island produced a pocketknife with "Diamond Edge" etched on the blade and "D.E." stamped on the shield in 1966.

The E. C. Simmons Company Hardware was organized in 1869 in St. Louis, Missouri. It adopted "Keen Kutter" as the trademark for a line of superior cutlery. It was manufactured to their specifications by other companies such as Camillus Cutlery of New York and by the Walden Knife Company of Walden, New York, of which they acquired control in 1902. The Winchester Arms Company's cutlery division merged in partnership, and the Walden Cutlery plant was moved to New Haven where they continued to make "Keen Kutter" and Winchester brand knives until 1940 when Winchester found it necessary to fill government contracts for guns used in WWII.

In 1940, the E.C. Simmons Company was taken over by the Shapleigh Hardware Company, which continued the "Keen Kutter" brand until 1960 but did not continue the Simmons name. As pointed out earlier, the Val Test Distributors bought the Shapleigh Hardware Company in 1960 which is still producing the "Keen Kutter" brand of pocketknives.

Collectible rating: High

Stampings were as follows:

Oak Leaf (under leaf)

Keen Kutter, E. C. Simmons Hdw. Co., St. Louis, Mo. (enclosed by a keystone emblem)

Keen Kutter, St. Louis, Mo.
Current Stamping: Keen Kutter, Chicago, USA
Keen Kutter, USA
Keen Kutter, E. C. Simmons Hdw. Co., St. Louis, Mo. (enclosed by a
    keystone emblem)
Keen Kutter, St. Louis, Mo.
Current stamping: Keen Kutter, Chicago, USA
(Note: See Winchester Arms Company)

Kattle Knife. 3⅝", celluloid handle, with steer's head, 1 clip, 1 spay point blade, 1 leather punch.

Balloon Jack, 3½", red and black celluloid handle, 1 spear, pen blade.

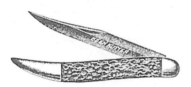

Fish Knife or Toothpick, 5", stag handle, single large saber clip blade.

Pruning Knife, 4⅛", heavy cocabolo handle, one large blade.

"Swell end Jack", 3½", celluloid handle.

Sow belly, 3", bone handle.

SHAPLEIGH POCKET KNIVES

Physican or Doctor's Knife, 3⁵/₈", bone handles.

Easy Open Jack, 2³/₄", fancy celluloid handles.

Barlow, 3¹/₂", rough sawed bone handles.

Serpentine Jack, 3", fancy celluloid handles.

Equal End Pen, 3¹/₈", bone handles.

Humpback Jack, 3³/₄", crown bolster, bone handles.

E.C. SIMMONS KNIVES

3¹/₄", smooth black fibre handle, one large eraser blade.

Barlow. 5", bone handle, one large blade.

4", stag handle, 1 clip and 1 pen blade.

Barlow. 3³/₈", bone handle,
one large blade.

285

SMITH & WESSON ARMS COMPANY
Springfield, Massachusetts C. 1974 –

In 1974 Smith & Wesson Arms Company, one of our country's great makers of side arms, produced a series of knives designed by the outstanding custom knifemaker Blackie Collins. These knives were 440 SS with Wessonwood handles, nickel silver bolsters, and guards. Only one of the series, the number 606 dropped point, was a folding hunter, and the other six were sheath knives. All are stamped with the famous Smith & Wesson logo and trademark and are fitting companions to the Smith & Wesson side arms. The series are already good collector items, though rather expensive for a new collector.

About 1980 a new series mostly consisting of lockback, folding hunter type knives was introduced at a more moderate price.

Collectible rating: High

Stampings and logo: Smith & Wesson (logo in circle)

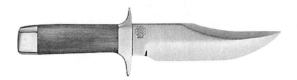

Bowie. Model 6010

Outdoorsman. Model 6020

Survival. Model 6030

286

SMITH & WESSON KNIVES

Sunfish.

Folding Hunter. Model 6060

SPYDERCO CUTLERY CO. INC.
P. O. Box 800
Golden, Colorado C. 1980 –

This company was originated by Sal Glesser, who introduced the first line of good quality "Clipit" knives, so called because they contained a permanent steel clip for securing them to one's clothing (belt, pocket, etc.). This is presumably the same reason it is labelled the "Spyder Knife."

The "Spyder," by most opinion, is by appearance a particularly ungainly knife. Perhaps its only original features are the high quality stainless steel and the conspicuous opening hole in its humpbacked blades.

Although the above features, along with the knives' efficient cutting ability, seem to constitute the main reasons for its rising popularity, it is still unlikely to take any ribbons in a beauty contest.

The second model, the "Mariner," came with an unusual two-step serrated "Spyder" edge. Since then, several new models have been added for particular type tasks.

These knives are designed for use, rather than as collector items. They are not cheap gadgets, but are rather expensive quality tools that are built for tough usage.

Collectible rating: Good

Stamping: Spyderco (with silhouette of spider)

The Spyderco Co. also imports the "Moki" Brand pocketknives from Japan. This is a limited, high-quality, hand-constructed line of art knives, designed to fill the gap between expensive custom-made knives and good, factory-made knives.

Collectible rating: High

Stamping: "Moki"

Civilian Survival, lockback blade, 5¹/₄" closed, serrated edge blade, Tuffram coated aluminum handles.

Miniature lockback, 2¹/₈" closed, serrated edge blade, abalone handles.

STAR SALES CO. INC.
Knoxville, Tennessee (Current)

Star Sales is a large import distributing firm in Knoxville, Tennessee, known chiefly to collectors as the exclusive U.S. importer of the high-quality "Kissing Cranes" (Robert Klaas) knives from Solingen, Germany. Howard Rabin is president.

Star Sales offers a wide range of merchandise from all over the world. They were among the first to import quality knives from the Orient and Japan through specifying design and material quality. When these knives are stamped with the "Star" trademark, the collector can be assured of quality.

Collectible rating: Very Good

Stamping: Star (Country of Origin)

(Note: See Robert Klaas, Kissing Cranes)

Interchangeable Clip Blade

Interchangeable Drop Point Blade

TAYLOR CUTLERY AND MANUFACTURING COMPANY
Kingsport, Tennessee C. 1975

Taylor Cutlery, located in Kingsport, Tennessee, began in 1975. The company was formed by Stewart Taylor. Taylor Cutlery's first knives were very low production items of only 600 pieces of one type. These first knives were made mostly with rosewood handles and brass bolsters. Taylor Cutlery's earlier knives carry the Bear Creek trademark with Taylor Cutlery, Kingsport, Tennessee, on the reverse side. The Bear Creek and Kingsport, Tennessee, trademarks were used until the middle of 1979.

A more common mark is the Elk Horn, of which Taylor Cutlery is the sole importer in the United States. This trademark started in 1979, and all of these knives are made with surgical steel blades. Most importantly, these Elk Horn knives are dated on the blade. Most major dealers carry the Elk Horn brand. These knives are reasonably priced and are of excellent value with the collector in mind. Taylor Cutlery knives are made of the finest materials; often the handles are genuine stag from India and genuine pearl. Taylor Cutlery is the first dealer in the world to import genuine stag handled knives from Japan.

Elk Horn also has a full line of Christmas Tree, stainless steel, and plastic handled knives. Some of these knives are original Taylor designs. A few names are Copper Indian, Pocket Rocket, Pumpkin Seed, Viper, Cobra, Shark, Panda, Stag Skinner, Stag Copperhead, and Phantom.

These knives can only enhance one's collection because of their originality, discontinued patterns, and dated blades. Many Taylor knives have been featured in the *National Knife Collector Magazine,* because Elk Horn brand was one of the main leaders in the commemorative knife field. These include:

The Hatfields and McCoys: 1,000 sets made

Virginia and West Virginia Copperheads, stag: 600 sets made

The Bad Guys, Kidd & James, stag canoes: 600 sets made

The Good Guys, Masterson & Earp, stag gunstocks: 600 sets made

Plain Series, stag: 2,000 sets made

Stag Fighting: 1,000 pieces

Robert E. Lee, stag folding hunter: 1,250 pieces

U.S. Constitution & Raleigh, Great American Ships: 1,000 sets made

Most importantly, the Tennessee, Kentucky, and Virginia Bicentennial Sunfish
   Set: 1,000 sets made

George Washington, Cherry Tree Chopper: 1,200 pieces

Other sets made are the American Indians, Great Western Explorers, Tennessee
   Presidents, Robert L. Lewis, Cowboy series; the list goes on and on.

Every commemorative set is a serial numbered, limited issue, and all have greatly increased in value.

Collectible rating: Very Good

Stampings: Bear Creek-Taylor Cutlery (on back)
Elk Horn–Taylor Cutlery (on back)
Taylor–Seto, Surgical–Japan
Taylor Cutlery (Current)
Taylor Cutlery w/Elk's head (Current)
Cherokee w/Indian profile (Current)

(See Appendix 6 for detailed Taylor price guide.)

Elk Horn Hunter (10-814). 5¼" in length, genuine deer stag handle, nickel silver bolsters, and stainless blade.

Viper (10-815). 3½" closed, genuine deer stag handles, stainless steel blade with nickel silver bolster.

TAYLOR CUTLERY KNIVES

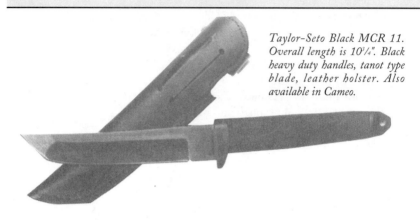

Taylor-Seto Black MCR 11. Overall length is 10¾". Black heavy duty handles, tanot type blade, leather holster. Also available in Cameo.

Taylor-Seto Brass Manila Folder. Solid brass handles, surgical steel blade, 5" closed.

Taylor-Seto Bone Butterfly. Smooth bone handles with brass on each end, surgical steel blade, 5" closed.

Taylor-Seto Butterfly Skinner. Features surgical steel blade with a gut hook, sandalwood handles.

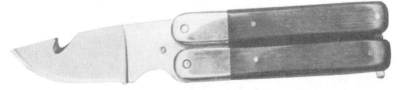

292

TAYLOR'S EYE WITNESS
Sheffield, England C. 1836 –

This company was established in 1836 in Sheffield, England, and is still active today. In 1948 they acquired Saynor, Cooke, and Ridal, and in 1951 they acquired Southern & Richardson cutlery firms.

They have now reduced the variety and patterns of their pocketknives to small numbers and use very little natural materials for handles, but older patterns are well made and actively sought by collectors.

Collectible rating: Very Good

Stampings: Taylor's Eye Witness (Written around an eye)

ULSTER KNIFE COMPANY
Ellenville, New York C. 1872

This company was founded by Sheffield Cutlers in Ellenville, New York, in 1872. It was acquired by Dwight Divine & Sons four years later in 1876. In 1947, it was again sold, this time to the Imperial Knife Company of Providence, Rhode Island, and placed under the leadership of "Uncle" Henry Baer, who also acquired the Schrade-Walden Cutlery Company. This accounts for the "Old Timer" shields found on some Ulster knives. However, both continue to produce knives under their respective trademarks.

Being one of our older American cutlery companies, the collectible rating for Ulster knives is: High

Their stampings were:

Ulster, Dwight Divine & Sons, USA

Ulster Cutlery Company

Ulster Knife Co.

Ulster, USA (current)

Ulster-Scout Knife. Genuine Staglon handle, four blades: spear, can opener, screwdriver, cap lifter & leather punch. Nickel silver oval shield, bolsters & shackle, 3³/₄" closed.

ULSTER KNIVES

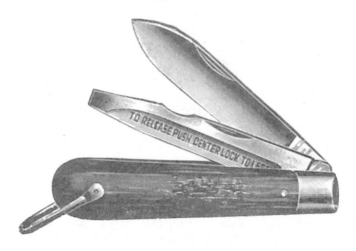

Ulster Electrician's Knife. Mahogany grained plastic handle with ring shackle attached, two blades: one spear cutting and one screwdriver, high carbon steel, polished finish, screwdriver blade etched.

Ulster Fruit & Meat Sampling Knife. One long stainless steel high carbon spear-shaped blade, full mirror polished. Molded plastic Ivoroid handle, 5" closed.

UNITED CUTLERY COMPANY
Sevierville, Tennessee C. 1985

A group of businessmen that included John Parker, Kevin Pipes, Phillip Martin, and David Hall established this company in 1985 as the Twin Mountain Distributing Company. The name was changed later to United Cutlery Corp.

In 1985 they began manufacturing a line of knives along with Boker, Germany. These knives were stamped United/Boker. The line was discontinued in 1990, and the firm reverted mostly to distributing fine old German-made brands.

However, they do own the "Rigid Trademark," and still produce knives bearing their own "United" stamping. Among their popular reproductions are the "movie" knives, such as the "Rambo III" and the "Indiana Jones" knives.

Collectible rating: Good

Stampings: "United/Boker"

"United" (with Globe outline)

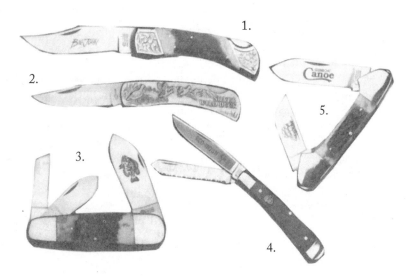

1. Big John
2. Silver Wild Duck
3. Sunfish Whittler

4. Red Injun, United/Boker
5. Gunboat Canoe

UTICA CUTLERY COMPANY
Utica, New York C. 1910

This company was established in Utica, New York, in 1910. It produced quality knives and used the best of the old-time handle materials. It also made contract and advertising knives for other companies.

They probably produced the "Blake & Lamp" muskrat as a contract knife.

About 1925, they changed their stamp from Utica Cutlery Co., Utica, NY, to Kutmaster USA.

In the past, Utica produced some of the finest American-made knives, but their overall production was not great. A "bullet" pattern Utica with a buffalo head shield is a rare and valuable prize for collectors today.

Collectible rating: Very High

Stampings: Utica Cutlery Co., Utica, N.Y.

Current stampings: Kutmaster, USA

VALLEY FORGE CUTLERY COMPANY
Newark, New Jersey C. 1892 – 1950

The Valley Forge Cutlery Company began making knives and other cutlery in 1892 in Newark, New Jersey. It was acquired by the Herman Boker & Company of New York in 1916.

The plant, under the management of Edward Grafmueller, president, continued to produce Valley Forge brand knives along with Boker, USA brands, until the Valley Forge trademark was discontinued in 1950.

Valley Forge logo (a VF inside a circle) was not used prior to 1916.

Collectible rating: High

Stamping & logo:

Valley Forge, Newark, N.J.

VF (inside circle)

(Note: See Boker Cutlery Company)

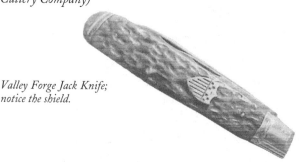

*Valley Forge Jack Knife;
notice the shield.*

VAN CAMP HARDWARE & IRON COMPANY
C. 1876 – 1960
CAPITAL CUTLERY CO.
Indianapolis, Indiana, C. 1904 – 1948

The Van Camp Hardware and Iron Company was established in 1876 by Cortland Van Camp. In 1904, they formed Capital Cutlery Company to make their own brand of knives. Though Van Camp Hardware is still in business, it ceased making its own knives in 1948. Contract knives under the Van Camp brand were discontinued in 1960.

There is no known connection between Van Camp knives and the "pork 'n beans" company.

Collector rating: Very Good

Stampings: Van Camp Hdw. Co.
   Capital Cut. Co.
   Van Camp USA
   Van Camp H&I Co.
   Vanco, Indpl.

Current stamping: None

"Moose", 3⅜", bone handles.

Whittler, 3¼", bone handles.

England Pen w/top bolsters, 3", bone handles.

Serpentine Stock Knife, 3¼", celluloid handles.

Cattle Knife, 3½", bone handles.

VICTORINOX
Ibach, Switzerland

Victorinox Cutlery is entering its second century as a manufacturer of what may very well be the most recognizable and most copied knife in the world. The multi-tooled knife, "The Swiss Army Knife," has been carried in the pockets of businessmen, Boy Scouts, Swiss soldiers (of course), conquerors of Mt. Everest, explorers of the tropics, adventurers and scientists on expeditions to both poles, on space shuttle missions, and to the moon. They have even found places for themselves in the New York Museum of Modern Art and the Munich State Museum of Applied Art.

Although most have red Delrin composition handles with the "Swiss Cross of Helvetia" as a shield, some do not. All 98 models, from the "Champ" to the one blade "BSA Sentry," have the same quality workmanship, metal, and lifetime warranty. Many seem like miniature tool boxes.

No knife collection is complete without at least one Swiss Army Knife.

Collectible Rating: Good

Current stampings: Victorinox, Switzerland
    Stainless, Rosterfi

Logo/shield: Cross of Helvetia

Swiss Champ. Mother-of-pearl handle.

Swiss Champ. 3½" closed.

Rocknife. Handle made of Andeer granite from Switzerland.

VICTORINOX IMPLEMENT ILLUSTRATIONS

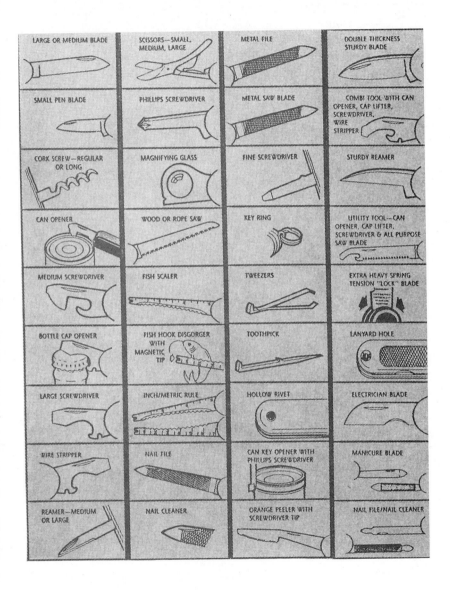

VOSS CUTLERY COMPANY
Solingen, Germany C. 1880 –

The Voss Cutlery Company was established about 1880 and for nearly a century was the exclusive distributor of the "Hen & Rooster" brand knives. Although the knives were made by Bertram Cutlery Company, the "Hen & Rooster" trademark became almost synonymous with the Voss Cutlery Company name since the Hen & Rooster logo was stamped on the front tang and Voss Cutlery Co., Solingen, on the back tang. Some collectors still say they believe the Voss Cutlery Hen & Rooster is superior because it had to meet Voss's specification. Some knives were stamped Voss Cut. Co., Solingen, only. In the early 1970s the Voss Cutlery Co. was acquired by Cole National Corporation and is still in operation.

Collectible rating: High

Stampings:

Hen & Rooster (With Voss Cut. Co., Solingen, on back)

Current stampings: Voss Cutlery Co.

No. 544
Pen.

No. 652 P. ST.
1/2 Whittler.

WADE AND BUTCHER
Sheffield, England C. 1819 –

This firm was established in 1819 in Sheffield, England, being one of the older original Sheffield cutlery firms. They specialized more in razors and fixed-blade cutlery but have produced pocketknives in limited numbers over the many years past. Being rare and of excellent quality, their knives bring high collector prices today.

Collectible rating: Very High

Stamping and logo: (An arrow and cross)

WALDEN KNIFE COMPANY
Walden, New York C. 1870 – 1923

This firm was formed by a group of workers from the New York Knife Company in 1870, and incorporated as the Walden Knife Co. in 1874. In 1902, the E.C. Simmons Co., a large hardware firm of St. Louis, Mo., took control of the firm to make their "Keen Kutter" brand knives. Simmons enlarged the plant, and during WWI, it ran to full capacity.

After the war, in 1922, Simmons merged with Winchester, and it was decided it would be more economical to make both "Keen Kutter" knives and Winchester knives in their New Haven plant. They proceeded to move both workers and machinery to New Haven, and although Walden and Keen Kutter brand knives were made until 1927, the plant was closed in 1923.

Collectible rating: Very High

Stampings: Walden Knife Co., Walden, N.Y.

(Note: See E. C. Simmons Co. and Winchester Arms Company)

WALLKILL RIVER WORKS
(See New York Knife Co.)

WENGER
Dele'mont, Switzerland

Reverend Theodore Wenger was a community leader in the Jura region of Switzerland during the latter part of the 19th century. This region is located in the French speaking section of the country around the village of Dele'mont. Reverend Wenger, trained as a journeyman cutler, had the skills of a diplomat, negotiator, mediator, and entrepreneur, and the respect given to a man of God. He used these skills and his position to convince local cutlers to work together instead of undercutting each other. He was able to organize them into a consortium, which allowed them to pool their resources and their knifemaking skills so that the community could prosper.

In 1893, Reverend Wenger was asked to head this consortium and by 1908 it began providing half of the knives for the Swiss Army. Today, it still produces 50% of the knives for the Swiss Army! It calls its knives "genuine" (Victorinox, the other producer of Swiss Army knives, calls its knives "original") Swiss Army Knives. Wenger cutlery includes some 200 different configurations, including 10 left-handed models. Their knives are handled in Teuite Butgrate scales, and the blades are hardened to "C" 54-56 on the Rockwell scale. About half of the company's production is exported to the United States each year. Currently, the Surees Buck line of multifunction pocketknives is being produced to Buck's specifications by Wenger. All their knives carry a lifetime guarantee.

There certainly is enough variety in Wenger knives to make collecting them a challenge even for the most seasoned collector.

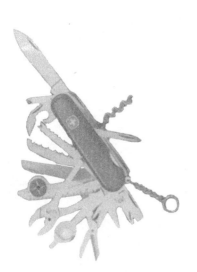
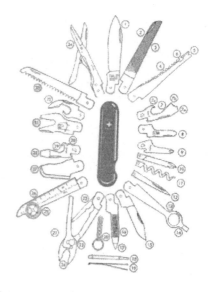

WESTERN CUTLERY COMPANY
Boulder, Colorado C. 1920 – 1991

The Western Cutlery Company was established as the Western States Cutlery Company in Boulder, Colorado, in 1920. It was founded by Harvey N. Platts, the husband of Deborah Case Platts of the Case Cutlery family. Harvey had worked for Case and Cattaraugus before his health necessitated a move west.

In 1940, H.N. retired and left his factory to his sons, Harlow and Reginald. They ran the business together until 1950 when Reginald left the company; Harlow and his son Harvey were left in charge.

About 1956, the Western States Cutlery Company changed its name to Western Cutlery Company. Their stamping was also changed to Western USA.

In 1978 the company moved from Boulder, Colorado, to Longmont, Colorado. Then in the spring of 1984, Harvey Platts retired, and the company was purchased by Coleman, the camping supply company. The existing management was retained as were the traditional stampings. Some changes were made in patterns and designs. During this time, Western had a custom knifemaking division with full-time custom makers and three full-time scrimshaw artists.

In the spring of 1990, Coleman relinquished their interests to a group of investors and the company operated again under the name of Western Cutlery. Though sales increased and the company began a new road to prosperity, the debts incurred in the '80s became too much to withstand. In the late summer of 1991, Western Cutlery went bankrupt and on August 22, 1991, its assets were sold at auction.

Camillus Cutlery purchased the Western trademarks and will continue to market Western brand knives.

Stampings:

Western States, Boulder, Colo.

Western, Boulder, Colo.

Westmark USA

West-Cut

Western-USA

Westaco-USA

Barlow
No. 6211. Overall size 3³/₈".
Smooth bone stag handles.

Stock
No. 2100 Overall size 5¹/₄". Heavy
pearl composition handles. Also made
with lighter pearl handles. No.
2100V. Assorted handles No. 3100.
Bone stag handles No. 6100.

Swell Center Pen/Stock
No. 2356F. Overall size 3". Pearl
composition handles. Also with bone
stag handles No. 6356F.

Folding Hunter
No. Y125 Overall size 5¹/₂". Amber
composition handles. Also made with
pearl composition handles No. 2125.

No. 105PB. Safety Push Button
Knife. Dagger type, 4" long. Brass
lined, assorted non-breakable pyralin
handles.

Folding Hunter
No. 6274C. Size 3⁷/₈". Nickel silver
bolsters and linings. Bone stag handles.

Office Pen
No. 2258. Overall size 3⁵/₈". Pearl
composition handles. Also made in
smaller sizes 3¹/₄" long No. 2259.

Muskrat
No. X2365. Overall size 3³/₈". Pearl
composition handles. Also with assorted
composition handles No. X365

Trapper
*No. 52094C. Overall size 4³/₈".
Genuine buckhorn handles. Also
made with pearl composition handles
No. 22094C.*

Stock
*No. X6342. Overall size 3¹/₂". Bone
stag handles.*

Folding Hunter
*No. 5230 Overall size 4¹/₂".
Genuine buckhorn handles. Also
with heavy pearl composition
handles No. 2230. Also with
single heavy sabre blade bone
stag handles No. 6130.*

Pen Springer
*Safety Push Button Knife.
Overall 3¹/₄". Assorted non-
breakable Pyralin handles. Also
supplied in smaller size. 2³/₄"
long our No. 1002 Jr.*

*No. 48BGH. Blade 4³/₈". Overall size
8¹/₄". Assorted orange, yellow and
green molded tenite handles. Finnish
type Hunting Knife with deep blood
groove in blade. Supplied with a fine
quality attractively embossed sheath
with an inside wooden lining to prevent cutting.*

Florist
*No. 4149F. Overall size 3³/₄". Ivory
composition handles.*

*No. 577 Blade 5". Overall size 9".
Genuine buckhorn handles. Deep
blood groove in blade. Supplied with
Finnish type sheath as shown. Also
made in leather handle No. L77. Also
made in heavy pearl composition handles No. 277.*

Folding Hunter
*No. 5227 Overall size 5¹/₄". Genuine
buckhorn handles. Also made with
bone stag handles No. 6227.*

Whittler
No. 2363. Overall size 3". Pearl composition handles. Also with bone stag handles No. 6363.

Swell Center Pen Stock
No. 6356. Overall size 3". Bone stag handles. Also with pearl composition handles No. 2356.

Granddaddy Barlow
No. 6111¹/₂". Overall size 5". Smooth bone stag handles.

No. Ax-Knife. Size of ax and handle 10¾". Blade 4¾". Finest construction and balance. Total weight in sheath 1¼ lbs. Pearl composition non-breakable handles. Ax and blade are interchangeable in the handle.

Stock
No. 6355. Overall size 3³/₈". Bone stag handles.

Folding Hunter
No. Y100BH Overall size 5¼". Amber composition handles. Also with pearl composition handles No. 2100BH.

Stock
No. X2374P. Overall size 3⁷/₈". Pearl composition handles. Also made with sheep foot blade in place of punch No. X2374.

No. 1001. Press button knife. Overall 4⁵/₈". Stag patterned handles. Made in 4¼" size No. 1001¹/₂.

Cherry Tree Chopper

No. 2219 Hatchet knife. Overall size 5". Pearl composition handles. Also with aluminum handles No. S219H.

Fish

No. A2075HSS. Overall 4⅜". Amber composition handles with hook sharpening stone. Stainless steel blades. Also made in larger size. 5" overall No. A275HSS. Also made with high carbon steel blades without stone on handle. 4⅜" size No. A2075D. 5" size No. A275D.

Scout

No. 64900. Size 3⅝". Ulster Official Scout knife. Also in less expensive knife No. X350ST with bone stag handle. With pearl composition handle X350 Comp.

No. S319. Gaff Knife. Size overall 5". Aluminum handles. Also made with pearl composition handles No. P319.

No. W49WP. Bowie Knife with Trophy Plaque.

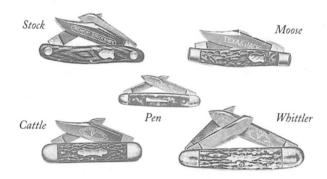

Stock

Moose

Cattle

Pen

Whittler

Stock No. R374. 3⁷/₈", brown composition handles.
Moose No. 6293J. 3⁷/₈", ender bone handles.
Cattle No. 06245¹/₂. 3⁵/₈", bone handles.
Whittler No. 53103. Stag handles, 4⁵/₈" closed.
Bullhead pen No. 9262. 3¹/₈", rainbow pearl
  Pyralin handles.

WINCHESTER ARMS COMPANY
New Haven, Connecticut C. 1919 – 1940

The Winchester Arms Company entered the cutlery business in 1919 in order to maintain their company's production capacities after World War I. They saw cutlery production as a way to offset the loss of government arms contracts. This same year they purchased the Eagle Knife Company of New Haven and the Napanoch Knife Company of Napanoch, New York. Both the men and machinery of the Napanoch Knife Company were moved to their New Haven location.

Winchester began mass production that year using the most advanced techniques of the time. Perhaps their methods were a little too far advanced because the public did not accept their use of chrome-vanadium-steel, new for knife blades. Even though vanadium steel was a better material, it did not polish like the more common high carbon steel and had to be discontinued.

In the early 1920s, Winchester, through their association with E. C. Simmons Hardware Company, gained control of Walden Knife Company of Walden, New York. Walden equipment and employees were also moved to Winchester's New Haven location. There, they continued to manufacture many of Walden's old patterns, including the one known today as the famous 1920 Winchester folding hunter.

It seemed their production of pocketknives was at last getting into full swing when once again government contracts for the manufacture of arms began coming in. With World War II in the wings, Winchester ceased their production of pocketknives and other forms of cutlery in the early 1940s in order to make arms for the government. Since then, they have considered it impractical to re-open a cutlery division.

Currently, the Winchester trademark is being used on knives produced by Blue Grass Cutlery. See pages 167 and 168.

Collectible rating: Top Priority
Stamping: Winchester Trademark, Made in USA
Current stamping: None, discontinued 1942
(Note: See Napanoch Knife Company, Eagle Knife Company, E. C. Simmons, and Walden Knife Company)

(See Appendix 7 for detailed Winchester price guide.)

WINCHESTER'S NUMBERING SYSTEM

The Winchester pattern numbering system is good, but you will not find it stamped on the blade of many of their knives. This is unfortunate since they rate top priority as collecting knives and number-stamped blades are very useful.

The first figure in Winchester's numbering system indicates the number of blades, while the second figure indicates type of handle material. The last two figures are pattern indicators only.

The second figure indicating handle materials is coded as follows:

0 or 1. Celluloid 6. Cocabolo Wood
2. Nickel Silver 7. Smooth Bone
3. Genuine Pearl 8 or 9. Jigged Bone

Physician's
No. 2380
Length closed 3½"
Pearl handle, two blades: one large spear and one pen, nickel silver bolster, cap and lining.

Congress
No. 4930
Length closed 3¼"
Stag handle, four blades: one large sheep foot, two pens and one file, nickel silver rat-tail bolsters, shield and lining.

Lobster
No. 4920
Length closed 3¼"
Stag handle, four blades: one large spear, two pens and one pick file, nickel silver tips, shield and milled lining.

Whittler
No. 3006
Length closed 3⅜"
Black celluloid handle, three blades: one large clip, one pen and one file, nickel silver bolsters, shield and lining.

Office
No. 2089
Length closed 3³/₄"
White celluloid handle marked "Office Knife," two large blades: one spear and one eraser, spear blade full polished, shadow ends, nickel silver lining.

Stock
No. 3014
Length closed 4"
Pearl gray celluloid handle, three large blades: one clip, one sheep foot, and one spay, nickel silver bolsters, shield and lining.

Four Blade Stock
No. 4962
Length closed 4"
Stag handle, four blades: one large clip, one large sheep foot, one large spay, and one patent leather punch blade, nickel silver bolsters, shield and lining.

Whittler
No. 3971
Stag handle, three blades: one large clip, one spay, and one pen, nickel silver bolsters, shield & lining.

No. 3903
Length closed 3³/₄"
Stag handle, three blades: one large clip, one large spay, and one patent leather punch blade, nickel silver bolsters, shield, and lining.

Boy's Jack
No. 2608
Length closed 3¹/₂"
Cocobola handle, two blades: one large point and one pen, steel bolster and lining, shackle, and chain.

Jack
No. 2660
Length closed 3½"
Ebony handle, two blades: one large spear and one punch blade, steel bolster, nickel silver shield, brass lining.

Capped Jack
No. 2982
Length closed 4"
Stag handle, two blades: one large spear and one pen, nickel silver bolster, cap, and shield, brass lining.

Jack
No. 2907
Length closed 4¼"
Stag handle, two blades: one large clip and one pen, nickel silver bolster, cap, and shield, brass lining.

Balloon Jack
No. 2098
Length closed 3⅛"
Green celluloid handle, two blades: one large clip and one pen, nickel silver bolster, cap, shield, and lining.

Coke
No. 2850
Length closed 3¼"
Stag handle, two blades: one large sabre clip and one pen, nickel silver bolster, cap, and shield, brass lining.

Easy Open
No. 1201
Length closed 3⅛"
Nickel silver handle, one large sheep foot blade, threaded bolster and cap, brass lining.

312

WINCHESTER POCKET KNIVES

3⅛" Equal End Jack Pattern. Spear and punch blades. Large blade fully polished. Nickel silver bolsters. Brass lining. Crest shield.
2855 – Stag handle.
2106 – Abalone blue celluloid handle.

4" Premium Stock Jack Pattern.
2928 – Clip and punch blades. Large blade fully polished. Nickel silver bolsters and lining. Stag handle. Crest shield.

2¾" Small Dog Leg Pattern. Spear and pen blades. Large blade fully polished. Nickel silver cap, bolster, and lining.
2962 – Stag handle.
2086 – Silvaleur celluloid handle.
2107 – Gold celluloid handle.

4⅛" Dagger Jack Pattern. Large sabre clip blade fully polished. Nickel silver bolster. Brass lining. Crest shield.
1923 – Stag handle.
1060 – Celluloid handle, red and black.

4" Premium Stock Jack Pattern.
2976 – Clip and pen blades. Large blade fully polished. Nickel silver bolsters and lining. Stag handle. Crest shield.

2¾" Small Dog Leg Pattern.
2361 – Spear and pen blades, fully polished. Pearl handle. Nickel silver cap, bolster, and lining.

3⅝" Equal End Jack Pattern.
2966 – Spear and pen blades. Large blade fully polished. Stag handle. Nickel silver bolsters. Brass lining. Crest shield.

4¼" Small Powder Horn Pattern. Long flat clip blade fully polished. Nickel silver bolster and cap. Brass lining. Crest shield.
1924 – Stag handle.
1051 – Celluloid handle (red and black).

2¼" Small Dog Pattern.
2856 – Small clip and pen blades. Large blade fully polished. Nickel silver cap and bolster. Nickel Silver cap and bolster. Nickel silver lining. Stag handle.

WINCHESTER POCKET KNIVES

3⁵/₈" Equal End Jack Pattern.
   2973 – Clip and pen blades. Large blade fully polished. Nickel silver bolsters. Brass lining. Stag handle. Crest shield.

5" Large Powder Horn Pattern. Large sabre clip blade. Glazed finish. Steel cap and bolster. Brass lining.
   1936 – Stag handle.
   1050 – Assorted celluloid handles: blue, red, gold

2³/₄" Curved or Serpentine Jack Pattern.
   2990 – Sabre clip and pen blades. Large blade fully polished. Stag handle. Nickel silver cap and bolster. Brass lining.

3⁵/₈" Swell End Jack Pattern.
   2994 – Spear and pen blades. Large blade fully polished. Stag handle. Steel bolster. Brass lining. Crest shield.

3³/₄" Swell Center Jack Pattern.
   2850 – Sabre clip and pen blades. Large blade fully polished. Stag handle. Nickel silver cap and long fluted bolster. Brass lining. Crest shield.

3⁷/₈" Curved Jack Pattern.
   2904 – Sabre clip and spey blades. Clip blade fully polished. Stag handle. Nickel silver cap and bolster. Nickel silver lining. Crest shield.

3⁵/₈" Swell End Jack Pattern. Spear and pen blades. Large blade fully polished. Steel cap and bolster. Brass lining. Crest shield.
   2612 – Cocabolo handle.
   2995 – Stag handle.

5¹/₄" Swell Center Hunting Jack Pattern.
   1920 – Sabre clip blade glazed finish. Nickel silver cap and bolster. Brass lining. Stag handle. Guimpe shield. Lanyard hole in cap.

3⁷/₈" Curved Jack Pattern.
   2993 – Sabre clip and pen blades. Sabre clip blade fully polished. Stag handle. Nickel silver cap and bolster. Nickel silver lining. Crest shield.

WINCHESTER POCKET KNIVES

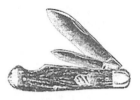

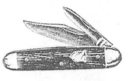

3⅝" Swell End Jack Pattern. Spear and pen blades. Easy opener. Large blade fully polished. Steel cap and bolster. Brass lining. Crest shield.
    2613 – Cocabolo handle.
    2930 – Stag handle.

3" Small Gun Stock Jack Pattern.
    2851 – Spear and pen blades. Large blade fully polished. Stag handle. Nickel silver cap and bolster. Brass lining. Crest shield.

3⅜" Equal End Jack Pattern. Sabre clip and pen blades. Large blade fully polished. Cocabolo handle. Nickel silver bolsters. Brass lining. Crest shield.
    2614 – Cocabolo handle.
    2853 – Stag handle.

3½" Swell Center Gun Stock Jack Pattern.
    2921 – Spear and pen blades. Large blade fully polished. Stag handle. Nickel silver octagon cap and bolster. Brass lining. Crest shield.

3⅞" Curved Jack Pattern.
    1937 – Sabre clip blade. Large blade fully polished. Nickel silver cap and bolster. Nickel silver lining. Stag handle. Crest shield.

3⅛" Equal End Jack Pattern. Spear and pen blades. Large blade fully polished. Nickel silver bolsters. Brass lining. Crest shield.
    2028 – Shell celluloid handle.
    2069 – Pearl blue celluloid handle.
    2665 – Ebony handle.
    2854 – Stag handle.

3⅜" Swell Center Balloon Equal End Pattern.
    2864 – Long flat clip and small clip blades. Large blade fully polished. Stag handle. Nickel silver bolsters. Brass lining. Crest shield.

3⅝" Swell Center Balloon Pattern. Long sabre clip, small clip, and pen blades. Large blade fully polished. Nickel silver bolsters and lining. Crest shield.
    3925 – Stag handle.
    3015 – Golden celluloid handle.

3⅝" Well Center Balloon Pattern.
    2908 – Long flat clip and pen blades. Large blade fully polished. Stag handle. Nickel silver bolsters and lining. Crest shield.

WINCHESTER POCKET KNIVES

3¹/₂" Swell Center Balloon Equal End Pattern.
2903 – Spear and pen blades. Large blade fully polished. Stag handle. Nickel silver bolsters. Brass lining. Crest shield.

3⁵/₈" Swell Center Balloon Pattern.
3971 – Long flat clip, spay, and pen blades. Large blade fully polished. Stag handle. Nickel silver bolsters and lining. Crest shield.

3⁷/₈" Swell Center Fluted Pattern.
2967 – Large spear and flat clip blades. Spear blade fully polished. Stag handle. Nickel silver fluted bolsters. Nickel silver lining. Crest shield.

3¹/₂" Swell Center Balloon Equal End Pattern.
3902 – Clip and two pen blades. Nickel silver bolsters. Brass lining. Stag handle. Crest shield.

3⁵/₈" Swell Center Balloon Pattern. Long flat clip, small clip and pen blades. Large blade fully polished. Nickel silver bolsters and lining. Crest shield.
3005 – Black celluloid handle.

3¹/₂" Small Balloon Cattle Pattern.
2969 – Large clip and large spay blades. Clip blade fully polished. Nickel silver fluted bolsters and lining. Stag handle. Crest shield.

3¹/₂" Swell Center Balloon Equal End Pattern.
2865 – Spear and clip blades. Spear blade fully polished. Stag handle. Nickel silver bolsters. Brass lining. Crest shield.

3¹/₂" Small Balloon Cattle Pattern.
3915 – Long spear, pen and punch blades. Large blade fully polished. Stag handle. Nickel silver bolsters and lining. Crest shield.

3⁵/₈" Swell Center Balloon Pattern. Long flat clip, spay, and punch blades. Large blade fully polished. Nickel silver bolsters and lining. Crest shield.
3972 – Stag handle.
3002 – Iridescent celluloid handle.

WOSTENHOLM (GEORGE) I-XL CUTLERY
Sheffield, England C. 1745 –

This old firm was established in 1745 by George Wostenholm in Sheffield, England. This was one of the first large makers of pocketknives. In 1787 they were granted the trademark I-XL, which is still in use today. When the founder died, his son, Henry Wostenholm, continued the business. Upon the death of Henry, his son, George, became the sole owner of the business. In 1848, he purchased the old Washington Works and moved the firm into that building.

In 1971, the firm was purchased by the Joseph Rodgers & Sons firm of Sheffield to form the Rodgers-Wostenholm firm, and in 1977 the firm was acquired by Schrade Cutlery Co., a division of Imperial Knife Co. of Providence, Rhode Island. The Sheffield firm is still in operation producing the I-XL brand knives, some of which are stamped the "Schrade-Wostenholm I-XL," and sold in the U.S.A. at the present time.

Collectible rating: High

Stampings:

George Wostenholm Cutlery Co., Shef., Eng.

Wostenholm, Sheffield, Eng.

George Wostenholm I-XL, England

I-XL Eng.

Schrade-Wostenholm, I-XL, Sheffield, Eng.

(Note: See Schrade Cutlery Company, Imperial Cutlery Company, and Joseph Rodgers & Sons)

*Pruner Pattern. Length 4¹/₈",
polished steel rat-tail bolsters.*

*Senator Pattern. Length 3³/₈",
German silver flush bolsters.*

*Warncliffe Pruning Pattern. Length
3⁷/₈", polished steel rat-tail bolsters.*

*Premium Stock Pattern. Length 3⁷/₈",
German silver scored bolsters.*

WOSTENHOLM CUTLERY

Gun Stock Pattern. Length 3⁵/₈",
polished steel rat-tail bolsters and
German silver flush caps.

Cattle Pattern. Length 3⁵/₈", German
silver flush bolsters.

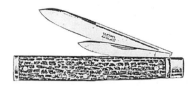

Physican
Patent stag handle, brass lining, flush
steel bolster, German silver cap, 3³/₄" long.

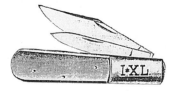

Barlow
Bone handle, steel lining and bolster,
3¹/₂" long.

Lockback
No. 17015. Patent stag handle, steel
lining and bolster. 4¹/₂" long.

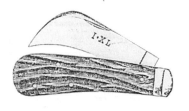

(Pruner)
No. 7690. Corn, genuine stag handle,
steel hollow glazed bolster, 3¹/₄" long.

(Pruner)
No. 14151. Corn, iron handle, steel
hollow glazed bolster, 3³/₄" long.

Congress
No. 15297. Ivory handle, brass lining,
3³/₄" long.

WOSTENHOLM CUTLERY

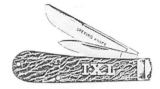

Boy's Knife
Iron handle and hollow bolster, 3¼" long.
No. 13786. One large spaying blade
No. 11169. One large spaying blade and one small spear blade.

Corn
No. 12825. Ivory handle, brass lining, 3¼" long.

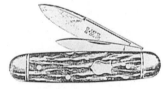

Equal End Jack
No. 2043. Patent stag handle, brass lining, German silver bolster and cap, 3½" long.

Capped Jack
No. 17011. Patent stag handles, brass lining, German silver bolster and cap, 3½" long.

Office
No. 16584. Celluloid ivory handle, brass lining, 3¼" long.

Congress
No. 2191. Stag handle, brass lining, steel bolsters. 3¼" long.
No. 2192. 3½" long.
No. 2193. 3¾" long
No. 2194. 4" long.

Congress
No. 17035. Patent stag handle, brass lining, German silver bolsters, 3¼" long.

Congress
No. 2158. Patent stag handle, brass lining, steel bolsters. 2⅞" long.
No. 2160. 3¼" long.
No. 2162. 3¾" long.
No. 2163. 4" long.

WOSTENHOLM CUTLERY

Physican
No. 17005. Patent stag handle, brass lining, flush steel bolster, German silver cap, 3¼" long.

Congress
No. 2152. Patent stag handle, brass lining, steel bolsters. 2" long.
No. 2153. 3" long.
No. 2154. 3¼" long.
No. 2156. 4" long.

Cattle
No. 17006G. Patent stag handle, brass lining, flush steel bolster, German silver cap, 3¼" long.

Crown Jack
No. 2054. Patent stag handle, brass lining, German silver bolsters, 3½" long.

Jack
No. 17003. Patent stag handle, brass lining, German silver bolster and cap, 3¼" long.

½ Hawk/Pruner
No. 6920. Genuine stag handle, steel lining and hollow bolster, 3¼" long.

Jack
No. 17001. Patent stag handles, brass lining, German silver bolster, 3¼" long.

Jack
No. 7030. Genuine stag handle, steel lining and hollow bolster, 3¼" long.

WOSTENHOLM CUTLERY

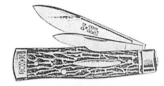

Gunstock Jack
No. 17061. Patent stag handle, steel lining and bolster, German silver cap, 3½" long.

Jack
German stag handle, 3½" long. No. 7001. Steel lining and flush bolster. No. 7005. Brass lining, German silver bolster.

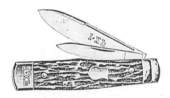

Gunstock Jack
No. 17009. Patent stag handle, steel lining and bolster, German silver cap, 3½" long.

Lockback Jack
No. 17063. Patent stag handle, steel lining and bolster, 4½" long.

Budding
No. 7691. Black buffalo handle, brass lining, German silver bolster, 4¾" long.

Pen
No. 2294. Patent stag handle, brass lining, German silver bolsters. 3¼" long.

Whittler Pen
No. 2144. Patent stag handle, brass lining, German silver tips, 3¼" long. Tip holsters

Pen
No. 2240S. Patent stag handle, brass lining, steel hollow bolsters, 3½" long.

321

WOSTENHOLM CUTLERY

Warncliffe
No. 2217. Patent stag handle, brass lining, German silver tips, 3¼" long.

Pen
No. 2141. Patent stag handle, brass lining, German silver tips, 3" long.

Whittler
No. 17023. Patent stag handle, brass lining, German silver bolsters, 3¼" long.

Pen
No. 2060. Brass lining, 3¼" long, patent stag handle. Also with handles of buffalo, ivory, or pearl.

Whittler
No. 17020. Patent stag handle, brass lining, steel hollow bolsters, 3½" long.

Congress
No. 6587T. Genuine stag handle, steel lining, and bolsters, 3¼" long.

Custom-made knives are great for the connoisseur collector, discerning art investor, and the user who must own the best. Since custom-made knives have also evolved into a new art form, collecting in this field is undoubtedly on the highest plane in cutlery collecting today.

In the early twentieth century, custom knifemaking almost became a lost art. This was because many of our reputable old American cutlery firms, such as John Russell, W.R. Case, Remington, and Winchester, were turning out an unprecedented number of variety and patterns of the finest knives ever known. Also, knives were inexpensive then, because American firms had to compete with English and German imports. One could buy anything from a big Russell "Buffalo Skinner" to a fancy pearl penknife for less than a buck. It is small wonder, then, that there was little demand for custom-made cutlery at the time.

Nevertheless, throughout the 1920s and 1930s and during the Depression years, such great artists as Bill Scagel worked on producing fine custom knives for little more than the pleasure derived from the art. Then in the 1940s, H.H. Buck and Bo Randall arrived on the scene to help as much as they could to supply the needs of our fighting men of WWII, men who had become very disenchanted with the GI knives they were given as a part of their equipment for combat.

In all fairness to our cutlery manufacturers, we believe the poor quality of GI knives was due to our government's crash production contracts. But knowing this did not allay our servicemen's desire for something better. Following the war, sheath knives became generally unpopular. The exceptions, of course, were times when those great custom-made knives (encountered on rare occasions) were remembered. Thus, the custom knifemaker found the field wide open, and filling this void during the 1950s and 1960s resulted in a virtual renaissance of cutlery crafting by American artists.

So it was from a very lonely beginning that custom knife-making has grown, until thousands of fine craftsmen are now working in the field. Knives made by Bill Scagel and sold for $30 or less have a collector value of well into the thousands today. Early-made Buck and Randall knives which sold for $30 to $50 will very handily bring many times these prices.

This folding hunter by Frank Centofante of Madisonville, Tennessee, is an excellent example of knives as artistic treasures.

When the art began to reawaken, production was confined almost entirely to fixed-blade knives, that is, with the notable exception of that of the old master who began it all, William Wales Scagel. Oddly enough, in many of Scagel's marvelous fixed-blade knives, he inserted an extra folding blade in the handle. Why he did this is not known, but Scagel was not only a master of design but an innovative genius as well. Certainly, there was no need to carry a folder in one's pocket for lighter work with these unique knives.

With the passing of time, more and more custom makers began adding folding knives to their line. Some switched to making only folding knives. Although construction is more complex and more parts are used, there is a wider market for folders, and in general, they bring a higher price. The earlier ones to appear were the large folding hunter types, with back lock blades for additional safety. This bulkiness, of course, played a large part in the present popularity of belt sheaths, because they were too hefty to carry in the pockets. Recently though, the trend seems to be veering toward lighter and smaller versions that are exquisitely art worked. Of course, all of the new artists working today will not make the grade. Some of their knives will not be top quality. But all are trying and, in many ways, each and every knife they produce will be "one of a kind."

Tommy McNabb (front) and Travis Daniel (back) of Carolina Custom Knives at work in their shop.

In the effort to meet consumer specifications, variations in materials will range from the ordinary to precious gems and metals. The grades of art work, artistry of design, and workmanship will be extremely wide. Therefore, a price guide for the custom knifemaker's knives would neither be fair to the maker nor would it achieve any degree of accuracy. Even with the growing number of makers and the beginning of competition, every custom maker is still entitled to set his own prices according to his customer's specifications. The value of the knife he produces cannot be judged until it is completed and in hand.

Because of this, it is difficult to provide you with a current price list on custom knifemaker's products. Instead we are providing you with a list of the names and addresses of the members of the Knifemakers Guild. We suggest that you contact the custom maker, and ask him for a brochure picturing some of his knives and a price list of his knives. Be sure to ask about anticipated delivery time on a custom knife. It may be that you will want to check the collector market if waiting time is too long.

Some guidelines for buying custom-made knives are as follows:

It is advisable to study the background of the maker as thoroughly as you would study a racing form before betting on a horse. Of course, the makers with the established reputations are the surest bets, but their knives will just as surely cost you more.

Contact the Knifemakers Guild of America, P.O. Box 1019, Madisonville, TN 35354-5019 for a brochure on the Knifemakers' Guild and its functions. Then, contact craftsmen you are interested in for their personal brochures. (Send postage.)

Read and study all you can on materials (steels, etc.) used in knife construction, and whether forging or grinding is used. By all means be familiar with the tempering and heat treating (drawing) processes used. (In many instances the collector makes a choice between the modern and the traditional.)

In the matter of art work (artistry of design and art materials), the collector should strive to build expertise. A good background in cultural history and frequent consultations with more experienced collectors should help. If it is art you are collecting, you must know how to distinguish classic art from sheer gaudiness.

Take as much time as you can to inspect the knife and the artist who made it. Then, if everything about them pleases you, the chances are that others will feel the same way. If these "educated hunches" are backed up by experience in the field, you may have picked a winner.

These guidelines may give you a little "edge" in collecting custom cutlery or at least increase your pleasure in the game.

KNIFEMAKERS GUILD

Adams, Les
6413 N.W. 200 St.
Hialeah, FL 33015
305-625-1699

Aida, Yoshihito
26-7, Narimasu 2-chome
Itabashi-Ku, Tokyo, Japan 175-0094
81-3-3939-0052
Fax: 81-3-3939-0058
web: http://riverside-land.com

Allen, Mike "Whiskers"
12745 Fontenot Acres Rd.
Malakoff, TX 75148
903-489-1026
e-mail: whiskersknives@aol.com
web: www.kmg.org/mallen

Alverson, R.V.
215 111 Street
Orofino, ID 83544
208-476-3999
e-mail: alversonknives@aol.com
web: rvalversonknives.com

Anderson, Michael
1741 Weiler Blvd.
Fort Worth, TX 76112
817-496-1964
Fax: 817-496-3706

Ankrom, W.E.
14 Marquette Dr.
Cody, WY 82414
307-587-3017
Fax: 307-587-3017

Arnold, Joe
47 Patience Cres.
London, Ontario, Canada N6E 2K7
519-686-2623
Fax: 519-686-9859
e-mail: j.arnold@odyssey.on.ca

Ashworth, Boyd
3135 Barrett Ct.
Powder Springs, GA 30127-1657
770-943-4963
e-mail: ashworthknives@aol.com

Atkinson, Dick
General Delivery
Wausau, FL 32463
850-638-8524
Fax: 850-638-8524

Bailey, Joseph D.
3213 Jonesboro Dr.
Nashville, TN 37214
615-889-3172
e-mail: jbknfemkr@aol.com

Bardsley, Norman
197 Cottage St.
Pawtucket, RI 02860
401-725-9132
Fax: 401-725-9132

Barnett, Van
168 Riverbend Blvd.
St. Albans, WV 25177
304-727-5512
e-mail: artknife@vanbarnett.com
web: www.vanbarnett.com

Barr, A.T.
P.O. Box 828
Nicholasville, KY 40340-0828
859-885-1042
Fax: 859-887-5400
e-mail: at-barr@worldnet.att.net
web: www.customknives.com

Barry, James J. III
115 Flagler Promenade No.
West Palm Beach, FL 33405
561-832-4197

Bartlow, John
5078 Coffeen Ave.
Sheridan, WY 82801
307-673-4941
e-mail: jbartlow@vcn.com

Baskett, Gene
427 Sutzer Creek Rd.
Eastview, KY 42732-9753
270-862-5019
web: www.geocities.com/baskettknives/

Batson, James
176 Brentwood Lane
Madison, AL 35758
256-971-6860 or 912-383-6776
e-mail: jbbatson@hiwaay.net

Beauchamp, Gaetan
125 de la Riviere Stoneham
Quebec, Canada GOA 4PO
418-848-1914
Fax: 418-848-6859
web: http://pages.infinit.net.couteau/

Beckett, Norman
1501 N. Chaco Ave.
Farmington, NM 87401
505-325-4468
e-mail: nbknives@yahoo.com

Beers, Raymond
8 Manor Brook Road
Monkton, MD 21111
410-472-2229; Fax: 410-472-9136
or 2501 Lake Front Dr.
Lake Wales, FL 33853
941-696-3036
Fax: 941-696-9421

Bennica, Charlie
Chemin du Salet
Moules et Baucels, France 34190
04-67-73-42-40
Fax: 04-67-73-42-40
e-mail: b-ni-k@club-internet.FR

Black, Tom
921 Grecian N.W.
Albuquerque, NM 87107
505-344-2549
Fax: 505-344-7581

Blackton, Andrew
12521 5th Isle
Bayonet Point, FL 34667
727-869-1406

Blanchard, Gary
3507 S. Maryland Pkwy. #E
Las Vegas, NV 89109
702-733-8333
Fax: 702-732-0333

Bloomer, Alan T.
P.O. Box 154, 116 E. 6th St.
Maquon, IL 61458
309-875-3583

Bojtos, Arpad
Dobsinskeho 10
98403 Lucenec, Slovakia
00421-863-4323214

Borger, Wolf
Benz Str. 8
Graben-Neudorf 76676, Germany
07255-72303
Fax: 07255-72306
e-mail: wolf.borger@t-online.de
web: www.wolf-borger-messer.de

Bose, Tony
7252 N. Co. Rd. 300 E.
Shelburn, IN 47879
812-397-5114

Bradley, Dennis
2410 Bradley Acres Rd.
Blairsville, GA 30512
706-745-4364

Brandsey, Edward
335 Forest Lake Dr.
Milton, WI 53563
608-868-9010
e-mail: edchar2@hotmail.com

Bray, W. Lowell Jr.
6931 Manor Beach Rd.
New Port Richey, FL 34652
727-846-0930
Fax: 727-847-8924
e-mail: brayknives@aol.com

Breshears, Clint
1261 Keats St.
Manhattan Beach, CA 90266
310-374-1398
Fax: 310-372-0739
e-mail: breshears2@earthlink.net

Britton, Tim
5645 Murray Rd.
Winston-Salem, NC 27106
336-922-9582
e-mail: tbritton@timbritton.com or
timbritton@yahoo.com
web: www.timbritton.com

Broadwell, David
P.O. Box 4314
Wichita Falls, TX 76308
940-692-1727
Fax: 940-692-4003
e-mail: david@broadwell.com
web: www.david.broadwell.com

Brown, David
500 E. Main St.
Steele City, NE 68440
402-442-2308

Brown, Harold
3654 NW Hwy. 72
Arcadia, FL 34266
863-494-7514
e-mail: brknives@desoto.net

Browne, Rick
980 W. 13th St.
Upland, CA 91786
909-985-1728
Fax: 909-946-2080
e-mail: knopfi@gte.net

Buckner, Jimmy
P.O. Box 162
Putney, GA 31782
912-436-4182

Busfield, John
153 Devonshire Circle
Roanoke Rapids, NC 27870
252-537-3949
Fax: 252-537-8704
e-mail: busfield@3rd door. com
web: www.busfieldknives.com

Caldwell, Bill
255 Rebecca Dr.
West Monroe, LA 71292
318-323-3025

Callahan, Errett
2 Fredonia Avenue
Lynchburg, VA 24503
804-528-3444

Cannady, Daniel
P.O. Box 301
Allendale, SC 29810
803-584-2813
e-mail: sdnaug@avl.com
web: www.scak.org

Canter, Ron
96 Bon Air Circle
Jackson, TN 38305
731-668-1780
Fax: 731-664-2583

Capdepon, Robert
829 Vatican Rd.
Carencro. LA 70520
318-896-8753

Carson, Harold J. "Kit"
1076 Brizendine Lane
Vine Grove, KY 40175
270-877-6300
Fax: 270-877-6338
e-mail: carsonknives@kvnet.org
web: www.kvnet.org/knives

Carter, Fred
5219 Deer Creek Rd.
Wichita Falls, TX 76302
940-723-4020
Fax: 940-723-0928

Casteel, Dianna
1205 Shady Lane
Manchester, TN 37355
931-723-0851
Fax: 931-723-1856
e-mail: dcasteel@charter.net
web: www.casteelcustomknives.com

Casteel, Douglas
1205 Shady Lane
Manchester, TN 37355
931-723-0851
Fax: 931-723-1856
e-mail: dcasteel@charter.net
web: www.casteelcustomknives.com

Centofante, Frank
P.O. Box 928
Madisonville, TN 37354-0928
423-442-5767
Fax: 423-442-5767
e-mail: cento@compfxnet.com

Chamblin, Joel
296 New Hebron Church Rd.
Concord, GA 30206
770-884-9055
Fax: 770-884-9292
e-mail: ccknives@accessunited.com
web: www.chamblinknives.com

Chapo, William
45 Wilridge Rd.
Wilton, CT 06897
203-544-9424
Fax: 203-544-1080

Chase, Alex
208 E. Pennsylvania Ave.
DeLand, FL 32724
386-734-9918

Chavar, Edward
1830 Richmond Ave.
Bethlehem, PA 18018
610-865-1806

Cheatham, William
P.O. Box 636
Laveen, AZ 85339
602-237-2786

Clark, Howard F.
115 35th Place
Runnells, IA 50237
515-966-2126

Clay, Wayne
Box 125
Pelham, TN 37366
931-467-3472
Fax: 931-467-3076

Coleman, Keith
5001 Starfire Place N.W.
Albuquerque, NM 87120-2010
505-899-3783
e-mail: keith@colemanmade.com
web: www.colemanmade.com

Coleman, Vernon
141 Lakeside Park Dr.
Hendersonville, TN 37075
615-824-7002
Fax: 615-822-9560
e-mail: vernonwc@home.com

Collins, Blackie
P.O. Box 100
North, SC 29112
803-247-2169
Fax: 803-247-2938

Conley, Bob
1013 Creasy Rd.
Jonesborough, TN 37659
423-753-3302

Corbit, Gerald
1701 St. John Rd.
Elizabethtown, KY 42701
270-765-7728
e-mail: gerald.corbit@gte.net
web: www.corbits.com

Corby, Harold
218 Brandonwood Dr.
Johnson City, TN 37604
423-926-9781

Cordova, Joe
P.O. Box 977
Peralta, NM 87042
505-869-3912
Fax: 505-869-2509

Corrado, Jim
255 Rock View Lane
Glide, OR 97443
541-496-3951
Fax: 541-496-3595
e-mail: jim@corradoknives.com
web: www.corradoknives.com

Cousino, George
7818 Norfolk Dr.
Onsted, MI 49265
517-467-4911
Fax: 517-467-4911
e-mail: geocousi@excite.com

Cover, Raymond
Rt. 1, Box 194
Mineral Point, MO 63660
573-749-3783

Cox, Colin
107 N. Oxford Dr.
Raymore, MO 64083
816-322-1977
e-mail: colin4knives@aol.com

Crawford, Pat & Wes
205 N. Center
West Memphis, AR 72301
870-735-4632
Fax: 870-735-4632
e-mail: pat@crawfordknives.com
web: www.crawfordknives.com

Crowder, Bob
Box 1374
Thompson Falls, MT 59873
406-827-4754

Cruze, Dan
14406 Winterset Dr.
Orlando, FL 32832
407-277-8848

Cutchin, Roy D.
960 Hwy. 169 South
Seale, AL 36875
334-855-3080

Dailey, George E.
577 Lincoln St.
Seekonk, MA 02771
508-336-5088
Fax: 508-336-5985
e-mail: gedaily@msn.com
web: www.magnus-design.com/dailey-knives/

Dake, Charles M.
19759 Chef Menteur Hwy.
New Orleans, LA 70129
504-254-0357
Fax: 504-254-9501

Daniels, Alex
1416 County Road 415
Town Creek, AL 35672
256-685-0943
e-mail: akdknives@aol.com

Davenport, Jack
P.O. Box 451
Crystal Springs, FL 33524
352-521-4088
e-mail: jdaven@innet.com

Davidson, Edmund
3345 Va. Ave.
Goshen, VA 24439
540-997-5651
Fax: 540-997-5651

Davis, Barry
4262 U.S. 20
Castleton, NY 12033
518-477-5036
Fax: 518-477-5036

Davis, Terry A.
Box 111
Sumpter, OR 97877
541-894-2307

Davis, Vernon M.
1006 Lewis
Waco, TX 76705
254-799-7671

Davis, W.C.
19300 S. School Rd.
Raymore, MO 64083
816-331-4491

Dean, Harvey
Rt. 2 Box 137
Rockdale, TX 76567
512-446-3111
Fax: 512-446-5060
e-mail: dean@majik-net.com
web: www.hdean.tripod.com

Defeo, Robert
403 Lost Trail Dr.
Henderson, NV 89014
702-434-3717

DeFreest, William G.
P.O. Box 573
Barnwell, SC 29812
803-259-7883
Fax: 803-259-1642
e-mail: gordonknives@barnwells.com

Derr, Herbert
413 Woodland Dr.
St. Albans, WV 25177
304-727-3866
e-mail: hkderrknives@netzero.com

Dietz, Howard
421 Range Road
New Braunfels, TX 78132
830-885-4662

Dellana
168 Riverbend Blvd.
St. Albans, WV 25177
304-727-5512
e-mail: dellana@knivesbydellana.com
web: www.knivesbydellana.com

Dennehy, Dan
P.O. Box 2-F
13321 Hwy 160
Del Norte, Co 81132
719-657-2545
Fax: 719-657-2699

Dietzel, William
P.O. Box 1613
Middleburg, FL 32068
904-282-1091

Dill, Robert
1812 Van Buren Ave.
Loveland, CO 80538
970-667-5144
Fax: 970-667-5144

Dilluvio, Frank
13611 Joyce
Warren MI 48093
810-775-1216
Fax: 810-775-3330
e-mail: fjdknives@home-com
web: www.fjdknives.com

Dippold, Al
90 Damascus Lane
Perryville, MO 63775
573-547-1119
Fax: 573-547-1119
e-mail: adippold@midwest.net

Dowell, T.M.
139 N. W. St. Helens Place
Bend, OR 97701
541-382-8924
Fax: 541-382-8924
e-mail: tmdkinves@webtv.net

Downing, Larry
12268 State Rt. 181 N.
Bremen, KY 42325
502-525-3523
Fax: 502-525-3372
e-mail: downing@muhlon.com

Downing, Tom
129 South Bank St.
Cortland, OH 44410
330-637-0623
e-mail: tomsblade@aol.com

Downs, James
35 Sunset Rd.
Londonberry, OH 45647
740-887-2099

Dozier, Bob
P.O. Box 1941
Springdale, AR 72765
501-756-0023
Fax: 501-756-9139
e-mail: bobdozier@aol.com
web: www.dozierknives.com

Duff, Bill
P.O. Box 694
Virginia City, NV 89440
775-847-0566

Dunn, Steve
376 Biggerstaff Rd.
Smiths Grove, KY 42171
270-563-9830
e-mail: dunndeal@gte.net
web: www.stevedunnknives.com

Duran, Jerry
P.O. Box 80692
Albuquerque, NM 87198-0692
505-873-4676
Fax: 505-873-4676
e-mail: jtdknives@unwest.net
web: www.kmg.org/jtdknives

Easler, Russell & Paula
P.O. Box 301
Woodruff, SC 29388
864-476-7830
Fax: 864-476-3940

Eaton, Rick
9944 McCranie Rd.
Shepherd, MT 59079
406-373-0901
Fax: 406-373-0901
e-mail: rleaton@earthlink.net
web: www.eatonknives.com

Edwards, Fain
P.O. Box 280
Topton, NC 28781
828-321-3127

Elishewitz, Allen
3960 Lariat Ridge
New Braunfels, TX 78132
830-227-5325
Fax: 830-899-4595
e-mail: allen@elishewitzknives.com
web: www.elishewitzknives.com

Elliott, Jim
18175 Hwy. 98 N.
Okeechobee, FL 34972-3904
863-763-3265

Ellis, David
3505 Camino Del Rio S. #334
San Diego, CA 92108
619-285-1305
Fax: 619-285-1326
e-mail: ellis@mastersmith.com
web: www.mastersmith.com or
www.exquisiteknives.com

Embretsen, Kaj
Falnuagen 67, S-82830
Edsbyn, Sweden
+46-271-21057
Fax: +46-271-22961
e-mail: kaj.embretsen@swipnet.se
web: http://welcome.to/embrestsen_knives

Emerson, Ernest
P.O. Box 4180
Torrance, CA 90510-4180
310-212-7455
Fax: 310-793-8730
e-mail: eknives@aol.com
web: www.emersonknives.com

Ence, Jim
145 South 200 East
Richfield, UT 84701
435-896-6206

England, Virgil
7133 Arctic Blvd. #5
Anchorage, AK 99518
907-274-9494

Engle, William
16608 Oak Ridge Rd.
Boonville, MO 65233
660-882-6277

Eriksen, James T.
3830 Dividend Dr.
Garland, TX 75042
972-494-3667
Fax: 972-235-4932
e-mail: vikingknives@aol.com
web: www.vikingknives.com

Fecas, Stephen
1312 Shadow Lane
Anderson, SC 29625
864-287-4834
Fax: 864-287-4834

Ferguson, Lee
R. 2, Box 109
Hindsville, AR 72738
501-443-0084

Fiorini, Bill
P.O. Box 237
Dakota, MN 55925-0237
507-643-6946
Fax: 507-643-7946
e-mail: kokgiron@clear.lakes.com
web: www.kokametalsmiths.com

Fisher, Jay
P.O. Box 267
Magdalena, NM 87825
505-854-2118
Fax: 505-854-2118
e-mail: jayfisher@gilanet.com
web: www.gilanet.com/jayfisher/index.html

Fisk, Jerry
145 N. Park Ave.
Lockesburg, AR 71846
501-289-3240
Fax: 501-289-5465
e-mail: jfisk@cswnet.com

Fister, Jim
5067 Fisherville Rd.
Simpsonville, KY 40067
502-834-7841
e-mail: rvkeys@yahoo.com

Flournoy, Joe
5750 Lisbon Rd.
El Dorado, AR 71730
870-863-7208
Fax: 870-864-1270
e-mail: flournoy@ipa.net

Forthofer, Pete
5535 Hwy. 93 S.
Whitefish, MT 59937
406-862-2674

Fowler, Ricky
P.O. Box 339
22080 9th St.
Silverhill, AL 36576
334-945-3289
Fax: 334-945-3290
e-mail: rfowler@gulftel.com
web: http://fowlerknives.com

Fox, Paul
4721 Rock Barn Rd.
Claremont, NC 28610
828-459-2000
Fax: 828-459-9200
e-mail: laser@twave.net

Frank, Henry
13868 NW Keleka Pl.
Seal Rock, OR 97376
541-563-3041
Fax: 541-563-3041

Franklin, Michael H.
9878 Big Run Road
Aberdeen, OH 45101
937-549-2598
Fax: 937-549-2598
e-mail: hawgman@bright.net
web: http://hawgknives.com

Frazier, Ron
2107 Urbine Rd.
Powhatan, VA 23139
804-794-8561

Freer, Ralph
114 12th St.
Seal Beach, CA 90740
562-493-4925
e-mail: ralphfreer@earthlink.net

Friedly, Dennis
12 Cottontail Lane – E
Cody, WY 82414
307-527-6811

Fronefield, Daniel
137 Catherine Dr.
Hampton Cove, AL 35763
256-536-7827
e-mail: dfronfld@hiwaay.net
web: www.hiwaay.net/~dfronfld

Fuegen, Larry
617 N. Coulter Circle,
Lynx Mountain View Estates
Prescott, AZ 86303-6270
623-523-4102
e-mail: fuegen@northlink.com

Fujikawa, Shun
977-18 Sawa
Kaizuka, Osaka, 597-0062 Japan
81-724-23-4032
Fax: 81-724-23-9229
e-mail: shun_2@mth.biglobe.ne.jp

Fujisaka, Stanley
45-004 Holowai Street
Kaneohe, HI 96744
808-247-0017
Fax: 808-247-0017

Fukuta, Tak
38 Umegae-Cho
Seki, Gifu, Japan
0575-22-0264
Fax: 0575-24-3835

Fuller, Bruce
1305 S. Airhart Dr.
Baytown, TX 77520
281-427-1840
e-mail: fullcoforg@aol.com

Furukawa, Shiro
1416-5 Yoshino Fujino
Tsukui, Kanagawa,
Japan, 199-0203
0426-87-4006
Fax: 0426-87-4007

Gamble, Frank
3872 Dunbar Place
Fremont, CA 94536
510-797-7970
Fax: 510-797-7970
e-mail: log10@pacbell.net

Gamble, Roger
2801-65th Way N.
St. Petersburg, FL 33710
727-384-1470
e-mail: rlgamble@aol.com
web: www.kmg.org/rlgamble/

Garner, William O. Jr.
2803 E. DeSoto St.
Pensacola, FL 32503
850-438-2009

Gaston, Ronald
330 Gaston Dr.
Woodruff, SC 29388
864-433-0807
Fax: 864-433-9958

Gault, Clay
Rt. 1, Box 287
Lexington, KY 78947
512-273-2873

Gibson, James "Hoot" Sr.
R.R. 1, Box 177F
St. Johns Park
Bunnell, FL 32110
904-437-4383

Goers, Bruce
3423 Royal Court South
Lakeland, FL 33813
941-646-0984
Fax: 941-647-3870

Goldberg, David
1120 Blyth Court
Blue Bell, PA 19422
215-654-7117
Fax: 215-628-4107
e-mail: kirzan3@aol.com
web: www.goldmountainforge.com

Goltz, Warren
802 4th Ave. E.
Ada, MN 56510
218-784-7721
e-mail: sspexp@loretel.net

Gottschalk, Greg
12 First St. (Ft. Pitt)
Carnegie, PA 15106
412-279-6692
e-mail: gottschalk2@home.com

Green, Roger M.
P.O. Box 1801
Joshua, TX 76058
817-447-2395
e-mail: green05@digitex.net
web: www.digitex.net/green05

Greiss, Jockl
Obere Muhlstrasse 5
Gutenberg, Germany
00-49-7026-3224
e-mail: info@jockl-greiss-misser.de
web: www.jockl-greiss-messer.de

Gurganus, Carol
2553 NC 45 South
Colerain, NC 27924
252-356-4831
Fax: 252-356-4650
mgurganus@coastalnet.com

Gurganus, Melvin
2553 NC 45 South
Colerain, NC 27924
252-356-4831
Fax: 252-356-4650
mgurganus@coastalnet.com

Guth, Kenneth
35 E. Wacker Dr., Suite 1840
Chicago, IL 60601
312-346-1760
Fax: 312-282-6890

Hagen, Philip L. (Doc)
P.O. Box 58
Pelican Rapids, MN 56572
218-863-5858
Fax: 218-863-1143
e-mail: phagen@prtel.com
web: www.dochagen.com

Hague, Geoffrey
The Malt House, Hollow Lane-Wilton
Marlborough, Wiltshire, England SN8 3SR
44-0-1672-870212
Fax: 44-0-1672-870212
e-mail: geoff@hagueknives.com
web: www.hagueknives.com

Halligan & Son, Ed
14 Meadow Way
Sharpsburg, GA 30277
770-251-7720
Fax: 770-251-8341
e-mail: ehkiss@bellsouth.net
web: www.halliganknives.com

Hammond, Jim
P.O. Box 486
Arab, AL 35016-0486
256-586-4151
Fax: 256-586-0171
e-mail: jhammond@mindspring.com

Hand, James E., M.D.
1001 Mockingbird Lane
Gloster, MS 39638
601-225-4197 or 225-655-2492
e-mail: je_cshand@eaglepc.net
web: www.kmg.org/hand

Hara, Kouji
Ohsugi 292-2
Seki-City, Gifu-Pref., Japan
81-575-24-7569
Fax: 81-575-24-7569
e-mail: koujih@aqua.ocn.ne.jp
web: www.knifehousehara

Harkins, J.A.
P.O. Box 218
Conner, MT 59827
406-821-1060
e-mail: kutter@rmdbs.net

Harley, Larry
348 Deerfield Dr.
Bristol, TN 37620
423-878-5368

Harris, Ralph D.
2607 Bell Shoals Rd.
Brandon, FL 33511
813-681-5293
Fax: 813-654-8175

Hawkins, Rade
110 Buckeye Rd.
Fayetteville, GA 30214
770-964-1177
Fax: 770-306-2877
e-mail: rade1938@aol.com
web: www.radehawkinscustomknives.com

Hehn, Richard
Lehnmuhler Str. 1
D-55444 Dorrebach, Germany
06724-3152
Fax: 06724-6287

Heitler, Henry
P.O. Box 15025
Tampa, FL 33684-5025
813-933-1645
Fax: 813-933-1645
e-mail: hheitler@tampabay.rr.com

Hendrickson, Earl Jay
4204 Ballenger Creek Pike
Frederick, MD 21703
301-663-6923
Fax: 301-663-6923
e-mail: jhendrickson@xecu.net

Hendrix, Wayne
9636 Burtons Ferry Hwy.
Allendale, SC 29810
803-584-3825
web: www.hendrixknives.com

Hensley, Wayne G.
2924 Glad Dale Drive S.E.
Conyers, GA 30094
770-483-8938
Fax: 770-483-5782
e-mail: rebwayhe@bellsouth.com

Herbst, Peter
Komotauer Strasse 26
91207 Lauf, Germany
09123-13315
Fax: 09123-13379
e-mail: messerherbst@web.de

Herman, Tim
7721 Foster
Overland Park, KS 66204
913-649-3860
Fax. 913-649-0603
e-mail: tai1000@qni.com
web: //www.qni.com/~tai1000

Herron, George
474 Antonio Way
Springfield, SC 29146
803-258-3914

Hethcoat, Don
Box 1764
Clovis, NM 88102-1764
505-762-5721

Hetmanski, Thomas S.
494 Orchard Dr.
Mansfield, OH 44903-9471
419-774-0165

Hibben, Gil
2914 Winters Lane
La Grange, KY 40031
502-222-1397
Fax: 502-222-2676
e-mail: gil_hibben@ntr.net
web: www.hibbenknives.com

Hill, Howard (Persuader Knives)
111 Mission Lane
Poison, MT 59860
406-883-3405
Fax: 406-883-3486
e-mail: knifeman@bigsky.net
web: www.kmg.org/persuader

Hill, Steve E.
40 Rand Pond Road
Goshen, NH 03752
603-863-4762
Fax: 603-863-4762
e-mail: kingpirateboy2@juno.com

Hinson & Son, R.
2419 Edgewood Road
Columbus, GA 31906
706-327-6801
Fax: 706-327-2602

Hirayama, Harumi
4-5-13 Kitamachi
Warabi-City Saitama-Ken, Japan 335-0001
048-443-2248
Fax: 048-443-2248
web: http://www.ne.jp/asahi/harumi/knives

335

Hitchmough, Howard
95 Old Street Rd.
Peterborough, NH 03458-1637
603-924-9646
Fax: 603-924-9595
e-mail: howard@hitchmoughknives.com
web: www.hitchmoughknives.com

Hoel, Steve
P.O. Box 283
Pine, AZ 85544
520-476-4278
Fax: 520-476-4278

Hoffman, Kevin
14672 Kristenright Lane
Orlando, FL 32826-5305
407-207-2643
Fax: 407-207-2643
e-mail: kevh052475@aol.com

Holder, D´Alton
7148 W. Country Gables Dr.
Peoria, AZ 85381
623-878-3064
Fax: 623-878-3964
e-mail: dholderknives@cs.com
web: www.dholder.com

Horn, Jess
2526 Lansdown Rd.
Eugene, OR 97404
541-463-1510
e-mail: jandahorn@aol.com
web: www.horn-net.com/knives

Howard, Durvyn
4220 McLain St. Sough
Hokes Bluff, AL 35903
256-492-5720
Fax: 256-492-5720

Hudson, Rob
22280 Frazier Rd.
Rock Hall, MD 21661
410-639-7273
Fax: 410-639-7273
e-mail: hudson@friend.ly.net

Hughes, Daryle
10979 Leonard
Nunica, MI 49448
616-837-6623
Fax: 231-773-0909

Humphreys, Joel
3260 Palmer Rd.
Bowling Green, FL 33834-9756
863-773-0439
Fax: 863-767-0739

Hytovick, Joseph
14872 S.W. 111th St.
Dunnellon, FL 34432-4731
352-489-5336
Fax: 352-489-3732
e-mail: triadedm@aol.com

Imel, Billy Mace
1616 Bundy Ave.
New Castle, IN 47362
765-529-1651

Irie, Michael
1606 Auburn Drive
Colorado Springs, CO 80909
719-572-5330

Jacks, Jim
344 S. Hollenbeck Ave.
Covina, CA 91723
626-331-5665

Jarvis, Paul
30 Chalk St.
Cambridge, MA 02139
617-547-4355

Jensen, John
P.O. Box 60547
Pasadena, CA 91116
626-449-1148
e-mail: jensen@magnus-design.com
web: www.magnus-design.com

Jernigan, Steve
3082 Tunnel Rd.
Milton, FL 32571
850-994-0802
Fax: 850-994-0802
e-mail: jerniganknives@home.com

Johanning, Tom
1735 Apex Rd.
Sarasota, FL 34240
941-371-2104 Ext. 23
Fax: 941-378-9427
e-mail: tjknife@gte.net
web: www.survivalknives.com

Johnson, Brad
41046 Rue Chend
Ponchatoula, LA 70454
225-294-0413
Fax: 225-294-4518

Johnson, Ronald
Box 11
Clearwater, MN 55320
320-558-6128
Fax: 320-558-6128
web: www.customknives.com/r.b.johnson

Johnson, Ruffin
215 La Fonda Dr.
Houston, TX 77060
218-448-4407
Fax. 218-445-5702
e-mail: ruffinj31@msn.com

Johnson, Steven R.
P.O. Box 5
Manti, UT 84642-0005
435-835-7941
Fax: 435-835-8052
e-mail: sr@srjknives.com or srjohnson@sisna.com
web: www.srjknives.com

Johnson, W.C.
225 Fairfield Pike
Enon, OH 45323
937-864-7802

Jones, Enoch D.
7278 Moss Lane
Warrenton, VA 20187
540-341-0292

Jones, Robert
6219 Aztec N.E.
Albuquerque, NM 87110
505-881-4472

Kalfayan, Edward N.
410 Channing
Ferndale, MI 48220
248-548-4882
e-mail: enkalfayan@excelonline.com

Keeton, William
6095 Rehoboth Rd., S.E.
Laconia, IN 47135
812-969-2836

Kennedy, Bill Jr.
P.O. Box 850431
Yukon, OK 73085
405-354-9150

Khalsa, Jot Singh
368 Village St.
Millis, MA 02054
508-376-8162
Fax: 508-376-8081
e-mail: jotkhalsa@aol.com
web: www.lifeknives.com

King, Bill
14830 Shaw Rd.
Tampa, FL 33625
813-961-3455

Klingbeil, Russell
1120 Shaffer Trail
Oviedo, FL 32765
407-366-3223
Fax: 407-977-0329
e-mail: russkk@aol.com

Knipschield, Terry
808 12th Avenue N.E.
Rochester, MN 55906
507-288-7829
e-mail: knipper@millcomm.com
web: www.millcom.com/~knipper

Knipstein, R.C.
731 N. Fielder
Arlington, TX 76012
817-265-2021
Fax: 817-265-3410

Koval, Mick
P.O. Box 492
New Albany, OH 43054
614-855-0777
Fax: 614-855-0945

Krause, Roy W.
22412 Corteville St.
Clair Shores, MI 48081
810-296-3995
Fax: 810-296-2663

Kressler, D.F.
Am Schlossberg 1
D-8063 Odelzhausen, Germany
08134-7758
Fax: 08134-7759

Kubasek, John
74 Northampton St.
East Hampton, MA 01027
413-527-7917

Lake, Ron
3360 Bendix Ave.
Eugene, OR 97401-5825
541-484-2683
Fax: 541-484-2693
e-mail: lake@televar.com

Lary, Edward M.
651 Rangeline Rd.
Mosinee, WI 54455
714-693-3940

Laurent, Kermit
1812 Acadia Dr.
La Place, LA 70068
504-652-5629
e-mail: klaurent@mindspring.com

Leach, Mike
5377 W. Grand Blanc Rd.
Swartz Creek, MI 48473
810-655-4850

Letcher, William
3909 South Trask St.
Tampa, FL 33616
813-837-5122
e-mail: lknives@aol.com
web: www.letcherknives.com

Levengood, Bill
15011 Otto Rd.
Tampa, FL 33624
813-961-5688

Levin, Yakov
7216 Bay Parkway
Brooklyn, NY 11204
718-232-8574
Fax: 718-232-8574

Levine, Bob
101 Westwood Dr.
Tullahoma, TN 37388
931-454-9943
e-mail: knife397@aol.com

Linklater, Steve
8 Cossar Dr.
Aurora, Ontario, Canada L4G 3N8
905-727-8929
Fax: 905-726-2349
e-mail: knifman@sympatico.ca

Loerchner, Wolfgang
P.O. Box 255
Bayfield, Ontario, Canada N0M 1G0
519-565-2196
web: www.wolfe.to

Lonewolf, Juan A.
481 Hwy. 105
Demorest, GA 30535
706-754-4660
Fax: 706-754-8470
e-mail: lonewolf@hemc.net
web: www.lonewolfknives.com

Loveless, R.W.
P.O. Box 7836
Riverside, CA 92503
909-689-7800

Lovestrand, Schuyler
1136 19th St. SW
Vero Beach, FL 32962
561-778-0282
Fax: 561-466-4426

Lozier, Don
5394 S.E. 168th Ave.
Ocklawaha, FL 32179
352-625-3576

Lum, Robert W.
901 Travis Ave.
Eugene, OR 97404
541-688-2737

Lyle, Ernest
P.O. Box 1755
Chiefland, FL 32644
352-490-6693

Malloy, Joe
1039 Schwabe St., P.O. Box 156
Freeland, PA 18224
717-636-2781
e-mail: jdmalloy@ptd.net

Maragni, Dan
1278 Old Route 80
Georgetown, NY 13072
315-662-7490
Fax: 315-662-3402

Martin, Peter
28220 N. Lake Dr.
Waterford, WI 53185
414-662-3629
Fax: 414-662-3629

Martin, Randall J.
1477 Country Club Rd.
Middletown, CT 06457
860-347-1161
Fax: 860-347-1161
e-mail: rfmartin@martinsite.com
web: www.martinsite.com

McConnell, Charles
158 Genteel Ridge
Wellsburg, WV 26070
304-737-2015

McConnell, Loyd
1710 Rosewood
Odessa, TX 79761
915-363-8344
Fax: 915-363-0643
e-mail: ccknives@apex2000.net
web: www.ccknives.com

McDonald, Richard
4590 Kirk Road
Columbiana, OH 44408
330-482-0007
Fax: 330-482-0007

McDonald, Robert J.
14730 61 Court N.
Loxahatchee, FL 33470
561-790-1470

McDonald, W.J.
7173 Wickshire Cove East
Germantown, TN 38138
901-756-9924
e-mail: wjmcdonaldknives@email.msn.com
web: www.mcdonaldknives.com

McFall, Ken
P.O. Box 458
Lakeside, AZ 85929
520-537-2026
Fax: 520-537-8066

McGowan, Frank
12629 Howard Lodge Rd.
Sykesville, MD 21784
410-489-4323

McGuane, Thomas
410 South Third Ave.
Bozeman, MT 59715
406-522-9739
Fax: 406-522-8348
web: www.thomasmcguane.com

McHenry & Williams (Metalsmiths)
Box 67
Wyoming, RI 02898-0067
401-539-8353
Fax: 401-539-0252

McNabb, Tommy
4015 Brownsboro Rd.
Winston-Salem, NC 27106
336-759-0640
Fax: 336-759-0641
e-mail: tommy@tmcnabb.com
web: www.carolinaknives.com

Meerdink, Kurt
120 Spla Rock Dr.
Barryville, NY 12719
845-557-0783

Mercer, Mike
149 Waynesville Rd.
Lebanon, OH 45036
513-932-2837

Merchant, Ted
7 Old Garrett Court
White Hall, MD 21161
410-343-0380
e-mail: tedmerchant@home.com

Merz, Robert L. III
20219 Prince Creek Dr.
Katy, TX 77450
281-492-7337
e-mail: Imerz77450@aol.com

Michinaka, Toshiaki
1-679, Koyamacho-nishi, Tottori-shi Tottori
Japan, 680-0947
0857-28-5911

Miller, James P.
9024 Goeller Rd., R.R. 2 Box 28
Fairbank, IA 50629
319-635-2294

Miller, Steve
1376 Pine St.
Clearwater, FL 33756
727-461-4180
e-mail: millknives@aol.com

Mills, Louis
9450 Waters Rd.
Ann Arbor, MI 48103
734-668-1839

Mink, Dan
P.O. Box 861, 196 Sage Circle
Crystal Beach, FL 34681
727-787-2477 or 727-786-5408
Fax: 727-786-5408
e-mail: dbmink@ij.net

Minnick, Jim
144 N. 7th St.
Middletown, IN 47356
765-354-4108

Momcilovic, Gunnar
Nordlys v.16
N-3305 Krokstadelva, Norway
47-328-73586

Moore, James B.
1707 N. Gillis
Ft. Stockton, TX 79735
915-336-2113

Morgan, Jeff
9200 Arnaz Way
Santee, CA 92071
619-448-8430

Morris, C.H.
1590 Old Salem Road
Frisco City, AL 36445
334-575-7425

Moulton, Dusty
135 Hillview Lane
Loudon, TN 37774
865-408-9779
e-mail: dusty@moultonknives.com
web: www.moultonknives.com

Nealy, Bud
1439 Poplar Valley Rd.
Stroudsburg, PA 18360
570-402-1018
Fax: 570-402-1019
e-mail: budnealy@ptd.net

Newcomb, Corbin
628 Woodland Ave.
Moberly, MO 65270
660-263-4639

Newton, Larry
1758 Pronghorn Ct.
Jacksonville, FL 32225
904-221-2340
Fax: 904-220-4098
e-mail: cnewton@aol.com

Newton, Ron
223 Ridge Lane
London, AR 72847
501-293-3001

Nolen, R.D. & Steve
1110 Lake Shore Dr.
Estes Park, CO 80517
970-586-5814
Fax: 970-586-8827
web: www.nolenknives.com

Nordell, Ingemar
Skarpa 2103
82041 Farila, Sweden
46651-23347
Fax: 46651-767370
e-mail: nordell.knives@tclia.com
web: www.nordellknives.com

Norfleet, Ross
3947 Tanbark Rd.
Richmond, VA 23235
804-276-4169 or 804-782-7682

Ochs, Charles F.
124 Emerald Lane
Largo, FL 33771
727-536-3827
Fax: 727-536-3827
e-mail: chuckandbelle@juno.com

Ogletree, Ben R. Jr.
2815 Israel Road
Livingston, TX 77351
409-327-5211
Fax: 409-327-3894
e-mail: mayor@livingston.net
web: www.livingston.net/mayor

Osborne, Warren
215 Edgefield
Waxahachie, TX 75165
972-935-0899
Fax: 972-937-9004
e-mail: ossiel@worldnet.att.net
web: www.osborneknives.com

Overeynder, T.R.
1800 S. Davis Dr.
Arlington, TX 76013
817-277-4812
Fax: 817-860-5485

Owens, John
13180 CR 280
Nathrop, CO 81236

Pachi, Francesco
Via Pometta, 1
17046 Sassello (SV), Italy
011-39-019-720086
Fax: 011-39-019-720086
e-mail: info@pachi-knives.com
web: http://www.pachi-knives.com

Page, Larry
165 Rolling Rock Rd.
Aiken, SC 29803-6626
803-648-0001
e-mail: capnknife@aol.com

Papp, Robert
7075 Eventide Dr.
Parma, OH 44129
440-888-9299
Fax: 440-451-2333

Pardue, Joseph
P.O. Box 693
Spurger, TX 77660
409-429-7074
e-mail: jrpardue444@aol.com
web: www.joeparxdueknives.com

Pardue, Melvin
Rt. 1 Box 130
Repton, AL 36475
334-248-2447
Fax: 334-248-2447
e-mail: mpardue@frontiernet.net

Pease, W.D.
Rt. 2, Box 37AA
Ewing, KY 41039
606-845-0387
Fax: 606-845-8058

Pendray, Alfred
13950 N.E. 20th St.
Williston, FL 32696
352-528-6124
Fax: 352-528-6124
e-mail: bpendray@aol.com

Perry, John L.
9 South Harrell Rd.
Mayflower, AR 72106
501-470-3043
e-mail: jpknives@cyberback.com

Peterson, Eldon
260 Haugen Heights Rd.
Whitefish, MT 59937
406-862-2204
e-mail: driano@digisys.net
web: www.kmg.org/egpeterson

Pfeiffer, Kenneth
P.O. Box 551
Hagaman, NY 12086
518-842-7018
e-mail: kpfeif6949@aol.com

Piergallini, Daniel
4011 N. Forbes Rd.
Plant City, FL 33565
813-754-3908
Fax: 813-754-3908
e-mail: coolnifedad@earthlink.net

Pitt, David
6812 Digger Pine Lane
Anderson, CA 96007
530-357-2393

Pittman, Leon & Tracy
661 Hubert Pittman Rd.
Pendergrass, GA 30567
706-654-2597

Polk, Clifton
4625 Webber Creek Road
Van Buren, AR 72956
501-474-3828

Polkowski, Al
8 Cathy Ct.
Chester, NJ 07930
908-879-6030
Fax: 908-879-6090

Prince, Joe
190 Bulman Rd.
Roebuck, SC 29376
864-576-7479
e-mail: princeknives@aol.com

Pugh, Jim
P.O. Box 711
Azle, TX 76098
817-444-2679
Fax: 817-444-5455

Pullen, Martin
1701 Broken Bow Rd.
Granbury, TX 76049
817-573-1784
e-mail: selmar@itexas.net
web: www.kmg.org

Pulliam, Morris (Knob Hill Forge)
560 Jeptha Knob Rd.
Shelbyville, KY 40065
502-633-2261
Fax: 502-633-5294
e-mail: mcknifepulliam@hotmail.com

Rados, Jerry
P.O. Box 531
Grant Park, IL 60940-0531
815-472-3350
Fax: 815-472-3944
e-mail: rados@favoravi.com

Ragsdale, James D.
3002 Arabian Woods Dr.
Lithonia, GA 30038
770-482-6739
e-mail: jimpegrags@att.net

Rapp, Steven
7273 S. 245 East
Midvale, UT 84047-2125
801-567-9553
Fax: 801-566-6342

Rardon, A.D.
1589 S.E. Price Dr.
Polo, MO 64671
660-354-2330

Reeve, Chris
11624 W. President Dr. #B
Boise, ID 83713-8971
208-375-0367
Fax: 208-375-0368
e-mail: creeve@micron.net
web: www.chrisreeve.com

Reynolds, John
#2 Andover HCR 77
Gillette, WY 82716
307-682-6076

Richard, Ron
4875 Calaveras Ave.
Fremont, CA 94538
510-796-9767

Ricke, Dave
1209 Adams
West Bend, WI 53090
414-334-5739

Rietveld, Bertie
P.O. Box 53 Magaliesburg
Gauteng 1791, South Africa
011-2714-5771294
Fax: 011-2714-5771294
e-mail: batavia1@mweb.co.za
web: www.batavia.co.za

Rigney, Willie
191 Colson Dr.
Bronston, KY 42518
606-561-5918

Roath, Dean
3050 Winnipeg Dr.
Baton Rouge, LA 70819
225-272-5562
e-mail: dean@roath.com
web: www.roath.com

Robbins, Howard
1407 S. 217 Ave.
Elkhorn, NE 68022
402-289-4121
Fax: 402-289-1723
e-mail: arobb1407@aol.com

Robinson, Rex III
10531 Poe St.
Leesburg, FL 34788
352-787-4587

Robinson, Robert
1569 N. Finley Point Rd.
Polson, MT 59860-9613
406-887-2259
Fax: 406-887-2259
e-mail: robby@polsol.net
web: www.skybusiness.com/celtic4u

Roe, Fred
4005 Granada Dr.
Huntsville, AL 35802
256-881-6847

Roulin, Charles
113 Brt.de Soral, 1232 Lully
Geneva, Switzerland
022-757-4479
Fax: 022-757-4479
web: www.coutelier-roulin.com

Russ, Ron
5351 N.E. 160th Ave.
Williston, FL 32696
352-528-2603
e-mail: russrs160@cs.com

Russell, A.G.
1705 N. Thompson St.
Springdale, AR 72764
501-751-7341
Fax: 501-751-4520
e-mail: ag@agrussell.com
web: www.agrussell.com

Saindon, R. Bill
11 Highland View Rd.
Claremont, NH 03743
603-542-9418

Sakakibara, Masaki
20-8 Sakuragaoka 2-Chome
Setagaya-ku, Tokyo, Japan 156-0054
03-3420-0375

Sakurai, Hiroyuki
Higashi-Senbo 15
Seki-City, Gifu Pref., Japan 501-32
011-81-575-22-4185
Fax: 011-81-575-24-5306
e-mail: nsk@mxl-ktroad.ne.jp

Sakmar, Mike
2470 Melvin
Rochester, MI 48307
248-852-6775
Fax: 248-852-8544

Salley, John
3965 Frederick-Ginghamsburg Rd.
Tipp City, OH 45371
937-698-4588
Fax: 937-698-4131

Sawby, Scott
480 Snowberry Lane
Sandpoint, ID 83864
208-263-4171

Schirmer, Michael
P.O. Box 534
Twin Bridges, MT 59754
406-684-5868
Fax: 406-684-5868
e-mail: schimer@3rivers.net
web: www.handforgedknives.com

Schneider, H.J.
14084 Apple Valley Rd.
Apple Valley, CA 92307-5467
760-946-9096
Fax: 760-946-9096
e-mail: genoruth@aol.com

Schrock, Maurice & Alan
1712 S. Oak St.
Pontiac, IL 61764
815-842-1628
Fax: 815-842-3288

Schwarzer, Steve
P.O. Box 4
Pomona Park, FL 32181
904-649-5026
Fax: 904-649-8585
e-mail: schwarzer@gbso.net
web: www.schwarzer.com

Sentz, Mark C.
4084 Baptist Rd.
Taneytown, MD 21787
410-756-6970
Fax: 410-756-2018
e-mail: sentzms@cct.infi.net

Shadley, Eugene W.
26315 Norway Dr.
Bovey, MN 55709-9405
218-245-3820
Fax: 218-245-1639

Shore, John I.
2901-A Sheldon Jackson St.
Anchorage, AK 99508
907-272-2253
e-mail: akknife@ptialaska.net
web: www.akknife.com

Simons, Bill
6217 Michael Lane
Lakeland, FL 33811
863-646-3783

Sims, R.J.
P.O. Box 772
Meridian, TX 76665
254-435-6240
Fax: 254-435-6240

Sinyard, Cleston
27522 Burkhardt Dr.
Elberta, AL 36530
334-987-1361

Siska, Jim
6 Highland Ave.
Westfield, MA 01085-4216
413-568-9787
Fax: 413-568-6341

Slee, Fred
9 John St.
Morganville, NJ 07751
732-591-9047

Slobodian, Scott
4101 River Ridge Dr., P.O. Box 1498
San Andreas, CA 95249
209-286-1980
Fax: 209-286-1982
e-mail: scott@slobodianwards.com
web: www.slobodianswords.com

Smith, J.D. (HammerSmith Knives)
516 East 2nd St., Box 38
South Boston, MA 02127
617-269-1699
Fax: 617-269-1699

Smith, John W.
1322 Cow Branch Rd.
W. Liberty, KY 41472
606-743-3599
Fax: 606-743-2578
e-mail: jwsknive@mrtc.com
web: http://members.tripod.com/~smithknives

Smith, Michael J.
2806 Manor Hill Dr.
Brandon, FL 33511
813-571-7347
e-mail: smithknife@hotmail.com
web: http://www.smithknife.com

Smith, Ralph
P.O. Box 1690
Greer, SC 29652-1690
864-848-1247
Fax: 864-281-6027

Snell, Jerry
235 Woodsong Dr.
Fayetteville, GA 30214
770-461-0586

Solomon, Marvin
23750 Cold Springs Rd.
Paron, AZ 72122
501-821-3170
Fax: 501-821-6541
e-mail: mardot@swbell.net
web: www.coldspringforge.com

Soppera, Arthur
Morgental Str. 37, P.O. Box 708
CH-8038 Zurich, Switzerland
41-1-482-86-12
Fax: 41-1-481-62-71
e-mail: esoppera@bluewin.ch

Sornberger, Jim
25126 Overland Dr.
Volcano, CA 95689
209-295-7819
Fax: 209-295-7819
e-mail: sierrajs@volcano.net

Steigerwalt, Ken
R.R. 1 Box 30
Orangeville, PA 17859
717-683-5156

Steinau, Jurgen
Julius-Hart-Str. 44
12587 Berlin, Germany
030-6452512
Fax: 030-6452512

Stephan, Daniel
2201 S. Miller Rd.
Valrico, FL 33594
813-684-2781
Fax: 813-684-5109

Sterling, Murray
693 Round Peak Church Rd.
Mt. Airy, NC 27030-8417
336-352-5110
Fax: 336-352-5105
e-mail: sterck@surry.net
web: www.sterlingcustomknives.com

Stevens, Barry B.
901 Amherst Rd.
Cridersville, OH 45806
419-221-2446
e-mail: bareknives@hotmail.com

Stout, Johnny
1205 Forest Trail
New Baunfels, TX 78132-4627
830-606-4067
Fax: 830-606-4067
e-mail: jlstout@stoutknives.com
web: www.stoutknives.com

Sugihara, Keidoh
4-16-1 Kamoricho
Kishiwada, Osaka, Japan 596-0042
81-724-44-2677
Fax: 81-724-2677

Summers, Arthur L.
8700 Brigner Road
Mechanicsburg. OH 43044
937-834-3776
e-mail: janrn@mgmainnet.com

Sutton, Russ
4900 Cypress Shores Dr.
New Bern, NC 28562
252-637-3963
e-mail: sutton@cconnect.net
web: www.suttoncustomknives.com

Syslo, Charles (Cisco Knives)
3418 S. 116 Ave.
Omaha, NE 68144
402-333-0647
e-mail: csyslo@radiks.net

Szilaski, Joseph
29 Carroll Drive
Wappinger Falls, NY 12590
845-297-5397
Fax: 845-297-5397
e-mail: joe@szilaski.com
web: www.szilaski.com

Tally, Grant
14618 Cicotte
Allen Park, MI 48101
313-381-0100

Terzuola, Robert
3933 Agua Fria
Santa Fe, NM 87507
575-473-1002
Fax: 575-438-8018
e-mail: terzuola@earthlink.net

Thompson, Leon
1735 Leon Dr.
Forest Grove, OR 97116
503-357-2573
e-mail: lthompson8@compuserve.com

Tighe, Brian
R.R. 1 Ridgeville
2305 Sulphur Spring Dr.
Ontario, Canada L0S IM0
905-892-2734
Fax: 905-892-2734
e-mail: tighe@netcom.ca
web: www.tigheknives.com

Tomes, P.J.
594 High Peak Lane
Shipman, VA 22971
804-263-8662
Fax: 804-263-4439
e-mail: tomesknives@aol.com

Tompkins, Dan
310 N. 2nd St., Box 398
Peotone, IL 60468-0398
708-258-3620
Fax: 708-258-6669

Toner, John E.
5202 N. 106 Dr.
Glendale, AZ 85307
623-872-1126
Fax: 23-872-1126
e-mail: cdknives@msn.com

Toole, Bobby L.
1022 S. 25th St.
Saginaw, MI 48601
517-753-2547

Towell, Dwight
2375 Towell Rd.
Midvale, ID 83645
208-355-2419

Treiber, Leon
P.O. Box 342
Ingram, TX 78025
830-367-2246
Fax: 830-367-2246

Trindle, Barry
1660 Ironwood Trail
Earlham, IA 50072-8611
515-462-1237
e-mail: trindle@dwx.com

Tschager, Reinhard
Piazza Parrocchia 7
1-39100 Bolzano, Italy
0471-970642
Fax: 0471-970642
e-mail: goldtschager@dnet.it

Turecek, Jim
P.O. Box 882
Derby, CT 06418
203-734-8406

Turnbull, Ralph
14464 Linden Dr.
Spring Hill, FL 34609
352-688-7089
e-mail: tbull2000@aol.com

Van Eldik, Frans
Hoflaan 3 3632 BT
Loenen A/D Vecht, Netherlands
029423-3095
Fax: 029423-3095

VanHoy, Edward T.
1826 McCallum Rd.
Candor, NC 27229
910-974-7955
Fax: 910-974-7955
e-mail: vanhoyknives@ac.net

Van Rijswijk, Aad
Cederdreef 28
3137 PB Vlaardingen, Netherlands
3110 4742952
Fax: 3110 2343648
e-mail: info@avrknives.com
web: http://www.avrknives.com

Veit, Michael
3289 E. 5th Rd., R.R. 1
Lasalle, IL 61301
815-223-3538
e-mail: veit@theramp.net

Velarde, Ricardo
746 E. 200 N.
Provo, UT 84606
801-375-0519
Fax: 801-375-2742

Viele, Howard
88 Lexington Ave.
Westwood, NJ 07675
201-666-2906
Fax: 201-666-8665

Vogt, Donald
9007 Hogans Bend
Tampa, FL 33647
813-973-3245
e-mail: vogtknives@aol.com

Walker, George
P.O. Box 3272
Alpine, WY 83128-3272
307-883-2372
Fax: 307-883-2372

Walker, James
22 Walker Lane
Morrilton, AR 72110
501-354-3175
e-mail: jwalker@mail.cswnet.com

Walker, John W.
Box 10620 Moss Branch Rd.
Bon Aqua, TN 37025
931-670-4754

Walker, Michael
P.O. Box 1924
Taos, NM 87571
505-751-1667
Fax: 505-751-0284
e-mail: lockers@newmex.com
web: www.ssdamascus.com

Ward, Charles B.
1010 East North St.
Benton, AR 72015
501-778-4329
e-mail: chuckbop@aol.com

Ware, Tommy
P.O. Box 488
Datil, NM 87821
505-772-5817

Warenski, Buster
P.O. Box 214
Richfield, UT 84701
435-896-5319
Fax: 435-896-8333
e-mail: bwar@gbasin.net

Warren, Daniel
571 Lovejoy Rd.
Canton, NC 28716
828-648-7351

Warther, Dale
418 E. 10th St.
Dover, OH 44622
303-343-5241

Watson, Thomas J.
1103 Brenau Terrace
Panama City, FL 32405
850-785-9209
Fax: 850-763-6034
e-mail: tomwatson@aol.com

Weeber, Charles
5285 E. Tu Ave.
Vicksburg, MI 49097
616-649-2486
e-mail: cweeber@ibm.net

Weever, John S.
107A Westmeadow Dr.
Cleburne, TX 76031
817-645-3974
Fax: 817-645-3998

Weiland, J. Reese (Custom Kraft)
P.O. Box 2337
Riverview, Fl 33568
813-671-0661
Fax: 813-972-5336
e-mail: rwphil413@earthlink.net
web: www.rwcustomknives.com

Weinstock, Robert
Box 39, 520 Frederick St.
San Francisco, CA 94117
415-731-5968

Weiss, Charles L.
18847 N. 13th Ave.
Phoenix, AZ 85027
623-582-6147
Fax: 623-582-6147

Whitley, Weldon
6316 Jebel Way
El Paso, TX 79912
915-584-2274
e-mail: wwhitley@flash.net
web: www.flash.net/~wwhitley

Whittaker, Wayne
2900 Woodland Court
Metamora, MI 48455
810-797-5315

Wicker, Donnie R.
2544 East 40th Ct.
Panama City, FL 32405
904-785-9158

Wilson, R.W.
P.O. Box 2012
Weirton, WV 26062
304-723-2771
e-mail: rwknives@hotmail.com
web: www.rwwilsonknives.com

Winkler, Daniel
P.O. Box 2166
Blowing Rock, NC 28605
828-295-9156
Fax: 828-295-0673
e-mail: winklerd@boone.net

Witsaman, Earl
B. 3957 Redwing Circle
Stow, OH 44224
330-688-4208
e-mail: eawits@aol.com
web: http://hometown.aol.com/eawits/index.html

Wolf, William
4618 N. 79th Ave.
Phoenix, AZ 85033
623-846-3585
Fax: 623-846-3585
e-mail: wolfknives@earthlink.com
web: www.customknives.net/wolf

Wojtinowski, Frank
Bahnhofstrasse 11
83417 Kirchanschoring, Germany
08685-1789
Fax: 08685-1729
e-mail: info@frank-wojtinowski.com
web: www.frank-wojtinowski.com

Wood, Owen
12639 W. 84th Dr.
Arvada, CO 80005
303-279-3751
e-mail: ow2knives@cs.com

Wood, Webster
22041 Shelton Trail
Altanta, MI 49709
989-785-2996
Fax: 989-785-2996

Wright, Tim
P.O. Box 3746
Sedona, AZ 86340
520-282-4180
Fax: 520-282-4180

Yeates, Joe
730 Saddlewood Circle
Spring, TX 77381
281-367-2765
e-mail: joeyeates291@cs.com

Yoshihara, Yoshindo, c/o Leon Kapp
49 Pt. San Pedro Rd.
San Rafael, CA 94901
415-457-6436
Fax: 415-459-4791

Young, George
713 Pinoak Dr.
Kokomo, IN 46901
765-457-8893

Yurco, Mike
P.O. Box 712
Canfield, OH 44406
330-533-4928
e-mail: shorinki@aol.com

Zinker, Brad
1591 N.W. 17th St.
Homestead, FL 33030
305-247-4507
Fax: 305-247-7142
e-mail: bzknives@aol.com

1999 Probationary Members

Ballestra, Santino
Via Domenico Tempesta 11/17
18039 Ventimiglia-Fraz.
Calvo (1M), Italy
0184-215228
Fax: 0184-215228

Largin, Ken
P.O. Box 151
Metamora, IN 47030
765-969-5012
e-mail: kelgin@pocketmail.com
web: www.kelgin.com

2000 Probationary Members

Booth, Philip
301 S. Jeffery Ave.
Ithaca, MI 44847
517-875-2844
Fax: 517-875-2844
e-mail: philipb@power-net.net

Cameron, Ron
P.O. Box 183
Logandale, NV 89021
702-398-3356
e-mail: cameron@comnett.net
web: www.cameronknives.com

Fraley, Derek
1355 Fairbanks Ct.
Dixon, CA 95620
707-678-0393

Gilbert, Chantal
291 Christophe Colomb St. #105
Quebec, Quebec, Canada G1K 3T1
418-525-6961
Fax: 418-525-4666
e-mail: gilbertc@medion.qc.ca
web: http://www.chantalgilbert.com

Gobec, Stefan
Weinserstr. 42
A-3680 Persenbeug Austria
43-7414-7675
Fax: 43-7414-7675
web: www.gobec.com

Green, Mark
P.O. Box 207
Graysdill, AL 35073
205-674-8080 or 205-647-9353
Fax: 205-674-3414

Hollett, Jeff
3077 Wildflower Way
Rockwall, TX 75032
972-771-8770
Fax: 972-772-0949
e-mail: bjhollett@mindspring.com
web: www.kustomknives.com

Hossom, Jerry
3585 Schilling Ridge
Duluth, GA 30096
770-449-7809
Fax: 770-446-0644
e-mail: knives@mediaone.net
web: www.hossom.com

Humenick, Roy
P.O. Box 55
Rescue, CA 95672-0055
530-677-2778

Lunn, Larry
6970 9th Ave. North
St. Petersburg, FL 33710
727-345-7455
e-mail: llunn@tampabay.rr.com or
  llunn@lunnknives.com

Nowland, Rick
3677 E. Bonnie Blvd.
Waltonville, IL 62894
618-279-3170
e-mail: ricknowland@waltonville.net

Rogers, Richard
P.O. Box 769
Magdalena, NM 87825
505-854-2567
Fax: 505-854-2567

Seto, Yoshinori
1-20 3-Chome
Asahigaoka, Seki-City, Gifu Pref., Japan 501-3828
0575-23-9519
Fax: 0575-23-9690
e-mail: seto@sage.ocn.ne.jp

Vagnino, Michael Jr.
38340 Rd 172
Visalia, CA 93292
559-538-2800
e-mail: mvknives@lightspeed.net
web: www.mvknives.com

2001 Probationary Members

Bradshaw, Bailey
17800 Dickerson St. #112
Dallas, TX 75252
972-381-0558
Fax: 972-381-1255
e-mail: nimbail@sprynet.com
web: www.bradshawcutlery.com

Burke, R.D. "Dan"
22001 Ole Barn Rd.
Edmond, OK 73003
Fax: 405-340-3333

Chaffee, Jeffrey
P.O. Box 1
Morris, IN 47033
812-934-6350
Fax: 812-934-6128
e-mail: jchaffee@seidata.com

Dodds, David
Rt. 1, Box 157
Belington, WV 26250
304-823-3503

Durio, Fred
144 Gulino St.
Opelousas, LA 70570
337-948-4831

Dushane, Dwayne
1010 N.W. 2nd
Andrews, TX 79714
915-523-6689
e-mail: ddushane@powr.net
web: www.lx.net/dushane

Faucheaux, Howard
P.O. Box 206
Loreauville, LA 70552
337-229-6467

Frederick, Aaron
302 Lyons Ave.
Morehead, KY 40351
606-780-0883
e-mail: aaronf@mrtc.com
web: www.frederickknives.com

Glover, Warren
P.O. Box 475
Cleveland, GA 30528
706-865-3998
Fax: 706-348-7176
e-mail: bubbaknives@bigplanet.com
web: www.bubbaknives.com

Hamada, Tomonori
5-12-83 Kaminagaya Kohonan-ku
Yokohama Kanagawa Pref. 233-0012 Japan
045-844-2567
Fax: 045-844-2567

349

Hansen, Shaun
15505 So. Camp Williams Hwy.
Bluffdale, UT 84065
801-254-7363

Hurst, Gerard
P.O. Box 8742
Albuquerque, NM 87198
505-828-0446
e-mail: gerardhurst@msn.com
web: www.gerardhurst.com

Jacks, Jason
Rt. 9, Box 4724
Lufkin, TX 75901
936-637-6181
e-mail: jacks@inu.net
web: www.jacksknives.com

Keller, Bill
12211 Las Nubes
San Antonio, TX 78233
210-653-6609
e-mail: bkeller@satx.rr.com
web: www.kellerknives.com

Lerch, Matthew J.
N88 W23462 North Lisbon Rd.
Sussex, WI 53069
262-246-4569
Fax: 262-246-4569
web: www.lerchknives.com

Lewis, Tom
1613 Standpipe Rd.
Carlsbad, NM 88220
505-885-3616
e-mail: lewisknives@carlsbadnm.com

Lightfoot, Greg
RR #2 Kitscoty
Alberta, Canada T0B 2P0
e-mail: pitbull@lightfootknives.com
web: www.lightfootknives.com

Massey, Roger
4928 Union Rd.
Texarkana, AR 71854
870-779-1018
e-mail: rmassey668@aol.com

Moon, Sidney "Pete"
982 Bellevue Plantation Rd.
Lafayette, LA 70503
337-981-7396
e-mail: knifeman@aol.com

Oldham, Raymond Frank
2129 Muskingum Ave.
Cocoa, FL 32926
321-633-4531
e-mail: knifemaker@earthlink.net

Patton, Robert
9330 Landmark St.
Boise, ID 83704
208-327-7641
e-mail: grpatton@mindspring.com

PROFESSIONAL KNIFEMAKER ASSOCIATION

Agnew, James K.
5260 S. Sherman
Littleton, CO 80121
303-789-3084

Anthon, John R.
P.O. Box 600
Getzville, NY 14068
800-548-7427

Beene, Lee
3340 S. Evanston St.
Aurora, CO 80014
303-690-3624

Bennett, Brett C.
1922 Morrie Ave.
Cheyenne, WY 82001
307-432-0985

Bliss, James E.
2900 Wild Rose Way
Fort Collins, CO 80526
970-266-0878

Bogg, Forrest W.
P.O. Box 52
McGirk, MO 65055
573-796-3817

Bradburn, Gary F.
1714 Park Pl.
Wichita, KS 67203
316-269-4273

Brahms, Larry
14216 SW 136th St.
Miami, FL 33186

Brock, Kenneth L.
P.O. Box 375
Allenspark, CO 80510
303-747-2547

Burger, David
3528 Clipper Road
Baltimore, MD 21211
410-366-8171

Burrows, Stephen R.
3532 Michigan Ave.
Kansas City, MO 64109
816-921-1573

Camerer, Craig
287 East Main
Hettick, IL 62649
618-778-5704

Cameron, Tim S.
1180 S. Madison St.
Denver, CO 80210
303-733-9828

Carter, Rod S.
7303 S. Costilla St.
Littleton, CO 80120
303-734-1019

Chaffee, Jeffrey L.
14314 N. Washington St.
Morris, IN 47033
812-934-6350

Cumming, Robert J.
35 Manana Dr.
Cedar Crest, NM 87008
505-286-0509

Darpinian, David V.
15219 W. 125th Street
Olathe, KS 66062
913-397-8914

Davis, Terry L.
P.O. Box 23255
Ketchikan, AK 99901
907-225-6619

Draper, Audra L.
10 Creek Dr.
Riverton, WY 82501
307-856-6807

Draper, Mike J.
10 Creek Dr.
Riverton, WY 82501
307-856-6807

Ennis, Ray W.
1220 S. 775 E.
Ogden, UT 84404
801-622-2406

Eriksen, James T.
3830 Dividend Drive
Garland, TX 75042
972-235-4910

Feder, Jack S.
P.O. Box 208
Westport, CT 06881
203-226-5211

Fowler, Ricky
P.O. Box 339
Silverhill, AL 36576
334-945-3289

Glesser, Sal
20011 Golden Gate Canyon Rd.
Golden, CO 80402
800-525-7770

Griffith, Pete
62 Breamore Ct.
Castle Rock, CO 80104
303-660-0357

Hartman, Marge
254 Amity St.
Meriden, CT 06450
800-682-5489

Hielscher, Guy E.
P.O. Box 992
Alliance, NE 69301
308-762-4318

Hockensmith, Dan
P.O. Box E
Drake, CO 80515
970-669-5404

Howell, Ronald D.
P.O. Box 393
South Fork, CO 81154
719-873-5578

Irie, Michael L.
1606 Auburn
Colorado Springs, CO 80909
719-594-4580

Jones, Donald
6133 Hunt Rd.
Pleasant Garden, NC 27313
910-674-5654

King, Jason M.
Eskridge, KS 66423
785-449-2683

Kohler, Gary
3005 Delta Dr.
Colorado Springs, CO 80910
719-391-0068

Kraft, Steve
315 S.E. 6th
Abilene, KS 67410
785-263-1411

Largent, James R.
107 E. South St.
Bayfield, CO 81122
970-884-4337

Lemcke, Jim L.
10649 Haddington #180
Houston, TX 77043
713-467-6272

Ludemann, Mike A.
2940 Fayette Ave.
Ionia, IA 50645
800-301-9774

Magee, James T.
707 Carriage Ct.
Salina, KS 67401
785-825-6892

Marlowe, Charles C.
510 E. 9th St.
Wayne, NE 68787
402-375-4928

McLaughlin, Larry D.
P.O. Box 241
Avon, MT 59713
406-492-7072

McLure, Jerry R.
3052 Isim Rd.
Norman, OK 73026
405-321-3614

Miller, Clayton
3314 Country Club Road
San Angelo, TX 76904
915-949-1707

Molnar, Mark S.
6714 County Road 3
Swanton, OH 43558
419-825-9993

Montell, Tyree L.
P.O. Box 781
Silver City, NM 88062
505-388-4463

Nolen, Steve D.
1110 Lakeshore Dr.
Estes Park, CO 80517
970-586-5814

Ott, Fred A.
1257 Rancho Durango Rd.
Durango, CO 81303
970-375-9669

Palmer, Taylor
Box 97
Blanding, UT 84511
435-678-2523

Patrick, Willard C.
P.O. Box 5716
Helena, MT 59604-5716
406-458-6552

Patton, Richard R.
1518 Sunrise Manor Way
Boise, ID 83713
208-377-5704

Patton, Robert
9330 Landmark St.
Boise, ID 83704
208-327-7641

Penfold, Mick E.
131 Mojave Court
Vacaville, CA 95688
707-668-0584

Poplin, James L.
103 Oak St.
Washington, GA 30673
706-678-2729

Porter, Charlie
206 Solar Way
Denton, TX 76207
940-382-9558

Rabie, Celia
P.O. Box 18006
Nelspruit, South Africa 1200

Rummell, Hank
10 Paradise Lane
Warwick, NY 10990
914-469-9172

Sampson, Clinton D.
2084 County Rd. 782
Woodland Park, CO 80863
719-687-9741

Sauer, Charles R.
68 Tahoe Drive
Kalispell, MT 59901
406-257-9310

Schepers, George B.
P.O. Box 395
Shelton, NE 68876
308-647-6489

Self, Ernie
950 O'Neil Ranch Rd.
Dripping Springs, TX 78620
512-858-7133

Self, Richard
Rt. 3 Box 2453
Nacogdoches, TX 75964
409-560-5891

Steketee, Craig
871 N. Hwy. 60
Billings, MO 65610
417-744-2770

Taylor, Mike D.
660 S. Ohio, P.M.B. #132
Salina, KS 67401
785-392-3122

Thomsen, Loyd W.
HRC-46 Box 19
Oelrichs, SD 57763
605-535-6162

Thrash, James D.
81 Vallecitos Loop
Tijeras, NM 87059
505-286-4779

Vallet, Louis M.
82 Palm Dr., Bay Point
Key West, FL 33040
305-745-1044

Waites, Dick
3315 Cooper Ave.
Broomfield, CO 80020
303-465-9970

Waldrup, Bill E.
30121 1st Ave. S.
Federal Way, WA 98003
253-839-3362

Weir, Jacque
2721 S. Arkansas Ave.
Russellville, AR 72801

Wheeler, Harold J.
1310 N. Broadway
Shawnee, OK 74801
405-273-0999

Wiggins, Marc E.
8552 N. Melody Ln.
Macedonia, OH 44056
330-468-2977

Zima, Michael F.
732 State Street
Fort Morgan, CO 80701
970-867-6078

Zronek, Daniel F.
45007 N. 16th St.
New River, AZ 85087
623-465-2727

In April of 1987, another field of knife collecting was formalized with the organization of the Miniature Knifemakers Society. It was formed in an effort to address the interests and needs of makers and collectors of miniature knives. The goals of the MKS are simply to promote miniature knife collecting, support displays at shows, share information, and insure customer trust by requiring that members guarantee their products.

These are admirable goals for any organization! Neither the value of the little knives nor the effort it takes to make them should be discounted. As with other custom knives, they are often an art form.

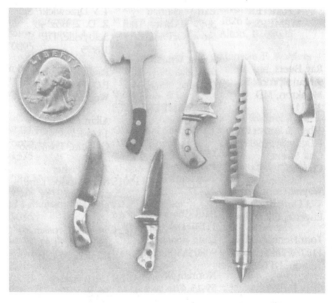

Terry Kranning's knives are excellent examples of the quality of work of the maker/members of the Miniature Knifemakers Society.

Directly after WWII, factory-produced sheath and hunting knives reached a low ebb in popularity. This came about because most of the combat knives issued to our troops were of notoriously poor quality. Our GIs would jump at a chance to exchange them, even for an English or German-made knife of better quality. An old line commercial or custom-made knife would elicit a fit of enthusiasm from the same GI trader.

Of course it does something to a man's pride if he is trapped in a situation where he has to open a can of beans with his sheath knife and later finds the blade grossly bent and distorted. Any doubt as to the accuracy of this description can be quickly dispelled just by asking someone who was there. Yet, the ever increasing interest in pocketknife collecting spread inevitably to include the fine old pre-WWII sheath knives that were made by old cutlery firms, and with the appearance of so many custom knifemakers during the last decades, these older blades, as well as the finer more recently manufactured ones, have increased tremendously in value.

It did take a crop of the best custom knifemakers the world has ever known nearly two decades to restore our pride, confidence, and self-esteem to where we once more felt that we could be the owners of a blade made of the best steel and design available anywhere. The rediscovered art of the custom makers has now been transferred to late model factory-produced knives. With their beauty of design, suitability, and higher price tags, these knives have begun competing once more with models from top line custom makers.

Models such as the Hibben designed Browning line, Colt/Wood design, Schrade-Walden/Loveless, and many others, have price tags well within range of the custom-made knife and are certainly just as good. Satisfying the owner's ego has become the chief variable to consider.

The W.R. Case Co.'s "Kodiak Hunter," though still in production, has already become a collector's prize. We have no reason at all to doubt that many other models in the commercial line will reach higher collector value in the future.

Naturally, the average collector of pocketknives cannot help becoming aware of and interested in these fixed-blade beauties. For this reason we are including a limited listing of sheath and hunting knives and their approximate values.

Since stable and fixed patterns for sheath knives are at best uncertain, our prices will approximate the collector value of each brand's average model in Excellent to Mint condition. Most firms generally made use of bone, wood, leather, and hard rubber for handle materials. The material did not make a great deal of difference in value. However, some did use fine stag and even pearl on their knives. In these cases, it is advisable to use the Handle Materials, Chart No. 3, to adjust the value. Also, if the knife is in less than Excellent condition, consult Condition Scale No. 4, and make the suggested reduction.

IDENTIFICATION	MINT
AERIAL (Disc.)	$300.00
BROWNING (c. 1969–) USA	250.00
BUCK	115.00
BUCK (General)	85.00
BUCK (Kalinga)	105.00
BUCK (Old)	250.00
CAMILLUS	65.00
CAMILLUS (Old)	155.00
CATTARAUGUS (Old)	365.00
CASE	125.00+
CASE (Old)	285.00
CASE (Astronaut commem.)	750.00
COLONIAL	55.00
COLONIAL (Old)	175.00
COLT (c. 1969–)	285.00
FRONTIER (Imperial)	65.00
GARCIA/HACKMAN	40.00
GARCIA (Survival)	70.00
GERBER	70.00
GERBER (Old)	115.00
GUTMANN (Old)	95.00
IMPERIAL	60.00
IMPERIAL (Old)	150.00
JAEGER BROS. (Disc.)	265.00
JEAN CASE (Disc.)	450.00

IDENTIFICATION	MINT
KABAR	125.00
KA-BAR (Old)	400.00
KUTMASTER (Utica)	65.00
KINFOLKS	445.00
MARBLES	65.00
MARBLES (Old)	410.00
NORMARK (Finland)	60.00
OLD (Colonial cut.)	85.00
OLSEN (Disc.)	85.00
PAL (Disc.)	165.00
PAL/REMINGTON (Disc.)	285.00
PARKER	55.00
PARKER-FROST	60.00
PUMA (White Hunter)	225.00
PUUKOO (Finland)	35.00
QUEEN	65.00
QUEEN (Old)	225.00
RANDALL (Survival) Sol., Ger.	650.00
REMINGTON (Disc.)	650.00
RIGID RUSSELL, A.G.	285.00
RUSSELL (Not John Russell), Canada	70.00
RUSSELL, J. (Disc.)	650.00
SCHRADE	55.00
SCHRADE-WALDEN	75.00
SCHRADE (Old)	185.00

IDENTIFICATION   MINT

SCHRADE-WALDEN/LOVELESS	210.00
SMITH & WESSON (c. 1974–)	150.00
SHAPLEIGH (Disc.)	200.00
SCHATT & MORGAN/S&M (Disc.)	215.00
TAYLOR CUT	50.00
THOMPSON/CENTER (Sewell)	85.00
UTICA (Disc.)	90.00
WESTERN STATES (Old)	95.00
WESTERN	75.00
WESTERNMARK (Western)	75.00
WINCHESTER (Disc.)	650.00

Excellent American Commercial Hunting Knives

Schrade-Walden – Uncle Henry
Heavy genuine leather sheath and piggy-back hone stone in handsome gift box. Length overall 10⅛".

Western Cutlery
Blade length 5½", overall length 10".

A book on cutlery is not complete without a section on the old stag, bone, and wood handled kitchen cutlery of our ancestors. Especially collectible are those old carving sets consisting of a fine carving knife, a fork, and a steel for sharpening. There are also many other examples so skillfully wrought that, even without showing a maker's mark, grab the eye with such grace and beauty that they were recognized as works of art. Some were of foreign origin, but most of them were made by such indigenous firms as Russell, Remington, Winchester, and Cattaraugus, from which any product is considered worthy of collecting. Most intriguing of all, those old sets are steeped in tradition, having graced homes and castles for centuries, associating themselves with many happy memories of family reunions, holidays, and gala occasions.

In truth, they stem from those early colonial and pre-colonial days when such things as individual knives, forks, and spoons were just not available for every person around the dining table. A boxed carving set consisting of knife, fork, and steel was the pride of every household. When skillfully applied to a main dish of roast pig, fowl, or leg of lamb by the lord master, compliments for the cook and the carver were often abundant.

Realizing this, where could we possibly find a person "with soul so dead" that he would not swell up with pride when given the oppportunity to use one of these fine old stag carvers instead of (hush your mouth!) that domesticated hedgeshear sometimes fortuitously called an "electric carving knife"?

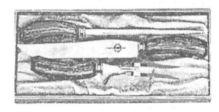

An example of a beautiful old stag carving set.

Wow! Those wonderous boxed and cased old sets are definitely top-line collector items. In fact, some of our better known custom knifemakers have added them to their line. We predict more will follow.

Aside from these, there are also many other old items of kitchen cutlery such as cooks' knives, butcher knives, steak sets, and plain old table knives that are zooming in value as collector items. The collector should look especially for those having handles of pearl, stag, bone, or exotic wood to authenticate age and value. Since so much emphasis at this time is being given to handle material, it is advisable to use the Value Rating Scale (Chart No. 3), and the Condition Scale (Chart No. 4) by the same system as applied to other old knives in this manual.

The items included in the following listing are mostly those from our older American cutlery firms. You will very likely find many English and other foreign brands. These are comparable but somewhat less desirable as collector items.

IDENTIFICATION   MINT

BOKER CUTLERY CO.
Stag Handles, 3-piece set w/box $225.00

BRIDGE CUTLERY CO.
Stag Handles, 3-piece set w/box   350.00

CAMILLUS CUTLERY CO.
Stag Handles, 3-piece set w/box   175.00

CASE CUTLERY CO.
Stag Handles, 3-piece set w/box   200.00

CATTARAUGUS CUTLERY CO.
Stag Handles, 3-piece set w/box   325.00

GOODELL CO. USA
Stag Handles, 3-piece set w/box   200.00

CHRISTY
Wire Handle, bread knife   55.00

W.C. HEIMERDINGER
Wood Handle   125.00

HIBBARD, SPENCER, BARTLETT & CO.
Bakelite Handles, 3-piece set w/box   120.00

JOHN RUSSELL & CO.
Stag Handles, 3-piece set w/box
(Sculptured animal pommels)   800.00

JOHN RUSSELL & CO.
Wood handles, butcher only   45.00
Wood Handles, paring knife only   15.00

LANDERS, FRARY & CLARK
Celluloid Handles, 3-piece set w/box   125.00

LANDERS, FRARY & CLARK
Wood Handles, butcher only   25.00
Wood Handles, paring knife only   15.00

IDENTIFICATION   MINT

LEWIS ROSE & CO. (LARKO)
Bone Handles, 3-piece set w/box — 200.00

MERIDIAN CUTLERY CO.
Stag Handles, 3-piece set w/box — 350.00

REMINGTON USA (DUPONT)
Stag Handles, 3-piece set w/box — 450.00

REMINGTON USA (DUPONT)
Wood Handles, butcher only — 45.00
Wood Handles, paring knife only — 20.00

ROYAL BRAND CUTLERY CO. (SHARP-CUT)
Bakelite (Rough Black) Handles, 3-piece set — 80.00

ULSTER KNIFE CO.
Bone Handles, 3-piece set w/box — 210.00

ULSTER KNIFE CO.
Wood Handles, butcher only — 25.00
Wood Handles, paring knife only — 10.00

UTICA KNIFE CO.
Stag Handles, 3-piece set w/box — 310.00

VALLEY FORGE CUTLERY CO.
Bakelite Handles, 3-piece set w/box — 50.00

WADE & BUTCHER, ENGLAND
Stag Handles, 3-piece set w/box — 300.00

WINCHESTER, TRADEMARK USA
Stag Handles, 3-piece set w/box — 675.00

WINCHESTER USA
Wood Handles, butcher only — 80.00
Wood Handles, cook's knife only — 55.00
Wood Handles, paring knife only — 15.00

NOTE: Most of the old kitchen cutlery was marked by etching only. This is usually erased or made illegible by use or exposure. This reduces the value of an item approximately 30%. Also, the short or two-piece set is reduced 30% in value from a full or three-piece set. Single pieces of original sets are valued at 50% for knife only, 15% for fork only, and 15% for steel only

A John Primble display of a variety of the kitchen knives they carried.

As the popularity of straight razors increases, prices of those razors also increase. This carries with it a lure of investment possibilities which can encourage the novice or speculator to make purchases that may later prove to be unwise. We recommend that before investing serious money in razors you become familiar with the elements which make a razor valuable. As with other collectibles, there are specific traits which are desirable and which have a major impact on the price of a piece.

The following information is based on our book, *The Standard Guide to Razors*, by Roy Ritchie and Ron Stewart (available from R&C Books, P.O. Box 151, Combs, KY 41729, or RBR Cutlery, 197 Royhill Rd. Hindman, KY 41822 @$9.95 +$2.50 S&H). It describes the elements most likely to influence a razor's collector value and the system of calculating that value. The book is a valuable reference guide for both the casual and serious collector of razors.

There are four major factors which determine a razor's collector value: the brand and country of origin; the handle material; the art work found on the handles and/or blades; and the condition of the razor. We freely admit that there are numerous other factors that may come into play with some collectors, but these are the major ones in determining value. However, our system of evaluation is based on those four factors.

The most important factor is the brand and country of origin, and the base value for a common razor with plain handles, probably plastic, no art work other than perhaps a simple blade etch, and in collectible condition. Hundreds of these values are provided in the Ritchie-Stewart razor book.

The second category is that of handle material. This covers a wide range of materials from fiber on the low end to ivory on the high end. The collector should be able to identify the different handle materials which takes practice since there are some very good plastics that mimic even ivory quite successfully. Also, the difference between genuine celluloid and plastic can become significant when determining value. A detailed chart of these values is supplied in the razor book, but the listing below can be used as a general guide.

The third category, artwork, is the most subjective, but is an extremely important factor in determining value. Art can include everything from logo art to carving and sculpture and may range from the highly ornate to the tastefully correct. Blade etching as well as artistic handles are to be considered. Perhaps what some call the "gotta have it" or the "neatness" factors properly fall into this category. You must determine just where your razor falls in evaluating this category. Again, the razor book provides a more complete listing of considerations than is used here.

Finally, the condition is considered. The book's scales run from Parts (10%+) to Good (150%+/-). Average (100%+/-) is classified as Collectible.

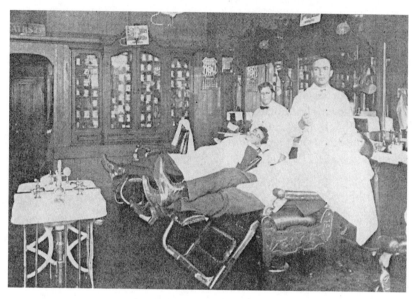

Barber shops as pictured above were commonplace. The straight razor was a common tool of that trade. Straight razor collecting is very popular today.

Chart A: Companies & Base Value

Abercrombie & Fitch, NY	$12.00
Aerial, USA	21.00
Boker, Henri & Co., Germany	13.00
Brick, F., England	11.00
Case Mfg. Co., Spring Valley, NY	35.00
Chores, James	9.00
Dahlgren, C.W., Sweden	11.00
Diane, Japan	10.00
Electric Co., NY	14.00
ERN, Germany	11.00

Faultless, Germany	10.00
Fox Cutlery, Germany	9.00
Golden Rule Cutlery, Chicago	12.00
Griffon XX, Germany	10.00
Heimerdinger	15.00
Henckels, Germany	15.00
Holley Mfg. Co., CT	27.00
International Cutlery Co., NY/Germany	8.00
I.X.L., England	14.00
Jay, John, NY	10.00
KaBar, Union Cut Co., USA	28.00
Kanner, J., Germany	6.00
Kern, R. & W., Canada/England	9.00
LeCocltre, Jacque, Switzerland	12.00
Levering Razor Co., NY/Germany	18.00
McIntosh & Heather, OH	12.00
Merit Import Co., Germany	8.00
National Cut. Co., OH	11.00
Oxford Razor Co., Germany	10.00
Owl Brand, England	9.00
Palmer Brothers, Savannah, GA	20.00
Primble, John, India Steel Works, Louisville, KY	22.00
Queen City, NY	30.00
Quigley, Germany	8.00
Rattler Razor Co., Germany	10.00
Robeson Cut. Co., USA	25.00

Salamander Works, Germany	11.00
Soderein, Ekilstuna, Sweden	11.00
Taylor, L.M., Cincinnati, OH	14.00
Tower Brand, Germany	10.00
Ulmer, Germany	10.00
U.S. Barber Supply, TX	11.00
Vinnegut Hwd. Co., IN	11.00
Vogel, E.D., PA	10.00
Wade & Butcher, England	24.00
Weis, J.H. Supply House, Louisville, KY	15.00
Yankee Cutlery Co., Germany	11.00
Yazbek, Lahod, OH	9.00
Zacour Bros., Germany	8.00
Zepp, Germany	8.00

Chart B: Handle Material

Ivory	550%
Tortise Shell	500%
Pearl	400%
Stag	400%
Bone	300%
Celluloid	250%
Composition	150%
Plastic	100%

Chart C: Art Work

Superior	550%
Good	400%
Average	300%
Minimal	200%
Plain	100%
Nonexistent	0%

Chart D: Condition

Good	150%	Does not have to be factory mint to fall within this category. However, there can be no visible flaws if it is calculated at 150%.
Collectible	100%	May have some flaws that do not greatly detract from the artwork or finish.
Parts	10%	Unrepairable — valuable as salvageable parts.

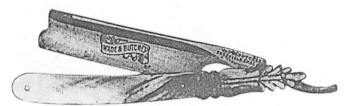

Courtesy of Smoky Mountain Knife Works

To determine the collector value of your razor, multiply A times B, then multiply A times C. Add these two answers and multiply that sum by D. The answer is your collector value. [(A x B) + (A x C)] x D = Collector Value. See example below:

(A) Brand and Origin Base Value	(B) Handle Material % Value	(C) Artwork % Value	(D) Condition % Value	Collector Value
Wade & Butcher England $24.00	Iridescent pearl handles 24x400%= $96.00	Carved handles 24x350%= $84.00	Cracked handle at pin Collectible– 80%	$96+$84=$180 $180x80%= $144.00

Chart samples from *The Standard Guide to Razors.*

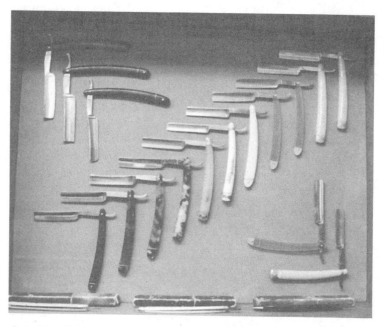

Impressive displays such as this collection of Heimerdinger razors contribute to the popularity of razor collecting. (C.E. Heimerdinger collection)

When the newly smitten collector acquires a dozen or so knives, he immediately begins thinking of some neat and attractive means of keeping his treasures together. It is quite normal for him to want a better way of storing them than unceremoniously dumping the knives into an old cigar box where they are free to rattle and roll around in amiable togetherness, to stain, scratch, chip, and rust at will.

There are numerous options to consider, most of which have been tried by both old and new collectors. These include knife rolls, packets that fold like books, display cases with glassed in departments, portable and stationary containers with small cubical drawers for individual knives, and, of course, boxes, plaques, and boards. If the collector is looking for something that will display his knives nicely and be easily accessible for cleaning, transporting, and storing them, he would be wise to consider a small, well-constructed knife roll.

In defense of the small rolls' superior usefulness for transporting, displaying, and storing knives, we would like to point out that they have been traditional since the days of the wagon jobber. The early salesman always carried his sample knives in small rolls and displayed them for merchants and others in hopes of securing orders for lot shipment.

Although portable covered display cases that hold knives in place with elastic loops or spring clips, plaques, and knife boards provide exceptionally beautiful displays, they are also invariably unwieldy to transport and limited in capacity.

TRANSPORTING

Some collectors transport large quantities of knives to knife shows, club meetings, etc., and many of them use boxes of various types, such as large, soft plastic trays with airtight covers. From these, they transfer their knives to display cases. Since it is necessary to use boxes or trays to transport large collections, it would be wise to insert thin sheets of foamed plastic material between the layers of knives. The large folding hunter patterns and fixed-blade knives can be nestled in slots or troughs cut to their size in thicker foam plastic slabs. This material is very inexpensive, but it is so strong and light in weight that it is ideal for the job.

With small and medium collections, it is more convenient to use packets, folding display cases, or small rolls, as shown below. All are easy to maneuver, but several small rolls will hold more knives and occupy less space than an equal number of packets or cases. And by leaving the tie loose, they will flatten out in a suitcase so as to occupy very little space.

If the need is present, you can also transport knives by U.S. mail, United Parcel Service, or freight, but make sure they are well packed and insured. When you do ship valuable old knives, you may be asked for a purchase or appraisal receipt, or another document to substantiate their value; be sure to have it. The shipping container should show no evidence that it contains knives. You can also transport knives by the airways, if they are in your baggage, but be sure you don't try taking them aboard in your personal luggage.

STORING

Since we have already discussed transportation, the reader has very likely concluded that good storage can be accomplished by the same methods. Some changes are necessary to make the collector's knives more accessible and convenient to locate. Once again we recommend the small rolls and packets.

Most collectors we know collect many varieties and patterns of knives, but even those who specialize in only one field will very soon find it convenient, and almost necessary, to have their knives sorted into groups of similar brand, size, handle materials, etc., for quick location. Because of this, the small rolls and packets are almost ideal. The small roll, holding a maximum of three dozen knives, can be labeled according to the type of knives they hold, and stored in drawers, boxes, or on bookshelves as you would books, but they do occupy more space than the larger rolls.

In selecting rolls, be sure that they are well made of heavy vinyl such as naugahyde or leatherette, and lined with velvet or other soft cloth. Good quality elastic bands should be well attached to hold knives in place, and there should be no loose cloth carrying straps. These are usually worthless on knife rolls, and a single strong strap of fabric for securing the roll when closed is usually sufficient. You will not need a handle for carrying these small sized rolls. There are rolls on the market that hold up to 200 knives, but you will find these about as handy as a restroom with no tissue paper.

Remember that when storing larger knives in plastic trays and boxes for a lengthy period of time, it is advisable to punch out some holes in the boxes for ventilation. And if available, throw in a few packets of silica gel to absorb condensation.

Should you possess any old knives with genuine celluloid scales be sure to store them individually, not in close proximity with other knives. This beautiful old handle material can become unstable with age and begin a process of sudden disintegration. When this happens, the celluloid gives off fumes that are very corrosive and will rapidly rust and corrode other knives nearby or in the same container. This happens, of course, only with genuine old celluloids and not with the modern plastic scales that are made to simulate the old celluloid types. These newer knives can be stored safely along with all other knives.

Finally, never store knives in leather or roll them in paper towels. Residual acids in the leather and paper will corrode even stainless steel and brass if stored for very long.

CLEANING AND LUBRICATING

No matter how knives are stored, they will need to be taken out and examined and very likely cleaned after only a few months. For knives that have been properly cleaned and stored, this involves little effort. First check the blades, backsprings, and bolsters for staining and beginning rust, and if you cannot remove these by wiping with an oiled cloth, try removing them with a pencil eraser. Many times light staining and rust specking can be erased without harming the polish. But if this doesn't work, don't reach for sandpaper or emery cloth; get one of the milder abrasive rubber block erasers. These abrasive erasers are made in several grades of abrasiveness, and the finer grade is much less likely to scratch your knives' finish.

When your blade is clean enough, use a little high grade penetrating oil on the joints. Just remember, though, that the penetrating oil is for cleaning and flushing out rust and dirt. It will evaporate in a short time. So before you store your knives again, go over them with a good silicone base lubricant, such as the ones used on guns. These have been thoroughly tested by gun owners and they are the best preservatives and rust preventing lubricants we know of. They are a little more expensive, but knives, like guns, are expensive, and your knives will definitely keep much longer in storage.

KEEPING TABS ON YOUR COLLECTION

The most overlooked aspect of the care and management of a knife collection is simply keeping tabs on the collection itself. There are those who can assure you, without hesitation, that they know the value, location, amount invested, condition, and collector value of every knife they own.

Well, perhaps they do. However, when your collection grows into the hundreds (and it can do so quicker than you might expect), it becomes more difficult to keep tabs on it.

A record keeping system can help you keep a handle on the amount of money you invest, the knives you trade or sell, and the growth of your collection's value. Records are also invaluable to the person who needs to account for his collection for insurance purposes. It is difficult to convince an insurance adjustor of the value of a collection referenced only from memory.

Some notes of caution:
•Do not store records with your collection!
•Keep records up to date.
•Do not store records where they are readily available to a thief; it would be like furnishing a list of what to look for.
•Do not store records (or knives) where they might burn.

• Although they are safe from fire and theft, safety deposit boxes are not ideal places to store knives unless they are checked with regularity. Rust happens!
• Date your entries; this adds validity to them when you're dealing with an insurance adjustor.
• Have your collection appraised annually, and keep a written record.

We suggest an adaptation of the following chart, either on cards or in a notebook, as a method of keeping records on your collection. Feel free to copy this chart, if you like.

COLLECTION RECORD

Brand: _____   Date Required: _____

Pattern: _____   Amount Invested: _____

Pattern Number (if available): _____

Handle Material(s): _____   Collector Value: _____
                                        (RE: RBR Scales)

# of Blades: _____   Appraised by: _____

Length Closed: _____   Date: _____

Approximate Age: _____   Where Stored: _____

Stampings: _____   Last Viewed: _____

Condition: _____   Other: _____

Comments or observations: _____

_____

_____

The authors do insurance and individual appraisals. Contact:

Ron Stewart
P.O. Box 151
Combs, KY 41729

Roy Ritchie
P.O. Box 384
Hindman, KY 41822

Knife sharpening is one of man's oldest survival skills and not at all the difficult and exacting task that the typical urban blade-bender describes it to be. In bygone days, even dummies knew this. But, in this age of electric toothbrushes, leg shavers, and mustache trimmers, it seems most people are scared out of their wits at the mere mention of sharpening their own knives. A cuckoo's nest of myths and fables have grown up about knife sharpening methods. Many people are under the illusion that they cannot hold a blade at the proper angle for sharpening without some type of device, a miracle stone, and a special kind of sharpening oil. That is mostly bunk.

As the knife user will soon learn with a little experience in knife sharpening, the art of holding the blade at the proper angle on the stone will become almost instinctive. Other than this, a little experience in setting the finished edge on the sharpened blade is about all the skill that is required.

The time and difficulty one is confronted with is determined by the type and tempered hardness of the steel of the blade. Some cutlery firms, and especially custom knifemakers, produce knives with very hard metal alloy blades. While a sharp edge on these knives will usually last longer before becoming dull, it is very difficult to resharpen. Since no edge will stand up long under a maximum of survival conditions, the owner of such blades should not expect to gain a great deal of advantage. The length of time any blade will hold its edge is almost in direct proportion to the difficulty required for resetting it to sharpness again. Let us say then that in our opinion, most of us will be better off if we stick to the types of steel standardized by commercial knifemakers, such as high carbon tool or 440C stainless. If tempered to about RC 56, these steels can be sharpened with a minimum of difficulty.

But different usage and the cutting of different materials require different degrees of sharpness and different edges. Most everyone knows that you don't use a razor for whittling, or an ax for shaving. These tools have specialized edges for specialized uses. One needs a thin, sharp blade for cutting soft, yielding material, and a thicker, stronger blade for hacking hard substances.

If you examine any edge, no matter how keen, under a powerful microscope, you'll find that it has tiny jags similar to the teeth of a very fine saw. Yet your blade is not gapped, because this is quite natural and useful in cutting if the blade is drawn or pushed through the material like the action used in sawing. Hence, when slicing bread, a tomato, or even whittling, the blade is drawn through, not pushed directly into the material.

So if you like to carry a really sharp knife and you find yourself in rough going, such as cutting and hacking hard material, your knife will soon become extremely dull regardless of the type of steel or hardness of your blade. You will need to resharpen it if you're going to continue using it for rough work; there is no need to restore that keen, thin edge immediately. If you've neglected to bring a "wonder gadget" or even a carborundum stone, you may, with just a little luck and experience, find a small rock that will serve well enough. We've known some experienced guides and hunters to use unglazed crockery, cast iron skillets, and even the scratch panels of a matchbox effectively.

Yet, most all people who habitually carry good knives want them to be very sharp at all times. For that reason (and because I prefer it myself), we'll do our best to direct you in acquiring this vital skill, and maybe we'll puncture a few myths in the telling.

In the first place, it is quite unnecessary to use oil on your stone. Use a dry stone. The only time your stone should be wet is when it becomes dirty and you wash it in lukewarm water. Then be sure to air dry it before using it again. Actually that gritty, oily slush you push your blade through can be scouring and gapping it to a degree where it is virtually impossible to obtain that keen edge you desire. To be sure, oil may make your stone cut a little faster, but at the same time it is cutting away and dulling your edge. It would be better to use the oil in your furnace this winter.

We know that leaving off the oil is a hard break with tradition, but the facts have been substantially proven by scientific laboratory testing. A few cutlery manufacturers such as The Queen Cutlery Company now recommend their blades be sharpened on dry stones only, and all their blades are 440C stainless steel which is more difficult to sharpen than high carbon tool steel.

Perhaps harder yet to digest is the fact that the very best sharpening stones in the world today are high grade, man-made carborundum stones. They can be far superior to any natural stone ever taken from a mine. In modern laboratories, man can duplicate any stone found in nature and, except for diamonds, improve on its texture and contents. Of course, natural stones are good, but they are much more expensive.

So forget tradition. Get yourself a good factory-made stone or two. Maybe for beginning, one good stone with a coarse grit on one side and fine grit on the other side will do. However, its minimum size should be at least 2" x 6" and approximately one inch thick. Now to save yourself the cost of a cradle to hold your stone stationary, place it on a block of wood that is a little larger in length and width than the stone. Trace around it with a marker and chisel out until it beds in no more than half the thickness of the stone, or you can just frame it with small strips of wood. Place it on your workbench and you have both hands free to work.

Then measure and cut an angle of approximately 22 degrees from a strip of stiff paper or plastic for your primary edge. Now, holding the angle guide upright on the stone with your left hand, lay the blade of your knife on the angle with its edge contacting the stone at the point. Now study this angle very carefully and do your best to hold it as you work. A little variation should do no harm and is to be expected. Then, lay your angle finder aside and begin drawing your blade edge forward across the stone with a little downward pressure as if slicing it. Work one side for any number of strokes, then the other an equal number until you can detect a tiny burr forming on the opposite side of the edge you are working, by gently stroking it flat against, and backwards, over your fingertips. Never do this point first unless you enjoy wearing band-aids. Then turn your blade over and work the other side until you find the burr has turned. You'll now need to finish your edge on a fine grit stone, carefully working both sides with an even number of strokes until the burr can no longer be detected on either side.

Now test your blade for sharpness. Some use the dry shave method of shaving hair off their arm. But better still use a soft wood whittle stick and compare your blade with another blade that is already sharpened. If it is sharp enough to suit you, give it a final setting by stroking or stropping it on leather such as your belt, an old razor strap, or the heel-cut of your boot, drawing the edge backward and away from the edge with even and alternate strokes. Some use the palm of their hands and this might help some if you don't wear shoes.

I still prefer the leather strap method my grandpa used on his fine old straight razor. Still, another method is to use a cutler's steel, and a few careful strokes (I mean careful, don't try that flashy stuff butchers use), and you can set an edge that will surprise a professional.

Many woodsmen carry their steels as religiously as they do their knives. Some very small ones being manufactured today can be carried in the same sheath as the knife, or in one's pocket.

Now, if you have succeeded in getting your blade sharp, you can use it many times and for a lengthy period by just resetting the edge occasionally before there is need for another sharpening job.

However, if you are the type who uses your knife consistently, you will eventually find it necessary to do a different type of sharpening. As a knife is used, the primary edge wears away gradually and a shoulder or secondary edge builds up just behind the true (or primary) edge.

This creates much difficulty in cutting very deep below the surface of the material, because your edge has become blunt or wedge shaped. Its thickness at the secondary edges or shoulders tends to spread or pry the material apart rather than slicing into it. Your next need then is to cut another angle guide of approximately twelve degrees. This will let your blade lie almost (but not quite) flat against the rough grit stone. By using the same sharpening method described at first, proceed to remove this secondary edge until you feel the burr beginning to form on the true edge from both sides. Then proceed to set your edge by whichever method you like. Keep in mind that you will not have to remove the secondary edge very often, and certainly not every time your knife becomes dull. Unless you have a very thick blade, such as some sheath knives have, just resharpening or setting the edge will do.

It seems many modern sheath and hunting knives derive their thick blade and other characteristics from old-style fighting knives, these are largely unsuited for jobs such as skinning and dressing game. Although there is not much game to skin now, we should take a lesson from the American Indians, plainsmen, and buffalo skinners. They chose the common old kitchen butcher knife such as those manufactured by John Russell, Green River Works. These were well suited for dressing game. With a thin, upswept blade, it was easy to keep sharp, and it required but little effort to send it "up to Green River" in whatever material was available. There is still a breed of men considered top-notch woodsmen who still use the old butcher for such task. So if you are a knife user, a collector, or just interested in knives, you should discover how easy it really is to sharpen knives naturally and instinctively without any gadgetry at all, because knife sharpening is truly a survival skill.

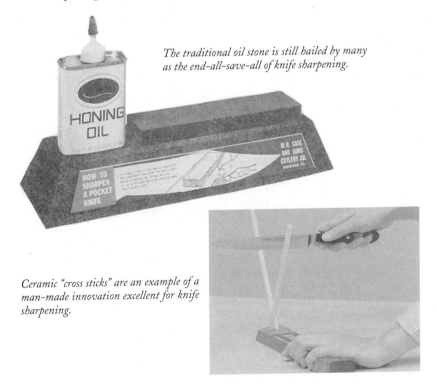

The traditional oil stone is still hailed by many as the end-all-save-all of knife sharpening.

Ceramic "cross sticks" are an example of a man-made innovation excellent for knife sharpening.

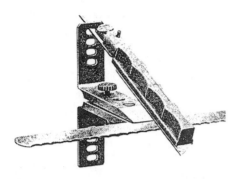

Sharpeners such as this one by Lansky allow you to rehabilitate an edge and sharpen it to a specific angle.

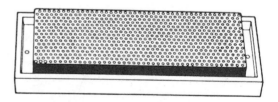

LANSKY SHARPENING ANGLES

17° ANGLE. A severe angle only recommended for razor blades, X-Acto® blades or similar tools. Provides an extremely sharp but highly delicate edge.

20° ANGLE. A commonly used angle for higher grade, quality blades. Provides an excellent edge for these types of knives. Ideal for kitchen knives.

25° ANGLE. The recommended angle for most knives that need a durable, sharp edge. Ideal for hunting and outdoor knives.

30° ANGLE. An outstanding angle for knives that see the heavy use of cutting cardboard, wire or carpets. Only for heavy duty use.

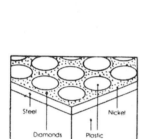

Manmade "stones" such as this one by "Diamond Whetstone" are very effective in honing an edge. The "stones" come in fine, coarse, and extra coarse.

378

Pocket and portable sharpeners are quite common and effective.

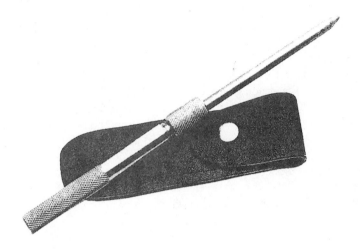

Model M Sportsman's Diamond sharpener. 8" overall, 3½" round rod.

Economy Diamond sharpener. 5⅞" long.

379

⚔ CUTLERY STORES, MAIL ORDER DEALERS, AND ON-LINE DEALERS ⚔

If the hobby of collecting cutlery is to grow and expand to the point where it takes its rightful place alongside stamp collecting and coin collecting, the appreciation of quality cutlery by the general public must be cultivated. The trend toward cheap cutlery products which "really, really work" and must be resharpened with the grinding wheel found on the back of the electric can opener (if even that method is successful) must be exposed for the rip-offs they are. Whether one is discussing kitchen knives, folding and pocketknives, or hunting knives, the end result is the same. A person blessed with an inferior product will develop a bad taste for that product in general.

Such is a valid fear, especially since the home computer and the Internet have become so popular. A recent search for pocketknife, using the search engine Google revealed 209,000 sites dealing with pocketknife. The search took 0.04 seconds.

Collectors can find literally thousands of knives on auctions sites such as eBay. In spite of some of the stories you may hear of people getting ripped off, you should not fear using these sites. They should be viewed simply as available sources of collectibles. You can find items in a few minutes that may take years to find elsewhere. You do need to know what you are looking for and ask questions about the product, including, "If the knife is not as advertised, can I return it?" Unsatisfactory answers should tell you volumes! Remember though, good reference guides are a must in finding what you want.

Perhaps the best and most effective way of learning the difference between shoddy and quality products is by comparison. The person interested in knife collecting has ample opportunity to see quality cutlery at knife shows, trade meets, etc. The person who is not particularly interested in the collection aspect of cutlery has the alternative of comparison at stores and cutlery shops which deal with all types of knives. For many years the local hardware store played an important role in supplying excellent quality cutlery for the consumer; many still do. However, the variety is generally not there anymore. Increased costs, heavy competition from discount houses, and, of course, interest rates, have precluded the variety which was once there.

In order to get a good look at the variety of cutlery products currently on the market, the non-collecting consumer must find a knife cutlery shop. There are a number of these businesses around some small towns, and in many mid-sized to major cities across the United States. Many are privately owned establishments, some relatively new, while others are well-established concerns.

We are listing a number of privately owned cutlery shops and mail order dealers which will appreciate your business. So either write for a catalog or drop in, look around, and buy something! Encourage them! They are the ones on the front line in teaching the public to appreciate quality cutlery products.

Of course, the following listing is by no means complete. No stores or reputable mail order businesses have been left out deliberately. If you know of one which we've not included, please drop us a line, and we'll try to get it in our next edition.

The Acorn Shop
Gatlinburg, TN

A.G. Russell
1705 Hwy. 71
Springdale, AR 72764

A&J Enterprises
Box 1343
Springfield, MO 65805

Americana LTD.
P.O. 170C. Hwy. #157
Smithfield, KY 40068

Antique Armament, Inc.
12859 Old Cutler Rd.
Coral Gables, FL 33156

Atlanta Cutlery
Box 389
Conyers, GA 30207

Roy Bayes Products
819 Binns Blvd.
Columbus, OH 43204

B & B Distributing
P.O. Box 374
Kingsport, TN 37662

Bill's for Knives
5 Dorchester Rd.
Collegeville, PA 19426

Blue Ridge Knife Co.
Rt. 6, Box 185
Marion, VA 24354

Blue River Knife Works
P.O. Box 244
Rushville, IN 46173

Boone Trading Co.
562 Coyote Rd.
Binnon, WA 98320

Buckley's Knives
RR #5, Box 28 A
North Vernon, IN 41265

Burnt Chimney Cutlery Co.
P.O. Box 188
Forest City, NC 28403

Paul Charles Busch Enterprises
W. Del Amo Blvd. Suite 1
Long Beach, CA 90805

Frank Buster
P.O. Box 936
Lebanon, TN 37087

C & R Knives
P.O. Box 8088
Chester, OH 45069

Cecil E. Clark Co.
1038 Monmouth St.
Newport, KY 41071

Classic Cutlery
Suite 195
Daniel Webster Hwy.
Nashua, NH 03060

Corrado Cutlery, Inc.
25. N. Clark St.
Chicago, IL 60602

Country Knives
4134 Old Phila. Pike
Intercourse, PA 17534

Crazy Crow
P.O. Box 314
Denison, TX 75020

Damascus-USA
149 Deans Farm Rd.
Tyler, NC 27980

Paul Davis Collector Cutlery
P.O. Box 9354
Chattanooga, TN 37412

Davidson's
2703 High Point Rd.
P.O. Box 5387
Greensboro, NC 27435-0387

J.W. Denton
Box 429
Hiawassee, GA 30546-0429

Duty-Bynum Company
Corinth, KY 41010

Eagle Brand Farm
Box 23522
Chattanooga, TN 37422

Edge of the World
Jack London Village
Oakland, CA 94607

EK Commando Knife Co.
601 Lombardy St.
Richmond, VA 23220

Roy Fazalare
P.O. Box 3373
Granada Hills, CA 91344

Fitz Cutlery
P.O. Box 227
Middlebranch, OH 44652

Forest Cruse & Son
Box 2122
Austin, TX 78768

Bob Freeman
4512 Foxfire Way
Fort Worth, TX 76133

Frost Cutlery
Box 21353
Chattanooga, TN 37421

Fulton Hardware
126 Main Street
Ripley, OH 45167

Garden State Surplus
301 Broadway
Camden, NJ 08103

Herb Gaynor
12859 Old Cutler Rd.
Coral Gables, FL 33156

Goodwin Enterprises
Box 4124 A
Chattanooga, TN 37405

Gorilla & Sons
Box 2309
Bellingham, WA 98227

Green's Cutlery
P.O. Box 55
Jackson, TN 38301

Hee's Enterprises
3810 S. 41st
Greenville, WI 53221

Joe Hillard
Box 1629
Marysville, CA 95901

H&S Farms & Knives
514 14th St.
Kenova, WV

Hard Hat Knives
P.O. Box 248
Owensboro, KY 42302

Heimerdinger's
4207 Shelbyville Rd.
Louisville, KY 40207
1-888-267-9572
http://www.heimerdingercutlery.com

Heritage Antique Knives
P.O. Box 22171
Chattanooga, TN 37422

Hickory Hill Cutlery
Rt. 2, Box 171 A
Chattanooga, TN 37343

Ed Landy
13230 S.W. 68th St.
Miami, FL 33183

J. Nielsen-Mayer & Sons
2441 Woodmere Dr.
Heights, OH 44106

J.W. Knife Co.
2422 Whirlaway
Owensboro, KY 42301

Knife City
Rt. 1, Box 269
Castallan Springs, TN 37301

Knife and Cutlery Products
Box 54275
Tulsa, OK 74155

The Knife Factory, Inc.
1000 Teaster Lane
Pigeon Forge, TN 37863

Knife and Gun Finishing Supplies
P.O. Box 13522
Arlington, TX 76094

The Knife Shop
Box 409
Whitesboro, NY 13492

Knives A' Plenty Inc.
Box 67
Pointe Claire
Dorval Quebec, Canada H9R458

Koval Knives
P.O. Box 26155
Columbus, OH 43226

James Lennard
1202 W. Samaria Rd.
Samaria, MI 48177

Magnum USA
1550 Balsam St.
Lakewood, CO 80215

Mastercraft Supply Co.
P.O. Box 423
Meriden, CT 06405

Matthews Cutlery
3845 P N Druid Hills
Decatur, GA 30033

Charlie Matton
P.O. Box 1565
Gallatin, TN 37066

M & M Ferris
225 Corte Madera Ave.
Corte Madera, CA 94925

MTM Enterprises
511 Bridge St.
Westbrook, ME 04092

New England Sportsman
Rt. 4, Box 97 A Hillcrest Ct.
S. Salem, NY 10599

Northwest Safari
Box 7172
Olympia, WA 98507

Noshoba Valley Knife Works
P.O. 35
Lancaster, MA 01523

Pacific Cutlery Corp.
3039 Roswell St.
Los Angeles, CA 90065

Parker's Knife Collector Service
P.O. Box 23522
Chattanooga, TN 37422

Patterson Cutlery
2721 South Perkins
Memphis, TN 38118

Peter Henry & Son
332 Nine Mile Ride
Workingham, Berkshire
RG 113 NJ, England

Randall Made Knives
Box 1988
Orlando, FL 32802

R&C Knives & Such
P.O. Box 1047
Manteca, CA 95336

RC Supply
P.O. Box 55
Rescue, CA 95672

Clarence Risner
56 Centerville Rd.
Spring Valley, OH 45307

Russ's Knives
Duncan Plains Rd.
Johnstown, OH 43031

S & D Products
P.O. Box 453
Maysville, KY 41056

San Diego Knives
P.O. Box 326
Lakeside, CA 92040

Santa Fe Knife Works
1209 Calle De Comercio
Santa Fe, NM 87505

Jean Sargent
1403 Chisholm Rd.
Florence, AL 35630

J. Seale
11711 Buckingham Rd.
Austin, TX 78759

Select Cutlery
Parkview Shopping Ctr.
Winston-Salem, NC 27107

Seven & Seven Trading Co.
222 W. 42nd St.
New York, NY 10036

The Sharp Shop
P.O. Box 3773
Calton, GA 30721

William Shockley
6500 Maysville Rd.
Scottsville, KY 42164

Jerry and Carolyn Skelton
Rt. 1 Box 225
Alamo, TN 38001

Smoky Mountain Knife Works
P.O. Box 4947
Sevierville, TN 37862

Tommy Souse
Rt. 7 Bunny Trail
Winston-Salem, NC 27105

Star Sales
1803 N. Central St.
P.O. Box 1503
Knoxville, TN 37901

Taylor Cutlery
P.O. Box 1638
Kingsport, TN 37662

Three Bears Cutlery
P.O. Box 1198
Crawfordville, FL 32327

The Sportsman's Guide
Attn. Gary Olen
900 Apollo Rd.
Eagan, MN 55121-0654

United Cutlery
1425 United Blvd.
Sevierville, TN 37862

White Oak Mountain Cutlery
P.O. Box 2845
Cleveland, TN 37320

Whited's Trading Post
Box 401-A-Hwy 421
Bristol, TN 37620

This Remington store is typical of shopping mall cutlery stores that can be found around the country.

Cutlery collecting supports a large number of businesses in addition to the flea markets, swap corners, hardware stores, and sporting goods establishments that were primary sources only a few years ago.

As the hobby continues to expand, retail cutlery outlets will play an even more important role in supporting the collector. However, these will never replace the thrill of "finding" a prize at an antique shop, yard sale, or estate auction!

Anyone who considers himself to be a collector or who has an active, or even passive, interest in a hobby owes it to him or herself to become as well informed as possible about that hobby. Knife collecting is no exception. Collecting pocketknives can and should be viewed as a type of investing. Surely you would not invest a significant amount of money in any project or product without first checking it out. Even the quasi-serious collector can invest quite a bit of money in knives before realizing it. Wise investing can yield good dividends at a rather rapid rate. However, unwise investing can cause a person to lose money equally as rapidly, if not more so. The name of the game is information.

There are a number of ways to stay abreast of the market. The most common of these is by observation and word of mouth. It is advisable to talk to reputable collectors and dealers, to visit knife shows at every available opportunity, to observe what is happening at flea markets and other trade markets, and to attend auctions which are selling collectible cutlery. These kinds of activities will give you some idea of what the real market is and what you can expect to realize from a particular investment. Many times you will have an opportunity to pick up real bargains while you are there.

Another method of becoming and staying informed is simply by reading! The well-rounded knife collector will want to read everything he can lay his hands on concerning his hobby. This is good. It is the fastest way to become knowledgeable in the field. There is much existing literature and more being written on knife collecting and knife trading. As the hobby has matured, information about the hobby has become more widespread. With the currently available range of publications on today's market, the collector can read to his heart's content.

We encourage you to stay current in your reading about knives and the marketplace. We freely advise you not to rely on any one book or publication, including this one, as the final word on pricing. There is no "final authority" or bible of information in the world of knives. By the time a book is researched, updated, and published, it is likely to be somewhat dated as a price guide. No newspaper or monthly publication can keep you up-to-date about what is happening in all sections of the country. Values change almost from week to week. Publications will help you keep up with trends. They will help you stay informed and sharp. They will help you become and remain a serious player in the hobby of knife collecting.

We have selected the following listings as recommended reading for the serious collector:

RECOMMENDED READING

A Collection of U.S. Military Knives, M. H. Cole, published the author, Birmingham, AL.

A History of Cutlery in the Connecticut Valley, Martha Van Hoesen Taber, Dept. of History, Smith College, Northampton, MA.

A History of the John Russell Cutlery Co., Robert Merriam, Bete Press, Greenfield, MA.

ABCA Price Guide to Antique Knives, Bruce Voyles, American Blade Books, Chattanooga, TN, 1990.

Advertising with a Sharp Edge, Ed Brady, published by author, Traverse City, MI.

Allied Military Fighting Knives, Robert A. Buerlein, American Historical Foundation, Richmond, VA.

American Handmade Knives of Today, R. B. Hughes, Pioneer Press, Union City, TN.

American Knives, Harold L. Peterson, Charles Schribner's Sons, New York, NY.

American Made Pocketknives, Union Cutlery catalog reproduction, Ka-Bar Cutlery, Cleveland, OH.

American Premium Guide to Pocketknives and Razors, Jim Sargent, Books Americana, Florence, AL.

An Introduction to Switchblade Knives, Ben and Lowell Meyers, American Eagle Publishing, Chicago, IL, 1982.

Big Book of Pocket Knives, Ron Stewart and Roy Ritchie, Collector Books, Paducah, KY, 2000.

Bowie Knives, William G. Keener, published by author, (a reprint of Robert Abels), 1988.

Case Brothers 1904 Catalog reproduction, Bob Cargill, Lockport, IL.

Case, The First 100 Years, James S. Giles.

Cattaraugus Cutlery Co., catalog reproduction, Dewey P. Ferguson, Fairborn, OH.

Cattaragus Cutlery, Identification and Values, Roy Ritchie and Ron Stewart, Collector Books, Paducah, KY, 2000.

Collection of Albert Blevins, Bernard Levine.

Combat Fighting Knives, J. E. Smith, Jr., EPJ & H. Enterprises, Inc., Statesboro, GA, 1987.

Custom Knifemaking, Tim McCreight, Stackpole Books, Harrisburg, PA, 1985.

E. C. Simmons & Winchester, American Reprints, St. Louis, MO.

Encyclopedia of Old Pocketknives, Roy Ehrhardt, Heart of America Press, Kansas City, MO, 1974.

Everybody's Knife Bible, Don Paul.

George Schrade – His Accomplishments to the Knife Industry, G. M. Schrade, Bridgeport, CT.

Goins Encyclopedia of Cutlery Markings, John E. Goin, Knife World Book, Knoxville, TN, 1986.

Gun Digest Book of Knifemaking, Jack Lewis & Roger Combs.

How to Make Knives, Richard Barney & Robert Loveless, American Blade Books, Chattanooga, TN, 1982.

IBCA Price Guide to Antique Knives, Bruce Voyles.

International Blade Collectors Association Price Guide to Commemorative Knives 1960–1990, Bruce Voyles, Krause Publications, 1995.

I-XL Catalog, reprint by Atlanta Cutlery Corp., Decatur, GA. (I-XL Means I Excel, William R. Williamson, published by author, 1974).

Joseph Rodgers & Sons, Cutlers, catalog reprint, Adrian Ban Dyk, Marietta, OH.

Kentucky Knife Traders Manual, Roy Ritchie and Ron Stewart, published by authors, Hazard, KY, 1980.

Knife Album, Col. Robert Mayes, published by author, Middlesboro, KY, 1975.

Knife and Tomahawk Throwing, Harry McEvoy.

Knife Digest, William L. Cassidy, Knife Digest Publishing Co., Berkeley, CA, 1974/1976.

Knifecraft, Sid Latham, Stackpole Books, New York, NY.

Knifemakers, an Official Directory of Knifemakers Guild, J. Bruce Voyles, American Blade Books, Chattanooga, TN.

Knifemakers of Old San Francisco, Bernard R. Levine, Badger Books, San Francisco, CA, 1977.

Knife Repair and Restoration, Adrian A. Harris, Columbia, TN.

Knives and the Law, James R. Neilsen, Knife World Books, Knoxville, TN, 1980.

Knives '81–'96, Ken Warner (editor), DBI Books, Northbrook, IL.

Knives of the World, Jean-Noël Mouret, Chartwell Books, Secaucus, NJ, 1994.

Knives, Points of Interest, Jim Weyer, published by author, Toledo, OH, 1984, 1987, 1990, 1993.

Levine's Guide to Knives and Their Value, Bernard Levine, DBI Books, Inc., Northbrook, IL, 1989, 1993, 1997.

Light but Efficient, Albert N. Hardin, Jr. & Robert W. Hedden, published by authors, 1973.

Marbles, Knives and Axes, Konrad F. Schreier, Jr., Beinfield Publishing, 1978.

Modern Handmade Knives, B. R. Hughes, Pioneer Press, Union City, TN, 1982.

Moran–Fire and Steel, Wayne V. Holter, published by author, 1982.

Napanoch, Rett C. Stidham, published by author.

New England Cutlery, Philip R. Pankiewicz, Hollytree Publications, Gilman, CT, 1986.

Official Price Guide to Collector Knives, C. Houston Price, House of Collectibles, NY, 1996, 1998, 2000.

Penknives and Other Folding Knives, Simon Moore, Shire Publications Ltd., Cromwell House Church St., Princes Risborough Buckinghamshire, UK, HP17 9AJ.

Pocket Cutlery, U.S. Tariff Commission, Washington, DC.

Pocketknives, Bernard Levine, Quintet Publishing, 1993.

Pocketknives, Markings, Manufacturers and Dealers, John E. Goins, ed., Knife World Publications, 1979.

Razor Edge Book of Sharpening, American Reprints, St Louis, MO, 1985.

Remington 1936 Catalog reprint, American Reprints, St. Louis, MO.

Romance of Knife Collecting, Dewey P. Ferguson, published by author, 1976.

Russell Green River Works Cutlery, Dewey P. Ferguson, published by author, 1972.

Scagel, the Man and His Knives, Harry McEvoy, World Books, Knoxville, TN, 1985.

Schrade Pocketknives, A.G. Russell, Knife Collector's Publishing House, Fayetteville, AR, 1971.

Standard Guide to Razors, Identification, and Values, Roy Ritchie and Ron Stewart, Collector Books, Paducah, KY, 1995.

Straight Razor Collecting, Robert A. Doyle, Collector Books, Paducah KY 1980.

Sunday Knives, John Roberts, published by author, Louisville, KY, 1984.

Survival Knives and Survival (2 volumes), J. E. Smith, Jr., EPJ & H Enterprises, Inc., Statesboro, GA.

The Best of Knife World (3 volumes), Knife World Books, Knoxville, TN, 1979, 1982, 1993.

The Book of Knives, Yvan A. de Riaz, Crown Publishers, New York, NY, 1981.

The Case Knife Story, Allen P. Swayne, Knife World Books, Knoxville, TN, 1987.

The Complete Book of Pocketknife Repair, Ben Kelly, Jr., American Blade Books, 1983, 1987.

The Gun Digest Book of Knives (3 editions), Jack Lewis & Roger Combs, Northfield, IL, 1973, 1982, 1988.

The Hand Forged Knife, Karl Schroen, Knife World Books, Knoxville, TN, 1984.

The Knife and Its History, from Victorinox Cutlery, Ibach, Switzerland, 1984.

The Knife Collection of Albert Blevins, Bernard Levine, Allon Schoener Associates, Grafton, VT, 1988.

The Knife in Homespun America, Madison Grant, published by author, 1984.

The Knifemaker Who Went West, Harvey Platts, Long Peak Press, 1978.

The Old Knife Book, Tracy Tudor, published by author, Speedway, IN, 1978.

The Pocketknife Manual, Blackie Collins, Benchmark Division, Jenkins Metal, Gastonia, NC, 1977.

The Practical Book of Knives, Ken Warner, Stoeger Publishing Co., So. Hackensack, NJ, 1976.

The Sheffield Knife Book, Geoffrey Tweedale, The Hallamshire Press, 1996.

The Standard Guide to Razors, Identification and Values, Roy Ritchie & Ron Stewart, Collector Books, Paducah, KY, 1995, 1999.

The Standard Knife Collector's Guide, Roy Ritchie & Ron Stewart, Collector Books, Paducah, KY, 1986, 1993, 1997.

United States Military Knives, Collector's Guide, Michael W. Silvey & Gary D. Boyd, published by authors, Sacramento, CA, 1989.

U.S. Military Knives, Bayonets, and Machetes, M.H. Cole, published by author, Birmingham, AL, 1979.

MAGAZINES AND PERIODICALS

Knife, a Japanese magazine dedicated to knifemaking and collecting (printed in Japanese). C/o Weyer International, 333 14th St., Toledo, OH 43624.

Knife World, Box 3395, Knoxville, TN 37927. www.knifeworld.com

Newsletter, The Canadian Knife Collectors Club, 2410 Lower Base Line, R.R #1 Milton, Ontario L9T-2X5 Canada.

Knives Illustrated, 2145 W. La Palma Ave., Anaheim, CA 92801.

The Blade Magazine, 700 E. State St., Iola, WI 54945.

Tactical Knives, Harris Publications, Inc., 115 Broadway, New York, NY 10010.

Theater Made Military Knives of WWII, Helwright.

As we said earlier, knife collecting has been around for a very long time. Without meaning to repeat ourselves, knives of quality have been collected since before King Arthur extolled the merits of his sword, Excalibur. Knife trading and collecting were not uncommon to the pioneer or the southern mountain trader in the earlier parts of our country's history. As a means of barter, knife trading goes hand in hand with the histories, written and unwritten, of mankind itself.

However, it was not until collecting clubs and organizations were formed that the pocketknife attained the status of a recognized hobby. Within this framework, knife collecting is still a relatively new hobby which has literally grown by leaps and bounds.

A great deal is owed to these organizations for their efforts and successes. In the United States, one is rarely more than a few hours from the location of a knife collecting club. There are also collecting clubs and organizations located in Canada, Japan, and several European countries. The interests of collectors may vary somewhat, but the appreciation of a fine cutting edge is the common thread found throughout the world of cutlery.

Perhaps the most noteworthy of the knife clubs is the National Knife Collectors Association. It was founded in 1972 and is made up of members who make their homes in all 50 United States, Canada, Europe, South Africa, Japan, Pakistan, India, Australia, and others.

The association provides its members with a newsletter, *The NKCA Gazette*, which helps keep them abreast of NKCA news and events. Featured in a typical issue are articles on the history of knives, future designs or issues of knives, show dates, machairology (knife collecting, see page 781) in general, and knife news. The purpose, of course, is to keep members' knowledge of the hobby current. The cost of the newsletter is included in the price of the club dues.

We highly recommend membership to any person who has more than a passing interest in knives or knife collecting. The $25 per year dues (first year $28) are reasonable, in light of the services it provides both the members and the hobby.

You may request additional information on the National Knife Collectors Association by writing NKCA, P.O. Box 21070, Chattanooga, TN 37421 or by e-mail: NKCA@aol.com (tell 'em you found their address in our book).

Perhaps the second best-known (this, of course, is open to debate) cutlery association is the American Blade Cutlery Association. This association sponsors knife shows, issues club knives "For Members Only," and produces *The Blade Magazine*. Additionally the association provides a variety of books about knives and related items for sale to members. Membership in ABCA certainly exposes the collector to current trends in collecting and helps keep him abreast of the market.

Another active national knife club that you should check out is The Knife Collectors Club. It offers its members a variety of quality collectible knives and regularly publishes an attractive and informative catalog. The club also maintains a website, http://www.AGRussell.com. Its e-mail address is AG@AGRussell.com

As you might have gathered, we believe that it is a good idea to be a member of a club or organization which promotes a hobby in which you are interested. In an attempt to recognize the efforts of knife clubs across the country, we are listing as many of these as we know. We believe our information is accurate, but sometimes things change between the time information is researched and it becomes a book. Also, since no listing is ever really complete, we ask that you send us any information on clubs which may have been left out of this edition that should be included in our next one. If you find a knife club in the following listing which is near you, make an effort to join and attend their meetings. If not, we suggest that you consider becoming a long-range member in one which may hold an interest for you.

ALLIANCE OF LOCAL KNIFE CLUBS

Alabama

Club: Heart of Dixie Cutlery Club
& Wheeler Basin Knife Club
Contact: Ann Britton
Address: 2303 Hwy. 20 Lot 7
Decatur, AL 35601
Phone: 256-353-7086

Alaska

Club: Alaska Knifemakers and Collectors
Contact: Brian Clem
Address: 8505 Jewel Lake Rd.
Anchorage, AK 99501
Phone: 907-245-0088

Arizona

Club: Arizona Knife Collectors
Contact: D'Alton Holder
Address: 7148 W. Country Gables Dr.
Peoria, AZ 85381
Phone: 623-878-3064

California

Club: Bay Area Knife Collectors
Association
Contact: Bob Lee
Address: 3533 Jamison Way
Castro Valley, CA 94546
Phone: 510-886-9778

Club: Southern California Blades
Contact: Lowell Shelhart
Address: 23204 Falena Ave.
Torrance, CA 90501
Phone: 310-326-3869

Colorado

Club: Rocky Mtn. Blade Collectors
Contact: Tom Gilroy
Address: P.O. Box 324
Westminster, CO 80230
Phone: 303-426-9004

Florida

Club: Florida Knife Collectors
Contact: Louie Rothman
Address: 5321 Holden Road
   Cocoa, FL 32927
Phone: 407-636-1876

Club: Fort Myers Knife Club
Contact: Russ Smegal
Address: P.O. Box 706
   St. James City, FL 33956-0706
Phone: 941-283-7253

Club: Gator Cutlery Club
Contact: Dan Piergallini
Address: 4011 N. Forbes Rd.
   Plant City, FL 33565
Phone: 813-754-3908

Club: Gold Coast Knife Club
Contact: Alan Weinstein
Address: 7490 NW 42nd Court
   Lauderhill, FL 33319
Phone: 954-747-1851

Club: Riverland Knife Collectors Club
Contact: Ann Piper
Address: 11155 S.W. 78th Ct.
   Ocala, FL 34476-3785
Phone: 352-861-4334

Club: South Florida Knife Collectors
Contact: Craig Bozorth
Address: Condo 1 3475 SW 1st Ave.
   Miami, FL 33145
Phone: 305-858-5635

Georgia

Club: Chattahoochee Cutlery Club
Contact: Michael Cowart
Address: P.O. Box 568
   Tucker, GA 30084
Phone: 770-963-6406

Club: Flint River Knife Club
Contact: Kevin Spell
Address: 2482 Clover Ct.
   Morrow, GA 30260
Phone: 770-961-4503

Club: Ocmulgee Knife Collectors Club
Contact: Joseph P. Wilson
Address: 263 Welker Circle
   Macon, GA 31211
Phone: 478-746-3181

Club: Three Rivers Knife Club
Contact: Jimmy Green
Address: 783 NE Jones Mill Rd.
   Rome, GA 30165
Phone: 706-234-2540

Idaho

Club: Miniature Knifemakers Society
Contact: Terry Kranning
Address: 1900 W. Quinn #153
   Pocatello, ID 83202
Phone: 208-237-9047

Illinois

Club: American Edge Collectors Assoc.
Contact: Louie Jamison
Address: 24755 Hickory Court
   Crete, IL 60417
Phone: 708-672-8838

Club: Bunker Hill Knife Club
Contact: Dale Rice
Address: 108 Pickett
   Bethalto, IL 62010
Phone: 618-377-8050

Indiana

Club: Circle City Knife Collectors
Contact: Daniel Grau
Address: 3302 Terra Vista Ln.
   Indianapolis, IN 46220
Phone: 317-259-1907

Club: Indiana Knife Collectors
Contact: Ed Etchason
Address: P.O. Box 101
Fountaintown, IN 46130-0101
Phone: 317-835-7487

Iowa

Club: Hawkeye Knife Collectors
Contact: Ton Hickcox
Address: 4209 E. Madison Ave.
Des Moines, IA 50317
Phone: 515-266-0910

Kansas

Club: Kansas Knife Collectors Assoc.
Contact: Bill Davis
Address: P.O. Box 1125
Wichita, KS 67201
Phone: 316-838-0540

Kentucky

Club: Central Kentucky Knife Club
Contact: G.T. Williams
Address: 4499 Muddy Ford Road
Georgetown, KY 40324-9280
Phone: 502-863-4919

Club: Kentucky Cutlery Association
Contact: Jim Haberman
Address: 6921 Woodrow Way
Louisville, KY 40228
Phone: 502-964-1814

Maryland

Club: Chesapeake Bay Knife Club
Contact: Ted Merchant
Address: 7 Old Garrett Ct.
White Hall, MD 21161
Phone: 410-343-0380

Massachusetts

Club: Northeast Cutlery Collectors
Contact: Cindy Taylor
Address: P.O. Box 624
Mansfield, MA 02048
Phone: 508-266-5157

Michigan

Club: Marble Plus Knife Club
Contact: Bob Schmeling
Address: P.O. Box 228
Gladstone, MI 49837-0228
Phone: 906-786-5186

Club: Mid-Michigan Knife Club
Contact: Bill McMall
Address: 13568 Geddes Rd.
Hemlock, MI 48626
Phone: 517-642-5750

Club: Wolverine Knife Collectors Club
Contact: Pat Donovan
Address: 14543 Yale Ct.
Sterling Heights, MI 48313-2982
Phone: 810-247-5883

Minnesota

Club: North Star Blade Collectors
Contact: Sid Zochert
Address: P.O. Box 20523
Bloomington, MN 55420
Phone: 612-866-8090

Missouri

Club: Gateway Area Knife Club
Contact: Mike Helms
Address: 310 Andrews Trail
St. Peters, MO 63376
Phone: 636-928-5775

Club: Knife Club of the Ozarks
Contact: Randy Long
Address: P.O. Box 1848
  Ozark, MO 65721
Phone: 417-581-2835

New York

Club: Empire Knife Club
Contact: Jan Muchnikoff
Address: 1203 E. 98th St.
  Brooklyn, NY 11236
Phone: 718-763-0391

North Carolina

Club: Tar Heel Cutlery Club
Contact: Clyde Ranson
Address: 2730 Tudor Rd.
  Winston-Salem, NC 27106
Phone: 336-725-1016

Ohio

Club: Buck Collectors Club, Inc.
Contact: W. Murray Andrews
Address: P.O. Box 3
  Enon, OH 45323
Phone: 937-767-7613

Club: Fort City Knife Collectors Club
Contact: Robert F. Wurzelbacher
Address: 5479 Haft Road
  Cincinnati, OH 45247
Phone: 513-574-9281

Club: Johnny Appleseed Knife Collectors
Contact: Kenneth Parker
Address: 990 Averill Ave.
  Mansfield, OH 44906-1606
Phone: 419-747-6939

Club: National Pike Knife Club
Contact: Jerry Stephen
Address: 34841 Hendrysburg Rd.
  Barnesville, OH 43713
Phone: 740-758-5727

Club: Western Reserve Cutlery Assoc.
Contact: Darlene Musgrave
Address: 2552 Edwin Ave.
  Akron, OH 44314-3445
Phone: 330-745-4242

Oregon

Club: Oregon Knife Collectors
Contact: Dennis Ellingsen
Address: P.O. Box 2091
  Eugene, OR 97402
Phone: 541-484-5564

Pennsylvania

Club: Allegheny Mtn. Knife Collectors
Contact: Ruth Trout
Address: P.O. Box 23
  Hunker, PA 15639
Phone: 724-925-2713

Club: Eastern Pennsylvania Knife
  Collectors
Contact: Ed Petro
Address: 4884 Limeport Pike
  Coopersburg, PA 18036
Phone: 610-965-9248

Club: Keystone Blade Assoc.
Contact: Marlyn A. Kepner
Address: P.O. Box 46
  Lewisburg, PA 17837
Phone: 570-584-4835

South Carolina

Club: Bechtler Mint Knife Club
Contact: Gerald Parker
Address: 3035 Old Georgia Hwy.
  Gaffney, SC 29340
Phone: 864-489-1469

Club: Palmetto Cutlery Club
Contact: Johnny Perry
Address: P.O. Box 1356
Greer, SC 29652
Phone: 864-472-3170

Tennessee

Club: Memphis Knife Collectors
Contact: Adron Tucker
Address: 9566 Blue Spruce Dr.
Lakeland, TN 38002
Phone: 901-372-1835

Club: Northeast Tennessee Knife Club
Contact: Bobby Beuris
Address: P.O. Box 562
Kingsport, TN 37662
Phone: 423-245-2096

Club: Soddy Daisey Knife Collectors
Association
Contact: Jim Morgan
Address: P.O. Box 1224
Soddy Daisey, TN 37379
Phone: 423-843-1635

Club: Williamson County Knife Club
Contact: Stephen Martin
Address: 5510 County Drive #119
Nashville, TN 37211
Phone: 615-401-2430

Texas

Club: Gulf Coast Knife Club
Contact: Mike Moeskau
Address: P.O. Box 265
Pasadena, TX 77501
Phone: 281-614-5995

Club: Permain Basin Knife Club
Contact: Fred Nolley
Address: 4309 Roosevelt
Midland, TX 79703-6133
Phone: 915-694-1209

Virginia

Club: Mason-Dixon Knife Club
Contact: Matthew Halterman
Address: P.O. Box 66
Toms Brook, VA 22660
Phone: 540-436-9425

Club: Northern Virginia Knife Clubs
Contact: Watt Stiffler
Address: P.O. Box 2754
Sterling, VA 20167
Phone: 703-444-3525

Club: Old Dominion Knife Collectors
Contact: John Riddle
Address: 224 Lakeridge Cir.
Troutville, VA 24175
Phone: 540-977-0242

Club: Shenandoah Valley Knife Collectors
Contact: Edmund Davidson
Address: P.O. Box 843
Harrisonburg, VA 22801
Phone: 540-997-5651

Washington

Club: Northwest Knife Collectors
Contact: Don Hanham
Address: 1911 SW Campus Drive Suite
Federal Way, WA 98023
Phone: 425-827-1644

Wisconsin

Club: Badger Knife Club
Contact: Robert G. Schrap
Address: P.O. Box 511
Elm Grove, WI 53122
Phone: 414-479-9765

Special Interest Knife Clubs

Buck Collectors Club
Star Rt. Box 40, Orland, CA 95963

Bull Dog Knife Collectors Club
P.O. Box 453, Maysville, KY 41056

Case Collectors Club
c/o Eddie Moreland, P.O. Box 2845,
Cleveland, TN 37320

Colonel Coon Collectors Club
Box 1676, Dyersburg, TN 38025

EK Commando Knife Collectors Club
601 N. Lombardy St., Richmond, VA
23220

International Fighting Rooster
Collector's Club
Box 936, Lenanon, TN 37087

KA Bar Knife Collectors Club
P.O. Box 688
1125 E. State St., Olean, NY 14760

Queen Cutlery Collectors, Inc.
P.O. Box 109, Titusville, PA 16354

Trappers Knife Collectors Club
Box 3507, Gastonia, NC 28052

National/Regional Collectors Associations

Alliance of Local Knife Clubs
4499 Muddy Ford Rd., Georgetown,
KY 40324

American Historical Foundation
1142 W. Grace Street, Richmond, VA
23220

Canadian Knife Collectors Club
2410 Lowey Baseline, RR #1, Milton,
Ontario L9T2Y5

International Blade Collectors
Association
700 E. State St., Iola, WI 54990
1-800-258-0929

The Knifemakers Guild
P.O. Box 17587, Tampa, FL 33682

The Knife Collector's Club, Inc.
1705 N. Thompson, Springdale, AK
72764
AG@AGRussell.com

Miniature Knife Collectors Association
1900 West Quinn, #153, Pocatello, ID
83202

National Knife Collectors Association
Box 21070
Chattanooga, TN 37424-0070
423-892-5007
NKCA@aol.com

New England Cutlery Collectors
Association
P.O. Box 677, Milldale, CT 06467

⊰ Bicentennials, Commemoratives, Reproductions, and Limited Editions ⊱

Looking back at our country's 200th birthday and the impact the bicentennial celebration has had on knife collecting gives us an objective perspective. Such insight can only be gained by reviewing a couple of decades of experience. The twists and turns that the hobby has taken over the past 20 years was unpredictable. Knife collecting all started as a simple and innocent pastime. Old pocketknives were rounded up and hung in dens or living rooms or were kept in cigar boxes to show friends and visitors. Condition didn't matter much; as long as a knife was usable, it was collectible.

As time went by and more people began playing the game, the older knives became scarce. Collectors began looking for new knives which they felt might become "tomorrow's antiques." Subjective reasoning led many to believe that new knives of limited number would have a better shot at increasing in value than new knives of common design and wide circulation. This same reasoning reckoned that if one could find an older knife in reasonable condition, he best grab it even if the cost seemed high.

In our society, it seems that if there is an adequate demand for almost anything, there will develop a willing supplier. So, not too surprisingly, by the mid 1960s, counterfeits began to appear on the market. Also, to no one's surprise, they were eagerly grabbed up by novice collectors. Later in the decade, fake Barlows stamped "Russell," "Remington," and "Winchester" (knives of good quality) were imported from Germany and were snatched up even by collectors who knew better! Manufacturers of cutlery, both here and abroad, began to enjoy a boom which had been started by knife collectors.

Custom knifemakers found that everything they produced was in great demand. Interestingly, both the number of custom patterns available and the number of custom makers began to immediately increase.

The coming of the 1970s brought with it an awareness about our nation's bicentennial celebration. Knife manufacturers were eager and ready to make sure that the event did not go unnoticed. The market was flooded with an almost countless number of bicentennial commemoratives, limited editions, and knives commemorating almost any event the maker/designer could find in his or her old high school history book.

Of course, commemorative knives are not new. Their origin runs far back to ancient and medieval times, to those grand old artisans who slaved with inferior tools to make superior swords, spears, and daggers from bronze, crude iron, and eventually steel. These were made to commemorate great events in the lives of the people, such as the winning of wars and battles, the crowning of kings, and the dubbing of knights. Masterpieces in cutlery were created by the best metal workers in the realms. They worked on commission, were supplied with choice, and sometimes precious materials, provided with a recognized position in the community, and given the time required to create the beautiful and graceful works of the cutler's art. It is this art which we can now see in many museums and in the collections of a few very lucky people.

It was during the industrialization of the 1700s and 1800s that folding knives began to appear as commemoratives. English cutlers began to produce them as inexpensive, novelty type knives to enhance their other products' sales appeal, both at home and abroad. They often used the profiles of heroes as the subject of the commemoration. Many of these knives were considered cheap, perhaps almost worthless, at the time. They have since, however, become precious historical mementos. Not all could be considered inexpensive by any measure though. An excellent, though relatively unknown, example is the Holley "Charter Oak," which was marketed in 1911 in two sizes, at three and six dollars (Does anyone care to calculate that amount in current dollars?). The company was well aware that they were producing an historical memento as the handles were made of wood from the famous "Connecticut Charter Oak." A notorized guarantee of genuineness was included with each knife. Needless to say, the number made was limited to the number of handles which could be made from the wood available from the tree. (See photo, page 428.) Do not overlook the popularity of the novelty knives of the '40s and '50s, when Mickey Mouse, Hopalong Cassidy, Buck Rogers, Roy Rogers, and Gene Autry were kings. These belong in the commemorative category and can command an amazing price on today's market.

The first of the relatively recent, pre-bicentennial commemoratives to really make a hit was Schrade Cutlery's "Kentucky Long Rifle." It was an attractive, well-built knife that captured the imaginations (and dollars) of collectors everywhere. Other manufacturers paid attention, too. Soon the collector saw an "authorized reproduction" of the "Russell Barlow." Then the "Liberty Bell," "Paul Revere," and "Minute Man" commemorative series. Case and Queen got into it with sets of Kentucky Bicentennials. The race was on!

While these developments were taking place, knife clubs, associations, guilds, and shows were blossoming all over the place. Many of these designed their own versions of commemoratives and annual knives for their members. Even knives commemorating knife shows and/or show locations almost became popular. The world of knives was well into the commemorating business. It may seem to the new collector that almost everything worth being commemorated has been commemorated. This just isn't so. We foresee many years of popularity for the commemorative and believe that this limited edition market will become the testing ground for new knife designs, handle materials, metals, etc., which will become standards in the future lines of cutlery manufacturers.

If you are interested in collecting commemorative knives and are a person who collects only for fun, we suggest that you go to it! There is a whole world out there waiting for you and you should go after anything within your means that gives you pleasure and satisfaction. Have fun! If, on the other hand, you are like most of the rest of us and like to combine the fun aspect with investment potential (profit), then perhaps you should pay close attention to the next few pages. We do not claim to have the corner on the advice market; however, if you are looking toward spending money on knives as an investment, we believe there is no safer area than the commemorative/limited edition area, if you use good judgment. Good judgment in knife investing, incidentally, is at least as rare as it is in any other field of investment. Hindsight always seems so much clearer than our well-thought-out foresight. With this in mind, as well as an awareness of the general value of "free advice," we have developed the following list of considerations which may be used as a guide for investing in commemorative/limited edition knives.

Quality

As with any knife, the quality of workmanship in a commemorative or limited edition is a very important aspect to be considered when speculating on its future value. Most manufacturers put their best foot forward for their commemorative line. We have seen companies which generally produce an average line produce some super quality commemorative and limited editions. On the other hand, we have seen some limited editions made by reputable manufacturers which are average or below average in quality of workmanship. Although we have seen some commemoratives of average to below average quality and workmanship increase by leaps and bounds, a general rule of thumb is that a well-constructed knife is likely to increase in value while the future of one made with less care is purely open to speculation.

Price

Commemorative knives are generally priced somewhat higher than comparable cutlery. Several factors can combine to make this justifiable. These include workmanship, the event commemorated, the appearance of the set, and the limit of the edition. Of course, a study of the value of similar commemoratives can be used as something of a guide with which to speculate on future value. Some collectors maintain that to buy a brand new commemorative is taking a chance because the price usually drops after the initial issue. To follow this advice may entail some risk, for if the knife "takes off," you have missed an opportunity to buy it at the cheapest price.

Number

Unlike some other publications, we don't get too excited about the particular number on a commemorative knife. We do, however, recommend that close attention be paid to the number of the total production. If enough copies of a particular knife are produced to supply every collector in the country with at least one, then the chances of a value increase "just ain't too great." A person buying such a knife darn well better like it, for he is likely to keep it for a while if he expects to make a profit on it. On the other hand, if there are only 27 or so made, who is going to know about them? We have observed that commemoratives, the total production of which falls between 600 and 6,000 and which are well advertised at issue, seem to be more likely to increase in value. A word of caution, however, is that all factors should be considered before investing. **Numbers alone are no assurance that the value will increase.**

Blade Engraving

If the commemorative knife is engraved, this can be a factor of value. There are two primary methods of engraving the blades of a knife. The most common is *photo engraving*. Although this is the most inexpensive method of etching a blade, it can produce an attractive and lasting scene. If photo engraving is deep and detailed, it should be considered a definite plus. If it is done in a "lick and promise" method, is shallow, and without detail, it adds little, if any, to the knife's value. The other method of blade engraving is *hand engraving*. When done by an artisan, this addition will be one of real value for the collector. You are, when buying a knife which has been custom engraved, purchasing two pieces of art work for the price of one. It is highly unlikely that you will ever see a cheaply made knife with a hand engraved blade. (These same observations can generally be applied for engraved bolsters.)

Scrimshaw

The art of carving or engraving on bone or ivory, developed by American whalers, has been introduced to the world of knives. The relatively recent reintroduction of smooth bone as a handle material for pocketknives has provided scrimshaw artists with a new surface upon which to practice their craft. Indeed, scrimshawed handles can make any knife a work of art. The care and detail with which the artist etches the handles can be truly beautiful. The collector should view these efforts as an art form.

One should ask him or herself questions before investing in scrimshaw work, such as, is the knife itself one which I would add to my collection if it did not have the art work? Is the art work of a quality that would merit collecting if

401

it did not have the art work? Are the etchings deep enough to tolerate common use or handling?

Also remember that scrimshaw on plastic or composition handles will never be as valuable as that on natural materials such as bone, ivory, and horn. Maclieve scrimshawing (whatever that is) will add little or no value to most knives.

Appearance

Appearance is a very subjective factor, but should not be overlooked by the collector. A few things many collectors look for which fall under this heading are: Does the design of the knife in any way seem to be connected with the event commemorated? Is the design of the knife unusual? Does the packaging and/or display add anything to enhance the event commemorated or the knife? If the answer to any of these questions is yes, then you may be safe in paying a somewhat higher price for the knife than you might feel you should. In any event, make sure that all packaging is included with the commemorative for which you pay full price. If it is not, you may be justified in offering as much as 20% less than normal, especially if the packaging was elaborate. (Some commemoratives, without the packaging, are worth no more than a normal knife of similar design and brand.)

Event Commemorated

This factor can override most everything we've said about investing in a collectible commemorative. For example, American Centennial commemorative items are now selling for a king's ransom. I recently watched a 1939 World's Fair knife sell at auction for $185.00. (I had estimated the value of the knife to be $25.00 to $35.00.) Even if knives from these events were cheaply made, the collector value is often high. We believe that bicentennial commemoratives are moving into this category. On the other hand, a knife commemorating General Cornpone's surrender or the local bowling league's championship is not going to have wide enough appeal to be successful, regardless of quality.

The bottom line is: If the knife is a quality product, the price is reasonable, the commemorating design reflects thought and effort, and the event commemorated is of significance, you have a prize worthy of investment. Although we are sure that we have left commemorative, limited editions, and collectibles out of the following list which some will feel should have been included, we believe that this assembled group gives the collector an excellent helping of what is available. To a large degree, we have included both the issue price and collector value on knives we have listed. Pictures are included on most of them. We hope you will collect wisely. Be willing to "dicker" when buying (that's part of the fun), but then realize that the dealer/ supplier or liquidating collector must have some room to realize a profit. And remember, no price guide's figures are etched in stone!

American Bald Eagle Commemorative – In 1782, despite Benjamin Franklin's urging to adopt the turkey, the United States adopted the bald eagle as its national bird. In 1982, on the 200th anniversary of this event, **Frost Cutlery** issued 2,400 knives to commemorate it. The knives have a hand scrimshawed, color picture of a bald eagle on their genuine stag handles. The knife fits into "excelsior" grade and is of top quality. It has worked backsprings and a front blade lock. Overall, this is a beautiful knife for the collector.

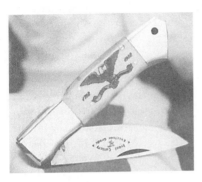

Collector Value: $90.00

African Big Five – One of the more ambitious non-bicentennial commemorative projects was **Puma's** African Big Five. The five most sought-after African game animals were commemorated on a series of ornately decorated Puma knives. An issue of 500 each at $2,000.00 per set made this set rather rare and expensive. Nonetheless, it is a beautifully done set and Puma knives are always top quality.

Official 1977 America's Cup Knife – This is, without a doubt, one of the most unusual knives ever associated with the America's Cup race. The Swedish **EKA Company** was commissioned by the America's Cup committee to produce 312 official knives for VIPs and crews of the race. The knife had to meet sailing standards and be a quality tool worthy of being used by crews during the race.

Years after the race was run, it was discovered that only about 150 of the knives had been distributed. The others were offered to the public in 1980 at $40.00 each. This knife and its story certainly would add color to any collection.

Collector Value: $150.00

American Civil War – This **Frost Cutlery** set of knives features General William T. Sherman of the Union army and General Stonewall Jackson of the Confederate army. The knives are 4½" folding hunter patterns with bone handles and an image of one of the generals on the face of the blade.

Issue Number: 1,200 sets
Collector Value: $110.00

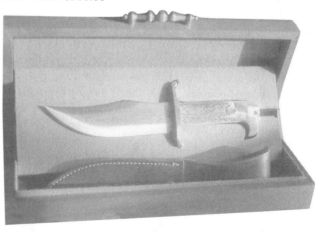

American Eagle Series – This set of **Parker-Frost** knives commemorated five outstanding individuals of the American Revolution. These men were Patrick Henry, Nathan Hale, John Adams, Thomas Jefferson, and George Washington. The knives are 4" three blade stock patterns with delrin handles, eagle shields, and stainless steel blades. Each set came with registration papers and a display plaque suitable for wall hanging.

Issue Number: 12,000
Issue Date: 1976
Collector Value: $185.00

The American Spirit Bicentennial – One of two outstanding knives made by **Case** for the Bicentennial, this one is a fighting type, Bowie style, sheath knife. It has stag handles, an etched blade, and an eagle head pommel. The edition limit of 2,500 combines with the workmanship of this presentation piece to make it a classy collectible.

Collector Value: $500.00

The American Spirit Bicentennial – A stag handled, one blade folding hunter pattern (5165) knife which was adapted and dressed up for the Bicentennial by **Case Cutlery**. The knife is beautifully etched on both the face of the blade and the gold bolsters. The display case, too, is pure class. A collector is indeed lucky to have one of these in his collection.

Collector Value: $300.00

Roy Acuff Signature Knife

W.R. Case and Sons honored Roy Acuff as the King of Country Music in 1985. The gunstock pattern number 52155S was placed in a solid cherry music box which played "The Wabash Cannonball" when opened.

Interest in and following of Mr. Acuff by country music lovers combine with an appreciation of fine cutlery to make the 5,000 piece edition very collectible.

Collector Value: $250.00

Anniversary Knife – **Schrade Cutlery**, USA, produced a 5" one blade folding hunter with embossed bolsters and shield, etched blade, and simulated stag handles.

Collector Value: $130.00

405

The Aviator – Four milestones in aviation history are displayed on this 1996 **Boker** collectible knife. The Zeppelin, Spirit of St. Louis, Concorde, and the Space Shuttle stand out in anodized aluminum against a blue sky. The Top Lock II knife, with aluminum handles and a 420 stainless blade, makes this an outstanding commemorative.

Issue Number: 1,500
Retail: $145.00

Apollo Moon Landing Commemorative

It seems only appropriate that **Victorinox** would issue a 20th Anniversary Commemorative of the Apollo moon landing since some of their knives made that trip.

The knife used in the commemorative is a current issue, 23 function, Space Shuttle issue. It has red handles (of course), an etched blade, a serial number, and a special shield representing an astronaut's moon-style EVA space suit.

Total Production: 2,000
Collector Value: $125.00

Astronaut Knife – Navy Commander John Young and Major Virgil Gus Grissom introduced this knife to the world when they carried it in their survival kits on their Gemini space flight, March 23, 1965. The **Case Knife Company** issued 2,494 of these knives for the collector market. They are made of 13 gauge carbon steel and are handled with a light plastic, polypropylene, which is fumeless. The collector issue is exactly like the knife which accompanied many of our astronauts on their space missions.

However, the knives included on the Apollo moon shots had their handles replaced with aluminum handles, probably as a safety measure resulting from the Gemini fire. The model on display at the Smithsonian Institution, an actual knife from an Apollo craft, has the gray metal handles.

The knife was discontinued at the end of 1971. All issues for the collector market came in an attractive display box with a color background depicting the Gemini spacecraft entering the earth's atmosphere.

Issue Price: $49.95

Collector Value: $800.00

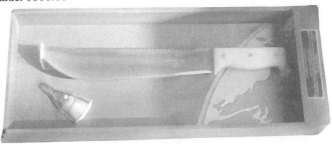

Astronaut Knife 25th Anniversary – This knife is identical to the original issue by **Case Cutlery** except that it has the NASA 25, Astronaut knife M-1 S/N XXX Model 1983 etched on the blade in bright orange, white, and blue. It comes on a plaque identifying it as the NASA 25th Anniversary Commemorative issue 1958-1983.

The knife is on an impressive display plaque. We predict that it will increase rapidly in value because of the predecessor and because only half of the intended originals were produced. Despite what we have said about serial numbers, matching ones for both knives would be unique enough, we believe, to add 15% to the total collector value for both.

Issue Date: 1983 (late)

Issue Number: 1,000

Issue Price: $250.00 (May have varied from dealer to dealer, most were limited to two knives)

Collector Value: $400.00 – 600.00

407

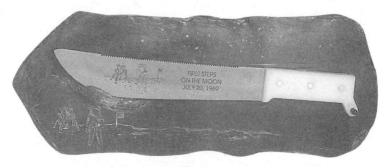

Astronaut's Knife, 20th Anniversary – Moon Landing

This knife continues the tradition of **Case** quality. It was issued commemorating man's first steps on the moon. It is displayed on a moonscape plaque with an engraving of "The Eagle," Neil Armstrong, the flag, and "Tranquility Base." This engraving is repeated on the moonscape plaque. This 1989 issue was limited to 1,000 copies.

Collector Value: $300.00 – 400.00

7 & 7 Commemoratives

Frost Cutlery announces that it is the exclusive producer of 7 & 7 commemorative cutlery. The 7 & 7 commemoratives will honor Richard Petty and Dale Earnhardt for their seven championships each. Retail on these items will range from $38.95 to $733.33, and they are available from dealers nationwide.

The Babe Ruth "Ball Bat Commemorative"

This knife is made in the shape of a baseball bat bearing Babe Ruth's signature on the handle. Most of them were made by the **Camillus Cutlery** during the 1930s, and sold for about $1.00 at the time of issue.

Collector Value: $150.00

The Babe Ruth Baseball Legends

These commemorative knives were issued in 1990 by the **Frost Cutlery Co.** and are based on 6240 **Case**/Red Pick Bone Trappers. At the same time, similar issues were released honoring also Ty Cobb, Dizzy Dean, and Lou Gehrig.

Each knife is packed in a walnut music box that plays "Take Me Out To The Ballgame."

Retail Price: $176.47

Collector Value: $210.00

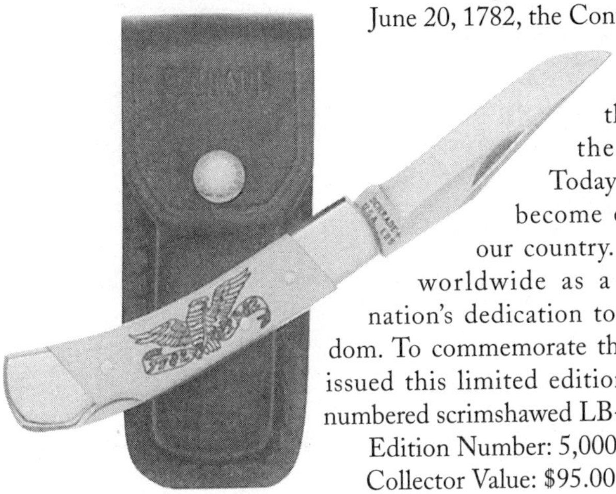

Bald Eagle Commemorative – On June 20, 1782, the Continental Congress selected the bald eagle for the Great Seal of the United States. Today this symbol has become one of pride for our country. It is recognized worldwide as a symbol of our nation's dedication to peace and freedom. To commemorate the event, **Schrade** issued this limited edition of 5,000 serial numbered scrimshawed LB-5SC knives.

Edition Number: 5,000 (numbered)
Collector Value: $95.00

Bicentennial Barlow

Queen Cutlery entered the bicentennial parade with a Barlow, the world's most popular pattern of folding knife. It used the bicentennial flag as a shield, a "crown Q" with '76 decorated the bolsters, and the dates 1776 – 1976 surrounded by stars decorated the face of the single blade. Fifteen thousand of these knives were made, each packed in a block of pine wood for display by the collector.

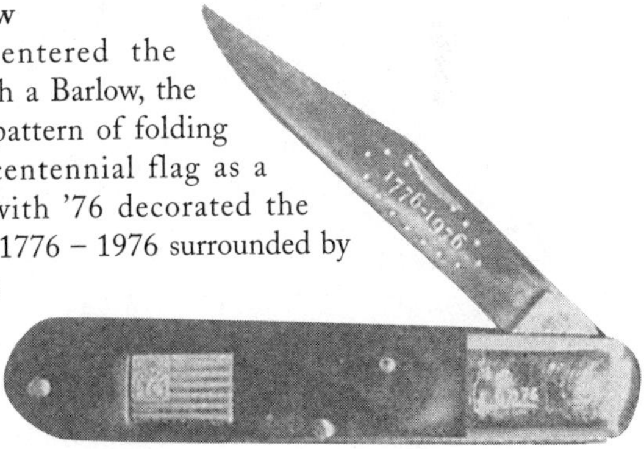

Issue Price: $15.00
Collector Value: $80.00

411

Belknap Hardware, USA, 1977 "Blue Grass Commemoratives"
A series of knives commemorating the **Blue Grass** trademark.

1st – 3½", 2 blade, stock pattern, 5,000 with white, sawed delrin handles, Blue Grass shield, etched blades.
Issue: $15.00
Collector Value: $85.00

2nd – ½", 2 blade Barlow pattern with a hammer shield, 5,000 with antique finish.
Issue: $15.00
Collector Value: $70.00

3rd – 3½", 2 blade Barlow pattern with a handsaw shield, 5,000 produced.
Issue: $20.00
Collector Value: $60.00

4th – 3½", 2 blade Barlow pattern with a screwdriver shield, 5,000 produced.
Issue: $20.00
Collector Value: $60.00

5th – 3½" , 2 blade stock, ax shield, 5,000 produced.
Issue: $25.00
Collector Value: $50.00

6th – 3½", 2 blade stock, wood handles with screwdriver shield, 750 produced.
Issue: $25.00
Collector Value: $50.00

7th – 3½", 2 blade stock, wood handles, laser engraved, 750 produced.
Issue: $25.00
Collector Value: $50.00

Blue Tick Hound – Near and dear to the hearts of Southerners everywhere, and Tennessee in particular, is the ole coon dog. Of this group of hunting dogs, the Blue Tick Hound is perhaps the most outstanding. A coon hunter will tell you that unless you have heard the music of the hounds on a trail as it drifts through the ridges and valleys of the Appalachian hills late at night, you can have no appreciation of the love of a coon hunter for his dog.

This **Tennessee Knife Works Colonel Coon** knife recognized this appreciation and the ole Blue Tick Hound with 500 quality Colonel Coon stock knives, each handled in blue bone. To round out the effort, each knife came packaged in an attractive display box.

Issue Number: 500

Collector Value: $95.00 – $105.00

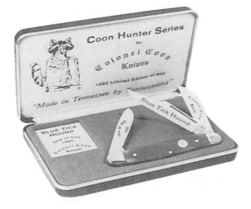

Boker 1993 LTD Tribute to Harley-Davidson and to the annual Harley meet at Sturgis, South Dakota.

The philosophy "Live to Ride/Ride to Live" as well as a 1911 Harley in cast is on the pewter handles. The blade engraving shows bikers on the way to Sturgis.

Issue Number: 9,999

Collector Value: $100.00

Boker Damast

It's "Gurantie" says this is "der Boker Damast Serie (Ein Messer pro Jahr)." It says more, but my high school German is too long unused. Loosely, this is the Boker Damast year knife for 1987. It is a canoe pattern and has beautiful pearl handles. It is of doubtless quality and should be treasured.

Collector Value: $400.00

Boker Damast, John un Messer, 1980

Boker's first Damascus year knife was produced primarily for the European market. It was an effort initiated by Ernest Felix, president of the German Boker operation, to spark the interest of knife collecting in Europe. The ivory-handled, 336 layer Damascus bladed lockback was a success.

Issue Number: 300

Issue Price: $400.00

Boker Damascus Year Knife, 1993 and 1994

Boker has continued its tradition of issuing a state-of-the-art Damascus bladed year knife. The 1993 version had interesting laminated wood handles which added both beauty and appeal. Its blade is 3¼" long, and it is 5" long closed.

The 1994 version features 300 layer Damascus steel blade, crafted by Manfred Sachse, and tetonium handles. It is claimed to be "as light as a feather." The blade length is 3⅛", and 5" long closed. Each edition was limited to 999 knives.

Issue Price: 1993 Version: $335.00
1994 Version: $250.00

Boker Fire Fighter Commemorative

The **Boker** Firefighter Commemorative is a find for any collection. After the events of September 11, 2001, and the heroism shown by the New York City firefighters, we suspect this particular commemorative will become hard to find (and perhaps harder to afford). This commemorative begins with a well-constructed, attractive, red-handled lockback knife. Then it adds an attractive and a unique feature: a siren which sounds when the button showing the fire bell is pushed.

Issue Date: 1994
Issue Price: $129.50

Boker Wiss Cutlery, USA & Germany

Began their yearly commemorative series in 1971. The first one was produced in Solingen, Germany.

1971 edition – a 4", 3 blade stock pattern with bone handles, two shields, and etched blade. Collector Value: $42.00.

1972 edition – 3½", 3 blade, stock pattern with two dated shields and etched blade. Collector Value: $42.00.

1973 edition – a 13¾", 4 blade congress pattern with delrin handles, two red shields, etched blade. Collector Value: $40.00.

1974 edition – a 4", 3 blade stock pattern with delrin bone handles, two shields, and etched blade. Collector Value: $40.00.

1975 edition – a 4", 3 blade, whittler pattern, with cracked ice handles, engraved "Sternwheeler" shield, etched blade. Collector Value: $40.00.

1976 edition – "American Bicentennial" commemorative, a 5" folding hunter, limited to 24,000, with a red, white, and blue flag etched on the blade and a silver eagle shield. Collector Value: $50.00.

1977 edition – 4", 2 blade canoe pattern with cracked ice handles, an Indian in a canoe shield, and an etched blade. Collector Value: $50.00.

1978 edition – a 4", 2 blade "Hillbilly Trapper" pattern with bone handles and etched blade. Collector Value: $60.00.

1979 edition – a 5" folding hunter, wood handled lockback recognizing hardware stores, the scene on the blade is of the inside of an old hardware store. Collector Value: $65.00.

1980 edition – a 5¼" blade folding hunter "recognizing the uncommon men who developed the American railroad system," the knife has stag handles and an etching of the C & O's Pacific Number 161 locomotive on the face of the blade. Collector Value: $100.00.

1981 edition – a large two blade trapper with a bar shield with the words "White Lightning" on it. Blades are etched with a scene of federal agent "revenuers" stalking a fine upstanding mountain gentleman practicing his trade. Collector Value: $52.00.

1982 edition – Along the Blue Ridge Mountains runs a walking path which extends from Maine to Georgia, The Appalachian Trail. This knife, a 3⁹⁄₁₆" canoe with rough uniquely jigged rosewood handles, brings attention to this national treasure. Scenes etched on the blades are from along the trail. Collector Value: $60.00.

1983 edition – "The Farm Boy," 2 blade stock, 8,000 issued. Collector Value: $35.00.

1984 edition – "Old Tom," 1 blade folding hunter, 8,000 issued. Collector Value: $45.00.

1985 edition – "Blackbeard," 4,100 issued, Collector Value: $150.00.

1986 edition – "The Forty-niner," Gold Rush Commemorative, 5,000 issued. Collector Value: $60.00.

1987 edition – "The Constitution," 4 blade congress, 8,000 issued. Collector Value: $60.00.

1988 edition – "The Titanic," Lockback folding hunter, 3,000 issued. Collector Value: $90.00.

1989 edition – "The Graf Zeppelin," 2 blade trapper, 3,000 issued. Collector Value: $60.00

1985 Edition, Blackbeard.

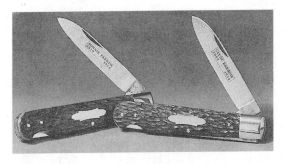

Bonnie and Clyde

In the late 1970s, knife dealers across America discovered that in addition to being a way of introducing or reintroducing old patterns to collectors, something or some event made their knives more marketable. **Battle Ax Cutlery,** Hardin Wholesale of Kenova, W. Va., was among the leaders of the pack. They produced some memorable and often unusual knife sets. Their knives were made in Germany and were top quality.

The Bonnie and Clyde Commemorative set was one of these. A one blade 4⅞" lockback with bone handles and black and gold etched blades was the foundation for this commemorative set. The movie about Bonnie and Clyde, even though old, prompted customers to remember the infamous pair and their exploits.

Production Number: 578 sets
Issue Price: $100.00 – 120.00
Collector Value: $150.00

Browning Limited Edition – This is the Big Game grade of this knife's three grades. They are designed by Michael Collins and limited to 5,000 per grade.

The Big Game grade has engraving on both sides of the blades which depicts the male deer and the whitetail deer as they appear on the B.A.R. Big Game rifles. The scenes are detailed in gold, and the handles are of exotic quince wood.

Grade 4 has handles of cocobola wood and features scenes found on Grade 4 B.A.R. rifles. Grade 1 features a polished blade and handles of mahogany.

These knives would doubtlessly enhance a Browning enthusiast's collection.

Issue Number: 5,000 per grade
Issue Price: Big Game: $125.00
Grade 4: $110.00
Grade 1: $85.00

Buck Rogers Knife

Buck Rogers of the twenty-fifth century was alive and well during the '30s. Rocketship knives were sold off cards, often for less than one dollar. This same knife has appreciated in value somewhat on today's collector market. (Caution: Watch for reproductions! There is usually a reason they look too good to be true.)

Collector Value: $125.00

Buck's Statue of Liberty Commemorative

The Statue of Liberty was presented to the United States by France in 1886. For the 100 years that followed, the Lady stood as a beacon of hope to immigrants from around the world.

Refurbishing the statue in time for her centennial anniversary became an obsession throughout the entire country. Several companies issued commemorative pocketknives which will serve as mementoes for years to come.

We selected the one issued by **Buck** to be representative of the event, partly because of its shield. A Miss Liberty Medallion was made from authentic materials from the Statue of Liberty/Ellis Island National Monument. The owner of one of these knives actually possesses a piece of the monument.

Collector Value: $100.00

Buffalo Bill

Produced by **Schrade Cutlery**, this knife was made as a 4" stock pattern knife with sawed delrin handles, a medallion shield, and an etched blade. Since the issue number was 15,000, it is very important for the collector to be sure that the box and medallion, which accompanied each new knife, are still with it.

Collector Value: $48.00

Camillus' 115th Year Anniversary Double Lockback Trapper

America's oldest continuous manufacturer of pocketknives celebrated its 115th anniversary in 1991 by producing a commemorative of its newest knife, the double lockback Trapper.

This special, limited edition featured genuine stag handles and detailed blade etchings. Only 1,000 were made. The knives were issued in a collector's presentation case.

Issue Number: 1,000
Collector Value: $150.00

Carvel Hall "Historical Knives"

Carvel Hall entered into the commemorative knife business in the late 1960s, with its historical knife series. These knives were not exact reproductions in that they were all made with stainless steel. They were reasonable facsimiles of the originals. The editions were limited, not by an arbitrary production number, but by market demand. They made impressive wall hangings and could be purchased with a wall plaque or a leather sheath or both. The knives are of such quality that the factory offered to hone them, upon request, for functional use. Even though they were not widely distributed through knife collecting circles, many were collected. Recently, they have now begun making appearances in collecting circles and bringing collector prices.

These were six models produced:

Buffalo Bill Knife

This replica of the knife used by William F. Cody "Buffalo Bill", is stainless steel with a walnut handle. It came with a 19½" mahogany plaque. It is easy to understand the need for such a knife in the buffalo hunting trade from which Buffalo Bill got his nickname.

Collector Value: $55.00

Bowie Knife

The Bowie knife certainly is among the most popular of the historical series. This is a three-quarter size replica of what is popularly thought to be the knife Jim Bowie carried at the Alamo. As his actual knife has never been identified and photography at the time of its use just wasn't around, this design is arguably an acceptable ideal of what his knife was thought to be. The overall length of the reproduction is 14½" (that would have made the original 19+"). In any event, the spirit and lore of the knife are captured in this beechwood handled representation of Colonel Bowie's knife. It came with a mahogany plaque and/or a cowhide sheath.

Collector Value: $60.00

Arkansas Toothpick

The Arkansas Toothpick was a long thin frontier throwing knife that was very popular in the early 1800s. The blade of this walnut handled 17½" knife tapers down to a dagger-like point. Interestingly, it is reputed to have been nicknamed by Jim Bowie. The knife came with a 21" mahogany plaque and/or cowhide sheath.

Collector Value: $55.00

Davy Crockett Knife

Davy Crockett was a rather interesting figure in the history of the U.S. in the early 1800s. His resumé included pioneer, scout, member of the Tennessee Legislature and of the U.S. House of Representatives. He was killed at the Alamo along with Jim Bowie. This knife is a reproduction of one reputed to have been his. It is 14¾" long, has a walnut handle, and came with a 19½" mahogany plaque and/or cowhide sheath.

Collector Value: $55.00

Daniel Boone Knife

This knife is the most exacting reproduction of the group. Daniel Boone's knife resides in the Museum of Kentucky History in Frankfort. The original was made for him by his brother, and he carried it throughout his career as a pioneer. This replica has a walnut handle, is 15¾" long, and came with a 19½" mahogany plaque and/or leather sheath.

Collector Value: $60.00

George Washington Knife

There are many historians who believe our nation's history would look very different had it not been for the contributions of George Washington. George Washington served as the General of the Continental Army during the Revolutionary War and our nation's first president. This 5½" Carvel Hall Commemorative knife is a reproduction of the one he carried throughout his military career. It came with a mahogany plaque and/or with a cowhide sheath. This is the rarest of the Carvel Hall Historical series.

Collector Value: $75.00

Note to the collector: Even though these knives were quality made, they were intended to be displayed. Because of that, the following considerations should be applied to their collector value.

- •Knives with plaque only = 100% of collector value
- *Knives with plaque and sheath = 125% of collector value
- *Knives with sheath only = 75% of collector value
- •Knives with neither sheath nor plaque = 50% of collector value
- • Original box adds 10% to the total collector value of the knife

Case Whittler Collector's Set

This collector's set consists of some of the most beautiful knives ever produced by **Case Cutlery**. The patterns used are 5308SSP, 5380SSP and 5383SSP. The scales are stag, the very best quality, of course. The bolsters are nickel-silver with a 14K gold-filled florentine design. The metal in the knife, the blades and backsprings are all mirror polished stainless steel.

Only 2,500 sets were produced, making this a sought after and appreciated set of knives.

Collector Value: $400.00

Case Auto Racing Commemoratives

There has been a proliferation of auto racing commemoratives in the last few years. In fact, there could easily be a book devoted exclusively to these knives. We have no intention of giving that much space to this category of knives. However, in fairness, we believe a sampling is required to provide our readers with an introduction to them and their values.

The pressure of auto racing memorabilia has generated an active market for these collectibles. Collectors of knives who do not actively move in race car memorabilia circles should proceed with caution. We advise that you apply the same criteria to these knives that you would to other commemorative pocketknife collectibles.

Mfg. Company	Pattern	Commemorating	Issue Number	Collector Value
Case	5254/Trapper	Awesome Bill Elliott	600	$350.00
Case	6254/Trapper	Handsome Harry Grant	1,000	$125.00
Hen and Rooster	Trapper	Tribute to Cale Yarborough	2,000	$75.00
Case	Big Coke	King Richard Petty	1,000	$350.00
Case	6265RPB	Dale Earnhardt's Time	2,000	$175.00
Case	52131 Canoe	Geoff Bodine's '86 Daytona 500 Victory	1,000	$125.00

Case's Damascus

The introduction of Damascus steel to **Case's** cutlery line indeed added a new dimension to Case collectibles. Perhaps the most outstanding examples are the stag Damascus Bowie and Kodiak hunter. The issue was limited to 500 each, serial numbered and stamped Case XX, Bradford, PA.

A collector is fortunate to have these knives in his collection.

Collector Value:

Kodiak $800.00

Bowie $550.00

Case Classics
(Distributed by Parker Collector Service)

Over the past ten or so years, older models of discontinued **Case** patterns and trademarks have been used for reproduction knives generally referred to as "Case Classics." The objective seemed to have been to reintroduce these old-style knives for collectors. After all, the genuine old ones, if and when you find them, are either in rough shape or very expensive.

The knives are well built, in varying quantities, with a wide variety of handle materials. They may well appreciate handsomely in the future. However, it is a little early to speculate about which ones collectors will want most or how much they'll pay for them.

The following is a listing of some of our favorites. The prices on them are the suggested retail at the time of issue. You should bear in mind that when issued, these prices would often be substantially discounted to dealers and collectors who bought in quantity. If you are willing to dicker, you should be able to do better than these prices, at least for now.

CS71050

ROG63043½

51072

5355BT

52094

Case Classics

Pattern Number	Quality Produced	Handle Material	Stamping	Retail
53043½	260	Stag	Case Tested	$100.00
ROG63043½	1,000	Red Bone	Case Bradford	$150.00
WF73043½	500	Waterfall	W.R. Case & Son	$65.00
TS73043½	500	Tortoise Shell	W.R. Case & Son	$65.00
ROG620465	1,000	Brown Bone	Case Bros.	$70.00
5488	500	Stag	Case Tested	$80.00
ROG6488	500	Brown Bone	Case Bros.	$80.00
51050	250	Stag	W.R. Case & Son	$140.00
CS71050	500	Candy Stripe	Case Tested	$120.00
83109X	269	Pearl	W.R. Case & Son	$200.00
51072	500	Stag	Case XX	$200.00
G61072	1,000	Green Bone	Tested	$300.00
5223	223	Stag	Case Bros.	$100.00
5355	500	Stag	Case Bros.	$140.00
52094	191	India Stag	W.R. Case & Sons	$175.00
5039	200	India Stag	Case Bros.	$170.00

The Case Indian Head Penny

This knife and coin set was introduced in 1990 by the Little River Knife Sales of Arden, North Carolina. It consists of a Rogers Jigged Bone **Case** Copperhead (ROGO6200SS) with etched blades and an Indian head penny inset in the handle just below the Case shield.

This knife and an authentic Indian head penny are included in a hard shell presentation box. The sets are limited to 1,500 and are individually numbered.

Collector Value: $90.00

Case's Stag Barlow Set

This limited edition of 5000 Case Barlow set contain some unique knives. It came in an oak glass topped display case. Together they made an impressive set.

Collector Value: $225.00

Johnny Cash Case Muskrat

Johnny Cash and trains have seemed to go together since the release of "Folsom Prison Blues." The **Case** Muskrat has been dressed with honeycomb bone handles, etched with a train and Cash's signature, and displayed in an etched glass-topped wood case. The issue of 1,000 makes this knife very interesting to the collector.

Collector Value: $165.00

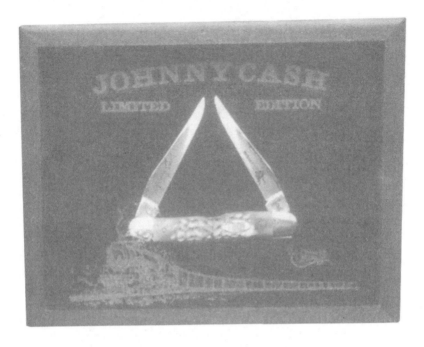

Butch Cassidy & The Sundance Kid Ride Again

The exploits of these colorful characters are commemorated with two 3⅝"
knives (closed) in a Bandits of the West display box. These stainless steel knives
have an engraved Colt pistol on the handles and etchings of Butch and
Sundance on separate blades. Total production was limited to 1,200.

Stamping: Frost Cutlery
Collector Value: $70.00

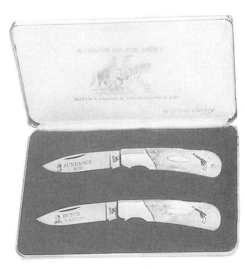

Connecticut Charter Oak

The handles of this knife were made from the wood of the Connecticut Charter Oak tree.

This tree played an important role in Connecticut's history. On October 31, 1687, John Wadsworth successfully hid the colony's Charter of Independence in the hollow of this tree. The Charter had been issued by King Charles II in 1662 and had granted Connecticut independence. When Sir Edmund Andros, appointed governor of all New England in 1686, attempted to revoke the Charter and thus the Colony's independence, the incident occurred. The Charter was recovered only after Governor Andros was deposed. Needless to say, this old tree, which was some 33 feet in circumference when it was blown down in 1856, was near and dear to the hearts of loyal Connecticuteans.

Holley Cutlery acquired a portion of the tree and used it for the handles of its Charter Oak Commemorative knives. A guarantee of genuineness of the wood used, attested to before a notary public, accompanied each knife. This seemed necessary because of the wide variety of items which laid claim to having been made from the Charter Oak's wood. Mark Twain, in his unique style, placed it into this perspective, "I've seen a walking stick, dog collar, needle case, three-legged stool, boot jack, dinner table, tenpin alley, toothpick and enough Charter Oak to build a plank road from Hartford to Salt Lake City."

Museums do, in fact, have a variety of chairs, gavels, and other odd items which were made from the tree. It seems only natural that knives with Charter Oak scales should be included in this listing.

The Charter Oak penknives were available in two sizes.

Date Issued: 1911

Stamping: **Holley Mfg. Co.**

Collector Value: Unknown. To our knowledge a Holley "Charter Oak" has not surfaced. If you locate one of these, please contact the authors.

Cherokee Council Reunion

At the Red Clay Historical Area in Cleveland, Tennessee, on April 6 and 7, 1984, Cherokee history was made, when the Cherokee peoples reunited after 147 years of separation.

To commemorate this event, a combination of fine art and cutlery craftsmanship was used by Hampton House Studios of Chattanooga. A poster featuring the famous Cherokee Folk Heroes "Raven," "Nancy Ward," and "Five Killer" was designed by the late world famous artist Ben Hampton in cooperation with the Tennessee Department of Conservation. Also a special issue of Case Canoes was released to commemorate the occasion.

This set of knives, the first-ever yellow-handled **Case** canoes, has the image of one of these Indian heroes etched in gold on the master blade of each knife. The set has a one blade canoe (a first!), a two blade canoe, and a three blade canoe. Each knife has a short description of the lore about the person whose image is on the blade. The three come in an attractive box stamped with the seal of the Cherokee nation.

The combination of the poster and knife set made an attractive addition to any den or office. The set of knives was distributed through Frost Cutlery dealers.

Issue Date: April, 1984
Edition Number: 1,500
Collector Value: $700.00, w/poster $750.00

Cherry Tree Chopper

This knife is perhaps the most successful yet produced by **Taylor Cutlery**. Orders exceeded the production run of 1,000 well before the knives arrived. The pattern was a reintroduction of the old knife hatchet pattern used by companies many years ago. The knife has an etched picture of George Washington on the hatchet blade and the name "Cherry Tree Chopper" on the knife blade. The handle material used was genuine stag.

Collector Value: $150.00

Cherry Tree Chopper II

Taylor Cutlery began a series of these knives with this spin-off from the Cherry Tree Chopper which is almost identical to the original. It came with both smooth and picked bone handles. There were 2,500 produced and distribution was successful from the outset. Even this copy became a knife to be considered a collector's item.

Collector Value: $85.00

(Photo Courtesy National Knife Collector's Magazines)

Miniature Cherry Tree Chopper

A continuation of the Cherry Tree Chopper series, there were 2,000 knives produced and sold in sets of two. The 3½" knives were handled in smooth and picked bone. They came in an attractive display box typical of **Taylor**.

Collector Value: $85.00 (set)

'57 Chevy Bel Air

The car won the hearts of teens and wannabes from the time it hit the showrooms. It was and is one of the most sought after cars in Chevrolet history. Commemorating this, the **Franklin Mint** has issued a rather interesting knife incorporating into its design the Chevy shield emblem and the Bel Air bumper guard. The trademarks are used under license to Franklin Mint from General Motors Corp. The knife was authorized by *Antique Quarterly Magazine*.

Issue Price: $37.50

Chief Crazy Horse Special Edition Commemorative

This special edition **Case** knife is the first produced in quantity with a deep gun metal blued blade. Both sides of the blade are etched in gold and have a photo of Chief Crazy Horse and the names of the eleven Sioux tribes in both English and Lakota.

The Kodiak pattern knife was produced as a companion piece for a Chief Crazy Horse rifle made by Winchester.

Issue Number: 5,000
Date of Issue: 1983
Issue Price: $225.00
Collector Value: $350.00

The People's Choice Set

This was the final set of **Taylor** knives in the Cherry Tree Chopper series. It featured three mini-chopper knives with the etched images of presidents Washington, Lincoln, and Reagan, one on each hatchet blade of the set.

Collector Value: $85.00

Civil War Set

This **Frost Cutlery** set of knives features the two most outstanding generals in the American Civil War, Robert E. Lee and Ulysses S. Grant. The knives are 4½" folding hunter patterns, having bone handles and an image of one of the generals on the blade.

Issue Number: 1,200 sets
Collector Value: $100.00

The Coal Miner

This set of knives, produced by **Boker Cutlery,** commemorates the phases of the development of the United Mine Workers of America. The set contains three knives, each with an engraved master blade depicting some part of the Union's struggle. Displayed in a wooden box, this set makes an interesting addition to any den or family room.

Collector Value: $325.00

Coal Miners of America

The occupation of coal mining is honored with this **Frost Cutlery** set of 4½" (closed) folding hunter knives. One is handled in pick bone, the other smooth bone. They have nickel and silver bolsters and surgical steel blades. The blades are etched, and the box for display has a picture of a coal miner surrounded by the set name on the inside of the lid cover. Overall, the set is impressive and should hold a special place in the home or collection of any person with an interest in coal mining.

Stamping: Frost Cutlery
Collector Value: $80.00

The Cowboy Commemorative

This knife set features two knives with pearl handles, worked inside liners and back springs, and blades engraved, one with a cowboy on a bucking horse, the other with a cowboy roping a steer. Six hundred sets were made at an issue price of $100.00.

Date Issued: 1980
Stamping: **Elk Horn** Taylor
Collector Value: $165.00

Dale Earnhardt

Knives riding in the beds of trucks is a current fad for collection. This version is a Dale Earnhardt commemorative loaded with a Case toothpick.

Collector Value: $100.00

The Damascus Rainbow Set (by Case)

This set was issued in 1989 by Smoky Mountain Knife Works and contains 5 one blade, Case Trapper Pattern knives consecutively handled in red, yellow, blue, green, and white jigged bone. The shields are gold colored, Case XX, with raised letters.

The knives are stamped with serial numbers and sets limited to 5,000.

Collector Value: $675.00

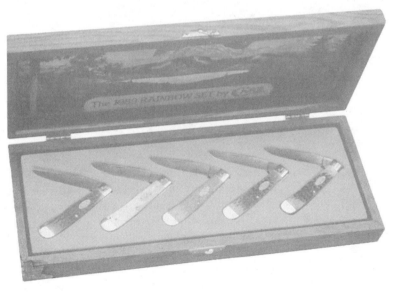

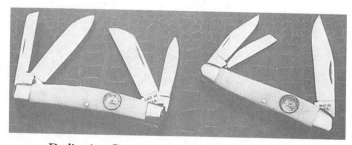

Dedication Commemoratives, N.K.C.A. Museum

On May 22, 1981 the National Knife Collector's Association dedicated the first museum for cutlery only. In order to pay for the expenses of building displays, the N.K.C.A. issued a dedication set of knives that was available to members for a period of only 45 days. During this time 1,700 sets were sold.

The knives were unique **Case patterns**, numbers 6488 and 6380. Each had stainless blades and smooth bone rose-colored handles. Shields were N.K.C.A. issue, one depicting the museum dedication, the other the reward fund.

Collector Value: $200.00

Deerslayer Limited

Produced for **Clarence Risner Cutlery,** this Japanese knife is a very impressive 4½", 1 blade lockback pattern with walnut handles. It has a finely etched drop-point blade and the pommel of this knife is artistically done in the graceful shape of a stag's head. Each knife is packed in a walnut box for display, making an impressive addition to any collection.

Total Produced: 1,200

Issue Price: $45.00

Collector Value: $175.00

Desert Storm "Victory Edition"

It should be said, if it hasn't already been observed, "The collector of commemorative knives is a student of history!"

I do not suspect there is an event of significance in U.S. history that has not been "commemorated" in some fashion for knife collectors. Remember, such actions only take place when there is a demand for the product. Otherwise some knife producers would be likely to go broke. I suspect that the talent for issuing a successful commemorative of a particular topic is knowing what is considered significant by collectors.

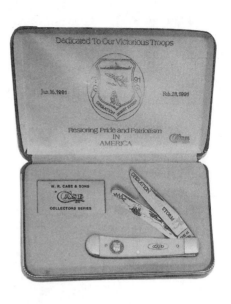

Well, a Desert Storm commemorative was a topic that several cutlery distributors and manufacturers took to heart. Several were issued. This one by Case was very well done and recognized the pride and patriotism of the American people. It came with a Desert Storm metal inlay and etched blades in a camouflage (desert style) hard shell display box.

Issue Price: $59.95

Dixie Commemorative

Produced by the Cooper Group, **Boker-Germany**, this impressively displayed set of knives honors the heroes of the Confederacy. When the lid is lifted, a music box displaying knives honoring Jefferson Davis, Robert E. Lee, and Stonewall Jackson plays "Dixie." A Confederate flag graces the inside of the lid. The knives are handled in a Rebel gray delrin.

Issue Price: $100.00
Collector Value: $300.00

A Yankee Hero Collection

These sets were produced by the Cooper Group in 1988 by **Boker of Germany.** Each set contains three knives, honoring Abraham Lincoln, Ulysses Grant, and William T. Sherman, heroes of the North during the Civil War.

The knife set is displayed in a walnut music box that plays "Battle Hymn of the Republic" when opened.

Collector Value: $300.00

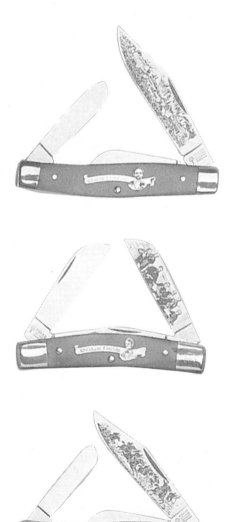

Dinosaur Bones

This is a unique line of presentation knives released by Santa Fe Stone Works of New Mexico in 1985, manufactured by **Camillus Cutlery**. They include several patterns and a letter opener and are handled in fossilized dinosaur bones which are claimed to be 150 million years old. The handles, due to the sediment in which they were found, show up in beautiful grain and coloration.

Each knife was packed in a presentation box.

Collector Value: $150.00

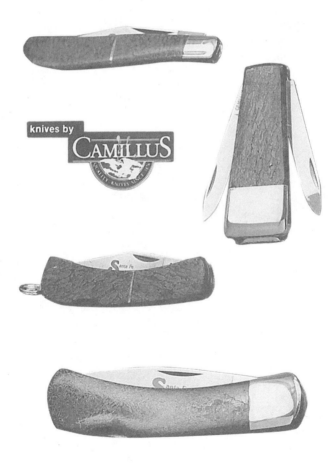

The Ducks Unlimited Collection

This consists of a series of collectible knives produced in a partnership of **W.R. Case & Sons** and Ducks Unlimited Organization, 1991. Each knife features a Ducks Unlimited etched blade and shield logo. A portion of the profit from each sale went to the Ducks Unlimited Organization to help maintain wetland habitat for waterfowl and other wildlife.

These knives were individually priced and should increase in value accordingly:

1. Camper #763 ....$29.99
2. Featherweight #733 ....$22.99
3. Executive #744 ....$24.99
4. Click 'N Clean #762 ....$48.99
5. Back Packer #742 ....$46.99
6. Companion #730 ....$24.99
7. Outdoorsman #741 ....$42.99
8. Mountaineer #760 ....$59.99
9. Golden Stag #759 ....$55.99
10. Folding Hunter #740 ....$46.99

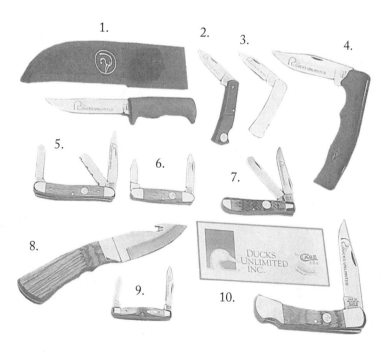

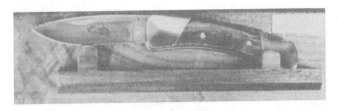

Ducks in Flight

Buck Cutlery in cooperation with Aurium Engravers of Garland, Texas, produced the Sears Roebuck exclusive "Ducks in Flight." The 1,000 number issue came with its own display stand and featured a beautiful 22 karat gold engraving on the face of the blade. The knives were distributed through Sears in 1984.

Issue Price: $75.00
Collector Value: $110.00

Drake Oil Well

Produced by Queen Cutlery commemorating the company's 50th birthday, this 1972 knife was one of the earlier modern commemoratives. The knife was a 3½" 2 blade Barlow pattern of which 5,000 were made. Each had bone handles, etched blades, and the Queen logo stamped on the bolsters.

Issue Price: $15.00
Collector Value: $75.00

Famous Men of Texas

A Taylor Cutlery issue featuring two stag handle, gunstock pattern knives honoring Sam Houston and Ben Milan. There were 450 produced and released, as indicated by the dated blades, in 1980.

Collector Value: $50.00

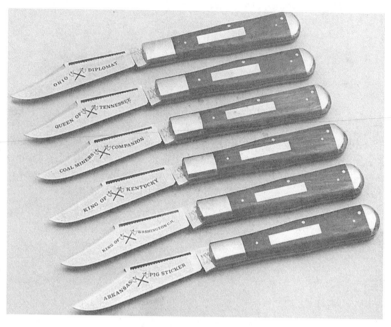

Folding Hunter Series

This series of 6 one blade, folding hunter-style knives by **Battle Ax Cutlery** makes an impressive display. Each knife has a name which commemorates an idea, profession or subject: King of Kentucky; Coal Miner's Companion; Ohio Diplomat; Queen of Tennessee; King of Washington Court House and Arkansas Pigsticker.

Collector Value: Complete set, $400.00

Fighting Cocks

This issue from **Smoky Mountain Knife Works**, 1981, honors the sport of cockfighting in a royal way. These 3½" gamecock knives have pewter handles crafted by the renowned artist Shaw Liebowets, and 24 kt. gold blade etching by Adrian Harris.

Collector Value: Set w/display box, $575.00

Founders Knife

Commemorating the founding of **Case Cutlery**, this Case 1 blade Daddy Barlow pattern is 5½" long and has stag handles and an etched blade. There were 10,000 of these knives made for each letter in the company's name. The knife is well constructed and comes in a nice display.

Collector Value: $160.00

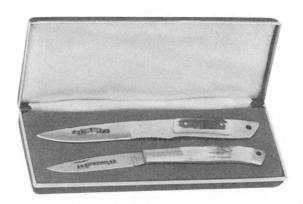

The Gamblers

This set of knives is distinctive because one knife is a fixed-blade knife and the other is a folding one. The fixed-blade knife, "The Ace," is 7" long, has stag handles and an etched blade. The closed length of the folding member of this set, "The Deuce," is 3¾" long and also has stag handles and an etched blade. Total number of sets was limited to 1,200.

Stamping: **Frost Cutlery**
Collector Value: $95.00

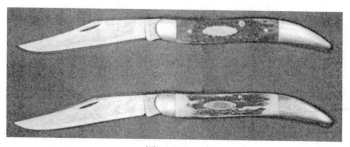

The Gators

These Texas Toothpick stag and bone handled **Case** knives were the thing to have when released by Time Tested Products of St. Petersburg, Florida in 1979. They were called "The Gators" and came in an attractive display box. The set was limited to 2,750 pairs of knives.

Collector Value: $150.00

The General

This three blade stock pattern knife was made by **Bowen Knife Company** to commemorate the Great Locomotive Chase and the train, "The General," which was used in that chase. A total of 1,200 of these knives was made. They were 3⅝" long and had rosewood handles. A picture of the train was etched on the main blade of each knife.

Collector Value: $75.00

Generals Robert E. Lee and Stonewall Jackson Commemorative Set
This set of two coke pattern 5½" folding hunter knives was produced by **Taylor Cutlery** to commemorate the exploits of the South's two greatest generals. The knives have stag handles and production was limited to 1,250 numbered sets in display boxes.
Collector Value: $210.00

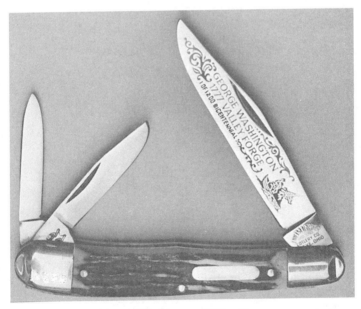

George Washington Valley Forge
This commemorative whittler was made by **Robert Klaas Cutlery** for J. Nielsen-Mayers. It is a 4" 3 blade whittler with stag handles, etched blades, and sequenced numbers.
Issue Date: 1976
Collector Value: $95.00

443

Gerber Bicentennial, Sportsman

Gerber Cutlery, 1976, 1 blade, lockback, folding hunter pattern, issued 200 with stag handles, etched blade, engraved bolsters, sheath, and walnut presentation box.

Issue Price: $195.00
Collector Value: $325.00

Gerber Mark II 20th Anniversary Commemorative

To quote from the Certificate of Authenticity, "This knife is one of 5000 produced in celebration of the 20th anniversary of the Gerber Mark II™ Survival Knife. This numbered limited edition knife is an exact replica of the Mark II™ as originally manufactured by Gerber Legendary Blades in 1966."

An enclosed flyer tells about the design suggestions and drawings of Army Captain C.A. (Bud) Holzmann. The most unique of its features was the "waspwaist" blade which was angled at 5 degrees. This allowed the knife to hug the soldier's body. Production of the knife began in 1966. A total of 2,747 of these knives with angled blades was manufactured for U.S. servicemen.

Collector Value: $160.00

Grand Dad's Old Timer Series

A **Schrade** issue of 4 knives:

•4" 3 blade, stock pattern, sawed delrin handles, worked backspring, and Old Timer shield. Collector Value: $40.00.

•3½" stock pattern, sawed delrin handles, worked backspring, Old Timer shield. Collector Value: $35.00.

•"Sharpfinger" sheath knife, sawed delrin handles, Old Timer shield. Collector Value: $40.00.

•3½" Barlow pattern with sawed delrin handles, embossed brass bolsters, slant shield. Collector Value: $40.00.

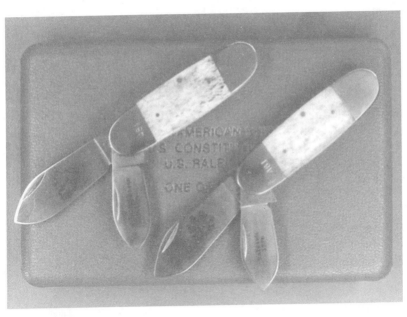

The Great American Ship Set

This knife set features two sunfish pattern knives commemorating the USS Constitution and the USS Raleigh. The 1,000 sets issued have smooth bone handles.

Date Issued: 1980
Stamping: **Elk Horn, Taylor**
Collector Value: $75.00

Granddaddy Barlow Commemorative, CM2

The Granddaddy Barlow Commemorative, made by **Camillus** Cutlery for **A.G. Russell** in 1973, came in three grades. The Premier (#1 – 18) had 14k gold bolsters, which were engraved and weighed more than an ounce. The blade was also engraved and partially plated in gold. The Excelsior grade (#19 – 300) had engraved bolsters and an etched blade. The Collector grade was plain. It had numbers over 1,000.

These knives were all of excellent quality and complimented both the designer and manufacturer.

Premier Grade: $1,500.00
Excelsior Grade: $450.00
Collector Grade: $125.00

Great American Story

A series of knives by **Boker Cutlery** which, beginning in 1974, was issued at a rate of one every three months until the set of 12 was complete. The knives were several different patterns, 4" to 4½" in length, with two to four blades. Delrin handles and shields symbolized specific events.

Series 2 was produced 1976 – 1978.

Collector Values: $20.00 – 40.00 each.

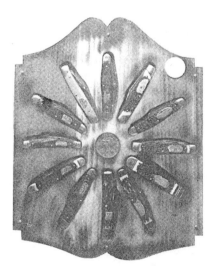

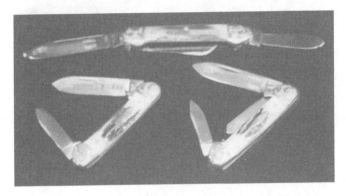

Gunboat Canoe

This is, in the opinion of at least one of this book's authors, a most impressive set of limited edition **Case** brand knives. Not only have the style and size of three blade canoes been introduced, the stag handles, engraved gold slated bolsters, and beautiful stag handles combine with the limit of the edition (5,000) to make the set extremely collectible (and of course a beautiful display). Case patterns used were Numbers 52131, 53131, and 5394.

Issue Price: $200.00

Collector Value: $575.00

The Hallamshire Knife

As if to confirm that traditional skills of quality cutlery manufacturing are still alive and well in Sheffield, **Steel City Manufacturing** of Sheffield, England, released this superb limited edition (50) knife of mother-of-pearl, Sheffield steel, and gold. This 1982 issue will undoubtedly become a multigenerational work of art.

Collector Value: $500.00

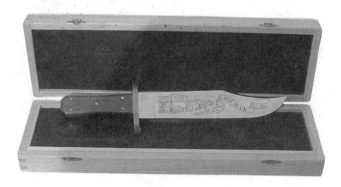

H.H. Buck

This knife is a 15" Bowie which has the blade etched with a scene of H.H. Buck working in his blacksmith's shop. This is a very impressive knife. It is well presented in its mammoth display box.

Collector Value: $325.00

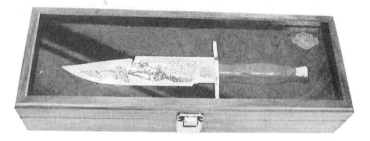

Harley-Davidson Black Hills Commemorative Limited Edition

No one who has been paying attention will call you more than a maker of understatement if you say "Harley riders take their bikes seriously." Anyone who doubts this or who wants to know just how widespread the Harley following is should take a trip to Sturgis, South Dakota, during the annual Harley gathering. Bikers from all over the United States and several foreign countries attend. Many display the "easy rider" biker's uniform. It is a memorable occasion!

It logically follows that there would be a need for lots of souvenirs and commemoratives to document the occasion. Knife manufacturers have never been accused of a lack of logic when there is a demand for knives to be met.

The "Black Hills Commemorative Knife" was no doubt produced to meet the demand of Harley fans. The Bowie came in an attractive glass-top display box with the Harley-Davidson trademark on the glass. The blade of the Bowie has etching of a couple riding a bike as they pass an overlook of Mount Rushmore. This 1990 edition did enthusiasts proud.

Issue Price: $299.00

Collector Value: $990.00

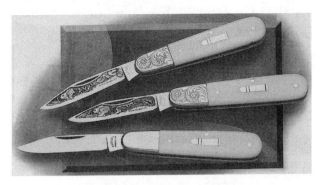

Photo courtesy A.G. Russell Cutlery

Hen & Rooster/A.G. Russell Baby Barlow

These knives were made in 1975 by **Hen and Rooster** for A.G. Russell. They are rather unique in that there were different grades of the same knife made in such a way that the quality of the basic knife was not compromised. The basic knife was enhanced by replacing the bolsters with 14k gold ones (premier grade), bolsters engraved by Ben Lane and blades etched by Shaw-Lieobowitz (Excelsior grade), and two collector grades A and B (based on serial numbers). These 2½" knives have genuine ivory handles. They were made in 1975, before the ban.

Total Production: 1,800
Premier Grade: (ss#s 1 – 25)
Issue Price: $250.00
Collector Value: $1,600.00

Excelsior Grade (ss#s 26 – 300)
Issue Price: $83.00
Collector Value: $525.00

Collector Grade A (ss#s 301 – 1000)
Issue Price: $24.00
Collector Value: $300.00

Collector Grade B (ss#s 1001 – 1800)
Issue Price: $19.00
Collector Value: $285.00

449

Ka-Bar's Commemoratives and Limited Editions

As a part of their member services, the KA-BAR Collector's Club issues knives for purchase by their membership. Both the club dues and the knives are priced very moderately, making membership a great bargain. The club has been issuing knives since 1975. The following is a list, to date, of the editions which KA-BAR has issued.

Year	Pattern	#Produced	Issue Price	Collector Value	Comments
1975	Fixed blade fighting knife	1,500	$100.00 – 300.00	$150.00 – 400.00	USMC 200-year commemorative
1976	4⅛" trapper	3,500	30.00 – 100.00	100.00 – 150.00	Arguably the most beautiful bicentennial commemorative knife produced. Red, white, and blue handles with dog's head shield
1977	5¼" folding	2,000	200.00/set	250.00	Two knives in set, 1 hunter and 2-blade knives, stag handles, dog's head shield
1978	Fixed blade	1,200	50.00 – 150.00	85.00 – 175.00	WWII Commemorative
	5½" folding hunter				
	1 blade, #1107	3,000	35.00	85.00	Stag handle with dog's head shield
	2 blade, #2107		40.00	100.00	
1979	CK-79, 3½", 1 bl LB	750	27.50	90.00	Oval Kabar shield, stag handles
	#1010, 4" Jack, 2 blade	500	31.50	75.00	Stag handles, dog's head shield
	#1015, 3⅝", 2 bl. Canoe	940	33.00	115.00	Pearl handles, bar shield
	#1020, 3⅝", 2 bl. Canoe	915	29.50	90.00	Stag handles, bar shield
	#401, 5", F. Hunter	331	80.00	250.00+	Genuine ivory
	#402, 5", F. Hunter	298	80.00	235.00	Mother-of-pearl
1980	CK-80, 3½", Gun Stock Jack	2,162	27.50	60.00	K-wood handles, man-fights-bear shield
	LBC, 3⅝", Cong.	806	25.00	110.00	Mother-of-pearl handles
	#2189, 5", L.B., folding hunter	585	65.00	100.00	Stag handles, engraved
		150	67.50	100.00	bolsters (with initials)
1981	CK-81, 5¼", Coke pattern folding hunter, #1 of 5	2,003	35.00	150.00	Stag handles, engraved blade
	3½" Gunstock Jack	358 sets	125.00 (sets of 3)	250.00	Pearl, stag, jigged bone handles, oval shield
1982	CK-82, 5½" Coke pattern, folding hunter, #1 of 5	1,752	37.50	135.00	Green jigged bone handles, oval shield
	RT-82, 4½", Trapper LB	1,308	35.65	70.00	Stag handles with dog's head shield

Year	Pattern	#Produced	Issue Price	Collector Value	Comments
	4⅛" Trapper	457 sets	125.00 (sets of 3)	250.00	Pearl, stag, and bone handles with oval shield
1983	CK-83, 5¼" Coke pattern folding hunter #3 of 5	1,328	37.50	80.00	Laminated wood with dog's head
	DH-83, 5¼", 1 blade folding hunter	885	37.50	70.00	Jigged bone with dog's head shield
	3½" Barlow	2,368	18.75	60.00	Stag handles with dog's head shield
1984	CK-84, 5¼" Coke pattern folding hunter, #4 of 5	1,500	37.50	125.00	Hickory bone with man-fights-bear shield
	DH-84, 5¼", 1 blade folding hunter	352	37.50	125.00	Jigged bone with dog's head shield
	Whittler DH-85	749	23.50	80.00	Jigged bone with nickel shield
	DH-85-G	251	50.00	80.00	Jigged bone with gold shield
	Texas Toothpick DH-86	875	22.50	75.00	Jigged bone with nickel shield
	DH-86-G	333	50.00	80.00	Jigged bone with gold shield
	4" Congress DH-87	783	25.50	85.00	Jigged bone with nickel D.H. shield
	DH-87-G	250	57.50	95.00	Jigged bone with gold D.H. shield
	3⅝" Stock DH-88	783	22.50	85.00	Jigged bone with nickel D.H. shield
	DH-88-G	249	55.50	95.00	Jigged bone with gold D.H. shield
1985	CK-85, 5¼" Coke pattern, folding hunter, #5 of 5	1474	45.00	150.00	Mother-of-pearl handles with gold man-fights-bear shield
	4½" Plowman Jack DH-89	814	29.00	70.00	Jigged bone with nickel D.H. shield
	DH-89-G	250	52.50	75.00	Jigged bone with gold D.H. shield
	4½" Sling guard lockback DH-90	999	28.50	95.00	Jigged bone with nickel D.H. shield
	DH-90-G	50	52.50	100.00	Jigged bone with gold D.H. shield

Year	Pattern	#Produced	Issue Price	Collector Value	Comments
	3¼" Sleeveboard pen				
	DH-91	736	20.00	65.00	Jigged bone with nickel D.H. shield
	DH-91-G	200	52.50	70.00	Jigged bone with gold D.H. shield
	3½" Barlow				
	DH-92	779	24.00	60.00	Jigged bone with nickel D.H. shield
	DH-92-G	200	47.00	70.00	Jigged bone with gold D.H. shield
	5¼" Folding hunter Coke pattern	62	72.50	125.00	Albermarle-Phenolic laminated wood handles, engraved bolsters, etched blade
1986	5" Grizzly, CK-86, #1 of 5	1,673	42.00	150.00	Stag handle, engraved blade
	LL-86, 4½", Lady's leg knife				
	LL-86	1,061	32.50	70.00	Multicolored handles
	LL-86-DL	250	75.00	150.00	Lace embedded in handles with 2 pt. cut diamonds as buttons; nicknamed "Diamond Lil"
	4¼" Swing guard lockbacks				
	SG-86-S	890	35.00	75.00	Stag handles, oval shield
	SG-86-P	251	45.00	95.00	Pearl handles, no shield
	SF-86, 4¼" Sunfish, 3 knives per set	426 sets	110.00	200.00	Stag with Union Razor Co. stamp, jigged chestnut bone with Union Cutlery stamp, Black Delrin with Kabar stamp
	4¼" Sunfish	747	32.50	75.00	Jigged chestnut bone handles with KA-BAR stamp
1987	5" Grizzly, CK-87, #2 of 5	1,640	42.00	150.00	Smooth chestnut bone handles with engraved bolsters
	3¹¹⁄₁₆" Pillbuster				
	PHD-101	684	25.00	65.00	Stag handles
	PHD-101-P	300	39.00	75.00	Pearl handles
	3¹¹⁄₁₆" "Bomb" Jack				
	UCC-87	600	28.00	55.00	Stag handles
	UCC-87-DL	500	33.00	60.00	Delrin handles with WWI Spad aircraft scrimshawed on handle
	4" Aerial Whittler				
	TT-201-S	698	32.00	60.00	Stag handles
	TT-201-AK	400	35.00	75.00	Aerial style picture handles
1988	5" Grizzly, #3 of 5	1,165	42.00	95.00	Bubinga wood handles, engraved blade, and large oval shield

Year	Pattern	#Produced	Issue Price	Collector Value	Comments
	LTD-88, 5" Grizzly	400	55.00	155.00	Scrimshaw handle, laser engraved blade
	13½" J. Bowie Knife				
	8001-ST	723	55.00	75.00	Stag with J. Bowie etched on blade
	8001-DL	389	67.50	75.00	Bone with laser engraving on blade
	5" Center Lock Jack				
	CL-88	673	31.00	90.00	Red jigged bone
	CL-88-DL	399	37.50	95.00	Smooth brown bone with engraved bolsters
	3½" Coffin Lid Jack				
	DMB-88	711	29.00	65.00	Stag handles "Gunfighter"
	DMB-88-DL	406	37.50	75.00	Briar root handles "Gunfighter"
	4³⁄₁₆" Congress				
	USC-88	686	32.50	65.00	Red jigged bone "Congressman"
	USC-88 "Senator"	401	37.50	65.00	"Ivory" white, engraved blade
1989	5¼" Grizzly, #4 of 5	1,566	42.00	150.00	Prairie jigged bone handles
	3½" Dolphin Pattern				
	Dol-89	784	33.00	70.00	Moss Green jigged bone handles
	Dol-89-DL	488	37.50	75.00	Cinnamon Red bone with engraved blade
	3¼" Humpback Jack				
	HMP-89	776	33.00	75.00	Prairie Brown jigged bone
	HMP-89-DL	475	38.00	85.00	Smooth Green bone with oval shield and engraved blade
	3¼" One Hand Opener				
	OHO-89	766	29.50	60.00	Polished briar root
	OHO-89-DL	431	32.50	65.00	Smooth red bone handles, oval shield and engraved blade
	4⅜" Whaler or Navy				
	WLR-89	774	31.00	60.00	Natural bone handles
	WLR-89-DL	496	38.50	65.00	Natural bone handles with brass bolsters and shackle
1990	4⅜" Grizzly	1,400	45.00	175.00	Picture handle, large club shield, engraved blade
	5⅜" Long John Pattern				
	LJN-90	762	38.00	75.00	Polished bleached bone, oval shield
	LJN-90-DL	501	43.00	85.00	Stag, dog's head shield
	4⅛" Rancher				
	WRA-90	720	39.00	75.00	Strawberry bone, oval shield

453

Year	Pattern	#Produced	Issue Price	Collector Value	Comments
	WRA-90-DL	527	42.00	95.00	Stag with dog's head shield
	3⅞" Boxcar Whittler				
	BXC-90	530	37.00	75.00	Mahogany bone with oval shield and sculptured bolsters
	BXC-90-DL	519	42.00	95.00	Stag with dog's head shield and engraved bolsters
	4" Bent Barlow				
	KLO-90	719	35.00	70.00	Blue jigged bone handles
	KLO-90-DL	480	40.00	80.00	Green smooth bone handles with dog's head shield and engraved bolsters
	Fixed Blade USMC fighting knife	?	45.00	65.00	USMC WWII 50th Anniversary with laser-engraved blade
1991	5⅝" center lock, #1 of 5	1,473	45.00	75.00	Bird's-eye maple handles, engraved, large club shield
	Classic Pen				
	CBS-91	775	35.00	65.00	Stag handles with oval shield
	CBS-91-DL	501	39.00	60.00	"Alternative Ivory" with dog's head shield and engraved blade
	4⅜" Swashbuckler				
	PTP-91	737	35.00	50.00	Delrin Maize with brass hinge bolster
	PTP-91-DL	426	39.50	50.00	Black Delrin with nickel silver bolster
	4⅜" Elephant's toenail whittler				
	ETN-91	740	44.50	85.00	Black swirl poly handles with oval shield
	ETN-91-DL	479	49.50	75.00	Alternative Ivory with oval shield, engraved blade
	Fixed Blade USMC				
	PH-1941	942	48.00	65.00	Pearl Harbor 50th Anniversary commemorative, engraved blade
	Fixed Blade UMC				
	DS-91	5,256	48.00	60.00	Desert Storm commemorative, engraved blade
1992	CK-92, 5⅝", center lock, #2 of 5	1,293	47.50	100.00	Stag handles
	4" Copperhead				
	WJK-91	791	37.50	65.00	Brown jigged bone
	WJK-91-DL	480	42.00	75.00	Stag handles, dog's head shield

Year	Pattern	#Produced	Issue Price	Collector Value	Comments
	3⅞" Muskrat Pattern				
	MP-92	802	37.50	65.00	Jigged brown bone, bar shield
	MP-92-DL	500	45.00	75.00	Stag with dog's head shield
	4¼" Coke Bottle				
	SBC-92	801	47.50	85.00	Brown jigged bone, bar shield
	SBC-92-D1	500	52.00	70.00	Brown smooth bone, dog's head shield, engraved blade
1993	5⅜" center lock, #2 of 5	1,293	47.50	95.00	Stag handles, engraved blade, club shield
	5" Cotton Sampler	802	42.50	75.00	Cherry wood handles, bar shield
	USMC fixed blade	1,200	60.00	85.00	Vietnam Commemorative 1965-1973, blade etched in 24K gold
	USMC fixed blade	1,244	60.00	85.00	D-Day 50th Anniversary Commemorative, gold engraving
1994	5¼" Center lock, #4 of 5	800	47.50	85.00	Smooth brown bone handles
	Texas Tooth Pick or Tickler				
	TR-94	400	31.00	50.00	Bone handles
	TR-94-DL	250 sets	67.00 (pair)	125.00	Stag handles
	Congress				
	CE-94	510	39.00	80.00	Bone handles
	CE-94 (pair)	367	83.00 (set)	125.00	Stag handles
	4½" Swing Guard	730	49.00	90.00	Brown jigged handle, oval shield
1995	5¼" Folding hunter, #1 of 5, 2 blades		52.50	95.00	2-blade stag handles, stainless blades, club shield
1996	5¼" Folding hunter, #2 of 5	850	47.50	85.00	Jigged bone, engraved blade, 2 blade
1997	5¼" Folding hunter, #3 of 5	650	47.50	85.00	Jigged wood, 2 blades, year on blade
	Pillbuster II				
	PHD-97	800	47.50	65.00	Alanté pearl handles, spatula and pen blades
	PHD-97 (pair)	400	100.00	135.00	Smooth bone handles, spatula and pen blades, physician's symbol etched on master blade
1998	5¼" folding hunter, #4 of 5	650	47.50	85.00	Smooth bown bone, oval club shield

Kabar Bicentennial Trapper

We have long maintained that the **KaBar** Bicentennial issue is among the most beautiful. The red, white, and blue handles set it off and make it special. The dog's head shield too is unique. Collector Value: $125.00

Kentucky's Bicentennial is a series of knives made to commemorate Kentucky's Bicentennial by W. R. **Case** & Sons Cutlery.

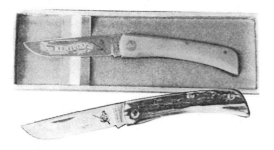

•1 blade, sodbuster Jr. pattern, 35,299 with green delrin handles, etched blade. Collector Value: $65.00

•1 blade sodbuster Jr. pattern, 30,000 with pakkawood handles, color etched blade. Collector Value: $65.00

•1 blade sodbuster Jr. pattern, 30,000 with stag handles, color etched blade. Collector Value: $100.00

The Kentucky Rifle

This knife is considered by many to be the knife which kicked off commemorative knife collecting. Athough it was by no means the first, this A. G. Russell product caught the imagination of collectors nationwide. And why not? The knife was made by **Schrade**, limited to 12,000 (although because of rejects, numbers may run as high as 15,000), was attractively made with a nickel silver replica of a Kentucky long rifle in the handle, and was generally a good quality knife. Gun collectors even liked it and many added them to their collections. The issue price of $12.50 for the collector grade was right, too.

The collector value began to skyrocket almost as soon as the knife was issued. Needless to say, the pace was set for commemorative knives to follow.

This knife was issued in three grades: Premier (#1 – 12) gold inlay bolsters and a highly engraved blade; Excelsior (#13 – 100), engraved bolsters and etched blade; and Collector (several numbers over 1,000), blade etch only.

Issue Date: 1971
Issue Price: $12.50
Collector Value:
    Premier Grade: $1,400.00
    Excelsior Grade: $500.00
    Collector Grade: $125.00

Kentucky and Tennessee Copperheads

Produced by **Robert Klass or Parker-Frost** Cutlery, this is a matched set of two 4" 2 blade copperhead pattern knives. Twelve hundred sets were made. Each knife has etched blades and stag handles.

Issue Number: 1,200 sets
Issue Date: 1976
Collector Value: $150.00

Kentucky Tennessee, Southern Belle

This set of knives clearly demonstrates the ability of **Fighting Rooster Cutlery** to produce an outstanding set of knives. The set contains 3, 3¾" 2 blade jack knives with plastic gold flake handles and gold etched blades.

Collector Value: $175.00

Kentucky and Tennessee Whittlers

This set of knives by **Schrade Cutlery** seems to reflect these two states' influence on knife collecting. The set of two 4" 3 blade whittlers had delrin handles, the old Schrade stamping and shields, and etched blades, and came in a nice presentation box.

Date Issued: 1976
Issue Number: 300 sets
Collector Value: $150.00
Distributed by: **Parker-Frost**

Kentucky & Tennessee Winchester

Trapper, produced by the **George Winchester Company.** This large (5½" closed) muskrat pattern knife has two gold etched blades and genuine bone handles.

Date Issued: 1975
Collector Value: $250.00 per set

The Kentucky Thoroughbred and Tennessee Walking Horse

Robert Klaas Cutlery. This German-made set of knives displayed two 5½" one blade lockback knives with stag handles and color etched blades. The quality of the knives is indicative of the country of origin and the company's reputation for excellence (Kissing Crane).

Issue Number: 1,000 sets
Issue Date: 1978
Distributed by: Parker-Frost
Collector Value: $175.00

Kershaw Kai Cutlery

"We want you to want what we are proud to make." This set of knives seems to be intended to show the customer/collector the quality of Kershaw Cutlery. The quality of the cutlery of this display set is certainly impressive. The carrying/display case is also unique and impressive. There are knives in this collection which are of superior quality!

Collector Value: $252.00 set

2100	Rotary Jack	$100.00
2120	Macho	$50.00
2110	Honcho	$40.00
2105	Lil Stud	$35.00
5100S	McKinley	$25.00
5200S	Ronner	$20.00
5300S	Shasta	$10.00
	Mint ME Engraved	$100.00
5800	Mt. St. Helen	$10.00
2205	Caper	$20.00
2210	Lil Skinner I	$20.00
2220	Catfish & Mallard	$30.00
2230	Lil Skinner II	$35.00

Kissing Crane Reproduction Series

This reproduction series of knives is probably the most ambitious since the bicentennial of the United States. It contains twelve **Kissing Crane knives**, reproduced from patterns used around the turn of the 20th century. The patterns vary greatly; however, the scales of each knife are either high-quality German stag or beautiful mother-of-pearl.

With a 600 limit on the edition, a machairologist would indeed be fortunate to have this 1983–84 issued set in his collection.

Collector Value, complete set: $1,500.00

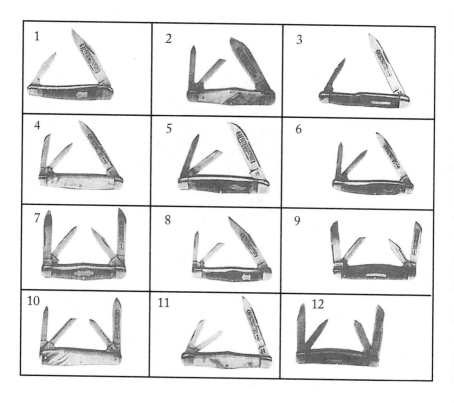

Number	Date	Handle	Issue Price	Collector Value
1	Circa 1901	Genuine Deer Stag	$50.00	$85.00
2	Circa 1893	Mother-of-Pearl	100.00	155.00
3	Circa 1902	Genuine Deer Stag	50.00	80.00
4	Circa 1900	Mother-of-Pearl	85.00	135.00
5	Circa 1895	Genuine Deer Stag	65.00	105.00
6	Circa 1894	Genuine Deer Stag	65.00	100.00
7	Circa 1891	Genuine Deer Stag	65.00	110.00
8	Circa 1899	Genuine Deer Stag	65.00	100.00
9	Circa 1897	Genuine Deer Stag	70.00	125.00
10	Circa 1892	Mother-of-Pearl	100.00	175.00
11	Circa 1896	Mother-of-Pearl	85.00	150.00
12	Circa 1883	Genuine Deer Stag	95.00	165.00

Kutmaster Commemorative
75th Anniversary

In 1985, **Utica Cutlery** proudly commemorated **Kutmaster's** 75 years of knife production. Uniquely, this was done with a knife with a variety of metal handles. The collector could select from copper, brass, nickel silver, and 24 karat gold.

The knives were distributed by Utica Cutlery Company.

Collector Value: $85.00

1st Edition

Knife World Limited Editions

Knife World Publications has produced six limited edition pocket knives over the past 17 or so years. These knives have all been unique and produced to Knife World's specifications by top notch manufacturers. They are very well made and highly sought after.

Edition	Date	Pattern	#Produced	Manufacturer	Value
1st	1982	Dogleg Trapper	2,000	**Cripple Creek**	$150.00
2nd	1987	Equal End Cigar	500	**Cripple Creek**	175.00
3rd	1992	Powder Horn/ Toothpick	500	**Frank Buster Cutlery**	100.00
4th	1997	5 blade Sowbelly/ stock	350	**Blue Grass/ Winchester**	125.00
1st Ambassador	1989	2 blade Sowbelly	150	**Frank Buster Cutlery**	190.00
2nd Ambassador	1992–93	3 Back Spring Whittler	150	**Cripple Creek**	175.00

Liberty Canoe

This solid brass handled commemorative canoe is unique as a bicentennial knife. The knife was encased in a red lined wooden tackle box. Production totaled 1,776. The handles were embossed with the words "Let Freedom Ring," and a gold liberty bell was etched on the face of the master blade. The knife was produced for **Star Sales**. This is a very collectible knife for those lucky enough to find one.

Collector Value: $125.00

Abe Lincoln Replica

The evening Abraham Lincoln was assassinated at Ford's Theater in Washington, D.C., he was carrying a six blade, pearl-handled pocketknife. Lincoln's knife was made by William Gilchrist's celebrated Razor Steel.

The commemorative, a close duplicate of Lincoln's knife, was produced by the **Frank Buster Co.** "Fighting Roosters" for the Kentucky Cutlery Association. The release date of the knife was December, 1981.

Collector Value: $185.00

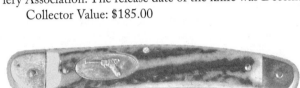

Luger Pistol

A.C. Russell contracted the third in the "CM" series of knives to **Puma** for manufacture. The "Luger Pistol" was a single blade jackknife with Warncliffe handles of India stag. Each knife had a shield inlay of a Luger pistol. The knife was produced in three grades. Total production was 2,650.

Premier Grade (#1 – 18), engraved 18k gold bolsters and gold shield, engraved blade. Collector Value: $1,200.00.

Excelsior Grade (#19 – 300), engraved bolsters.
Collector Value: $375.00

Collector Grade (#301 – 1,000), plain bolsters.
Collector Value: $135.00.

The Marine Raider Stiletto, WWII Commemorative

This knife, produced by **Camillus Cutlery**, the original and only company to manufacture this WWII knife, was issued as a special limited edition, the highly collectible combat knife.

It is assembled from parts produced with original WWII tooling, with high luster blue finish blade and pewter handle. USMC in 18 karat gold inlay etching is on the knife. It comes in a genuine oak display case with a brass plaque, and is limited to 2,000 sets.

Collector Value: $250.00

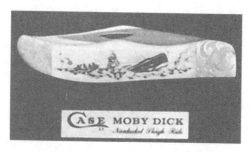

Moby Dick & Nantucket Sleighride

These knives were made by **Case** to recognize the American whaler. They have smooth bone handles which have been scrimshawed with scenes from whaling history. The knives are a folding hunter 6265 Case pattern. The display boxes also had different color liners.

Moby Dick (10,000 produced): $225.00

Nantucket Sleighride (7,500 produced): $225.00

Mountaineers Are Always Free

This set of **Battle Ax** gunstock pattern knives comes with pearl, stag, and bone handles. Black and gold etched blades really make these 1980 knives unique.

Issue Number: 400 sets

Issue Price: $150.00

Collector Value: $175.00

National Knife of the Cherokee Nation

This limited edition knife was authorized by Ross O. Swimmer, principal chief of the Cherokee Nation of Oklahoma. It has smooth bone handles and the blade is etched with the Cherokee Nation's seal. The knife was produced by **Standing Stone Cutlery.** The Cherokee Nation received $10.00 royalty on each knife sold.

Collector Value: $165.00

The Nelson Pocketknives, Centenary of Trafalgar, 1805 – 1905

These Sheffield-made knives were used as limited edition presentations, fêtes, and general souvenirs. They were made with ivory handles and a handle material, which was probably an alloy of platinum called platinoid. The original price of the 3¼" ivory handled model was 2.2 British pounds and the larger 3¾" platinoid handle models were 1.8 British pounds. This knife was produced as a souvenir of the Naval Expedition in London, England, 1905. Remember, this was during a time when Britannia ruled the waves and the sun never set on the British Empire.

Issue Date: 1905
Issue Price: 1.8 pounds and
        2.2 pounds
Collector Value: Unknown

The Old Man and the Sea

This special run of two sailor knives was made by **Case** for Smoky Mountain Knife Works. Utilizing discontinued patterns with etched blades, this limited edition knife set was made especially for collectors.

Issue Number: 600 sets
Collector Value: $120.00

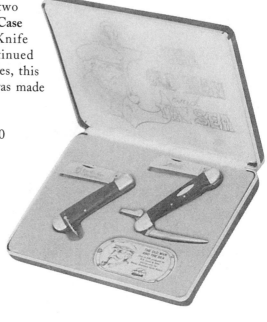

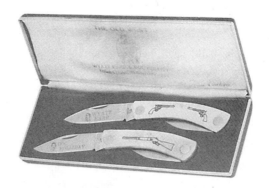

The Old West

Wyatt Earp & Doc Holliday – Tombstone Territory 1881. This set of knives is similar to the Jesse James/ Billy the Kid set. Both bone and micarta are used as handle materials in this set which is limited to 600 serialized copies. The serious collector might try to get both sets of the same number.

Stamping: **Frost Cutlery**
Collector Value: $75.00

1980 Olympic Commemorative, Lake Placid Winter Games

February 1980 saw the Winter Olympics held at Lake Placid, New York. A limited quantity of the OL278SS pocketknives was produced.

The handles were embossed by the Shaw-Liebowitz studios with a downhill skier, a ski jumper, a figure skater, a speed skater, and a hockey player. The knife has become scarce and as a result, very collectible.

Collector Value: $110.00

1992 Presidential Race

Campaign materials from presidential campaigns and races are so popular that they have generated their own classification of collectibles. When you marry a campaign with a commemorative knife, you have an item which becomes valuable in both collecting classifications. That is what has happened with this set of knives.

The 1992 Presidential campaign generated three viable candidates, Bill Clinton, George Herbert Walker Bush, and Ross Perot. The knives in the set are 3⅛" stainless steel **Case** knives with picture handles of Bush, Perot, and Clinton and an American flag in the background. These photos are covered with a clear Lucite handle. The knives come individually packed in a plastic blister package.

Collector Value: $100.00, unopened set of three

1996 Atlanta Olympics

The Olympics, like World's Fairs, always generate their own version of commemorative collectibles. Some fall into the tourist category (cheap) while others are reserved for the most serious collector (expensive). Interestingly, the knives used for the official licensed commemorative of the '96 Olympics feature both quality and affordability.

Made by **Victorinox** and distributed by Swiss Army Brands of Switzerland, these souvenir knives can be used effectively as the tools they really are. They make a good addition to any collection.

Issue Price: $23.95

Collector Value: $30.00

One Hundred Year Anniversary, Camillus Cutlery

A large bronze medallion was included in the display boxes with these two knives to commemorate 100 years of knifemaking.

•A 4" 3 blade stock pattern, white delrin handles, gold shield, etched blade.

Collector Value: $50.00

•A 3½" 2 blade stock pattern, white delrin handles, gold shield, etched blade.

Collector Value: $45.00

Operation Desert Storm
Presidential Dedication

This knife was introduced for July 4, 1991, by **Little River Knife Sales,** and is perhaps the most outstanding commemorative issued for this event.

The knife is a reproduced **Remington** mini trapper bullet with quality stag delrin handles, containing an inlaid Desert Storm design and silver bullet shield. The blades are color etched with a 4th of July Flag and the Presidential Dedication.

It comes complete in a hard shell, presentation jewelry box and is limited to 2,000.

Collector Value: $120.00

Opinel D-Day Commemorative

Somehow it seems fitting to feature a French commemorative of D-Day. There are other knives commemorating this occasion, of course, but the fact that **Opinel** is French makes their June 6, 1944 D-Day commemorative a bit different. It includes a laser-engraved blade (in French), numbered knife with rosewood handles, and a presentation box. A good collectible!

Issue Price: $34.95

Collector Value: $40.00

Original 13 Colony Series

This series of knives came about as a result of one of the most ambitious ventures undertaken by knife collectors done for knife collectors. Jim Parker and Jim Frost collaborated to form Parker Frost Cutlery and contracted with **Schrade** to produce 42,000 knives – 3,000 sets of 14 knives — to commemorate America's Bicentennial. This kind of commitment takes imagination, a willingness to take risk, and just plain guts. These two men should be respected for their initiative in this project which produced the finest set of bicentennial knives available for America's 200th birthday.

Although 3,000 sets of the knives were produced, the method of distribution resulted in several hundred sets which were never completed. The customer could reserve a number and could then purchase a knife each month until the set was complete. This, of course, makes the remaining completed sets even more valuable. These knives came in an impressive display case ready for wall hanging. Handle materials included brass, copper, silver, pewter, and stag. The knife for each state had artwork handles which incorporated the name of the state. The centerpiece was a beautiful grizzly patterned stag handle knife with the blade etched with a scene commemorating our nation's birthdate.

Collector Value: $650.00

Knife	Type	Size	Blades	Handle Finish	State
1	Premium Stock	4"	3	Antique Coin Silver	Delaware
2	Trapper	4"	2	Antique Brass	Pennsylvania
3	Muskrat	4"	2	Antique Copper	New Jersey
4	Congress	3⅜"	4	Antique Coin Silver	Georgia
5	Muskrat	4"	2	Antique Brass	Connecticut
6	Trapper	4"	2	Antique Copper	Massachusetts
7	Congress	3⅜"	4	Antique Brass	Maryland
8	Premium Stock	4"	3	Antique Copper	South Carolina
9	Trapper	4"	2	Antique Coin Silver	New Hampshire
10	Muskrat	4"	2	Antique Coin Silver	Virginia
11	Congress	3⅜"	4	Antique Copper	New York
12	Premium Stock	4"	3	Antique Brass	North Carolina
13	Muskrat	4"	2	Antique Copper	Rhode Island
14	Clasp Knife or Folding Skinner	5½"	1	The Finest Genuine Stag Money Can Buy	United States

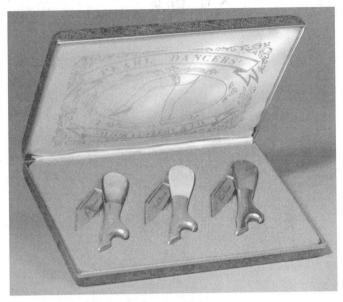

Pearl Dancers

This may be the most impressive and unique set of knives ever made by **Taylor Cutlery**. The set is composed of three leg knives, each handled in a different color of pearl. The white, black, and brown pearl handles make the display a truly beautiful one. Twelve hundred sets of these knives were made.

Collector Value: $100.00

President Carter – Mr. Peanut

This commemorative knife was produced by **Taylor Cutlery** in honor of President Carter. It is a novelty knife with brass handles made in the shape of a peanut. "Carter" is embossed on one handle, and "Mr. Peanut, Nov. 2, 1976" is on the other. Although the knife is an inexpensive one, its subject will perhaps make it collectible in circles other than knife collecting.

Collector's Value: $25.00

Presidential Scrimshaw Collection

In 1984, American Express, in cooperation with **Schrade Cutlery** and the American Historical Foundation, produced and distributed a series of individually scrimshawed knives honoring five of our greatest Presidents: Washington, Lincoln, Jefferson, Teddy Roosevelt, and Andrew Jackson.

The Presidents honored were men of character, principle, vision, and strength. History also records that each of them appreciated a good pocketknife.

The knives were sold through American Express. There were 6,000 sets of these knives produced.

Collector Value: $750.00

Rawhide 1875 – 1975
This knife was made for Parker-Frost by **Schrade**. It is a stock/cattleman's pattern and has a special "Longhorn" shield.
Production Total: 3,000
Collector Value: $65.00

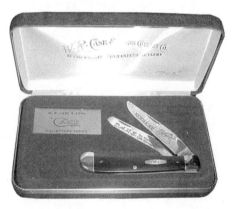

Recognition-Presentation Knife
From time to time an organization will have a knife engraved and placed in a presentation case to be given to someone as a token of recognition or appreciation. Often these are editions which are limited to "one of one." When properly done, the recipient will likely hang this on the wall of his office or place it in a conspicuous place for the notice of all who visit. They are an object of pride.

This knife was presented to William "Bill" Gorman, Mayor of Hazard, Kentucky, for his support of the Kentucky D.A.R.E. program. This program was designed to help keep kids off drugs.

Collctor Value: (You may have to ask the Mayor!)

(For someone interested in a unique series of collectibles, this field would certainly be a challenge.)

Remington UMC Reproductions (by Remington)

Hunter 1986

Beginning in 1982, a limited number of **Remington** knives was initially reproduced for the collector market. Generally, these knives are referred to as year knives and consist largely of updated versions of the Remington Bullet patterns. These patterns are appreciating rapidly in value, and the advertising posters that were used in conjunction with them are being updated and reproduced. These, too, are increasing rapidly in value.

These knives are all marked with the original Remington trademarks, pattern numbers, etchings, and stamping, and are also stamped with the year of their release. They generally retailed at the time of release from $40.00 to $60.00. Below, you will notice the appreciation for each year.

From 1982 – 1997, an "Outdoors" four-color poster was issued at the time of release, featuring each of these knives in use. All these posters except one were done by artist Larry Duke; in 1988, Bruce Wolfe did the poster. These posters have appreciated in value handsomely.

Year	Pattern	Collector Value
1982	R1123 Hunter 2 bl.	$675.00
1983	R1173 Baby Bullet	$350.00
1984	R1173L Baby Bullet	$220.00
1984	R1303 Lg. Lockback	$200.00
1985	R4353 Woodsman	$165.00
1986	R1263 Hunter 2 bl.	$250.00
1987	R1613 Fish Knife	$185.00
1988	R4466 Muskrat	$100.00
1989	R1128 Trapper 2 bl.	$95.00
1990	R1306 Tracker 1 bl.	$55.00
1991	R1178 Baby Bullet 2 bl. Mini Trapper	$55.00
1992	R1253 Guide 1 bl.	$75.00
1993	R4356 Muskrat	$60.00

Year	Pattern	Collector Value
1994	R4243 Camp Knife 4 bl. (4½")	$80.00
1995	R1273 Master Guide 2 bl. (5¼") Trapper	$60.00
1996	R3843 Trail Hand 5 bl./tools Utility Pat.	$75.00
1997	R4468 Lumberjack Bullet/Coca. hdls	$60.00
1998	R293 Hunter-Trader-Trapper	$60.00
1999	R103 Ranch Hand	$60.00
2000	R1630 Navigator	$65.00
2001	R897 Mariner	$55.00
2002	R898 Apprentice	$65.00

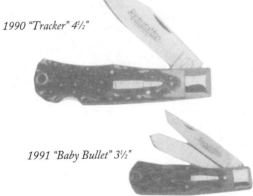

1988 "Muskrat" 3¾"

1989 "Trapper" 4⅜"

1990 "Tracker" 4½"

1991 "Baby Bullet" 3½"

Remington Baby Bullet Knife

Model R1126
Collector Value: $135.00

Remington 10th Anniversary of the Bullet

Question: How does a company commemorate the 10th anniversary of the successful reintroduction of one of its most popular series of knives? With a commemorative knife, of course.

This commemorative is the old trapper bullet pattern but with a colorful handle commemorating the event, covered in clear plastic. It then is placed in an attractive lunchbox style tin with a copy of the 1982 "Bad Time for a Snag" poster on the lid.

It looked good (and sold well)!
Collector Value: $150.00

10th Anniversary of the Bullet

Model Trapper
Collector Value: $150.00

Puma Commemorative

This knife was issued to commemorate **Pumawerk's** 300th anniversary of knifemaking. It is a beautiful 5" lockback pattern with gold embossed bolsters, a gold etched blade, and stag handles. The 1,769 of these knives which were made did an excellent job of bringing honor and recognition of what is truly a master knife company.
Collector Value: $375.00

477

Riders of the Silver Screen

Camillus Cutlery Company is often willing to take on new projects and try new things. This 1991 set of commemorative movie cowboy knives was certainly ambitious. Using their pattern #23, they made a series of knives which brought back memories to lots of collectors from age 8 to 80. The Riders of the Silver Screen tickled long dormant memories of the matinee and television heroes of the '30s, '40s, and '50s. The eleven knives in this set commemorate the entertainment provided by Hopalong Cassidy (CM8000); Tom Mix (CM8001); Tonto (CM8002); Red Ryder (CM8003); Little Beaver (CM8004); Roy Rogers (CM8005); Dale Evans (CM8006); Lone Ranger (CM8007); Lash Larue (CM8008); Zorro (CM8009); and Gene Autry (CM8010).

An individual movie character is displayed under special acrylic handles on one side and the entire group shows on the other. Of course, licensing from each character's owner was required for this set to be produced.

Issue retail: $49.99 each (Many dealers gave the collector of this set of knives a free poster.)

Collector Value: $60.00

Russell Barlow Commemorative Issue

Released to commemorate 100 years of popularity, the Russell Harrington Company reproduced the **Russell** Barlow pocketknife. The new commemorative model was limited to 12,000 issues. It was produced to close specifications to imitate the original. Exceptions included the use of brass rivets and stainless (non-corrosive) blades.

To uphold the traditions, the original hob was used to reproduce the solid nickel silver bolster with the famous arrow R (➤) trademark. Generally the appearance and feel of this Barlow is much the same as the one produced from 1875 to just before World War II.

The first 2,000 of these serial numbered knives were packaged in leatherette cases and boxed in redwood. These sold for ten dollars more than the other 10,000. This was one of the fastest moving commemoratives of the past several years. The collector who can add one of these to his collection certainly should do so.

Issue Number: 12,000
Collector Value (boxed): $250.00
Collector Value (unboxed): $175.00

Russell's Green River Works Bicentennial

A set of historical Russell Green River Works frontier knives was issued to commemorate the United States Bicentennial. It seems appropriate as knives of these patterns were used by trappers, pioneers, and frontiersmen to lay the foundation of our country. We suspect that the velvet case these knives are displayed in would have seemed peculiar to the frontiersmen who used the originals.

Collector Value: $300.00

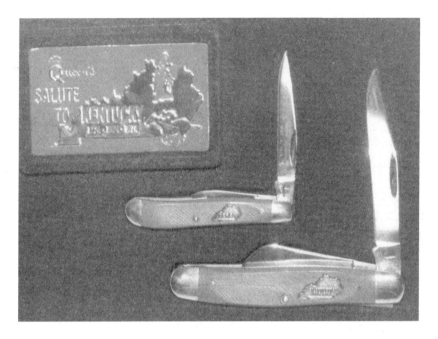

"Salute to Kentucky"

Queen Cutlery's entry into the Kentucky bicentennial commemorative was indeed a beautiful effort. They produced two knives which came in a special display case.

•Commemorating the 200th birthday of Fort Harrod, Kentucky's first settlement; 4", 2 blade, stock pattern, cardinal red handles with Kentucky-shaped shield, etched blade.

•Commemorating the 100th running of the Kentucky Derby, a 3", 2 blade, peanut pattern, cardinal red handles with Kentucky-shaped shield, etched blade.

Collector Value with box: $175.00. (Some sets were issued with the wrong Derby date on them. These were recalled. However, all of them were not turned back in. The collector value of one of these sets is $250.00.)

Jim Bowie Stock Commemorative

This **Schrade** stockman has a unique shield and is one of the earlier 1970s commemorative knives. It has not significantly increased in price, we suspect, because of the 18,000 production run. Nonetheless, it is an interesting addition to a collection.

Issue Price: $20.00
Collector Value: $25.00

"Custer" and "The Trail of Tears"

Custer and "The Trail of Tears" generally do not come to mind as a pair. However, the events of Custer's last stand and the mass move of the Cherokee nation from the Smokey Mountains to Oklahoma were paired in this beautiful set of **Schrade** knives, made for Parker-Frost around 1977. They were sold both in sets and separately. The knives were serial numbered. Beautiful stag handles and artistic blade etchings made these knives special.

Total Production: 1,200 sets
Collector Value of sets with matching numbers: $350.00 – 400.00
Collector Value of individual knives: $150.00 – 175.00

Schrade Cutlery Classics

"Honoring those Americans who supplied the muscle and determination that made America great...The Farmer, Rancher and Fisherman who fed a growing and hungry nation, the Lumberman who cut wood that built our homes and towns and the Miner who supplied the raw materials that fed our factories."

This commemorative set is made of basic Schrade patterns, the trapper, the stock/cattle (2 used), the moose, and the jack. Each knife is of quality production and has jigged bone handles. On the face of each blade is an etching of the trade represented, and a shield further identifies that trade with the name etched on it. The set comes in an impressive walnut display case designed to hang on the wall of a den, office or most any other room in the home. Each knife in the set has matching serial numbers.

Collector Value: $250.00

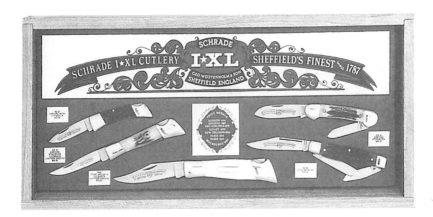

Schrade's IXL Cutlery

In November 1980, Schrade Cutlery introduced its new IXL line to America with an impressive display of five knives. This display was hand crafted in England by the workers at Geo. Wostenholm and Sons. It contained three lockbacks, a canoe, and a stockman. Handle materials were genuine wood, bone, antler, stag, and other exotic materials. The wooden display box resembled an old English crate, which added a unique flavor to the issue.

Collector Value: $300.00

Schrade-IXL Giant Stockman

This three blade stockman measured 5" closed! Handles are of wood and the knife came with a custom display box.

Production Total: 8,000

Issue Price: $125.00

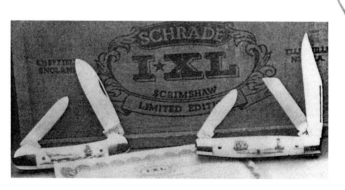

IXL Custom Limited Edition Scrimshaw

A canoe and stock pattern with bone handles make up this set. The handles are scrimshawed with scenes of a ship and a lighthouse.

Issue Price: $150.00

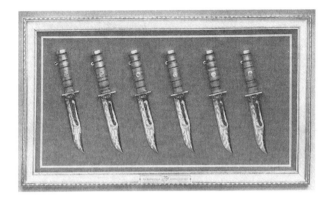

The Semper Fidelis Ka-Bar Collection

This issue of presentation grade **Ka-Bar** commemoratives is made to the exacting standards of the American Historical Foundation. Each knife has been embellished with 24 karat gold to honor the Marines of each of the six Marine Corps divisions. Each knife bears the Marine Corps symbol which is flanked by the battle honors of the respective division. In recognition of the year the Marine Corps was founded, 1,775 of these knives will be produced for each division. Each knife is serial numbered.

Collector Value: $240.00

Schrade's Liberty Bell, Paul Revere, and Minute Man

This series was rather interesting as it was released around America's bicentennial. Made by **Schrade**, all three 3⅝" stock patterns were identical except for shield designs and blade etching. Handle colors varied; the Paul Revere was red while the Minute Man and Liberty Bell were both black. The issue price of $12.50 was reasonable for the time. The knife has not yet risen to astronomical values, primarily because of the 24,000 knives issued. We believe, however, that they are currently among the best buys on the collector market.

Collector Value: $40.00 each

Per set w/identical numbers: $100.00 – 150.00

The Shady Lady

This slightly risque set of knives was issued by **Frost Cutlery**. The abalone handles alone make this set of knives particularly special. Add to this the blade engraving and the fact that the knives were featured in **Playboy** magazine, and you have a formula for a series of 600 that sold out quickly. Included was a simulated alligator hide display box, if anyone noticed.

Issue Price: $60.00

Collector Value: $105.00

Smith and Wesson Commemorative

Issued in 1995, this set of anniversary knives (40th anniversary of the .44 Magnum and 60th anniversary of the .357 Magnum) is an excellent example of how almost any event can be commemorated.

The investment potential of such a set should be considered. In spite of the fact that the event commemorated is of debatable importance, the set may well appreciate because of the pattern (they are styled from the popular Remington bullet trapper pattern) and the quality of workmanship of the knives.

Handle Materials: Cocobola and bone
Issue Number: 3,000 sets
Collector Value $85.00 each

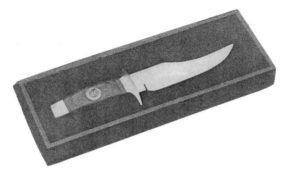

Smith and Wesson's Texas Ranger Commemorative

This beautiful 10½" bowie knive was used for commemorative recognition of the Texas Rangers. It came with a Texas Ranger shield and in a custom wood presentation box with the shield of the Texas Rangers inlaid on its top. Five hundred of these knives were matched with an S & W pistol to make a super presentation set.

Collector Value (knife only): $300.00

Smith and Wesson Collector Set

The quality of Smith and Wesson's firearms only served to set a standard that cutlery bearing its name would have to live up to. They rose to the occasion.

This collector's set was produced in the mid '70s. There were 1,000 of each knife produced. Blackie Collins, the renowned custom knifemaker, custom treated each knife. The set is made up of S & W patterns: "Skinner," "Outdoorsman," and "Bowie." Each knife has an etched outdoor scene on the face of the blade. The guards and pommels are sterling silver with deep oak leaf etching. Escutcheons are hand inlaid the hardwood handles of each knife.

Issue Price: $1,400.00

Spirit of '76 Bicentennial

Buck Cutlery, USA. This knife was Buck's entry into the bicentennial derby. It was a sheath knife with a beautifully etched blade and inlaid handle. It came with a medallion and a nice display box.

Issue Date: 1976
Collector Value: $275.00

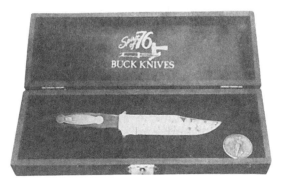

Spirit of St. Louis

Released by **Schrade-Walden** in 1974 as a commemorative of the Lindbergh flight, this three blade stock knife has rough cut delrin black handles with three shields. These include one with the old Keen Kutter design, an airplane, and on the reverse handle, the dates of the Lindbergh flight. Schrade released 12,000 knives with this edition.
Collector Value: $75.00

The Squirrel

The artistic creations of Shaw-Leibowitz Studios should be included in any account of limited edition knives. The unique handles cast in high relief by the lost wax method make every edition special.

The Squirrel, pictured at right, used a 1981 **Queen** pen knife as a base. It was available in bronze handles at $46.00, sterling silver at $65.00, and sterling silver with gold plated squirrels at $90.00. Six hundred sets of these knives were produced.

Collector Value:
  Bronze: $75.00
  Sterling silver: $100.00
  Sterling silver with gold plate: $125.00

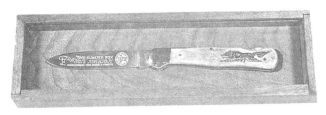

The Swamp Fox

By **Robert Klaas Cutlery**, this is a tribute to Francis Marion and his activities in the Revolutionary War. The knife is a 5", 1 blade lockback with slick bone handles. It has a unique running fox shield and an etched blade. "One of 1,200" etched on the blade tang clearly identifies the edition. This Klaas knife, made for Messer-Gullette, exhibits the abilities of German craftsmen.

Collector Value: $115.00

Statue of Liberty Commemorative

What could be more appropriate than a commemorative of the 100th anniversary of the gift of the Statue of Liberty to the United States than a knife made for the occasion by France. **Opinel** is identified as closely to France in the world of cutlery as the Eiffel Tower is in tourism. This Opinel knife was made especially for the 100th Anniversary celebration. It has a cherry handle, a 3½" blade, and a special commemorative logo on the handle. It is certainly a handsome addition to any knife collection, especially one with a patriotic theme.

Issue Date: 1986
Issue Price: $19.95
Collector Price: $25.00

Storytellers

The legends of Davy Crockett, Jesse Chisholm, and Jim Bridges live in this **Boker** commemorative issue. It is dedicated to storytellers and the subjects of their stories.

The knives are displayed in an attractive rosewood box. Patterns are a trapper with stag scales, a congress with rosewood handles, and a stockman handled in green bone.

Boker's edition limit of 8,000 serialized sets adds to the likelihood that this 1983 issue is investment grade.

Collector Value: $150.00

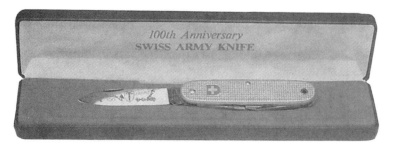

Swiss Army Knife Centennial Edition

In 1891, Swiss cutlers began producing a specialized knife for the Swiss Army. This knife was the first of what has evolved into perhaps the world's most recognizable military knife.

The 100th anniversary of this knife was commemorated by the Swiss Collector's Guild, which issued the **Wenger** Soldier's Issue Knife in limited quantity. The Soldier's Issue commemorative bears the Cross of Helvetia on anodized metal handles and has an engraved master blade. The master blade bears the inscription "100 JAHRE," goats on a mountain side, and a shield with a crossbow on its face.

This knife comes in a handsome display box and adds interest to any collection.

Collector Value: $75.00

The Teddy Roosevelt Commemorative Bowie

This knife was issued in 1988 by The American Historical Foundation to honor Theodore Roosevelt, the 25th and youngest president of the United States, one of the greatest outdoorsmen of his time.

The knife, a massive bowie pattern, was crafted by **H.G. Long & Co.** of Sheffield, England, of tempered sword steel, deeply etched, and plated with 24 karat gold.

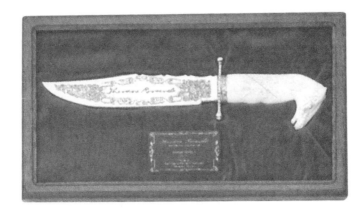

The grip is a sculptured horsehead design of ivory combined with polymers to create a near splitproof material. The knife was issued in a limited edition of 2,500.

Collector Value: $300.00

Tennessee and Kentucky Muskrats

Parker-Frost Cutlery produced this set of knives, two 4" muskrat pattern knives with a choice of genuine pearl or plastic handles. Each knife has etched blades. The edition was limited to 600 sets of each handle material.

Issue Date: 1978
Genuine Pearl Handles: Collector Value: $150.00
Plastic Handles: Collector Value: $120.00

Tennessee, Kentucky, and Virginia

The Kentucky and Tennessee knives in this set have rosewood handles. The Virginia knife has stag scales. There were 1,000 sets made.

Date Issued: 1977
Collector Value: $85.00
Stamping: Bear Creek, **Taylor**

The Trail Blazers

Throughout the history of our country, nothing has been more important to its development than the avenues of transportation which were blazed by our earliest settlers. These paths, which later became wagon trails (many times following the

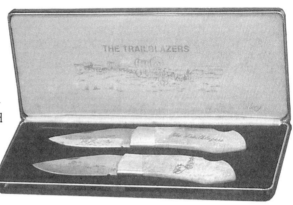

routes of the buffalo and other wild animals), were crucial to the settlement of the West. This set of knives recognizes the efforts of those who blazed the trails.

The **Frost Cutlery** set features knives, one with blade etchings of an Indian scene and the other with a mountain man leading a wagon train. The edition was limited to 1,200 sets. The knives have smooth bone handles and came in an attractive display box.

Issue Number: 1,200

Collector Value: $60.00

United's Indiana Jones's Khyber Bowie

This knife was not made as a commemorative or even a limited edition but is simply a reproduction of a knife from the Indiana Jones movie, "Temple of Doom." It was intended to SELL and SELL it has! We placed this knife in this section of the book because collecting reproductions can just be fun! This knife displayed on a wall plaque, with a bullwhip and a fedora, will generate conversation about as quickly as anything we know. Will it increase in value? Probably, if given some time. Despite its movie relationship, the knife has quality and will certainly hold a keen edge!

Original Issue Price: $185.99 + poster $7.99 + plaque $62.99 (Currently, the entire set can be acquired at a much better price. However, as the movies continue to be made, the value may well appreciate.)

United's "The Young Indiana Jones Chronicles"

As with the Khyber Bowie, this knife was generated by a popular movie character. It is fun and is certainly collectible! The collector should take a page from the past and look at "Johnny Carver" and other "boy's knives" to speculate about this knife's future as a collectible. Be sure to retain the certificate of authenticity, the use and care handbook, and of course, the box.

Issue price: $36.99

U.S. Armed Forces Commemoratives

Eight thousand sets of these knives were produced by **Imperial** to commemorate the 200th anniversary of the Army, Navy, and Marines. The use of hammer forged blades contributes to the unique appearance of these knives. When displayed in their presentation box, this commemorative issue is indeed impressive.

Produced For: **Parker-Frost**
Issue Number: 8,000 sets
Collector Value: $90.00

The USMC Beirut Commemorative Fighter

I'm sure you remember, as do Americans everywhere, the shock and dismay you felt when you heard the news that 253 American Marines were killed while they slept in Beirut, Lebanon. The story of the car bombing of the Marine barracks which took place October 23, 1983 should never be forgotten. It should never be forgotten that the Marines were there on a peace-keeping mission. The National Knife Collector's Association wanted to do something to help the families of the servicemen who had lost their lives in this tragic event.

A knife was commissioned by the association to be made by the late **Jim Pugh**, a reknowned custom knifemaker from Azle, Texas. Copies of the knife were to be ordered and made on a per order basis. The total was not to exceed 1,000. The knife is a fighting design which is engraved on one side with the words "Semper Fi" in the scrawl, as it was written by Corporal Jeffrey Nashton from his hospital bed, to General Paul X. Kelley, Marine Corps Commandant. On the reverse side there is a sketch drawn exclusively for the NKCA by Bill Mauldin, the Pulitzer Prize winning World War II artist of "Willie and Joe Up Front" fame. The overall quality of the knife is exactly what collectors had come to expect from Jim Pugh – EXCELLENCE.

Victory Collection War in Europe

The American Historical Foundation issued, beginning in 1981, a World War II Victory Collection which commemorated the major allied victories in Europe and the Pacific. The Victory in Europe series commemorated the Desert War — North Africa, the Battle of the Rhineland, the Battle of the Bulge, the Invasion of Italy, the D-Day Invasion, and, of course, the final Victory in Europe.

The knife used in the commemoration is a Fairbairn-Sykes Fighting Knife which was designed in 1940 for British commandos and later adopted by most of the war elite Allied Special Forces/Commando Units. It was made by **Wilkinson Sword,** the same company which produced the original. There were six knives in the European Series. The issue was limited to 2,500 of each knife. It is collectible both as a quality series of knives and as a WWII commemorative.

Collector Value: $200.00

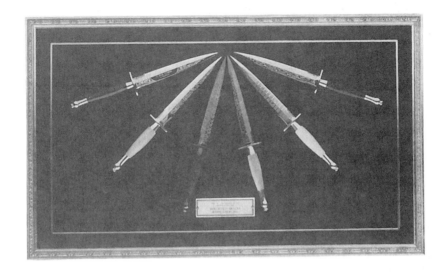

Village of Walden

This **Schrade**-made office knife pattern commemorates the town that was the home of three of our major knife companies: New York Knife Company, Walden Knife Company, and the Schrade Cutlery Company. It has written on the handle, "New York Knife Works, Walden New York." It is a fitting tribute to American knifemakers.

Collector Value: $50.00

The Warrior

This knife was produced for **Smoky Mountain Knife** Works in an edition of 600. It is a folding hunter pattern, 5¼" long, similar to the Case Buffalo. It has Honduras rosewood handles and a blade which is well detailed with a scene of an Indian warrior.

Issue Number: 600
Collector Value: $85.00

495

George Washington's Knife

Commemorative knife production is not a "Johnny-come-lately" proposition. It has been around for quite a while. This copy of George Washington's knife, by **Camillus**, was produced during the 1930s. It is evidence that knives with a history are of interest to the public. "Sharp" manufacturers have long known this, and these kinds of knives can be found in many old cutlery catalogs.

Discovering one of these knives would be quite a find!

Collector Value: $175.00

*In 1998, **Camillus** issued another edition of this knife. The knife came in a nice display box with information regarding the historical significance of the knife and how George had acquired it (an interesting story). The issue price was $89.00. (Incidentally, the original is housed in the Masonic Lodge Hall in Washington.)*

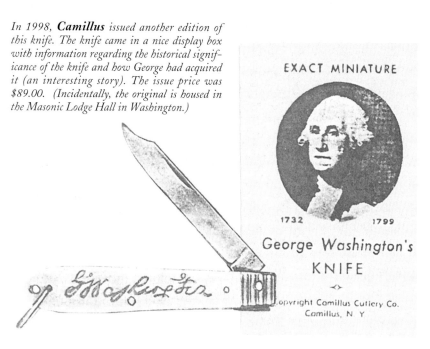

Western's Series 54 Collector's Edition

Western's entry into the limited edition collector's market was production of a matched pair of its No. 54 pattern lockback knives. With a limited edition of 2,000, they put half together in an impressive gift boxed set of knives. Pattern 541 is a lockback with hardwood handles, while 542 has delrin handles. The knives are 5" long and have 440 steel 3½" blades.

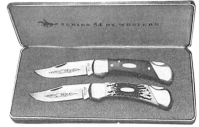

Collector Value: $110.00

Actual size

Official Royal Wedding
Commemorative Pocketknife

To celebrate the wedding of Prince Charles to Lady Diana Spencer on July 29, 1981, **Stud Custom Knives LTD** offered a pocketknife marking the occasion. The knife was hallmarked sterling silver and was handmade and engraved with the Prince of Wales' coat of arms.

One thousand five hundred fifty-five were made for worldwide distribution, with 500 of these reserved specifically for the U.S. market.

The marriage officially ended August 28, 1996. "Lady Di" was killed in an automobile accident about a year later. The princess's popularity is still on the rise.

In our last edition, we predicted this wedding commemorative would be valued at 10 times its $45.00 issue price. Now, because of the events that have transpired, we believe we were too conservative with our estimate.

The Wilderness, Limited Editions

These knives were produced for **Smoky Mountain Knife Works**. There are three sets of two knives each. Sets one and two were made by **Queen Cutlery**. Set three was made by **Case**. The first and second sets each have one pearl and one stag handled knife. Set one utilizes a gunstock pattern, while set two is a Texas toothpick pattern. The third set utilizes bone handled Case patterns with blade etchings by "Col. Coon" (Adrin Harris).

Issue Number: 600 sets each

Issue Price: $100.00

Winchester Commemoratives

Bluegrass Cutlery of Winchester, Ohio, has been authorized by the Olen Corporation to produce Winchester trademarked knives.

Bluegrass strives to produce a quality, American-made knife, utilizing old Winchester dies and original handle materials and techniques.

These are excellent knives worthy of investment consideration. The chart below is a sampling of the limited editions they have produced. (These are by no means the entire list. This is just some of our favorites.)

Number	Pattern	Handle	Produced	Collector Value
1901	Bow Tie	Pearl	317	$150.00
2857	Tear Drop Jack	Rogers Jig Bone	3070	90.00
3904	Whittler	Pearl	296	250.00
1927	F. H. Lockback	Bone with Peach Seed Jigging	3234	110.00
3949	Sowbelly	Stag	982	125.00
39049½	Sowbelly	Waterfall	250	100.00
1950	F. H. Lockback	Stag	2,511	125.00
1920	F. H. Coke	Bone with Peach Tree Jigging	1,594	150.00
3995	Whittler	Bone with Peach Seed Jigging	1,440	100.00

The Winchester Case XX Replica

The legend of the **Winchester/Case** XX knife was proven when one of the knives was found to exist in the Case Factory Collection. It is said to have come into being when Winchester Knives contracted during the 1920s with W.R. Case & Sons for a special knife containing the Winchester name to be manufactured by Case.

This replica was then reproduced by the **Case** Company for the American Blade Collectors Association.

Issue Date: 1990

Collector Value: $135.00

Wiss Whittler

This **USA Boker** commemorates the universal whittler pattern and one of Boker's subsidiary companies, Wiss. There were 24,000 made and white delrin was used as handle material. The shield, a double "Boker-Wiss," is perhaps the most unique feature of this knife.

Collector Value: $40.00

The Winchester Scouts

These knives by **Blue Grass Cutlery** consist of two 4½" 2 blade Jack Knives, authentic authorized Winchester stamping, one with "Wild Bill Hickok" etched on the blade, the other with "Buffalo Bill Cody."

Both knives feature genuine peach seed handles. One has a shield featuring the shape of a Winchester repeating rifle, and the other shield features a horse and rider. The sets were issued in 1987.

Collector Value: $225.00

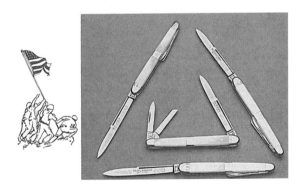

World War II Commemoratives

This group of **Battle Ax** whittlers commemorates the Pacific battles of Okinawa, Iwo Jima, Pearl Harbor, and Guadalcanal. The knives are beautiful and well made. They are of special interest to the collector who saw action in the Pacific Theater.

Collector Value: $250.00

World War II Commemoratives, Set Number 2

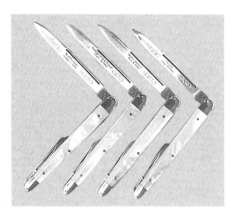

This group of **Battle Ax** whittlers is a continuation of the first set. This group commemorates battles in the European Theater. Included are Normandy, North Africa, Battle of the Bulge, and Sicily. The knives have pearl handles and etched blades, several are numbered and they are handcrafted in Solingen, Germany.

Issue Number: 300 sets

Collector Value: $250.00

World War II Commemoratives

Camillus's salute to the U.S. Armed Forces who served in World War II consists of four knives with patterns used by our servicemen. They are:

U.S. Navy Mark II Knife

U.S. Air Force Pilot Survival Knife

U.S. Army Mark III Trench Knife

U.S. Marine Corps Fighting Knife

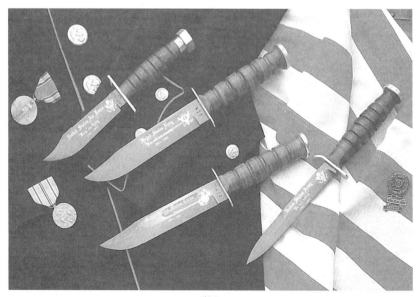

Each knife is inlaid with a gold etching of the respective branch of the military it served. They all have blued finishes, high luster blades, leather handles, and gold plated hand guards and butts. An attractive oak display is provided with each set of these knives.

Collector Value: $500.00

Yellowhorse Buck

With this pair of knives, David Yellowhorse again did himself proud! He has again taken a popular Buck knife and turned it into a treasured collectible.

David used a process he describes as channel inlay to blend native turquoise, coral, and other stones and metals. The bolsters are hand tooled. Truly, the finished product is a work of art.

Yellowhorse knives are often displayed in boxes which are in themselves works of art. We believe these knives are displayed in boxes made by Brookfield, Inc. of Battle Creek, Michigan. Up to 25% of the collector value of a knife such as these should be deducted if the box is missing.

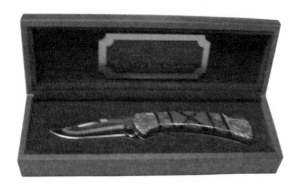

Confederate Flag Knife
Collector Value: $600.00

United States Flag Knife
Collector Value: $600.00

Yellowhorse Cuthair

The joint efforts of David Yellowhorse, Bill Cheatham, and **Buck Cutlery** resulted in this beautiful knife which honors specifically David Yellowhorse's grandfather, Cuthair, and the Navajos in general. Both handle and blade are works of art. The handle is a mosaic of turquoise, brass, ironwood, coral, and mother-of-pearl. The blade is chipped flint steel which gives the appearance of a genuine flint knife.

The display box further enhances the aesthetic value of the knife. All in all, it is a beautiful addition to any collection.

Collector Value: $1,500.00 – 2,000.00

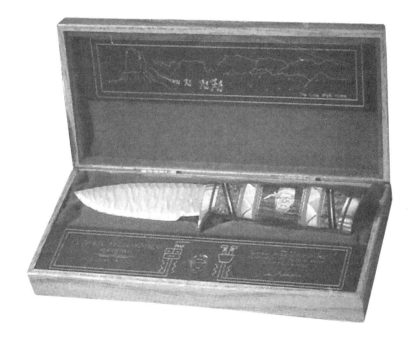

Mother of Pearl Company, Inc., premier manufacturer and supplier of rare and exotic materials, has provided knifemakers and manufacturers with quality handle material for over 20 years.

Mother of Pearl Company, Inc.
293 Belden Circle
P.O. Box 445
Franklin, NC 28734
www.knifehandles.com

There are many different types of mother-of-pearl, but they have, for the most part, the same working characteristics and all are stable and will not warp, shrink or enlarge regardless of humidity, altitude or time.

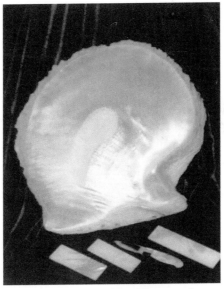

Courtesy of Mother of Pearl Company, Inc.

White mother of pearl

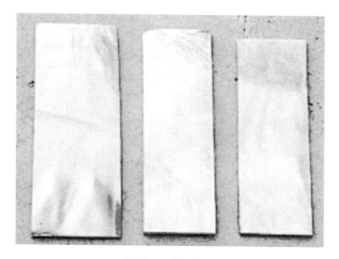

Goldlip mother of pearl
(taken from reverse side of white mother of pearl)

Raw material   *Polished shell*

Blacklip mother of pearl

Brownlip mother of pearl polished shell

Pink freshwater pearl

Raw pink

Finished pink

Examples of Handle Materials used on AG Russell Knives

Smoked pearl, pearl, smooth bone, India stag.

Clockwise, from far left: mammoth ivory scales; elephant ivory scales; brown jigged bone scales; India stag scales; black rucarta scales; coral (red) rucarta scales; ivory rucarta scales.

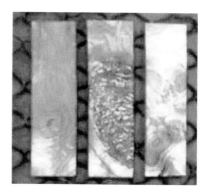

Abalone

Mosaic (laminated) Abalone

Paua Select

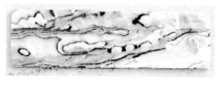

Green Select

Green Heart

Green Ripple

Red Heart

Crushed Abalone

506

Dyed Bone

Various Horns

Ram's horn

Buffalo horn

Longhorn steer

508

Various corals

Various stones

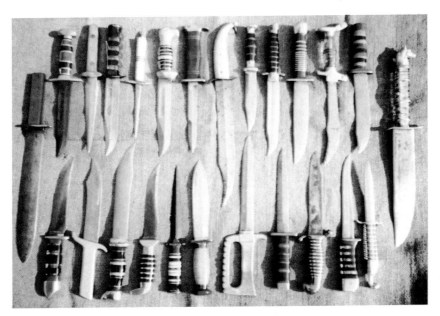

A fairly new area of interest in the military arena is that of Theater Knives. These are knives which soldiers make in the field from materials on hand. These knives vary enough in material, quality, and design to keep collector interest alive for years to come.

509

HANDLE MATERIALS

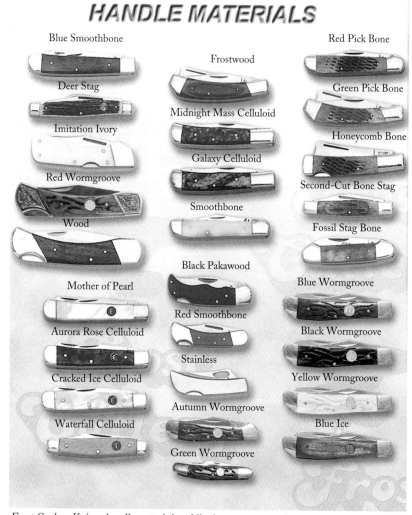

Blue Smoothbone

Frostwood

Red Pick Bone

Deer Stag

Midnight Mass Celluloid

Green Pick Bone

Imitation Ivory

Galaxy Celluloid

Honeycomb Bone

Red Wormgroove

Smoothbone

Second-Cut Bone Stag

Wood

Fossil Stag Bone

Black Pakawood

Blue Wormgroove

Mother of Pearl

Red Smoothbone

Black Wormgroove

Aurora Rose Celluloid

Stainless

Yellow Wormgroove

Cracked Ice Celluloid

Autumn Wormgroove

Blue Ice

Waterfall Celluloid

Green Wormgroove

Frost Cutlery Knives handle material and jigging.

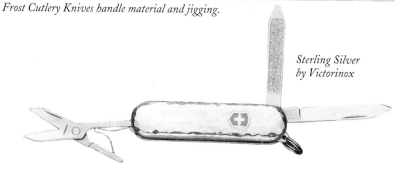

*Sterling Silver
by Victorinox*

510

From top:
Japanese-style checkered jigging (Starlite)
Boker-style jigging (Boker, Germany)
Water buffalo horn (Buffalo Creek, Sheffield)

From top:
Sambar or India stag, old (Remington)
India stag (Case)
Sambar or India stag (Kabar)
German or American stag, NKC & DA 1977 club knife (Kissing Crane)

From top:
Old style Case stag (Case XX Tested)
Stag-like composition (Dunlap)
2nd cut India stag (Case)
German stag (Buck Creek)
German stag (Puma)

From top:
Smooth "dyed" Delrin (Russell)
Jigged bone-like Delrin (Buck Creek)
Rough-sawed Delrin (Queen)
Rough-sawed Delrin (Schrade)
Simulated jigged bone Delrin (A.G.R. Co./Camillus)

From top, alternate left and right:
Bone with English style jigging (C. Johnson)
Faded out orange bone (Bridge)
Jigged camel bone (Buffalo Creek)
Rough-sawed bone, dark color (Russell)
Rough-sawed bone, light color (Russell)
Rough-sawed bone (Robeson)
Rough-sawed bone with marrow groove (Case)

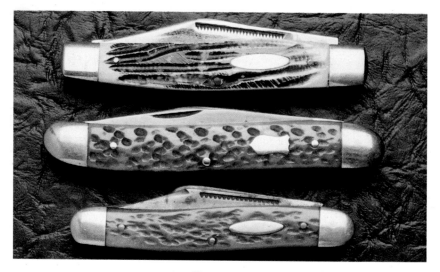

From top:
White bone with winter bottom jigging (Buck Creek)
Honeycomb bone (German Eye)
Old jigged bone (Henry Sears & Son, 1865)

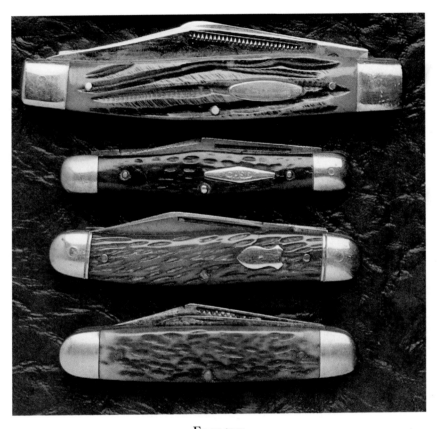

From top:
Green bone with winter bottom jigging (Buck Creek)
Old jigged bone (Case Tested)
Green bone with peach seed jigging (Schrade)
Old jigged bone (Pal Cutlery)

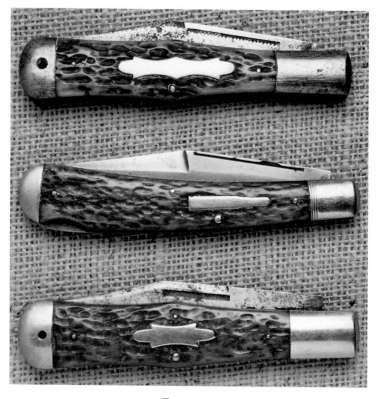

From top:
Old bone, Schrade-style jigging (Schrade)
Old bone, Remington-style jigging (Remington)
Old bone, Winchester-style jigging (Winchester)

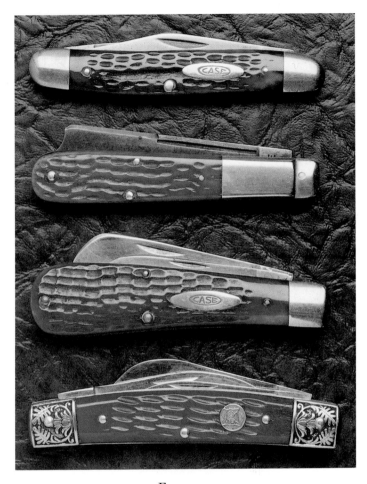

From top:
Red bone with worm groove (Case)
Red bone, strawberry (Case)
Red bone (Case)
Red bone cherry (Owl Head)

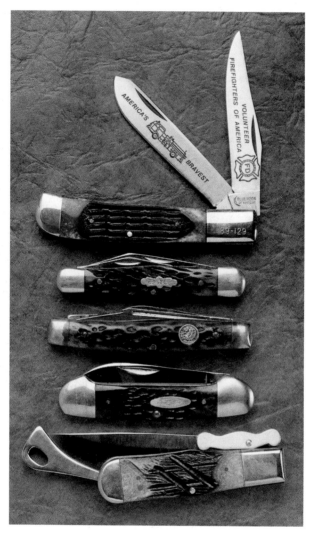

From top:
Dyed bone, Modern-style jigging (Blue Moon of Ky.)
Tree bark jigging (Star)
Brown bone with aged jigging (Buck Creek)
Brown bone with Case-style jigging (Case)
2nd cut bone, possibly dyed (Marbles, reproduction)

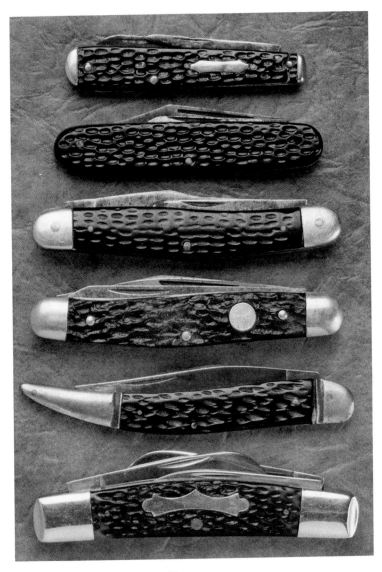

From top:
Jigged black composition (Winchester)
Jigged black composition (Colonial)
Jigged black composition (I.K.C.)
Imitation boker-style jigged bone (Boker)
Jigged black composition (Syracuse Knife Co.)
Imitation jigged bone (John Primble)

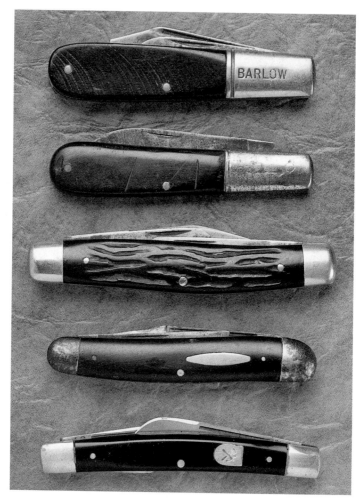

From top:
Rough sawed black (CAMCO)
Smooth black (Russell)
Rough black (Henri Boker)
Smooth black (Henri Sears)
Smooth black composition (Buck Creek)

From top:
Stained wood (B.M.W.)
European walnut (Buck Creek)
Laminated wood (Cherokee)
Stained wood (Cherokee)

From top, alternate right and left:
Old rosewood (Russell)
Pakkawood (Case)
Wood with jigging (Taylor)
Impregnated laminated wood (Taylor)
Rosewood (Thompson Center)

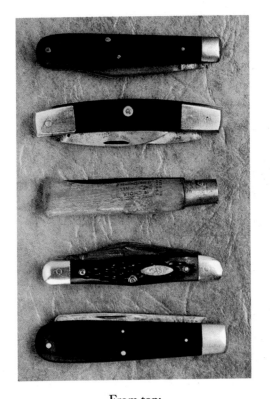

From top:
Ebony (Keen Kutter)
Cocabolo (Browne & Pharr)
European Beech (Opinel)
Simulated jigged bone Delrin (Case)
Cocabolo (Stainless Cutlery)

From top:
Old bone, smooth (Brown Bros.)
Smooth bone, old, unfinished (Electric Knife Co.)
Smooth bone, old, stained (Walden Knife Co.)
Old smooth bone, Whittler (Miller Bros. Cutlery)*
Smooth bone, fish shape (Southern Richardson)*
Smooth bone, modern (Frost)

From the Finley Begley Collection

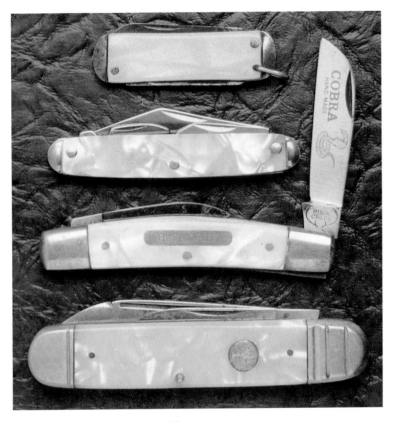

From top:
Cracked ice, old (Colonial)
Cracked ice (Colonial)
Cracked ice, imitation pearl (Buck Creek)
Cracked ice, imitation pearl, old (Boker)

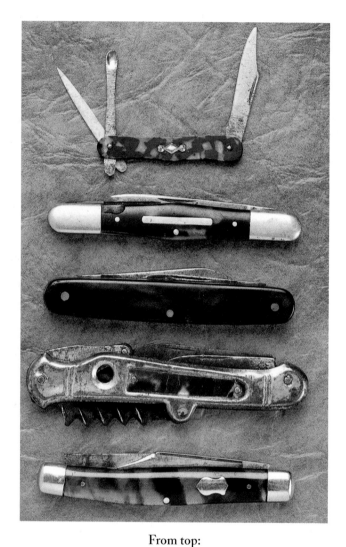

From top:
Tortoise shell, simulated, Cracker Jack (?) (Czechoslovakia)
Genuine tortoise shell (Friedmann Lauterjung)
Genuine tortoise shell (Winchester)
Plastic simulated tortoise shell (Dixon)
Simulated tortoise shell (Remington)

From top:

Ivory (Russell)
Simulated ivory, old (Remington)
Ivory (Queen)
Simulated ivory with scrimshaw (Parker Frost)
Simulated ivory, micarta (Schrade KY Rifle)
Ivory (Challenge Cutlery Co.)

From top:
Mother-of-pearl and silver fruit knife
Carved or grooved pearl (no brand)
Abalone, Elk Horn
White pearl (Brückmann)
Fiery mother-of-pearl (Brückmann)

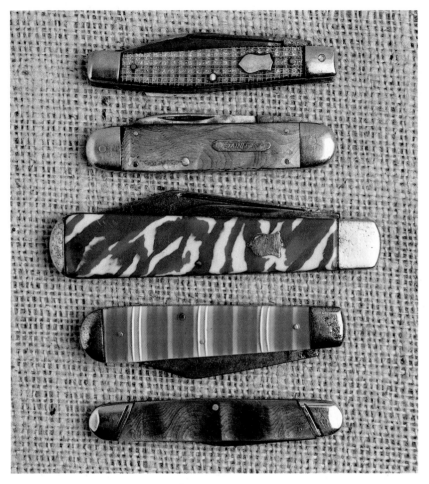

From top:
Celluloid, checkered (Van Camp)
Celluloid, waterfall (Landers, Farley & Clark)
Candy celluloid (Pal)
Celluloid, candy stripe (Walkill River Works)
Celluloid, waterfall (Hibbard, Spencer & Bartlett)

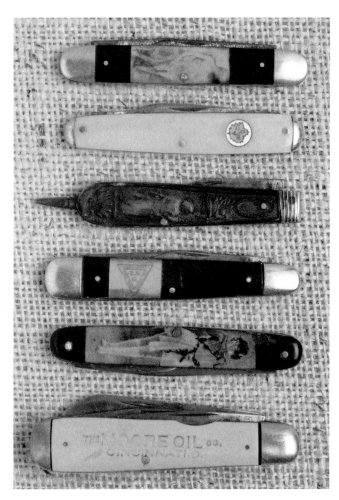

From top:
Clear celluloid with picture (Aerial Cutlery Co.)
Celluloid, imitation ivory (Western States)
Amber handles with pen knife, c. 1765, English note, quill splitter*
Clear celluloid with advertising logo (Wabash Cutlery Co.)
Clear celluloid with photo (Aerial Cutlery Co.)
Celluloid, advertising, 3 blade (Robeson, Suredge)*

*From the Finley Begley Collection

Center, from top:
Plastic wrapped metal, R.C.M.P. (Richards)
Plastic wrapped metal (Hammer Brand)
Plastic wrapped metal (Imperial)
Plastic wrapped metal (Diamond Edge)
Plastic wrapped metal (Imperial)
Plastic wrapped metal (Sabre)
Left:
Plastic wrapped metal (Hammer Brand)
Right:
Plastic wrapped metal, Davy Crockett promotion (Imperial)

From top:
High impact modern plastic, composition, camouflage (Imperial)
High impact modern plastic, composition, black (Buck/Wenger)
High impact modern plastic, composition, red (Victorinox)
High impact modern plastic, composition, black (Cut Co.)
Rubberized composition (Beretta)
Right:
High impact modern plastic, "Grilon" (Smith and Wesson)

534

From top:
Black micarta (Schrade)
Jigged plastic (Kent)
Picture under clear plastic, modern, U.S.A.
Plastic wrapped metal (Richards)
Red micarta (Schrade)
Gray laminated micarta (Smith and Wesson)

From top, alternate right and left:
Blue stripe, KSP (Buck Creek)
High impact eye glass material (Buck Creek)
Gold sparkle (Buck Creek)
Christmas tree (Buck Creek)
Copper sparkle (Buck Creek)
Christmas tree sparkle, old (Buck Creek)

From top:
Blue marble composition (Fighting Rooster)
Clear plastic composition over photo (United)
Composition basketweave (Winchester)
Composition, "Angry Sky" (Utica)
Yellow composition (Case)
Yellow composition (Buck Creek)

From top, left:
Ornate brass (Case)
Sterling silver* (Van Cleft)
Gold-plated king's knife (EKA)

From top, right:
Brass relief
Coin silver fruit knife, English*
14k gold fob knife, USA

Bottom, left to right:
Sterling silver 1933 World's Fair knife
Nickel silver (Remington)
Aluminum alloy figural knife
Brass, Remington reproduction
Brass lady and wildcat (Sheffield Steel)

From the Finley Begley Collection

538

From top:
Jigged metal boy's knife (Swanwerks/Ohlings)
Stainless, loop handle (Christy)
Embossed metal, President Roosevelt (Lion)
Jigged metal (Lik. Co.)
Nickel silver advertising knife (Anheuser Busch)
Plain metal handles (Imperial)
Silver pen knife with blade handles* (J.A.
   Henckels)
Copper handles (Schrade)

539

From top:
Brass (Wade & Butcher)
Brushed stainless (FES)
Brushed aluminum (Taylor)
Stainless steel (Kut Master)
Aluminum Swiss officer's knife (Victorinox)
Stainless steel, "Paul Knife" (Gerber)

From the Finley Begley Collection

From top:

Nickel silver (Victorinox)
Blued steel (A.W. Wadsworth)
Stainless steel, official Boy Scout (Imperial)
Steel handled Scout with ruler* (Eagle Knife Co.)
Wire handle, military knife* (Schrade)
Motorist's knife* (Baumann)

From the Finley Begley Collection

541

A serious effort to catalog and develop a price guide for Buck Creek Knives was first made in our 1980 book, *The Kentucky Knife Trader's Manual.* As we stated in that book, detailed information often is just not available on such specifics as quantity produced, variety of handle materials, and dates of production. We felt, however, that enough information was available to make reasonably accurate estimates. Interestingly, during the 22 years since 1980, gathering accurate information has been as difficult as it was during the company's first 12 years.

The following section is the most comprehensive collector's guide in print on Buck Creek. It revises the earlier information which has been published and brings the collector up to date on later developments. Since 1980, the company has changed hands as a result of the death of Millard Burns, its founder. The knives are currently produced by Frost Cutlery of Chattanooga, Tennessee.

The standard of Buck Creek quality is being well maintained by Frost Cutlery. Evolutionary changes have taken place over the years which are of interest to collectors and help date the knives. The following charts are based on our research; we believe they will serve the collector well as an informational resource and a price guide to the knife that has been called "the best German 'carryin' knife' on today's market."

Information which would help update these charts will be greatly appreciated and heartily received.

10. Rosewood (disc. 1991)
11. Walnut
12. Christmas tree (green), fish scales imbedded in clear plastic (disc. 1976), material made prior to WW II.

Handle Material Codes

1. India stag
2. German stag
3. Genuine mother-of-pearl
4. Buffalo horn (disc. 1973)
5. Winterbottom jigged bone (white) (disc. 1973)
6. Winterbottom jigged bone (green) (disc. 1973)
7. Smooth bone
8. Jigged bone, Picked bone (discontinued 1991)
9. Camel bone, jigged

13. Imitation stag
14. Imitation bone
15. Imitation pearl or cracked ice
16. Black composition
17. Yellow composition
18. Dark red composition
19. Green composition
20. Brazil, brown stripe composition (disc. 1991)
21. Brown marble
22. Gray marble
23. Yellow marble
24. Red marble
25. Blue marble
26. Green marble (disc. 1991)
27. Christmas tree, predominantly red
28. Christmas tree, predominantly blue
29. Christmas tree, predominantly pink
30. Transparent, yellow (disc. 1979)
31. Transparent, red (disc. 1979)
32. Transparent, purple (disc. 1979)
33. Transparent, blue (disc. 1979)
34. Transparent, green (disc. 1979)
35. Transparent, white (disc. 1979)
36. Gold sparkle
37. Red sparkle
38. Green sparkle
39. Blue sparkle
40. Copper sparkle
41. Waterfall
42. White composition (milk color)
43. Bark brown
44. Swirl brown
45. Swirl green
46. Swirl red

BUCK CREEK
Frost Cutlery
(Current Production)

3½"

4"

Buck Creek Trapper
2, 3, 4, 5, 6, 7, 8

Little Diamond Back
1, 2, 5, 6, 7

3¾"

Copperhead
2, 3, 4, 5, 6, 7

4½"

Diamondback Kentucky
Flintlock
4, 5, 7

4½"

Diamond Back
1, 2, 3, 4, 5, 6, 7, 8

3⅝"

Bobcat
1, 2, 4, 6, 7, 9, 10

3½"

Whittler
1, 2, 3, 4, 5, 7, 8

4"

Bear and Bull
1, 2, 4, 5, 6

3½"

Bear and Bull
1, 2, 3, 4, 5, 6, 7, 8

2⅞"

Baby Diamondback
1, 2, 4, 5, 6

Handle Materials

1. Deer Stag	6. Yellow
2. Red Pick Bone	7. Waterfall
3. Red Marble	8. Blue Marble
4. Cracked Ice	9. Red Pearl
5. Pink Ice	10. Blue Pearl

BUCK CREEK KNIVES

Pattern Large Stockman, Diamondback

Etching On Face Of Master Blade	Shield	Blades	Length Closed	Stampings	Date of Manufacture	Handle Materials/ Scales	Mint Value	Comments
Diamondback Hand made	Smooth oval	Clip spay sheep foot	4¼"	Buck Creek (enclosed by antlers Solingen Germany)	1970–1973	15, 16, 17	$130	
Diamondback Hand made	Official with crossed swords	as above	as above	Buck Creek (enclosed by antlers)	1974–1975	15, 16, 17, 18, 20	$115	
Diamondback Hand made	Official with antlers a line & Solingen	as above	as above	as above	1976–1989	15, 16, 17, 18, 20, 21, 23, 24, 25, 26, 36, 37, 38, 39, 40	$70	
						10	$75	
Diamondback Snake picture Hand made	Official with antlers and Buck Creek	as above	as above	as above (1992–add Stewart A. Taylor Co.)	1990–1994	15, 16, 17, 18, 20, 24, 25, 41	$65	

545

BUCK CREEK KNIVES

Pattern Large Stockman, Diamondback

Etching On Face Of Master Blade	Shield	Blades	Length Closed	Stampings	Date of Manufacture	Handle Materials/ Scales	Mint Value	Comments
Diamondback Snake pictured	Prancing horse	Clip, Spay, Sheep foot	4¼"	Buck Creek (enclosed by antlers) Solingen Germany Oil the joints	1990	23, 24, 25, 26	$75	
Coal Miner Black Gold	Circle, with miner profile	as above	as above	as above	as above	8	$75	

BUCK CREEK KNIVES

Pattern Large Stockman

Etching On Face Of Master Blade	Shield	Blades	Length Closed	Stampings	Date of Manufacture	Handle Materials/ Scales	Mint Value	Comments
Blade face is blank	smooth Oval	clip, Spay Sheep foot	4¼"	Buck Creek (enclosed by by antlers) Nippon Rostfrei	1973	5-(Winterbottom jigged white bone) 6-(Winterbottom jigged green bone)	$125 $135	These are the ONLY Japanese made Buck Creeks
Sheffield Steel XL Handmade XL	Smooth Oval (brass)	Clip Spay Sheep foot	4¼"	Buffalo Creek (enclosed by antlers) Sheffield Steel Pakistan Oil the joints	1973	4 (Water Buffalo horn)	$110	Rare knife with brass bolsters and shield
Blade face is blank	Smooth Oval (brass)	as above	as above	as above	1973	9 (jigged camel bone)	$135	Very rare knife, brass bolsters and shield

547

BUCK CREEK KNIVES

Pattern Large Stockman

Etching On Face Of Master Blade	Shield	Blades	Length Closed	Stampings	Date of Manufacture	Handle Materials/ Scales	Mint Value	Comments
Blade face is blank	smooth Oval	clip, Spay Sheep foot	4¼"	Buck Creek (enclosed by antlers) Nippon Rostfrei	1973	5-(Winterbottom jigged white bone) 6-(Winterbottom jigged green bone)	$125 $135	These are the ONLY Japanese made Buck Creeks
Sheffield Steel XL Handmade XL	Smooth Oval (brass)	Clip Spay Sheep foot	4¼"	Buffalo Creek (enclosed by antlers) Sheffield Steel Pakistan Oil the joints	1973	4 (Water Buffalo horn)	$110	Rare knife with brass bolsters and shield
Blade face is blank	Smooth Oval (brass)	as above	as above	as above	1973	9 (jigged camel bone)	$135	Very rare knife, brass bolsters and shield

BUCK CREEK KNIVES

Pattern Medium Stockman

Etching On Face Of Master Blade	Shield	Blades	Length Closed	Stampings	Date of Manufacture	Handle Materials/ Scales	Mint Value	Comments
*Premium Stock knife	Smooth, oval	Western Clip, Spay, Sheep foot	3¾"	Buck Creek Solingen Germany	1968-1970	17	$200	Original, few were collected Only use of Western Clip blade on a stock knife
*Hand made Germany	Smooth Official	Clip, Spay, Sheep foot	3¾"	as above	1970-1975	10	$125	
Premium Stock knife	Smooth, Official	Clip, Spay,	3⅞"	Buck Creek, (enclosed by antlers) Solingen Germany	1971-1973	15, 16, 17	$130	Sheep foot blade unique to this knife
Hand made		Sheep foot w/ slightly curved or hooked blade				2 (rare!)	$225	Only 300 made with stag handles

*Pictured

549

BUCK CREEK KNIVES

Pattern Medium Stockman, Rattler

Etching On Face Of Master Blade	Shield	Blades	Length Closed	Stampings	Date of Manufacture	Handle Materials/ Scales	Mint Value	Comments
Premium Stock Knife Hand made	Official with crossed swords	Clip, Spay, Sheep foot	3⅞"	Buck Creek, (enclosed by antlers) Solingen Germany oil the joints	1974-1975	15, 16, 17, 18, 20	$80	
Rattler Hand made	Official with antlers, a line & Solingen	as above	as above	as above	1976-1990	2 10 15, 16, 17, 18, 19, 20, 21, 23, 24, 25, 26, 27, 28, 29, 36, 37, 38, 39, 40	$100 $70 $50	
Rattler Snake picture Hand made Date	as above	as above		as above	discontinued 1990	2	$85	last of stag Rattlers

BUCK CREEK KNIVES

Pattern Medium Stockman, Rattler

Etching On Face Of Master Blade	Shield	Blades	Length Closed	Stampings	Date of Manufacture	Handle Materials/ Scales	Mint Value	Comments
Rattler Snake picture	Official with antlers & Buck Creek	Clip, Spay, sheep foot	3⅞"	Buck Creek, (enclosed by antlers)	discontinued 1991	8	$65	
Hand made Date (1992)						17	$60	600 made– dated 1992

BUCK CREEK KNIVES

Pattern Medium Stockman

Etching On Face Of Master Blade	Shield	Blades	Length Closed	Stampings	Date of Manufacture	Handle Materials/ Scales	Mint Value	Comments
Indian Head Buck Creek	Miniature 1902 Indian Head Penny	Clip, Spay, Sheep foot	3⅞"	2 Indian Chief Heads, with Buck Creek Curved beneath Solingen Germany	1976–1989	13, 14, 15, 16, 17, 20, 27, 28, 29, 30, 31, 32, 33, 34, 35, 36, 37, 38, 39, 40, 42, 43, 44, 45, 46	$75	Earliest production runs have master blade long pull which almost reaches to the blade tang.
						1 – India stag	$135	
						2 – German stag	$125	
						3 – Mother-of-pearl	$160	
						7 – Smooth bone	$110	
						8 – Rogers jigged bone	$115	
						12 – * Green Christmas tree	$135	Handles have fish scales embedded in clear plastic.

* It is the most beautiful of Christmas Tree scales on a modern knife. Colors are a combination of glitter green, red, silver, and yellow. Handles were made from a cache of material produced prior to World War II. The process is banned today because of the explosive nature of the method of manufacture. Colors are unstable if exposed to light for prolonged periods. See color photo in Handle Materials chapter.

BUCK CREEK KNIVES

Pattern Medium Stockman

Etching On Face Of Master Blade	Shield	Blades	Length Closed	Stampings	Date of Manufacture	Handle Materials/ Scales	Mint Value	Comments
Owl Head Hand made Germany	Round w/owl head image	Clip, Spay, Sheep, foot	3⅞"	2 owl heads, with Buck Creek curved beneath	1979	15, 16, 17, 20, 21, 27 28, 29, 30, 31, 32, 33, 34, 35, 36, 37, 38, 39, 40	$60	Identical to Indian Head Stock Knife Did not catch on.

553

BUCK CREEK KNIVES

Pattern Small Stockman, Little Diamondback

Etching On Face Of Master Blade	Shield	Blades	Length Closed	Stampings	Date of Manufacture	Handle Materials/ Scales	Mint Value	Comments
Little Diamondback	Official with antlers, a line, & Solingen	Clip, Spay, Sheep foot	3¾"	Buck Creek (enclosed by antlers) Solingen Germany Oil the joints	1976-1978	10 / 15, 16, 17, 18, 19, 20, 23, 24, 25, 26, 27, 36, 37, 38, 39, 40	$55 $50	
Little Diamondback Snake picture Hand made	as above	as above	as above	as above	1978-1989 (10)	as above / as above (10)	$42 $48	
Little Diamondback Snake picture Hand made Date	as above	as above		as above	1990-present	2 / 10 / 15, 16, 17, 18, 19, 20, 23, 24, 25, 26, 27, 28, 29, 36, 37, 38, 39, 40	$75 $50 $42	Current Production
As above	Train	as above	as above	as above	1990-present	15, 16, 17, 18, 24, 25, 26, 40	$45	

BUCK CREEK KNIVES

Pattern Little Diamondback

Etching On Face Of Master Blade	Shield	Blades	Length Closed	Stampings	Date of Manufacture	Handle Materials/ Scales	Mint Value	Comments
Coal Miner Black Gold	Coal Miner	Clip, Spay, Sheep foot	3¾"	Buck Creek (enclosed by antlers)	1985	8	$65	Current
Little Diamondback Stainless	as above	as above	as above	Buck Creek (enclosed by antlers) Solingen Germany Stainless	1976-1978	15, 20	$55	limited production
Little Diamondback Surgical Steel	Official with antlers & SS beneath	as above	as above	as above

Surgical Steel, Solingen Germany | 1978-1990 | 10, 15, 16, 17, 26, 27, 28, 35, 36, 37, 38, 39 | $60 $55 | |

BUCK CREEK KNIVES

Pattern Indian Head Stockman

Etching On Face Of Master Blade	Shield	Blades	Length Closed	Stampings	Date of Manufacture	Handle Materials/ Scales	Mint Value	Comments
Hand made Germany	Smooth official	Clip, spay, sheep foot	3⅜"	Buck Creek	1970	10	$275	Market test knife, only 100 made, preceded small slim Indian Head stockman
Indian Head Solingen, Germany	Miniature 1902 Indian Head Penny (there seem to have been two sizes of this shield no value difference)	as above	3½"	2 Indian chief profiles, with Buck Creek beneath	1977-1984	8	$75	
				Solingen Germany		15, 16, 20, 27, 29, 30, 31, 32, 33, 34, 35, 36, 37, 38, 39, 40, 43, 44, 45, 46	$55	

BUCK CREEK KNIVES

Pattern Large Congress, Bobcat

Etching On Face Of Master Blade	Shield	Blades	Length Closed	Stampings	Date of Manufacture	Handle Materials/ Scales	Mint Value	Comments
Bobcat, cat picture, Hand made	Bar style with Buck Creek imprint	Sheep foot, pen Sheep foot, cut-off pen or copin	3⅝"	Buck Creek (enclosed by antlers) Solingen Germany oil the joints	1974-75	15, 16, 17, 18, 19, 20	$85	1st large congress
As above	as above plus Official with antlers, a line & Solingen	as above	as above	as above	1976-1990	2	$125	Stag introduced 1978
						8	$100	Stag & Bone have official style shields
						14, 16, 17, 18, 19, 20, 22, 23, 24, 25, 26, 28, 35, 36, 37, 38, 39, 40	$65	oil the joints moved from pen to copin blade

557

BUCK CREEK KNIVES

Pattern Large Congress, Bobcat

Etching On Face Of Master Blade	Shield	Blades	Length Closed	Stampings	Date of Manufacture	Handle Materials/ Scales	Mint Value	Comments
Coal Miner	Miner Profile	as above	as above	as above	1983-88	10, 14	$75	
Black Coal						13	$80	
						16	$65	
						8	$100	

BUCK CREEK KNIVES

Pattern Slim Congress

Etching On Face Of Master Blade	Shield	Blades	Length Closed	Stampings	Date of Manufacture	Handle Materials/ Scales	Mint Value	Comments
Bear and Bull Hand made	Bar w/ Buck Creek imprint or Official with antlers, a line, and Solingen	Sheep foot, Sheep foot, pen, cut-off pen or copin	3⅝"	Bear & Bull (Wall Street style)	1979-1989	15, 16, 17, 18, 20, 24, 26, 27, 28, 36, 37, 38, 39, 40	$75	
				Solingen Germany		14	$75	
				oil the joints		8	$90	
As above	no shield	as above	as above	as above	1982	3	$135	
As above	E. KY Cutlery Assn. engraved on handle	as above	as above	as above	1983	3	$165	only 30 numbered knives made

BUCK CREEK KNIVES

Pattern Slim Congress

Etching On Face Of Master Blade	Shield	Blades	Length Closed	Stampings	Date of Manufacture	Handle Materials/ Scales	Mint Value	Comments
Coal Miner Black Gold	Spade shape w/miner profile	as above	as above	as above	1986	16	$85	
I Dig Coal	Spade shape w/pick and shovel imprint	as above	as above	as above	1984	16	$90	
Wildcat Fever	Ky. wildcat head	as above	as above	as above	1987	15, 25	$100	300 sets of these were also produced w/a presentation box with matching #'s set value $175

BUCK CREEK KNIVES

Pattern Long Slim Congress

Etching On Face Of Master Blade	Shield	Blades	Length Closed	Stampings	Date of Manufacture	Handle Materials/ Scales	Mint Value	Comments
Bear & Bull Hand made	Official with antlers, a line and Solingen	Sheep foot, Sheep foot, pen Cut off pen or Copin	3⅞"	Image of wall Wall Street style Bear & Bull w/Bear & Bull beneath Solingen Germany Oil the joints	1984	20, 27	$50	fairly rare

561

BUCK CREEK KNIVES

Pattern Slim Congress

Etching On Face Of Master Blade	Shield	Blades	Length Closed	Stampings	Date of Manufacture	Handle Materials/ Scales	Mint Value	Comments
Bear & Bull Hand made date	Bar w/ Buck Creek imprint or Official w/antlers and Buck Creek	Sheep foot, Sheep foot, pen, Cut-off pen or Copin	3⅝"	Bear & Bull (Wall Street style) Solingen Germany	1990-1991	15, 16, 17, 18, 20, 24, 26, 27, 28, 36, 37, 38, 39, 40, 41	$46	
				oil the joints		8	$65	
				1992 add: Stewart A. Taylor Co.	1992	2	$75	
						15, 16, 17, 18, 20, 27, 28, 29	$48	

BUCK CREEK KNIVES

Pattern Large Senator, Cobra

Etching On Face Of Master Blade	Shield	Blades	Length Closed	Stampings	Date of Manufacture	Handle Materials/ Scales	Mint Value	Comments
Cobra Hand made	Bar w/ Buck Creek imprint	Sheep foot, pen	3⅝"	Buck Creek (enclosed by antlers), Solingen Germany, oil the joints	1976-1989	2 10 15, 16, 17, 20, 22, 23, 24, 25, 26, 28, 27, 36, 37, 38, 39, 40	$110 $70 $67	
As above	KY map w/ KY imprinted	as above	3⅝"	as above	1976	15, 16, 17,	$80	300 produced
As above	TN map w/state name on shield	as above	3⅝"	as above	1976	15, 16, 17	$80	300 produced
As above	West Virginia map w/ W. VA on shield	as above	3⅝"	as above	1976	15, 16, 17	$80	300 produced

563

BUCK CREEK KNIVES

Pattern Large Senator, Cobra

Etching On Face Of Master Blade	Shield	Blades	Length Closed	Stampings	Date of Manufacture	Handle Materials/ Scales	Mint Value	Comments
Indy 500 w/race car picture		Sheep foot, pen	3⅝"	Buck Creek (enclosed by antlers), Solingen Germany, oil the joints	1976	24, 15, 16, 17, 20	$80	300 produced
My Old Kentucky home w/house pictured	KY map outline w/KY on shield	as above	as above	as above	1976	36, 37, 19, 16	$80	as above each handle color
Alabama	University of AL symbol	as above	as above	as above	1988	24	$80	*Value

*Value of knife depends on how dedicated a fan the customer may be! (It could be worth hundreds or more!)...but only to a "Crimson Tide" supporter.

BUCK CREEK KNIVES

Pattern Large Senator, Cobra

Etching On Face Of Master Blade	Shield	Blades	Length Closed	Stampings	Date of Manufacture	Handle Materials/ Scales	Mint Value	Comments
Kentucky state police w/official KSP shield imprint	Shield of KY State Police	Sheep foot, pen	3¾"	Buck Creek (enclosed by antlers) Solingen Germany oil the joints	1985–1991	25	$75	Beautiful knife carried by many KSP troopers – Knives are sometimes found in a paper display box. Add $5
Merry Christmas Hand made	Santa Profile	as above	as above	as above	1990–Current	24	$35	
Cobra w/picture of coiled snake Hand made	Bar w/ Buck Creek imprint	as above	as above	as above	1990–1991	15, 16, 17, 18, 20, 24, 25, 26, 41	$40	
Date					1992	15, 16, 17, 18	$40	
As above	Duck in flight	as above	as above	as above	1989	15, 16, 17, 18, 20	$42	

565

BUCK CREEK KNIVES

Pattern Large Senator, Cobra

Etching On Face Of Master Blade	Shield	Blades	Length Closed	Stampings	Date of Manufacture	Handle Materials/ Scales	Mint Value	Comments
Cobra w/picture of coiled snake Hand made Date	church	Sheep foot, pen	3¾"	Buck Creek (enclosed by antlers) Solingen Germany oil the joints	1989	15, 16, 17, 18, 20, 24, 25, 26, 41	$42	
As above	train	as above	as above	as above	1989	as above	$42	
Coal Miner Black Gold	Miner Profile	as above	as above	as above	1983	16	$50	
Black Gold Hand made	as above	as above	as above	as above	1985-1988	16	$42	

566

BUCK CREEK KNIVES

Pattern Slim Senator

Etching On Face Of Master Blade	Shield	Blades	Length Closed	Stampings	Date of Manufacture	Handle Materials/ Scales	Mint Value	Comments
Bear & Bull Hand made	Bar w/ Buck Creek imprint	Sheep foot, pen	3⅝"	Bear & Bull (Wall street style) Solingen Germany oil the joints	1979-1989	8 15, 16, 17, 18, 20 24, 26, 27, 28, 36 37, 38, 39, 40	$55 $45	
Bear & Bull Hand made Date	as above	as above	as above	as above	1990-	as above	$45	
I Dig Coal	Spade shape w/pick & shovel imprint	as above	as above	as above	1986	8 16	$55 $45	
Bear & Bull Hand made Date	Steam train	as above	as above	as above	1990	15, 16, 17	$45	

BUCK CREEK KNIVES

Pattern Copperhead

Etching On Face Of Master Blade	Shield	Blades	Length Closed	Stampings	Date of Manufacture	Handle Materials/ Scales	Mint Value	Comments
Copperhead Hand made	Official with antlers, a line & Solinger	Clip Skinner	3¾"	Buck Creek (enclosed by antlers) Solingen Germany Oil the joints	1976-1989	2 10 8 15, 16, 17, 18, 19, 20 21, 22, 23, 24, 25, 26 27, 28, 29, 36, 37, 38 39, 40	$75 $60 $65 $50	
Snake picture w/ Copperhead Hand made Date	Official with antlers & Buck Creek	as above	as above	as above plus Stewart A. Taylor Co.	1990-current	15, 16, 17, 18, 41, 20	$50	
					(Disc. 1991) (Disc. 1991) (Disc. 1991)	8 26 24	$60 $45 $45	

BUCK CREEK KNIVES

Pattern Copperhead

Etching On Face Of Master Blade	Shield	Blades	Length Closed	Stampings	Date of Manufacture	Handle Materials/ Scales	Mint Value	Comments
Snake Picture w/ Copperhead Hand made	Farm Tractor	Clip, skinner	3¾"	Buck Creek (enclosed by antlers) Solingen Germany Oil the joints	current	15, 16, 17, 18, 24, 25, 26, 40	$44	
As above	Dozer	as above	as above	as above	current	as above	$44	
As above	Coal Miner Profile	as above	as above	as above	current	8 16, 18, 24	$58 $44	
Copperhead Hand made	Smooth official	Clip, Skinner	3¾"	as above	1974-1975	15, 16, 17	$90	
As above	Official with crossed swords	as above	as above	as above	1974-1975	10 15, 16, 17, 18, 20	$65 $60	

BUCK CREEK KNIVES

Pattern Whittler

Etching On Face Of Master Blade	Shield	Blades	Length Closed	Stampings	Date of Manufacture	Handle Materials/ Scales	Mint Value	Comments
Whittler Snake picture Hand made	Official with antlers, a line & Solingen	Clip, Pen & Cut-off Pen or Copin	3½"	Buck Creek, (enclosed by antlers) / Solingen Germany / Oil the joints	1976-1984	10 / 15, 16, 17, 18, 19, 20 / 35, 36, 37, 38, 39	$90 / $70	Stamping on pen and cut pen blade tangs reverse with production runs
As above	no shield	as above	as above	as above	as above	3 (mother of pearl)	$175	use of pearl limited — outstanding knife!
Whittler Snake picture Hand made	as above	as above	as above	as above	1984-1989	as above, plus stag (#2)	$135	

BUCK CREEK KNIVES

Pattern Whittler

Etching On Face Of Master Blade	Shield	Blades	Length Closed	Stampings	Date of Manufacture	Handle Materials/ Scales	Mint Value	Comments
Whittler Snake picture Hand made	Official with antlers, a line & Solingen	Clip, Pen & Cut-off Pen or Copin	3½"	Buck Creek, (enclosed by antlers) Solingen Germany Oil the joints	1990 (only)	as above except no pearl (#3) 2 others	$135 $80	Excellent investment potential as these were dated only 1 year with official style Solingen shield
As above	Official with antlers & Buck Creek	as above	as above	as above plus Stewart A. Taylor Co. as of 1992	1991-Current	2 16, 15, 17, 20	$90 $42	Shield double stamped

BUCK CREEK KNIVES

Pattern Half-Whittler

Etching On Face Of Master Blade	Shield	Blades	Length Closed	Stampings	Date of Manufacture	Handle Materials/ Scales	Mint Value	Comments
Indian Head Hand made Germany	Miniature 1902 Indian Head Penny	Clip, Pen	3½"	2 Indian Chief profiles with Buck Creek beneath,	1977–1984	15, 17, 20	$50	
Surgical Steel Indian Head Hand made Germany	as above	as above	as above	Solingen Germany As above plus Surgical Steel	1977–1984	as above	$48	

BUCK CREEK KNIVES

Pattern Trapper

Etching On Face Of Master Blade	Shield	Blades	Length Closed	Stampings	Date of Manufacture	Handle Materials/ Scales	Mint Value	Comments
Trapper Hand made Germany	Official with antlers a line & Solingen	Western Clip Spay	4"	Buck Creek (enclosed by antlers) Solingen Germany Oil the joints	1984-1990	15, 16, 17, 24	$52	
As above, plus date	Official with antlers & Buck Creek	as above	as above	as above plus Stewart A. Taylor Co.	1991-current	15, 16, 17, 24	$49	
As above	KY Flintlock Rifle	as above	as above	Buck Creek (enclosed by antlers) Solingen Germany Oil the joints	1989-current	15, 17, 24, 25	$58	used in silver edition sets- w/silver Buck Creek medallion value $85
As above, plus date As above	K.K.K. Coal truck	as above as above	as above as above	as above as above	1989-1991 1989-current	16 15, 16, 17	$47 $47	

573

BUCK CREEK KNIVES

Pattern Canoe

Etching On Face Of Master Blade	Shield	Blades	Length Closed	Stampings	Date of Manufacture	Handle Materials/ Scales	Mint Value	Comments
Engraving of Indian in a canoe	Official with antlers, a line & Solingen	Spear, Pen	3¼"	Buck Creek (enclosed by antlers) Solingen Germany	1991	15, 16, 17, 18, 24, 25, 26, 40	$39	
As above	Official with antlers & Buck Creek	as above	as above	as above plus Stewart A. Taylor Co.	1992	as above	$39	
Merry Christmas Hand made	Santa Claus image	as above	as above	as above	1991–present	24	$50 w/ box $40 w/o box	The box is a "must" for collectors!

BUCK CREEK KNIVES

Pattern Lockback Canoe

Etching On Face Of Master Blade	Shield	Blades	Length Closed	Stampings	Date of Manufacture	Handle Materials/ Scales	Mint Value	Comments
Buck Creek Hammer Forged Solingen, Germany Hand made Date	Official with antlers, a line & Solingen	Clip	3¼"	Buck Creek (enclosed by antlers) Solingen Germany	1984-1991	15, 16, 17, 18, 20, 24, 25	$46	

575

BUCK CREEK KNIVES

Pattern Large Canoe

Etching On Face Of Master Blade	Shield	Blades	Length Closed	Stampings	Date of Manufacture	Handle Materials/ Scales	Mint Value	Comments
Indian in a Canoe	Official style w/ antlers and Buck Creek	Spear & pen	4"	Buck Creek (enclosed by antlers) Solingen Germany, Oil the joints, Stewart A. Taylor Co.	Introduced 1992	15, 16, 17, 18, 24, 25, 41	$55	

BUCK CREEK KNIVES

Pattern Stiletto, Folding Guard

Etching On Face Of Master Blade	Shield	Blades	Length Closed	Stampings	Date of Manufacture	Handle Materials/ Scales	Mint Value	Comments
Buck Creek Hammer Forged Solingen Germany Hand made Date	Official with antlers, a line, & Solingen	Clip	4½"	Buck Creek (enclosed by antlers) Solingen Germany	1990	15, 16, 17	$55	
						2	$100	
						10	$65	
As above	K.K.K.	as above	as above	as above	as above	16	$65	
As above	Official with antlers & Buck Creek	as above	as above	as above	1991– 1990 1991	15, 16, 17 2 8	$50 $100 $75	
As above	Bullet Shield	as above	as above	as above	1991–	10	$60	
As above	K.K.K.	as above	as above	as above	as above	16	$65	K.K.K. shield only on knives w/ black handles

BUCK CREEK KNIVES

Pattern Folding Hunter

Etching On Face Of Master Blade	Shield	Blades	Length Closed	Stampings	Date of Manufacture	Handle Materials/ Scales	Mint Value	Comments
Skinner, etched inside snake picture, Hand made	Bar w/ Buck Creek imprint	Drop point skinner	3¾"	Buck Creek (enclosed by antlers) Solingen Germany	1979	15, 16, 24, 27, 11	$60	Fairly rare made only one year
Buck Creek, Hammer Forged, Solingen Germany, Surgical Stainless	as above	Clip	as above	as above	1978	15	$65	Very few produced w/clip blade & these etchings

BUCK CREEK KNIVES

Pattern Fixed-Blade Hunting Knife

Etching On Face Of Master Blade	Shield	Blades	Length Closed	Stampings	Date of Manufacture	Handle Materials/ Scales	Mint Value	Comments
Buck Creek Hammer Forged	None	Fixed	Overall Blade 4¼"	Etching on face of blade "Buck Creek" hammer forged Solingen Germany surgical stainless and antlers	1988	German Stag (8)	$175	This knife comes w/a two-piece, German-style sheath. This is the only fixed-blade Buck Creek knife produced. Only 600 were made. It is a MUST for a Buck Creek collection!

A book on cutlery pricing in general is incomplete and will be a disappointment to many collectors if Case brand knives are not given prominent treatment. After all, Case brand knives are the most collected pocketknife on the American market. This collector interest, we believe, is due in part to the vast amount of information which has been published on Case products. The Case trademark, too, is one of the oldest under which pocketknives are still being produced. The Case numbering system, which has been stamped on the blades of most all Case knives since the Case XX stamping appeared in the early 1940s, makes different patterns of Case knives easy to identify. Despite the contribution these combined factors make to the collection of Case knives, interest would not exist to its present extent without the quality of workmanship and materials which all Case knives have in common.

When studying a price guide, most collectors are interested in determining the price of a particular knife or a group of particular knives. In the following charts, we have tried to go a step beyond just listing the numbers of knives as they might be found in catalogs or according to pattern. We have, with some exceptions, placed the knife numbers in numerical order, using the first two digits of the number as the primary key to their positioning. In this way any particular knife's number can be found quickly by reading the numbers from right to left. Also, where possible, we have included the pattern name after the number to help identify the knife and its features.

Our Case price guide has an added feature which will allow the collector a quick-glance method of determining the collector value for each Case knife pattern from the "Circle XX" to the "Lightning Case." The collector can determine the approximate dates of the pattern's beginning and ending.

The different values of patterns as determined by stamping changes are also indicated on these charts. We are not suggesting that you can use the charts to accurately predict the value of a particular knife 15 years from now by simply looking at one which is presently 15 years old. Instead, the charts are designed to demonstrate established trends in the market for particular knives. Our experience has shown that with fluctuating prices and inflation, most old standby methods of predicting the future value of pocketknives do not always work. So, when guessing what will increase and what will not, just use your own "horse sense" and hope for a little luck.

The prices and values quoted in our charts are not intended to be "Official Blue Book" prices. They are only realistic prices that you can usually use to buy or sell a knife without going (or being taken) to the cleaners. We advise that you keep this in mind and make adjustments accordingly.

In Case knives, the pattern numbering system was first stamped on the tang of their knives in 1949. The first figure (other than zero) indicates the handle material. The second figure indicates the number of blades, and the last two (or sometimes three) figures indicate the pattern number. Thus:

1 or 01:	Walnut, Hardwoods
2 or 02:	Rough Black, Hard Rubber, Gutta Percha, etc
3 or 03:	Yellow Composition
4 or 04:	White Composition
5 or 05:	Genuine Stag
6 or 06:	Genuine Bone (*Delrin, Wood Laminate/Beach Pattern)
7 or 07:	Genuine Tortoise Shell (also used to designate
7/P	curly maple on Sharkstooth knives, Rosewood, and Laminated Hardwood)
8 or 08:	Genuine Mother-of-Pearl
0 or 09:	Imitation Pearl
10:	Micarta
M:	Stainless Steel or Synthetic

The letters stamped after the pattern numbers indicate the type of blades and/or bolsters:

½–Clip Blade	P–Punch
CG–Concave Ground	PEN–Pen Blade
B&G–Budding & Grafting	RAZ–Razor Blade/One Arm Man Blade
CI–Cracked Ice	R–Bail
DR–Drilled for Lanyard	R–Redbone
EO–Easy Open	SAB–Saber Blade
F–File Blade	SCIS–Scissors
G–Green Bone	SSP–Stainless Steel, polished blade edge
GS–Gold Metal Flake	SH–Sheepfoot Blade
J–Large Spay Blade	SHAD–Shadow Ends, No Bolsters
K–Corkscrew or Caplifter	SP–Spay Blade
L–Lock Open	SS–Stainless Steel
M–Metal	T–Tip Bolsters
P–Pakkawood	

It should be noted that in some small knives, Case leaves off the first two numbers and stamps the pattern indicating numbers only on these knives. In knives with all metal construction, the pattern indicators are stamped in letters instead of numbers. While it is uncommon, some knives such as the Muskrat are stamped by name.

Case's innovation for collectors, beginning in 1970, was a row of ten dots under the U.S.A. stamping. In 1971 there were only nine dots and from there on one dot was removed per year until 1979 when a new row of ten dots in a different location began all over again. The 1980 dots are situated between the "Case XX" and the "U.S.A." Case is stamped with a lightning bolt ($), and when stainless steel is used, a double lightning bolt ($$) is centered between the dots.

From 1990 through 1993, the date was stamped on the blade. The dot system was reintroduced from mid. 1993 through 1999. In 2000, a new tang stamp/dating system was introduced. There are 5Xs and 5 dots on the tang of a year 2000 knife. Each year through 2005 an X will disappear. From 2006 through 2009 a dot will disappear. See illustration on page 191. When using these charts, keep in mind that these prices are for Mint knives only. If your knife is not MINT, please refer to Chart 4 of the RBR Cutlery Scales to determine its Condition Value.

Delrin handles have been used on Case knives since 1967. Until 1974, they had a shield with the word "CASE" with a circle around it, the same as bone handled knives. Since 1974, the shield circle has been removed on knives with Delrin handles, leaving only CASE on the shield. Bone handled knives still have the circle or the shield.

CASE KNIFE CHART
One Blade

Pattern Number	Name	Handle Material	CASE XX 1940–1965	CASE XX U.S.A. 1965–1970	10 Dots, 1970	CASE XX USA 1971–1979	CASE XX USA 1980–1989	Comments
M-100		Gold Plate	$200.00					
M-100		Silver Plate	$170.00					
4100 SS	Melon Tester	White Composition	$225.00	$165.00	$125.00			
4100	Melon Tester	White Composition	$160.00	$200.00	$165.00*			*Serrated edge
6104 B	Budding Knife	Green Bone	$575.00					
6104 B	Budding Knife	Bone	$375.00					

6104B. Budding Knife. 3³/₈" closed.

4100SS. Melon Tester/Citrus. 5¹/₂" closed.

M-100. 3¹/₄" closed.

583

CASE KNIFE CHART
One Blade

Pattern Number	Name	Handle Material	CASE XX 1940–1965	CASE XX U.S.A. 1965–1970	CASE XX U.S.A. 10 Dots, 1970	CASE XX U.S.A. 1971–1979	CASE XX USA 1980–1989	Comments
2109B	Budding Knife	Black Composition	$150.00	$125.00				
M110	Spaying Knife	Nickel Silver	$125.00					
11011	Hawkbill	Walnut	$85.00	$45.00	$40.00	$30.00	$25.00	Discontinued
61011	Hawkbill	Green Bone	$275.00					
	Hawkbill	Bone	$125.00	$125.00				
	Hawkbill	Laminated Wood	$125.00	$50.00	$40.00	$25.00	$25.00	Discontinued
	Hawkbill	Red Bone	$225.00					

11011. Hawkbill. 4" closed.

M-110. Spaying Knife. 3⅛" closed.

2109B. Budding Knife. 3¼" closed.

CASE KNIFE CHART
One Blade

Pattern Number	Name	Handle Material	CASE XX 1940–1965	CASE XX U.S.A. 1965–1970	CASE XX USA 10 Dots, 1970	CASE XX USA 1971–1979	CASE XX USA 1980–1989	Comments
5111½	Lockback				$1,000.00	$450.00		
6111½L	Lockback	Bone	$400.00	$185.00	$255.00	$125B/75D	$60.00 (B)	
6111½L	Lockback	Green Bone	$1,500.00					
1116 SP	Budding Knife	Walnut	$70.00	$50.00	$40.00	$35.00		
5120 SSP	Budding Knife	Stag					$50.00	
31024½	Budding Knife	Yellow Composition	$75.00	$65.00				
61024½	Budding Knife	Bone	$80.00	$50.00				
11031 SH	Budding Knife	Walnut	$65.00	$40.00	$25.00	$25.00	$18.00	Discontinued 1981
2136	Budding Knife	Black Composition	$162.00					

5120 SSP. 3¾" closed.

31024½. 3" closed.

2136. Budding Knife.

1116 SP. Budding Knife. 3½" closed.

11031 SH.

6111½. Stiletto. 4⅜" closed.

585

CASE KNIFE CHART
One Blade

Pattern Number	Name	Handle Material	CASE XX 1940–1965	CASE XX U.S.A. 1965–1970	CASE XX U.S.A. 10 Dots, 1970	CASE XX U.S.A. 1971–1979	CASE XX U.S.A. 1980–1989	Comments
2137	Sod Buster Jr.	Black Composition			$85.00	$30.00	$25.00	Bade Engraved "Sod Buster Jr."
2137 SS	Sod Buster Jr.				$40.00	$35.00	$30.00	Stainless Blade
G137	Sod Buster Jr.	Green				$65.00		Kentucky Bicentennial
P137 SS	Sod Buster Jr.	Pakka Wood				$65.00		Kentucky Bicentennial
5137 SS	Sod Buster Jr.	Stag				$100.00		Kentucky Bicentennial
2138	Sod Buster	Black Composition		$42.00	$38.00	$35.00	$25.00	Blade Engraved, "Sod Buster"
2138 SS	Sod Buster				$40.00	$35.00	$25.00	Stainless Blade
2138 SS L	Sod Buster				$45.00	$40.00	$40.00	Lockback
1139	Banana Knife	Walnut	$150.00					

1139. Banana Knife. 4½" closed.

2138. Sod Buster. 4⅝" closed.

2137. Sod Buster Jr. 3⅝" closed.

CASE KNIFE CHART
One Blade

Pattern Number	Name	Handle Material	CASE XX 1940–1965	CASE XX U.S.A. 1965–1970	CASE XX USA 10 Dots, 1970	CASE XX USA 1971–1979	CASE XX USA 1980–1989	Comments
6143	Daddy Barlow	Bone	$135.00	$95.00	$85.00	$65.00		
	Daddy Barlow	Green Bone	$325.00					
	Daddy Barlow	Smooth Black	$150.00					
	Daddy Barlow	Delrin				$40.00	$40.00	Discontinued
	Daddy Barlow	Red Bone	$210.00					
B1048	Florist	Onyx Composition	$125.00					
61048	Slim Trapper	Bone	$150.00					
	Slim Trapper	Delrin			$40.00	$36.00		Blade Polished 70
61048	Slim Trapper	Red Bone	$200.00					
61048	Slim Trapper	Green Bone	$300.00					
61048 SP	Slim Trapper	Green Bone				$550.00		

61048. Slim Trapper. 4⅛" closed.

6143. Daddy Barlow. 5" closed.

CASE KNIFE CHART

One Blade

Pattern Number	Name	Handle Material	CASE XX 1940–1965	CASE XX U.S.A. 1965–1970	CASE XX U.S.A. 10 Dots, 1970	CASE XX U.S.A. 1971–1979	CASE XX USA 1980–1989	Comments
31048	Slim Trapper	Yellow Composition	$100.00	$75.00	$60.00	$35.00	$25.00	
31048 SP	Slim Trapper	Yellow Composition	$95.00	$70.00	$60.00			
31048 SH R	Florist	Yellow Composition	$115.00					
61048	Slim Trapper	Bone	$105.00	$85.00			$25.00	
61048 SSP	Slim Trapper	Bone		$85.00			$85.00	Surgical Steel w/Polished Blade
61048 SP	Slim Trapper	Bone	$105.00	$75.00				
61048 SP	Slim Trapper	Red Bone	$200.00					
61048 SP	Slim Trapper	Green Bone	$450.00					
61048 SP	Slim Trapper	Delrin		$48.00	$33.00			
61048	Slim Trapper	Red Bone	$200.00					
61048	Slim Trapper	Green Bone	$375.00					
	Slim Trapper	Delrin		$45.00				
61048 SSP	Slim Trapper	Delrin		$50.00	$40.00			

31048. Slim Trapper.

31048 SHR. Florist. 4¹¹/₁₆" closed

CASE KNIFE CHART
One Blade

Pattern Number	Name	Handle Material	CASE XX 1940–1965	CASE XX U.S.A. 1965–1970	CASE XX USA 10 Dots, 1970	CASE XX USA 1971–1979	CASE XX USA 1980–1989	Comments
C61050 SAB	Coke Bottle	Bone	$250.00	$300.00				
	Coke Bottle	Laminated Wood	$150.00	$95.00	$75.00			
	Coke Bottle	Green Bone	$600.00					
	Coke Bottle	Red Bone	$500.00					
C51050 SAB	Coke Bottle	Stag					$175.00	1989
C61050 L SAB	Coke Bottle	Bone						Lockback
1050	Coke Bottle	Horn					$150.00	1989

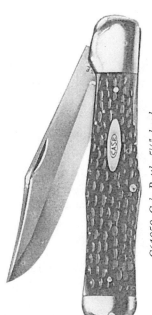

C61050. Coke Bottle. 5½" closed.

CASE KNIFE CHART
One Blade

Pattern Number	Name	Handle Material	CASE XX 1940–1965	CASE XX U.S.A. 1965–1970	CASE XX U.S.A. 10 Dots, 1970	CASE XX U.S.A. 1971–1979	CASE XX U.S.A. 1980–1989	Comments
M1051 L SSP	Horned Lockback	Brushed Aluminum					$55.00	Lockback Dish
21051 L SSP	Horned Lockback	Black Plastic					$55.00	Discontinued
61051 L SSP	Horned Lockback	Brown Laminated Wood					$55.00	Discontinued
P10051 SSP	Horned Lockback	Black Laminated Wood					$60.00	
061051 L SSP	Horned Lockback						$55.00	Discontinued
05051 L SSP	Horned Lockback						$75.00	Discontinued
M1054 SSP	Lockback	Brushed Stainless					$35.00	
M1056 L SSP	Lockback	Brushed Stainless					$35.00	
M1057 L SSP	Lockback	Duranel					$35.00	

M1057 L SSP. 2½" closed.

M1056 L SSP. 2½" closed.

M1054. 2½" closed.

M1051. Horned Lockback. 4¾" closed.

CASE KNIFE CHART
One Blade

Pattern Number	Name	Handle Material	CASE XX 1940–1965	CASE XX U.S.A. 1965–1970	CASE XX U.S.A. 10 Dots, 1970	CASE XX U.S.A. 1971–1979	CASE XX U.S.A. 1980–1989	Comments
P158 L SSP	Mako	Pakka Wood				$75.00	$70.00	Sheath Included
5158 L SSP	Mako	Stag				$125.00	$100.00	Stainless
P159 L SSP	Hammerhead	Pakka Wood					$65.00	
2159 L	Hammerhead						$55.00	
5159 L SSP	Hammerhead	Stag					$125.00	Blade Etched

2159 L. Hammerhead. 5" closed.

P158 L.

P158. Mako. 4¼" closed.

591

CASE KNIFE CHART
One Blade

6165 L. Folding Hunter. 5¼" closed.

Pattern Number	Name	Handle Material	CASE XX 1940–1965	CASE XX U.S.A. 1965–1970	CASE XX U.S.A. 10 Dots, 1970	CASE XX USA 1971–1979	CASE XX USA 1980–1989	Comments
5165	Folding Hunter	Stag	$600.00					Flat Ground
5165 SAB	Folding Hunter	Stag	$300.00	$350.00				
5165 SAB DR	Folding Hunter	Stag	$400.00	$360.00				
5165SSP	Folding Hunter	Stag				$275.00		American Spirit Bicentennial
6165 SAB DR	Folding Hunter	Bone		$300.00				.
6165 SAB	Folding Hunter	Bone	$250.00	$250.00				
6165	Folding Hunter	Bone	$500.00					Flat Ground
6165 SAB	Folding Hunter	Green Bone	$600.00					
6165 SAB	Folding Hunter	Green Bone	$600.00					
6165 SAB	Folding Hunter	Rough Black	$400.00					
6165 SAB DR	Folding Hunter	Wood	$125.00	$100.00	$75.00	$65.00	$50.00	Discontinued
6165	Folding Hunter	Red Bone	$500.00					Flat Ground
6165 SAB	Folding Hunter	Red Bone	$350.00					
6165 DR L SSP	Folding Hunter					$65.00		Lockback
W165 SAB SSP	Folding Hunter	White Smooth Scrimshawed Bone				$225.00		Moby Dick & Nantucket Sleighride, 1977, 1978.
4165	Folding Hunter	White Composition				$80.00		Texas Special, 1977.

CASE KNIFE CHART
One Blade

Pattern Number	Name	Handle Material	CASE XX 1940–1965	CASE XX U.S.A. 1965–1970	CASE XX U.S.A. 10 Dots, 1970	CASE XX U.S.A. 1971–1979	CASE XX U.S.A. 1980–1989	Comments
P172	Buffalo	Pakka Wood		$110.00		$100.00		Buffalo Engraved on Blade, Box Included.
P172	Buffalo	Pakka Wood		$250.00				No Etch. Box Included.
P172 L SSP	Buffalo	Laminated Wood					$125.00	"Boss" etched on Blade.
P172	Buffalo						$100.00	Discontinued 1980
5172	Bulldog	Stag	$500.00	$350.00		$180.00		English Bulldog Engraved on Blade. Box Included.
5172 SSP	Bulldog	Stag				$110.00		"Case Razor Edge" Etched on Blade. Box Included.

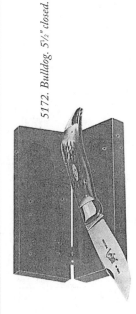

5172. Bulldog. 5½" closed.

P172. Buffalo. 5½" closed.

CASE KNIFE CHART
One Blade

Pattern Number	Name	Handle Material	CASE XX 1940–1965	CASE XX U.S.A. 1965–1970	CASE XX U.S.A. 10 Dots, 1970	CASE XX U.S.A. 1971–1979	CASE XX U.S.A. 1980–1989	Comments
3185	Doctor's/Physician's	Yellow Composition	$175.00	$135.00	$135.00	$50.00		
6185	Doctor's/Physician's	Bone	$225.00	$150.00	$125.00	$85.00		
	Doctor's/Physician's	Delrin				$45.00		
	Doctor's/Physician's	Red Bone	$350.00					
31093	Toothpick	Yellow Composition	$175.00					
61093	Toothpick	Bone	$225.00	$150.00	$110.00	$85.00		
	Toothpick	Green Bone	$550.00					
	Toothpick	Red Bone	$350.00					
	Toothpick	Delrin				$35.00		

61093. Toothpick. 5" closed.

6185. Doctor's or Physician's. 3⅝" closed.

594

CASE KNIFE CHART
One Blade

Pattern Number	Name	Handle Material	CASE XX 1940–1965	CASE XX U.S.A. 1965–1970	CASE XX U.S.A. 10 Dots, 1970	CASE XX U.S.A. 1971–1979	CASE XX U.S.A. 1980–1989	Comments
7197 L SSP	Shark Tooth	Black Pakka Wood				$80.00		Sheath included
	Shark Tooth	Curly Maple				$150.00		
5197 L SSP	Shark Tooth	Stag				$150.00	$150.00	
P197 L SSP	Shark Tooth	Black Pakka Wood				$75.00	$60.00	
1199	Whaler or Sailor	Walnut	$75.00	$55.00	$45.00	$45.00	$100.00	

Two Blade

Pattern Number	Name	Handle Material	CASE XX 1940–1965	CASE XX U.S.A. 1965–1970	CASE XX U.S.A. 10 Dots, 1970	CASE XX U.S.A. 1971–1979	CASE XX U.S.A. 1980–1989	Comments
Muskrat	Muskrat	Bone	$300.00	$250.00	$200.00	$75.00	$45.00	
	Muskrat	Green Bone	$800.00					
	Muskrat	Red Bone	$500.00					
	Muskrat	Rough Black	$1,000.00					
	Muskrat	Stag				$100.00		1979

Muskrat. 3⅛" closed.

1199. Whaler or Sailor. 4⅛" closed.

7197. Shark Tooth. 4½" closed.

CASE KNIFE CHART
Two Blade

Pattern Number	Name	Handle Material	CASE XX 1940–1965	CASE XX U.S.A. 1965–1970	CASE XX USA 10 Dots, 1970	CASE XX USA 1971–1979	CASE XX USA 1980–1989	Comments
Muskrat	"Improved Muskrat" Hawkbaker Special	Bone	$335.00	$750.00	$950.00	$750.00		
Muskrat	"Improved Muskrat" Hawkbaker Special	Delrin			$800.00	$50.00		
4200	Citrus/Melon Tester	White Composition	$800.00	$200.00	$150.00	$85.00		Discontinued 1974
	Citrus/Melon Tester	Serrated blade		$750.00				Master blade serrated
3201	Pen	Yellow Composition	$75.00	$75.00	$50.00	$35.00		
6201	Pen	Bone	$85.00*	$60.00	$40.00	$35.00		Discontinued 1975
6201	Pen	Delrin				$20.00		
6201 SS	Pen						$30.00	
8201	Pen	Pearl	$150.00					
9201	Pen	Imitation Pearl	$65.00	$45.00	$40.00	$25.00	$25.00	*With bail add 10%
9201 R	Pen	Imitation Pearl	$65.00					
		Cracked Ice	$60.00					With bail

6201. Pen. 2⅝" closed.

4200. Citrus or Melon Tester.

"Improved Muskrat," Hawkbaker Special. 3⅞" closed.

CASE KNIFE CHART
Two Blade

Pattern Number	Name	Handle Material	CASE XX 1940–1965	CASE XX U.S.A. 1965–1970	10 Dots, 1970	CASE XX U.S.A. 1971–1979	CASE XX USA 1980–1989	Comments
S2	Lobster	Sterling Silver	$150.00	$150.00				
2202½	Jack	Black Composition	$150.00					
6202½	Jack	Bone	$65.00	$50.00	$40.00	$25.00		
	Jack	Delrin			$30.00*			Discontinued 1978
6205		Bone	$225.00					Discontinued 1963
		Green Bone	$350.00					
		Red Bone	$275.00					
6205 RAZ	One Arm	Bone	$250.00	$135.00	$75.00	$60.00		
		Green Bone	$625.00					
		Delrin				$45.00*		Discontinued 1978 (?)
		Red Bone	$250.00					

6205 RAZ.

6202½ Jack.
3⅛" closed.

52. Lobster.
2¼" closed.

CASE KNIFE CHART
Two Blade

Pattern Number	Name	Handle Material	CASE XX 1940–1965	CASE XX U.S.A. 1965–1970	CASE XX U.S.A. 10 Dots, 1970	CASE XX U.S.A. 1971–1979	CASE XX U.S.A. 1980–1989	Comments
6206½	Jack	Rough Black	$150.00					Discontinued 1949
2207	Jack	Black Composition	$350.00					
6207	Jack	Rough Black	$350.00					
	Jack	Green Bone	$500.00					
	Jack	Red Bone	$300.00					
	Jack	Bone	$150.00	$105.00	$85.00	$50.00	$35.00	
	Jack	Delrin				$35.00		
6207 SS P	Jack						$35.00	
6208	Half Whittler	Bone	$110.00	$85.00	$70.00	$50.00	$35.00	
	Half Whittler	Red Bone	$150.00					
	Half Whittler	Green Bone	$275.00					
	Half Whittler	Rough Black	$150.00					
	Half Whittler	Delrin				$30.00		
A6208	Half Whittler					$30.00	$30.00	

6208. Half Whittler. 3¼" closed.

6207. Jack. 3½" closed.

6206½. Jack. 2⅝" closed.

598

CASE KNIFE CHART
Two Blade

Pattern Number	Name	Handle Material	CASE XX 1940–1965	CASE XX U.S.A. 1965–1970	CASE XX U.S.A. 10 Dots, 1970	CASE XX U.S.A. 1971–1979	CASE XX U.S.A. 1980–1989	Comments
62009	Barlow	Black Composition	$150.00					
	Barlow	Red Bone	$150.00					
	Barlow	Green Bone	$200.00				$30.00	
	Barlow	Bone	$100.00	$65.00	$50.00			
	Barlow	Delrin			$40.00			
62009 SH	Barlow	Black Composition	$160.00					
62009 RAZ	Barlow	Bone	$115.00	$100.00	$60.00			One Arm Knife or Razor
	Barlow	Delrin			$60.00	$30.00*		
	Barlow	Green Bone	$325.00					
62009½	Barlow	Black Composition	$150.00					
	Barlow	Green Bone	$300.00					
	Barlow	Red Bone	$200.00					
	Barlow	Bone	$100.00	$75.00	$55.00			
	Barlow	Delrin		$75.00	$65.00	$25.00		
A62009½	Barlow	Slick Bone				$25.00	$30.00	
A62009½ SS	Barlow	Slick Bone					$25.00	

62009. Barlow. 3³/₈" closed.

62009½. Barlow. 3³/₈" closed.

599

CASE KNIFE CHART
Two Blades

Pattern Number	Name	Handle Material	CASE XX 1940–1965	CASE XX U.S.A. 1965–1970	CASE XX U.S.A. 10 Dots, 1970	CASE XX U.S.A. 1971–1979	CASE XX U.S.A. 1980–1989	Comments
6214	Large Jack	Rough Black	$125.00					
	Large Jack	Green Bone	$200.00					
	Large Jack	Red Bone	$150.00					
	Large Jack	Bone	$100.00	$65.00	$60.00			
	Large Jack	Delrin			$45.00*	$30.00*		
6214½	Large Jack	Rough Black	$125.00					
	Large Jack	Green Bone	$200.00					
	Large Jack	Bone	$100.00	$50.00	$42.00			
	Large Jack	Red Bone	$150.00					
	Large Jack	Delrin			$40.00*	$35.00*		Discontinued 1975

6214. Large Jack. 3⅛" closed.

6214½. Large Jack. 3⅛" closed.

6216. Open End Jack.

CASE KNIFE CHART
Two Blade

Pattern Number	Name	Handle Material	CASE XX 1940–1965	CASE XX U.S.A. 1965–1970	CASE XX U.S.A. 10 Dots, 1970	CASE XX U.S.A. 1971–1979	CASE XX U.S.A. 1980–1989	Comments
6216½	Open End Jack	Bone	$75.00	$50.00				Discontinued 1968
2217	Half Hawkbill	Black Composition	$235.00*					
6217	Half Hawkbill	Red Bone	$200.00*					
	Half Hawkbill	Green Bone	$350.00*					
	Half Hawkbill	Bone	$125.00*	$100.00	$75.00			
	Half Hawkbill	Laminated Wood		$55.00	$55.00	$35.00		
2220	Peanut	Black Composition	$75.00	$80.00	$50.00	$35.00		
3220	Peanut	Yellow Composition	$75.00	$70.00	$65.00	$40.00		
5220	Peanut	Stag	$125.00	$100.00	$65.00	$45.00*		*1979 Only
6220	Peanut	Bone	$100.00	$75.00	$75.00	$75.00*		1971 Only

5220. Peanut.
2¾" closed.

2217. Half Hawkbill.
4" closed.

6216½. Open End Jack.
3⅛" closed.

CASE KNIFE CHART
Two Blade

Pattern Number	Name	Handle Material	CASE XX 1940–1965	CASE XX U.S.A. 1965–1970	CASE XX U.S.A. 10 Dots, 1970	CASE XX U.S.A. 1971–1979	CASE XX U.S.A. 1980–1989	Comments
6220	Peanut	Red Bone	$250.00					
	Peanut	Green Bone	$400.00					
	Peanut	Rough Black	$190.00					
	Peanut	Delrin			$125.00*	$35.00*	$25.00*	
9220	Peanut	Imitation Pearl	$175.00					
	Peanut	Cracked Ice	$175.00					
A6620	Peanut	Slick Bone				$60.00		Appaloosa 1979
2224 SP	Jack	Black Composition	$185.00					
2224 SH	Jack	Black Composition	$185.00					
2224 RAZ	Jack	Black Composition	$225.00					

2224. Jack. 3" closed.

CASE KNIFE CHART
Two Blade

Pattern Number	Name	Handle Material	CASE XX 1940–1965	CASE XX U.S.A. 1965–1970	CASE XX U.S.A. 10 Dots, 1970	CASE XX U.S.A. 1971–1979	CASE XX U.S.A. 1980–1989	Comments
220024½	Little John Carver	Black Composition	$1,400.00					With box
620024½	Jack	Bone	$95.00	$65.00				1965 – 1968
6225 RAZ	Coke	Bone	$250.00					Master Blade, RAZ
6225½	Coke	Rough Black	$175.00					
	Coke	Green Bone	$350.00					
	Coke	Red Bone	$225.00					
	Coke	Bone	$115.00	$60.00*	$55.00	$35.00	$30.00	
6227	Jack	Green Bone	$165.00					
	Jack	Bone	$75.00	$45.00	$40.00	$30.00*	$30.00*	*Redbone 79 & 80
	Jack	Delrin			$35.00*	$20.00*		Discontinued 1978
62027	Jack	Delrin				$25.00*		1978 – 1979
SR 62027	Jack	Red Bone				$30.00	$25.00	1979 – 1980

6227. Jack. 2¼" closed.

6225½. Coke. 3" closed.

SR 62027. Jack.

220024. Little John Carver. 3" closed.

603

CASE KNIFE CHART
Two Blade

Pattern Number	Name	Handle Material	CASE XX 1940–1965	CASE XX U.S.A. 1965–1970	CASE XX U.S.A. 10 Dots, 1970	CASE XX U.S.A. 1971–1979	CASE XX U.S.A. 1980–1989	Comments
62027½		Bone	$95.00					
92027½		Cracked Ice	$85.00					
6228½	Easy Open Jack	Red Bone	$200.00					Easy Open Jack
22028½ EO	Easy Open Jack	Black Composition	$115.00					
62028½	Serpentine Jack	Rough Black	$200.00					
	Serpentine Jack	Bone	$200.00					
2229½	Jack	Black Composition	$125.00					
6229½	Jack	Bone	$100.00	$75.00*				*Tadpole
6229½	Jack	Rough Black	$200.00					

6229⅞. Jack. 2⅞" closed.

62028½. Serpentine Jack. 3½" closed.

22028. Serpentine Jack. 3½" closed.

62027½. 2¼ closed.

604

CASE KNIFE CHART
Two Blade

Pattern Number	Name	Handle Material	CASE XX 1940–1965	CASE XX U.S.A. 1965–1970	CASE XX U.S.A. 10 Dots, 1970	CASE XX U.S.A. 1971–1979	CASE XX U.S.A. 1980–1989	Comments
6231	Jack	Bone	$175.00	$400.00				Discontinued 1966
	Jack	Red Bone	$250.00					
	Jack	Green Bone	$350.00					
	Jack	Rough Black	$200.00					
12031 L.H.R.	Electrician	Walnut				$18.00		
12031	Electrician	Walnut	$55.00	$35.00	$30.00	$25.00	$22.00	
62031	Jack	Bone	$145.00					Discontinued 1960
	Jack	Green Bone	$275.00					
	Jack	Red Bone	$200.00					
	Jack	Rough Black	$175.00					

62031. Jack. 3¾" closed.

12031. Electrician. 3¾" closed.

6231. Jack. 3¾" closed.

CASE KNIFE CHART
Two Blade

Pattern Number	Name	Handle Material	CASE XX 1940–1965	CASE XX U.S.A. 1965–1970	CASE XX U.S.A. 10 Dots, 1970	CASE XX U.S.A. 1971–1979	CASE XX U.S.A. 1980–1989	Comments
2231½	Jack	Black Composition	$90.00					
2231½ SAB	Jack	Black Composition	$90.00	$45.00	$40.00	$32.00	$30.00	
4231½	Jack	White Composition	$200.00					
6231½	Jack	Bone	$150.00	$65.00	$45.00	$35.00	$30.00	
	Jack	Red Bone	$225.00					
	Jack	Green Bone	$325.00					
	Jack	Rough Black	$200.00					
5232	Jack	Stag	$250.00	$95.00	$100.00	$100.00		
6232	Jack	Green Bone	$250.00					
	Jack	Red Bone	$150.00					
	Jack	Rough Black	$150.00					
	Jack	Bone	$125.00	$85.00	$65.00	$40.00	$30.00	
	Delrin					$25.00*		

2231½ SAB. Jack.

5232. Jack. 3⅝" closed.

3233. Pen. 2⅝" closed.

CASE KNIFE CHART
Two Blade

Pattern Number	Name	Handle Material	CASE XX 1940–1965	CASE XX U.S.A. 1965–1970	CASE XX U.S.A. 10 Dots, 1970	CASE XX U.S.A. 1971–1979	CASE XX U.S.A. 1980–1989
3233	Pen	Yellow Composition	$75.00	$50.00	$40.00	$35.00	
5233	Pen	Stag	$200.00	$175.00	$125.00		
5233SP	Pen	Stag				$50.00	
DU 5233 SS	Pen	Stag					$60.00
52033	Pen	Stag				$75.00	
6233	Pen	Rough Black	$165.00				
	Pen	Red Bone	$165.00				
	Pen	Green Bone	$275.00				
	Pen	Bone	$75.00	$60.00	$60.00	$25.00	
	Pen	Delrin		$60.00*	$45.00*	$25.00*	
62033	Pen	Delrin				$25.00*	
A 62033	Pen	Smooth Bone				$35.00	$30.00
8233	Pen	Pearl	$150.00	$90.00	$60.00	$55.00	
9233	Pen	Imitation Pearl	$75.00	$50.00	$50.00	$25.00	
	Pen	Cracked Ice	$65.00				
92033	Pen	Cracked Ice				$25.00	

CASE KNIFE CHART
Two Blade

6235. Swell End Jack. 3¼" closed.

6235½. Jack. 3¼" closed.

Pattern Number	Name	Handle Material	CASE XX 1940–1965	CASE XX U.S.A. 1965–1970	CASE XX U.S.A. 10 Dots, 1970	CASE XX U.S.A. 1971–1979	CASE XX U.S.A. 1980–1989	Comments
6235 EO	Swell End Jack	Rough Black	$350.00					
6235 EO	Jack	Red Bone	$350.00					
	Swell End Jack	Bone	$250.00					
6235	Swell End Jack	Bone	$125.00					
	Swell End Jack	Rough Black	$125.00					
6235	Jack	Red Bone	$225.00					
	Swell End Jack	Green Bone	$250.00					
620035	Swell End Jack	Imitation Bone	$65.00					
620035 EO	Swell End Jack	Imitation Bone	$70.00					
6235½	Jack	Bone	$100.00	$85.00	$55.00	$40.00		
	Jack	Smooth Bone						
	Jack	Green Bone	$275.00				$40.00	
	Jack	Rough Black	$125.00					
6235½	Jack	Red Bone	$200.00					
6235½ SS	Jack	Smooth Bone					$40.00	
62003 5½	Jack	Imitation Bone	$55.00					

608

92042. Pen Knife. 3" closed.   *6244. Jack. 3¼" closed.*

CASE KNIFE CHART
Two Blade

Pattern Number	Name	Handle Material	CASE XX 1940–1965	CASE XX U.S.A. 1965–1970	CASE XX U.S.A. 10 Dots, 1970	CASE XX U.S.A. 1971–1979	CASE XX U.S.A. 1980–1989
52042 RSSP	Pen Knife	Stag					$35.00
62042	Pen Knife	Bone	$80.00	$65.00	$65.00	$40.00	
62042	Pen Knife	Delrin				$40.00*	
	Jack	Red Bone	$110.00				
	Pen Knife	Green Bone	$175.00	$75.00			
	Pen Knife	Rough Black	$75.00	$35.00			
A 62042	Pen Knife	Smooth Bone				$40.00	$35.00
92042	Pen Knife	Imitation Pearl	$40.00	$35.00	$35.00	$30.00	
	Pen Knife	Cracked Ice	$40.00				
92042 R	Pen Knife	Imitation Pearl	$40.00	$35.00	$35.00		
6244	Jack	Bone	$75.00	$55.00	$45.00		
6244	Jack	Red Bone	$135.00				
	Jack	Green Bone	$160.00				
	Jack	Delrin			$70.00*	$25.00*	$25.00*
SR 6244	Jack	Smooth Bone				$40.00	$30.00
SR 6244 SS	Jack						$25.00

CASE KNIFE CHART
Two Blade

Pattern Number	Name	Handle Material	CASE XX 1940–1965	CASE XX U.S.A. 1965–1970	CASE XX U.S.A. 10 Dots, 1970	CASE XX U.S.A. 1971–1979	CASE XX U.S.A. 1980–1989	Comments
06244	Pen	Green Bone	$175.00					
	Pen	Red Bone	$125.00					
	Pen	Bone	$85.00	$50.00	$50.00	$30.00		
	Pen	Delrin			$35.00*	$30.00		
2245 SHSP	Grafting Knife	Black Composition	$140.00					
06245	Grafting Knife	Green Bone	$300.00					
3246 R	Rigger's Knife	Yellow Composition	$275.00					
3246R SS	Rigger's Knife	Yellow Composition	$300.00	$200.00				
6246 SS	Rigger's Knife	Bone	$225.00	$100.00	$65.00	$45.00		
6246 SS	Rigger's Knife	Red Bone	$300.00					
6246R SS	Rigger's Knife	Delrin					$35.00*	

3246. Rigger's Knife. 4⅛" closed.

06245. Grafting Knife.

06244. Pen. 3¼" closed.

CASE KNIFE CHART
Two Blade

Pattern Number	Name	Handle Material	CASE XX 1940–1965	CASE XX U.S.A. 1965–1970	CASE XX U.S.A. 10 Dots, 1970	CASE XX U.S.A. 1971–1979	CASE XX U.S.A. 1980–1989	Comments
4247 K	Greenskeeper Knife	White Composition	$525.00	$400.00	$400.00	$300.00		
04247 SP	Texas Jack	White Composition	$150.00	$125.00				
05247 SP	Texas Jack	Stag	$250.00	$225.00				
06247 PEN	Texas Jack	Bone	$160.00	$85.00	$60.00	$50.00	$45.00	
	Texas Jack	Delrin				$35.00*		
	Texas Jack	Green Bone	$375.00					
	Texas Jack	Rough Black	$325.00					
	Texas Jack	Red Bone	$300.00					

05247 SP. Texas Jack. 3 ⅞" closed.

4247. Greenskeeper Knife. 4" closed.

611

32048. Serpentine Jack.
4" closed.

6249. Copperhead/Vietnam.
4" closed.

CASE KNIFE CHART
Two Blade

Pattern Number	Name	Handle Material	CASE XX 1940–1965	CASE XX U.S.A. 1965–1970	CASE XX U.S.A. 10 Dots, 1970	CASE XX U.S.A. 1971–1979	CASE XX U.S.A. 1980–1989
32048	Serpentine Jack	Yellow Composition					$25.00
32048 SP	Serpentine Jack	Yellow Composition	$100.00	$60.00	$50.00	$35.00	
62048	Serpentine Jack	Bone			$125.00		
62048 SP	Serpentine Jack	Bone	$125.00	$60.00			
	Serpentine Jack	Delrin		$40.00*	$40.00*	$25.00*	
		Red Bone	$200.00				
	Serpentine Jack	Green Bone	$300.00				
62048 SP SSP	Serpentine Jack	Bone		$70.00			
	Serpentine Jack	Delrin		$35.00*	$35.00*	$30.00*	$25.00*
62048	Serpentine Jack						$25.00
76248 SS	Serpentine Jack		$50.00			$25.00	
6249	Copperhead/Vietnam	Bone	$250.00	$125.00	$150.00	$75.00	
	Copperhead/Vietnam	Delrin				$35.00*	$35.00
	Copperhead/Vietnam	Green Bone	$600.00				
6249	Copperhead/Vietnam	Red Bone	$300.00				
	Copperhead/Vietnam	Rough Black	$500.00				
	Copperhead/Vietnam	Stag				$60.00	

CASE KNIFE CHART
Two Blade

Pattern Number	Name	Handle Material	CASE XX 1940–1965	CASE XX U.S.A. 1965–1970	CASE XX U.S.A. 10 Dots, 1970	CASE XX U.S.A. 1971–1979	CASE XX U.S.A. 1980–1989	Comments
6250	Sunfish or Elephant's Toenail	Bone	$425.00	$400.00				
	Sunfish/Ele. Tn.	Laminated Wood	$185.00	$125.00	$100.00	$65.00	$55.00	
	Sunfish/Ele. Tn.	Red Bone	$600.00					
	Sunfish/Ele. Tn.	Green Bone	$1,000.00					
62052	Congress	Bone	$135.00	$100.00	$85.00	$50.00		
	Congress	Delrin				$40.00		1971 – 1976
	Congress	Green Bone	$500.00					
	Congress	Red Bone	$350.00					
	Congress	Rough Black	$500.00					
5253	Congress	Stag	$225.00					
6253	Congress	Rough Black	$150.00					
9253	Congress	Imitation Pearl	$100.00					

6250. Sunfish or Elephant's Toenail. 4⅛" closed.

5253. 3¼" closed.

62052. Congress.

613

CASE KNIFE CHART
Two Blade

Pattern Number	Name	Handle Material	CASE XX 1940–1965	CASE XX U.S.A. 1965–1970	CASE XX U.S.A. 10 Dots, 1970	CASE XX U.S.A. 1971–1979	CASE XX U.S.A. 1980–1989	Comments
62053 SS		Bone	$85.00	$175.00				
82053		Pearl	$110.00					
82053 SS		Pearl	$85.00					
82053 SR		Pearl	$80.00					
82053 SR SS		Pearl	$95.00					
3254	Trapper	Yellow Composition	$225.00	$125.00	$125.00	$75.00	$35.00	
5254	Trapper	Stag	$425.00	$225.00	$175.00	$70.00		
5254 SSP	Trapper					$75.00		
6254	Trapper	Bone	$365.00	$175.00	$125.00	$65B/55D	$45.00	
		Red Bone	$750.00					
		Green Bone	$1,000.00					
6254 SSP	Trapper			$210.00	$125.00	$70B/50D	$40.00	

6254. Trapper.

82053 SR. 3 ¼" closed.

CASE KNIFE CHART
Two Blade

Pattern Number	Name	Handle Material	CASE XX 1940–1965	CASE XX U.S.A. 1965–1970	CASE XX U.S.A. 10 Dots, 1970	CASE XX U.S.A. 1971–1979	CASE XX U.S.A. 1980–1989	Comments
22055	Equal End Jack	Black Composition	$75.00	$210.00				
62055	Equal End Jack	Bone	$115.00	$75.00	$70.00	$50.00		
	Equal End Jack	Delrin				$25.00*	$20.00*	
	Equal End Jack	Rough Black	$275.00					
	Equal End Jack	Green Bone	$385.00					
	Equal End Jack	Red Bone	$225.00					
92055	Equal End Jack	Imit. Pearl	$350.00					
42057	Office Pen	Imit. Ivory/imprint	$135.00					Etched
	Office Pen	Imit. Ivory/plain	$75.00					Plain
4257	Office Pen	Imitation Ivory	$100.00					Etched
	Office Pen	Imitation Ivory	$50.00					Plain
5260	Office Pen	Stag	$225.00					

5260. 3 ¼″ closed.

42057. Office Pen.

62055. Equal End Jack.

615

CASE KNIFE CHART
Two Blade

Pattern Number	Name	Handle Material	CASE XX 1940–1965	CASE XX U.S.A. 1965–1970	CASE XX U.S.A. 10 Dots, 1970	CASE XX U.S.A. 1971–1979	CASE XX U.S.A. 1980–1989	Comments
8261	Pen	Pearl	$90.00	$80.00	$70.00	$60.00		
9261	Pen	Imitation Pearl	$45.00	$40.00	$35.00	$25.00		
05263	Equal End Pen	Stag	$165.00					
05263 SS	Equal End Pen	Stag	$125.00	$80.00	$70.00			
06263	Equal End Pen	Bone	$100.00					
	Equal End Pen	Green Bone	$150.00					
06263 SS	Equal End Pen	Green Bone	$175.00					
06263 SS	Equal End Pen	Red Bone	$125.00					
	Equal End Pen	Bone	$85.00	$60.00	$40.00			
06263 SSP	Equal End Pen	Bone		$60.00		$40.00		
	Equal End Pen	Delrin		$50.00*	$45.00*	$25.00*	$25.00*	

05263. 3 ⅛" closed.

8261. Pen. 2 ⅛" closed.

CASE KNIFE CHART
Two Blade

Pattern Number	Name	Handle Material	CASE XX 1940–1965	CASE XX U.S.A. 1965–1970	CASE XX U.S.A. 10 Dots, 1970	CASE XX U.S.A. 1971–1979	CASE XX U.S.A. 1980–1989	Comments
82063 SHAD	Sleeveboard Pen	Pearl	$90.00					
82063 SHAD SS	Sleeveboard Pen	Pearl	$100.00					USA Uncommon
62063½	Sleeveboard Pen	Green Bone	$135.00	$275.00				
62063½ SS	Sleeveboard Pen	Green Bone	$135.00					
62063½	Sleeveboard Pen	Bone	$110.00					
90063½	Sleeveboard Pen	Imitation Pearl	$100.00					

62063 ½ SS. 3" closed.

82063. 3⅛" closed.

617

CASE KNIFE CHART
Two Blade

Pattern Number	Name	Handle Material	CASE XX 1940–1965	CASE XX U.S.A. 1965–1970	CASE XX U.S.A. 10 Dots, 1970	CASE XX U.S.A. 1971–1979	CASE XX U.S.A. 1980–1989	Comments
5265	Folding Hunter	Stag	$600.00					
5265 SAB	Folding Hunter		$400.00	$155.00	$115.00			
5265 SS	Folding Hunter					$90.00		Set
5265 SSP	Folding Hunter					$90.00		Set
6265	Folding Hunter	Green Bone	$700.00					
6265 SAB	Folding Hunter	Red Bone	$400.00					
	Folding Hunter	Rough Black	$400.00					
	Folding Hunter	Green Bone	$650.00					
	Folding Hunter	Laminated Wood	$125.00	$80.00	$80.00	$50.00	$40.00	
	Folding Hunter	Bone	$210.00	$250.00				
6265 SAB SS	Folding Hunter	Laminated Wood					$30.00	
06267	Swell Center Pen	Bone	$135.00	$110.00				

06267. Swell Center Pen.
5 1/4" closed.

5265. Folding Hunter.

CASE KNIFE CHART
Two Blade

Pattern Number	Name	Handle Material	CASE XX 1940–1965	CASE XX U.S.A. 1965–1970	CASE XX U.S.A. 10 Dots, 1970	CASE XX U.S.A. 1971–1979	CASE XX U.S.A. 1980–1989	Comments
6269	Congress	Bone	$110.00	$80.00	$65.00	$35.00	$25.00	
	Congress	Delrin				$30.00		
	Congress	Green Bone	$210.00					
	Congress	Red Bone	$159.00					
	Congress	Rough Black	$135.00					
6271 SS	Senator Pen	Bone	$135.00					
8271	Congress	Pearl	$210.00					
8271 SS	Congress	Pearl	$215.00					
5275 SSP	Moose	Stag				$65.00		
6275 SSP	Moose	Bone	$150.00	$110.00	$80.00	$55.00	$35.00	
	Moose	Delrin				$35.00*		
	Moose	Green Bone	$650.00					
	Moose	Red Bone	$350.00					
	Moose	Rough Black	$300.00					

6271. Senator Pen. 3 ¼" closed.

6269. Congress. 3" closed.

6275. Moose. 4 ¼" closed.

CASE KNIFE CHART
Two Blade

Pattern Number	Name	Handle Material	CASE XX 1940–1965	CASE XX U.S.A. 1965–1970	CASE XX U.S.A. 10 Dots, 1970	CASE XX U.S.A. 1971–1979	CASE XX U.S.A. 1980–1989	Comments
M 279 SS	Senator Pen	Stainless Steel	$50.00	$35.00	$35.00	$30.00	$25.00	
M 279 FSS	Senator Pen		$55.00	$45.00	$40.00	$35.00	$30.00	
5279	Senator Pen	Stag	$300.00					
5279 SS	Senator Pen	Stag	$110.00	$165.00		$45.00		
6279	Senator Pen	Bone	$100.00					
6279	Senator Pen	Green Bone	$200.00					
6279	Senator Pen	Rough Black	$150.00					
6279 SS	Senator Pen	Bone	$95.00	$55.00	$55.00	$35.00		
	Senator Pen	Delrin				$25.00*	$20.00*	
8279	Senator Pen	Pearl	$120.00					
8279 SS	Senator Pen	Pearl	$110.00					
9279	Senator Pen	Imitation Pearl	$80.00					
	Senator Pen	Cracked Ice	$80.00					

6279. Senator Pen. 3 1/8" closed.

CASE KNIFE CHART
Two Blade

Pattern Number	Name	Handle Material	CASE XX 1940–1965	CASE XX U.S.A. 1965–1970	CASE XX U.S.A. 10 Dots, 1970	CASE XX U.S.A. 1971–1979	CASE XX U.S.A. 1980–1989	Comments
82079½	Sleeveboard Pen	Pearl	$110.00	$90.00				
92079½	Sleeveboard Pen	Imitation Pearl	$85.00					
22087	Serpentine Jack	Black Composition	$50.00				$20.00	
52087	Serpentine Jack	Stag	$140.00	$90.00	$60.00			
52087 SS	Serpentine Jack	Stag				$50.00		
52087 SSP	Serpentine Jack	Stag				$50.00		
62087	Serpentine Jack	Bone	$75.00	$60.00	$30.00	$30.00		
	Serpentine Jack	Delrin		$50.00			$22.00*	
	Serpentine Jack	Green Bone	$140.00					
	Serpentine Jack	Red Bone	$120.00					
	Serpentine Jack	Rough Black	$100.00					

52087 SSP. Serpentine Jack.

82079½ SS. Sleeveboard Pen.
3 ½" closed.

CASE KNIFE CHART
Two Blade

Pattern Number	Name	Handle Material	CASE XX 1940–1965	CASE XX U.S.A. 1965–1970	CASE XX U.S.A. 10 Dots, 1970	CASE XX U.S.A. 1971–1979	CASE XX U.S.A. 1980–1989	Comments
5292 SSP	Texas Jack					$50.00		
6292	Texas Jack	Bone	$135.00	$115.00	$85.00	$35.00	$30.00	
	Texas Jack	Red Bone	$160.00					
	Texas Jack	Green Bone	$345.00					
	Texas Jack	Rough Black	$175.00					
6294	Equal End Jack	Bone	$365.00					
	Equal End Jack	Red Bone	$450.00					
	Equal End Jack	Green Bone	$550.00					
32095	Fish Knife	Yellow Composition	$90.00	$75.00	$65.00	$40.00	$35.00	

32095. Fish Knife.

6294. Equal End Jack. 4¼" closed.

6292. Texas Jack. 4" closed.

CASE KNIFE CHART
Two Blade

Pattern Number	Name	Handle Material	CASE XX 1940–1965	CASE XX U.S.A. 1965–1970	CASE XX U.S.A. 10 Dots, 1970	CASE XX U.S.A. 1971–1979	CASE XX U.S.A. 1980–1989	Comments
6296 X SS	Citrus Knife	Bone	$450.00	$400.00				
	Citrus Knife	Green Bone	$850.00					
6299	Jack	Rough Black	$200.00					
	Jack	Green Bone	$400.00					
	Jack	Bone	$300.00					
3399½	Swell End Jack	Yellow Composition	$100.00	$100.00	$100.00	$55.00	$40.00	$40.00
5299½	Swell End Jack	Stag	$175.00	$100.00	$200.00			
62109 X	Baby Copperhead	Bone	$95.00	$75.00	$40.00	$30.00	$25.00	
	Baby Copperhead	Delrin				$35.00*		
	Baby Copperhead	Rough Black	$200.00					
	Baby Copperhead	Green Bone	$300.00					

62109 X. Baby Copperhead. 3″ closed.

6299. Jack. 3″ closed.

5299½. Swell End Jack. 4″ closed.

6296 XSS. Citrus Knife. 4 ¼″ closed.

CASE KNIFE CHART
Two Blade

Pattern Number	Name	Handle Material	CASE XX 1940–1965	CASE XX U.S.A. 1965–1970	CASE XX U.S.A. 10 Dots, 1970	CASE XX U.S.A. 1971–1979	CASE XX U.S.A. 1980–1989	Comments
52131	Canoe	Stag	$300.00	$250.00	$175.00	.		
52131 SS	Canoe	Stag				$150.00		1978
62131	Canoe	Bone	$325.00	$135.00	$100.00	$65.00	$40.00	

Three Blade

Pattern Number	Name	Handle Material	CASE XX 1940–1965	CASE XX U.S.A. 1965–1970	CASE XX U.S.A. 10 Dots, 1970	CASE XX U.S.A. 1971–1979	CASE XX U.S.A. 1980–1989	Comments
6308	Whittler	Bone	$200.00	$150.00	$85.00	$55.00	$40.00	
	Whittler	Delrin				$25.00*		
	Whittler	Red Bone	$300.00					
	Whittler	Green Bone	$500.00					
	Whittler	Rough Black	$300.00					
3318 SH PEN	Stock	Yellow Composition	$85.00	$65.00	$75.00			
3318	Stock					$40.00	$30.00	
4318	Stock	White Composition	$95.00					
4318 SH SP	Stock		$75.00	$85.00	$65.00	$35.00		
4318 SSP	Stock		$95.00					

52131. Canoe.

6308. Whittler.
3 ¼" closed.

4318 SSP. Stock.
3 ½" closed.

CASE KNIFE CHART
Three Blade

6318 SH SP.
3½" closed.

Pattern Number	Name	Handle Material	CASE XX 1940–1965	CASE XX U.S.A. 1965–1970	CASE XX U.S.A. 10 Dots, 1970	CASE XX U.S.A. 1971–1979	CASE XX U.S.A. 1980–1989	Comments
6318 SH SP	Stock	Bone	$95.00	$100.00	$80.00	$40.00	$25.00	
		Delrin				$25.00*		
		Green Bone	$350.00					
		Red Bone	$250.00					
		Rough Black	$250.00					
6318 SH PEN		Bone	$100.00	$90.00	$65.00	$40.00	$25.00	
		Delrin				$25.00*		
		Green Bone	$400.00					
		Red Bone	$250.00					
		Rough Black	$195.00					
6318 SSP		Bone	$125.00	$95.00	$80.00	$35.00	$25.00	
		Green Bone	$275.00					
		Red Bone	$225.00					
		Rough Black	$200.00					
6318 SH SP SSP		Bone		$110.00	$95.00	$50.00	$25.00	

CASE KNIFE CHART
Three Blade

Pattern Number	Name	Handle Material	CASE XX 1940–1965	CASE XX U.S.A. 1965–1970	CASE XX U.S.A. 10 Dots, 1970	CASE XX U.S.A. 1971–1979	CASE XX U.S.A. 1980–1989	Comments
6327		Bone	$100.00	$70.00	$60.00	$40.00	$30.00	
		Delrin			$70.00	$45.00*		
9327		Imitation Pearl	$70.00	$50.00	$35.00	$35.00		
63027		Delrin				$15.00*	$15.00*	
13031 SRT	Electrician	Walnut	$75.00	$65.00	$50.00	$40.00		
5332		Stag	$200.00	$110.00	$85.00	$115.00		
6332		Bone	$115.00	$90.00	$75.00	$40.00	$40.00	
		Delrin				$25.00*		
		Red Bone	$225.00					
		Green Bone	$335.00					
		Rough Black	$200.00					
63032		Bone					$25.00	
		Black Composition		$35.00				

13031 SRT. Electrician. 3¼" closed.

6332. 3 ⁵⁄₈" closed.

6327. 2 ³⁄₄" closed.

CASE KNIFE CHART
Three Blade

Pattern Number	Name	Handle Material	CASE XX 1940–1965	CASE XX U.S.A. 1965–1970	CASE XX U.S.A. 10 Dots, 1970	CASE XX U.S.A. 1971–1979	CASE XX U.S.A. 1980–1989	Comments
6333	Small Stock	Bone	$150.00	$85.00	$65.00			
		Delrin				$40.00*	$30.00*	
		Green Bone	$400.00					
		Red Bone	$250.00					
		Rough Black	$200.00					
9333		Imitation Pearl	$75.00	$40.00	$35.00	$30.00		
63033		Delrin				$30.00*	$25.00*	
93033						$30.00		

6333. 2 ⅝″ closed.

CASE KNIFE CHART
Three Blade

Pattern Number	Name	Handle Material	CASE XX 1940–1965	CASE XX U.S.A. 1965–1970	CASE XX U.S.A. 10 Dots, 1970	CASE XX U.S.A. 1971–1979	CASE XX U.S.A. 1980–1989	Comments
6344 SH SP	Stock	Bone	$1250.00	$75.00	$70.00	$50.00	$38.00	
	Stock	Delrin				$35.00*	$30.00	
	Stock	Green Bone	$375.00					
	Stock	Red Bone	$275.00					
6344 SH PEN	Stock	Bone	$150.00	$70.00	$60.00	$45.00		
	Stock	Delrin			$35.00	$25.00*		
	Stock	Green Bone	$300.00					
	Stock	Red Bone	$225.00					
6344 SH PEN SS	Stock	Delrin					$22.00*	

6344. Stock. 3 ¼" closed.

CASE KNIFE CHART
Three Blade

Pattern Number	Name	Handle Material	CASE XX 1940–1965	CASE XX U.S.A. 1965–1970	CASE XX U.S.A. 10 Dots, 1970	CASE XX U.S.A. 1971–1979	CASE XX U.S.A. 1980–1989	Comments
33044 SH SP	Birds Eye	Yellow Composition	$110.00	$85.00	$65.00	$35.00		
	Birds Eye	Imitation Onyx			$65.00			
2345½	Cattle Knife	Black Composition	$150.00	$160.00				
6345½	Cattle Knife	Bone	$225.00					
	Cattle Knife	Green Bone	$450.00					
	Cattle Knife	Red Bone	$350.00					

6345 ½. Cattle Knife.
3 ⅝" closed.

33044 SH SP. Birds Eye.
3 ¼" closed.

629

CASE KNIFE CHART
Three Blade

Pattern Number	Name	Handle Material	CASE XX 1940–1965	CASE XX U.S.A. 1965–1970	CASE XX U.S.A. 10 Dots, 1970	CASE XX U.S.A. 1971–1979	CASE XX U.S.A. 1980–1989	Comments
3347 SH SP	Stock	Yellow Composition	$150.00	$125.00	$100.00	$65.00	$35.00	
5347 SH SP	Stock	Stag	$300.00	$200.00	$175.00			
5347 SSP	Stock	Stag				$65.00		
5347 SS	Stock	Stag				$65.00		
5347 SH SP SS	Stock	Stag	$350.00	$250.00	$250.00			
5347 SH SP SSP	Stock	Stag				$125.00		
53047	Stock	Stag	$300.00	$250.00	$150.00			
6347 SHP	Stock	Bone	$185.00	$115.00				
	Stock	Green Bone	$450.00					
	Stock	Rough Black	$325.00					
6347 SPP	Stock	Bone	$275.00	$135.00	$100.00	$70.00		
	Stock	Green Bone	$450.00					

CASE KNIFE CHART
Three Blade

Pattern Number	Name	Handle Material	CASE XX 1940–1965	CASE XX U.S.A. 1965–1970	CASE XX U.S.A. 10 Dots, 1970	CASE XX U.S.A. 1971–1979	CASE XX U.S.A. 1980–1989	Comments
6347 SPP	Stock	Red Bone	$300.00					
6347 SH SP SS	Stock	Green Bone	$600.00					
6347 SH SP SSP	Stock	Bone	$250.00	$150.00			$50.00	
	Stock	Red Bone	$375.00					
	Stock	Green Bone	$500.00					
53047	Stock	Stag	$300.00	$200.00	$150.00			
63047	Stock	Bone	$225.00	$200.00	$125.00	$50.00	$50.00	
	Stock	Delrin				$25.00*		
93047	Stock	Imitation Pearl	$350.00					
6347½	Stock	Bone					$50.00	

6347. Stock.

CASE KNIFE CHART
Three Blade

Pattern Number	Name	Handle Material	CASE XX 1940–1965	CASE XX U.S.A. 1965–1970	CASE XX U.S.A. 10 Dots, 1970	CASE XX U.S.A. 1971–1979	CASE XX U.S.A. 1980–1989	Comments
23055P	Congress Whittler	Black Composition	$500.00					
63055		Rough Black	$400.00					
8364TSS		Pearl	$200.00					
8364SCIS-SS		Pearl	$200.00	$150.00	$125.00	$100.00		
5375		Stag	$325.00	$200.00	$165.00			
		2nd Cut Stag	$1,000.00	$850.00				
6375		Bone	$250.00	$200.00	$150.00	$65.00	$40.00	
		Delrin				$35.00		
		Green Bone	$600.00					
		Red Bone	$375.00					
		Rough Black	$485.00					

5375. 4 ¼" closed.

8364 SCIS SS. 3 ⅛" closed.

CASE KNIFE CHART
Three Blade

Pattern Number	Name	Handle Material	CASE XX 1940–1965	CASE XX U.S.A. 1965–1970	CASE XX U.S.A. 10 Dots, 1970	CASE XX U.S.A. 1971–1979	CASE XX U.S.A. 1980–1989	Comments
4380	Whittler						$225.00	NKCA Whittler
6380	Whittler	Bone	$400.00	$250.00	$160.00	$90.00		
	Whittler	Delrin				$50.00*		
	Whittler	Green Bone	$1,000.00					
	Whittler	Red Bone	$425.00					
2383	Whittler	Black Comp.	$250.00	$200.00				
2383 SAB	Whittler	Black Comp.	$400.00					
5383	Whittler	Stag	$500.00	$225.00	$160.00			
6383	Whittler	Bone	$350.00	$200.00	$160.00	$55.00	$40.00	
		Delrin				$50.00*		

CASE KNIFE CHART
Three Blade

Pattern Number	Name	Handle Material	CASE XX 1940–1965	CASE XX U.S.A. 1965–1970	CASE XX U.S.A. 10 Dots, 1970	CASE XX U.S.A. 1971–1979	CASE XX U.S.A. 1980–1989	Comments
6383 SAB	Whittler	Bone	$500.00					
	Whittler	Red Bone	$675.00					
	Whittler	Rough Black	$450.00					
	Whittler	Green Bone	$1,200.00					
9383	Whittler	Imitation Pearl	$500.00					
9383 SAB	Whittler	Imitation Pearl	$500.00					

6383. Whittler. 3 ½" closed.

4380. Whittler. 3 ⅞" closed.

CASE KNIFE CHART
Three Blade

Pattern Number	Name	Handle Material	CASE XX 1940–1965	CASE XX U.S.A. 1965–1970	CASE XX U.S.A. 10 Dots, 1970	CASE XX U.S.A. 1971–1979	CASE XX U.S.A. 1980–1989	Comments
23087 SH		Black Composition	$125.00	$75.00	$45.00	$50.00	$35.00	
53087		Stag	$175.00	$150.00	$150.00	$100.00		
63087 SP		Bone	$125.00	$85.00	$70.00	$35.00	$25.00	
		Delrin				$25.00*	$20.00*	
		Green Bone	$275.00					
		Red Bone	$200.00					
		Rough Black	$200.00					
83088 SS	Lobster	Pearl	$200.00					
83089 SC FSS	Lobster	Pearl	$200.00	$275.00				
83090 SC RSS	Lobster	Pearl	$225.00					

83090 SC RSS.
Lobster. 2 1/4" closed.

83089 SC FSS.
Lobster. 3" closed.

83088 SS. Lobster.
3" closed.

53087 SH PEN.
3 1/4" closed.

CASE KNIFE CHART
Three Blade

Pattern Number	Name	Handle Material	CASE XX 1940–1965	CASE XX U.S.A. 1965–1970	CASE XX U.S.A. 10 Dots, 1970	CASE XX U.S.A. 1971–1979	CASE XX U.S.A. 1980–1989	Comments
5391	Whittler	Stag	$2,200.00					
5392	Stock	Stag	$300.00	$200.00	$200.00			
6392	Stock	Bone	$300.00	$200.00	$125.00	$75.00	$35.00	
	Stock	Green Bone	$425.00					
	Stock	Red Bone	$350.00					
	Stock	Rough Black	$325.00					
33092	Birds Eye	Yellow Composition	$110.00	$95.00	$80.00	$80.00	$45.00	
6394½	Cattle	Red Bone	$2,200.00					
	Cattle	Green Bone	$2,500.00					

5391. Whittler. 4½" closed.

6392. Stock. 4" closed.

33092. Birds Eye. 4" closed.

6394½. Cattle.

CASE KNIFE CHART
Three Blade

Pattern Number	Name	Handle Material	CASE XX 1940 – 1965	CASE XX U.S.A. 1965 – 1970	CASE XX U.S.A. ..... 10 Dots, 1970	CASE XX U.S.A. ..... 1971 – 1979	CASE XX U.S.A. ..... 1980 – 1989	Comments
M 3102 RSS	Lobster	Metal	$50.00	$45.00	$45.00	$40.00	$35.00	
83102 SS	Lobster		$180.00					
T 3105	Toledo Scale (old)		$310.00			$150.00		
	Navy Knife	Metal	$110.00					
53131	Gunboat					$250.00	$200.00	

53131. Gunboat.

Navy Knife.

T3105. Toledo Scale.

83102 SS. Lobster. 2 3/4" closed.

M3102 RSS. Lobster. 2 3/4" closed.

CASE KNIFE CHART
Four Blade

Pattern Number	Name	Handle Material	CASE XX 1940–1965	CASE XX U.S.A. 1965–1970	CASE XX U.S.A. 10 Dots, 1970	CASE XX U.S.A. 1971–1979	CASE XX U.S.A. 1980–1989	Comments
6445 R	Fly Fisherman	Stainless Steel	$255.00	$235.00	$235.00			
	Scout	Bone	$120.00	$110.00	$120.00	$125.00		
	Scout	Delrin				$75.00	$25.00	
	Scout	Red Bone	$250.00					
	Scout	Green Bone	$325.00					
	Scout	Rough Black	$175.00					
	Scout	Black Composition	$175.00					
640045	Scout	Brown Composition	$75.00	$60.00	$40.00	$35.00	$25.00	
	Scout	Black Composition	$60.00					

640045. Scout.

6445 R. Scout.

CASE KNIFE CHART
Four Blade

Pattern Number	Name	Handle Material	CASE XX 1940–1965	CASE XX U.S.A. 1965–1970	CASE XX U.S.A. 10 Dots, 1970	CASE XX U.S.A. 1971–1979	CASE XX U.S.A. 1980–1989	Comments
64047 P		Bone	$350.00	$200.00	$175.00	$50.00		
		Delrin				$45.00*		
		Rough Black	$450.00					
		Green Bone	$850.00					
54052	Small Congress	Stag	$550.00	$265.00	$325.00			
64052		Bone	$300.00	$225.00	$200.00	$165.00		
		Green Bone	$900.00					
		Red Bone	$600.00					
DR 64052		Dark Red					$65.00	

54052.

64047 P.

CASE KNIFE CHART
Four Blade

Pattern Number	Name	Handle Material	CASE XX 1940–1965	CASE XX U.S.A. 1965–1970	CASE XX U.S.A. 10 Dots, 1970	CASE XX U.S.A. 1971–1979	CASE XX U.S.A. 1980–1989	Comments
5488	Large Congress	Stag	$700.00	$400.00	$600.00			
6488		Bone	$600.00	$300.00	$400.00	$150.00		
		Delrin				$125.00		
		Rough Black	$1,000.00					
		Red Bone	$1,200.00					
		Green Bone	$2,800.00					

5488.

CATTARAUGUS CUTLERY

Numbering System

The numbering system for Cattaraugus knives is one of the finest in the field. When you become familiar with them, you can tell at a glance if the knife is original.

The problem with the system, though, is that the same code numbers represent several different knife patterns. The appearance is that the company just did not follow their codes.

This is fairly unlikely. Quality control was always a priority of Cattaraugus Cutlery. It is more likely that numbers 00 through 99 are not adequate to represent all the patterns the company had produced. Instead of adding a sixth digit to the knife's number, they simply assigned new patterns to a number as a knife pattern was phased out. This conclusion is based on speculation. If records supporting this exist, the authors have not had access to them. We are, however, comfortable with this speculation.

The knife's number code translates:
•The first number is the number of blades
•The second number is the number and placement of bolsters.
•The third and fourth digits are the pattern.
•The fifth number is the handle material.

Simply put, 32164:

3 – blades

2 – bolsters on both ends of knife

16 – whittler

4 – celluloid handles

Letter codes, in any, which also described types of blades, patterns or handles followed the number.

The following charts have been developed to attempt to crack the codes even further. The pattern chart is not yet complete (we're certain), but it is probably the most complete currently available.

With these, you should be able to determine a good deal about your knife.

Blade and Bolster Codes

Blade Codes – Blade codes told the number of blades, represented by the first digit of the knife's number.

Bolster Codes – Bolster codes were the second digit of the knife's number.
0   No bolster
1   Front (or open ended)
2   Bolsters
3   Tip (or shadow)
5   Slant bolsters

Knife Type Codes

The third and fourth digits indicated the particular type of knife.

00 Lobster pen	23 Sleeveboard pen/whittler/bartender
01 Open end jack	24 Folding hunter/cattle
02 Open end jack	25 Jack
03 Jack/hogback stock	26 Coke/large jack (folding hunter)
04 Folding hunter/lobster	27 Swell center jack
05 Congress/pruner/whittler	28 Swell center jack
06 Senator pen/corn knife/pruner	29 Stock
07 Equal end pen/cotton sampler	30 Open end jack
08 Dog leg jack	31 Open end jack/lobster
09 Swell center whittler/lobster	32 Swell center pen
10 Tickler/florist	33 Open end jack/swayback jack/hawk-bill pruner/moose
11 Fish knife	34 Jack/pen
12 Open end jack	35 Open end jack
13 Warncliffe whittler	36 Swell end jack
14 Large open end jack	37 Equal end jack
15 Warncliffe whittler/Warncliffe pen	38 Serpentine jack
16 Open end jack/serpentine pen/dog leg jack/whittler	39 Balloon jack/easy open
17 Folding hunter/serpentine pen	40 Large whittler/easy open jack
18 Serpentine stock jack	41 Diner's knife/tear drop jack
19 Cattle	42 Gun stock
20 Cattle/scout	43 Dog leg jack
21 Pen	44 Congress whittler
22 Sleeveboard pen/whittler/gelding jack	45 Swayback/congress whittler

46 Congress whittler
47 Jack (open end?)
48 Open end jack
49 Large folding hunter/slim jack
50 Congress whittler/senator pen/
   orange blossom gunstock whittler
51 Congress
52 Dog leg jack
53 Dog leg jack
54 Dog leg jack
55 Equal end whittler
56 Plumber whittler/humpback
   whittler
57 Equal end open
58 Large pen/budding knife
59 Pen/whittler/congress
60 Equal end pen
61 Pen
62 Jack
63 Slim congress
64 Equal end whittler
65 Large whittler
66 Congress pen/fob
67 Pen/whittler/congress
68 Congress pen
69 Congress pen
70 Office pen/trapper
71 Slim jack
72 Crown jack

73 Gunstock jack
74 Doctor's knife
75 Doctor's knife
76 Equal end pen
77 Congress pen/senator/cattle whittler
78 Pen/butter bean
79 Equal end congress
80 Jack knife/bays knife
81 Open end jack
82 Large folding hunter/coke
83 Open end jack
84 Swell center pen
85 Pen/corn
86 Carpenter whittler
87 Carpenter whittler
88 Jack/scout
89 Balloon jack
90 Large pen
91 Large folding hunter Yukon/Large
   equal end jack
92 Sunfish/elephant toenail
93 Swell center whittler/half whittler
94 Large equal end pen/half whittler
95 Board pen
96 Half whittler
97 Swell center jack/whittler/half
   whittler
98 Swell center whittler
99 Small stock, cattle

Handle Codes

Number handle codes were the fifth digit of the knife's number.

0 Metal/iron
1 White fiberloid
2 French pearl/tortoise shell
3 Genuine mother-of-pearl
4 Celluloid/colored fiberloid

5 Genuine stag
6 Ebony
7 Cocoabolo
8 White bone
9 Bone, Rogers jigging

Letter Codes

These codes followed the knife's number.

Blades

L	lockback or springlock
SS	stainless steel
Sta	stainless stell
C	clip blade
G	punch blade
S	scribing blade or spear point blade
Spat.	spatula blade
SH	sheepfoot blade
P	pen blade
Pl	pencil
D	combination: screwdriver, caplifter and scraping blade
W	nail file

Pattern

BW	Barlow
WH	whittler
W	wrench
JR	junior

Other

B	bale
F	flat bolsters/scale
LB	lockback
TL	thumblock
S	shield

Handle

Gold	gold
Silver	silver
O	metal-nickel silver or iron (i.e., boy's knife)
ORI	Oriental pearl
G	gambler pearl
OP	opal pearl
PP	peacock pearl
B	burnt bone
R	red fiberloid
B	blue fiberloid
Y	yellow fiberloid
C	candy stripe

Reprinted with permission from Cattaraugus Cutlery, Identification and Values

P-1	Pencil Knife	96.00
1-W	Wrench Knife	425.00
3-W	Wrench Knife	425.00
200-OP	Lobster	80.00
200-PP	Lobster	80.00
201-R	Lobster	130.00
203-G	Lobster	135.00
203-Ori	Lobster	135.00
203-O	Lobster	130.00
206-Shrine	Pen	110.00
206-32nd	Pen	110.00
231-OP	Whittler	255.00
300-Ori	Lobster	100.00

300 G

300-G	Lobster	77.00
300-OP	Lobster	190.00
301	Lobster	125.00
301-100F	Lobster	125.00
301-BPOE	Lobster	125.00
301-Shrine	Lobster	125.00
303-G	Lobster	174.00
303-D-Ori	Lobster	179.00

304-Ori	Lobster	118.00
304-G	Lobster	123.00
305-F&AM	Lobster	154.00
305-FOE	Lobster	164.00
305-KT	Lobster	164.00
305-Shrine	Lobster	169.00
305-K of P	Lobster	164.00
305-100F	Lobster	164.00
305-BPOE	Lobster	154.00
309-Ori	Lobster	138.00
309-OP	Lobster	133.00
309-R	Lobster	138.00
1012	Pen	138.00
1159	Barlow	225.00
2000	Veterinary Knife	210.00
2013	Lobster	241.00
2014	Lobster	165.00
2022	Pen (Emblem Shield)	205.00
2022-OP	Pen (Emblem Shield)	205.00
2022-PP	Pen (Emblem Shield)	200.00
2043	Flat Pen (open end)	174.00
2059-Ori	Office Pen	164.00
2059-OP	Office Pen	164.00
2059-PP	Office Pen	164.00
2066-Ori	Pen	123.00
2066-G	Pen	123.00

2066-O	Pen	123.00
2066-OP	Pen	123.00
2066-PP	Pen	128.00
2073	Lobster Pen	236.00
B2109	Copperhead Jack	241.00
2139-(BW)	Barlow	216.00
2149-(BW)	Barlow	216.00
2159-(BW)	Barlow	226.00

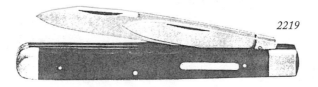

2219

2219	Big Slim Jack	282.00
B2219	Big Slim Jack	282.00
2224-B	Jack	169.00
2227	Equal End Jack	154.00
2239	Big FH Jack	586.00
2249	Big FH Jack	513.00
2259	Board Jack Large)	246.00
B2259	Board Jack (Large)	241.00
2261-OP	Stock Pen	160.00
2269	Board Jack (Large)	264.00
2279	Stock Pen (Large)	264.00
2279-P	Stock Pen (Large)	264.00
2281-OP	Stock Pen (Small)	155.00

2284	Stock Pen (Large)	318.00
2284-C	Stock Pen (Large)	318.00
2284-G	• Stock Pen (Large)	308.00
2289	Jack	185.00
2313	Lobster Pen	236.00
2314	Lobster Pen	164.00
2319	Lobster Pen	210.00
2342	Pen (Small)	128.00
2343	Pen (Small)	72.00
2344	Pen (Small)	135.00
2349	Pen (Small)	295.00
2379	Stock Pen (Large)	267.00
2389	Serp. Jack (Medium)	190.00
C2589	Scout	241.00
D2589	Scout	246.00
B2672	Stock Jack	231.00
B2874-Y	Stock Jack	215.00
B2879	Stock Jack	235.00
2909	Half Whittler	236.00
B2909-(SS)	Half Whittler	241.00
2919	Half Whittler	236.00
B2919-(SS)	Half Whittler	246.00
2929	Half Whittler	241.00
3003	Lobster	310.00
3009	Lobster	225.00
3093	Lobster	215.00

3094	Lobster	165.00
3099	Lobster	195.00
3216-OP	Serp. Whittler	325.00
3229	Stock (Medium)	246.00
3233	Bartender	246.00
3239-H	Bartender	190.00
3289	Whittler	290.00
3293	Cattle (Medium)	384.00
3299	Cattle (Medium)	297.00
3343	Pen (Small)	185.00
3349	Pen (Small)	295.00
3373	Spatula Pen	265.00
3913	Pen (Medium)	246.00
4003	Lobster Pen	335.00
4059	Lobster (Large)	215.00
4303	Lobster (Large)	282.00
4309	Lobster (Large)	215.00
4503	Lobster (Large) (Orange Blossom Gunstock)	335.00
4509	Lobster (Orange Blossom Gunstock Whittler)	335.00
5003	Lobster (Large)	295.00
5009	Lobster (Large)	325.00
10101	Florist	164.00
10484	Budding	169.00
10851	Corn Knife	179.00

11047	Jack	185.00
11057	Pruner (Hawkbill)	165.00
11067-S	Corn Pruner	133.00

11079

11079	Cotton Sampler	200.00
11099	Doctor's Knife	175.00
11227	Gelding Knife	144.00
11247	Open End Jack (Large)	176.00
11339	Open End Jack (Large)	246.00
11404	Budding	205.00
11486	Budding	164.00
11704-(L)	Slim Trapper	210.00
11709	Slim Trapper	241.00
11709-(G)	Slim Trapper	595.00
11709-L	Slim Trapper/Liner Lock	300.00
11804	Cartoon Jack (Medium)	165.00
11827	Open End Jack (Large)	113.00
11837	Open End Jack	175.00
11844	Big FH Jack	513.00
11849	Big FH Jack	533.00

11996-S	Big FH Jack	410.00
12099	Big FH Jack King of the Woods	550.00
12099-L	Big FH Jack King of the Woods	625.00
12109	Tickler (Large)	300.00
12114	Tickler (Large)	308.00
12719	Big Doctor's Knife	290.00
12719-CP	Big Doctor's Knife	251.00
12819	Big FH Coke King of the Woods	716.00
12829	Big FH Coke King of the Woods	716.00

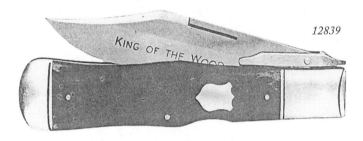

12839

12839	Big FH Coke King of the Woods	750.00
12849	Big FH Coke King of the Woods	650.00
12919	Big FH Yukon King of the Woods	900.00
12919-L	Big FH Yukon King of the Woods	1,000.00
20090	Jack/Boy's Knife	185.00
20222	Sleeveboard Pen (No bolsters)	175.00
20223	Sleeveboard Pen (No bolsters)	170.00
20224	Sleeveboard Pen (No bolsters)	190.00
20228	Sleeveboard Pen (No bolsters)	215.00
20229	Sleeveboard Pen (No bolsters)	170.00
20232	Pen (Small)	87.00

20233	Pen (Small)	180.00
20234	Pen (Small)	118.00
20603	Pen (Small)	179.00
20613	Open End Pen (Small)	174.00
20663	Pen (Small)	169.00
20664	Pen (Small)	118.00
20673	Pen (Small)	169.00
20677	Pen (Small)	92.00

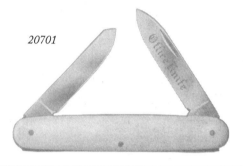

20701

20701	Office Pen (Large)	190.00
20706	Office Pen (Large)	148.00
20773	Pen (Medium Open End)	130.00
20803	Pen (Medium Open End)	244.00
20833	Pen (Small)	174.00
20853	Pen (Small)	190.00
21019	Open End Jack (Medium)	190.00
21027	Open End Jack (Medium)	160.00
21029	Open End Jack (Medium)	190.00
21039	Open End Jack (Medium)	195.00

21046	Open End Jack (Large)	225.00
21049	Open End Jack (Large)	241.00
21087	Electrician	128.00
21089	Electrician	190.00
21129	Open End Jack	200.00
21166	Open End Jack	170.00
21169	Open End Jack	210.00
21169-G	Open End Jack	195.00
21177	Open End Jack	154.00
21229	Gelding Jack	225.00
21246	Open End Jack	128.00
21249	Open End Jack	189.00
21259	Large Open End Jack	241.00
21266	Large Folding Hunter	461.00
21269	Large Folding Hunter	664.00
21269-C	Large Folding Hunter	664.00
21269-CC	Large Folding Hunter	664.00

21286

21286	Large Folding Hunter	461.00

21306	Big Jack	205.00
21309	Big Jack	250.00
21319	Jack (Medium)	190.00
21336	Jack (Medium)	255.00
21339	Jack (Medium)	235.00
21346	Jack (Medium)	165.00
21349	Jack (Medium)	195.00
21356	Open End Jack (Large)	169.00
21359	Open End Jack (Large)	246.00
21396	Equal End Pen	190.00
21399	Open End Jack	240.00
21411	Open End Jack (Medium)	169.00
21419	Diner (Take Apart)	374.00
21474	Open End Jack (Medium)	164.00
21476	Open End Jack (Medium)	133.00
21479	Open End Jack (Medium)	195.00
21484	Open End Jack (Medium)	181.00
21486	Open End Jack (Medium)	128.00
21489	Open End Jack (Medium)	190.00
21709	Slim Trapper	300.00
21709-G	Slim Trapper	300.00
21559	Jack	300.00
21759	Slim Trapper	450.00
21804	(Cartoon) Jack	179.00
21809	(Cartoon) Jack	205.00
21816	Open End Jack (Large)	179.00

21817	Open End Jack (Large)	174.00
21819	Open End Jack (Large)	291.00
21826	Open End Jack	128.00
21829	Open End Jack	190.00
21837	Open End Jack (Large)	133.00
21839	Open End Jack (Large)	190.00
21899-C	Open End Jack (Medium)	184.00
21899-S	Open End Jack (Medium)	190.00
22029	Dog Leg Jack (Medium)	195.00
22039	Dog Leg Jack (Medium)	190.00
22053	Congress Pen (Small)	200.00
22059	Congress Pen (Small)	185.00
22059-B	Congress Pen (Small)	285.00
22059-N	Congress Pen (Small)	185.00
22069	Congress Pen (Large)	350.00
22079	Dog Leg Jack (Medium)	195.00

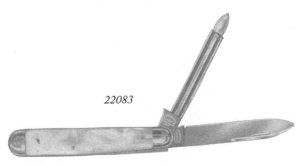

22083

22083	Dog Leg Jack (Medium)	251.00
22084	Dog Leg Jack (Medium)	179.00
22089	Dog Leg Jack (Medium)	190.00
22099	Open End Jack	185.00

22099-F	Open End Jack	200.00
22104	Open End Jack	169.00
22109	Open End Jack	225.00
22109-F	Open End Jack	225.00
22119	Dog Leg Jack (Large)	246.00
22139	Warncliffe Pen	282.00
22149	Stock Jack (Large)	241.00
22153	Warncliffe Pen	241.00
22156	Warncliffe Pen	160.00

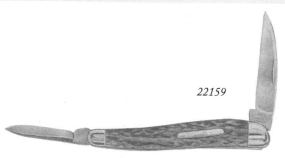

22159

22159	Warncliffe Pen	235.00
22162	Serpentine Pen (Small)	128.00
22163	Serpentine Pen (Small)	179.00
22167	Serpentine Pen (Small)	145.00
22169	Serpentine Pen (Small)	170.00
22179	Stock Jack (Large)	241.00
22182	Stock Serpentine Jack	179.00
22182-(SS)	Serpentine Jack	179.00
22186	Serpentine Jack	128.00

22187	Serpentine Jack	128.00
22199	Cattle Pen	395.00
22209	Board Pen	184.00
22213	Sleeveboard Pen (Medium)	246.00
22219	Sleeveboard Pen (Medium)	190.00
22222	Sleeveboard Pen (Medium)	179.00
22223	Sleeveboard Pen (Medium)	251.00
22226	Sleeveboard Pen (Medium)	195.00
22229	Sleeveboard Pen (Medium)	190.00
22233	Small Sleeveboard Pen	246.00
22239	Small Sleeveboard Pen	190.00
22246	Big Jack	210.00
22247	Big Jack	190.00
22249	Big Jack	292.00
22256	Big Jack	205.00
22257	Big Jack	205.00
22258	Big Jack	292.00
22259	Big Jack	297.00
22269	Big Jack	292.00
22276	Jack (Small)	145.00
22278	Jack (Small)	133.00
22279	Swell Center Jack (Small)	210.00
22286	Swell Center Jack	165.00
22287	Swell Center Jack	138.00
22289	Swell Center Jack	205.00
22292	Stock Pen (Medium)	179.00
22294	Stock Pen (Medium)	165.00

22299	Stock Pen (Medium)	186.00
22329-(SS)	Half Whittler (Small)	190.00
22336	Big Swell Center Pen	390.00
22339	Big Swell Center Pen	282.00
22346	Big Jack	220.00
22347	Big Jack	245.00
22349	Big Jack	292.00
22356	Big Jack	200.00
22357	Big Jack	200.00
22359	Big Jack	200.00
22366	Small Center Pen (Large)	203.00

22369

22369	Small Center Pen/Moose (Large)	392.00
22376	Eq. End Jack (Large)	186.00
22378	Eq. End Jack (Large)	287.00
22379	Eq. End Jack (Large)	292.00
22389	Serpentine Jack (Large)	292.00
22389-(SS)	Serpentine Jack (Large)	287.00
22396	Jack (Large)	185.00
22399	Jack (Large)	192.00
22406	Jack (Large)	105.00

22409	Jack (Large)	128.00
22416	Balloon Jack	180.00
22426	Gunstock (Large)	190.00
22429	Gunstock (Large)	290.00
22436	Jack (Medium)	97.00
22439	Jack (Medium)	118.00
22449	Jack (Large)	154.00
22459	Jack (Large)	159.00
22463	Jack (Large)	175.00
22469	Jack (Large)	195.00
22469-N	Jack (Large)	159.00
22474	Open End Jack (Large)	87.00
22476	Open End Jack (Large)	180.00
22479	Open End Jack (Large)	154.00
22486	Big Jack	165.00
22489	Big Jack	190.00
22509	Congress Pen (Large)	195.00
22509-N	Congress Pen (Large)	205.00

22519

22519	Congress Pen (Large)	128.00
22526	Dog Leg Jack (Large)	87.00
22529	Dog Leg Jack (Large)	225.00
22536	Dog Leg Jack (Large)	103.00

22539	Dog Leg Jack (Large)	205.00
22546	Board Pen (Medium)	200.00
22549	Dog Leg Jack	292.00
22551	Board Pen (Medium)	190.00
22554	Eq. End Pen (Medium)	190.00
22556	Eq. End Pen (Medium)	149.00
22557	Eq. End Pen (Medium)	149.00
22559	Eq. End Pen	165.00
22559-(SS)	Eq. End Pen	215.00
22569	Whittler Pen (Large)	241.00
22576	Board Pen (Large)	164.00
22579	Cattle	241.00
22586	Board Pen (Large)	166.00
22589	Board Pen (Large)	246.00
22594-(SS)	Pen (Small)	118.00
22599-(SS)	Pen (Small)	133.00

22603

22603	Pen (Small)	174.00
22609	Pen (Small)	135.00
22612	Pen (Small)	128.00
22613	Pen (Small)	174.00

22614	Pen (Small)	118.00
22622	Sleeveboard Jack (Medium)	179.00
22624-Y	Sleeveboard Jack (Medium)	164.00
22628-(SS)	Sleeveboard Jack (Medium)	190.00
22629	Sleeveboard Jack (Medium)	190.00
22629-(SS)	Sleeveboard Jack (Medium)	195.00
22633	Congress Pen (Small)	174.00
22639	Congress Pen	185.00
22642	Eq. End Jack	179.00
22643-(SS)	Eq. End Jack	246.00
22649-(SS)	Eq. End Jack	185.00
22652	Dog Leg Jack (Small)	128.00
22653	Dog Leg Jack (Small)	179.00
22654	Dog Leg Jack (Small)	118.00
22659	Dog Leg Jack (Small)	138.00
22659-(SS)	Dog Leg Jack (Small)	138.00
22663	Congress Pen (Small)	123.00
22664	Congress Pen (Small)	118.00
22679	Board Pen (Medium)	190.00
22682-(SS)	Eq. End Pen (Large)	205.00
22683	Eq. End Pen (Large)	155.00
22684	Eq. End Pen (Large)	189.00
22686	Eq. End Pen (Large)	160.00
11689	Eq. End Pen (Large)	185.00
22689-(SS)	Eq. End Pen (Large)	200.00
22716	Slim Jack	180.00

22719	Stock Pen	295.00
22726	Crown Jack	295.00

22729

22729	Crown Jack	295.00
22733	Bent Serpentine Jack (Large)	308.00
22736	Gunstock	290.00
22739	Bent Serpentine Jack (Large)	240.00
22749	Bent Serpentine Jack (Large)	425.00
22752	Doctor's Knife	380.00
22753	Doctor's Knife	425.00
22754	Doctor's Knife	215.00
22759	Doctor's Knife	390.00
22761	Pen (Large)	189.00
22762	Pen (Large)	205.00
22763	Pen (Large)	185.00
22766	Pen (Large)	160.00
22769	Pen (Large)	215.00
22772	Board Pen (Medium)	179.00
22773	Board Pen (Medium)	246.00
22779	Board Pen (Medium)	210.00
22783	Pen (Small)	174.00

22793	Pen (Medium)	251.00
22793-(SS)	Pen (Medium)	251.00
22794	Pen (Medium)	149.00
22796	Pen (Medium)	164.00
22799	Pen (Medium)	185.00
22799-N	Pen (Medium)	185.00
22813	Swell Center Pen (Small)	160.00
22814	Swell Center Pen (Small)	118.00
22819	Swell Center Pen (Small)	140.00
22822	Congress Pen (Small)	128.00
22823	Congress Pen (Small)	174.00
22833	Pen	175.00
22849	Jack (Medium)	190.00
22859	Board Jack (Medium)	190.00
22869	Gun Stock	144.00
22874	Serpentine Jack (Medium)	169.00
22877	Serpentine Jack	129.00
22879	Serpentine Jack	235.00
22879-(SS)	Serpentine Jack	195.00
22882	Equal End Jack (Small)	128.00
22883	Equal End Jack (Small)	174.00
22884	Equal End Jack (Small)	133.00
22886	Equal End Jack (Small)	110.00
22889	Equal End Jack (Small)	150.00
22893	Teardrop Jack (Medium)	256.00
22894	Teardrop Jack (Medium)	169.00

| 22896 | Teardrop Jack (Medium) | 150.00 |
| 22899 | Teardrop Jack (Medium) | 190.00 |

22899

22899	Jr. Teardrop Jack (Medium)	185.00
22906	Swell Center Jack (Medium)	190.00
22909	Swell Center Jack (Medium)	195.00
22911	Big Equal End Jack	256.00
22916	Big Equal End Jack Regulator	225.00
22919	Big Equal End Jack Regulator	300.00
22929	Big Sunfish/Elephant Toenail	495.00
22936	Big Sunfish/Elephant Toenail	400.00
22939	Half Whittler	325.00

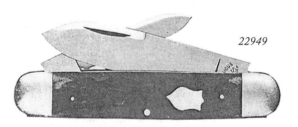

22949

22949	Big Equal End Pen	300.00
22952	Sleeveboard Pen (Large)	205.00
22959	Sleeveboard Pen (Large)	250.00

22963	Board Pen (Medium)	282.00
22964	Board Pen (Medium)	190.00
22967	Board Pen (Medium)	148.00
22969	Board Pen (Medium)	215.00
22979	Whittler Pen	292.00
23009	Stock Pen (Large)	267.00
23156	Warncliffe Pen	185.00
23224	Sleeveboard Pen	246.00
23229	Sleeveboard Pen	185.00
23232	Sleeveboard Pen (Medium)	179.00
23232-C	Sleeveboard Pen	179.00
23232-(SS)	Sleeveboard Pen	179.00
23234	Sleeveboard Pen	246.00
23236	Sleeveboard Pen	129.00
23642-(SS)	Sleeveboard Pen	179.00
23649	Sleeveboard Pen (Medium)	185.00
23662	Pen (Small)	128.00
23663	Pen (Small)	175.00
23669	Pen (Small)	165.00
N23672	Pen (Small)	128.00
23673	Pen (Small)	174.00
23679	Pen (Small)	133.00
23689	Pen (Medium)	185.00
23799	Pen (Medium)	185.00
24316	Open End Jack	129.00
24376	Easy Open Jack (Medium)	129.00

24377	Easy Open Jack	129.00
24379	Easy Open Jack	185.00
24396	Easy Open Jack (Large)	180.00
24397	Easy Open Jack (Large)	180.00
24399	Easy Open Jack (Large)	241.00
24409	Easy Open Jack	185.00
24889	Easy Open Jack	185.00
25152	Warncliffe Pen	179.00
30663	Pen (Open End)	200.00
30669	Pen (Open End)	165.00
30673	Pen (Open End)	215.00
30679	Pen (Open End)	265.00

30683

30683	Pen (Open End Medium)	210.00
30689	Pen (Open End Medium)	270.00
30693	Pen (Open End Medium)	240.00
30699	Pen (Open End Medium)	295.00
30773	Whittler Pen (Medium Open End)	241.00
32009	Stock (Large)	400.00
32019-C	Stock (Large)	405.00
32019-S	Stock (Large)	405.00

| 32029 | Stock (Medium) | 318.00 |

32039

32039	Hogback Stock	375.00
32049	Stock (Medium)	318.00
32053	Congress Whittler	385.00
32059	Congress Whittler	385.00
32059-B	Congress Whittler	385.00
32073	Equal End Pen (Medium)	255.00
32079	Equal End Pen (Medium)	235.00
32093	Swell Center Whittler	325.00
32096	Whittler	300.00
32097	Whittler	226.00
32099	Whittler	320.00
32109	Swell Center Stock	325.00
32153	Warncliffe Whittler	325.00
32125	Whittler (Small)	364.00
32126	Whittler (Small)	200.00
32129	Warncliffe Whittler	600.00
32131	Warncliffe (Large)	350.00
32133	Warncliffe Whittler	625.00
32136	Warncliffe (Large)	360.00

32139

32139	Warncliffe	349.00
32141	Stock (Premium)	282.00
32144	Stock (Premium)	282.00
32145	Stock (Premium)	393.00
32149	Stock (Premium)	275.00
32149-G	Stock (Premium)	275.00
32149-SH & G	Stock (Premium)	320.00
32149-P & Sh	Stock (Premium)	320.00
32153	Warncliffe Whittler	320.00
32156	Stock Whittler	220.00

32163

32159	Stock Whittler	350.00
32163	Whittler	265.00
32164	Whittler	256.00

32169	Whittler	325.00
32173	Stock (Premium)	395.00
32174	Stock (Premium)	285.00
32175	Stock (Premium)	395.00
32179	Stock (Premium)	355.00
32183	Stock (Serpentine)	385.00
32184	Stock (Premium)	279.00
32189	Stock (Premium)	323.00
32189-S	Stock (Equal End)	400.00
32189-G	Stock (Premium)	292.00
32189-S & G	Stock (Premium)	298.00
32199	Stock (Premium)	323.00
32203	Cattle (Large)	522.00
32204	Cattle (Large)	354.00
32204-G	Cattle (Large)	349.00
32204-C & G	Cattle (Large)	354.00
32205	Cattle (Large)	492.00
32206	Cattle (Large)	335.00
32206-C & G	Cattle (Large)	302.00
32206-G	Cattle (Large)	318.00
32209	Cattle (Large)	400.00
32209-G	Cattle (Large)	400.00
32209-C & G	Cattle (Large)	425.00
32209-G & P	Cattle (Large)	400.00
32209-S	Cattle (Large)	400.00
32209-S & C	Cattle (Large)	405.00

32209-S & G	Cattle (Large)	410.00
32223	Sleeveboard Pen	315.00
32233	Whittler (Small)	308.00
32243	Cattle/Stock (Medium)	349.00
32244	Cattle/Stock (Medium)	236.00
32245	Cattle/Stock (Medium)	328.00
32249	Cattle/Stock (Medium)	275.00
32294	Cattle/Stock	235.00
32389	Serpentine Jack	267.00
32401	Whittler (Large)	283.00
32403	Whittler (Large)	400.00
32404	Whittler (Large)	300.00
32406	Whittler (Large)	300.00
32409	Whittler (Large)	350.00
32443	Congress Whittler (Medium)	410.00
32449	Congress Whittler (Medium)	295.00
32459	Congress Whittler	390.00
32463	Congress Whittler	384.00
32469	Congress Whittler	385.00
32566	Whittler (Small)	345.00
32567	Whittler (Small)	350.00
32569	Whittler, Plumber's Knife	390.00
32575	Whittler (Large)	492.00
32576	Whittler (Large)	277.00
32579	Whittler (Large)	400.00
32586	Whittler (Large)	282.00

32589	Whittler (Large)	405.00
32593	Whittler (Medium)	225.00
32596	Whittler (Medium)	295.00
32599	Whittler (Medium)	310.00
32603	Board Pen (Medium)	295.00
32609	Board Pen (Medium)	300.00
32633	Board Pen (Medium)	313.00
32639	Board Pen (Medium)	385.00
32643	Whittler (Large)	350.00
32644	Whittler (Large)	354.00
32646	Whittler (Large)	300.00
32649	Whittler	320.00
32653	Whittler (Medium)	384.00
32654	Whittler (Medium)	354.00

32656

32656	Whittler	325.00
32659	Whittler-Engineer	390.00
32683	Whittler Pen (Medium)	313.00
32689	Whittler Pen (Medium)	292.00
32733	Gunstock Whittler	425.00
32734	Stock Whittler (Large)	282.00

32739	Gunstock Whittler (Large)	350.00
32743	Gunstock	425.00
32749	Gunstock	300.00
32775	Whittler Pen (Large)	320.00
32779	Whittler Pen (Large)	308.00
32793	Whittler Pen (Medium)	313.00
32794	Whittler Pen (Medium)	256.00
32799	Whittler Pen (Large)	308.00
32866	Whittler (Large)	350.00
32869	Whittler, Carpenter's Knife	441.00
32875	Whittler (Large)	492.00
32876	Whittler (Large)	350.00
32879	Whittler (Large)	410.00
32889	Big Whittler	460.00
32916	Big Whittler	282.00
32919	Big Whittler	410.00
32936	Whittler (Medium)	300.00
32937	Whittler (Medium)	300.00
32939	Whittler (Medium)	360.00
32956	Whittler (Medium)	300.00
32959	Whittler (Medium)	335.00
32963	Whittler (Medium)	315.00
32964	Whittler (Medium)	297.00
32969	Whittler (Medium)	297.00
32973	Whittler (Medium)	384.00
32976	Whittler (Medium)	277.00

32979

32979	Whittler (Medium)	297.00
32989	Swell Center Whittler	255.00
33073	Pen (Medium)	245.00
33079	Pen (Medium)	225.00
33669	Whittler Pen (Medium)	297.00
33673	Whittler Pen	220.00
33674	Whittler Pen	235.00
33679	Whittler Pen	297.00
33683	Whittler Pen	308.00
33689	Whittler Pen (Medium)	297.00
33693	Whittler Pen (Medium)	300.00
33699	Whittler Pen (Medium)	270.00
33773	Whittler Pen (Medium)	200.00
33793	Whittler Pen (Medium)	225.00
33794	Whittler Pen (Medium)	265.00
33799	Whittler Pen (Medium)	297.00
34399	Whittler Pen (Medium)	297.00
35141	Stock (Large)	282.00
35144	Stock (Large)	287.00
35151	Stock (Large)	282.00
40503	Equal End Pen (No bolster, Medium)	365.00
40593	Pen (No bolster, Medium)	246.00

40633	Pen (No bolster, Medium)	300.00
40663	Pen (No bolster, Medium)	210.00
40669	Pen (No bolster, Medium)	295.00
40673	Pen (No bolster, Medium)	300.00
40679	Pen (No bolster, Medium)	240.00
40683	Pen (No bolster, Medium)	185.00
40689	Pen (No bolster, Medium)	275.00
40693	Pen (No bolster)	241.00
40699	Open End Pen	275.00
40773	Pen (Equal End)	246.00

42049

42049	Congress (Medium)	310.00
42049-N	Congress (Medium)	325.00
42053	Congress	300.00
42059	Congress Whittler	295.00
42059-B	Congress Whittler	300.00
42069	Congress (Medium)	300.00
42070	Congress (Large)	308.00
42079	Congress (Large)	400.00
42093	Congress (Large)	275.00
42099	Congress (Large)	349.00
42109	Stock (Large)	355.00
42172	Stock (Large)	308.00

42179	Stock	282.00
42209-B	Cattle	323.00

42363

42363	Bartender	400.00
42369	Bartender	360.00
42453	Congress (Small)	325.00
42459	Congress (Small)	300.00
42463	Congress	295.00
42469	Congress	295.00
42503	Congress (Medium)	349.00
42509	Congress (Large)	385.00
42519	Congress (Large)	346.00
42559	Senator Pen (Large)	290.00
42633	Congress (Medium)	349.00
42639	Congress (Medium)	315.00
42689	Pen (Large)	215.00
42793	Senator Pen	246.00
42795	Pen (Medium)	215.00

42799

42799	Pen (Medium)	225.00
43073	Pen (Medium)	300.00
43559	Pen (Medium)	185.00
43593	Pen (Medium)	251.00
43663	Pen (Small)	179.00
43673	Pen (Small)	185.00
43679	Pen (Small)	325.00
43683	Board Pen (Medium)	190.00
43689	Board Pen (Medium)	240.00
43693	Equal End Pen (Medium)	285.00
43699	Equal End Pen (Medium)	325.00
43773	Equal End Pen (Medium)	200.00
221039	Open End Jack (Large)	241.00
221049	Open End Jack (Large)	241.00

The Robeson numbering system is excellent, perhaps the best. It is stamped on all Robeson-made knives except for some of the late contract knives.

The first figure in the number indicates the handle materials:

1. Black Composition
2. Rosewood
3. Yellow Composition
4. White Composition
5. Genuine Stag (or Metal)

6. Bone or Stag
7. Genuine Pearl
8. Mottled Composition
9. Gun Metal

The second figure indicates the number of blades:

1. One Blade
2. Two Blades
3. Three Blades

The third figure indicates the lining and bolsters:

1. Steel Liners and Bolsters
2. (or 6.) Brass Liners, Nickel Silver Bolsters
3. Nickel Silver Lining and Bolsters
9. Stainless or Chrome, Liners and Bolsters

The last figures indicate the pattern number.

Example: 211035
2 – Rosewood
1 – One blade
1 – Steel lining and bolsters
035 – Pattern number

211035. Gelding.

These are six of the 13 known stampings used by Robeson between 1895 and 1977.

ROBESON **PREMIER**	**ROBESON** *ShurEdge* **ROCHESTER**	**ROBESON** **CO.** **CUTLERY**
Circa 1895 – 1900	*Circa 1901 – 1948*	*Circa 1900 – 1948*

ROBESON *ShurEdge* **U.S.A.**	**ROBESON** **SHUREDGE** **U.S.A.**	**ROBESON** 0 0 0 0 0 0 **U.S.A.**
Circa 1920 – 1945	*Circa 1945 – 1965*	*Circa 1965 – 1977*

Number	Pattern Name	Collector Value

026319	Father & Son Set (Gift Boxed)	350.00
	622026-622319	
033750	Cattle (Large)	114.00
126056	Straight Jack (Large)	100.00
126240	Open End Jack (Large)	78.00
126636	Teardrop Jack (Large)	95.00

128105	Pen	65.00
132433	Cattle (Large)	107.00
2027	Easy Open Jack (Large)	155.00
211007	Hawkbill Pruner	56.00
211008	Open End Corn	65.00

211035	Gelding	65.00

Number	Pattern Name	Collector Value
222030	Gelding	67.00
222050	Equal Open End Broad Jack	227.00
22229	Teardrop Jack (Large)	113.00
226056	Open End Jack (Large)	188.00

322013	Equal End Jack (Large)	121.00
322286	Straight Jack	60.00
323404	Serpentine Pen (Small)	63.00
323480	Serpentine Jack	97.00
323617	Senator Pen	60.00

323646	Jack	116.00
323657	Serpentine Jack	69.00
323669	Dog Leg Jack	87.00
323675	Half Whittler	80.00
323676	Board Pen	80.00

Number	Pattern Name	Collector Value

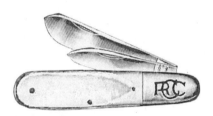

323817	Sleeveboard Pen	95.00
323826	Sleeveboard Pen (Large)	82.00
323865	Equal End Jack (Large)	80.00
324004	Equal End Pen	61.00
326011	Open End Jack (Small)	

326015	Equal End Jack	56.00
326245	Equal End Jack (Large)	69.00
333633	Cattle (Large)	126.00
33750	Stock	134.00
421179	Barlow	134.00

421200	Barlow	107.00

Number	Pattern Name	Collector Value
422064	Senator Pen	81.00
422174	Office Pen	80.00
422274	Office Pen	67.00
423405	Serpentine Pen	97.00

Number	Pattern Name	Collector Value
423480	Serpentine Jack	57.00
432868	Cattle	113.00
433594	Stock	100.00
435595	Cattle	108.00
433727	Stock	78.00

Number	Pattern Name	Collector Value
4525	Pen (Ger.)	47.00
4821	Equal End Pen (Ger.)	47.00
4822	Jack (Ger.)	50.00
4833	Stock (Ger.)	87.00
4864	Swiss Army (Ger.)	80.00

Number	Pattern Name	Collector Value

Number	Pattern Name	Collector Value
511168	Barlow	125.00
511178	Barlow	168.00
511179	Barlow	165.00
511224	Daddy Barlow	273.00
512224	Daddy Barlow	280.00
512872	Daddy Barlow (Stag)	169.00
512874	Daddy Barlow (Stag)	354.00
521168	Barlow	160.00
521178	Barlow	160.00
521179	Barlow	193.00
521199	Barlow	147.00
522027	Barlow	153.00

Number	Pattern Name	Collector Value
522482	Trapper	325.00
523858	Jack (Small)	118.00

Number	Pattern Name	Collector Value
529003	Pen	42.00
529007	Pen	48.00
529404	Pen	38.00

529735	Lobster (Small)	71.00
529740	Lobster (Small)	48.00
533167	Lobster	90.00
533278	Lobster	74.00
533279	Serpentine Pen	77.00
533750	Stock	121.00

533858	Pen	117.00
539445	Lobster	45.00
612060	Big FH Jack	234.00
612118	Big Coke FH	544.00
612246L	Big FH Coke	576.00

Number	Pattern Name	Collector Value

Number	Pattern Name	Collector Value
612407	Fish Knife	225.00
612610	Big FH Jack	288.00
616407	Tickler	210.00
621105	Board Pen	77.00
621177	Congress Pen	83.00
62232	Big FH Jack	358.00
622001	Equal End Pen (Large)	108.00
622003	Senator Pen	78.00

Number	Pattern Name	Collector Value
622013	Big Equal End Jack	111.00
622020	Straight Jack (Large)	128.00
622022	Sleeveboard Pen	108.00
622026	Sleeveboard Pen (Small)	77.00

Number	Pattern Name	Collector Value
622027	Easy Open End Jack (Large)	147.00
622037	Big Equal End Jack	211.00
622048	Equal End Jack (Small)	58.00
622056	Straight Jack (Large)	102.00
622061	Big Jack	147.00

Number	Pattern Name	Collector Value
622062	Big Jack	195.00
622064	Board Pen (Small)	78.00
622083	Straight Jack	89.00
622088	Senator Pen	148.00
622102	Sleeveboard Pen (Large)	102.00
622105	Sleeveboard Pen (Large)	83.00
622119	Big Jack FH	198.00

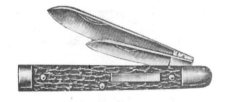

Number	Pattern Name	Collector Value
622138	Doctor's Knife (Large)	240.00
622151	Big Jack FH	275.00

Number	Pattern Name	Collector Value
622167	Senator Pen (Large)	90.00
622183	Peanut Jack	95.00

622187	Moose (Large)	235.00
622193	Senator Pen	125.00
622195	Doctor	205.00
622225	Doctor	210.00
622253	Board Pen	83.00
622299	Board Pen (Small)	70.00
622225	Serpentine Jack (Small)	58.00
622229	Serpentine Jack (Small)	58.00
622253	Serpentine Jack (Small)	70.00

622295	Serpentine Jack	110.00
622299	Board Pen (Small)	70.00
622319	Serpentine Jack	83.00

Number	Pattern Name	Collector Value

Number	Pattern Name	Collector Value
622331	Dog Leg Jack	87.00
622358	Dog Leg Jack (Large)	128.00
622382	Dog Leg Jack (Large)	210.00
622393	Peanut	102.00
622457	Straight Jack (Large)	143.00

Number	Pattern Name	Collector Value
622597	Straight Jack (Large)	85.00
622636	Straight Jack	77.00
622730	Straight Jack (Large)	108.00
622841	Sleeveboard Pen (Large)	128.00
62292	Big Jack	160.00
622847	Sleeveboard Pen	102.00
622317	Board Pen	90.00
623191	Board Pen	79.00
623405	Serpentine Pen	69.00
623422	Board Pen (Large)	108.00

Number	Pattern Name	Collector Value

623480	Serpentine Jack	110.00
623500	Warncliffe Pen	140.00
623501	Swell Center Pen	90.00
623505	Equal End Pen	83.00

623595	Muskrat	135.00
623603	Equal End Pen (Small)	64.00
623605	Equal End Pen (Small)	64.00
623662	Equal End Pen	83.00

623667	Jack	85.00
623671	Board Jack	90.00
623681	Equal End Pen	77.00
623698	Board Jack (Large)	102.00

Number	Pattern Name	Collector Value
623777	Senator Pen (Large)	98.00
623851	Senator Pen (Large)	90.00
623858	Sleeveboard Pen (Small)	90.00

Number	Pattern Name	Collector Value
623875	Woodcraft Pen	135.00
626041	Straight Jack	140.00
626052	Straight Jack (Large)	111.00
626054	Straight Jack (Large)	112.00
626056	Straight Jack (Large)	110.00
626094	Open End Jack	69.00
626104	Open End Jack	69.00

Number	Pattern Name	Collector Value
626204	Open End Jack	78.00
626240	Open End Jack	83.00
626241	Straight Jack	83.00
626242	Straight Jack	90.00
626285	Straight Jack (Large)	230.00
626331	Straight Jack (Small)	90.00

Number	Pattern Name	Collector Value

Number	Pattern Name	Collector Value
626636	Straight Jack	90.00
626637	Straight Jack	92.00
626639	Straight Jack	92.00
626765	Straight Jack	96.00

Number	Pattern Name	Collector Value
626766	Easy Open End Jack	85.00
629005	Equal End Pen	77.00
629675	Equal End Pen (Large)	100.00
632102	Equal End Pen (Large)	150.00
632167	Equal End Pen (Small)	155.00

Number	Pattern Name	Collector Value
632225	Whittler	190.00

Number	Pattern Name	Collector Value
632295	Stock	150.00
632319	Whittler (Small)	140.00
632596	Whittler (Large)	131.00
632750	Stock	220.00
632751	Stock	220.00
632768	Cattle (Small)	90.00

Number	Pattern Name	Collector Value
632831	Stock	141.00
632838	Stock (Small)	96.00
632868	Stock (Small)	95.00
632882	Stock (Large)	108.00
632992	Stock (Large)	128.00
633295TC	Stock (Large)	128.00
633593	Stock (Large)	128.00
633594	Stock (Large)	125.00
633595	Stock (Large)	160.00
633596	Stock (Large)	150.00
633662	Stock (Large)	125.00
633670	Stock (Small)	160.00
633681	Equal End Pen	110.00

Number	Pattern Name	Collector Value
633727	Stock (Small)	110.00
633728	Stock (Small)	118.00
633750	Stock (Small)	120.00
633830	Stock (Small)	158.00
633850	Stock Pen	92.00

Number	Pattern Name	Collector Value
633865	Cattle	156.00
633866	Cattle	140.00
633875	Stock	152.00
633880	Stock	132.00
633881	Stock	132.00
633884	Stock	150.00
633885	Stock	150.00

Number	Pattern Name	Collector Value
633886	Stock	110.00

Number	Pattern Name	Collector Value
642088	Stock (Large)	175.00
642208	Congress (Large)	200.00
642214	Scout	96.00
642385	Scout (Large)	110.00

Number	Pattern Name	Collector Value
643453	Congress (Large)	160.00
643594	Congress (Large)	140.00
643645	Congress (Large)	140.00
643777	Congress	205.00
722007	Senator Pen w/b	110.00
722064	Senator Pen	77.00
722083	Serpentine Jack	85.00
722105	Senator Pen	77.00
722110	Congress Pen	77.00
722167	Open End Pen	85.00

Number	Pattern Name	Collector Value
722183	Peanut	95.00

Number	Pattern Name	Collector Value
722319	SI	90.00
722363	Open End Pen	77.00
723167	Senator Pen (Small)	95.00
723273	Lobster Pen	95.00
723317	Open End Pen (Small)	95.00
723681	Open End Pen (Small)	95.00
732167	Open End Pen (Small)	105.00
732319	Whittler	120.00
733077	Sleeveboard Pen	105.00
733505	Senator Pen	105.00
733727	Stock	152.00

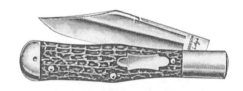

Number	Pattern Name	Collector Value
812118	Large FH Coke	197.00
812872	Big FH Coke	210.00
822023	Equal End Jack	75.00
822048	Jack (Small)	65.00
822061	Jack (Large)	155.00
822064	Senator Pen (Small)	65.00
822094	Open End Jack	75.00
822183	Dog Leg Jack (Small)	65.00
822253	Board Pen	65.00
822295	Serpentine Jack	70.00

Number	Pattern Name	Collector Value
822319	Serpentine Jack (Small)	65.00
822355	Serpentine Jack (Small)	65.00
822393	Serpentine Jack (Small)	60.00
822407	Fish Knife	70.00
822482	Tickler	207.00
822497	Tickler	135.00
822728	Moose	94.00
822850	Peanut	70.00
823505	Board Pen	75.00
823724	Board Pen	87.00
823850	Board Pen	69.00
823881	Cattle Pen	100.00
832597	Stock	128.00
837726	Stock	100.00
832838	Stock	108.00
832868	Stock	108.00

Number	Pattern Name	Collector Value
832883	Stock	108.00
833295	Stock	105.00
833594	Stock	105.00
833595	Stock	108.00
833850	Stock	115.00
833865	Stock	100.00
833867	Cattle	135.00
833880	Cattle	135.00
833881	Cattle	122.00
833887	Stock	100.00
922253	Cattle Pen	95.00
922295	Cattle Pen	95.00
922296	Open End Pen	68.00
922407	Fish Knife	68.00
922497	Tickler	127.00
929007	Open End Pen	52.00
939003	Open End Pen	52.00
939004	Open End Pen	52.00
939445	Lobster	71.00

Appendix 5
Remington Arms Company

While Remington's numbering system is stamped on nearly every knife they made, it is limited in the amount of information it gives about the knife.

The letter "R" which precedes all numbers simply denotes that the knife is a pocketknife, but don't be surprised if you find it on a small sheath knife also. There is no figure in the pattern to indicate the number or type of blades, but the last figure in the pattern number does indicate the handle material:

1. Redwood
2. Black Composition
3. Genuine Bone
4. Genuine Pearl
5. Pyremite or Celluloid
6. Genuine Stag
7. Ivory or White Bone
8. Cocobola Wood
9. Metal
10. English Buffalo Horn

The figures R1 to R2999 indicate Jack knives; R3000 to R5999 indicate knives in such classes as Cattle, Stock, Mechanic, etc.; and R6000 to R9999 indicate Pen knives.

*Numbers on the following chart indicate Bullet Shield Remingtons.

Number	Pattern Name	Collector Value
R01	Open End Jack (1 Blade)	165.00
R03	Open End Jack (1 Blade)	240.00
RA1	Open End Jack (1 Blade)	165.00
R1	Open End Jack	160.00
R3	Open End Jack	240.00
R5	Open End Jack	230.00
R015	Leg Knife	150.00
R 15	Leg Knife	315.00
R21	Open End Jack	145.00

Number	Pattern Name	Collector Value
R21CH	Open End Jack	150.00
R22	Open End Jack	155.00
R23	Open End Jack	170.00
R23Ch	Open End Jack	170.00
R25	Open End Jack	164.00
R31	Open End Jack	135.00
R32	Open End Jack	150.00

Number	Pattern Name	Collector Value

Number	Pattern Name	Collector Value
R33	Open End Jack	175.00
R33CH	Open End Jack	185.00
R35	Open End Jack	165.00
RB040	Barlow (1 Blade)	240.00
RB041	Barlow (1 Blade)	240.00
RB042	Barlow (1 Blade)	240.00
RB43 (and W)	Barlow	250.00
RB44 (and W)	Barlow	400.00
RB45	Barlow	230.00
RB46	Barlow	300.00
R52	Jack	200.00
R53	Jack	240.00
R55	Jack	230.00
R63	Jack	225.00
R65	Jack	130.00
R71	Open End Jack	165.00
R72	Open End Jack	200.00
R73	Open End Jack	240.00
R75	Open End Jack	230.00
R81	Open End Jack	165.00
R82	Open End Jack	210.00

Number	Pattern Name	Collector Value
R83	Open End Jack	240.00
R85	Open End Jack	235.00
R91	Open End Jack	165.00
R92	Open End Jack	210.00
R93	Open End Jack	250.00
R95	Open End Jack	225.00
R101	Jack	165.00
R102	Jack	211.00
R102CH	Jack	210.00
R103	Jack	240.00
R103CH	Jack	240.00
RI05	Jack	225.00
RI08CH	Jack	170.00
R111	Jack	165.00
R 112	Jack	210.00
R115	Jack	225.00
R123	Jack	240.00
R133	Jack	250.00
R135	Jack	225.00
R152	Jack (Teardrop)	215.00
R153	Jack (Teardrop)	240.00
R155	Jack (Teardrop)	225.00

Number	Pattern Name	Collector Value

Number	Pattern Name	Collector Value
R161	Jack (Teardrop)	170.00
R162	Jack (Teardrop)	210.00
R163	Jack (Teardrop)	250.00
R165	Jack (Teardrop)	225.00
R171	Jack (Large Teardrop)	175.00
R172	Jack (Large Teardrop)	215.00
R173	Jack (Large Teardrop)	250.00
R175	Jack (Large Teardrop)	225.00
R181	Jack	200.00
R183	Jack (Large Teardrop)	320.00
R185	Jack (Large Teardrop)	225.00
R191	Jack (Large Teardrop)	212.00
R192	Jack (Large Teardrop)	275.00
R193	Jack (Large Teardrop)	310.00
R195	Jack (Large Teardrop)	295.00
R201	Easy Open Jack	215.00

Number	Pattern Name	Collector Value

Number	Pattern Name	Collector Value
R203	Easy Open Jack	310.00
R205	Easy Open Jack	295.00
R211	Easy Open Jack	215.00
R212	Easy Open Jack	275.00
R213	Easy Open Jack	310.00
R219	Easy Open Jack	225.00
R222	Jack (Large Teardrop)	215.00
R223	Jack (Large Teardrop)	315.00
R225	Jack (Large Teardrop)	295.00
R232	Jack (Large Teardrop)	270.00
R233	Jack (Large Teardrop)	307.00
R232	Jack (Large Teardrop)	270.00
R235	Jack (Large Teardrop)	295.00
R242	Easy Open Jack	270.00
R243	Easy Open Jack	307.00
R245	Easy Open Jack	295.00
R252	Jack (Large Teardrop)	270.00
R253	Jack (Large Teardrop)	310.00
R255	Jack (Large Teardrop)	295.00
R262	Serpentine Jack	270.00

Number	Pattern Name	Collector Value
R263	Serpentine Jack	300.00
R265	Serpentine Jack	290.00
R272	Serpentine Jack (Large)	275.00
R273	Serpentine Jack (Large)	305.00
R275	Serpentine Jack (Large)	295.00
R282	Copperhead	275.00
R283	Copperhead	307.00
R293	Trapper	614.00
R303	Open End Trapper (1 Blade)	375.00
R305	Open End Trapper (1 Blade)	360.00
R313	Trapper	380.00

Number	Pattern Name	Collector Value
R315	Large Jack	361.00
R323	Equal End Jack	307.00
R325	Equal End Jack	290.00
R328	Equal End Jack	215.00
R333	Equal End Jack (Large)	315.00
R341	Equal End Jack (Acorn Shield)	215.00
R342	Equal End Jack	271.00
R343	Equal End Jack	350.00
R353	Equal End Jack	315.00
R355	Equal End Jack	290.00

Number	Pattern Name	Collector Value
R363	Equal End Jack	315.00
R365	Equal End Jack	295.00
R372	Equal End Jack (Acorn Shield)	280.00
R373	Equal End Jack (Acorn Shield)	350.00
R375	Equal End Jack (Acorn Shield)	300.00
R378	Equal End Jack (Acorn Shield)	250.00
R383	Big Equal End Jack	315.00
R391	Jack (Teardrop)	215.00
R392	Jack (Teardrop)	275.00
R395	Jack (Teardrop)	295.00
R402	Easy Open Jack (Acorn Shield)	295.00
R403	Easy Open Jack (Acorn Shield)	310.00
R405	Easy Open Jack (Acorn Shield)	300.00
R412	Easy Open Jack	270.00
R413	Easy Open Jack	300.00
R415	Easy Open Jack	290.00
R423	Easy Open Jack	295.00
R432	Doctor's	350.00
R433	Doctor's (Spatula)	400.00
R434	Doctor's	500.00
R435	Equal End Jack	365.00
R443	Doctor's	375.00

Number	Pattern Name	Collector Value

Number	Pattern Name	Collector Value
R444	Doctor's	425.00
R453	Doctor's	400.00
R455	Doctor's	360.00
R463	Equal End Jack (Acorn Shield)	310.00
R465	Equal End Jack (Acorn Shield)	295.00
R473	Equal End Jack	300.00
R475	Equal End Jack	280.00
R482	Equal End Jack	270.00
R483	Equal End Jack	300.00
R485	Equal End Jack	275.00
R488	Equal End Jack	215.00
R493	Equal End Jack	300.00
R495	Equal End Jack	295.00
R503	Equal End Jack	300.00
R505	Equal End Jack	295.00
R512	Equal End Jack	270.00
R513	Equal End Jack	300.00
R515	Equal End Jack	290.00
R523	Equal End Jack	305.00
R525	Equal End Jack	290.00
R551R	Equal End Jack	215.00
R552	Equal End Jack	270.00

Number	Pattern Name	Collector Value
R553	Equal End Jack	300.00
R555	Equal End Jack	295.00
R563	Equal End Jack (Acorn Shield)	310.00
R572	Equal End Jack	270.00
R573	Equal End Jack	300.00
R575	Equal End Jack	295.00
R583	Equal End Jack (Acorn Shield)	310.00
R585	Equal End Jack (Acorn Shield)	290.00
R590	Equal End Jack	300.00
R593	Equal End Jack	305.00
R603	Serpentine Jack (Medium)	240.00
R605	Serpentine Jack (Medium)	230.00
R609	Serpentine Jack (Medium)	190.00
R623	Serpentine Jack (Large)	305.00
R625	Serpentine Jack (Large)	290.00
R633	Serpentine Jack (Large)	310.00
R635	Serpentine Jack (Large)	290.00
R643	Stiletto (1 Blade)	300.00
R645	Stiletto (Switchblade)	600.00
R653	Stiletto (1 Blade)	350.00

Number	Pattern Name	Collector Value

Number	Pattern Name	Collector Value
R655	Automatic Stiletto (1 Blade)	400.00
R662	Big Jack (Teardrop)	335.00
R663	Big Jack (Teardrop)	400.00
R668	Big Jack (Teardrop)	320.00
R672	Big Jack (Teardrop)	335.00
R673	Dogleg Jack	310.00
R674	Dogleg Jack	400.00
R675	Dogleg Jack	295.00
R679	Dogleg Jack	190.00

Number	Pattern Name	Collector Value
R682	Gunstock	325.00
R683	Gunstock	400.00
R684	Gunstock	550.00
R693	Hawkbill (1 Blade)	230.00

Number	Pattern Name	Collector Value

Number	Pattern Name	Collector Value
R698	Hawkbill (1 Blade)	165.00
R703	Hawkbill	235.00
R708	Hawkbill	165.00
R713	Hawkbill	245.00
R718	Hawkbill	175.00

Number	Pattern Name	Collector Value
R723	Cobbler's Hawkbill (1 Blade)	245.00
R728	Cobbler's Hawkbill (1 Blade)	165.00
R733	Jack (Teardrop) (Acorn Shield)	310.00
R735	Jack (Teardrop) (Acorn Shield)	300.00
R743	Jack (Teardrop) (Acorn Shield)	320.00
R772	Jack (Teardrop)	210.00
R773	Jack (Teardrop)	250.00
R775	Jack (Teardrop)	230.00
R783	Jack (Teardrop)	305.00
R803	Serpentine Jack	300.00

Number	Pattern Name	Collector Value
R823	Serpentine Jack	300.00
R833	Stock Jack (Spay Blade)	305.00
R835	Stock Jack	295.00
R843	Serpentine Jack	295.00
R845	Serpentine Jack	300.00
R855	Serpentine Jack	300.00
R863	Serpentine Jack (Large)	310.00
R865	Serpentine Jack (Large)	300.00
R873	Sleeveboard Jack	240.00
R874	Sleeveboard Jack	315.00
R875	Sleeveboard Jack	225.00
R881	Open End Jack (Acorn Shield)	212.00
R883	Open End Jack (Acorn Shield)	238.00
R901	Open End Jack	212.00
R913	Equal End Jack	307.00
R921	Budding Knife	220.00
R933	Toothpick	410.00
R935	Toothpick	400.00
R943	Toothpick	360.00
R945	Toothpick	425.00
R953	Toothpick	440.00

R955	Toothpick	350.00

Number	Pattern Name	Collector Value
R963	Easy Open Jack	585.00
R965	Easy Open Jack	300.00

Number	Pattern Name	Collector Value
R971	Cotton Sampler	500.00
R982	Copperhead Jack	271.00
R983	Copperhead Jack	307.00
R985	Copperhead Jack	295.00
R992	Straight Jack	215.00
R993	Straight Jack	240.00
R995	Straight Jack	230.00
R1002	Straight Jack	215.00
R1003	Straight Jack	240.00
R1005	Straight Jack	230.00
R1012	Straight Jack (Large)	270.00
R1013	Straight Jack (Large)	308.00
R1022	Straight Jack (Large)	350.00
R1023	Straight Jack (Large)	400.00
R1032	Jack (Straight)	215.00
R1033	Jack (Straight)	240.00
R1035	Jack (Straight)	230.00
R1041	Jack (Straight)	165.00
R1042	Jack (Straight)	210.00

Number	Pattern Name	Collector Value
R1043	Jack (Straight)	240.00
R1045	Jack (Straight)	215.00
R1061	Open End Jack	165.00
R1062	Open End Jack	212.00
R1063	Open End Jack	230.00
R1065	Open End Jack	200.00
R1071	Open End Jack (Large)	212.00
R1072	Open End Jack (Large)	270.00
R1073	Open End Jack (Large)	307.00
R1083	Open End Jack (1 Blade)	200.00
R1085-W	Open End Jack (1 Blade)	200.00
R1093	Open End Jack (1 Blade)	200.00
R1103	Open End Jack	230.00
R1112	Open End Jack	212.00
R1113	Open End Jack	230.00

Number	Pattern Name	Collector Value
R1123	Folding Hunter Bullet (2 Blade)	2,350.00
R1128	Folding Hunter Bullet (1 Blade)	2,500.00
R1133	Big Open End Jack (1 Blade)	375.00

Number	Pattern Name	Collector Value
R1143	Folding Hunter Open End Jack	750.00
R1153	Big Folding Hunter Jack	750.00
R1163	Big Folding Hunter Jack	700.00

Number	Pattern Name	Collector Value
R1173	Baby Bullet (2 Blade)	2,700.00
R1182	Swell Center Jack (Large)	332.00
R1183	Swell Center Jack (Large)	375.00
R1192	Swell Center Jack (Large)	322.00
R1193	Swell Center Jack (Large)	375.00
R1202	Swell Center Jack	278.00
R1203	Swell Center Jack	310.00
R1212	Equal End Jack	350.00
R1213	Equal End Jack	375.00
R1222	Board Jack (Large)	335.00
R1223	Board Jack (Large)	380.00
R1225	Board Jack (Large)	360.00
R1232	Big Swell Center Jack	220.00
R1233	Big Swell Center Jack	310.00
RB1240	Daddy Barlow	410.00
RB1241	Daddy Barlow	400.00
RB1242	Daddy Barlow	380.00

Number	Pattern Name	Collector Value
RB1243	Daddy Barlow	400.00

R1253	Trapper, Bullet (Lock Blade)	2,000.00
R1263	Trapper, Bullet (2 Blade)	2,200.00

R1273	Trapper, Bullet (2 Blade)	2,300.00
R1283	Jack (Swell Center)	310.00
R1284	Jack (Swell Center)	305.00
R1285	Jack (Swell Center)	295.00
R1293	Toothpick	310.00
R1295	Toothpick Bullet	1,150.00

R1306	Folding Hunter Bullet	2,800.00
R1315	Slim Open End Trapper	360.00
R1323	Dogleg Jack	240.00

Number	Pattern Name	Collector Value
R1324	Dogleg Jack	312.00
R1333	Equal End Jack	240.00
R1343	Straight Jack (Large)	420.00
R1353	Dogleg Jack (Large)	375.00
R1363	Dogleg Jack (Large)	375.00
R1383	Stiletto Lockback	500.00
R1379	Open End Jack	200.00
R1389	Open End Jack	185.00
R1399	Open End Jack (1 Blade)	150.00
R1409	Open End Jack	200.00
R1413	Serpentine Jack	235.00
R1423	Serpentine Jack	235.00
R1437	Pruner (1 Blade)	185.00
R1447	Budding (1 Blade)	185.00
R1457	Budding (1 Blade)	250.00
R1465	Budding (1 Blade)	185.00
R1477	Budding (1 Blade)	185.00
R1483	Serpentine Jack	230.00
R1485	Serpentine Jack	200.00
R1493	Serpentine Jack	235.00
R1495	Serpentine Jack	200.00
R1535	Florist	230.00
R1545	Budding	230.00
R1555	Budding	230.00

Number	Pattern Name	Collector Value
R1568	Florist	235.00
R1572	Jack (Open End)	220.00
R1573	Jack (Open End)	235.00
R1573Ch	Jack (Open End)	250.00
R1582	Jack (Open End)	210.00
R1592	Jack	225.00
R1593	Jack	240.00
R1595	Jack	230.00
R1608	Banana	220.00

R1613	Fish Knife	2,500.00
R1615	Round B. Shield	615.00
R1623	Jack (Open End)	243.00
R1623Ch	Jack (Open End)	250.00
RB1630	Daddy Barlow Lockback	650.00
R1643	Jack	240.00
R1644	Jack	312.00
R1645	Jack	230.00
R1653	Peanut	175.00
R1655	Peanut	156.00
R1668	Peanut	150.00
R1671	Budding	170.00
R1673	Budding	240.00

Number	Pattern Name	Collector Value
R1687	Budding	360.00
R1697	Budding	360.00
R1707	Budding	360.00
R1717	Budding	360.00

Number	Pattern Name	Collector Value
R2403	Automatic	900.00
R3003	Cattle (Acorn Shield)	400.00

Number	Pattern Name	Collector Value
R3013	Cattle	419.00
R3033	Cattle (Acorn Shield)	400.00
R3050	Stock	350.00
R3050-Buf	Stock	420.00
R3053	Stock	410.00
R3054	Stock	540.00
R3055	Stock	500.00
R3056	Stock	510.00
R3059	Stock	300.00
R3062	Stock	378.00

Number	Pattern Name	Collector Value
R3063	Stock	410.00
R3065	Stock	400.00
R3073	Stock	405.00
R3083	Stock	410.00
R3093	Stock	410.00
R3103	Stock	410.00
R3113	Stock Pen	305.00
R3115	Stock Pen	300.00
R3123	Moose	415.00
R3133	Stock (4 Blade Acorn Shield)	515.00
R3143	Stock (5 Blade Acorn Shield)	1,550.00
R3153	Cattle	375.00
R3155	Cattle	360.00
R3163	Cattle	360.00
R3173	Cattle	380.00

Number	Pattern Name	Collector Value
R3183	Cattle	375.00
R3185	Cattle	360.00
R3193	Cattle	375.00
R3203	Cattle	380.00
R3213	Stock (Large)	410.00

Number	Pattern Name	Collector Value
R3233	Stock (Large)	375.00
R3243	Cattle	375.00
R3253	Cattle	375.00
R3263	Cattle	375.00
R3273	Cattle	511.00
R3274	Cattle	500.00
R3283	Cattle	375.00
R3293	Cattle	380.00
R3303	Cattle (4 Blade)	511.00
R3313	Cattle (4 Blade)	515.00
R3322	Scout	275.00

RS3333	Official Scout	310.00
R3335	Scout	300.00
R3353	Cattle Pen	310.00
R3363	Cattle Pen (Large)	325.00
R3372	Cattle Pen (Large)	300.00
R3373	Cattle Pen (Large)	325.00
R3382	Cattle Pen (Acorn Shield)	290.00

Number	Pattern Name	Collector Value
R3383	Cattle Pen (Acorn Shield)	310.00

Number	Pattern Name	Collector Value
R3393	Birdseye Pen	275.00
R3395	Birdseye Pen	260.00
R3413	Cattle	375.00
R3414	Cattle (Acorn Shield)	525.00
R415	Cattle (Acorn Shield)	361.00
R3423	Cattle (Acorn Shield)	400.00
R3424	Cattle (Acorn Shield)	525.00
R3432	Birdseye (2 Blade)	250.00
R3433	Birdseye (2 Blade)	275.00
R3435	Birdseye (2 Blade)	260.00
R3442	Board Pen (Large)	250.00
R3443	Board Pen	275.00
R3445	Board Pen	260.00
R3453	Cattle (Large)	512.00
R3455	Cattle	450.00
R3463	Cattle	400.00
R3465	Cattle	400.00
R3475	Cattle	360.00
R3483	Stock (Large Acorn Shield)	410.00
R3484	Stock (Large Acorn Shield)	435.00
R3485	Stock (Large Acorn Shield)	395.00

Number	Pattern Name	Collector Value
R3489	Stock (Large Acorn Shield)	260.00
R3493	Stock (Large)	345.00
R3494	Stock (Large)	550.00
R3499	Stock (Large)	275.00
R3500	Stock	300.00
R3503	Stock	350.00
R3504	Stock	500.00
R3505	Stock	330.00
R3513	Stock (Large Acorn Shield)	410.00
R3514	Stock (Large Acorn Shield)	450.00
R3515	Stock (Large Acorn Shield)	400.00
R3520	Stock	200.00
R3523	Stock	350.00
R3524	Stock	500.00
R3525	Stock	330.00
R3533	Stock Pen	310.00
R3535	Stock Pen	295.00
R3553	Stock	350.00

Number	Pattern Name	Collector Value
R3555	Stock	375.00
R3563	Stock (Large Acorn Shield)	410.00

Number	Pattern Name	Collector Value
R3565G	Stock (Large Acorn Shield)	400.00
R3573	Stock (Acorn Shield)	350.00
R3593	Stock (Lock)	375.00
R3600	Stock	275.00
R3603	Stock	350.00
R3604	Stock	500.00
R3613	Stock	350.00
R3643	Stock	340.00
R3644	Stock	495.00
R3645	Stock	330.00
R3653	Stock (Acorn Shield)	350.00
R3655	Stock (Acorn Shield)	345.00
R3665	Stock (Acorn Shield)	345.00
R3675	Stock (Large)	490.00

Number	Pattern Name	Collector Value
R3683	Cattle	320.00
R3693	Cattle (Large Acorn Shield)	510.00
R3704	Stock (4 Blade)	670.00
R3713	Stock (4 Blade)	520.00
R3714	Stock (4 Blade Acorn Shield)	675.00
R3722	Big Whittler	395.00

Number	Pattern Name	Collector Value
R3723	Big Whittler	600.00
R3732	Big Whittler	400.00

R3843	Scout	300.00
R3853	Hawkbill Pruner	307.00
R3863	Scout (Acorn Shield)	400.00
R3873	Stock	345.00
R3874	Stock	450.00
R3875	Stock	330.00
R3883	Stock Pen	275.00

R3893	Stock Pen	270.00
R3895	Stock Pen	265.00
R3903	Moose	410.00
R3923	Stock	345.00
R3926	Stock	420.00

Number	Pattern Name	Collector Value
R3932	Big Whittler	400.00
R3933	Big Whittler	410.00
R3942	Big Board Pen	400.00
R3943	Big Board Pen	310.00
R3952	Board Pen (Large)	250.00
R3953	Board Pen (Large Punch Lock)	275.00
R3955	Board Pen (Large)	270.00
R3963	Board Pen (Large)	275.00
R3965	Board Pen (Large)	270.00
R3973	Stock	345.00
R3975	Stock	330.00
R3983	Whittler (Acorn Shield)	410.00
R3985	Whittler (Acorn Shield)	395.00
R3993	Stock	345.00
R4003	Stock Pen	295.00
R4005	Stock Pen	295.00
R4013	Moose	415.00
R4023	Stock (Acorn Shield)	510.00
R4033	Stock	285.00
R4043	Stock	290.00
R4053	Stock (Acorn Shield)	300.00
R4063	Stock (4 Blade Acorn Shield)	375.00
R4073	Stock (Acorn Shield)	340.00
R4075	Stock (Acorn Shield)	425.00

Number	Pattern Name	Collector Value
R4083	Stock	290.00
R4085	Stock	328.00
R4093	Stock (Acorn Shield)	300.00

Number	Pattern Name	Collector Value
R4095	Stock (Acorn Shield)	310.00
R4103	Serpentine Pen	251.00
R4105	Serpentine Pen	280.00
R4113	Stock	320.00
R4114	Stock	545.00
R4123	Stock	350.00

Number	Pattern Name	Collector Value
R4124	Stock	545.00
R4133	Stock	340.00
R4134	Stock	480.00
R4135	Stock	295.00
R4143	Stock Pen	230.00
R4144	Stock Pen	357.00

Number	Pattern Name	Collector Value
R4145	Stock Pen	290.00
R4163	Stock (Acorn Shield)	340.00
R4173	Stock (Acorn Shield)	340.00
R4175	Stock (Acorn Shield)	328.00
R4203	Stock	290.00
R4213	Stock	340.00

R4223	Scout (Official)	341.00
RS4233	Scout (Official)	341.00
R4235	Scout (Official)	330.00

R4243	Big Scout (Bullet)	2,300.00
R4253	Stock Pen	231.00
R4263	Cattle	375.00
R4273	Cattle	375.00
R4274	Cattle	500.00
R4283	Cattle (5 Blade)	800.00
R4293	Stock (Acorn Shield)	341.00

Number	Pattern Name	Collector Value
R4303	Stock (Acorn Shield)	341.00
R4313	Stock (Bowback)	410.00
R4323	Girl Scout	307.00

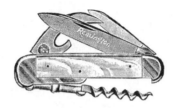

Number	Pattern Name	Collector Value
R4334	Bartender	357.00
R4336	Bartender	390.00
R4343	Board Pen (Large)	231.00
R4345	Board Pen (Large)	262.00

Number	Pattern Name	Collector Value
R4353	*Cattle (Bullet 2 Blade)	2,500.00
R4363	*Cattle (Bullet)	2,500.00
R4365	Cattle (Acorn Shield)	361.00
R4373	Girl Scout (Official)	310.00
R4383	Scout (Acorn Shield)	310.00
R4384	Scout (Acorn Shield)	402.00
R4393	Scout	300.00
R4394	Scout	400.00

Number	Pattern Name	Collector Value
R4403	Stock	290.00
R4413	Cattle (Small)	231.00
R4423	Cattle (Small)	231.00
R4425	Cattle (Small)	262.00
R4433	Whittler	320.00
R4443	Board Pen (Large)	260.00

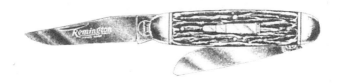

Number	Pattern Name	Collector Value
R4466	*Muskrat (Bullet 2 Blade)	2,800.00
R4473	Cattle Pen (Large)	252.00
R4483	Cattle (Large)	328.00
R4495	Florist Pen	262.00
R4505	Stock (Medium)	295.00
R4506	Stock (Medium)	355.00
R4513	Stock (Large)	341.00
RC4523	Scout (Official)	310.00
RC4533	Scout	300.00
R4548	Electrician (Pen)	225.00
R4555	Stock (Medium)	295.00
R4563	Stock (Large)	450.00
R4573	Cattle	310.00
R4583	Cattle	300.00
R4593	Muskrat	295.00

Number	Pattern Name	Collector Value
R6013	Congress Pen	231.00
R6014	Congress Pen	357.00
R6015	Congress Pen	262.00
R6023	Pen	318.00
R6024	Pen	500.00
R6032	Congress	301.00
R6033	Congress	350.00
R6034	Congress	485.00
R6043	Congress	350.00
R6053	Congress	450.00
R6063	Congress Pen (2 Blade)	300.00
R6073	Congress	475.00
R6083	Congress	400.00
R6093	Congress Pen	280.00
R6103	Congress Pen	280.00
R6104	Congress Pen	360.00
R6105	Congress Pen	262.00
R6113	Congress	280.00
R6123	Congress	277.00
R6133	Whittler	318.00
R6143	Congress Pen	275.00
R6145	Congress Pen	262.00
R6153	Congress Pen	231.00
R6155	Congress Pen	262.00
R6163	Congress Pen	231.00

Number	Pattern Name	Collector Value

Number	Pattern Name	Collector Value
R6175	Office	182.00
R6182	Pen (Medium)	200.00
R6183	Pen (Medium)	202.00
R6184	Pen (Medium)	312.00
R6185	Pen (Medium)	229.00
R6192	Pen (Medium)	200.00
R6193	Pen (Medium)	202.00
R6194	Pen (Medium)	312.00
R6195	Pen (Medium)	230.00
R6203	Pen (Medium)	202.00
R6204	Pen (Medium)	310.00
R6205	Pen (Medium)	230.00
R6213	Whittler Pen	231.00
R6214	Whittler Pen	357.00
R6215	Whittler Pen	263.00
R6223	Whittler Pen	231.00
R6224	Whittler Pen	355.00
R6225	Whittler Pen	300.00
R6233	Whittler Pen (4 Blade)	300.00
R6234	Whittler Pen (4 Blade)	470.00
R6242	Lobster Pen	211.00

Number	Pattern Name	Collector Value
R6244	Lobster Pen	311.00
R6245	Lobster Pen	228.00
R6249	Lobster Pen	145.00
R6255	Lobster Pen	228.00
R6259	Lobster Pen	140.00
R6265	Whittler Pen (2 Blade)	350.00
R6275	Whittler	360.00
R6285	Whittler	361.00
R6293	Whittler	316.00
R6303	Whittler Pen (2 Blade)	300.00
R6313	Whittler	310.00
R6323	Whittler	316.00
R6325	Whittler	250.00
R6330	Whittler	300.00
R6333	Whittler	320.00
R6334	Whittler	490.00
R6335	Whittler	360.00
R6340Buf	Whittler	231.00
R6343	Whittler	300.00

Number	Pattern Name	Collector Value
R6344	Whittler	490.00
R6353	Whittler	320.00

Number	Pattern Name	Collector Value
R6363	Whittler Pen (2 Blade)	320.00
R6390	Whittler	310.00
R6393	Whittler	325.00
R6394	Whittler	500.00
R6395	Whittler	350.00
R6403	Whittler	325.00
R6404	Whittler	500.00
R6423	Lobster Pen	200.00
R6424	Lobster Pen	300.00
R6429	Lobster Pen	146.00
R6433	Lobster	200.00
R6434	Lobster	300.00
R6439	Lobster	145.00
R6443	Lobster	231.00
R6444	Lobster	350.00
R6445	Lobster	600.00

Number	Pattern Name	Collector Value
R6454	Whittler (Lockback)	600.00
R6456	Lobster Pen	270.00
R6463	Equal End Pen	203.00
R6464	Equal End Pen	310.00
R6465	Equal End Pen	220.00

Number	Pattern Name	Collector Value
R6473	Pen (Medium)	203.00
R6474	Pen (Medium)	300.00
R6483	Pen (Medium)	200.00
R6484	Pen (Medium)	312.00
R6494	Pen (No bolsters)	150.00
R6495	Pen (No bolsters)	131.00
R6499	Pen (No bolsters)	100.00
R6504	Pen (Medium)	300.00
R6514	Pen (Medium)	145.00
R6519	Pen (Medium)	145.00
R6520	Whittler	210.00
R6523	Whittler	317.00
R6524	Whittler	490.00
R6533	Whittler	320.00
R6534	Whittler	500.00
R6535	Whittler	360.00
R6543	Whittler (Acorn Shield)	340.00
R6545	Whittler (Acorn Shield)	375.00

R6554	Lobster Pen	300.00
R6559	Lobster	147.00
R6563	Sleeve Board Pen	202.00

Number	Pattern Name	Collector Value
R6565	Sleeveboard Pen	230.00
R6573	Sleeveboard Pen	190.00
R6583	Sleeveboard Pen	202.00
R6585	Sleeveboard Pen	230.00
R6593	Whittler	320.00
R6603	Whittler	325.00
R6604	Whittler	500.00
R6605	Whittler	360.00
R6613	Whittler	317.00
R6623	Board Pen	231.00
R6624	Board Pen	350.00
R6625	Board Pen	260.00
R6633	Board Pen	225.00
R6634	Board Pen	345.00
R6635	Board Pen	225.00
R6643	Board Pen	235.00
R6644	Board Pen	355.00
R6645	Board Pen	262.00
R6653	Sleeveboard Pen	230.00
R6654	Sleeveboard Pen	310.00
R6655	Sleeveboard Pen	225.00
R6663	Congress Pen	230.00
R6664	Congress Pen	350.00
R6673	Congress	235.00

Number	Pattern Name	Collector Value

Number	Pattern Name	Collector Value
R6674	Congress	580.00
R6683	Congress	344.00
R6693	Congress	350.00
R6694	Congress	580.00
R6695	Congress	428.00
R6703	Board Pen (4 Blade)	260.00
R6704	Board Pen (4 Blade)	401.00
R6705	Board Pen (4 Blade)	295.00
R6713	Board Pen (4 Blade)	275.00
R6714	Board Pen (4 Blade)	402.00
R6723	Whittler	320.00
R6724	Whittler	490.00
R6725	Whittler	360.00
R6733	Equal End Pen	231.00
R6735	Equal End Pen	262.00
R6744	Sleeveboard Pen (No bolsters)	312.00
R6745	Sleeveboard Pen (No bolsters)	225.00
R6754	Whittler	490.00
R6755	Whittler	360.00
R6763	Congress Whittler	288.00
R6764	Congress Whittler	445.00
R6773	Congress Whittler	285.00

Number	Pattern Name	Collector Value

Number	Pattern Name	Collector Value
R6785	Office	229.00
R6793	Pen	144.00
R6795	Pen	165.00
R6803	Whittler	325.00
R6805	Whittler	360.00

Number	Pattern Name	Collector Value
R6816	Whittler Lockback	1,525.00
R6823	Whittler	1,100.00
R6825	Whittler	900.00
R6834	Whittler	950.00

Number	Pattern Name	Collector Value
R6835	Whittler	800.00
R6836	Whittler	800.00
R6843	Pen (No bolsters)	115.00
R6844	Pen (No bolsters)	150.00

Number	Pattern Name	Collector Value
R6845	Pen (No bolsters)	131.00
R6854	Pen (No bolsters)	150.00
R6859	Pen (No bolsters)	85.00
R6863	Pen (Small)	115.00
R6864	Pen (Small)	175.00
R6865	Pen (Small)	130.00
R6872	Pen (Small)	68.00
R6873	Pen (Small)	100.00
R6874	Pen (Small)	165.00
R6875	Pen (Small)	105.00
R6883	Warncliffe (2 Blade)	260.00
R6885	Warncliffe (2 Blade)	295.00
R6893	Warncliffe Whittler	425.00

Number	Pattern Name	Collector Value
R6894	Warncliffe Whittler	525.00
R6903	Pen (Small)	150.00
R6904	Pen (Small)	170.00
R6905	Pen (Small)	105.00
R6914	Pen (Small No bolsters)	150.00
R6919	Pen (Small)	84.00
R6923	Congress Pen (2 Blade)	183.00
R6924	Congress Pen (2 Blade)	312.00

Number	Pattern Name	Collector Value
R6925	Congress Pen (2 Blade)	229.00
R6933	Congress	341.00
R6934	Congress	446.00
R6949	Congress	745.00
R6954	Whittler Pen	350.00
R6956	Whittler Pen	315.00
R6964	Pen (Medium)	308.00
R6966	Pen (Medium)	275.00
R6973	Whittler Pen (4 Blade)	317.00
R6974	Whittler Pen (4 Blade)	490.00
R6984	Whittler Pen (Worked Back 4 Blade)	825.00
R6993	Warncliffe Pen (2 Blade)	317.00
R6994	Whittler Pen (1 Blade)	325.00
R6995	Whittler Pen (2 Blade)	360.00
R7003	Whittler	317.00
R7004	Whittler	490.00

R7005	Whittler (Swell Center)	394.00
R7023	Whittler	318.00
R7024	Whittler	490.00
R7026	Whittler	460.00
R7034	Lobster	300.00

Number	Pattern Name	Collector Value
RG7039/5	Lobster	147.00
RG7039/6	Lobster	275.00
RG7039/7	Lobster	220.00
RG7039/8	Lobster	165.00
R7044	Pen (Small Fob)	175.00

Number	Pattern Name	Collector Value
RG7049/21	Pen (Small Fob)	110.00
RG7049/22	Pen (Small Fob)	105.00
RG7049/23	Pen (Small Fob)	100.00
RG7049/24	Pen (Small Fob)	125.00
R7054	Pen (Small Fob)	135.00
RG7059/17	Pen (Small Fob)	100.00
RG7059/18	Pen (Small Fob)	110.00
RG7059/19	Pen (Small Fob)	110.00
RG7059/20	Pen (Small Fob)	105.00
RG7059/38	Pen (Small Fob)	100.00
RG7059/39	Pen (Small Fob)	100.00
RG7059/40	Pen (Small Fob)	110.00

Number	Pattern Name	Collector Value
R7064	Pen (Small Fob)	178.00

739

Number	Pattern Name	Collector Value
RG7069/25	Pen (Small Fob)	100.00
RG7069/26	Pen (Small Fob)	125.00
RG7069/27	Pen (Small Fob)	110.00
RG7069/28	Pen (Small)	105.00
R7074	Lobster (Small Fob 2 Blade)	135.00
RG7079/9	Lobster (Small Fob 2 Blade)	100.00
RG7079/10	Lobster (Small Fob 2 Blade)	100.00
RG7079/11	Lobster (Small Fob 2 Blade)	100.00
RG7079/12	Lobster (Smal] Fob 2 Blade)	100.00
RG7079/35	Lobster (Small Fob 2 Blade)	105.00
RG7079/36	Lobster (Small Fob 2 Blade)	105.00
RG7079/37	Lobster (Small Fob 2 Blade)	100.00
R7084	Lobster (Small Fob 2 Blade)	140.00
RG7089/13	Lobster (Small Fob 2 Blade)	85.00
RG7089/14	Lobster (Small Fob 2 Blade)	100.00
RG7089/15	Lobster (Small Fob 2 Blade)	90.00
RG7089/16	Lobster (Small Fob 2 Blade)	105.00
RG7089/32	Lobster (Small Fob 2 Blade)	85.00
RG7089/33	Lobster (Small Fob 2 Blade)	85.00
RG7089/34	Lobster (Small Fob 2 Blade)	95.00
R7094	Lobster Pen (Small Fob)	100.00
RG7099/1	Lobster Pen (Small Fob)	90.00
RG7099/2	Lobster Pen (Small Fob)	95.00
RG7099/3	Lobster Pen (Small Fob)	100.00
RG7099/4	Lobster Pen (Small Fob)	110.00
RG7099/29	Lobster Pen (Small Fob)	95.00

Number	Pattern Name	Collector Value
RG7099/30	Lobster Pen (Small Fob)	100.00
RG7099/31	Lobster Pen (Small Fob)	95.00
R7103	Pen (Medium)	202.00

Number	Pattern Name	Collector Value
R7104	Pen (Medium)	312.00
R7114	Whittler Pen (2 Blade)	312.00
R7116	Whittler Pen (2 Blade)	275.00
R7120Buf	Board Pen (Medium 4 Blade)	260.00
R7124	Board Pen (Medium 4 Blade)	300.00
R7126	Board Pen (Medium 4 Blade)	275.00
R7134	Board Pen (Medium 4 Blade)	300.00
R7144	Board Pen (Medium 4 Blade)	300.00
R7146	Board Pen (Medium 4 Blade)	275.00
R7153	Board Pen (2 Blade)	205.00
R7163	Board Pen (2 Blade)	206.00
R7176	Board Pen (2 Blade)	200.00
R7183	Whittler	315.00
R7196	Whittler	410.00
R7203	Whittler	320.00
R7216	Whittler	400.00
R7223	Whittler (2 Blade)	202.00
R7224	Whittler (2 Blade)	310.00
R7225	Whittler (2 Blade)	230.00

Number	Pattern Name	Collector Value
R7234	Whittler (2 Blade)	312.00
R7236	Whittler (2 Blade)	275.00

Number	Pattern Name	Collector Value
R7244	Whittler	490.00
R7246	Whittler	430.00
R7254	Pen (Small 2 Blade)	200.00
R7264	Lobster (2 Blade)	200.00
R7274	Lobster (2 Blade)	200.00
R7284	Lobster	222.00
R7284/5	Lobster	222.00
R7293	Whittler (Large)	550.00
R7309	Pen (Medium)	147.00
R7319	Pen (Medium)	147.00
R7324	Lobster (3 Blade)	200.00
R7329	Lobster (3 Blade)	147.00
R7339	Pen (Medium)	147.00
R7343	Jack (Medium)	200.00
R7344	Jack (Medium)	312.00
R7353	Pen (Medium 4 Blade)	200.00
R7364	Lobster Pen (4 Blade)	202.00
R7366	Lobster Pen (4 Blade)	275.00
R7374	Lobster (Small 3 Blade)	220.00
R7384	Lobster (Small 3 Blade)	223.00
R7394	Lobster (Small 3 Blade)	222.00
R7396	Lobster (Small 3 Blade)	195.00

Number	Pattern Name	Collector Value
R7403	Pen (Medium 3 Blade)	200.00
R7404	Pen (Medium 3 Blade)	310.00

Number	Pattern Name	Collector Value
R7414	Pen (Medium 2 Blade)	313.00
R7423	Pen (Medium 2 Blade)	200.00
R7433	Whittler	231.00
R7443	Whittler Pen (Medium)	200.00
R7453	Whittler Pen (Medium)	200.00
R7463	Whittler Pen (Medium)	200.00
R7465	Whittler Pen (Medium)	290.00
R7473	Whittler Pen (Medium)	200.00
R7475	Whittler Pen (Medium)	295.00
R7483	Whittler	315.00
R7485	Whittler	460.00
R7493	Whittler Pen	250.00
R7495	Whittler Pen	275.00
R7500Buf	Whittler	231.00
R7503	Whittler	315.00
R7513	Whittler	316.00
R7526	Warncliffe Pen	350.00
R7536	Warncliffe Pen	300.00
R7544	Whittler Pen	312.00

Number	Pattern Name	Collector Value
R7546	Whittler Pen	275.00
R7554	Whittler Pen	312.00
R7564	Warncliffe Pen	312.00
R7566	Warncliffe Pen	352.00
R7574	Warncliffe Pen	312.00
R7576	Warncliffe Pen	350.00
R7584	Whittler (Small)	312.00
R7586	Whittler (Small)	275.00
R7594	Whittler (Small)	312.00
R7596	Whittler (Small)	275.00
R7604	Whittler Pen (Small 4 Blade)	300.00
R7606	Whittler Pen (Small Blade)	350.00
R7613	Whittler Pen (Medium)	212.00
R7614	Whittler Pen (Medium)	300.00
R7623	Whittler Pen (Medium)	212.00
R7624	Whittler Pen (Medium)	312.00
R7633	Whittler	317.00
R7643	Whittler Pen (2 Blade)	230.00
R7645	Whittler Pen (2 Blade)	225.00
R7653	Whittler	318.00
R7654	Whittler	360.00

Number	Pattern Name	Collector Value
R7663	Whittler	318.00
R7664	Whittler	368.00
R7674	Pen (Small)	223.00
R7683	Pen (Small)	144.00
R7684	Pen (Small)	220.00
R7696	Whittler (Medium)	460.00
R7706	Whittler (Medium)	460.00
R7713	Pen (Small)	144.00
R7725	Budding Knife (2 Blade Pen)	130.00
R7734	Pen (Small No Bolsters)	220.00
R7744	Pen (Small No Bolsters)	221.00

Number	Pattern Name	Collector Value
R8055MW	Automatic Pen	550.00
R8065	Automatic Pen "Zip"	500.00

⊰ APPENDIX 6 ⊱
TAYLOR CUTLERY

Taylor Cutlery has been responsible for introducing a variety of knives to the market since it began importing them in 1977. To our knowledge, no attempt has been made to identify these knives in such a way that a legitimate collector value could be established for them.

All Taylor knives through 1981 were dated as to the year of manufacture. Handle materials and patterns have been as varied and as interesting as that of most large companies. The Elk Horn and Bear Creek stampings have long been discontinued. These then, now 20+ years old, have become collectible.

We have developed a Taylor Cutlery pricing guide using the RBR Evaluation Scales and information on production totals. We may have missed a few of Taylor's knives but hope you will find the information in the following charts useful.

Pattern/Name Handle Material	Date Produced	Total Produced	Tang Stamp	Collector Value
"Falcon" Stag	1980	4,000	Elk Horn	50.00
"Falcon" Bone	1980	3,600	Elk Horn	40.00
"Doctor's Knife" Stag	1980	3,600	Elk Horn	50.00
"Doctor's Knife" Stag	1980	1,200	Elk Horn	48.00
"Doctor's Knife" Pearl	1980	1,200	Elk Horn	60.00
"Skinner" Bone	1981	3,500	Elk Horn	33.00
"Caribou" Stag	1980	6,000	Elk Horn	55.00
"Coon" Stag	1979	3,000	Elk Horn	82.00
"Gunstock" Stag	1980	6,000	Elk Horn	50.00
"Barlow" Pearl & abalone	1981	800	Elk Horn	60.00
"Barlow" Stag	1981	4,000	Elk Horn	40.00
"Indian Head" Pearl	1981	1,000	Elk Horn	40.00
"Hunter" Stag	1980	3,500	Elk Horn	45.00
"Sidewinder" Stag	1981	1,000	Elk Horn	50.00

Pattern/Name Handle Material	Date Produced	Total Produced	Tang Stamp	Collector Value
"Shark" Stag	1981	1,000	Elk Horn	41.00
"Tennessee Shark" Stag handles	1980	6,000	Elk Horn	18.00
Tennessee Shield Tenn. orange handles	1981	3,000	Elk Horn	10.00
"Doctor's Knife" Stag handle	1981	1,000	Elk Horn	48.00
"Doctor's Knife" Pearl	1981	1,000	Elk Horn	55.00

"Doctor's Knife" Buffalo horn	1983	1,000	Elk Horn	28.00
"Skinner LB" Brown pearlite	1979	1,500	Elk Horn	50.00
"Skinner LB" White pearlite	1979	1,500	Elk Horn	50.00
"Copper Indian LB" Stainless handles	1980	6,000	Elk Horn	35.00
"Pocket Rocket LB" Stainless handles	1980	3,504	Elk Horn	35.00

Pattern/Name Handle Material	Date Produced	Total Produced	Tang Stamp	Collector Value

Pattern/Name Handle Material	Date Produced	Total Produced	Tang Stamp	Collector Value
"Elk Hunter" Bone handles	1981	4,008	Elk Horn	50.00
"2 Blade Pen" Wood handles	1977	1,200	Bear Creek	12.00
"Cheetah" Wood handles	1977	600	Bear Creek	12.00
"Cobra" Wood handles	1977	1600	Bear Creek	18.00
"Pumpkin Seed" India stag	1979	1400	Bear Creek	30.00
"Pumpkin Seed" Stag 7	1979	3,000	Elk Horn	38.00
"Gun boat" Stag	1981	3,000	Elk Horn	35.00
"Country Squire LB" Stag handle	1980	3,500	Elk Horn	30.00
"Wood Chuck" Stag handles		3,000	Elk Horn	30.00
"Peanut" Stag handles	1981	1,000	Elk Horn	30.00
"Peanut" Pearl	1981	1,000	Elk Horn	40.00

Pattern/Name Handle Material	Date Produced	Total Produced	Tang Stamp	Collector Value

Pattern/Name Handle Material	Date Produced	Total Produced	Tang Stamp	Collector Value
"Panda"				
India Stag		9,008	Elk Horn	45.00
Rough cut bone		1,200	Elk Horn	32.00
Smooth bone		3,016	Elk Horn	30.00
Abalone		600	Elk Horn	60.00
Christmas Tree (assorted)		3,000	Elk Horn	20.00
"Canoe"				
Stag	1979	1,000	Taylor Cutlery	35.00
"Baby Canoe"				
Red handles	1978	1,500	Bear Creek	15.00
"Canoe"				
Stag	1980	1,000	Elk Horn	60.00
"Canoe"				
Stag	1979	1,000	Bear Creek	60.00
"Baby Canoe" (Butter Bean)				
Stag	1980	3,000	Elk Horn	40.00
"Canoe"				
Plastic handles				
Black	1979	1,500	Bear Creek	22.00
Gray	1979	1,500	Bear Creek	22.00
White	1979	1,500	Bear Creek	22.00
Red & black	1979	1,500	Bear Creek	22.00
Brown	1979	1,500	Bear Creek	22.00

Pattern/Name Handle Material	Date Produced	Total Produced	Tang Stamp	Collector Value
"Copperhead" Small, ebony wood handles	1977	1,200	Bear Creek	25.00
"Copperhead" Regular size wood handles	1977	600	Bear Creek	25.00
"Copperhead" Stag 19	1979	1,000	Bear Creek	45.00
"Copperhead" Assorted plastic handle colors	1979	6,000	Bear Creek	20.00
"Copperhead" Pearl & abalone	1980	800	Elk Horn	60.00
"Copperhead" or "Shark" Assorted plastic handle colors	1977	3,960	Bear Creek	10.00
"Shark" Assorted plastic handle colors	1978	3,600	Bear Creek	10.00
"Shark" Assorted plastic handle colors (no shield)	1979	3,960	Bear Creek	12.00
"Shark" Plastic handles	1979	5,000	Elk Horn	12.00
	1979	5,000	Elk Horn	12.00
	1979	5,000	Elk Horn	12.00
	1979	5,000	Elk Horn	12.00

Pattern/Name Handle Material	Date Produced	Total Produced	Tang Stamp	Collector Value
"Shark" Stag handles	1979	3,000	Elk Horn	22.00
"Shark" Christmas handles				
Large stripes	1980	5,000	Elk Horn	12.00
Small stripes	1980	5,000	Elk Horn	12.00
Blue metal flake	1980	5,000	Elk Horn	12.00
Red metal flake	1980	5,000	Elk Horn	12.00
"Shark" Plastic handles				
Yellow	1981	5,100	Elk Horn	12.00
Black	1981	10,260	Elk Horn	12.00
White	1981	5,100	Elk Horn	12.00
Red	1981	5,100	Elk Horn	12.00
Green	1981	5,100	Elk Horn	12.00
Brown	1981	2,520	Elk Horn	12.00
Blue	1981	2,520	Elk Horn	12.00
"Kentucky Shark" Kentucky blue handles				
Kentucky shield	1981	3,000	Elk Horn	12.00

The Winchester pattern numbering system is good, but you will not find it stamped on the blade of many of their knives. This is unfortunate since they hold top priority as collectible knives, and number stamped blades are very useful for proper identification.

The first figure in Winchester's numbering system indicates the number of blades; the second figure indicates handle material. The last two figures are simply pattern indicators.

Handle Material Numbers

0 or 1.	Celluloid
2.	Nickel Silver
3.	Genuine Pearl
6.	Cocabolo Wood
7.	Smooth Bone
8 or 9.	Jigged Bone

Number	Pattern Name	Collector Value
1050	Tickler	290.00
1051	Tickler	292.00
1060	Slim Trapper	330.00
1201	Easy Open Jack	165.00
1605	Open End Jack	144.00

1610	Hawkbill	105.00
1611	Whaler	110.00
1613	Straight Jack	135.00
1614	Corn Knife	175.00
1621	Budding Knife	105.00
1632	Open End Jack	165.00
1633	Hawkbill	132.00
1701	Barlow	295.00
1703	Daddy Barlow	458.00
1704	Daddy Barlow	495.00
1785	Barlow	295.00
1905	Big Straight Jack	410.00

Number	Pattern Name	Collector Value

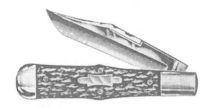

Number	Pattern Name	Collector Value
1920	Big Coke F.H.	2,200.00
1921	Open End Jack	220.00
1922	Open End Jack	220.00
1923	Slim Trapper (Large)	343.00
1924	Tickler (Large)	231.00
1925	Serpentine Jack	290.00
1936	Tickler	230.00
1937	Dog Leg Jack (Large)	275.00
1938	Dog Leg Jack (Large)	290.00
1950	Big F.H. Lock	2,238.00
2028	Equal End Jack	133.00
2037	Equal End Pen (Medium)	134.00
2038	Equal End Pen	134.00

Number	Pattern Name	Collector Value
2039	Equal End Pen (Medium)	133.00

Number	Pattern Name	Collector Value
2040	Equal End Pen (Medium)	133.00
2047	Big Board Jack	345.00

Number	Pattern Name	Collector Value
2051	Senator Pen (Small)	132.00
2052	Senator Pen (Small)	132.00
2053	Senator Pen (Large)	210.00
2054	Open End Pen (Medium)	130.00
2055	Open End Pen (Medium)	135.00
2057	Board Pen	170.00
2058	Senator Pen (Medium)	155.00
2059	Senator Pen (Medium)	110.00

Number	Pattern Name	Collector Value
2067	Serpentine Jack	170.00
2068	Sleeveboard Pen	258.00
2069	Equal End Jack (Large)	330.00
2070	Jack (Large)	330.00
2078	Warncliffe Pen	330.00
2079	Office Pen (Medium)	255.00

Number	Pattern Name	Collector Value
2082	Small Pen	180.00
2083	Serpentine Jack (Large)	245.00
2084	Sleeve Board Pen	185.00
2085	Dog Leg Jack	187.00
2086	Dog Leg Jack (Small)	148.00
2087	Dog Leg Jack (Small)	155.00
2088	Serpentine Jack	235.00

2089	Office Pen (Medium)	183.00
2090	Serpentine Jack	215.00
2094	Easy Open Jack (Large)	300.00
2098	Teardrop Jack (Large)	320.00
2099	Serpentine Jack (Large)	250.00
2106	Equal End Jack (Large)	190.00
2107	Dog Leg Jack (Small)	190.00

2109	Sleeveboard Pen	200.00

Number	Pattern Name	Collector Value
2110	Teardrop Jack (Large)	200.00
2111	Straight Jack (Large)	200.00
2112	Straight Jack (Large)	200.00
2113	Dog Leg Jack (Small)	150.00
2114	Dog Leg Jack	168.00
2115	Sleeveboard Pen (Small)	167.00
2116	Sleeveboard Pen	210.00
2117	Serpentine Jack (Large)	255.00
2201	Pen (Small)	100.00
2202	Serpentine Pen (Small)	100.00

Number	Pattern Name	Collector Value
2204	Pen (Small)	100.00
2205	Pen (Small)	105.00
2207	Easy Open Jack	200.00
2208	Senator Pen (Small)	170.00
2215	Senator Pen (Small)	105.00
2301	Senator Pen (Small)	190.00
2302	Senator Pen (Small)	180.00
2306	Senator Pen (Small)	180.00
2307	Senator Pen (Small)	130.00

Number	Pattern Name	Collector Value

2308	Senator Pen (Small)	150.00
2309	Senator Pen (Medium)	250.00
2314	Senator Pen (Medium)	300.00
2316	Warncliffe Pen (Medium)	300.00
2317	Warncliffe Pen (Medium)	225.00
2319	Sleeveboard Pen (Small)	230.00
2320	Sleeveboard Pen (Small)	225.00
2331	Congress Pen	280.00
2335	Sleeveboard Pen	295.00
2337	Congress Pen	325.00
2338	Senator Pen (Medium)	315.00
2344	Senator Pen (Medium)	320.00
2345	Sleeveboard Pen (Medium)	318.00

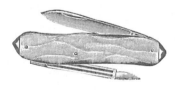

2346	Lobster (Serpentine)	250.00
2352	Serpentine Jack (Medium)	310.00
2356	Lobster (Serpentine)	330.00

Number	Pattern Name	Collector Value
2361	Dog Leg Jack (Small)	222.00
2363	Congress Pen	225.00
2365	Congress Pen	225.00
2366	Sleeveboard Pen (Large)	300.00
2367	Sleeveboard Pen	250.00

2368	Sleeveboard Pen	250.00
2369	Sleeveboard Pen	235.00
2374	Senator Pen	225.00
2375	Senator Pen (Small)	200.00
2376	Senator Pen (Small)	215.00
2377	Senator Pen (Small)	220.00

2380	Serpentine Doctor (Large)	600.00
2603	Open End Jack (Large)	205.00
2604	Open End Jack (Large)	235.00
2605	Easy Open Jack (Large)	265.00
2606	Easy Open Jack (Large)	225.00

Number	Pattern Name	Collector Value

2608	Open End Jack (Large)	245.00
2610	Open End Jack (Large)	225.00
2611	Dog Leg Jack	190.00
2612	Teardrop Jack (Large)	265.00
2613	Teardrop Jack (Large)	265.00
2614	Equal End Jack (Large)	265.00
2627	Serpentine Jack (Large)	265.00
2629	Serpentine Jack (Large)	260.00

2630	Teardrop Jack (Large)	265.00
2631	Sleeveboard Pen (Large)	193.00
2633	Serpentine Pen	195.00
2635	Open End Jack (Medium)	170.00
2636	Serpentine Jack (Large)	240.00

Number	Pattern Name	Collector Value
2638	Dog Leg Jack (Large)	216.00
2649	Jack (Large)	265.00
2660	Open End Jack (Large)	260.00
2661	Serpentine Jack (Large)	265.00
2662	Serpentine Jack (Large)	250.00
2665	Equal End Jack (Large)	245.00
2666	Open End Jack (Large)	225.00

Number	Pattern Name	Collector Value
2681	Electrician	168.00
2701	Barlow	325.00
2702	Barlow	350.00
2703	Barlow	325.00

Number	Pattern Name	Collector Value
2820	Open End Jack (Large)	250.00
2830	Senator Pen (No bolsters)	185.00
2840	Senator Pen (No bolsters)	250.00

Number	Pattern Name	Collector Value
2841	Senator Pen (No bolsters)	205.00

Number	Pattern Name	Collector Value
2842	Senator Pen (Large)	235.00
2843	Senator Pen (Medium)	206.00
2844	Big Open End Jack	320.00
2845	Big Jack	325.00
2846	Stock Pen (Large)	275.00
2847	Stock Pen (Large)	300.00
2848	Jack (Large)	250.00
2850	Big Coke/Jack	500.00
2851	Gunstock Jack (Small)	275.00

Number	Pattern Name	Collector Value
2851	Gunstock Jack (Large)	315.00
2852	Cattle Jack (Large)	350.00
2853	Equal End Jack (Large)	225.00
2854	Equal End Jack (Large)	220.00

Number	Pattern Name	Collector Value
2855	Equal End Jack (Large)	250.00
2856	Dog Leg Jack (Small)	225.00

Number	Pattern Name	Collector Value
2857	Dog Leg Jack	250.00
2858	Warncliffe Pen	250.00
2859	Sleeveboard Pen	200.00
2860	Straight Jack (Large)	250.00
2861	Straight Jack (Large)	250.00
2862	Sleeveboard Pen (Large)	190.00

Number	Pattern Name	Collector Value
2863	Congress Pen	220.00
2864	Swell Center Pen (Large)	325.00
2865	Swell Center Pen (Large)	350.00
2866	Senator Pen (Small)	185.00
2867	Pen (Medium)	200.00
2868	Cattle Pen (Large)	250.00
2869	Gunstock Pen (Large)	400.00
2870	Stock Jack (Large)	400.00

Number	Pattern Name	Collector Value

2871	Stock Pen (Large)	400.00
2872	Senator Pen (Large)	355.00
2873	Jack (Large)	250.00
2874	Jack (Large)	225.00
2875	Stock Pen (Large)	250.00

2876	Muskrat	375.00
2877	Muskrat	450.00

2878	Big Equal End Jack	300.00
2879	Big Sleeveboard Pen	650.00
2880	Big Straight Jack	550.00
2881	Big Straight Jack	550.00
2901	Open End Jack (Large)	225.00
2902	Senator Pen (Small)	150.00

Number	Pattern Name	Collector Value
2903	Swell Center Pen (Large)	325.00

Number	Pattern Name	Collector Value
2904	Trapper (Large)	600.00
2905	Big Straight Jack	500.00
2906	Big Straight Jack	525.00
2907	Big Straight Jack	550.00
2908	Swell Center Pen (Large)	250.00
2910	Lobster (Medium)	185.00
2911	Straight Jack (Large)	200.00
2914	Sleeveboard Pen (Large)	275.00

Number	Pattern Name	Collector Value
2917	Dog Leg Jack	300.00
2918	Serpentine Pen	200.00

Number	Pattern Name	Collector Value

Number	Pattern Name	Collector Value
2921	Coke Jack (Large)	525.00
2923	Stock Pen (Large)	300.00
2924	Congress Pen	250.00
2925	Jack (Large)	235.00

2928	Jack (Large)	265.00
2930	Teardrop Jack (Large)	275.00
2931	Straight Jack (Large)	225.00
2932	Congress	275.00
2933	Sleeveboard Pen	200.00
2934	Cattle Pen (Large)	225.00

2938	Sleeveboard Pen (Large)	250.00
2940	Teardrop Jack (Large)	275.00

Number	Pattern Name	Collector Value

Number	Pattern Name	Collector Value
2943	Sleeveboard Pen (Large)	245.00
2945	Senator Pen	200.00
2948	Slim Senator Pcn	190.00
2949	Straight Jack (Large)	275.00
2950	Open End Jack (Large)	225.00
2951	Open End Jack (Large)	250.00
2952	Straight Jack (Large)	265.00
2954	Straight Jack (Large)	270.00
2956	Dog Leg Jack (Large)	260.00
2958	Open End Jack (Large)	250.00

Number	Pattern Name	Collector Value
2959	Easy Open Jack (Large)	265.00
2961	Open End Jack (Large)	245.00
2962	Dog Leg Jack (Small)	190.00
2963	Senator Pen	160.00
2964	Straight Jack (Large)	265.00

Number	Pattern Name	Collector Value
2966	Equal End Jack (Large)	300.00
2967	Swell Center Pen (Large)	500.00
2969	Swell Center Pen (Large) (Moose)	475.00
2973	Equal End Jack (Large)	275.00

Number	Pattern Name	Collector Value
2974	Dog Leg Jack (Large)	250.00
2976	Stock Jack (Large)	325.00
2978	Serpentine Doctor's (Large)	500.00
2980	Cattle Pen (Large)	380.00
2981	Senator Pen	275.00
2982	Big Jack	325.00

Number	Pattern Name	Collector Value
2983	Open End Jack (Large)	250.00
2988	Big Jack	325.00
2990	Dog Leg Jack (Small)	200.00

Number	Pattern Name	Collector Value
2991	Cattle Equal End	375.00

Number	Pattern Name	Collector Value
2992	Stock Pen (Medium)	225.00
2993	Trapper	400.00
2994	Easy Open End Jack	250.00
2995	Big Swell End Jack	250.00
2996	Congress Pen (Large)	240.00
2997	Warncliffe Pen	275.00
2998	Open End Jack (Large)	265.00

Number	Pattern Name	Collector Value
2999	Dog Leg Jack (Medium)	250.00
3001	Swell Center Cattle	450.00
3002	Whittler	383.00
3003	Stock (Small)	345.00

Number	Pattern Name	Collector Value

Number	Pattern Name	Collector Value
3005	Whittler	375.00
3006	Warncliffe Whittler	395.00
3007	Stock (Large)	465.00
3008	Cattle (Large)	465.00

Number	Pattern Name	Collector Value
3009	Cattle (Large)	475.00
3010	Cattle Whittler	500.00
3014	Whittler	450.00
3015	Whittler	400.00
3016	Cattle	400.00
3017	Stock (Large)	425.00

Number	Pattern Name	Collector Value

Number	Pattern Name	Collector Value
3018	Stock (Large)	425.00
3019	Swell Center Cattle	400.00
3020	Swell Center Cattle	400.00
3023	Cattle Whittler	395.00
3024	Cattle Whittler	385.00
3025	Stock (Small)	295.00

Number	Pattern Name	Collector Value
3026	Stock (Small)	335.00
3027	Stock Whittler	300.00
3028	Stock Whittler	305.00

Number	Pattern Name	Collector Value

Number	Pattern Name	Collector Value
3029	Stock Whittler	305.00
3030	Cattle Whittler	350.00
3031	Cattle Whittler	325.00

Number	Pattern Name	Collector Value
3033	Cattle Whittler	325.00
3034	Cattle Whittler	300.00
3035	Cattle Whittler	300.00
3036	Cattle (Large)	400.00
3040	Stock Whittler	375.00
3041	Stock Whittler	375.00
3042	Cattle Whittler	360.00
3043	Cattle Whittler	300.00

Number	Pattern Name	Collector Value

Number	Pattern Name	Collector Value
3044	Cattle Whittler	300.00
3045	Stock Whittler	335.00
3046	Stock Whittler	350.00
3047	Stock (Small)	250.00
3048	Stock (Large)	360.00
3049	Stock (Large)	400.00

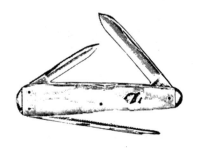

Number	Pattern Name	Collector Value
3331	Lobster (Pen)	225.00
3338	Lobster (Sleeveboard)	275.00
3341	Cattle (Large)	450.00
3347	Stock (Medium)	445.00
3348	Stock (Serp.)	450.00
3349	Whittler (Sleeveboard)	375.00

Number	Pattern Name	Collector Value

3350	Whittler	425.00

3352	Whittler (Open End)	385.00
3353	Pen (Equal End)	220.00
3357	Pen (Medium)	314.00

3359	Pen (Large)	365.00
3360	Bartender	350.00
3366	Whittler (Pen)	400.00
3370	Lobster (Pen)	260.00
3371	Lobster	250.00
3373	Stock (Medium)	300.00

Number	Pattern Name	Collector Value

Number	Pattern Name	Collector Value
3376	Stock (Large)	525.00
3377	Pen (Sleeveboard)	300.00
3378	Whittler (Pen)	325.00
3379	Whittler (Pen)	300.00
3380	Lobster (Large)	225.00
3381	Lobster (Small)	200.00

Number	Pattern Name	Collector Value
3382	Lobster (Medium)	225.00
3949	Sowbelly (Stock)	325.00
3950	Cattle (Large)	375.00
3953	Bartender	300.00
3959	Stock (Serp.)	375.00
3960	Stock (Serp.)	350.00
3961	Stock (Serp.)	350.00

Number	Pattern Name	Collector Value

Number	Pattern Name	Collector Value
3962	Stock (Serp.)	350.00
3967	Whittler (Serp.)	350.00
3968	Whittler (Serp.)	375.00

3969	Stock (Medium)	350.00
3971	Whittler (Classic)	400.00
3972	Whittler (Classic)	435.00

3973	Stock (Serp.)	300.00

Number	Pattern Name	Collector Value

Number	Pattern Name	Collector Value
3975	Stock (Medium)	300.00
3977	Cattle	350.00
3978	Whittler (Serp.)	325.00
3979	Cattle	375.00

3980	Sowbelly (Stock)	375.00
3991	Pen (Sleeveboard)	275.00
3992	Melon Tester	300.00
3993	Stock (Serp.)	350.00
3995	Whittler	380.00
4001	Stock (Large)	460.00

Number	Pattern Name	Collector Value

4301	Lobster Pen (Medium)	275.00
4313	Pen (Large)	275.00

4320	Lobster (Gunstock/Orange Blossom)	400.00
4340	Lobster (Large)	390.00
3341	Pen (Large)	390.00
4901	Scout (Medium)	300.00
4910	Stock (Large)	475.00
4918	Congress	381.00
4920	Lobster (Pen/Orange Blossom)	275.00
4930	Congress (Large)	405.00
4931	Congress (Medium)	350.00
4935	Congress (Large)	400.00

Number	Pattern Name	Collector Value
4950	Scout (Medium)	375.00
4951	Scout (Large)	395.00
4961	Cattle (Serp.)	435.00
4962	Cattle (Serp.)	485.00
4963	Stock (Large)	435.00

4975	Bartender	325.00

4990	Scout	345.00
4991	Scout	335.00

Knife collecting is the fastest growing hobby in the United States and is even gaining worldwide attention. It has grown from the street corner/courthouse knife swapping of the '50s and '60s into an entrenched hobby supported by publications, organizations, and a national museum devoted only to knives which displays the crown jewels of the hobby. Knife collecting even has a Latin name, "machairology."

Trading and investing are part of the hobby. Many maintain that these elements are as much fun as building a collection. There are many collectors we know who have made (and/or lost) significant sums of money in this hobby. So you should be well informed as you enter the world of knife collecting. This book is intended to point you in that direction. To further assist you, we are willing to:

- Forward your name and address to monthly publications about knives.
- Forward your name and address to mail-order dealers who publish catalogs.
- Attempt to answer your questions (provided you enclose a self-addressed, stamped envelope with your inquiry).

We also offer these services:

- Provide certified appraisals of knives/collections. (Fee varies with size and value of collection. Inquire at addresses below before shipping knives for appraisal.)
- Assist insurance companies with appraisals and adjustment evaluations.
- Sell autographed copies of this book for $14.95, plus $3.00 shipping and handling.

You may contact us at:

RBR Cutlery   R & C Books
197 Royhill Rd.   or   P.O. Box 151
Hindman, Ky 41822   Combs, KY 41729

Check out these other Cutlery books by Roy Ritchie and Ron Stewart

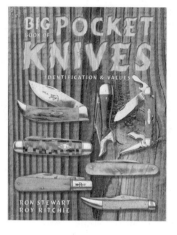

Big Book of Pocket Knives highlights knife and cutlery products from more than 20 cutlery companies. Hundreds of illustrations allow the collector to look directly at the original company materials used to advertise and promote the knives of past manufacturers. Companies and brands represented include Belknap, Case, Winchester, Remington, Robeson, Northfield, Imperial, John Primble, Russell, Shapleigh Diamond Edge, Schrade, and Marble.

#5616 • ISBN: 1-57432-178-1 • 8½ x 11 • 344 Pgs. • PB • $19.95

This original Cattaraugus Company catalog reprint from the early years of this century showcases pocket knives, razors, whittler, fishing and hunting knives, scissors, tableware, and even shaving brushes. The authors have also included an interesting historical overview of this classic American company.

#5355 • ISBN: 1-57432-137-4 • 8½ x 11 • 144 Pgs. • PB • $19.95

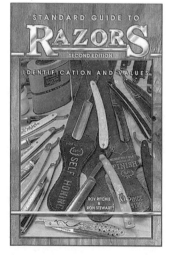

Over 200 companies, base values, hundreds of new pictures and illustrations, the history of shaving and a chapter to aid in determining razors' ages are included in this heavily revised and updated second edition. There are also tips on appraising your razor and an appraisal chart, as well as care and management of a razor collection. Hundreds of American, German, English, and even French razors are represented.

#5166 • ISBN: 1-57432-091-2 • 5½ x 8½ • 224 Pgs. • PB • $9.95

COLLECTOR BOOKS
Informing Today's Collector

GLASSWARE & POTTERY

4929 **American Art Pottery**, 1880 – 1950, Sigafoose $24.95
5907 Coll. Ency. of **Depression Glass**, 15th Ed., Florence.$19.95
5748 Collector's Encyclopedia of **Fiesta**, 9th Ed., Huxford..$24.95
1358 Collector's Encyclopedia of **McCoy Pottery**, Huxford $19.95
5921 Collector's Encyclopedia of **Stangl Artware**, Runge ...$29.95
2339 Collector's Guide to **Shawnee Pottery**, Vanderbilt.....$19.95
5528 Early American **Pattern Glass**, Metz $17.95
5257 **Fenton Art Glass** Patterns, 1939 – 1980, Whitmyer .$29.95
5261 **Fostoria Tableware**, 1924 – 1943, Long/Seate.........$24.95
5899 **Glass & Ceramic Baskets**, White............................$19.95
5279 **Glass Toothpick Holders**, Bredehoft/Sanford............$24.95
5679 Collector's Ency. of **Red Wing Art Pottery**, Dollen $24.95
5691 **Post86 Fiesta**, I.D. & Value Guide, Racheter.............$19.95
5924 **Zanesville Stoneware** Co., Rans/Ralston/Russell......$24.95

OTHER COLLECTIBLES

5898 Ant. & Contemporary **Advertising** Mem., Summers .$24.95
5731 **Auction Tracker** $14.95
5814 Antique **Brass & Copper** Collectibles, Gaston $24.95
1880 Antique **Iron**, McNerney $9.95
3872 Antique **Tins**, Dodge..$24.95
1128 **Bottle** Pricing Guide, 3rd Ed., Cleveland....................$7.95
3718 Collectible **Aluminum**, Grist $16.95
5681 Collector's Guide to **Lunchboxes**, White $19.95
3881 Collector's Guide to **Novelty Radios**, Bunis/Breed $18.95
4652 Collector's Gde to **Transistor Radios**, 2nd Ed., Bunis$16.95
1629 **Doorstops**, Identification & Values, Bertoia $9.95
5683 **Fishing Lure** Collectibles, 2nd Ed.Murphy/Edmisten.$29.95
5911 **Flea Market Trader**, 13th Ed., Huxford $9.95
3819 **General Store** Collectibles, Wilson $24.95
5912 The **Heddon** Legacy, Roberts/Pavey $29.95
2216 **Kitchen Antiques**, 1790–1940, McNerney $14.95
6028 Modern **Fishing Lure** Collectibles, Lewis $24.95
2026 **Railroad** Collectibles, 4th Ed., Baker $14.95
1632 **Salt & Pepper Shakers**, Guarnaccia...........................$9.95
5091 **Salt & Pepper Shakers** II, Guarnaccia $18.95
3443 **Salt & Pepper Shakers** IV, Guarnaccia......................$18.95
5007 **Silverplated Flatware**, Revised 4th Edition, Hagan ...$18.95
3892 **Toy & Miniature Sewing Machines**, Thomas...........$18.95
3977 Value Guide to **Gas Station Memorabilia**, Summers $24.95
4877 Vintage **Bar Ware**, Visakay $24.95
5923 Vin. **Jewelry** for Investment & Casual Wear, Edeen ..$24.95

TOYS & MARBLES

2333 Antique & Collectible **Marbles**, 3rd Ed., Grist.............$9.95
2338 Collector's Encyclopedia of **Disneyana**, Longest, Stern$24.95

4566 Collector's Guide to **Tootsietoys**, 2nd Ed, Richter $19.95
4945 **G-Men and FBI Toys**, Whitworth..............................$18.95
5593 Grist's Big Book of **Marbles**, 2nd Ed. $24.95
5267 **Matchbox Toys**, 3rd Ed., 1947 to 1998, Johnson.....$19.95
5830 **McDonald's** Collectibles, 2nd Ed., Henriques/DuVall $24.95
5673 Modern **Candy Containers** & Novelties, Brush/Miller$19.95
1540 Modern **Toys** 1930–1980, Baker $19.95

DOLLS, FIGURES & TEDDY BEARS

2079 **Barbie Doll** Fashion, Volume I, Eames.....................$24.95
3957 **Barbie Exclusives**, Rana...$18.95
3810 **Chatty Cathy** Dolls, Lewis......................................$15.95
4559 Collectible **Action Figures**, 2nd Ed., Manos $17.95
4863 Collector's Encyclopedia of **Vogue Dolls**, Stover/Izen$29.95
5599 **Dolls of the 1960s and 1970s**, Sabulis $24.95
6025 **Doll Values**, Antique to Modern, 6th Ed., Moyer......$12.95
1799 **Effanbee Dolls**, Smith..$19.95
6032 **Madame Alexander** Price Guide #27, Crowsey........$12.95
6033 **Modern Collectible Dolls**, Volume VI, Moyer $24.95
5689 **Nippon Dolls** & Playthings, Van Patten/Lau.............$29.95
5920 Schroeder Collectible **Toys**, 8th Ed., Huxford...........$17.95
5253 Story of **Barbie**, 2nd Ed., Westenhouser $24.95
1513 **Teddy Bears & Steiff Animals**, Mandel....................$9.95
1817 **Teddy Bears & Steiff Animals**, 2nd Series, Mandel..$19.95
1808 Wonder of **Barbie**, Manos $9.95
1430 World of **Barbie Dolls**, Manos $9.95
4880 World of **Raggedy Ann** Collectibles, Avery...............$24.95

INDIANS, GUNS, KNIVES, TOOLS, PRIMITIVES

1868 Antique **Tools**, Our American Heritage, McNerney $9.95
1426 **Arrowheads & Projectile Points**, Hothem $7.95
2279 **Indian Artifacts** of the Midwest, Hothem $14.95
5685 **Indian Artifacts** of the Midwest, Book IV, Hothem $19.95
6132 Modern **Guns**, 14th Edition, Quertermous................$14.95
2164 **Primitives**, Our American Heritage, McNerney $9.95

PAPER COLLECTIBLES & BOOKS

5902 **Boys' & Girls' Book Series**, Jones $19.95
4710 Collector's Guide to **Children's Books**, Jones $18.95
5153 Collector's Guide to **Children's Books**, Vol. 2, Jones $19.95
5596 Collector's Guide to **Children's Books**, Vol. 3, Jones $19.95
1441 Collector's Guide to **Post Cards**, Wood $9.95
2081 Guide to Collecting **Cookbooks**, Allen $14.95
5825 Huxford's **Old Book** Value Guide, 13th Ed......$19.95
6041 Vintage **Postcards** for the Holidays, Reed $24.95
4733 **Whitman Juvenile Books**, Brown............................$17.95

This is only a partial listing of the books on collectibles that are available from Collector Books. All books are well illustrated and contain current values. Most of our books are available from your local bookseller, antique dealer, or public library. If you are unable to locate certain titles in your area, you may order by mail from COLLECTOR BOOKS, P.O. Box 3009, Paducah, KY 42002-3009. Customers with Visa, MasterCard, or Discover may phone in orders from 7:00–5:00 CST, Monday–Friday, Toll Free 1-800-626-5420, or online at www.collectorbooks.com. Add $3.00 for postage for the first book ordered and 50¢ for each additional book. Include item number, title, and price when ordering. Allow 14 to 21 days for delivery.